INTRODUCTION TO REFERENCE WORK

VOLUME I *Basic Information Sources*

INTRODUCTION TO REFERENCE WORK

Volume I **Basic Information Sources**

Seventh Edition

William A. Katz
State University of New York at Albany

The McGraw-Hill Companies, Inc.
New York   St. Louis   San Francisco   Auckland
Bogotá   Caracas   Lisbon   London
Madrid   Mexico City   Milan   Montreal   New Delhi
San Juan   Singapore   Sydney   Tokyo   Toronto

McGraw-Hill

A Division of The **McGraw·Hill** *Companies*

Introduction to Reference Work
Volume I Basic Information Sources

3 4 5 6 7 8 9 0   DOC   DOC   9 0 9 8

ISBN 0-07-034277-6

This book was set in Baskerville by ComCom, Inc.
The editors were Bill McLane and Ronda S. Angel;
the production supervisor was Leroy A. Young.
The cover was designed by Christopher Brady.
The cover illustration was done by Gregory E. Stadnyk.
R. R. Donnelley & Sons Company was printer and binder.

Library of Congress Cataloging-in-Publication Data

Katz, William A., 1934-
    Introduction to reference work / William A. Katz—7th ed.
        p.   cm.
    Includes bibliographical references (p.) and index.
    ISBN 0-07-034277-6 (v. 1).—ISBN 0-07-034278-4 (v. 2)
        1. Reference services (Libraries)   2. Reference books-
    -Bibliography.   I. Title.
    Z711.K32   1997
    025.52—dc20

96-1741
CIP

ABOUT THE AUTHOR

WILLIAM A. KATZ is a professor at the School of Information Science and Policy, State University of New York at Albany. He was a librarian at the King County (Washington) Library for four years and worked in the editorial department of the American Library Association. He received his Ph.D. from the University of Chicago and has been the editor of *RQ*, the journal of the Reference and Adult Services Division of the American Library Association, and the *Journal of Education for Librarianship*. Professor Katz is now editor of *The Reference Librarian*, a quarterly devoted to issues in modern reference and information services, and *The Acquisitions Librarian*, concerned with collection development. He is the editor of *Magazines for Libraries* and has compiled a second edition of *The Columbia Granger's Guide to Poetry Anthologies*. He is editor of a series on the history of the book for Scarecrow Press including his *A History of Book Illustration* and *Dahl's History of the Book*. Presently, he is writing a cultural history of reference books.

To Will, Chris, and Randy

CONTENTS

PREFACE

As in previous editions, this seventh edition of *Introduction to Reference Work: Volume 1, Basic Information Sources* is almost totally rewritten. It is the author's conviction that the revolution in reference sources and the reference process requires virtually complete revision.

NEW TO THIS EDITION

Today reference libraries turn to indexes, encyclopedias, or directories for the same type of information as they did decades ago. The essential difference is threefold, and this is reflected in the text's revisions. First, one may use not only a print source, but also an electronic database, whether it be a CD-ROM, online, or over the Internet. Second, the library offers access not only to local resources, but also to all that has been published since the beginning of printing. There is little information that is not within the reach of a computer keyboard in almost every library in the United States and Canada. Third, the reference librarian uses traditional basic reference works and now acts as mediator as well, a middle person between masses of information and the user who is unable to discriminate the good from the poor, the best from the better. More and more the reference librarian has become the key professional information expert. Today she or he is necessary to filter the mass of undifferentiated information that flows over national and international networks.

Other trends in this revision are based upon probable reference services in the next decade. The changes represent a consensus among working reference librarians:

1. Networks, from local ones to international systems such as Internet, literally open up the whole globe as one impressive, for the most part disorganized, source of information. The role of the reference librarian is to mediate between this mass of data and the uses of specific clients.

2. Public, school, and academic libraries will make more databases available over networks. The reference librarians will be called upon to solve problems as they arise for individual users.

3. The new technologies are likely to increase the amount of reference services.

4. Thanks to constant changes in technology and resources, the librarian will have to continually renew, sharpen, and master new skills.

5. Subject expertise is increasingly important, particularly as the number of reference sources become more specific and the users more sophisticated.

6. Demand for instruction in the use of everything from computers to networks to pamphlets and, more particularly, online CD-ROM searching will continue to grow.

This first volume is by way of a basic-training manual. No one can move into the finer points of reference services (present and future) without an understanding and mastery of basic reference forms, no matter in what packages they are delivered. The primary purpose, as in past editions, is to offer a lucid, accurate description of basic reference sources.

PLAN OF THE BOOK

The organization is much the same as in previous editions. There seems to be no reason to change since the text is dealing with basics which, no matter what the information highway looks like or where it wanders, are essential to information understanding and mediation.

The first section, Introduction, considers the reference services process in Chapter 1 and, in Chapter 2, the parameters and meaning of the electronic library. Both chapters are expanded. They are an introduction to the second volume of this text, *Reference Services and Reference Processes*. The initial chapters serve as an explanation to two vital areas of reference services—the community served and the technologies employed in service.

As in the previous edition, Part II, Information: Control and Access, is concerned with bibliography and indexes. At this point, though, the basic layout changes. In previous editions the focus was first on the print version of a basic reference work, with a nod to CD-ROMs and online. No more. Now, because it is the author's firm conviction that in a decade most reference works will be available primarily in an electronic format, the focus is on CD-ROMs and on-line. These are highlighted. Print is secondary.

Emphasis here is on form, not on specific titles. Each form, from bibliographies to biographies, is discussed. Examples are given of titles—and particularly those titles likely to be found in most public, academic, or school libraries.

In describing each reference title the primary focus is on content, and how that content differs from, say, similar titles. The use of the reference work is indicated. Where print is highlighted, the arrangement is stressed. Where an electronic format is considered, the search patterns at the computer keyboard, or with a mouse, are the primary interest.

No exhaustive effort is made to show how to search X or Y database. Basic search patterns, especially where they are found in similar databases, are considered, but sophisticated searching is not discussed. Why? First, most schools and libraries have separate, necessary courses on database searching—whether this be a CD-ROM or an Internet point. Second, software (in which the search is found) is as likely to change as rapidly as means of delivery of information. Third, the rapid advance of software for easy-to-use searching may eliminate most, if not all need to master complex search patterns. Speed and sophistication of searches may require more skill for librarians, but even that may change. What may be a valid explanation of a search today may be nothing but history tomorrow. On the other hand, the basic content, the basic search approach is not likely to change. And that is why both are stressed.

Part III, Sources of Information, follows the pattern of previous editions. Again, entries are as they were outlined for the first section. Here, though, the focus is on using "one-stop" information sources as well as how these fit into the average reference services arrangement.

A typical entry for a given reference work begins with the CD-ROM version. Under that is given the print version and under that the online version. (Where there is no electronic database format, this is so indicated and the print version is given by itself.)

For each title, basic bibliographical information is given, including prices. It is important to recognize that prices are representative of relative costs. They change each and every year. Still the basic price difference, say, between an index in print and on CD-ROM is at least suggested. Note, too, that online costs are given primarily for DIALOG and in the per hour fashion. DIALOG and other online services are going to other methods of charging but, again, at least the per hour figures give a relative idea of cost.

Bibliographical data are based on publishers' catalogs, *Books In Print*, *Gale Directory of Databases*, and examination of the titles. Online and CD-ROM titles, for the most part, have been used at a computer terminal. Also, the author has turned to excellent reviews for support and assistance—particularly those in the *Library Journal, Online, Database, RQ*, and *Choice*. The information is applicable as of late 1995 and, like price, is subject to change.

Suggested Reading

In both volumes, suggested readings are found in the footnotes and at the end of each chapter. When a publication is cited in a footnote, the reference is rarely duplicated in the "Suggested Reading" section. For the most part, these readings are limited to publications issued since 1990. In addition to providing readers with current thinking, the more recent citations have the added bonus of making it easier for the student to locate the readings. It is beyond argument, of course, that *all* readings need not necessarily be current and that many older articles and books are as valuable today as they were when first published. Thanks to many teachers who have retained earlier editions of this text it is possible to have a bibliography of previous readings.

Thanks are due to the reviewers who critiqued this book. Eileen Abels, University of Maryland; Bahal El-Hadidy, University of South Florida; Ellen Getleson, University of Pittsburgh; Doug Raeber, University of Missouri; and Antonio Rodriguez-Buckingham, University of Mississippi. Thanks are also due to the editors of this volume, Bill McLane and particularly Ronda Angel whose diligence and imagination have vastly improved this edition. Thanks also to the indexer.

William A. Katz

INTRODUCTION TO REFERENCE WORK

VOLUME I *Basic Information Sources*

PART I
INTRODUCTION

CHAPTER ONE
REFERENCE LIBRARIANS ON THE INFORMATION HIGHWAY

Reference librarians answer questions. Queries may come from presidents or grade school children. The answer may be in a complex gathering of materials or may be a simple fact. Librarians act as mediators between the puzzled user and too much, or too little, information. As experts in matching questions with answers they are necessary navigators of an information highway which increasingly becomes more labyrinthine. Tortuous to follow, to discover the on- and off-ramps, the information highway's perplexities require an experienced, intelligent guide. The reference librarian is that guide.

The Sumerian librarians of some 5000 years ago responded to questions by consulting their cuneiform clay tablets. Today, the librarian turns to a computer and to a vast and growing technology for acquiring, storing, and retrieving data. A computer monitor, a keyboard, and a printer are found in the modern reference library. The librarian, or user, types in a subject, key word, author, or a multiple of other signals. The computer searches in the database(s) for what matches the signal terms. The response appears on the screen. Usually it is in the form of a citation to a specific article in a magazine (often with a description of that article, i.e., "abstract"). The user may then move on to another bit of data or print out what is on the screen. The user may download the material as well. "Download" is self-explanatory; it is a method of transfer of data from the main online computer source to the user's computer. The copy is made usually on a disc or diskette which can be viewed or printed.

CD-ROMs and online processing and communication networks such as Internet are at the heart of this textbook and discussed in detail throughout. Most readers will know what these are and, indeed, will have worked actively with one or all of the format. Still, as a brief reminder: a CD-ROM ("compact disc–read-only memory") appears to be a CD from which one plays music. It holds up to 250,000 pages of text. Also, if "multimedia" programmed, it can hold pictures, sound, music, and so on. "Online" refers to information gathering from a server or mainframe computer's "database." Internet is a good example. Information in digital form is impressive. For example, the Library of Congress has taken 195 years to collect close to 14 million books. The Internet's World Wide Web has added about 10 million electronic documents at a quarter million Web sites in less than three years. The importance of quality and selection aside, there is no question about the future of digitalized information.

All of the various electronic information databases are accessed at a computer, either a home PC (personal computer) or a library terminal. At a minimum even the smallest library will have one computer with a popular, general index on a CD-ROM. In 1996 approximately 80 percent of American libraries, regardless of type or size, have some type of CD-ROM reference work, usually an index. Online and additional CD-ROMs are found in about 50 percent of the medium to large libraries. The larger, the richer the library the more evidence there is of electronic forms of information. Small- to medium-sized libraries still rely primarily on printed reference works. No matter what type or size the library, all reference sections still rely on printed materials. Most reference questions are answered from such works, particularly as the electronic databases rarely cover data published before the mid-1980s.

The confusion is the degree of choice. Now reference librarians not only have countless reference sources to select from, but almost as many potential delivery systems, from print to CD-ROMs and magnetic tapes to online. Which format is best? Which CD-ROM, out of a half dozen possible choices of the same reference work, is best? Each question requires an individual decision. There is some compensation: "Countless choices mean complexity and, sometimes, even chaos. But choices, complexity, and even chaos mean that (librarians) have the opportunity to be in control. This control may be manifested in the search engines and interfaces we use; the pricing options we select (or if we don't like any of them, getting the information elsewhere); and the form, format, and appearance of the information we retrieve. Our ultimate form of control is always having the choice to select which . . . systems we choose to continue to search."[1]

Reference librarians do a number of things besides mastering electronic formats. They teach how to use CD-ROMs and online; are experts on acquisition of information sources; and are equally skilled in knowing what should be discarded from the collection. From day to day they take part in countless meetings and often act as administrators. Then there are the nitty-gritty aspects of the profession. Fixing the jammed printer next to the computer terminal or

---

[1]Carol Tenopir, "Changes and Choices," *Library Journal*, December 1994, p. 34.

putting more paper in the copy machine may take as much time as attending meetings. There are times when librarians wonder why it is necessary to answer the telephone when there are 10 or more people waiting about for service.

> Reference librarians need to balance a broad range of tasks—desk services, consultations, instruction, collection development, and involvement in implementing new technologies. This list of assignments reflects the need to maintain traditional desk and instructional services as well as to add consulting services and program and project development activities, especially with electronic products and services.[2]

Major Changes

If answering questions remains the primary role of the reference librarian, there have been sea changes in precisely what that implies. Among the more obvious modifications and changes in reference services, now as well as a few years ahead:

1. The reference desk in its present form no longer is important. Granted a central point is needed to answer directional queries, as well as short reference questions, but beyond that the old reference desk will be modified into an electronic data center.

2. Reference librarians will become highly developed subject experts. As mediators between the user and information, they weigh the good, the bad, and the indifferent data. They help clients determine what they need out of the ever-growing masses of information. This, in turn, implies a librarian who is associated with a subject area of the library. This means not only a thorough knowledge of the traditional materials but skills with electronic databases, and Internet communications with users and fellow librarians.

3. Reference librarians will be associated with the numerous new technologies, and as questions arise, particularly in subject areas of their expertise, they will instruct and assist the user (where it is requested) in finding the information at a computer terminal in the library or at the user's home.

4. At least a small group of working reference librarians will assume more research advisory positions. Librarians know, after all, what is required to filter information for particular needs. Librarians know what information sources to use and not to use. They know, in fact, a wide range of subject areas related to a specialized core of knowledge which will help the software/hardware/network organizations better serve the public. The reference librarian will be someone to whom all turn for battle line data on information needs.

In smaller libraries, and in most school libraries the reference librarian will continue to follow the established patterns of reference service, but always

---

[2]David Lewis, "Making Academic Reference Services Work," *College & Research Libraries*, no. 5, 1994, p. 647.

influenced by the four roles indicated above. What may have been a relatively static, predictable type of work is turning into a fast-growing ever-changing profession at each and every level of service.

Who Uses Reference Services?

Patrons, clients, users—the people who wander in and out of libraries and reference sections—generally are of three or four basic types. A small percentage, probably under 1 percent in academic libraries and negligible in public libraries, are researchers who are seeking raw data. Other than the need to be pointed in the direction of what they are looking for or to find quickly what they require, they generally fall outside the working circle of the average reference librarian.

The next large group are those seeking specific answers (resources to short facts) to equally specific questions. This is the primary audience for the reference librarian as mediator. Most of these people know little or nothing about the library and are interested only in the response, which should be precise, brief, and right on target. Again, this is probably no more than 5 to 10 percent of the users, at least in academic and special libraries. Public librarians will find a smaller percentage of such types, but these normally can be categorized as involved in business.

The largest group who need the reference librarians are those who have an undifferentiated requirement for information. They may range from the student who has to write a paper on the hobbies of Lincoln to the doctor who may be looking for hobbies to take his mind off medicine. Neither requires specific answers. Both want a variety of material, at various levels of depth and sophistication. The danger here is that the reference librarian will see these people as those who should be finding the information on their own, who should, at best, be turned over to someone in the general reading room. The librarian, then, has given up a process of information mediation where it may be needed the most. The student and the layperson not only want to know what to read, but what not to read. They both require an analysis that some reference librarians might consider not really part of their professional job. Wrong.

At the Reference Desk

Two experienced academic reference librarians, from different settings, College of William and Mary and Georgia State University, compare entries in their respective reference desk logs. The logs are maintained to aid in staff communication, but along the way they reflect the typical day of a reference librarian. The quotations are indicative of the problems and delights: "Occasionally patrons will complain that the copier in the front is printing blank pages" (contact copy center). "Patron reported a biology book as stolen" (called campus police). And "just noticed the Middle East map by the water fountain is missing." "Best question of the week—I need a picture of a camel showing its feet. I'm dressing as a camel for Halloween and I can't find how their feet look." (We found him what he needs.) "I just found someone playing a computer game on the Infotrac terminal." (He brought his own software.) "I've noticed people have trouble with parts A and B of *Historical Abstracts* as one is from modern history and one for the 20th century." (Why not separate the A and B volumes instead of having them all together?) "A student asked me tonight if we were starting to take the books off the shelves for the summer." (No.) "An early English Christmas Carol is identified as Sans Day Carol. What could 'sans' mean in this context. It could mean 'without day' but I doubt it." (The "sand day" is another way of putting "St. Day," so named because the melody and the first three verses were taken down at St. Day in Cornwall.)[3]

Taking the Highway

Anecdotal views of reference service are valuable, but out there is a digital information highway. The road is worldwide, and it will completely change the process of reference service. "Process" should be stressed. The goal (the answer to a query) remains a constant. Technology has made it possible to reach that goal faster and with added efficiency.

Until a few years ago if you wanted to read a page from the *Oxford English Dictionary*, which traces the history of words, you had to pull the heavy volume from the shelf, hunt up the information, and possibly copy it down or photocopy the page. If you were in a library without this reference work, it was necessary to have the page sent, or go to a library that had the set. There were other problems: the volume you needed might be missing, the page you needed might be torn out, and so on. Enter the electronic OED (*Oxford English Dictionary*) in a digitized form. Now one may search for the same word at a computer terminal. Furthermore, it is possible to do such things as search for your word in the millions of quotations in the complete set. There are numerous other points of data one may extract electronically in seconds. Using the print version the same quest might take hours, even months. Similar shortcuts are now possible with countless reference works.

The "information highway," "information superhighway," "information infrastructure," and "communications network" are a few descriptors indicative of change and confusion. Whatever it may be called, the necessary approach requires a vast amount of technology. Consider, for example, the reference desk of the future where one will find "a wide range and ever-expanding range of equipment including cameras, scanners, keyboards, telephones, fax machines, computers, switches, compact disks, video and audio tape, cable wire, satellites,

[3]Bettina Manzo and Elizabeth Cooksey, "Panic Is Setting In," to be published in *The Reference Librarian*. (Quotations are from the unpublished manuscript.)

optical fiber transmission lines, microwave nets, switches, televisions, monitors, printers, and much more."[4]

Today's reference desk will be called the "teledesk" or "multimedia desk" or simply be blown away in favor of one-to-one service from a strolling reference librarian.[5] Then, too, users may no longer be library dependent. They will get all the information at their personal computers. Still, there will be those moments when they need assistance. Then the slogan will be: "Reference librarian—will travel."

Problems on the Highway

Among the players in this information plan is some confusion. (1) What technologies are going to make all of this possible? (2) How about cost and such things as copyright? (3) Is information going to be available only in libraries, or in every home? (4) How long is this going to take? Meanwhile, should the librarian keep purchasing and mastering one form of communication or wait a month (year, decade) for the ultimate system design? (5) Will the information highway reduce the knowledge gap between the rich, the middle classes, and the poor? Will it be like the first railways and automobiles, offering open travel to everyone, not just a few? (6) Will monopolies control information to a point where lack of competition will mean lack of the free flow of data? Well-developed fiber-optic grids, for example, cost billions. Who is to pay for this, and if it is private companies— as seems to be the case—how much regulation or deregulation will be required? (7) With everyone having the potential to tap the resources of not one, but all libraries throughout the world, what is the place of the reference librarian in the future? Will a librarian be necessary? The answer is a resounding YES.

Reference librarians will be needed, as is demonstrated through this text. They (1) determine what, among the tons of information, is the ounce necessary and useful for the individual; (2) determine the organization and access of data in such a way as to be exploited by the specialist and the generalist; (3) assist everyone in the use of databases and information systems too involved for the average person to either purchase or use at home. Databases, for example, tend to duplicate one another; the software for one is not the same as for an-

[4]Information Infrastructure Task Force, *The National Information Infrastructure* (Washington, DC: 1993), quoted in Peter Young and Jane Williams, "Libraries and the National Information Infrastructure," *The Bowker Annual* (New York: R. R. Bowker, 1994), p. 35. Young and Williams offer a short, excellent overview of where libraries will fit in the new age of information. The summary concludes with an eight-page legislation plan. The federal organization engineering the information highway is the U.S. National Advisory Council on the National Information Infrastructure. Usually this is abbreviated as NII.

[5]Joanne Euester. "Take Charge of the Future," *C&RL News*, February 1993, p. 90. This is a detailed and, for the most part, realistic appraisal of the reference desk and reference services in the next decade or so.

other; and access to related sources is not all that evident. Expert advice, even for subject experts, often is required.

The reference interview, and the human communication patterns involved, is a necessary part of most detailed reference services. Even the finest computer system, even one such as "Hal" from the movie *2001,* is unlikely to replace human-to-human interaction. A simple example: The best automatic telephone program can drive a person mad when there is a constant flow of requests to push this or that button and one ends up with music or a dial tone. A human voice is much needed.

In summary, "it is ironic that the new information services simultaneously increase user need for assistance of [reference librarians] and reduce the contact they have with them."[6] Still, librarians can't wait until such time as the layperson or expert recognizes that an information specialist is needed. Reference librarians need to function "more like consulting information engineers, than traditional, passive information resource custodians. . . . Those who are successful in this endeavor will enjoy satisfying careers."[7]

If tomorrow's hope is in technology, the real monster for reference librarians is not the ubiquitous computer, but the ubiquitous budget slasher. Budget cutbacks eliminate positions, hours, and, yes, the new technologies. Michael Gorman, dean of Library Services at CSU, Fresno, puts it this way: "Librarians are buffeted by the endemic financial crisis . . . ; afflicted by existential angst; and under pressure to move away from traditional . . . services into something that no one can define. . . . Dealing with both can lead to despair and paralysis—the danger of us acting like deer caught in the highlights of history. We need practical, long term strategic plans that take into account the rapidly changing information environment."[8]

Libraries will be necessary for two sometimes overlooked reasons: (1) Browsing and the enjoyment of books—no matter what their form—will remain a constant. Most people use a library today for relaxation and amusement, not to find the answer to who or what set off the big bang. (2) Cost of information will remain high, and the majority will look to the library for materials they cannot afford to access.

Beyond the engineers arguing about the plans for the information highway there are numerous librarians and laypersons who have a normal response: "I don't like all this techie talk. After all, technology is just a tool. Let's just use it to serve people. We don't have to make it our only theme."[9] Conversely, those running large research libraries, whether they are public, academic, or special,

[6]S. Michael Malinconico, "Information's Brave New World," *Library Journal,* May 1, 1992, p. 38.

[7]Ibid. The author spells out in detail why more librarians, rather than fewer, will be needed in future years.

[8]*California Librarian,* February 1993, p. 2.

[9]Richard Dougherty, "Exercising Our Options," *Journal of Academic Librarianship,* March 1993, p. 3.

are more concerned with the new technologies. There is far from consensus on either the direction, commitment, or proper use of technology among librarians. Be that as it may, one can't turn back history, and like it or not, the new technologies will change reference services.

This author believes the change will ultimately be for the good, particularly as it will speed and refine the process of finding answers to questions. The new technologies mean new masses of undifferentiated information. This requires a mediator. The reference librarian is the mediator between the confused layperson and useful data. As such, the librarian will be required as never before.

THE REFERENCE PROCESS

The reference process consists of three primary elements:

1. *Information.* This comes in many formats. It may be in a traditional book or magazine or from a book or magazine as an electronic database, accessible by a computer. There is often too much of it, or not enough. It can be difficult to locate and even more challenging to interpret.

2. *The user.* This is the person who puts the question to the librarian, and often he or she is not quite sure how to frame the query. A basic problem in reference work is trying to determine precisely what type of answer is required.

3. *The reference librarian.* The key individual in the equation, the librarian, is the person who interprets the question, identifies the precise source for an answer, and, with the user, decides whether or not the response is adequate. The same librarian, when asked, will instruct the user on how to find information in an electronic or printed reference source.

Although a simple description of the reference process has been given here, this can never be definitive. Because of the rapid changes occurring in information technology, the reference process will continue to change too. But its goal remains the same—to answer questions.

Success as a Reference Librarian

Will you be a good reference librarian?

The answer depends as much upon the library as the individual. For example, on a large staff someone who delights in technology will find a position assisting with computer searches (either by the librarian or by the individual users) as well as keeping others advised of the best hardware, software, and the twists, turns, and off- and on-ramps of the information highway. Where the librarian is the only professional within four towns, the opportunities to master technological skills are checked by lack of money, lack of space, lack of time, and lack of the luxury of concentration on reference work. More likely, the average reference librarian is somewhere in between. On an average staff, there are a limited number of electronic databases. Much of the focus remains on print sources as well as help of individuals from student to geriatric veteran.

Reference librarians are unanimous about what the successful librarian needs: (1) Subject area knowledge. This means not only having a skilled appreciation of reference sources in general, but understanding better than anyone else how to dig out data from a given subject field. A generalist with a particular expertise is much sought after. (2) Conversational skills. This means an ability to talk to all types of people, to find out what they need. Furthermore, one should know whether a formal reference interview is required or whether it is easier to simply find the citation or answer. (3) Competence in selecting and acquiring materials—from computers and databases to print almanacs and biographical sources—is an absolute requirement.

Given the support of the proper information sources, a skill in interviewing, and a knowledge of a particular field, reference librarians should have an added dimension of sometimes hard-to-define values. Using quotations "directly from our own job ads," librarians have determined that the individual should have the following traits in addition to those previously discussed. The qualities are: "Flexibility, vision, leadership, commitment, ability to work collaboratively, understanding of the internal and external environment, potential for scholarly and professional achievement . . . good judgment, candor, sense of proportion and the practical, and commitment to excellence."[10] This paragon of all the virtues exists only, of course, in advertisements. Still, it is a useful list of possibilities and at the least indicates the responsibilities involved when dealing with information and people.

Public service is one of the most pleasurable aspects of the profession. There are drawbacks. Sometimes the questions asked will be repetitive, dull, or simple, although important to the person asking. Not everyone wants to know either the meaning of art or the best approach to ending the drug problem. In fact, the majority of reference queries are of a ready-reference type which require a quick, fact answer. These tend to be less than world shaking: What is the velocity of a sneeze? (Answer: Nearly 85 percent of the speed of sound.) What is the purpose of the half-moons on the base of our fingernails? (Answer: Apparently no purpose since they, the lunules, are little more than trapped air.) The most popular question put to *RO* (a magazine for reference librarians) concerns the history of the peace symbol. (Answer: It was originally used by a British group to protest nuclear war in the 1950s.)

[10]"Values and Qualities of Librarianship," discussion draft, January 18, 1992. The American Library Association's Strategic Visions Steering Committee, which first met in 1991, was organized to discuss critical issues facing, among others, reference librarians.

Reference Service Guidelines

The Reference and Adult Services Division of the American Library Association offers reference librarians a set of guidelines that help both to define their work and chart, if only in a tentative way, a philosophy of service. The guidelines are called "Information Services for Information Consumers: Guidelines for Providers" and "Behavioral Guidelines for Reference and Information Services."[11] Directed to all those who have any responsibility for providing reference and information services, the guidelines' most valuable contributions are the succinct description of a reference librarian's duties.

The guidelines address information services from six points of view: services, resources, access, personnel, evaluation, and ethics. The primary service is "to provide an end product: the information sought by the user." In a day when teaching people how to find information from a CD-ROM or online, instruction becomes a second important duty. "Such instruction can range from the individual explanation of information sources or creation of guides and appropriate media to formal assistance." There is a stress on the need for current, accurate resources as well as easy access to those sources and the reference librarian. A section on personnel underlines the importance of being "thoroughly familiar with and competent in using information sources." There is much more, but the statement concludes with an emphasis on the American Library Association's Code of Ethics which "governs the conduct of all staff members."

The ethics code leads to the next set of guidelines on evaluation of reference librarians and their services. In order to ensure "we collectively succeed" in the highly complex reference process, the "Behavioral Guidelines" urge librarians: (1) *Be approachable.* "The initial verbal and non-verbal responses of the librarian will influence the depth and level of the interaction between the librarian and the patron." (2) *Show interest.* "A successful librarian must demonstrate a high degree of interest in the reference transaction." (3) *Conduct a reference interview.* Here behavioral attributes which lead to a good interview are noted as well as methods of clarifying the patron's question. (4) *Conduct a search.* Again behavioral measures to aid in the search are listed, because "without an effective search, accurate information is unlikely to be found. (5) *Follow up.* "The reference transaction does not end when the librarian walks away from the patron. The librarian is responsible for determining if the patron is satisfied with the results of the search."

REFERENCE SERVICE AND THE LIBRARY

The reference librarian does not function alone in a library, but is part of a larger unit, a larger mission. Today the library is considerably more than a ware-

[11]"Information Services for Information Consumers: Guidelines for Providers," *RQ,* Winter 1990, pp. 262–265. "Behavioral Guidelines for References and Information Services," draft copy, 1994.

house of print materials. It is a media resource with promise for almost everyone.

The specific purpose of any library is to obtain, preserve, and make available the recorded knowledge of human beings. The system for achieving this goal can be as intricate and involved as the organizational chart for the Library of Congress or General Motors or as simple as that used in the one-person smalltown library or corner barbershop.

Regardless of organizational patterns or complexities, the functions of the system are interrelated and common to all sizes and types of libraries. They consist of administrative work, technical services (acquisitions and cataloging), and reader services (circulation and reference). These broad categories cover many subsections. Each is not an independent unit but rather a part of larger units; all are closely related. They form a unit essential for library service in general and for reference in particular. If one part of the system fails, the whole system suffers.

Administrative Work. Administration is concerned with library organization and communication. The better the administration functions, the less obvious it appears—at least to the user. Reference librarians must be aware of, and be prepared to participate in, administrative decisions ranging from budget to automation.

Technical Services: Acquisitions. The selection and acquisition of materials are determined by the type of library and its users. Policies vary, of course, but the rallying cry of the nineteenth-century activist librarians, "The right book for the right reader at the right time," is still applicable to any library today, as long as one understands "book" to include nonprint material. Reference librarians are responsible for the reference collection, but their responsibility extends to the development of the library's entire collection—a collection which serves to help them answer questions.

Technical Services: Cataloging. Once a library has acquired a piece of information, the primary problem becomes its retrieval from among the hundreds, thousands, or millions of other bits of information. A number of retrieval avenues are open, from oral communication to abstracts; but for dealing with larger information units such as books, recordings, films, periodicals, or reports, the normal finding device is the catalog. The catalog is the library's main bibliographical instrument. When properly used, it (1) enables persons to find books for which they have the author, the title, or the subject area; (2) shows what materials the library has by any given author, on a given subject, and in a given kind of literature; (3) assists in the choice of a book by its form (e.g., handbook, literature, or text) or edition; (4) assists in finding other materials, from government documents to films; and, often most important, (5) specifically locates the item in the library. It is a primary resource for reference librarians, and it is essential they understand not only the general aspects of the catalog but also its many peculiarities.

Most libraries now have replaced or augmented the familiar card catalog with an online public access catalog. This is constantly referred to in the literature as OPAC.[12] Today these catalogs often carry other data and are among the first facilities to be included in local or international networks. Most of the large 225 academic library catalogs in 10 countries are accessible through Internet and other linking devices. The librarian, or user, sits down before a computer terminal, types in a few key letters or parts of words, and is given immediate access to the holdings of the library or other libraries—often with additional data.

Technology. The rapid development of new technologies in information storage and retrieval has meant that larger libraries often have a special office, division, or section devoted to (1) keeping the administration and librarians advised of developments from new methods of networking to improved computer screens; (2) evaluating hardware, software, and other components of the modern information systems; and, in many cases, (3) determining what to buy, what to avoid, and how to work within a given budget.

Reader Services: Circulation. Circulation is one of the two primary public service points in the library. After a book has been acquired and prepared for easy access, the circulation department is concerned with (1) checking out the material to the reader, (2) receiving it on return, and (3) returning it to its proper location.

Adult Services: Reference. An important component of reference service is adult services, often used as a synonym for "adult education." This is a specialized area, although in daily work the average reference librarian will be involved in a range of adult services such as giving assistance with job and occupational information or providing service for the handicapped.

REFERENCE QUESTIONS

There are two or three traditional library approaches to analyzing reference questions. The usual is to count how many questions are asked, and how long it takes to give an answer. This is noted for statistical reports and, not incidentally, to rationalize need for more money and personnel. The practice continues today, but there is equal focus on types of questions. Not that categorization is easy. Given access by users to CD-ROMs or online searches, it is difficult

---

[12]Nicholson Baker, "Discards," *The New Yorker,* April 4, 1994, pp. 64–86. The novelist, who apparently at one time worked in a university library, deplores the scrapping of catalog cards in favor of online service. Most of his effort is spent on a relatively clear explanation of OCLC and networking.

at times to determine what kind of questions they are asking, other than how to use the equipment. Still, where analysis is employed the framework for queries remains much the same. This can be divided into two general types:

1. *The user asks for a known item.* The request is usually for a specific document, book, article, film, or other item, which can be identified by citing certain features such as an author, a title, or a source. The librarian has only to locate the needed item through the catalog, an index, a bibliography, or a similar source—and, often, all are searchable at a computer terminal.

2. *The user asks for information without any knowledge of a specific source.* Such a query triggers the reference interview—an important consideration in reference services discussed throughout this text and most particularly in the second volume. Most reference questions are of a general type, particularly those in school and public libraries where the average user has little or no knowledge of the reference services available.

Handling the two broad types of questions may not be as easy as it seems. For example, the person who asks for a specific book by author may (1) have the wrong author, (2) actually want a different book by that author, (3) discover that the wanted book is not the one required (for either information or pleasure), or (4) ask the librarian to obtain the book on interlibrary loan and then fail to appear when the book is received. All this leads most experienced reference librarians to qualify the "known-item" type of question. The assumption made by the librarian is usually correct, and the user really needs more information or help than indicated. Therefore, librarians tend to ask enough questions to clarify the real needs of the user rather than accept what may be only a weak signal for help.

A more finely drawn categorization of reference questions can be divided into four types:

1. *Direction.* "Where is the catalog?" "Where are the indexes?" "Where is the telephone?" The general information or directional question is of the information booth variety, and the answer rarely requires more than geographical knowledge of key locations. The time required to answer such questions is negligible, but directional queries can account for 30 to 50 percent of the questions put to a librarian in any day. The percentages given here and in what follows are relative and may vary from library to library.

2. *Ready reference.* "What is the name of the governor of Alaska?" "How long is the Amazon River?" "Who is the world's tallest person?" These are the typical ready-reference or data queries that require only a single, usually uncomplicated, straightforward answer. The requested information is normally found without difficulty in standard reference works, ranging from encyclope-

dias to almanacs and indexes. Many of these may be accessed through a computer terminal.

Ready-reference queries may be divided and subdivided in many ways. Crossing almost all subject lines, one can construct a classification scheme similar to the news reporter's five W's. These are (*a*) *Who?* Who is . . . ; Who said . . . ; Who won . . . ; and so forth. (*b*) *What?* What is the speed of sound? What are the qualities of a good swimmer? What does coreopsis look like? (*c*) *Where?* Where is the center of the United States? Where is the earth's core? (*d*) *Why?* Why does water boil? Why, why, why . . . almost anything. (This, the favored beginning of all children's queries, continues with most of us through life.) (*e*) *When?* When was *Coriolanus* written? When was the automobile invented? Most of these queries require only a specific piece of data. Also, many might be modified or rephrased in such a way as to get a yes, no, or maybe answer: Is aspirin harmful? Was America discovered in 1492?

It usually takes more than a minute or two to answer this type of question. The catch is that while 90 percent of such queries are simple to answer, another 5 to 10 percent may take hours of research because no standard reference source in the library will yield the necessary data. Apparently simple questions are sometimes complicated, such as "What are the dates of National Cat Week?" (Answer: Flexible, but usually in early November.) "When and where was Russian roulette first played?" (Answer: Cambridge University in 1801. Lord Byron describes the incident in his memoirs.) Difficult questions of this type are often printed in a regular column in *RQ*, the official journal of reference librarians, and are a popular Internet Listserv as STUMPERS.[13]

The percentage of ready-reference questions will differ from library to library, but about 50 to 60 percent of the questions asked in a public library are of the ready-reference type. Public libraries, which may have a well-developed phone service for reference questions as well as a high percentage of adult users, tend to attract the ready-reference question. Requests for background information make up the other 40 to 50 percent or so of the queries.

In academic, school, and special libraries, specific-search questions account for a larger percentage of the total.

3. *Specific-search questions.* "Where can I find information on sexism in business?" "What is the difference between the conservative and the liberal views on inflation and unemployment?" "Do you have anything on the history of atomic energy?" "I have to write a paper on penguins for my science class. What do you have?" The essential difference between the specific-search and the ready-reference question is important. Ready-reference queries usually can be answered with data, normally short answers from reference books. Specific-search answers almost always take the form of giving the user a document, for example, a list of citations, a book, or a report.

---

[13]The column, called "The Exchange," has various editors. It is devoted to "tricky questions, notes on unusual information sources, [and] general comments concerning reference problems. . . . "

More information is required if the user is writing a school paper, is preparing a speech, or is simply interested in learning as much about a subject as necessary for his or her needs. This query often is called a *bibliographical inquiry*, because the questioner is referred to a bibliographical aid such as the catalog, an index, or a bibliography. Most of these, even in small libraries, are available on CD-ROM or online, and makes searching much easier—*if*, and the "if" should be stressed, the user knows how to get information from the electronic database. At this point the librarian may have to step in to offer help.

Of course, not all specific-search questions involve bibliographies. At a less sophisticated level, the librarian may merely direct the user to an article in an encyclopedia, to a given section of the book collection, or to a CD-ROM newspaper index.

The time it takes to answer a user's question depends not only on what is available, but also on the librarian. If the librarian offers a considerable amount of help, the search can take from 10 minutes to an hour or more. Conversely, a less helpful or busier librarian may turn the question into a directional one by simply pointing the user to the catalog or the computer.

Some types of specific-search questions are treated by librarians as reader advisory problems. These are questions that, in essence, ask "What is the best source of information for my needs?" Questioners may be seeking everything from fiction and poetry to hobby magazines. Depending on the size and the organizational pattern of the library, their queries may be handled by subject or reader advisory librarians or by reference librarians. In a small library these are one and the same person.

4. *Research.* Almost any of the types of questions described in the "specific-search" section above may be turned into research questions. A research query is usually identified as that coming from an adult specialist who is seeking detailed information to assist in specific work. The request may be from a professor, a business executive, a scientist, or other person who needs data for a decision or additional information about a problem. With the exception of some academic and special libraries, this type of inquiry is a negligible part of the total reference pattern in libraries.

Ready-reference and specific-search queries presuppose specific answers and specific sources, which, with practice, the librarian usually can locate quickly. Research questions differ from other inquiries in that most involve trial-and-error searching or browsing, primarily because (*a*) the average researcher may have a vague notion of the question but usually cannot be specific; (*b*) the answer to the yet-to-be-completely formulated question depends on what the researcher is able to find (or not find). The researcher recognizes a problem, identifies the area that is likely to cover the problem, and then attempts to find what has been written about the problem.

There is another useful method of distinguishing types of queries. The first two types of queries (directional and ready-reference) may be classified as *data retrieval,* that is, individuals have specific questions and expect answers in the form of data. The specific-search and research questions might be classified as *document retrieval* in that the users want information, not just simple answers, and the information is usually in the form of some type of document, for example, book, report, or article.

Few situations require or, indeed, even allow opportunity to categorize questions in this manner; and this is just as well. A ready-reference query can quickly turn into a specific-search question, and someone embarked on research may have a few ready-reference questions related to that quest.

The difficulty with the categorization of reference questions is that few are that easy to label. True, when someone asks for the bathroom, this is a simple directional query. True, when another person needs material on the salmon, this is a specific-search question. At the same time, a directional question may turn into a ready-reference query, and a specific-search need may develop into research.

For example, the young person who asks for material on the salmon actually may be interested in knowing where one can catch salmon in the immediate area. Hence a supposed search question is really a ready-reference query. Conversely, someone may ask where to catch salmon, although that person really wants to know about fishing conservation. A ready-reference question has been turned inside out into a search or even a research problem.

Who Is to Answer?

The fascinating result of analyses of types of questions is that (1) the majority of queries are directional or ready-reference pure and simple; (2) generally, the queries and sources used are basic and easy to understand; and (3) most questions, therefore, could be answered by a well-trained person with a bachelor's degree.

But that does not necessarily mean that the trained nonprofessional can or should replace the professional librarian for the purpose of answering directional and ready-reference queries. Often the simple questions can develop into complex ones requiring professional aid. Even where nonprofessionals are used sparingly, the average library can depend on nonreference librarians to help at the reference desk.

Does it make any difference whether a professional librarian or a clerk answers a reference question? No—if the question is answered to the satisfaction of the user. Yes—if either the clerk or the librarian fails to follow through with enough of the right information, or totally strikes out. If the clerk is better-educated, more personable and, yes, more experienced than the librarian, it may be that the clerk scores higher. Odds are, though, that the professional will do better because of superior knowledge. In fact, professionals score higher because they know what and how much is needed for individual requests. This hardly resolves the problem of using nonprofessionals, but study after study indicates that the trained librarian (like the trained mechanic, doctor, postal worker, or writer) will do better than the casual employee.[14]

Many, perhaps too many, librarians believe that the student, whether a child in grade school or a graduate student in university, fits into a special category. As they have come to learn, they should learn how to use the library. They should be able to answer their own queries. Hence the reliance on bibliographical training (covered in Chapter 9 of the second volume of this text) for students. Teaching is rare for businesspeople and regular library readers, although these days they may be taught the fundamentals of how to use a CD-ROM system.

Reference Interview

The most common complaint heard among reference librarians about their work is that few people know how to ask reference questions. There are many reasons why the public may not appreciate the need for clarity at the reference desk, and these reasons are considered throughout this text. The reference interview has several objectives. The first is to find out what and how much data the user needs. This should be simplicity itself, except that most people do not know how to frame questions. The child looking for information on horses may be interested in pictures, an encyclopedia article, or possibly a book on riding. No matter what the scope of the query, it probably will come out as "Do you have anything on horses?"

Once the actual needs of the library patron are understood, the next step is to formulate a search strategy of possible sources. To do so requires translating the terms of the question into the language of the reference system. If a basic book on gardening is required, the librarian will find it readily enough in the catalog under a suitable subject heading or a key word. At the other extreme, the question may involve searching print, online, or CD-ROM indexes, such as the *Biological & Agricultural Index,* to find the latest information on elm blight, or perhaps checking out various bibliographies, such as *Subject Guide to Books in Print* or a union catalog, to find what may be available on elm blight in other libraries. Once the information is found, it has to be evaluated. That is, the librarian must determine whether it is really the exact kind and level of information that the patron wants: Is it too technical or too simple? Is it applicable in this geographical area?

The user has some notion of what is wanted, both in terms of quantity and quality. Yet, that same user may be vague about whether or not an article

[14]This is not to endorse second-grade "citizenship" for nonprofessionals. Quite the contrary. No library could function without these valuable individuals, and they deserve all the fringe benefits enjoyed by professional librarians.

should be used from a particular journal. The qualifications of the author and publisher are better known to the librarian than to the average user. For example, in a string of 10 citations about solar energy, would a high school senior, a college senior, or a layperson be happier with citations from *Time, Reader's Digest,* and *Newsweek,* or from the *Monthly Energy Review, EPRI Journal,* and *Solar Energy*? These fundamental decisions of the librarian will be of great help to the average user.

The reference interview often, all too often, is short-circuited by lack of interest on the part of the librarian, lack of knowledge of such help by the user, and lack of patience by user or librarian as the interview begins.

Users who have become acquainted with the ease of searching at a library computer terminal, often will avoid the librarian. Type in a few key words, a personal name, a subject heading, and if the database matches the query, four or five citations come up on the screen. That's quite enough for the average student or layperson who believes this is the end of the quest. It may be only the beginning or a total dead end, and it is here, or better, before the search begins, that the interview is extremely useful.

Information, Computers, and the Public

Of the 190 to 195 million adults (in about 96 million households) in the United States, about 40 percent have personal computers (PCs) in 1996. Forty-five to 55 percent of high school and college students have home computers (for minorities the figure is 15 to 25 percent). A late 1995 survey showed "5.8 million American adults are connected directly to the Internet. Another 3.5 million American adults use only commercial on-line services, like America Online."[15]

Why an interest in the PC? Unfortunately, most are purchased for something less than information seeking. First and foremost, they are seen as vehicles for word processing and to carry on conversations over the Internet by means of e-mail and through news groups. Second, they afford better definition for the fastest growing use of CD-ROM for multimedia games and entertainment. Third, they can be used for home shopping, spreadsheets, and business activities. Last, and often least, they are seen as methods of gaining information from the Internet, commercial networks, CD-ROMs, and so forth.

If only about half the public uses a library, an even smaller group has access to a computer. A public poll commissioned in late 1993 by the Institute of Electrical and Electronics Engineers found that new technologies are of minor interest to most Americans. Only 15 percent of those questioned think the information revolution holds any interest. In fact only 7 percent thought the in-

---

[15]"Digital Services Draw Consumers," *The New York Times,* January 7, 1995, p. 39. "Who Uses Internet?" *Ibid.* September 27, 1995, p. D2. Home sales of computers have risen about 20 percent each year since and as the price of the hardware comes down, some believe that by the turn of the century at least one-half of American homes will have computers and interactive televisions.

teractive promises of computers would change entertainment and leisure time. Close to half thought health and medical care would do more to change their lives than any other scientific development. "Of course people are not so much ignorant of the grand visions of the future clogged relentlessly by high-tech experts as they are skeptical that the promised benefits will materialize."[16]

INFORMATION SOURCES

Less than a decade ago information sources were synonymous with the printed book. Today the definition is turned on its electronic head. Basic reference sources are available online or as CD-ROMs. It is unusual to use only printed reference works unless one is seeking information before the early 1980s. Few electronic sources are retrospective. Some believe that before or slightly after the turn of the century all major information sources, and particularly those used daily by reference librarians, will be in electronic form. Many, in fact, will not be available in print.

Be that as it may, the content, if not methods of retrieval, remains the same no matter what format the publisher chooses. It is essential that the professional librarian be able to turn to X or Y source for the proper answer to X or Y question. How many titles should the new librarian be familiar with when taking over a reference position?

The basic guides, directories, and bibliographies of reference sources— such as *Guide to Reference Books* or *Gale Directory of Databases*—list and annotate from close to 10,000 databases to 15,000 printed reference books. Selected guidelines for a given subject or size of library may range in number from a few hundred to about 2000. "Best Reference Books of 19–," a regular annual selection in *Library Journal,* normally selects 30 to 40 titles as the "best" of the year.

The public has its own list. Regular "reference best sellers" include standard types if not always specific titles. In late 1993, for example, among the 20 best sellers were books familiar to most students: *The Old Farmer's Almanac, The Chicago Manual of Style, The World Almanac, Writer's Market, Leonard Maltin's Movie and Video Guide, MLA Handbook for Writers, Lazar's Shop by Mail, Places Rated Almanac, Great Speeches,* and *The People's Almanac.* Guides to the law, animal care, maps, colleges, quotations, first aid, and almost anything likely to bisect the average person's life are favored.[17] An average American home will have at least a dictionary, an encyclopedia, and possibly an almanac.

[16]"Americans See Future and Say, So What?" *The New York Times,* October 7, 1993, p. D4.

[17]"Reference Best Sellers," *Library Journal,* December 1993, p. 107. "The list includes titles most in demand by libraries and bookstores from Baker & Taylor Books nationwide for six months prior to the week ending November 9, 1993." Specific titles change from year to year, but the subject matter is pretty much of a constant.

How many reference titles in print, CD-ROM, online, and in yet-to-be-revealed formats should the student master? There is no single answer. There are numerous variables. Also, each library has its own "core" collection, its own "canon." In this text about 400 to 500 titles are considered basic. At the other extreme, in his *Distinguished Classics of Reference Publishing*, which moves from quotations to encyclopedias, James Rettig and friends agree that there are at least 31 "major reference works" which anyone worthy of the name of reference librarian should know.[18] As a rule of thumb, the beginner should be familiar with the much-used titles, from bibliography and indexes to encyclopedias and almanacs, found in every library. This amounts to mastering between 100 to 300 reference works. Beyond that is the universe of 15,000-plus titles.

The Control-Access-Directional Type of Source

The first broad class or form of reference sources is the bibliography. This form is variously defined, but in its most general sense it is a systematically produced descriptive list of records.

Control. The bibliography serves as a control device, a kind of checklist. It inventories what is produced from day to day and year to year in such a way as to enable both the compiler and the user to feel they have a control, through organization, of the steady flow of knowledge. The bibliography is prepared through research (finding the specific source), identification, description, and classification.

Access. Once the items are controlled, the individual items are organized for easy access to facilitate intellectual work. All the access types of reference works can be broadly defined as bibliographies; but they may be subdivided as follows:

1. Bibliographies of reference sources and the literature of a field, of either a general or a subject nature, for example, *Guide to Reference Books* or *The Information Sources of Political Science*.

2. The library catalog or the catalogs of numerous libraries arranged for easy access at a computer or through a union list. Technically, these are not bibliographies but are often used in the same manner.

3. General systematic enumerative bibliographies, which include various forms of bibliography, for example, *The National Union Catalog*.

4. Indexes and abstracts, which are usually treated separately from bibliographies but are considered bibliographical aids—systematic listings

---

[18]James Rettig, ed., *Distinguished Classics of Reference Publishing* (Phoenix, AZ: Oryx Press, 1992).

which help identify and trace materials. Indexes to the contents of magazines and newspapers are the most frequently used types in the reference situation. Examples: *The Readers' Guide to Periodical Literature* and *The New York Times Index*.

Direction. Bibliographies themselves normally do not give definitive answers, but serve to direct users to the sources of answers. For their effective use, the items listed must be either in the library or available from another library system.

These days most access and control sources of reference works are available not only in print, but also in electronic digital form. This is not so true for the next form, the source type.

Source Type

Works of source type usually suffice in themselves to give the answers. Unlike the access type of reference work, they are synoptic.

Encyclopedias. The single most-used sources are encyclopedias; they may be defined as works containing informational articles on subjects in every field of knowledge, usually arranged in alphabetical order. They are used to answer specific questions about X topic or Y person or general queries which may begin with "I want something about Z." Examples: *Encyclopaedia Britannica; World Book Encyclopedia.* Today, most are available in CD-ROM as well as in print. A few are available online.

Fact Sources. Yearbooks, almanacs, handbooks, manuals, and directories are included in this category. All have different qualities, but they share one common element: They are used to look up factual material for quick reference. Together, they cover many facets of human knowledge. Examples: *World Almanac; Statesman's Year Book.*

Dictionaries. Sources that deal primarily with all aspects of words, from proper definitions to spelling, are classified as dictionaries. Examples: *Webster's Third New International Dictionary; Dictionary of American Slang.*

Biographical Sources. The self-evident sources of information on people distinguished in some particular field of interest are known as biographical sources. Examples: *Who's Who; Current Biography.*

Geographical Sources. The best-known forms are the atlases, which not only show given countries but may illustrate themes such as historical development, social development, and scientific centers. Geographical sources also include gazetteers, dictionaries of place names, and guidebooks. Example: *The Times Atlas of the World*.

Government Documents

Government documents are official publications ordered and normally published by federal, state, and local governments. Since they may include directional and source works, their separation into a particular unit is more for convenience and organization than for different reference use. Examples: *Monthly Catalog of United States Government Publications* (access type); *United States Government Manual* (source type).

The neat categorization of reference types by access and by source is not always distinct in an actual situation. A bibliography may be the only source required if the question is merely one of verification or of trying to complete a bibliographical citation. Conversely, the bibliography at the end of an encyclopedia article or a statement in that article may direct the patron to another source. In general, the two main categories—access and source—serve to differentiate among the principal types of reference works.

Enter the Computer

Today, as in the past, a convenient method of mastering reference sources is to divide them into the aforementioned categories. Information may now be stored electronically in such a way that divisions among encyclopedias, biographies, and government documents are no longer needed. A vast electronic database of reference material includes all these. Sitting at a computer one is able to search not just an index, not just a bibliography, but many forms of reference works at the same time.

With that, though, it is necessary to appreciate the reference librarian who can differentiate sources of information (index or encyclopedia, yearbook or government document) and is able to ascertain what is likely to be best for the individual with a query. Forms, therefore, remain and will continue to remain important as guides to types of content, reliability, relative currency, and so on. So no matter how the sources are bunched together electronically, it is imperative to be able to differentiate fruit as an orange, an apple, or a pear.

EVALUATING REFERENCE SOURCES

A thorough understanding of the day-to-day sources of answers requires some evaluation of those sources. How does the librarian know whether a reference source is good, bad, or indifferent? A more detailed answer will be found throughout each of the chapters in this volume. Simply stated, however, a good reference source is one that answers questions, and a poor reference source is one that fails to answer questions. Constant use in practice will help in identifying any source (whether a book or a database) with one of these two categories.

What follows is primarily concerned with traditional reference books, but much of it is applicable to other reference forms, including computer, online, and CD-ROM. At the same time these various electronic reference sources have their own particular evaluation problems.

Because of the expense of most reference sources, the typical practice is to read one or more reviews before deciding whether to buy them, or in the case of many CD-ROMs, lease them. Groups of databases available online require some decision as to which vendor to use, or how many vendors, in order to gain access to online titles.

Large libraries usually request, or automatically receive examination copies of print reference works before purchase. Similar arrangements for trials of CD-ROMs, tapes, vendors, and so forth, may be arranged as well. Smaller libraries usually have no choice but to accept the word of the reviewer and order, or not order, the work. Ideally, the reference source should be examined by a trained reference librarian before it is incorporated into the collection. No reviewer, review, or review medium is infallible.

Evaluation of Databases

Effective evaluation of the content of electronic databases depends on methods similar to those employed for evaluating the content of printed works. Purpose, authority, and scope are to be tested.

There are additional considerations. One must evaluate the various formats: How are the data accessed? Does it meet the specific needs of the average user? How is the work to be updated and how often? What hardware and software are necessary to make use of the database to its fullest? Is the search easy or difficult for a beginner, for a trained librarian? Is there documentation, that is, manuals, and so on? Is someone on call when help is needed?

One must also size up the comparative costs of the different vendors, various formats, and individual database charges against the speed and efficiency of the computer search. One should also scrutinize pricing policies.

Evaluative measures are considered throughout the text as each database or group of databases is examined, whether on a CD-ROM, online, or in print. This is to say that there are general valuative rules, but every reference source must be judged individually.

Evaluative Points: Content

Whether in print or an electronic database, there are basic evaluative points concerning the all-important content. The librarian must ask at least four basic questions about a reference work: What is its purpose? Its authority? Its scope? Its proposed audience? Finally, the format of the work must be considered. These questions are as applicable to the *World Almanac* in print as the CD-ROM index, *ABI/Inform.*

1. *Purpose.* The purpose of a reference work should be evident from the title or form. The evaluative question must be posed: Has the author or compiler fulfilled the purpose? In an encyclopedia of dance, for example, has the purpose of capturing essential information about the dance been achieved? But immediately the librarian must ask other questions: What kind of dance and for what period? For what age group, experience, or sophistication in dance? For what countries? Is the emphasis on history, biography, practical application, or some other element?

The clues to purpose are found in:

a. The contents

b. The introduction or preface, which should give details about what the author or compiler expects this work to accomplish

c. The index, the sampling of which will tell what subjects are covered

A printed reference book without an index is usually of little or no value. Exceptions are dictionaries, indexes, directories, and other titles where the index is built into an alphabetical arrangement. This system is suitable for the data type of reference work, but not for running prose, where an index is absolutely essential.

Other hints about the purpose of a specific work are often given in the publisher's catalog, in advance notices received in the mail, and in the copy on the jacket or cover of the book. Such descriptions may help to indicate purpose and even relative usefulness, but are understandably less than objective.

In electronic format one will rely more on the publisher's or vendor's descriptive material than on actual examination of, say, the CD-ROM. Here, particularly because of high cost and lack of immediate access, reviews are of major importance.

2. *Authority.* The question of purpose brings one close to a whole series of questions that relate to the author:

a. What are the author's (or compiler's) qualifications for the fulfillment of his or her purpose? If the writer is a known scholar, there is no problem with authority. The difficulty arises with the other 95 percent of reference works prepared by experts, but not by those experts who make the best-seller lists. Here the librarian must rely on (1) the qualifications of the author given in the book; (2) the librarian's own understanding and depth of knowledge of the subject; and (3) a check of the author in standard biographical works such as *Who's Who* or *American Men and Women of Science.*

b. The imprint of the publisher may indicate the relative worth of a book. Some publishers have excellent reputations for issuing reference works; others are known for their fair-to-untrustworthy titles. Again, the librarian's expertise and experience are important.

c. Objectivity and fairness of a work are important considerations, particularly in reference works that rely on prose rather than simple statistics or collections of facts. Does the author have a bias about politics, religion, race, sex, or the proper type of color to paint a study? No one is totally objective, but those who write reference books must indicate the worth of both sides when there is a matter of controversy.

All these questions hold for CD-ROMs, online databases, and so on. Again, it is worth emphasizing that the format is incidental to the content and certainly to the authority of the author, compiler, or editor.

3. *Scope.* Other questions of major importance in selecting a reference work: Will this book (CD-ROM) be a real addition to our collection, and if so, what exactly will it add? The publisher usually will state the scope of the book (online database) in the publicity blurb or in the preface, but the librarian should be cautious. The author may or may not have achieved the scope claimed. For example, the publisher may claim that a historical atlas covers all nations and all periods. The librarian may check the scope of the new historical atlas by comparing it against standard works. Does the new work actually include *all* nations and *all* periods, or does it exclude material found in the standard works? If an index claims to cover all major articles in certain periodicals, a simple check of the periodicals' articles against the index will reveal the actual scope of the index.

a. What has the author contributed that cannot be found in other bibliographies, indexes, handbooks, almanacs, atlases, dictionaries, and so on? If the work is comprehensive within a narrow subject field, one may easily check it against other sources. For example, a who's who of education which limits itself to educators in the major colleges and universities in the Northeast may easily be checked for scope by comparing the current college catalog of P & Q University against the new who's who. If a number of faculty members are missing from the new work, one may safely conclude that the scope is not what is claimed.

b. Currency is one of the most important features of any reference work, particularly one used for ready reference. Data change so quickly that last year's almanac may be historically important but of little value in answering today's queries. An electronic database should be more current, but this is not always true. Online, it usually is up to date, but a CD-ROM may be issued quarterly, and actually well behind, say, the printed monthly title.

Most reference works (in print, CD-ROMs, etc.) contain some dated information. The best method of ascertaining whether the dated material is of value and of checking the recency factor is to sample the work. This is a matter of looking for names currently in the news, population figures, geographical boundaries, records of achievement, news events, and almost any other recent fact consistent with the purpose and scope of the work. It is important to remember that no reference work should be accepted or rejected after sampling only one or two items.

If the work purports to be a new edition (an updated CD-ROM), the extent of claimed revisions should be carefully evaluated. This can easily be done by checking the work against the earlier edition (disc) or by noting any great discrepancy between the dates of the cited materials and the date of publication.

4. *Audience.* With the exception of juvenile encyclopedias, most reference works regardless of format are prepared for adults. When considering the question of audience, the librarian must ask one major question: Is this work for the scholar or student of the subject, or is it for the layperson with little or no knowledge? For example, in the field of organic chemistry, Beilstein's *Handbuch der Organischen Chemie* is as well known to chemists as the "top 10" tunes are to music fans. It is decidedly for the student with some basic knowledge of chemistry. Often the distinction in terms of audience is not so clear-cut.

A useful method of checking the reading level of a given reference work is for the librarian to examine a subject well known to him or her and then turn to one that is not so well understood. If both are comprehended, if the language is equally free of jargon and technical terminology, if the style is informative yet lively, the librarian can be reasonably certain the work is for the layperson. Of course, if the total work is beyond the subject competency of the librarian, advice should be sought from a subject expert. Still, this is an unlikely situation, since reference librarians tend to be experts in fields within which they operate.

Other Evaluation Factors

Beyond the basic evaluation of content, no matter what the format, there are other major evaluative points to consider. Briefly, they include:

1. *Cost.* A major factor of frustration in the evaluation and purchase of reference works is the expense involved. This is particularly true of the ubiquitous electronic reference sources whose price and cost patterns seem to be constantly in flux. The only thing certain is that they cost much more than print, at least at the present. In time this will change and prices will drop. Meanwhile many of the new technologies are often quite beyond the budget of underfinanced libraries. Budget, rather than client need, may determine whether a particular work is purchased.

Reference service, even on a minimum scale, can be a luxury. Approximately 80 percent of the public libraries in the United States serve a population of under 25,000. Although not all rural communities are financially starved, the majority are poor. Most libraries in these areas, with or without state or federal aid, suffer from a lack of reference materials, and 75 percent lack any user education in reference services.

2. *Format.* One of the most meaningful questions about printed works concerns arrangement, treated here as part of the format. Arrangement is of major importance for print reference works. In electronic databases, which can be searched by the user, the arrangement per se is of no real importance. How to search the database, however, is of major concern.

Some reference works (e.g., the citation indexes and online databases) are complicated and difficult to use. When this is the case, some librarians tend to avoid them, resulting in poor service to the user as well as a feeling of incompetence on the part of the librarian.

Even the most carefully designed print work can be a nuisance if it is bound so that the pages do not lie flat or if it makes no clear distinction between headings on a page and subheads within the page. The apparatuses of abbreviation, typography, symbol, and indication of cross-reference must be clear and in keeping with what the user is likely to recognize. The use of offset printing from computerized materials has resulted in some disturbing complexities of format. For example, it may be impossible to tell West Virginia, when abbreviated, from western Virginia. Uniform lowercase letters would be equally confusing. Lack of spacing between lines, poor paper, little or no margins, and other hindrances to reading are all too evident even in some standard reference works.

A word regarding illustrations: When photographs, charts, tables, and diagrams are used, they should be current, clear, and related to the text. They should be adjacent to the material under discussion or at least clearly identified. In multimedia CD-ROMs and online services, a major problem tends to be the clarity of the pictures, photographs, films, and animation. Depending on the particular software, illustration may be better than most printed works or it may be much worse. Generally, it is the latter, although this is improving.

The last word on evaluation may sound as cynical or as simplistic as the reader cares to interpret it, but it is this: Trust no one. The reviewer, the publisher, and the author do make mistakes, sometimes of horrendous proportions. The librarian who evaluates reference sources with constant suspicion is less likely to be the victim of those mistakes. Whenever possible examine and use the work in question. Make your own evaluation!

To Publish or Not To Publish

An evaluative method that is rarely considered is a totally effective one. It is the refusal of a publisher to proceed with a reference work that is found wanting. Essentially the decision to publish a particular text is one of determining whether a market for the title exists and whether there is duplication of the proposed effort in another published work. Perhaps because the market for reference titles is largely institutional and libraries are the primary buyers, publishers field-test ideas with librarians. If little or no market seems possible, the idea, no matter how useful it may be to a few librarians, is dropped.

CONCLUSION

What should one learn in basic training for reference work or, for that matter, the profession as a whole?

Getting to feel at home behind a reference desk requires that the beginner master reference works. One must feel comfortable at a computer terminal as well as talking with a less-than-verbal user who is looking for a jam recipe or a way to get through to the next day.

In time the beginner becomes a veteran. And veteran librarians never quit, or are fired, or die. They simply gain fame as being among the wisest people in the world. One could do worse.

SUGGESTED READING

Campbell, Jerry, "Shaking the Conceptual Foundations of Reference: A Perspective," *Reference Services Review*, Winter 1992, pp. 25–29. Examining the new electronic library, a university librarian adopts the idea that librarians should now be called "access engineers" (or the equivalent). He thinks this indicates their true role, implying a reduction in the need to answer questions, which can be done by computers, and an appreciation for the intellectual capacities of the librarian.

Childers, Tom, "California's Reference Crisis," *Library Journal*, April 15, 1994. A hard look at what is happening in one state when budgets are cut. The California nightmare seems to be more the pattern than the exception. A sobering, objective view of American attitudes.

Crawford, Walt, and Michael Gorman, *Future Libraries*. Chicago: American Library Association, 1995. Is technology the beginning and end of reference services? No, say the authors and they show how librarians can embrace new technologies while retaining their traditional humanistic roles. A valuable counterargument to what the authors term "technovandals."

Cromer, Donna, and Andrea Testi, "Integrated Continuing Education for Reference Librarians," *Reference Services Review*, Winter 1994, pp. 51–58. The authors point out the necessary ingredients of a program to keep librarians current in their subject fields. While the focus here is on science, most of the points are applicable to other subject areas.

Eberhart, George, ed., *The Whole Library Handbook*, 2d ed. Chicago: American Library Association, 1995. In this second edition, the editor brings together a mass of facts and statistics about American libraries. The 10 sections open with "some basic figures," move on to "who works in libraries," and discuss day-to-day operations, technologies, and so forth. Little is overlooked and it is an excellent reference source, particularly for out-of-the-way data. Beginners will find that even a cursory look will give them much basic information on the profession.

Information for a New Age. Englewood, CO: Libraries Unlimited, 1994. A series of papers presented at an American Library Association meeting; the collection considers everything from bibliographic instruction to the future of the reference librarian. Answers are sought to the universal query, "How will the librarian's role change in the new information age?" The answers are literate, well-informed, and current.

Katz, Bill, "Opportunities for Reference Services: The Bright Side of Reference Services in the 1990s," *The Reference Librarian*, no. 33, 1991. James Rettig begins this issue with the keynote article, "Joy Is Bustin Out All Over." Other experts point out the delights of being a reference librarian, particularly in the 1990s. An upbeat, yet realistic view of a great profession.

Lipow, Anne G., ed., *Rethinking Reference in Academic Libraries*. Berkeley, CA: Library Solutions Press, 1993. Some 35 different experts respond to the question of the shape of future reference services. While the focus is on academic libraries, much of the material is applicable to other types of libraries.

Nugent, Amy, "The Best Library Jobs in America?" *Library Journal*, March 15, 1994, pp. 32–35. Eight different library jobs are considered and the opinion is that these represent the best, at least according to the 50 librarians surveyed. While the specific positions are not available, certainly similar positions are open. Reference librarians, as might be expected, are often considered to be in the best library position.

Plum, Terry, "Academic Libraries and the Rituals of Knowledge," *RQ*, Summer 1994, pp. 496–508. An imaginative approach to what will and will not work in bringing new technology to libraries. Gradual change, conforming with older methodologies of obtaining information, and appreciation of hierarchy will help in the transformation.

"The Publishing and Review of Reference Sources," *The Reference Librarian*, Fall 1986. The entire 336-page issue is devoted to this subject and includes a variety of viewpoints from reviewers, publishers, and librarians.

Rettig, James, ed., *Distinguished Classics of Reference Publishing*. Phoenix, AZ: Oryx Press, 1992. The one-man guide to the best in reference books (a monthly feature in *The Wilson Library Bulletin*) as well as an experienced librarian, Rettig asked for essays on outstanding works in the field. The result is this informative, charming, and witty look at the history and use of 31 famous titles, as well as a few cousins and aunts. A marvelous introduction.

"Rothstein on Reference," *The Reference Librarian*, nos. 25/28, 1990. The 650-page issue of the journal includes: (1) writings by the world's leading expert on the history and function of reference services, and (2) writings by his friends on the same subject. Rothstein should be required reading for any student or working reference librarian. His work is a basic point of departure for a clear, intelligent view of the whole problem of answering questions, whether it be in a small public library or in the largest specialized information center. Of all the readings in this book, let this be the first.

Short, Randall, "You Can Look It Up," *The New York Times Book Review*, January 27, 1991, pp. 1, 16. A popular writer gives an equally popular definition of a reference work and then goes on to discuss the "stranger animals" that make up much of any reference section. "Everything in the world exists in order that it may end up in a book," he says. That fairly well summarizes the scope of the reference library.

Stam, Deirdre, "What Reference Librarians Need to Know," *The Bookmark*, Winter 1992, pp. 173–179. An informal survey of working librarians reveals the practical aspects of what one has to know. Most agree that first and foremost the librarian must be able to get along with people, and second be able to match questions with sources.

CHAPTER TWO
THE ELECTRONIC LIBRARY

The day of seeking answers has not ended. Only the process has changed. Now a librarian may find answers, often with greater speed and usually with considerably less difficulty, by using a computer rather than a standard printed source. Taking only minutes, the librarian can search thousands of periodicals, scores of books, reports, and studies to discover answers.

At a computer terminal a user may weigh the implications of the greenhouse effect, decide when the term itself was first employed, and pinpoint who in Washington, D.C., is an authority on the subject. Multiple-entry points on an electronic database allow one to retrieve brief facts, names, headlines, or statistics as well as the complete text of an article, report, or even a book.

Electronic information accessing has two basic dimensions which distinguish it from the printed book. The first is an almost unlimited storage capacity that continually expands. The second aspect is the ability to select from a mass of data only what is needed. Almost instantly one may read the material, print it out, or, in the near future, listen to the computer speak. The technological alternatives and changes are characteristic of a gradual move from a writing culture to one that has still to be thoroughly defined and explained.

Mass storage and specific retrieval are both a wonder and a curse. The wonder is evident, but consider the curse. Publishers store masses of undifferentiated information, which means there are now thousands of citations for a given subject. "Information overload" is one very good descriptor of the process.

The ability to store data without much evaluation can result in piling up more and more junk, but among the data there may be a gem or two. The problem is finding ways to discover the jewels in the garbage. Here, the reference librarian becomes the trained magician who is able to extract the desired data.

It all adds up to a self-evident truth. Today, an individual has access to more information, but this does not necessarily mean he or she has more knowledge. Is anyone any wiser because of the availability of masses of data? The answer depends on the individual, not the computer.[1]

ELECTRONIC REFERENCE FORMATS

Before computer technology advancements in the late 1960s, the only way for most librarians to find information was to consult a standard printed reference work—from an index to a biographical source. Then electronic database sources arrived and allowed the retrieval of information at a computer terminal.[2] The next option, available since the mid-1980s, was the shiny compact disc called CD-ROMs. And there are other developing information channels, from television to handheld miniature books.

The database, or the reference work in a machine-readable form, is searched in much the same manner one would look for answers in a printed work. The essential difference is that the technology offers numerous added avenues of searching. Instead of being dependent on assigned subject headings, one may use a dozen or more different approaches in the search. One can, for example, look for key words in the title, abstract, or text. The search may be limited by date, language, format, and so forth.

Among the most-often-cited reasons for using the computer is speed of searching. A computer-aided search may take only a fraction of the time needed for a manual search, particularly when it is retrospective and requires examination of several years of material. A considerable amount of time and effort is saved in not having to look up the same term in each volume of the printed service. Another time savings is realized in the computer's ability to print out the citations, which sidesteps the need to photocopy or laboriously write out the retrieved data.

Many databases now offer the complete text of the indexed article. Books, reports, and almost all other forms of printed works are available in full text. This hardly means *all* printed works, but the number grows each year, and particularly those in the reference section.

---

[1]The tremendous advances in science and medicine, for example, conclusively demonstrate the importance of the computer in storing, sorting, and computing raw data which, with careful analysis, may offer solutions to century-old problems. Nevertheless, the use of information rests entirely with the individual. Granted, one day the computer may analyze its own vast databases, but for now at least, important conclusions require human interpretation.

[2]Technically, *database* is a collection of information (of any type) in a computerized format, that is, digitally encoded data on a magnetic tape, CD-ROM, and so forth. This means an electronic index or an encyclopedia may be described as a "database." Actually, some librarians and many laypersons may use the term to mean any collection of data, regardless of format, for example, a printed almanac may be called a database.

An electronic reference work may be different in format than the printed versions, but remains essentially the same in purpose and scope. A government document, a physics manual, a sociological journal, an online bibliography, Listserv, bulletin board, or news group serves the purpose of helping the librarian answer a question. One may argue that e-mail and conversations over a network have no immediate equivalent in a printed reference work, but conversation (person to person, by phone, letter, fax, or network) has always remained a valuable source of reference help. Ability to chat or plug into a group discussion on a network differs only in efficiency and numbers from the past.

The new technologies expand the oldest reference search rule: If the immediate reference section is exhausted, turn to the contents of the whole library. Where this fails, turn to the libraries in the immediate community-region-state-nation-world. A few years ago this was done by laborious searching in printed bibliographies, indexes, and guides. Often a telephone call to a distant librarian would solve the problem. The new technologies serve the major purposes of making the steps easier, considerably more efficient, and certainly more comprehensive. Nice touches, such as e-mail and news groups, have been added. Still, the process has changed little. The major difference is that one may travel for information at a single terminal and bring up not one or two sources, but hundreds. Furthermore, the text may be joined by sound, pictures, motion, and anything else likely to improve the answer.

It is as ridiculous to fight for a format such as print, for example, as for any old way of doing things (using only a telephone, for example). Conversely, it is of utmost importance to know when to turn to a print index, when to use the e-mail, or when to avoid both in favor of a bibliographical electronic network. If it helps the working librarian to slot these into memory channels for ease of matching with questions, fine. It all adds up to whether the right information is found for the individual. That should be the result of the successful reference encounter.

Online Databases

The online database is information transferred to hard discs or magnetic tape or their technological equivalents and "read" by being mounted on a computer. A few years ago this was a large, mainframe computer; today it may be smaller with an unusual amount of storage capacity. The use of less expensive computers has allowed numerous individuals to start their own database online services. As a source of information to others, the main computer today is often called a "server," which usually is part of a network.

The library accesses the database over a communication network using a phone line, a modem, a microcomputer, a monitor, or a printer. The process explains the term *online* and network. The librarian is, through the *online* wires, directly in communication with the computer's database which, as part of a *network*, can be as close as a few miles or as far as a continent away.

All of this adds up to what many call "open systems," a catchall term for the new order of information technology. There are three advantages to open systems. First, the computer can store an unlimited amount of information and, more important, can make it readily available to the library in a matter of seconds. Second, it can search with lightning speed. The third advantage of online is that material may be added to the database anytime, by the minute. Normally, additions are made every few days or once a week. Thus, for rapid access to current information, there is nothing to compare with online database searching.

CD-ROMs

The "compact disc–read-only memory" or CD-ROM was once described by the English writer Anthony Burgess as a "metallic coaster." Most will recognize it as looking just like the more ubiquitous CD music disc. It can carry up to 250,000 pages and can be formatted to include illustrations, music, animation, films, sound, and so on.

Driven by the strong sale of multimedia personal computers, the CD-ROM title market more than tripled in 1995 to 1996. Today the purchase of a computer without a CD-ROM drive is almost impossible. The leaders in the CD-ROM field include, pretty much in order: Microsoft, Mindscape, Electronic Arts and Broderbund—Well over 90 percent of units are for games, but reference works are becoming increasingly important, at least in terms of sales. Here Grolier has about 10 percent of the total CD-ROM market, an impressive figure for an encyclopedia-oriented CD-ROM publisher.

A CD-ROM can compress a whole library.[3] For example, a single disc with 57 million words of text represents 99 percent of extant Greek literature by 3157 authors from Homer to A.D. 600 authors. The *Thesaurus Linguae* (Irvine: University of California TLG Project) is frequently updated and a five-year subscription—including the updates—costs a mere $500. Work on a *Thesaurus Lingua Latinae* (Los Altos, CA: Packard Humanities Institute) contains virtually all extant Latin literature up to A.D. 200. Another example indicates how one day it will be possible to have on a few CD-ROMs (or their equivalent) a small library of retrospective literature. *The Classic Library* published by Andromeda of Oxford, offers 2000 classics from Plato and Aristotle to Dickens, along with pertinent biographical data, speeches, commentary, and so on, for under $100.

Compact size, relative low price, and ease of use make the majority of CD-ROMs ideal for reference work. Their golden promise, as well as the promise of online searching, is realized when one considers how they speed research. The

---

[3]Super-density discs are to be manufactured, for much the same cost as the standard CD-ROM, and will hold 15 times the amount of data on the present CD-ROM and deliver it 20 times as fast. (Currently a CD-ROM contains about 640 million bytes, as compared with the envisioned 3.7 billion to 4.8 billion bytes of the new discs.)

aforementioned TLG project, which captures Greek literature on a disc, offers a primary example of what one professor calls "techno-philological wizardry." After countless years of intensive labor a Greek scholar succeeded in identifying 53 papyrus fragments as containing a section of Sophocles' *Oedipus Tyrannus.* By contrast, in 1986 a computer search through the TLG databank for the seven letters on one of the smallest (unassigned) pieces produced a match *within three seconds.* "Professor Willis—arguably the doyen of American papyrologists— waxes lyrical at the possibilities of this computer philology, the ability to make joins of a few scraps and thereby revive a document from the dead."[4]

There are several other versions of the traditional CD-ROM: (1) CD-I which means a disc that is interactive "I," but for most purposes CD-ROM is used by itself to indicate interactive potential. (2) *Super Density Discs:* The tentative name for a disc of about the same size and shape as a CD-ROM, but able to hold up to eight to 15 times as much information. In late 1995 the major consumer electronics manufacturers agreed on a single format for the new disc— but not on a name. Eventually the super density disc may replace the CD-ROM for storage. Its main target is the videocassette which it will supercede, particularly for finer definition movies, animation, and so forth. Sales of the new disc will begin in late 1996 or early 1997. (3) CD-Recordable allows the users with the proper equipment to create a disc to be read on any standard CD-ROM drive. This can be used by organizations as prototypes of information distribution. More important, libraries can use it for distributing information.

The real question of the late 1990s is whether or not CD-ROMs will be replaced by online services. Many, including experts at Microsoft, believe the ultimate source of information will be a master computer with servers which will pipe information directly to home and library computers. Today's PC, for example, will not require software or a CD-ROM player—only a connection to an online service.

Multimedia and Hypertext[5]

Multimedia is the combination of text, sound, and numerous illustrations from animation, motion pictures, and videos, to graphs and charts. A related term, *hypertext,* is the technology of organizing the computer database for the nonsequential retrieval of data, which, in simpler terms, means one can be lead from one bit of text to another related piece of text (or music, sound, graphics, etc.) by a logical, although not sequential, electronic path. For example, someone looking for information on Bach may be taken from an encyclopedia, to a periodical, to a biography, to a music store in one search pattern.

The multiple approach to education, information, and primarily fun and

---

[4] *Times Literary Supplement,* December 11, 1992, p. 11.

[5] Librarians, particularly in elementary through high school libraries, use *multimedia* in a broader context. There reference is not simply to electronic data, but to separate items from books and globes to charts and videos.

games is by now familiar to most Americans. Particularly adaptable to CD-ROMs, multimedia games make up a large proportion of the CD-ROMs now available.[6] In the reference world, encyclopedias are the leaders in multimedia.

Substance, a CD-ROM magazine issued in 1994 offers, with a point of the mouse and a click, such items as a story about a band ("Nine Inch Nails"), a question and answer session with the group's frontman, and various music videos.[7] *Compton's Multimedia Encyclopedia* follows a similar pattern of presentation. It supports at least a few items with sound and music, but its real strength consists of the improved graphics (from high resolution illustrations to maps) to accompany the text. All of this can be called up by an average computer literate young person.

Between entertainment and education one finds a vast number of CD-ROMs dedicated to particular subjects, for example, *American Visions*, which gives fair to good reproductions of the work of 210 leading American artists. Unlike reproductions in a book (which can often be better), the system allows one to not only see Jackson Pollock's famous *Number 8,* but watch, in an insert video, Pollock demonstrating his drip technique. Impressive as this may be, there are so many glitches, so much poor and unimaginative work in many for-fun CD-ROMs that they tend to be a disappointment. As one critic put it: "There's all this stuff I call coffeetable multimedia . . . titles that are dry assemblages of text and images."[8]

Music on demand is another promise and example of an interactive multimedia communication system. The listener calls up the database with the listing of classical music by composer on a computer screen. After browsing, she chooses *Rheingold* by Richard Wagner. A glance at the reviews of the piece confirms that the best rendition is by Roger Norrington. Also, on command the Schwann database "dumps the music data, the music score, the reviews and a musicological commentary into your CD recorder, which you had previously loaded with a blank high density CD-ROM." Note: There will be a charge which is handled when you first enter your credit card number into the Schwann database.[9]

Delightful as this may seem for those who never can find the CD they want

---

[6]Of the over 3000 CD-ROM titles, less than one-fourth by the mid-1990s were multimedia. Conversely, these are the discs that tend to be less expensive, more popular, and sold in bookstores, department stores, and anywhere one finds computers. As a result they are the ones that lead the "bestseller" lists; for example, in 1996 two best sellers were *Myst* and *Jump Raven,* two relatively sophisticated entertainment disks that have received critical praise.

[7]The market potential of popular multimedia CD-ROM periodicals has problems such as informing potential readers of availability of magazines (and by 1996 there were fewer than a dozen), selling advertising, and finding a way to distribute the titles. Ingram, the book jobber, has created a division to focus on CD-ROM magazines and distributes them in bookstores and newsstands.

[8]"Multimedia Gulch . . . ," *The New York Times,* September 4, 1994, p. 46.

[9]"As We See It," *Stereophile,* February 1994, p. 3. This is *not* going to be available next year. It introduces the problems involved with downloading not only music, but also any copyrighted information. "The subsidiary issues need to be resolved. How does the copyright owner of the music being squirted down a fiber-optic link into your home get compensated . . . ?"

in a record store, it has a major drawback—the quality of the sound. It will be much less sophisticated than a manufactured CD. The same problem is evident in multimedia music works, for example, the *Multimedia Beethoven* features information on the composer, the score of the Ninth Symphony, and the sound of the music. Unfortunately the glorious ninth appears to be coming from the bottom of a cracked barrel.

Still another twist on the multimedia CD-ROM, is suggested by new firms which will make up a personalized CD-ROM. Everyperson's multimedia is offered by several companies. Bring them up to 650 bytes of data and they promise to send you home with an original CD-ROM—audio, hybrid, or mixed mode. The cost ranges from $100 to $200.

The vast development of entertainment, whether online or on CD-ROMs or the Net, leads to a new term, *info-tainment*, in which real information as understood by reference librarians makes the rarest appearance. Rather than substantive facts, publishers have learned to feed the public with a diet of insignificance.

Hypertext

Defined as the ability to move through a subject by selecting data from a series of sources, hypertext is another form of the familiar index. At its basic performance level it relates terms; for example, if one finds "librarian" it will highlight key words, often in other texts and in other places, from "education of" to "status of." Again, this is the same basic principle of an index. Hypertext directs the user both to primary and secondary pieces of information about the wanted subject. Still, it is more than another name for an index. Hypertext serves the same purpose, but allows one to move in a nonsequential fashion (unlike an alphabetically arranged index) in search not only for text, but also for related matters. One may search for Alexander the Great in text, and in various sources from encyclopedias to history books, and with the same search find graphics, audio, animation, and video. [Of course, this assumes that these are embedded in the database(s) being searched for Alexander.]

In a typical hypertext encyclopedia one might move freely from a mention of Marie Antoinette to the French Revolution to the history of the guillotine. Depending on the system, one might see photographs of a guillotine, a painting of Marie Antoinette, or a film recounting the fall of the French monarchy. The multimedia give rise to hypermedia that allow the reader to hear and to see the material related in the text.

The word *hypertext* was coined in the 1960s, but it did not become part of the jargon vocabulary until the late 1980s. The term *hyper* is from the Greek "more at." The idea is hardly new. From the Alexandria Library to the Britannica's *Propaedia*, it has always been a dream to link all knowledge and to make the world's literature available through association of key words and concepts. *Hypermedia* is a term often linked with hypertext (i.e., hypertext/hypermedia).

Quite simply it is another term for multimedia and simply means consideration of all forms of communication. It is by way of counterpoint to hypertext.

Essentially, the so-called hypermedia library would link all of the senses to a computer or its equivalent. One, for example, might look up information on London and hear the noises of street traffic, the voices of citizens and politicians, and the sights of the city on a screen at the same time. Here, in effect, one would call up television as a link in the process of information. Obviously other forms of media might be linked from music and films to art and text.

The Perseus Project, which originated at Harvard, allows a reader of a Greek play (in either Greek or English) to locate references in other texts, see visual representations and relevant place names on a map, look up Greek words in a dictionary, and read the encyclopedia entry. It can also access pictures of sites and buildings.

SEARCHING WITH THE COMPUTER

CD-ROM or online search begins when the librarian, or user, sits down at a terminal and keyboard that is connected to the database. In order to get information from the database the user must know a series of commands that allow one to find needed information. The commands are usually typed. Subject terms and, or key words, and author names are the primary keys to unlocking or retrieving data. There are subtle variations, and the actual search can be a complicated procedure.

When one finds what is needed, a command is typed to view citations or to have them printed out. If the sample is satisfactory, one may then ask for more citations; if it is not satisfactory, one can switch tactics and try a new search pattern.

While the technology of the process is mind-boggling, the actual search and the end result are much the same as those carried on in a traditional way at the reference desk. The two essential differences are that the user gets information not from a printed source but from data consigned to a computer's memory, where the necessary data are found through electronics, rather than by hand-turning a page. Also, a mastery of searching skills are required which, while much the same in principle to manual searches, differ in the command structures.

There are two basic types of searches at a computer terminal. The first is the familiar ready-reference type or one- or two-source quest. Thanks to simplified search patterns, the average layperson may find what is needed without difficulty. The information may not always be the best, but at least it is something.

The second is the search or research query. This requires a good deal of skill on the part of the user. Here one may be looking, say, for everything on radon gas published over the past six months, only in the United States, or only by the government; or for radon gas in residential communities, and so on. Use of print sources is difficult enough, but to use online or CD-ROM requires added ability.

The typical point of entry into any printed reference work is usually (but not always) subject, author, or, less frequently, title. Not so with a computer-assisted search. Here one may search by all of these, *plus*. The plus is important because the computer allows one to look for a key word in the text of an abstract, in a title, or even in the full text of the article or book.

For example, a cataloger gives only one subject heading to the article on the history of women in Rome. (The title of the article is "The Mother in Rome as a Manager.") The computer permits one to search the title by key words such as "women," "Rome," "mother," "manager," and any other important word that may be found in the title or any major word in the text of the article itself. All the points of entry ensure that one is no longer confined to a single subject heading, as valuable as that may be, or the author or title. Other tags or points of departure can be language, date, publication, and so forth. Finally, one can combine these to limit or expand a search.

Boolean Logic

The key to subtle searching is *boolean logic*. Without getting into the details, it is enough to say that the term allows one to combine words and phrases to either limit or expand the search. Boolean logic is a synonym for sophisticated searching patterns, and may or may not be available on various CD-ROM versions of indexes. Normally, it is a part of almost all online searching patterns.

The ideal system should allow the user to (1) enter a command at any time; (2) retrieve data by date, language, geographical location, or other qualifiers; (3) have unrestricted use of boolean operators and a number of search terms; (4) link search statements and words; (5) query the material in the database by typing in terms which are as natural as possible; and (6) have the use of a thesaurus or dictionary.

The patterns of search are important because most laypersons who use CD-ROM prefer the simple, direct route. The librarians, conversely, prefer the more sophisticated paths such as those provided by boolean logic and its cousins. At any rate, it is of major importance in evaluating a CD-ROM or online index whether it allows the use of boolean logic or is more simplified in its approach.

Currency is another plus because, while the printed volumes are usually produced from a modified machine-readable database, the actual database may be ready for delivery weeks or months before the printed version. The time elapsed between indexing and the published index is a constant problem that can be overcome with the database. For example, *The New York Times Index,* which in printed form is two or three months behind, may be updated daily and weekly online.

As with any technology, there are numerous difficulties with the online or CD-ROM search. The basic three are: (1) cost, (2) lack of standardization, and (3) complexity of searching.

Cost

Most librarians think the cost of a computer search is higher than the manual print search. There are so many variables that it is difficult to generalize, but most online searches cost a minimum of $1 per minute. Until the mid-1990s online searches were charged at so much per minute, and this charge is quoted throughout the text on a per hour basis. There is a movement toward a subscription fee based on use. Other plans have been suggested to encourage more online use. Still, the gross cost to libraries and the profit to vendors and publishers will remain probably much the same until wider use of online searches brings that cost down.

Between the equipment and the database discs, the cost of installation of a CD-ROM setup will be from $4000 to $6000. (After the equipment is purchased, the usual annual cost of discs is approximately $500 to $1400, with a low of only $100 and a high of close to $20,000.)

An example can be found in *The Readers' Guide to Periodical Literature* available both online and on CD-ROM directly from the publisher. A subscription to *Readers' Guide* includes the disc, plus monthly cumulative updates. The cost is $1095 a year, compared with about $230 for the printed version and about $35 an hour online.

There is no absolute saving between CD-ROM and online. Individual searches may cost less with CD-ROM, but the initial purchase and continuing maintenance of the system are likely to cost more, possibly much more, than for online services.

Lack of Standardization

While differing in particulars, the basic organization and retrieval apparatus for most groups of printed reference works may be mastered quickly. The majority of encyclopedias, for example, have alphabetical indexes, and most bibliographies are arranged by title, author, and subject. Unfortunately, this standard approach is foreign to electronic databases. There is no standard, no one single method of locating information in all databases.

Each database distributor offers a separate software program that must be mastered in order to use the system. Once the basic commands are understood, the user has to appreciate that each database has peculiar retrieval problems. For example, on X database an author may be found with one command, on Y database it will require two, three, or even four commands.

Complexity of Searching

Asked what are the worst problem areas in using databases, reference librarians inevitably point to the necessity for mastering multiple retrieval languages, learning about new databases, and learning the unique features of each database. The consequence of using such a vast number and variety of unique retrieval commands is predictable. Librarians, and particularly laypersons, who have become familiar with the command structure of one type of CD-ROM or online search tend to use that work first, and often do not go any further, although there may be better databases to search. At best the user may confine searches only to several databases in a single subject area.

What is really needed to make all the databases potentially useful is a common search command language. Master one system and master them all. A partial answer is found in the gateway front-end software systems.

The alternatives offered by gateway, or front-end software, sometimes called *end user software*, or *user-friendly software* is to offer a common command structure. This makes it possible, among other things, to search a number of databases without learning the codes for each. While primarily designed for laypersons, many of the systems are employed by librarians to overcome the complex search problem.

Using the menu approach, the systems take the user step by step from the problem to the solution. There are now numerous examples of menu systems. Again, no matter how excellent, no two menu systems are similar, at least in detail. Even at its most simple, one must search the screen for "print" or "new search" for each new menu system. It is as ridiculous as it is frustrating and wasteful of time.

Vendors and Publishers

When one searches online, the cost of the search is billed to the user by a vendor, a private publisher, or the government. It all depends on who has jurisdiction over the database(s) being searched. In the case of CD-ROM, the disc is purchased or leased from the publisher of the printed version or from a second party who is acting for the publisher.

An online vendor, as the middle person between the library and the database, supplies the larger, more powerful computer (or server) software, and other necessary elements for a search. The library, or individual, pays the vendor for using the system. Individual vendors offer access to scores, even hundreds of different databases. The amount of payment varies, but usually is based on a set rate per hour of use or a fee based on the amount of information viewed or printed out.

In the United States, the major commercial vendor for general reference services is DIALOG. Other players include ORBIT, Data-Star, CDP (formerly BRS), and about 850 listed, among other places, in the "Online Services" section of the *Gale Directory of Databases*. The same directory lists well over 2000 database and CD-ROM publishers and producers.

Generally, the publisher or producer is the one who gathers the information and publishes it (online, on a CD-ROM, in print, on a magnetic tape, or a combination of these). The vendors, who may be the publishers as well, make the material available to libraries. Sometimes confusion arises about who is doing what; for example, for a time. The H. W. Wilson Company, both on CD-ROM and online, distributed the *MLA Bibliography*, published by the Modern Language Association. Wilson is a publisher, a vendor, and a sales point for CD-ROMs. Therefore, the producer, the vendor, and the distributor may be the same, or they may differ. (Later, Silver Platter, who simply produces other people's information on CD-ROMs, took over the *MLA Bibliography*.)

Government is in a category by itself. One may either buy the database directly from the government for use on one's own computer, or (and this is the more usual case with librarians) access the government database through a vendor. A government agency such as the National Library of Medicine offers direct access to a file, but most use is made of the medical file through a vendor.

Access may be provided to a library by other means by joining a bibliographical utility such as OCLC or RLIN, or a local network consortium that provides such services.

NETWORKS[10]

A system of computers, from large mainframes to servers to laptops, are linked to share information. That is a network. There are many other types of networks, from a network of friends to a network of local librarians who may meet to discuss acquisitions. In the reference service world, though, network is now equated with computers and the rapid delivery of data.

There are two basic types of networks. One processes information and a second communicates the data to users. DIALOG, for example, processes databases that are widely used while Internet offers access to DIALOG and thousands of other networks. There are bibliographical utility networks, such as OCLC, that provide cataloging information. There are regional or state networks that link libraries.

---

[10]See Chapters 2 through 6 of the second volume of this text for a more detailed discussion of networks, in general, and bibliographical networks as well as Internet, in particular.

There are scores of variations on these basic types, but another handy method of definition is cost. The majority of databases and connecting networks are operated at a profit and are expensive to use. Even nonprofit bibliographical databases, such as RLIN, are far from inexpensive. The other type, as typified by the ubiquitous Internet, is operated at cost, and can—in part—be free to users.

The technology of networks that link the individual with the world is yet to be refined, yet to be fully developed. Some speak of using computers, others of simply turning to the television set, while still others envision voice commands and responses that will use a new, yet to be discovered technology. Meanwhile, of course, libraries are profiting from their ability to seek information not only from their own shelves, but also from anyplace their networks—and they are multiple—reach. Much more about networks is woven through this text. Suffice it to say they are as important a part of library reference service these days as the paste pot was a century ago. Networks primarily are used by reference librarians to locate information in sometimes elusive databases; to verify and find books, periodicals, and any other form of communication in a specific library catalog; to speed along interlibrary loan and rapid transmittal (by fax, online, etc.) of full texts of materials; and to connect one librarian with others, particularly when problems arise. Networks, too, imply education of users. Most people must be given at least basic instruction where a network, or fragment of it, is open to public use.

Bibliographical Networks

Essentially a bibliographical network (or *bibliographical utility*, as it is sometimes called) puts a massive number of catalogs at the fingertips of the librarian. With bibliographical networks the reference librarian is able to quickly answer three basic types of questions:

1. *The bibliographical query.* One is able to gain complete information about a given book, journal, recording, or other type of library material. The network systems normally give the librarian complete cataloging data, as well as added information, on the terminal's screen. The librarian may find data on as many as 50 million books and a comparable number of periodicals, reports, recordings, and so on. By the turn of the century it is quite possible that a librarian will have access to virtually all information throughout the world.

2. *The verification query.* One can determine the proper spelling of an author's name, the name of the publisher, the date the book was published, the number of pages, and so forth.

3. *The location query.* The system indicates which libraries have the material. There is usually also a method of requesting the wanted title on interlibrary loan.

Major Bibliographical Networks

The largest network, which offers access to hundreds of separate, individual library catalogs, is Internet. This is discussed in the next section.

Two major networks, OCLC and RLIN, combine the holdings of the Internet individual catalogs as well as masses of other material. Normally, whether for verification or interlibrary loan, the reference librarian will turn to OCLC or RLIN before consulting Internet. These two networks are faster, more complete, and easier to use than Internet.

OCLC

Located in Dublin, Ohio, the Online Computer Library Center (OCLC) has the greatest number of members, from all types and sizes of libraries, than any of the bibliographical networks. By 1996 OCLC claimed over 18,000 member libraries throughout the world, although most are in the United States and Canada.

The system supports a database of over 40 million books, films, reports, or monographs derived from the Library of Congress and merged catalogs of the member libraries. It grows each year, month, and day. Approximately 2 million records a year are added. In 1996 the system contained over 23 million books, 1.5 million serials, and 700,000 audiovisual media, as well as 600,000 recordings.

Moving into other areas of information, OCLC introduced First Search in the mid-1990s. Here OCLC acts as a vendor of databases, in addition to its vast catalog, and the user will find up to 60 electronic databases, from indexes to standard bibliographies. Menus and simple directions lead one through the holdings of the main OCLC database (here called World Cat) as well as into such indexes as ERIC, PAIS, MEDLINE, and ABI/INFORM (all discussed in subsequent chapters). In 1995 OCLC reported that somewhat over 2000 libraries had signed on for First Search, but of these only 8 percent were public. The remainder were academic. More than 45,000 to 50,000 searches online are done each day.

RLIN

Located in Mountain View, California, RLIN (Research Libraries Information Network) is the up-market bibliographical network. In addition to the records of the "ivy league" universities, it includes records from the major research centers such as The New York Public Library and the California State Library. Membership is limited to only the largest of systems (about 126), but there are over 500 partial members.

While the membership is limited, the actual number of records is over 40 million. The small homogeneous membership has two things in common: (1)

huge collections of materials, often of esoteric data; and (2) comparably large staffs in reference, acquisitions, and cataloging.

CitaDel is the RLIN equivalent of OCLC's First Search in that it is a package of databases from ABI/INFORM to *Newspaper & Periodical Abstracts*. As of the mid-1990s, the number of databases available was considerably less than from OCLC.

. . . And

There are now scores of other bibliographical networks, none of which even begin to approach the size of OCLC or RLIN, yet are valuable for particular specializations such as in-depth collections of material in given subject areas to ready access of the full text of periodical articles. Among the better known:

1. CARL, the Colorado Alliance of Research Libraries, is located in Denver, Colorado. Its bibliographical database numbers over 7 million. Items are drawn as much from the University of Colorado as from member libraries both in the West and scattered throughout the country. It offers access to individual library catalogs (much as Internet). Through UNCOVER it gives access to the title pages of over 15,000 journals and makes articles available electronically (or by regular mail). It gives access to some current databases such as ERIC and encyclopedias. (Note: The system in 1995 was purchased by a private firm. See volume 2 of this text for details.)

2. WLN, Western Library Network, located in Olympia, Washington, provides computer services to over 450 libraries in Washington, Arizona, Alaska, Idaho, Oregon, and Montana. A division of the Washington State Library, WLN has a database of close to 6 million records.

3. ISM Library Information Services is located in Canada and has a membership of over 2500 libraries, including some in the United States. Although originally established to serve Canadian libraries, it soon expanded its services south of the border. The services are similar to those offered by OCLC, but sometimes at a lower cost. (Note: This was called UTLAS, but the designation is now used only for the catalog system.)

There are numerous types and sizes of bibliographical networks, many of which are explained in the second volume of this text. Suffice it to say here, no matter the size or location, they have one thing in common and that is an access to the world's information.

THE INTERNET

The ubiquitous Internet is the ultimate communication network. It links thousands of other communication and data networks with one another and with individual users. It is somewhat like a vast telephone-television-radio cable network that covers the world. The essential difference is that the Internet is interactive, allows a dialog, while the radio network offers only monologue.

As an amalgamation of thousands of individual computer networks, Internet has the magic routing language and technology to permit them all to exchange messages and share data. Information ranges from a research report on cancer to a lover's conversation. Users have virtual instantaneous access to a mass of usually unedited, unpublished data. One may find on a personal computer screen the ultimate response to the meaning of life, or masses of unconsidered, thoughtless opinion on the same subject.

There are millions (some say 20 to 30 million) who travel the information superhighway in quest of company (e-mail), news groups, data (library catalogs and databases), and reading matter (electronic journals and newspapers). Graphics, sound, and text make the Net a type of television entertainment center.

Internet developed from the United States military who in 1969 started it to test how computer networks might survive nuclear attacks. It moved from the Pentagon to the National Science Foundation where it was expanded to allow high-speed communication among a group of supercomputers at various research centers. The NSF grew inward (with regional, intermediate, and local networks) and outward (with international ties). Today a campus network may be tied to a regional and state system, which, in turn, offers access to supercomputers in Washington, D.C., and London or Paris. In the 1990s commercial and individual networks entered the larger system offering everything from games and discussion groups to full-text newspapers and shopping services. Today it is almost impossible to say where the Internet begins or where it ends.[11]

Released by Columbia Pictures in 1995, the film *The Net* is the first of what promises to be a whole new group of movies devoted to various aspects of the Internet and its users. The critics considered the film good to bad, but agreed that everyone in the audience who had ever used the Net appreciated the sometimes confusing plot. The point is that movie producers believe enough people are involved with networks to be drawn to such a film. Next? Television, comic books, and so on.

Library Use of Internet[12]

In the typical reference situation, the Internet has four primary reference uses: (1) E-mail helps bring questions to the library and, with time, the librarian may

---

[11]For a brief and informative summary of the history, present, and future aspects of Internet, see the profile "For Father of the Internet . . . ," *The New York Times,* September 25, 1994, p. 4F.

[12]Robin Kinder, ed., "Librarians on the Internet: Impact on Reference Services," *The Reference Librarian,* nos. 41–42, 1994. This 385-page issue (also in book form) covers aspects of the system and reference services. A basic guide for anyone who wants to know the nitty-gritty about Internet and the reference desk. For a more theoretical approach see, too, Charles McClure et al., *Libraries and the Internet/NREN* (Westport, CT: Mecklermedia, 1994).

respond in the same fashion. Essentially it allows an individual to chat with another individual or group across town or across the world. At the reference desk some libraries accept questions by e-mail and regularly respond. This type of service is likely to expand, limited only by staff time. (2) Also e-mail is the vehicle for using news groups, and searching for specific data over one of the networks. For example, one can link up with business directories, Federal Reserve Board files, the Institute for East-West Studies European Center in Atlanta, or a menu offering data compiled by the White House staff. Vocational information flows from the U.S. Department of Education and data on the latest NASA shuttle payload are available from other files. (3) The Internet should be available for use by the public. By 1996, many public, academic, and school libraries were integrating free Internet use into the regular reference services section. (4) Listserv mailing list discussion groups. This consists of active groups which have a topic or interest in common. A similar system for discussion groups is known as *Usenet*. This is a shared network of thousands of separate bulletin boards that tie, as does Listserv, like groups together for purposes of queries and discussion.

Listserv and Usenet news groups have distinctive differences and audiences, but both are used in reference services at two levels.[13] Usenet is another way of having a meeting with librarians with similar problems and solutions; for example, a Usenet group considers reference and government documents, another is involved with (yes) Internet, and a third with acquisitions. The second approach is to turn to these services for specific answers to specific questions. For example, someone looking for the source of a quotation would put the quotation query to reference librarians involved with ready-reference queries, or academic librarians, English department specialists, and so on. The response would be the answer.

One Listserv of use to reference librarians is STUMPERS Archives. This is a Listserv to help answer difficult reference questions. Primarily for librarians, it accepts the questions for regular e-mail delivery. Those who can answer respond. The response is sent to the person who made the query and to STUMPERS. The replies are grouped by query. Searching can be done by (1) key word of the entire archive—usually employed for a month or so; (2) download of a past month's, or previous month's archive; (3) key word for a specific answer to a question.

Typical questions that have been answered: "What is the name of the disease in which a person ages prematurely?" (Progeria). The exact citation for a quotation is a favored, common query. "Who were the *Life* magazine photographers who gained fame in World War II?" (Robert Capa, for one). "What is

[13]Listserv tends to be more specific, more narrow in its interests. Usenet is made up of newsgroups (i.e., news about everything and everyone, and not confined to newspapers). Queries and answers come through a mainframe computer or server which the individual must then tap.

the largest city without a four-year college?" (Amarillo, Texas, with a population of 157,000). Normally, although not always, answers are supported with citations to sources.[14]

FTP (file transfer protocol) permits the individual to not only read, but also copy down, or download, material in the particular database or network reached. The material may range from everything from software to standard texts to parts of library catalogs. Through FTP one may literally borrow a good deal of the information on the Internet. One can move, for example, a complete file to London from San Francisco or from San Francisco to Oakland. It is done with extreme speed. Some files, of course, are not free.[15]

Popular Net Use

Two developments popularized the Internet. (1) The World Wide Web makes it possible to use hypertext across the world. A layperson simply selects a highlighted word or figure and the Web connects that individual with the source of the needed information. The key to the Web is superlinking which permits the user to move from information on one computer to another and to another, no matter where in the world they are located. For example, someone reading a Web article on encyclopedias might click on a highlight phrase referring to *Britannica,* and be automatically connected to a computer in England that offers information on *Britannica* maps. And that source can provide not only text, but also sound and graphics. (2) Netscape is a major software used on the Web to find specific data from vivid paintings to sound and video of major world events. The two transformed the Net into a device that is relatively easy to use. Netscape now has scores of cousins and aunts who serve to direct the user to sources of information. Two of the most popular are Yahoo and Java.

About 2 to 4 million people regularly use the Web; but commercial networks plan to increase the number substantially by offering easy access and shopper items from contact lenses to films. Also, more than 2000 businesses on the Web plan to bypass the commercial networks and offer their services directly to customers. The Forrester Research Inc. of Cambridge, Massachusetts, estimates that by 1998 the Web will have more than 11.2 million users.

Given this type of networking, commercial ventures see the eventual downloading of live television shows and films, in fact, the opportunity of full choice to view what one will. "If homes eventually have cheap video cameras

---

[14]For a detailed discussion, see Ann Feenye, "Internet Applications: Stumpers-L," *Computers in Libraries,* no. 13, 1993, pp. 40–42.

[15]The question about Internet is whether or not it is faster, easier, and less expensive to use than other networks or vendors. For example, it may be more efficient to turn to OCLC or RLIN for verification; and it may be easier to use MEDLINE through DIALOG than the Internet. There are cost and technological factors, such as downloading and speed of data, which must be considered before a decision is made as to the best avenue.

linked to the superhighway then the world will truly have shrunk. You will be able to talk to, and be seen by, a television show host or a university professor or a doctor anywhere in the world. You could have your house guarded by a security firm in New Zealand with instant access to your local police."[16]

Reference Librarians on the Internet

The greatest contribution of the Internet is not the technology, as impressive as it may be, but the sense of connection it makes possible between individual and individual, group and group. In the information rush it may be forgotten that people are more involved with e-mail (or over 200,000 subjects of common interest) than, say, isolating a citation from a given index or catalog. Where information, rather than companionship is sought, it tends to be the "back fence variety" of what do you know about X or what has been your experience with Y. Taken to the research level the same procedure is employed when concerned about an experiment, a social trial, or the results of a meeting. And at still another level, people play games of various intellectual strain, over a wide period of time and place.

Where does the reference librarian fit into this subtle shift of interests made possible by Internet? In two or three potential ways: (1) First, and in operation today, is the ability of the librarian to assist the average person to use the Internet. Granted the uses tend to be to locate information, but why not expand instruction to include all facets of communication? An electronic reader's adviser, if you will. (2) Second, but hardly yet noticed, there should be reference librarians available on the Internet itself to answer calls for help, not only about how to do this or that, but to assist directly with reference questions. Also, as a mediator, the librarian on the Net would be able to advise what is or is not useful for a particular problem. A librarian-to-librarian Listservs are a step in this direction, but it is too slow and too parochial. A broader scope is needed. (3) Librarians have Listserv and Usenet news groups, but these should be on a national and international scale offering free information about vital activities (from employment to education) to anyone who needs the data. Everything from commonly used bibliographies to tips on how to use the Internet should be readily available. There are many other potential roles for tomorrow's librarian— few of which take much money, but most of which require imagination and ingenuity.

[16]"Taking the Highway . . . ," *Guardian Weekly*, August 29, 1994, p. 12. While Netscape and World Wide Web helped to popularize the Net, neither solved the problem of the electronic traffic jam of busy signals that can hold up results from minutes to hours. Another problem is the slow rate of printout with average PCs as well as the related low receiving rate of the PC. And add, too, the virtual lack of control over what flows over the Net and one can see the difficulties for the average John and Jane Doe with family at home on the Net.

CONSUMER NETWORKS

Online consumer networks which reach into American homes, as well as households abroad, primarily provide easy access to information bulletin boards, e-mail, news information databases, financial aids, and first and foremost, entertainment. There are four to six primary networks: CompuServe, Prodigy, America Online, and the latest (i.e., 1996) Microsoft Network and Ziff-Davis Interactive. There are a half dozen others with their number growing. Each offers relatively low-price access to entertainment, and data.

Using windows with a point and click computer mouse the consumer services are easy to use. They require no more than a computer terminal, modem, and phone line to connect. Today the greatest use is for games, e-mail, bulletin boards, and discussion groups which consider everything from sex to submarines. By 1996 the major networks moved from promoting individual information service superiority to their competitive edge as gateways to publicly accessible information, and particularly to Internet and World Wide Web.

In terms of users, Prodigy has about 1 million, CompuServe 3.8 million, and America Online 4 million. The new Microsoft MSN is estimated to attract as many as 9 million users by 1996 to 1997.[17] Methods of charging differ, but most have a flat monthly fee of about $10 plus, for some, $3.50 per hour after a given amount of "free time." Total gross profits for online services (1995) are estimated to be between $1.4 and $2 billion per year. Comparatively, book sales in America average in total about $15 to $17 billion.

Despite the prodigious advertising efforts of consumer services they may not grow as quickly as expected. Subscribers find that e-mail, various bulletin boards, and other means of community chatter with strangers have a thrill in the beginning. Later, after a few expensive sessions, it becomes apparent, to paraphrase Oscar Wilde, that the brotherhood of man is a most depressing reality. Ubiquitous games may be purchased and played for much less on equally ubiquitous CD-ROM players.

Still, there is considerable hope that the consumer services will grow, that the number of users will double or triple by the turn of the century. Easy connections to the Internet will provide vast amounts of information and, for commercial purposes, even greater numbers of bulletin boards and talk groups through Listservs and Usenet. Thanks to World Wide Web, the consumer services will be able to offer multimedia sources.

All consumer networks have good and bad points, but few of them are organized to serve the needs of reference librarians. Information in each system varies dramatically. All offer some general news and the *Academic American En-*

---

[17]In 1995, an estimated 11 million customers worldwide subscribed to a commercial online service. This number is expected to grow dramatically over the next few years. In 1995 alone online business grew 30 percent. *The New York Times*, November 22, 1995, p. D5.

cyclopedia (i.e., the *Electronic Encyclopedia*), but few have or offer access to specific information databases. Those who see consumer networks replacing reference libraries have little understanding of their real purpose and goal, which is to be another mass media entertainment network. Even those offering "hard" information depend more on multimedia games, e-mail, and conversations than on answering questions.

DOCUMENT DELIVERY—FULL TEXT

One of the bonuses of gathering information through a library terminal or personal computer at home is the potential access to the articles, chapters from books, and reports themselves. There are three basic approaches to document delivery: (1) The most satisfactory, fastest, and unfortunately, costliest, is online. In a one- or two-step process the viewer calls up the magazine article for viewing. It may then be printed out in part or in full; or it may be ordered from the publisher or another source and arrive a few hours later through e-mail, fax, or other electronic methods. (2) The second prevalent system is to find the necessary citation and then, either at the terminal itself or through the reference librarian (or interlibrary loan office), request the article. It may be sent, again, by e-mail or fax, or through the mail. Arrival time will be from 24 hours to two or three days. (3) The traditional approach, which remains the most prevalent, is to print out or copy down the citation and then try to find the article, book, or report in the library. If it is not owned by the library then the next step is to (4) submit a request to the interlibrary loan office and wait from a few days to several weeks for the material to arrive by mail. (The interlibrary loan librarian, of course, can speed all of this up by doing the transaction over a computer.)

The ultimate document delivery system will allow anyone at anyplace (with access to the necessary technology) to call up on a computer screen and download, if desired, the entire contents of the world's libraries. This system is in place. Online searches may be made of over 6000 databases, many of which contain massive amounts of information, including books, magazine articles, and so forth. Bibliographical utilities, such as OCLC and its feeders, from the Library of Congress to member libraries, make it possible to find virtually any book published since the invention of printing.

The ultimate system was suggested in late 1994 when the Library of Congress announced its plans to put its full contents (over 104 million items) online by the turn of the century.[18] Other national libraries, from the British Library to the Bibliotheque Nationale have, or plan to have, similar document delivery systems available. Large research libraries such as Harvard and Cornell have plans for their collections.

[18]"Library of Congress Offering to Feed Data Superhighway," *The New York Times,* September 12, 1994, p. A10.

Out of this, the emerging National Information Infrastructure, or the information superhighway, would make it possible to navigate not one, but dozens of libraries at virtually the same time. Someone doing research on the American Civil War could look at books from the Library of Congress, as well as valuable manuscript material from Harvard, and draw upon films from X or Y library. And so it would go until, regardless of location or format, the researcher would have gathered all needed data from around the world without leaving a library or study.[19]

Meanwhile, the average indexing publisher or vendor does offer full text services. University Microfilms International, for example, allows the librarian or client to search its *Periodical Abstracts* for necessary citations to articles. Then one can turn to the companion *General Periodicals* to see the article(s). Almost all urban newspapers may be viewed in this fashion, as may numerous general reference works.

The Information Access Company, a publisher of electronic indexes, makes available at about $8 each, fax articles from some 100 periodicals. Writing about this service in late 1994 the author Nicholson Baker found it far from perfect: "The service is expensive (a single faxed article for the price of a paperback), it is troubled by typos . . . it is not dependable (I was charged for pieces I never received). . . ."[20] Be that at it may, the day is near when almost all electronic indexes will have the full text of everything indexed readily available for immediate searching, print out, and delivery.

THE FUTURE OF AUTOMATION AND REFERENCE SERVICE

Experts on the future of libraries generally have been no more accurate than stock brokers, horse experts, and weather forecasters. For example, it was predicted that today's society would be a paperless society with all of us reading the newspaper on a computer screen and getting our books on CD-ROM or the equivalent. But the reality is that the production of paper has increased and so has the number of books.

One prediction is likely to be certain. Electronic databases, and particularly online, within a decade will replace current printed reference works—or at the very least replace frequently consulted bibliographical tools and indexes. Increased networking and cooperation between libraries and within the library

---

[19]The National Digital Library project hopes to convert the most important documents in the Library of Congress by the year 2000. The cost of converting a page in a book to digital form averages $2 to $6 now, although this is expected to come down with mass conversion. It will take time, to say the least, to digitize all Library of Congress materials. Plans are to convert about a million items each year. This number must be increased, or it will take over a century just to convert the present holdings, let alone the new material coming in each day.

[20]Nicholson Baker, "Infohighwaymen," *The New York Times*, October 18, 1994, p. A25.

community mean that the distinction between the library and other sources of information will disappear.

It is entertaining and sometimes instructive to try to predict reference events in the coming years. Here are some of today's common predictions (probably to be trusted only as much as those of the past).

1. In the future there will be less dependence on the library. The individual may tap information sources at home by means of a computer or whatever new technology is around the corner. Although this has been a theme for many years, library use, if anything, seems to have increased. Why?

    a. The cost of online, CD-ROM, and so on, is too high for most people. Moreover, they can get the same information at less cost from the library. (Fees, to be sure, are often charged, but they are not as high as home-use charges.)

    b. The most important reason the use of the library will continue to increase is often forgotten because of the technology mania. Most books and magazines are there not for information. Most people read for amusement and aesthetic reasons, or both.

2. The cost of gathering information and making it available is growing, too. Sooner than most people expect, the public is going to have to decide whether or not it wants to spend money on information, in spite of the fact that those who have made a living betting on the "dumbing" of America are pessimistic. One hopes that the decision will be a wise one.

3. Information needs are great and getting greater. They arc also becoming more complex. The result is that the use of the trained specialist in the library is likely to increase, not decrease. More expert reference librarians are going to be needed, not fewer, and this need will be so for all types and sizes of libraries.

    a. Computer searching is not easy. An expert can find data in a sixth of the time (and at less cost) than a lay user. Also, the librarian can differentiate between what is useful and what is not, thus saving the user considerable time and effort. The exception is a subject expert who searches a database and may equal the librarian in approach; but the number of experts is small when compared to the general public.

    b. The reference librarian will become more professional, more important, and, let us hope, better paid. Technological complexities on the information highway will require more, not fewer, librarians to direct traffic.

4. Tied to reference services, many librarians may forget that the new information age is big, big business. For example, hardly a day or week goes by without a story such as "MCI Plan a Big Stake in the News Corporation." Why? To serve up a combination of entertainment and information products for millions of otherwise computer-ignorant Americans. The next day it is announced "Wall Street Sees Time Warner in AT&T Deal." Why? An effort is made to integrate telephone lines and television and information for profit. Then "Microsoft and NBC in Multimedia Alliance," and so on, and so on.

Digital technology has opened vast uncharted ways of moving information; it has introduced new ways of selling everything from jewelry to a president. Advertising, more or less forbidden on the Internet, is now common because advertisers use their own server (i.e., computer), which allows access to anyone on the Net—and particularly over the World Wide Web. Cyberspace, in fact, has shattered the monopoly media owners had on advertising space. Now anyone can sell almost anything.

Information may seem the heavyweight in the electronic systems. This is to misunderstand the role that everything from interactive television to visual reality is likely to play among laypersons who are less involved with data and more concerned with fun and games.

A Note on Terminology

The term *computer* is used throughout this text to signify the hardware that gives access to data. Technically, the following terminology is essential. (1) Most libraries have "dumb" terminals at the user's desk, which can only receive and send simple text-based commands. (2) The "desktop client" computer or *personal computer* (PC) can act as a dumb terminal, but more likely is connected to outside sources of data in a network. (3) What was once called a *mainframe computer* or one with a gigantic memory that matched the actual size of the machine, is now termed a *server*.[21] It has a much larger memory than the PC and can be the primary "server" of information to thousands of individual PCs. For example, in a library with CD-ROMs a dumb terminal is normally used. Where there is access to a network such as OCLC or DIALOG, the desktop client computer is usually employed.

Platforms for the various CD-ROM databases are not given in the bibliographical descriptions of information sources. These change constantly. The lack of standardization and uniformity of the platform have made it difficult to exchange even simple CD-ROMs and documents. There is consensus that, within the next decade, the idea of the platform will blur. There will be complete exchangeability of databases.

---

[21]Mainframe computer giants have and are giving way to what computer companies call "servers." Depending on the size of the job, a server can do anything from a glorified PC to an IBM mainframe, although servers tend to be less reliable or as fast. Compaq's servers, introduced in late 1994, sell from $11,600 to $50,000. Others go as low as $4000 and double or triple $50,000.

Information Science

An interesting thing happened on the way to the next century. Information science took over the library. A few years ago a competent librarian might have had to explain why he or she took up such a strange profession, more suited, after all, to recluses and bookworms than to warm-blooded American fans of Forrest Gump. No more. "I am an information scientist," or "I a computer pundit," serves to strike awe into the individual who a few months or years ago would have sneered at "librarian" as a profession. Most of the credit goes to the technomania that has swept the United States and a good part of the world. The computer, Internet, and a CD-ROM game have been endorsed by everyone, including political members of the cybertribe from Newt Gingrich to Al Gore. Now, the wired library is the center of the universe, and its keepers are as "awesome" as any member of the fleet of Star Wars.

On this side of the hype there is an information revolution taking shape. It remains to be seen whether the library or the shopping networks will benefit most from the high-speed communication systems. How much of all this is for amusement and a substitute for a television overdose is not clear. How much of the American or the world population will benefit from laptops and interactive communications is a question few are willing to address in more than general terms. In a recent poll it was found that 70 percent of those questioned were anxious to learn to use computers and the new technology, while 45 percent said they use a computer almost every day.[22] The question, of course, is for what purpose do people want to master a keyboard or the mouse clicks? The payback of a wired nation for commercial purposes is obvious. In some people's minds it is not so clear.

SUGGESTED READING

Bentley, Stella, et al., "Reference Resources for the Digital Age," *Library Journal*, August 1995, pp. 45–48. Experts select a "core" reference list of about 40 titles arranged by form, that is, dictionaries, directories, ready reference, and so forth, available on CD-ROM. Full bibliographical information is given for each with a short descriptive annotation. This offers a splendid overview of selection from about 3000 or so available CD-ROMs. The listing is updated each August in *LJ*. See, too: Patrick R. Dewey *303 CD-ROMs To Use In Your Library*. Chicago: American Library Association, 1995. Organized by subject, this is a detailed description of basic CD-ROM packages and series for the average small-to-medium-sized library. The compiler offers lively notes on the good and bad points of each service.

Birkerts, Steve, *The Gutenberg Elegies*. London: Faber & Faber, 1994. A discussion of the shift the author sees occurring between print and the electronic media. He moves from the technological to the sociological, that is, the form of the book in the future and how it will fit into the community. "We may even now be in the first stages of a process of social collectivization

---

[22]*Newsweek*, February 27, 1995, p. 48.

that will . . . vanquish the ideal of the isolated individual." The author's thesis is flawed, but it sets the reader to thinking about the consequences of online information.

"The CD-ROM in Transition: A Medium in Search of Its Message," *The New York Times,* December 13, 1994, pp. C14–15. A two-page exploration of current CD-ROMs, primarily for laypersons, and the possible fate of the disks in the decade ahead.

Cory, Kenneth, "The Information Standard," *Journal of Education for Library and Information Science,* Fall 1994, pp. 320–327. Subtitled "What It Is, How It Affects Librarianship, and Why It Has Been Overlooked," the article shows how digital signals have changed the world. The author urges the profession to "concentrate on preparing graduates for private sector placement." Without that, the so-called new class ethos will dominate and destroy. Not everyone will agree, but it is a most useful challenge to normal notions about information and its employment.

Cotton, Bob, and Richard Oliver, *The Cyberspace Lexicon.* New York: Phaidon, 1994. While this is a computer dictionary with excellent illustrations and definitions there are a number of in-depth articles which do much to explain everything from multimedia to virtual reality. A good, reliable source of information, as is the authors' *Understanding Hypermedia* from the same publisher in 1993.

Davis, Erik, "Cyberlibraries," *Lingua Franca,* February/March 1992, pp. 45–51. In this magazine for university faculty, a journalist explains the ins and the outs of the new electronic library. From the point of view of a layperson he sees what is good and bad in the promise of the future. A pleasant excursion into a sometimes difficult concept.

Dickinson, Gail, *Selection and Evaluation of Electronic Resources.* Englewood, CO: Libraries Unlimited, 1994. A basic guide to equally basic electronic databases, this is an excellent opener for anyone. There is practical advice, too, on searching and general use. Note the detailed bibliography.

"The Future of Libraries," *Wired,* December, 1995, p. 68. Five experts discuss the library of tomorrow and conclude that by about 2016 there will be the "first virtual large library." It will be 2043 before only half of the Library of Congress is digitized. They agree: "No software application will replace a good human reference librarian anytime soon."

Gates, Bill, *The Road Ahead.* New York: Viking, 1995. The man who built Microsoft explains the information age—its history and its future. While much of this is hype, there is enough material to warrant at least a cursory reading. Incidentally, the book comes with a CD-ROM which will not run on MacIntoshes. It is much easier and much faster, to read the book.

Gleick, James, "The Information Future Out of Control," *The New York Times Magazine,* May 1, 1994, pp. 54–57. A thoughtful discussion of the Internet and related technologies that have changed the face of middle America. "In the confusion, everyone is an information provider . . . for multimedia." The consequences of so many people involved in information are spelled out.

Huang, Samuel, ed., "Modern Library Technology and Reference Services," *The Reference Librarian,* no. 39, 1993. Experienced reference librarians explore the meaning of the new technologies from CD-ROMs and Internet to online indexes. An excellent overview of almost every facet of the technologies that are changing the reference process.

Kantor, Andrew "Ain't It the Truth?," *Internet World,* October 1995, pp. 16–20. Various misconceptions about the Internet and its use by laypeople are put to rest in a question-and-answer format; for example, "Isn't the Internet run by the government? No . . ." and a short, accurate answer. A useful piece for both those familiar or not so familiar with the system.

Kantor, Andrew, "Making On-Line Services Work for You," *PC Magazine,* March 15, 1994, p. 152. An overview of the subject for laypersons, this explains in easy-to-understand terms about getting online and how it can be "a productive experience." As much emphasis is put on games as on information.

Kinder, Robin, "Librarians on the Internet," *The Reference Librarian,* no. 41–42, 1994. A group of working experts on the joys and problems of the Internet contributed articles to this outstanding issue. It is an initial source for a day-to-day overview of what the Internet, and related automated areas, mean for the average librarian.

"The Learning Revolution," *Business Week,* February 28, 1994, pp. 80–86. A popular article on the technologies that are changing the face of education (and libraries). A clear explanation of various approaches to information.

Lubeski, Greg, "Multimedia to Go: Circulating CD-ROMs . . . ," *Library Journal,* February 1, 1995, pp. 27–39. A public librarian demonstrates the use of multimedia CD-ROMs not just for reference, but for the general entertainment of the public. He explains how a lending collection of CD-ROMs may be developed. See, too, other articles in the same issue concerning CD-ROMs.

Meeks, Brock, "Fueling the Net Porn Hysteria," *Wired,* September 1995, p. 80. A concise, although biased, summary of the debate over how to control, if at all, pornography on the Net. The writer is a journalist for *Interactive Week.* He opposes government intervention.

Negrouponte, Nicholas, *Being Digital.* New York: Knopf, 1995. The author, a frequent contributor to *Wired* magazine, explains the future in digital terms—where we are, and where we are going with computers. An intelligent, imaginative, and always judicious approach, this is a book for both beginner and expert who wish to see the probable results of computers in today's world.

    Frazen points out real flaws in the Negrouponte and Birkerts (listed above) books, particularly, that neither author likes to read. For a critical review of this book, as well as the Birkerts title, see Jonathan Frazen, "The Reader in Exile," *The New Yorker,* March 6, 1995, pp. 119–124.

Smith, Linda, et al., *Designing Information: New Roles for Librarians.* Urbana-Champaign, IL: Graduate School of Library and Information Service, 1993. Although the papers in this collection are somewhat dated they do serve to offer the always-present problems about technology as it relates to reference services and the library. Policy statements seem particularly useful.

Swan, John, "The Electronic Straitjacket," *Library Journal,* October 15, 1993, pp. 41–45. Not all librarians think the electronic library is ideal. Here the author asks librarians to "resist an electronic vision in which the mind is shaped rather than liberated by the computer."

Vinney, Gemma, "Visions," *The Journal of Academic Librarianship,* May 1994, pp. 91–92. A short piece which makes the point that the electronic library is far from perfect, particularly for the daily needs of students. A useful article in that most such pieces applaud rather than hiss the electronic future.

PART II
INFORMATION: CONTROL AND ACCESS

CHAPTER THREE
INTRODUCTION TO BIBLIOGRAPHY

American publishers issue approximately 40,000 to 50,000 books each year. About the same number are published in England and in each western European country. The so-called third-world nations do not have such a vigorous publishing program, but they nevertheless add to the international total. The result is a mass of hundreds of thousands of new titles. One must add to this pile of books the informative articles in over 140,000 periodicals, reports, studies, audiovisual materials, software programs, movies, recordings, and so forth, which gives one a graphic idea of what is meant by information overload.

The bibliography brings order out of chaos. How can one person even imagine the contents of a small portion of this mass of information? Does a person approach it with delight *and* frustration? A partial answer to the query, as well as a method of at least controlling the fear of abundance, is the bibliography. Whether in printed form, or online, or on CD-ROM, the bibliography gives the vital facts needed to locate X or Y item.

There are many definitions of bibliography, but no single definition is suitable for all situations. To most people, a *bibliography* is "a list of books." Experts give it a different meaning: the critical and historical study of printed books. In France, particularly during the late eighteenth century, the term emerged as a form of library science, that is, the knowledge and the theory of book lists. The Americans and the British now tend to divide it into critical, analytical, and historical designations, as differentiated from a simple listing. The definition problem is not likely to be resolved, but for most purposes it is enough to say that when Americans are talking about bibliography they are concerned with the study of books and lists of books, or other forms of information.

A bibliography tells, among other things, who is the author of a book, who published it and where, when it was published, and how much it will cost to purchase, in either hardback, paperbound, or another form.

Bibliographies are not necessarily confined to books. They may list, too, other forms of communication from films and recordings to computer software and photographs. A bibliography of, say, railroads could well include books about railroads as well as films and photographs of railroads.

The emergence of electronic formats (some would say the "explosion" of such formats) has resulted in bibliographies that keep up with the latest developments in online databases, CD-ROMs, networks, and other forms. Still, the basic idea and purpose of a bibliography remains the same, no matter what it lists or whether that list is available in print or electronically.

Once an item is located in a bibliography, the user wants to know (1) whether it is in the library and available to be read or (2) if not in the library, whether it is on order or can be obtained. The ideal library catalog answers all but one of these queries. Consultation will be necessary with a librarian to know whether it can be obtained through interlibrary loan, or by another form of document delivery.

Bibliography has assumed a major role because of technological developments. Online (through OCLC, RLIN, Internet, etc.), it is possible to literally view the holdings of not one, but thousands of libraries from the United States to Australia. The proliferation of information and the ability to locate and acquire such data through bibliography is impressive. One should appreciate (1) how a bibliography is constructed, (2) how a bibliography can be used, and, possibly most important, (3) how to discover among thousands of items the dozen or so that will really assist the user.

SYSTEMATIC ENUMERATIVE BIBLIOGRAPHY

The average librarian, when speaking of bibliography, is referring to systematic enumerative bibliography, that is, a list of books, CD-ROMs, films, recordings, and so on. An effective bibliography needs several elements if it is to adequately meet the need for control and access.

Completeness. Through either a single bibliography or a combination of bibliographies, the librarian should have access to the complete records of all areas of interest, not only what is now available, but also what has been published in the past, what is being published today, and what is proposed for publication tomorrow. Also, the net should be wide enough to include the world, not only one nation's works.

Access to a Part. Normally the librarian is apt to think of bibliographies in terms of the whole unit—a book, periodical, CD-ROM, manuscript, or the like.

But an ideal bibliography should also be analytical, allowing the librarian to approach the specific unit in terms of the smallest part of a work.

Various Forms. Books are considered the main element of most bibliographies,[1] but a comprehensive bibliographical tool will include all forms of published communication from reports and documents to the various types of electronic databases.

With the bibliography ready at hand, how does the reference librarian use it on a day-to-day basis? Regardless of form, a bibliography is used primarily for three basic purposes: (1) to identify and verify, (2) to locate, and (3) to select.

1. *Identification and verification.* The usual bibliographical citation gives standard information similar to that found in most catalogs: author, title, edition (if other than a first edition), place of publication, a collation (i.e., number of pages, illustrations, size), and price. Another element added to many bibliographies is the International Standard Book Number, abbreviated as ISBN or simply SBN, which is employed by publishers to distinguish one title from another. The ISBN number usually is on the verso of the title page. A similar system, the International Standard Serial Number (ISSN) is employed to identify serials.

In seeking to identify or verify any of these elements, a librarian will turn to the proper bibliography, usually beginning with a general source, such as *Books in Print* or *The National Union Catalog,* and moving to the particular, such as a bibliography in a narrow subject area. On the other hand, where the library has access to a bibliographical utility such as OCLC or RLIN, the librarian is likely to turn to one of these first since it is likely to include both broad and narrow subject areas.

2. *Location.* Location may be in terms of where the book is published, where it can be found in a library, or where it can be purchased.

3. *Selection.* The primary aim of a library is to build a useful collection to serve users. This objective presupposes selection from a vast number of possibilities. In order to assist the librarian, certain bibliographies indicate what is available in a given subject area, by a given author, in a given form, or in a form suitable for certain groups of readers. A bibliography may give an estimate of the potential use of the particular work for the needs of a reader.

Forms of Systematic Enumerative Bibliography: Universal Bibliography

A true "universal" bibliography would include everything published, issued, or pressed in the field of communications from the beginning through the present

---

[1]Despite the fascination with and importance of electronic databases, consider that in the mid-1990s there were from 10,000 to 12,000 such databases. Compare this to about 1.2 to 1.3 million books in *Books in Print* alone. Individual documents on the Internet number over 10 million, but most of these are one to 10 pages, not complete books.

to a look at the future. Today, such universality is an impossible dream, although there is a strong possibility that, through electronic databases, most and certainly all *major* items are now available at a computer terminal if published since the late 1980s. In practice, the term is employed in a narrower sense. *Universality* generally means that a bibliography is not necessarily limited by time, territory, language, subject, or form. National library catalogs, some book dealers' catalogs, and auction catalogs are the nearest thing to a universal bibliography now available.

Ready access to the world's information is growing closer. If "complete" may never be realized, at least "almost complete" is near at hand. This will be accomplished by having online access to the national bibliographies. For example, the *National Union Catalog* from the Library of Congress offers access to millions of books, periodicals, recordings, films, and other materials. When combined with similar national bibliographies from England, Germany, and other world nations online, on CD-ROM, or in other forms, the dream of universal bibliography comes close to realization.[2]

National and Trade Bibliographies[3]

Trade bibliographies are limited to materials published within a given country. They may be further narrowed to a section of the country, a city, or even a hamlet. For ease of use and convenience, national bibliographies normally are divided by time, form, and origin.

Time. This is a matter of listing works previously published, works being published, or works to be published. Such bibliographies are normally labeled as either retrospective or current.

Form. This classification may be in terms of bibliographical form: collections of works, monographs, components (e.g., essays, periodical articles, poems); physical form (books, databases, recordings, pamphlets, microfilm); or published and unpublished works (manuscripts, dissertations).

---

[2]One may claim that universal bibliography is a reality today, only to be frustrated by a country, region, or individual who refuses to methodically list what is issued. Eventually, most of the world will recognize standard bibliographical procedures to allow for universal bibliography, but that probability is far in the future.

[3]*Trade* bibliography is often used synonymously with *national* bibliography. *Trade bibliography* refers to a bibliography issued for and usually by the booksellers and publishers of a particular nation. The emphasis of a trade bibliography is on basic purchasing data. Information for a trade bibliography is gathered from the publishers, and the individual item listed is *not* examined by the compiler of the trade bibliography. A *national bibliography*, which includes additional information (often complete cataloging data), is compiled by librarians. The data are taken directly from the item which is examined by the cataloger. Result: National bibliographies are more complete and more accurate than trade bibliographies.

A typical trade bibliography will set itself limits of time, form, and, obviously, origin. For example, *Books in Print* is limited to books available for purchase (time); it includes only printed books, both hardbound and paperback, and some monographs and series (form); and it is a trade bibliography, that is, issued by a commercial organization (origin). There is no limit to the possible subdivisions of a national bibliography.

A distinction must be made between national bibliography and national library catalogs. A *national bibliography* often is the product of the government and is at a minimum an effort to include everything published within the boundaries of that nation. An example is the *British National Bibliography*, which, weekly since 1950, has listed and described every new work published in Great Britain. The important limitation is that the work must be published in Great Britain. Nothing else is included. A national catalog considerably broadens the scope. A *national library catalog*, such as our United States *National Union Catalog*, lists all works which are cataloged by the Library of Congress and other member libraries of the system. A bibliography of this type normally has many books *not* published in the country of origin. The NUC, for example, lists Chinese, French, Russian, and other foreign language titles as long as they have been cataloged.

Subject Bibliography

The subject bibliography is intended for research workers and others in special areas. Once a subject is chosen, the divisions common to national bibliographies may be employed—time, form, origin, and others. However, unlike most national bibliographies, a subject work may use all the divisions. For example, a definitive bibliography on railroad engines may be retrospective, current (at least at date of publishing), inclusive of all forms from individual monographs to government publications, and reflective of various sources of origins.

Guides to Reference Materials

Theoretically, lists that include the "best" works for a given situation or audience are not bibliographies in the accepted definition of the term. In practice, however, they are normally so considered. They include guides to reference books (in print, CD-ROM, online, magnetic tape, etc., formats), special reading lists issued by a library, and books devoted to the "best" works for children, adults, students, businesspeople, and other specific groups.

Analytical and Textual Bibliography

Analytical bibliography is concerned with the physical description of the book. Textual bibliography goes a step further and highlights certain textual variations between a manuscript and the printed book or among various editions. Often the two are combined into one scientific or art form. This type of research is designed to discover everything possible about the author's ultimate intentions; the goal is to recover the exact words that the author intended in expressing his or her work. One group of bibliographers may be experts in nineteenth-century printing practices and bookbinding, for example, and another group in paper watermarks or title pages. There are differences between analytical and textual bibliographies. Analytical bibliography is more concerned with the physical aspects of the book and textual bibliography with the author's words, that is, the exact text as the author meant it to appear in printed form.

Daily Use

Returning to the standard enumerative bibliography, one can apply two basic approaches to look for a particular work. Experts and laypersons who know a subject well look up X or Y by its title or by the author's name. Those who are not experts tend to use subject headings. The more sophisticated and knowledgeable a person is in any field (whether it be automobiles or psychology), the more likely the individual is to try to search a bibliography by author. This is a very precise approach because one does not have to guess the subject headings in the bibliography. For example, is automobile under "Automobiles" or "Cars" or "Transportation"? The most complex search is a subject search.

EVALUATION OF BIBLIOGRAPHY

When considering the relative merits of a bibliography, one applies the general criteria used for evaluation of all reference works: purpose, authority, and scope. (See the discussion on "Evaluating Reference Sources" in Chapter 1.) Beyond the general considerations, one should evaluate a bibliography in the following manner:

1. *Purpose.* It is important that the bibliography fill a real need and that it not be a repetition of another work or so esoteric that it is of little or no value. The subject is stated clearly in the title and well defined in the preface.

2. *Scope.* The bibliography should be as complete as possible within its stated purpose. For example, a bibliography of books and periodical articles about nineteenth-century American railroads will include contemporary magazine reports about the construction of railroads. Where there are different forms, such as magazines and books, these must be clearly identified.

3. *Methodology.* The method of compiling the bibliography should be straightforward and should make clear that the compiler has exam-

ined all material listed. The items are to be described in a standard bibliographical style, and include the basic elements of a bibliographical entry.

4. *Organization.* The bibliography should be organized in a clear, easy-to-use fashion, and indexes (from subject and author to geographical location) should be included where multiple access is desirable. At the same time, look for material arranged in a logical fashion so that it is not always necessary to use the index, for example, alphabetical by author, by date, by subject, and so forth. You want to see that the author offers a clear explanation of how to use the work as well as definitions, a key to abbreviations, and the like.

5. *Annotations and abstracts.* Where descriptive and critical notes are used for entries, these should be clear, succinct, and informative.

6. *Bibliographical form.* This is a standard entry with the information one needs to identify and locate the item.

7. *Current.* The material should be current, at least where this is the purpose of the bibliography. It is conceivable that one would list only eighteenth- or nineteenth-century publications, and in such a case timeliness would not be a factor.

8. *Accuracy.* It goes without saying that the material must be accurate. There should be some arrangement, if possible, for corrections to be made after publication, should the need arise.

9. *Format.* Is the bibliography available in print, on CD-ROM, online, and so forth? If in machine-readable form, is the software adequate to easily retrieve the necessary data? If only in print, is it easy to read?

NOTE: Throughout this text the reference works are listed by format:

CD: Biography and Man
    Print: Biography and Mankind
    Online: Biography
    Where available, the CD-ROM format comes first, followed (and indented) by *Print* and *Online* entries. Where only *Print, CD-ROM,* or *Online* is available, this is indicated.

GUIDE TO REFERENCE SOURCES: PRINT FORMAT ONLY

Balay, Robert. *Guide to Reference Books,* 11th ed. Chicago: American Library Association, 1996, 2000 pp. $275.

Walford, Albert John. *Guide to Reference Materials*, 6th ed. London: The Library Association, 1994–1997. 3 vols. $195 to $225 each.

Wynar, Bohdan. *American Reference Books Annual*. Englewood, CO: Libraries Unlimited, Inc., 1970 to date, annual. $85.

The basic purpose of a bibliographical guide to reference material is to introduce the user to (1) general reference sources for assistance in research in all fields and (2) specific reference sources to help in research in particular fields. These guides take a number of forms, but primarily are either (1) annotated lists of titles with brief introductory remarks before each section or chapter or (2) handbooks which not only list and annotate basic sources, but also introduce the user to investigative tools in a discursive, almost textbooklike, approach. There are numerous research guides of this latter type.

The general bibliographical guide to reference materials is the starting point for answering many questions. There are several guides helpful in the selection and use of reference books.

1. *Guide to Reference Books* lists and annotates some 16,000 titles considered basic for the large library. Titles are arranged under main sections, from the social sciences to the humanities. There is an excellent 400-page index. Smaller libraries use the *Guide* frequently to ascertain what to choose for particular subject areas or for forms. For example, a smaller library might use the *Guide* to select the best dictionaries in French and English as well as for an encyclopedia on France, and at the same time ignore other French material as not necessary for the collection.

The problem with *Guide to Reference Books* is the lack of current material. The cutoff date for the 1996 edition is the start of 1994, or titles that are a good two years behind publication of the 11th edition. It is hoped that the work will become available online and on CD-ROM, which should help to make it more current and, indeed, more useful.

The British *Guide to Reference Materials* (or "Walford") is more current than its American cousin and is therefore favored in many larger libraries. The three volumes are under constant revision and are published on a three-year schedule.

2. *Guide to Reference Materials* follows the same procedure as its American counterpart, although since the bibliography is in three volumes the total number of titles is at least one-third or more greater than in *Guide to Reference Books*. The annotations tend to be more lively than those in the American work. There are often citations to reviews with judicious quotations from those reviews. The focus is more involved with England and the European Union.

Walford's three volumes, issued about once every eighteen months with the process starting again when the third volume is published, cover science and technology, social sciences, and the humanities. The organizational pattern follows the UDC, that is, Universal Decimal Classification. (This means, for example, that the science volume includes anthropology which is not found under science in the American work.)

The high point of the three-volume work is the annotation style. The critical notes are written with a flair that has made Walford famous. They are not only descriptive, but include well-directed barbs and praise when necessary. Most are a delight to read.

While much of the focus in Walford's guide is on British and European Union works, it is broad enough to include basic American titles as well. This is evident in the second volume covering the social sciences, philosophy, and religion which offers a fine selection of international reference works.

Walford has a one-book revision each year until the cycle is complete and the revision begins once again. (By the time the next edition of *Guide to Reference Books* is available, Walford will have gone through two editions). Plans are to have the British work available online and on CD-ROM.

Both works begin with a broad subject and then are subdivided by more specific subjects and by forms. For example, *Guide to Reference Books* has a section on economics under the social sciences. This is subdivided by forms: guides, bibliographies, periodicals, dissertations, indexes and abstract journals, dictionaries and encyclopedias, atlases, handbooks, and so on. The economics section is later broken down into even more specific subjects and often, within a subject entry, a further division is made by country as, for example, in the political science section. *Guide to Reference Materials* subdivides economics by bibliographies, thesauruses, encyclopedias and dictionaries, dissertations, and so on, generally following the Balay pattern. In practice, the arrangement is not really important. Each volume has an excellent title, author, and subject index.

Both guides include limited information on electronic reference sources, clearly indicating what is available in various formats.

The January issue of *College & Research Libraries* (Chicago: American Library Association) offers a section, "Selected Reference Books." The 50 to 75 titles are carefully selected, annotated, and arranged by broad subject. This helps update the previous edition of *Guide to Reference Books*.

3. *American Reference Books Annual* (usually cited as *ARBA*) differs from both *Guide to Reference Books* and *Guide to Reference Materials* in three important respects: (1) It is limited to reference titles published or distributed in the United States and Canada; (2) it is comprehensive for a given year and makes no effort to be selective; (3) the annotations are written by more than 320 subject experts and are both more critical and more expository than those found in Balay or Walford. Depending on the extent of American publishing, the annual volume, usually available in March or April of the year following the year covered in the text, analyzes some 1300 to 1500 separate reference titles. The work is well organized and well indexed. Every five years the publisher issues a cumulative index to the set.

4. *Guide to Reference Materials for Canadian Libraries,* 8th ed. (Toronto: University of Toronto Press, 1992, 595 pp.) is edited by Kirsti Nilsen and includes about 3000 primary reference books. Most of these, although not all, have a particular interest for Canadian libraries. And while there is repetition of titles among this and the American and English works, enough is different to warrant its purchase by all Canadian libraries and larger libraries outside Canada.

Guides for Smaller Libraries

Most libraries are in the small- to medium-size category. The larger guides are too inclusive. A small library needs works that are considerably less exhaustive. *Reference Sources for Small and Medium Sized Libraries,* 5th ed. (Chicago: American Library Association, 1992) affords a useful list of some 2000 basic titles. The standard titles, from dictionaries to indexes, remain much the same as in *Guide to Reference Books;* electronic formats are included. It can be updated and supplemented by G. Kim Dority's *A Guide to Reference Books for Small and Medium Sized Libraries, 1984–1994* (Englewood, CO: Libraries Unlimited, 1995). This lists and annotates about 1000 titles including more than 400 books priced lower than normal, yet suitable for reference work. Nonprint formats are noted.

Considerably more ambitious, the American Library Association's *Guide to Information Access* (1994) considers some 3000 of "the best standard and electronic sources in the 36 most researched subject categories." Ably edited by Sandy Whiteley, the ALA guide is primarily an annotated listing of titles under subjects from "general reference sources" to "writing." The first 90 or so pages offer an introduction to research and electronic databases. Each of the numerous contributors is an expert in a field. The guide may be used by both librarians and laypersons.

Recommended Reference Books for Small and Medium Sized Libraries and Media Centers (Englewood, CO: Libraries Unlimited, 1980 to date) is a cut-down version of the same publisher's *American Reference Books Annual.* The reviews are under major subject categories, and codes indicate use by academic, public, or school libraries. It includes from 500 to 550 reference works published the previous year which meet the needs of the smaller- to medium-sized reference collection.

Subject Bibliographies

A cursory glance at any subject area in either *Guide to Reference Books* or *Guide to Reference Materials* will reveal hundreds of subject bibliographies. Most of these follow the same pattern of organization and presentation, but are for a particular area of interest. The various disciplines and large areas of knowledge have their own bibliographies, their own versions of *Guide to Reference Books.*

Random examples of subject bibliographies include: Nena Couch and Nancy Allen, *The Humanities and the Library* 2d ed. (Chicago: American Library

Association, 1993). This is both a listing of preferred books as well as discussion of the professional aspects of organizing collections in fine arts, literature, and so forth. Then there is Bernard Schlessinger and Rashelle Karp's *The Basic Business Library Core Resources,* 3d ed. (Phoenix, AZ: Oryx Press, 1994), which is an annotated listing of 200 basic titles. This type of bibliography differs from the humanities in that it must be more current. As a consequence it is updated every two or three years.

There are similar bibliographies and guides (as even a cursory glance at *Guide to Reference Books* will show) in all other fields. In history, for example, there is *The American Historical Association's Guide to Historical Literature,* 3d ed. (New York: Oxford University Press, 1995, 2 vols.). Some thirty years after the second edition, this is the basic bibliography in its field, covering historical writing from the ancient Near East to modern times. The 27,000 entries, arranged chronologically and by area, are critically annotated. An author and extensive subject index makes this easy to use. It is a first place to seek background information, and as reliable as its hundreds of scholarly editors. (Note: As of 1995, only in a print version for $150.)

The Internet offers a wide access to bibliographies and individual library catalogs. These cover as broad a range as the topics in *Guide to Reference Books.* While material considered is wide and useful, the problems of accuracy and completeness remain, as with much Internet information. The Internet bibliographies per se are useful, but they are not a substitute for a considered, often annotated listing. Interestingly enough, if the Internet's strength is not in general bibliographies, the various bulletin boards, e-mail, and so forth, offer hints on where to turn for highly specialized, highly regarded bibliographies.

CURRENT SELECTION AIDS

The selection of reference sources is a highly individualized process. The character and distribution of the elements which constitute the needs of users differ from library to library. Consequently, the first and most important rule when considering the selection of reference materials, or anything else for the library, is to recognize the needs, both known and anticipated, of the users.

How is a satisfactory selection policy reached? First and foremost, there must be a librarian who has some subject competence; that is, one who knows the basic literature of a field, or several fields, including not only the reference works but also the philosophy, jargon, ideas, ideals, and problems that make up that field. There is no substitute for substantive knowledge. Second, the librarian must have in-depth awareness of the type of writing and publishing done in that special field. Where is there likely to be the best review? Who are the outstanding authors, publishers, and editors in this field? What can and cannot be answered readily?

Selection is charted, rather than dictated, by the following:

1. Knowing as much as possible about the needs of those who use the reference collection.

2. Calling upon expert advice. In a school situation the expert may be the teacher who is knowledgeable in a certain area. In a public library it may be the layperson, skilled practitioner, or subject specialist who uses the library. Most people are flattered by a request that draws upon their experience and knowledge, and one of the best resources of reference materials is the informed user.

3. Keeping a record of questions. This is done to determine not only what materials the library has but what it does not have. Most important, a record of *unanswered* queries will often be the basis for an evaluation of the reference collection.

4. Knowing what other libraries have, and what resources are available. For example, the small library contemplating the purchase of an expensive run of periodicals or a bibliography would certainly first check to see whether the same materials are readily available in a nearby library.

These four points only begin to suggest the complexity of selection. Many libraries have detailed selection policy statements that consider in depth the necessary administrative steps merely hinted at here.

Reference Resources Reviews

CD: Books in Print with Book Reviews Plus. New York: R. R. Bowker, 1992 to date, monthly. $1600.[4]
Print: "Reference Books Bulletin," in *The Booklist.* Chicago: American Library Association, 1905 to date, semimonthly. $56.
Print: Choice. Chicago: American Library Association, 1964 to date, monthly. $160.
Print: Library Journal. New York: R. R. Bowker Company, 1876 to date, semimonthly. $79.
Print: RQ. Chicago: American Library Association, 1960 to date, quarterly. (Nonmembers, $42).

---

[4]The "catch" is not only the cost of reviews on CD-ROM, but the fact that the package includes all of *Books in Print*, and *only the reviews*, but none of the text found in the review magazines. Another, less expensive, more restrictive CD-ROM from the same publisher is *Books in Print Plus* ($1095), but this includes only reviews from three of the periodicals listed: *Booklist, Choice* and *Library Journal*.

Most libraries, regardless of size, will subscribe to at least two or three of these standard review journals. Larger libraries will have three of the reviews available as part of the larger database *Books in Print with Book Reviews Plus.* The three available on CD-ROM include *Booklist, Library Journal,* and *Choice,* as well as related and useful journals: *Publishers Weekly, Kirkus, BIOSIS, School Library Journal, Reference and Research Book News, University Press Book News, Sci-Tech Book News,* and a half dozen others. There are now close to 200,000 book reviews (not all of them of reference works by any means) available on this CD-ROM.

None of the journals is entirely satisfactory in the review of CD-ROMs and online offerings, but at least they cover the basics of interest to the majority of libraries—and certainly to students. Most of the periodicals also review books ranging from fiction to technical publications.

"Reference Books Bulletin," a center section in the twice-a-month issue of *The Booklist,* is the single most important place for a librarian to turn for accurate, current, and in-depth reviews of general reference works. Each section is prefaced by a series of notes about publishing, reference services, and new works. This is followed by unsigned reviews. The names of the members who write the reviews and serve on the committee (librarians and teachers) are given in each issue.

In the course of a year, the service reviews about 100 to 150 major works, and about double that number of more conventional, less expensive titles. From time to time a whole issue, or a good part of an issue, is dedicated to an overview of encyclopedias, dictionaries, children's reference works, and the like. The reviews are cumulated in a separate publication each year. Reviews appear no more than six months after publication of the reviewed book, and sometimes even sooner.

There are detailed reviews as well, of CD-ROMs and other forms of databases most likely to be used in the average library. The analysis is useful particularly for the layperson who wishes to learn the good and bad points about searching. In fact, the reviews of databases are among the best now available.

Other current reviews of reference books and information sources include:[5]

1. *Choice.* While specifically geared to college libraries, this professional journal evaluates a number of reference titles of value to all libraries. These are listed under "Reference." *Choice* reviews electronic databases in each issue under "Electronic Media" in the section on reference works. Nonreference databases are scattered throughout the various subject areas. Also, from time to time bibliographical essays in the front of the magazine highlight reference titles. There are approximately 6800 reviews a year, of which about 500 cover reference books. The

---

[5]Until 1995 the *Wilson Library Bulletin* was a major source of reviews. Unfortunately, after 81 years of continuous publication it ceased publication in mid-1995.

reviews are usually 120 to 500 words in length and are signed. Almost all reviewers make an effort to compare the title under review with previously published titles in the same subject area, a feature which is particularly useful but rarely found in the other reviews. When budgets are tight and choices must be made, it is of great importance that comparisons be available.

2. *Library Journal.* Again, the general book review section leads off with "Reference." There are about 450 reference reviews each year. These are 100 to 150 words long, usually written by librarians or teachers, and all are signed. Also, *School Library Journal* includes reviews of reference titles.

Some of the best reviews of CD-ROMs for reference purposes are found in *Library Journal.* Cheryl LaGuardia of Harvard compares four or five CD-ROMs in the same subject area. In a methodical, systematic way she points out the good and bad points of each and ends by suggesting the "best" for a given reference situation. The column alone is enough for most librarians to make decisions about CD-ROM reference titles.

3. *RQ.* The last section of this quarterly is given over entirely to the review of reference books. A few other related titles are considered, but, unlike *Library Journal* and *Choice, RQ* makes no effort to review general books. About 140 to 150 reference titles are considered each year. Reviews average about 200 words each.

In addition to the section, "Reference Books," four to five databases (including CD-ROM) are evaluated. These are excellent, critical reviews which consider the most often used online services. Finally, under "Professional Materials," about 10 to 12 books are usually considered for librarians involved in reference work.

Individual periodicals that carry reviews are becoming available on CD-ROM and sometimes online. The benefit is a one-stop cumulation and a quick, easy search pattern. But the great drawback is price. Is it worth $600 a year for *Choice* on CD-ROM, even with quarterly updates, when the monthly magazine is about $150? The query seems rhetorical. Two examples of other CD-ROM offerings: (1) *Booklist/Reference Book Bulletin* (Middletown, CT: Choice, 1990 to date, quarterly, price varies) is a CD-ROM which duplicates, at least for *Booklist,* what is found in the *Books in Print with Book Reviews Plus.* It includes only reviews in *Booklist* from 1990. (2) *Choice* (Middletown, CT: Choice, 1987 to date, quarterly, $600) offers the same service for their periodical on CD-ROM. Also, this is available online as *CHOICE Reviews Database* (1987 to date, monthly; CARL, rate varies).

Consumer networks offer limited reviews. One available in the mid-1990s, although quantitatively lower than those discussed here: *Book Review Database*

(Middletown, NY: Cineman, 1990 to date, 12 reviews every two weeks; Online: America Online, rate varies). Primarily this consists only of brief reviews of best sellers or would-be best sellers and is for domestic use rather than for libraries.

American Libraries, the monthly magazine of the American Library Association, does not regularly review reference books, but it does have an annual feature of interest: The "Outstanding Reference Sources of 19–," appearing in the May issue, is a compilation of the best reference titles of the year selected by the Reference Sources Committee of the ALA. Choice is based on quality and suitability for small- to medium-sized libraries. Selection includes CD-ROMs, although as of the mid-1990s only in a limited way. Some 35 to 45 titles are selected, and the result, usually with each work annotated, appears in various other library publications. *Library Journal* offers a competitor, "Reference Books of 19–," with titles selected by its book review editors. This appears in the April 15 issue which is devoted almost entirely to reference services. *Library Journal* has another helpful feature which appears at irregular intervals. This is "Reference Best Sellers," a listing of titles "most in demand by libraries and bookstores from Baker & Taylor Books nationwide for six months prior to the week." In December 1994, the perennial best seller *The Old Farmer's Almanac* topped the list with *Chilton's Truck and Van Manual* in the twentieth and last spot.

There are other approaches to reference works and news of the reference and information services field. One leader is *Reference Services Review* (Ann Arbor, MI: Pierian Press, 1972 to date, quarterly). This does not so much review new books as offer a dozen or more bibliographies. These may include an annotated listing on AIDS or one on the joys of mountain climbing. All the authors or compilers are experts in their respective fields. From time to time, too, there are general overviews of reference services.

While there are no reviews, *The Reference Librarian* (New York: Haworth Press, 1981 to date, semiannual) features 25 or more articles on a single subject of interest to reference librarians. The topics may range from online searching, to ethics, to the Internet. The authors are working librarians who offer a unique approach to various subject interests.

INDEXES TO REVIEWS

CD: Book Review Digest. New York: The H. W. Wilson Company, 1983 to date, quarterly. $1,095.
  Print: 1905 to date, monthly. Service.
  Online: 1983 to date, semiweekly. Wilsonline, $25 to $40 per hour. Note: This is free when the subscriber purchases the CD-ROM version.

CD: Book Review Index On CD-ROM. Detroit: Gale Research Inc., 1965 to date, annual. $1,250. Annual update. $495.

Print: Book Review Index. 1965 to date, bimonthly. $215. Cumulations: 1965–1984, $1,270; 1985–1992, $895.
Online: 1969 to date, 3 times a year. DIALOG file 137, $57 per hour.

The titles considered here are specialized. Their sole purpose is to list book reviews. They are used by students and others seeking background material on a given work as well as by the reference librarian on the lookout for notices about specific reference books. The reviews are *limited* to printed books. With few exceptions, electronic formats are not considered.

The long-standing, well-known *Book Review Digest* is a place where experienced librarians first look for reviews—at least if the book is by a well-known or controversial writer. Lesser-known authors are rarely found here because the publisher requires (1) that at least four reviews of a novel are published before the novel is listed and (2) that a minimum of two reviews of nonfiction are published before inclusion. This solves the problem of space, at least in print, but poses one difficulty—rarely is a first novel reviewed. Much the same is true of important but less-than-popular nonfiction titles.

Still, if the book is relatively noticed, then the *Book Review Digest* is an ideal source. Why? Because it gives a brief summary of the content of the reviewed title and, more important, it gives enough of an excerpt from a review for the reader usually to know whether the book is worth considering. This type of annotation saves much looking up of the original review(s). Another distinct advantage is that the print work goes back to 1905, thus giving the researcher an important resource for contemporary reviews of many titles which by now have become classics. Also, there is a subject approach to many of the titles reviewed. This can be valuable when someone is looking for a book, say, on pirates and has no idea of the author or title.

The librarian must know the approximate date that the book was published. The fastest method is simply to search *The Book Review Digest Author/Title Index, 1905–1974.* For reviews published after 1974, one must go to the annual index volumes or, from 1983, to the CD-ROM or online service. If the date cannot be found in these indexes, the librarian should turn to the catalog where the title may be entered or to one of the national or trade bibliographies such as *Books in Print.* Another possibility is to search for a title by using a bibliographical network, such as OCLC.

Book Review Index covers reviews in more than 900 periodicals from 1965 to date. As of 1996 the publisher claims over 3 million citations for some 1 million separate titles. Unlike the *Book Review Digest,* there is only a citation to the review, not a summary of the review's content. Therefore, the user must hunt down the review before any decision may be made about the quality and desirability of the book. On the other hand there are many more sources than those found in *Book Review Digest* (900 vs. *BRD's* 100). It is the first place to turn for titles which may be noticed in only one or two periodicals.

The print reviews are listed in two sections: the first by author, and the second by title. Unfortunately, there is no subject approach. On an average, about 75,000 books are covered each year, with about one to two reviews per title. This contrasts sharply with the other basic key to reviews, *The Book Review Digest*. Here one finds only about 6000 titles considered.

A useful feature of the index for reference librarians is that all reference works are marked with an "r." Thus one can look through the bimonthly issues for updated information on new works otherwise missed. Other codes include a "p" for a periodical review; and a "c" and a "y" for children and young people.

The CD-ROM version, obviously a better buy than the print cumulations, offers a straightforward method of searching from 1965 to the present. Points of entry include, of course, the author and the title; but in addition one may select a search by periodical where the review appeared, publication year, and the like. Also, unlike the print version, here one may search by subject as well as key words in titles. The catch to the CD-ROM is that it appears only once each year as compared with the print version every two months. The solution, at least for larger libraries, is to take both.

Modest reference budgets will dictate the *Book Review Digest* as a first choice, particularly as part of the subscription on CD-ROM allows the user to turn to free online searching for material not found on the CD-ROM. Larger libraries will have both review services.

The majority of periodical and newspaper indexes, discussed in Chapter 4, include citations to reviews of books. When one is looking for a review, say, of a current best seller, a general magazine index, particularly online, would be a first place to turn.

Bibliographies of Bibliographies

Print: Bibliographic Index. New York: H. W. Wilson Company, 1993 to date, triannual. Service.
    Online: 1984 to date. WilsonLine, $43 to $60 per hour. Also available on OCLC.

A bibliography of bibliographies is, as the name suggests, a listing of bibliographies. One may find a bibliography on dogs at the end of an article in a periodical, at the conclusion of an essay in an encyclopedia, or as part of a book on pets. If one lists these three bibliographies and adds from a dozen to a thousand more on dogs, one has a bibliography of bibliographies about dogs.

The primary example of a bibliography of bibliographies is *Bibliographic Index*. Under numerous headings, one may find bibliographies about subjects, persons, and places. The entries represent (1) separate published books and pamphlets that are normally bibliographies in a specific subject area, for example,

East European and Soviet Economic Affairs: A Bibliography . . . ; (2) bibliographies that are parts of books and pamphlets, such as the bibliography which appears at the end of David Kunzle's book *The Early Comic Strip;* and (3) bibliographies published separately or in articles in approximately 3000 English and foreign language periodicals. Emphasis is on American publications and a bibliography must contain more than 50 citations to be listed.

The inevitable catch to many reference works is applicable here: (1) The bibliographies are not listed until six months to a year after they have been published, and (2) although books, and to a lesser degree pamphlets, are well covered, the index cannot be trusted to include many periodical bibliographies. Why? Because over 120,000 periodicals are issued, often with bibliographies, and the index includes analysis of only 3000.

CD-ROM AND ONLINE DATABASES[6]

CD: Gale Directory of Databases. Detroit: Gale Research Inc., 1993 to date, semi-
    annual. $600.
    Print: 1993 to date, semiannual, 2 vols. $315.
    Online: 1994 to date, semiannual. ORBIT, $75 per hour.

The single best guide to electronic databases, from CD-ROMs and on-line services to magnetic tape is the comprehensive *Gale Directory of Databases.* There is nothing quite like it, and it is a necessary purchase for any library where there are questions about the content and availability of CD-ROMs and family. More than 10,000 databases are described in detail.

An important point: This is a bibliography of current databases. It lists what is available. It is nonevaluative, and can't be used for "best" or "better" anymore than one could turn to *Books in Print* for such help. To determine which is the most useful database for a given library requires reading in other places, and more particularly evaluations found in periodicals discussed throughout this text.

The print version consists of two volumes. The first covers online databases only. The second is primarily made up of CD-ROMs, but there are other sections on diskettes, magnetic tape, handheld products, and batch-access items. Both volumes have three helpful indexes: Database producers (about 3500)

---

[6]The directory represents a merger of titles described in the last edition of this text: *Cuadra's Directory of Portable Databases, Gale's Directory of Online Databases,* and *Gale's Computer-Readable Databases.*

    CD-ROMs in Print (Westport, CT: Meckler, 1987 to date, annual) is limited to CD-ROMs and describes over 5000. The descriptions are neither as full nor as accurate as those in the Gale directory. It sometimes has items not found in Gale, but other than that it is of little real value in any but the largest of libraries. Note: On CD-ROM it has a semiannual update for $165. There is no online version.

with their names and addresses and all of their products which, in turn, are numbered and refer to the first part of the guide. Online services (about 1900) which is primarily a listing of vendors and a geographical index. A subject index is a bit too broad, but is of some aid. Finally the complete master index covers everything in the book(s).

An introductory essay (repeated in each volume) gives an overview of the state of the art of databases for the previous year. This should be required reading. Often written by the expert of experts, Martha Williams, it highlights quantity and quality in electronic information sources.

Within each volume are individual entries for the formats arranged in alphabetical order. A systematic approach gives similar basic information for each item. There are 21 different pieces of data from the address and fax and phone number of the producer to "alternate electronic formats" for the product when available. The heart of the information is the "Content" note which gives precise information on what is included in the database. Years of coverage, frequency, price, and other information are part of each descriptive entry.

The online and CD-ROM versions are, of course, much easier to search than the two volumes; but the information in both is much the same. Where possible the library should have the CD-ROM, which at $600 is about twice the cost of the print volumes. At any rate, the reference guide is likely to be used as much by laypersons as librarians, and, in whatever form, it should be found in most libraries.

There are a growing number of guides to the "best" and "better" of CD-ROMs, but the majority are concerned with popular rather than reference-type discs. Among the guides is *CD-ROMs Rated* (New York: McGraw Hill, 1995 to date). Within the 304 pages are hundreds of reviews with one-paragraph descriptions of the contents. The discs are rated on a scale of 0 to 100 and are grouped under major subject categories. The book is packaged with a 650-megabyte demo disc containing a portion of the book.

Buying Guide Periodicals

There are numerous buying guides to help the librarian make decisions about the best types of computers and software. In a general way, the logical approach is to consult current issues of any of the computer magazines. (See the eighth edition of *Magazines for Libraries* for an evaluative, descriptive list of such titles.) *The New York Times* each Tuesday publishes a section on computers and "peripherals," which often considers software and hardware, both descriptively and in terms of what is best.

For a running account of both hardware and software see almost any issue of *Microcomputer Abstracts* (Medford, NJ: Learned Information, Inc., 1987 to date, monthly), which covers over 75 titles and includes sections on evaluation. Then, too, detailed judgments appear in numerous books such as the annual Harris

Publications *Computer Buyer's Guide.* A computer store is likely to have a dozen or more books which may be examined.

Reviews of software as well as notices about the latest books, hardware, searching techniques, and so forth, occur in the standard library journals from *RQ* and *Choice* to *Library Journal.* See, too, the *Microcomputer Software Guide* (New Providence, NJ: Reed Reference Publishing, 1990 to date, monthly) for descriptions of software from over 4000 publishers. In addition, at least four basic periodicals cover not only online searching but also new technologies. The four are: *Online,* which includes general material; *Database,* by the same publisher, which concentrates on specific databases; *Online Review,* a British-based periodical which is more scholarly than its American counterparts and covers a good deal of related territory; and *Computers in Libraries* which, as the title suggests, is directed almost exclusively to libraries. The articles are easy to understand and the material is directed primarily to beginners, not experts. All are fine sources of current material on various database reference guides and bibliographies, and they often run both critical and noncritical reviews of such materials.

A popular newsstand magazine can be recommended for a wide range of interest and for helping the librarian keep up with current traffic on the information highway. *Wired* (San Francisco, 1993 to date, monthly) has a wry sense of humor and features experienced writers. A single issue may move from a discussion of technical advantages of CD-ROMs to a look at the latest scandal about information in Washington. The only drawback is the flamboyant makeup which sometimes makes it hard to read.

BIBLIOGRAPHIES: NONPRINT MATERIALS

The previous discussion has been limited to guides and indexes to print and electronic bibliographies. There is another large group of reference works called "nonprint." Under this less-than-precise umbrella term one finds digital databases, discussed throughout these two volumes, and two universally familiar formats: (1) motion pictures, whether they be animation or videos or part of hypertext CD-ROMs; (2) sound, from music on CDs to voice-overs on CD-ROMs. Aside from these two everyday nonprint communication sources, there are items such as globes, overhead projector materials, and models. These items and the more traditional nonprint materials are an essential part of reference service, particularly in school libraries or, as they are called, "school media centers" or "learning centers."

When working with resources other than books, the reference librarian functions much as she or he would when working with the traditional media:

1. In schools, universities, and colleges, the librarian will be called upon by the classroom teacher for information on media that are available

in the library and may be ordered, or even borrowed, from other libraries.

2. The students will want information and advice about multimedia for the primary learning process.

3. The layperson's needs will be somewhat similar, although here most of the emphasis is likely to center on advice about the library's videos, recordings, and so on, which may extend knowledge (or recreational interests) beyond the traditional book.

The reference librarian should be conversant with at least the basic bibliographies and control devices for the media. Knowledge of bibliographies and sources is important for answering questions dealing directly with audiovisual materials: "Where can I find [such and such], a catalog of films, records, tapes?" "Do you have anything on video that will illustrate this or that?" "What do you have on recordings or video pertaining to local history?" In large libraries, such questions might be referred to the proper department, but in small- and medium-sized libraries, the questions usually will have to be answered by the reference librarian.

Guides and Bibliographies

CD: BiblioFile: NICEM AV MARC. Inwood, WV: The Library Corporation, 1991 to date, quarterly. $995.
   Print: NICEM Media Indexes. Albuquerque, NM: Access Innovations, 1967 to date. Various services, prices.
   Online: AV Online, 1964 to date, quarterly. DIALOG file 46, $70 per hour. Also available on CompuServe.

Print: The Video Source Book. Detroit: Gale Research Inc., 1978 to date, annual, 2 vols. $270.
   No electronic format.

CD: Variety Video Directory Plus. New York: R. R. Bowker, 1991, to date, quarterly. $395.
   Print: Bowker's Complete Video Directory, 1986 to date, annual, 3 vols. $230.

Print: Words on Cassette. New York: R. R. Bowker, 1994 to date, annual, 1880 pp. $145.
   No electronic format.

Print: Schwann Opus. Santa Fe, NM: Stereophile, 1949 to date, quarterly. $29.95.
   No electronic format.

There are no entirely satisfactory bibliographies for nonprint materials. The bibliographical utilities, OCLC and RLIN, may be used to trace specific items from films to videos, as long as they have been cataloged by member libraries or the Library of Congress. Still, this hardly gives an overview of the material as found, for example, in *Books in Print* or *Guide to Reference Books* for printed materials. Lacking overall bibliographical control, the materials are difficult to track. The lack of such tools accounts in no small way for the development of media experts who are familiar with the many access routes.

The closest thing to *Books in Print* for audiovisual materials is the *NICEM Media Indexes,* or *NICEM AV MARC* on CD-ROM. The purpose of these indexes, which are really bibliographies, is to provide noncritical information on what is available in nonprint materials. And, although directed at elementary and secondary school needs, a good deal of the data are applicable to other types of libraries. Hence they can be used to answer such queries as "What transparencies are available for geography?" "What educational films are there on animals?" "On environmental studies?" And so on.

The nonprofit National Information Center for Educational Media (NICEM) publishes a number of nonprint, audiovisual bibliographies on a regular time schedule. The print version is sold through NICEM, while the CD-ROM is from a private company. Essentially the database contains more than 800,000 records, often with abstracts, to educational materials. "Educational" must be stressed. There is nothing here which would pass, say, for a standard grade-B motion picture. The database includes: 16- and 35-millimeter filmstrips; transparencies; audio and video tapes; records, from early presses to advanced CDs; slides; 8-millimeter motion picture cartridges. CD-ROMs and software are indexed, too, but not thoroughly.

The *NICEM Print Indexes* are really a series of individual indexes, *not* a single work. Each item is briefly annotated, but only as description, not evaluation. Full information is given as to cost, rental (when available), and necessary bibliographical information for identification and order.

The index is updated quarterly in digital formats. As such the **CD-ROM** or online is preferable, particularly as the cost is only a bit more than the print format. Also, of course, searching a single **CD-ROM** is much easier than thumbing through individual volumes.

In libraries, videocassettes have replaced the traditional 16-millimeter films. The VCR is the most popular general tool for film viewing. There are now numerous guides to the "best" and "better" films on discs and tapes, as well as by subject, age, interest, and so forth. Selected lists of the "best" movies for home entertainment are common.

Unlike the NICEM indexes and bibliographies, the *Video Source Book* (available only in print) is not limited to educational materials, although they are included among the 100,000-plus listings. Each of the videos is described in terms of content, audience, use, genre, and the like. The publisher states that 35,000 of the entries are primarily for educational purposes and another 16,000 for business and technology, that is, for closed-circuit broadcast. About 57,000 titles represent what many people enjoy viewing in their homes. Arrangement is alphabetical by title with full bibliographical information and numerous indexes. Titles are assigned one of eight main categories from "Children" and "Business" to "Movies/Entertainment." Within these broad groups are over 400 more specific subject divisions. By far the most comprehensive index of its type, it is a basic necessity for any library with a large video collection.

Gale publishes a series of *VideoHound's* which are brief reviews and listings of videos and motion pictures for particular situations—situations explained in the titles: *VideoHound's Golden Movie Retriever* (23,000 films for entertainment); . . . *Family Video Retriever* (4000 flicks to offend no one); . . .*Pocket Movie Guide* (the top 106 favorites of all times); . . . *Nightmares;* and so on. Priced from $5 to $20 the guides are useful for the public more than for the librarian. They are reliable and current. Most are updated each year. All are in the style of the familiar paperback guides to movies and videos such as *Leonard Maltin's Movie and Video Guide* (New York: Penguin Books, 199–, annual).

The CD-ROM *Variety's Video Directory Plus* is a detailed listing of some 92,000 videocassettes—as well as related laserdisks and interactive CD-ROMs. Complete bibliographical information is given from title and price to ISBN number. More important, the descriptive annotations give the reader an excellent idea of content, if not always quality, although quality is implied by the small group of 92,000 entries. About 8000 entries, which, primarily, were first motion pictures and are most likely to be used in the home, have complete reviews from *Variety,* the "bible" of the entertainment industry. This latter feature of the directory gives it a special role in larger public libraries, where both librarians and laypersons may wish to refer to the detailed reviews before buying or renting the video.

In print, as in the CD-ROM, one finds not only entertainment videos (in the first of three volumes), but also educational and special interest videos (in the other two volumes). Here, however, the reviews from *Variety* are not included. Another important difference is that the CD-ROM is published and updated every quarter, while the three volumes in print come out only once each year. An obvious difference is that one may search the digital database from title of video to genre and related key words. The printed volumes have numerous indexes as well, but nothing as complete a search can be made as on the CD-ROM.

Libraries with audiocassettes, or users who want to find out what is available in this format should turn to the self-explanatory *Words on Cassette.* This lists 60,000 audiocassettes covering over 150 subjects with numerous indexes. The producers and distributors are dutifully listed, and there are four indexes from title to subject to authors, performers, and level of listeners.

The "books in print" of recorded sound, *Schwann Opus* offers primarily a listing of classical music on CDs. Cassettes and available laser discs are included. The paperback guide is well-known to classical music lovers, and to anyone who has ever wandered into a music section of a store. Listings are under "Composers" and "Collections." The same publisher's listing of popular music is the quarterly Schwann *Spectrum* for $24.95 per year.

A useful guide is available for those confused and lost in the world (swamp?) of multimedia. This is Pat Dillon and Dave Leonard's *Multimedia Technology from A to Z* (Phoenix, AZ: Oryx Press, 1995). Both a dictionary and text the clearly organized guide covers all terms and problems from the visual arts to telecommunications. Note, too, the excellent bibliography.

Index to Reviews

Print: Media Review Digest. Ann Arbor, MI: The Pierian Press, 1970 to date, annual. $245.
    No CD-ROM version, but available on magnetic tape.

Media Review Digest indexes reviews of media which have appeared in over 135 periodicals. The 40,000 or so indexed reviews include full citations by type of medium. Some excerpts from reviews are given and an evaluative sign shows whether the comments were favorable or not. A librarian can use it in almost the same way as the indexes to book reviews, that is, to check reviews, probably for purposes of buying or renting a given item. The information provided is full, and often includes descriptions of the material as well as cataloging information.

Again, as with book reviews, the librarian may turn to a periodical index, preferably one online for current reviews of media from videos to films and CDs. This is particularly wise as the *Digest* is published only once a year and is of little value for current reviews.

Precision One MediaSource (Williamsport, PA: Brodart Automation, 1994 to date, annual, $395) is a CD-ROM which gives the user access to thousands of media items from CD-ROMs and videos to films and recordings. These represent the holdings and the efforts of the Consortium of College & University Media Centers who worked with Brodart to produce the database. Full bibliographical information is given for each item as well as information on the costs to purchase or rent. The bibliography may be accessed by title, subject, run time, producer, and the like. More limited than the other sources noted here, it serves a useful purpose for identification and verification.

Microform

Print: Guide to Microforms in Print: Author-Title. New Providence, NJ: Reed Reference Publishing, 1961 to date, annual, 2 vols. $400.
    No electronic format.

While there is every reason to believe that in a decade or so microform will be entirely replaced by full texts in digital form (Online, CD-ROM, etc.), today it remains an important part of many library collections. Microform is used in libraries to preserve space, keep bibliographies and other reference aids relatively current, and provide easy access to users.

Microform exists in two formats: the roll and the flat transparency or card. The familiar 35-millimeter reel or roll has been in libraries for so long that many librarians and users think only of this form when microform is mentioned. The flat microform comes in several basic varieties: (1) Microfiche, or fiche, is available in different sizes, but the favored is the standard 4 by 6 inches, with an average of 98 pages per sheet. Various reductions may either increase or decrease the number of pages on a sheet. (2) Ultrafiche, as the name implies, is an ultrafine reduction, usually on a 4- by 6-inch transparency. One card may contain 3000 to 5000 pages. (3) Micropoint is a 6- by 9-inch card which contains up to 100 pages of text in 10 rows and 10 columns.

For purposes of storage and convenience, most librarians with substantial holdings in periodicals and newspapers store them on microform. Books, particularly those hard to locate or out of print, are on microform as are various other printed works, from reports to government documents.

The equivalent of *Books in Print* for microform is the ever-expanding *Guide to Microforms in Print*. It lists alphabetically over 100,000 titles from some 500 publishers, including international firms. Arranged by title and author in one alphabetical listing, the guide lists books, journals, newspapers, government publications, and related materials. Sixteen different types of microform are considered, and the types, with explanation, are listed in the preface. Not all materials on microform are listed, including theses and dissertations. The second volume is a supplement which is published six months after the main volume.

SUGGESTED READING

Baker, Nicholson, "Discards," *The New Yorker*, April 4, 1994, pp. 64–87. A novelist explains why some, at least, are unhappy with the discard of the old card catalog. Along the way he explores the use of OCLC and other technologies—all in an amusing, generally accurate fashion. One of the few articles, by the way, on libraries to appear in *The New Yorker*.

Bellarby, Liz, "A Comparison of Two Personal Bibliographic Software Packages: EndNote and Pro-Cite," *The Law Librarian*, March 1993, pp. 22–23. These types of study, and they are numerous, not only indicate what to look out for in electronic bibliographies but indicate general rules of the art. See, too, Sue Sigleman, "Papyrus . . . ," *Database*, June 1993, pp. 82–87.

Brown, Christopher, "Creating Automated Bibliographies," *Database*, February 1994, p. 67–71. The author explains how to compile a bibliography using Internet's access to catalogs. The method of editing and examples of downloaded bibliographical citations are given. A useful guide for electronic-originated bibliographies.

Harmon, Robert, *Elements of Bibliography*. Metuchen, NJ: Scarecrow Press, 1989. This is a revised edition of a basic guide to the fundamentals of bibliography for beginners. It is particularly good in its discussion of the often-used enumerative bibliographies. Some attention is given to the electronic forms of bibliography.

Henige, David, "When Bad Is Good Enough: The Lowest Common Denominator in Reference Publishing and Reviewing," *Reference Services Review*, Spring 1991, pp. 7–14. An African specialist uses a less-than-perfect reference work to test what reviewers have to say about the book. Most find it acceptable. Much the same is found for other titles tested. He concludes that reviewers are not given adequate space for reviews or are often not qualified in the subject area. "Perhaps what is needed is a new serial publication dedicated to providing analyses of the worst reference books."

Huston, Mary, and Maureen Pastine, eds., "In the Spirit of 1992: Access to Western European Libraries and Literature," *The Reference Librarian*, no. 35, 1992. Bibliographical paths to the resources of libraries outside the United States are studied by the various contributors. The larger questions of international cooperation are spotlighted.

Landau, Herbert, "Microform vs. CD-ROM: Is There a Difference?" *Library Journal*, October 15, 1990, pp. 56–59. The question is answered in the affirmative. However, the author believes there is a place for both forms in the modern library. The article stresses the importance of different types of format for data.

McCombs, Gillian, ed., "Access Services: The Convergence of Reference and Technical Services," *The Reference Librarian*, no. 34, 1991. An experienced technical service expert pulls together various points of view and various topics of interest which involve both technical services and reference work. A good deal of this carefully edited issue concerns the convergence of bibliography and technical services.

Stephens, Andy, *The History of* The British National Bibliography. Boston Spa: British Library, 1994, 159 pp. $30. While not an easy book to read, the author does trace the history of the national bibliography from its beginnings in 1950 until the mid-1970s. The *BNB* led the world in the use of computers.

Stokes, Roy, *A Bibliographical Companion*. Metuchen, NJ: Scarecrow Press, 1989. This is a dictionary of terms employed in bibliography. The descriptions, terminology, and general approach are as literate as they are a delight to read. Highly recommended for both beginners and would-be experts.

Studies in Bibliography. Charlottesville, VA: University of Virginia, various dates. Published for the Bibliographic Society of the University of Virginia, this annual publication contains articles of particular interest to textual and analytical bibliographers. A cursory glance at any of the contributions will give the student an excellent idea of what the process is about. Besides that, many of the pieces are fine reading in themselves.

CHAPTER FOUR
BIBLIOGRAPHIES: NATIONAL LIBRARY CATALOGS AND TRADE BIBLIOGRAPHIES

Someone wants to know how much information is available on a given sub-ject, such as eighteenth-century gardens or nuclear-waste dumping facilities. Thanks to Internet and the bibliographical utilities, OCLC and RLIN, it is now possible to search gigantic databases. Under normal circumstances the search will reveal all primary and many minor publications. The problem no longer is locating *everything* available. The problem is determining what is *relevant.* Rele-vancy, discussed throughout this text, is the major hurdle for both laypersons and librarians. The ability to locate precisely what is needed distinguishes the reference librarian as a professional. Bibliographies are the primary profes-sional tools for precision selection.

Bibliographies offer a type of coordination, a kind of fitting together of different pieces of a puzzle, which allows an overview of what is available from many parts of the world. Since OCLC, RLIN, and a national library catalog are not limited by time, territory, language, subject, or forms of communica-tion, combined they come close to the ideal bibliography. And although none claim to be universal in scope, collectively they do offer a relatively compre-hensive record of international publishing. The Library of Congress, for exam-ple, catalogs materials from around the world, and a good proportion of its hold-ings consists of books, magazines, music, and the like from international publishers. Numerically, an idea of the scope of the Library of Congress hold-ings may be gathered from the fact that the Library contains more than 14 mil-lion books and 100 million discrete items. About 5 to 6 million new items are added each year. Comparatively speaking, the average number of books pub-lished in America each year hovers around 40,000 to 50,000 titles, a small part of the overall annual acquisitions of the Library of Congress net, which sweeps in books as well as other published items from around the world. Quite similar figures apply to all national libraries.

In order to be properly qualified as a national bibliography, the system must have two elements: (1) It needs a legal deposit system which ensures that the national library receives a copy of everything to be listed in the bibliography; and (2) the records must be from direct examination of the materials, not from the publisher or author. Most western countries now have depository and direct examination as the foundation for national bibliography.

Form

Bibliographies and other reference works may be accessed online, through CD-ROM, print, or microfiche. Today the online/CD-ROM approach is favored. It will lead to two results:

1. By the end of this century, few national or general bibliographies will be available in print. The majority will be accessible only in an electronic form. This is not only less expensive but allows for faster updating of material and for easier searching.

2. There will, however, be "esoteric" printed bibliographies. These will be detailed scholarly works dealing with a specific subject. It is unlikely that analytical or textual bibliographies will be limited to electronic access because they are less frequently used and as of now are less costly to produce in print form.

Meanwhile, one must learn about the scope of bibliographies. Why? Although the form may be transferred to an electronic system, the content is similar. The method of compilation and the problems involved are the same. The basic theory behind the intellectual approach to bibliography does not differ. What is more important to consider, no matter in what format, is that the bibliography has definite uses, uses which can only be understood when one appreciates the scope and purpose of a particular type of bibliography.

UNION CATALOGS

A term associated with national catalogs is *union catalog* as, for example, the Library of Congress's *National Union Catalog.* A union catalog indicates who has what. A fuller, often-repeated definition is this: an inventory common to several libraries that lists some or all of their publications maintained in one or more orders of arrangement. The user turns to a union list to locate a given book, CD-ROM, periodical, or newspaper in another library, which may be in the same city or thousands of miles away. Given the location and the operation of an interlibrary loan or copying process, the user can then have the particular book or item borrowed from the holding library.

National Union Catalog (MARC)[1]

CD: CDMARC Bibliographic. Washington, DC: Library of Congress, 1968 to date, quarterly. $1200.
Online: LCMARC: Book All, 1968 to date, monthly. DIALOG file 426, $57 per hour. (DIALOG file updated weekly.) Also available in numerous services including WilsonLine, $32 to $45 per hour.[2]
Online: OCLC's First Search, World Cat. Update varies according to period covered. Rate varies.
Online: RLIN. Update varies according to period covered.[3] Rate varies.
Microform: The National Union Catalogs in Microfiche. Washington, DC: Library of Congress, January 1983 to date. Monthly issues and quarterly cumulations: (1) *NUC Books,* $580. (2) *NUC Audiovisual Materials,* quarterly, $95. (3) *NUC Cartographic Materials,* quarterly, $175. (4) *NUC Register of Additional Locations,* quarterly, $295.

The *National Union Catalog,* or *NUC* as it is often called, is a bibliography that is frequently consulted. Today the *NUC* is as much a part of online/CD-ROM searches as any reference work in the library. Normally the search is through OCLC or RLIN. Except for unusual cases, the microfiche or the printed volumes (which were used before electronic databases) are not used. Any library large enough to want the *NUC* has it available online, on CD-ROM or both. The microfiche is, to say the least, awkward and cumbersome as a cursory glance at the instructions issued by the Library of Congress will show.

Anyone looking for a book (by author, by subject, or by title) in the local library catalog can understand the scope and purpose of the *National Union Catalog.* Published by the Library of Congress, the *NUC* is no more than a vastly

---

[1]Before 1983 the *NUC* was issued in paperback volumes and then cumulated in hardbound volumes from 1956 to 1983. The various-colored bound cumulations are found in many libraries to this day, although they are rarely used. The printed set is in two parts: (1) *The National Union Catalog: A Cumulative Author List* (from 1956 to 1983) and (2) *Library of Congress Catalogs: Subject Catalog* (from 1950 to 1983). Subject access was available only from 1945. A third set, *Pre-1956 Imprints,* is discussed in the text. There were volumes, too, for audiovisual and other media.

[2]The *NUC* is referred to online in two parts: (1) MARC, an acronym for *machine-readable cataloging,* has reference to the *NUC* from 1968 through today, and now consists of over 2.5 million records. It is updated monthly with about 15,000 new records a month. (2) REMARC, an acronym for *retrospective machine-readable cataloging,* or retrospective MARC has reference primarily, although not exclusively, to many of the records in the *Pre-1956 Imprints* set.

[3]*Online via OCLC and/or RLIN.* OCLC and RLIN allow member libraries to share cataloging information. This information includes the basic Library of Congress cataloging on MARC tapes. The utilities offer catalog and reference information for about 40 million works.

expanded version of the local university, public, or school catalog. Here the librarian turns for three basic types of information: (1) The traditional bibliographical data from how authors spell their names to available books on Kenya. (2) Having located a book on Kenya which is not in the local catalog, the librarian is given enough information from the *NUC* to order the title on interlibrary loan. (3) If the librarian is a cataloger, the data called up for a book may be used for the local library catalog, thus avoiding the necessity of cataloging the book in the local library. There are numerous other ways the *NUC* is employed by librarians including equally excellent access to other communication formats from recordings to software.

Background

The National Union Catalog began in card form in 1901. By 1926, the *NUC* had over 2 million cards, physically located in the Library of Congress. Anyone who wanted to consult the *NUC* had to query the Library of Congress or go there in person. The problem was solved, or so it was thought, by sending duplicate cards to the *NUC* to key research libraries throughout the United States. This procedure proved as costly as it was inefficient. Beginning therefore, in the early 1940s, work started on the printed-book catalog. The individual cards were reproduced in the familiar *NUC* book form instead of being sent to libraries card by card. However, it was not decided until January 1, 1956, that the book catalogs should be expanded to include not only Library of Congress holdings but also the imprints of other libraries.

What was to be done with *The National Union Catalog* prior to 1956, that is, with the card catalog in the Library of Congress which was not in book form? The answer came in 1968 when *The National Union Catalog: Pre-1956 Imprints* began to be published.

The *Pre-1956 Imprints* (London: Mansell, 1968–1981, 754 vols. $35,000. Microform: $11,750) is a cumulative *National Union Catalog* up to 1956. The more than 11 million entries represent the *NUC* holdings prior to 1956. The rapid development of technology, from microfiche to online catalogs, makes it unlikely that there will ever be another printed bibliography of this size. (Balanced one upon the other, the 13.6-inch-tall volumes in a single set would stack higher than the Pan American Building in New York.)

Scope

What is the scope of the *NUC?*

At a computer terminal one may call up the full bibliographical description of over 20 million books, most of which are in the Library of Congress and have been cataloged since the founding of the collection. At the same time one is able to find titles unique to one or more of the 1500 other libraries who feed information into the *NUC.* Essentially, the scope is wide enough to include virtually every book published from the first printing press in the Colonies to the present. It is much wider in that it includes, too, titles from the world around.

In addition to books, there are approximately 85 to 90 million items in different formats, from maps and periodicals to manuscripts and recordings. All may be located through the same *NUC*. These are available online as part of the LCMARC family, that is, after *LCMARC: Books All*, there are *LCMARC: Maps* (with close to 140,000 maps); music (110,000 or so printed music and manuscript music); serials (700,000 plus serials); visual materials (120,000 AV items). Also, these are part of the magnetic tapes issued by the Library of Congress. They are, for the most part, accessed in libraries through OCLC or RLIN.[4]

Generally, the *National Union Catalog* offers the average individual all the bibliographical information needed. Still, there comes a time when more detail is required, when an item is so scarce, so elusive, and so esoteric that it may not be fully described (particularly in terms of its importance in the development of a subject) in *NUC*. At this point the search leads toward one of numerous retrospective enumerative, analytical, or textual bibliographies. The basic bibliographies of this type are dutifully listed in both *Guide to Reference Books* and *Guide to Reference Materials*, as well as in specialized bibliographies dealing with everything from the history of printing to the history of medicine.

Use

How is *The National Union Catalog (NUC)* used in reference work? (What follows relates in particular to the printed format, but content is the same in the digitalized forms.)

1. Since this is a union catalog that shows not only the holdings of the Library of Congress but also titles in over 1500 other libraries, it allows the reference librarian to locate a given title quickly. Hence users who need a work that is not in their library may find the nearest location in *The National Union Catalog*. For example, the first edition of *I Remember* by J. Henry Harper is identified as being in eight other libraries. Location symbols for the eight are: OOxM, TxU, OCU, OCL, MnU, NIC, ViBibV, and WU. The initials stand for libraries in various parts of the country and are explained in the front of cumulative volumes. Depending on the policy of the holding library, the librarian may or may not be able to borrow the title on interlibrary loan. Failing a loan, it may be possible to get sections copied. All titles without indication of a contributing library are held by the Library of Congress. (The symbol of the Library is DLC.) Books are listed chronologically by the Library of Congress catalog card number.

[4]On CD-ROMs, either from private publishers or the Library of Congress, the bibliographical data are limited primarily to books and to serials—at least for the present.

2. *The National Union Catalog* amounts to virtually a basic, full author bibliography. Anyone wanting to know every book (magazine articles and other such items aside) that author X has published has only to consult the author's name.

3. There is no end of the subject search possibilities, particularly of the digital databases where it is possible to search not only for assigned Library of Congress subject headings, but key words in the title and descriptive matter. Unless it is an extremely esoteric subject the librarian inevitably will need to modify by place, time, and so forth, or be swamped with too much material.

4. The *NUC* gives details on a book (e.g., when it was published, by whom, and where) and helps the reference librarian verify that it exists—an important matter when there is a question as to whether a particular publisher actually did publish this or that. Verification, however, is even more important when the reference librarian is attempting to straighten out the misspelling of a title or an author's name. In other words, the *NUC* sets the record straight when there is doubt about the validity of a given bit of information.

5. In terms of acquisitions, particularly of expensive or rare items, *NUC* permits a library to concentrate in subject areas with the assurance that the less-developed areas may be augmented by interlibrary loan from other libraries.

6. In terms of cataloging (which is basic to reference service), the *NUC* offers a number of advantages. The primary asset is central cataloging, which should limit the amount of original cataloging necessary.

7. The seventh advantage of *The National Union Catalog* is as much psychological as it is real. Its very existence gives the librarian (and more-involved lay users) a sense of order and control which would otherwise be lacking in a world that cries for some type of order.

Searching

Through a series of simple commands, the searcher uses the *NUC* usually on OCLC and RLIN. In addition, one may access the online version of the *NUC* (1) by accessing it through a commercial vendor such as DIALOG, (2) by the individual library which has *NUC* as part of the online library catalog, or (3) by simply buying the tapes as issued by the Library of Congress for various uses, private and public.

The cost of accessing the *NUC* online may be so high (it varies from service to service but is now around $50 an hour) that the library finds it more economical to get the same data on a CD-ROM from the Library of Congress, or from a commercial firm. There are several firms that offer MARC or RE-MARC, or both, on CD-ROM. Turn to the *Gale Directory of Databases* for publishers, or consult advertisements and mailings which inundate libraries each time a new service is made available by a publisher of CD-ROM.[5]

The future of bibliographic services is tied closely to cataloging which, in turn, has become truly national and international in scope and operation. "To reduce the workload on our technical services departments, release librarian for more public service tasks, and yet ensure the quality of catalog records . . . a high quality centralized cataloging facility, operating at standards set by the library community, is very likely to emerge over the next decade."[6]

Internet

The *NUC* and over 700 different library catalogs are available through various channels of the Internet. Many people these days simply want to find out what is available in their own library catalog(s), either at home or at work. They search on a PC through the Internet.

Using bibliography formatting software (such as End Note and End Link) one may build a file of up to 32,000 or more references. For example, one might tap into the University of California's Online Catalog *MELVIL* and tag records for a bibliography on environment or Jack London or whatever is needed. Records are displayed, the user tags what is wanted (and can even specify what to include or exclude from the record, such as a call number). The completed bibliography may then be downloaded or sent from the *MELVIL* by e-mail.

NATIONAL BIBLIOGRAPHIES OUTSIDE THE UNITED STATES

European national libraries follow much the same pattern as the Library of Congress. Each nation has its own bibliography. These are listed in detail in the *Guide to Reference Books*, and can only be suggested here. Today all are in several forms from the traditional printed book to online and CD-ROM.

More important, all are available through a bibliographical utility such as OCLC and RLIN. Both of these have many of the millions of titles listed in the other national bibliographies, and most Americans turn to European and

---

[5]The Library Corporation (Inwood, WV) is one of a half dozen or so private vendors of the *NUC* under the name Bibliofile. There are numerous divisions such as *BiblioFile: LCMARC English Language,* a weekly CD-ROM for $3000 a year. This is limited to English language records from books to music.

[6]Joan Segal, "Library Cooperation and Networking," in *The Bowker Annual* (New York: R. R. Bowker, 1994), p. 68.

other national bibliographies only when they have exhausted the content of OCLC and RLIN.

Meanwhile, the Canadian and the British national bibliographies are put to great use. The reason, of course, is that they are primarily concerned with books in the English language. Scholars and those with knowledge of other languages turn to the other bibliographies.

National Bibliography in Canada[7]

CD: CD-CATSS. Etobicoke, ON: ISM Library of Information Services, 1983 to date, quarterly. $2,532.
  Print: Canadiana: Canada's National Bibliography. Ottawa, ON: National Library of Canada, 1867 to date, monthly, annual cumulations. Price varies. (Available on microfiche.)
  Online: DOBIS Canadian Online Library System. Ottawa, ON: National Library of Canada, 1951 to date, weekly. Rate varies.

The Canadian equivalent of the online LCMARC series, DOBIS has more than 9 million bibliographical records. Only part of these are found in either the magnetic tape format or the print version. In other words, DOBIS is the first, the best, and for some, the only place to turn for titles found in the National Library of Canada as well as in about 1000 cooperating libraries. Some 45,000 serials are in the social sciences and humanities, as well as close to 70,000 in sciences. A wide variety of other materials are dutifully cataloged. Through DOBIS one may search the files in the standard way, as well as by Library of Congress numbers. Much of the material is a repetition of what is found in the Library of Congress records and is available, too, through OCLC and RLIN.

The Canadian cousin to OCLC/RLIN is the *ISM Library Information Services* (formerly *UTLAS International Canada*) or, as it is called more specifically, the CATSS (Catalogue Support System) which has 60 million records from the National Library of Canada, the Library of Congress, British Library, and all major national libraries. At its heart, of course, is the DOBIS system as well as all other basic Canadian bibliographies. Updated daily, it is an excellent service which is used by many larger American libraries as well as most Canadian libraries.

Some retrospective and most ongoing records from the online bibliographical utility are available on CD-ROM as CD-CATSS. This contains about 2 million (vs. 9-plus million online) records and is updated quarterly. It serves the purpose of the ongoing LCMARC database in the United States.

---

[7]For detailed descriptions of the variations on Canadian bibliography see Kirsti Nilsen, *Guide to Reference Materials for Canadian Libraries*, 8th ed. (Toronto: University of Toronto Press, 1992).

National Bibliography in Great Britain

CD: BLGC on CD-ROM. Boston Spa: British Library, 1991. Not updated. $18,500.
Print: The British Library General Catalogue of Printed Books. London: Bingley, 1980–1987. 360 vols. 1975 (after 1975 supplements bring the set up to 1994). Price varies.
Online: British Library Catalogue, 1975 to date, updated irregularly. BLAISE-LINE, $15 per hour.

CD: BNB on CD-ROM. Boston Spa: British Library, 1950 to date, monthly. $1,600.
Print: The British National Bibliography, 1950 to date, weekly. Rate varies.
Online: BNBMARC, 1950 to date, weekly. BLAISE-LINE, $15 per hour.

The *British Library Catalogue,* like the *National Union Catalog,* covers various types of materials with separate databases for print, music, maps, and so on. Online they may be searched as a single unit. The basic *Catalogue* contains citations to items in what was known as the *British Museum Department of Printed Books.* (The 360 volumes of this catalogue are still much in use at the British Library Reading Room.) There are about 3.8 million titles acquired to 1976. After that the *Catalogue* is supplemented, both in print and online, by current acquisitions. In total there are well over 10 million citations.

The CD-ROM version, which is not updated, has about 8.5 million citations representing the majority of material acquired by the Library before 1976. It serves primarily as a resource for those who do not wish to turn to the more comprehensive, updated version online.

Published on CD-ROM since 1950, the *British National Bibliography* by the mid-1990s had cumulated more than 1 million bibliographical records. It is the source of information on current titles and, for catalogers, essentially the equivalent of the United States *NUC.* The *BNB* includes only titles published in Great Britain and deposited as copyright evidence. As such it includes all types of printed and digital records from books, music, and government documents to serials and textbooks. Online, the BNBMARC database is precisely the same in content, but it is updated weekly. From 1977 on, the service includes an equivalent of "forthcoming books." The last issue each month of the printed version has a complete cumulative author, title, and subject index.

As in North America, the British and Europeans search primarily in bibliographical utilities in which the national bibliographies are an important core. While British librarians and laypersons use OCLC and RLIN and the Canadian CATSS (which includes much of the British bibliographical work), they have their own online aid in the British Library-National Bibliographic Service or BLAISE-LINE. This includes all of the records on BNBMARC, as well as current and retrospective records from the *British Library General Catalogue,* LCMARC online material, and other bibliographical data. Coverage is relatively complete for titles in the English language. There is more emphasis on European Union publications than on American services.

How much duplication is there between the massive British catalog and *The National Union Catalog?* Walford did a sampling and found that 75 to 80 percent of the titles in the British work are not in the American equivalent, and for titles published before 1800 that number increases to 90 percent. Some experts estimate that there are from 900,000 to over 1 million titles in the British Library catalog not found in other national bibliographies. With increased interest in capturing worldwide titles in *The National Union Catalog,* the amount of duplication is bound to increase in the years ahead. Meanwhile, no large research library can afford to be without the British Library's *General Catalogue* online or on CD-ROM. Better yet, the researcher should have access to holdings of the British Library through BLAISE-LINE or CATSS, the Canadian service.

In 1994 the Americans and British decided to create a single authoritative list of their collections. The decision is based on the need for rules covering both the British and American catalogs because many more people access the catalogs through computer networks. Lacking standard rules, to find a book in both catalogs had become laborious. The decision to standardize the names of authors, as well as spelling (color is now "color" instead of the English "colour"), should help matters.

TRADE BIBLIOGRAPHY

Most of the enumerative bibliographies found in libraries can be classified as national or trade bibliographies. The distinction between the types is not always clear, if indeed there is a distinction. There are numerous definitions and possible combinations. The important consideration is not so much where the bibliography falls in the sometimes esoteric reference scheme but, rather, how it is used.

The pragmatic function of a trade bibliography is to tell the librarian what was, what is, and what will be available either by purchase or by possible loan from another library. The bibliographies give necessary bibliographical information (e.g., publisher, price, author, subject area, and Library of Congress or Dewey numbers), which is used for a number of purposes ranging from clarifying proper spelling to locating an item by subject area. Also, the trade bibliography is a primary control device for bringing some order to the books published in the United States each year, not to mention pamphlets, reports, recordings, films, and other items.

The process of compiling trade bibliographies differs from country to country, but there is a basic pattern. An initial effort is made to give a current listing of titles published the previous week, month, or quarter. These data are then cumulated for the annual breakdown of titles published, and beyond that, those which are in print, those which are out of print, and those which are going to be published. (The same process applies to forms other than books.)

Thanks to electronic databases online and on CD-ROMs the whole process has been speeded up as well as made easier for the user. A single keyboard and monitor may be used to search countless possibilities for a given title, author, subject, and the like. This not only improves searching, but lowers the price of those searches. All of this is illustrated by the Reed Reference Publishing (i.e., R. R. Bowker) series which is the heart of American trade bibliography.

United States Trade Bibliography[8]

All titles listed below are published by R. R. Bowker Company, a subsidiary of Reed Reference Publishing.

CD: Books in Print Plus. 1986 to date, monthly. $1,095.
> *Print: Books in Print,* 1948 to date, 10 vols., annual. $475. *Supplement,* 1973 to date, 3 vols., annual. $245. *Subject Guide to Books in Print,* 1957 to date, 5 vols., annual. $330.
> *Print: Forthcoming Books,* 1966 to date, bimonthly. $240.
> *Print: Paperbound Books in Print,* 1955 to date, 3 vols., biannual. $350.
> *Online: Books in Print Online* (BIP), 1991 to date, monthly. DIALOG file 470, $60 per hour. Also available on CDP, CompuServe, at various rates.

These bibliographies list the books that can be purchased from American publishers (i.e., are in print), in what forms (hardbound, paperback), and at what prices. Depending on the individual title, additional information is given as to the date of publication, the number of pages, the subjects covered, and other data necessary for proper and easy use of the bibliography.

All are bunched together as a group and become a CD-ROM or an online electronic database. In order to understand how the individual titles fit into the group, consider each as it appears in print.

It is worth emphasizing that libraries may prefer the print volumes because (1) they want only one unit, not the whole group; or (2) they wish to save cost by paying for only one or two print units rather than for the group as a whole.

---

[8]Before the widespread use of OCLC, RLIN, and their easy access to the *National Union Catalog* (and Library of Congress cataloging), two trade bibliography publications were used widely in libraries. Both maintain a running monthly record of English language books published in the United States. They are now of no value to reference librarians (catalogers may not agree). They are: (1) *American Book Publishing Record* (New Providence, NJ: Reed Reference Publishing, 1961 to date, monthly, $225; cumulations back to 1985). (2) *Cumulative Book Index* (New York: H. W. Wilson Company, 1898 to date, monthly; service). (The *CBI* casts a wider net, and includes books from England, Canada, etc.). Both are of interest for historical purposes, particularly the *CBI* which goes back to the late nineteenth century. *Note:* The *CBI* is available online through WilsonLine at $34 to $50 per hour, and is available, too, on OCLC.

Print

The most frequently consulted titles are *Books in Print* (*BIP*) and the *Subject Guide to Books in Print*. More than 1.5 million in-print books of all kinds (hardbounds, paperbacks, trade books, textbooks, adult titles, juveniles) are indexed by author and by title in *Books in Print*. (*In print* is a term that indicates the book is still available from a publisher. If not available, it is called "out of print.") The set is in four parts: (1) authors, (2) titles, (3) O.P. (out of print) and O.S. (out of stock), and (4) publishers. Actually the last volume may be used independently, as noted later, as a handy guide to publishers.

Besides telling the user whether the book can be purchased, from whom, and at what price, the trade bibliography also answers such questions as: "What books by William Faulkner are in print, including both hardbound and paperbound editions at various prices?" "Who is the publisher of *The Old Patagonian Express?*" "Is John Irving's first novel still in print?"

Almost every entry in *BIP* includes the author, coauthor (if any), editor, price, publisher, year of publication, number of volumes, Library of Congress card number, and the International Standard Book Number (ISBN).

The majority of titles listed in *BIP* are similarly found in *Subject Guide to Books in Print*. In the subject approach, no entries are made for fiction, poetry, or bibles. (Note, though, that the guide does list books *about* fiction under the name of the author of the fiction; criticism of the works of Henry James, for example, is found under James.) The use of the subject guide, which virtually rearranges *BIP* under 77,000 Library of Congress subject headings, is self-evident.[9] It not only helps in locating books about a given subject but may also be used to expand the library's collection in given areas. If, for example, books about veterinarians are in great demand, the guide gives a complete list of those available from American publishers. An important point: The list is inclusive, not selective. No warning sign differentiates the world's most misleading book about veterinarians from the best among, say, 20 titles listed. The librarian must turn to other bibliographies and reviews for judgments and evaluations of titles in any subject area.

A fifth volume lists and cross-references all headings from the *Subject Guide*. The fact that sometimes the inquiry cannot be answered is not always the fault of the questioner's incorrect spelling of the title or the author's name. *Books in Print,* through either filing errors or misinformation from the publishers, may fail to guide a user to a title which the user knows to be correct.

Issued in September of each year, *Books in Print* is supplemented by three volumes in March of the following year. Publishers list some 250,000 newly pub-

[9]Library of Congress subject cataloging is used only as a guide, and Bowker or the publisher frequently assigns modified Library of Congress headings. This, coupled with only about 1.1 subject headings per book, results in less than satisfactory retrieval. Often, too, a vast number of titles may be assigned under a heading so broad that a search is almost impossible. The solution is an electronic database which allows for both subject and keyword searching.

lished titles, price changes not included in the basic *BIP*, as well as titles that are out of print or are to be issued before the next annual *BIP* volumes. These listings are arranged by author and by title as well as by subject; thus the *Books in Print Supplement* is also a supplement to *Subject Guide to Books in Print*. The *Supplement* includes an updated list of all publishers, with any address changes. For normal purposes, *BIP* is enough for most questions. When the original publishing date is more than one or two years old, when there has been a spurt of inflation, or when the librarian cannot find a title, a double check in the *Books in Print Supplement* is wise.

A definitive approach to what is going to be published is found in *Forthcoming Books*. This is likely to be of more value to acquisitions and cataloging personnel than to reference, but it does answer queries about a new book or possibly about a book the patron may have heard discussed on a radio or television program before it is actually published. The bimonthly lists books due to be published within the next five months by author and by title. Each issue of some 75,000 titles includes a separate subject guide.

Paperbound Books in Print, takes the paperbound titles out of *Books in Print* and, again, arranges them by author, title, and subject. The end result is a separate work with about 500,000 in-print titles. It has two distinct advantages over its parent volumes: (1) It is updated twice each year, spring and fall. The spring update, includes about 25,000 new titles, plus 100,000 entry updates. (2) It is limited to paperbacks and therefore removes any confusion about the various forms in which the title may appear.

As in the *Books in Print* series, all western countries have much the same system for keeping track of titles published and in print. In England, for example, there is the well-known *Whitaker's Cumulative Book List* (London: Whitaker, 1924 to date, quarterly), which is cumulated annually. The annual volume, has about 600,000 titles arranged in one alphabet, by author, title, and subject.

For Canada there is *Canadian Books in Print* (Downsview, ON: University of Toronto Press, 1967 to date, annual). This is in two volumes. The first covers author and title; the second, subjects. A microfiche edition of the author-title volume is issued each quarter. *Books in Print Plus—Canadian Edition* provides information on 1.6 million Canadian titles and follows the same pattern as *Books in Print Plus*, discussed below.

CD-ROM and Online

The four basic trade bibliographies—*Books in Print, Books in Print Supplement, Subject Guide to Books in Print*, and *Forthcoming Books*—are grouped together on a CD-ROM as *Books in Print Plus* (or online, *Books in Print Online*).[10] There are numer-

---

[10]In addition, the service includes the full text of reviews from Reed Reference Publishing, e.g., *Publisher's Weekly, Library Journal*, and *School Library Journal*. For about $400 more the reviews are expanded many times over, and if reviews are a consideration then the CD-ROM *Books in Print with Book Reviews Plus* should be a first choice. This is discussed earlier in the text.

ous advantages to this arrangement, advantages found for many reference works available on electronic formats. Among these are the following: (1) Price: The cost of slightly over $1000 for the CD-ROM and $60 per hour online is several hundred dollars less than print. (2) Space: Aside from the computer, printer, and screen the only space occupied is by a half dozen or so CD-ROMs, or, if on-line, nothing. (3) Ease of use: The librarian does not have to go from volume to volume and from photocopying machine to photocopying machine. (4) Time: The digital databases are updated monthly as compared with every six months for the printed work. (5) Most important, the search: There are more methods of finding material than by scanning the printed volumes.

Thanks to a series of easy-to-follow menus that appear on the computer screen, one may search the file with a minimum of difficulty. Standard search patterns are followed. One may locate a title by one of the primary elements in the printed work such as author, title, publishing date, or ISBN. Possibly the greatest advantage for the reference librarian is the ability online to search by key words, in terms of author, subject, and title. Thus, someone with only a vague notion of the name of a book may be satisfied by being offered not one, but some-times a half dozen or more closely related titles for consideration. Specifics are imperative; if one only enters basic words such as *economics*, the search result may show 3000 or more such works used in a title. This problem can be overcome by using multiword titles and phrases. One can modify the quest by stipulating a given price, audience, with or without illustrations, date of publication, and the like.

The CD-ROM database of the above group includes spin-offs from the basic *Books in Print*. These are found in some libraries as separate bound volumes. They are: *Scientific and Technical Books & Serials in Print, Medical and Health Care Books & Serials in Print,* and *Children's Books in Print*. Libraries that have purchased these, rather than the full *Books in Print*, continue to do so, but a much wiser move is simply to take the CD-ROM and forget the individual spin-offs.

The CD-ROM version and the online access help speed book orders. Many book jobbers (Baker & Taylor, Ingram Book Company, Brodart, etc.) allow the library to transmit information found in *Books in Print* directly to them. With a push of a few computer keys, the order is electronically moved from the library to the book wholesaler. This saves the laborious typing of multiform order slips and is much faster and likely to be more accurate.

PUBLISHING AND LIBRARIES

All titles listed below are published by R. R. Bowker Company.

CD: Publishing Market Place Reference Plus. 1994 to date, annual. $795.

    Print: Publishers, Distributors and Wholesalers of the United States. 1988 to date, annual, 2 vols. $185.

Online: Publishers, Distributors and Wholesalers of the United States. 1990 to date, monthly. DIALOG file 450, $66 per hour.
Print: American Book Trade Directory. 1915 to date, annual. $235.
Print: Bowker Annual Library and Book Trade Almanac. 1965 to date, annual. $160.
Print: Literary Market Place. 1940 to date, annual, pap. $148.50. (*International Literary Market Place,* 1950 to date, annual. $162.)
Print: American Library Directory. 1923 to date, annual, 2 vols. $245. (*World Guide to Libraries.* 1983 to date, annual. $350.)
Online: American Library Directory. 1991 to date, annual. DIALOG file 460, $75 per hour.

Those seeking a quick answer to the address or phone number of a publisher or name of an editor need only turn to several print sources. The most logical one for basic information is the last volume of *Books in Print* which includes 41,000 names, distributors, and publishers. There are numerous other sources, but the overall, umbrella for such information is the CD-ROM *Publishing Market Place.* Here are grouped together basic sources of directory-type information on publishers, libraries, suppliers, and booksellers. The disc contains the following, which are found, too, in individual print volumes:

1. *Publishers, Distributors and Wholesalers of the United States* offers convenient access to 80,000 publishing companies in one alphabet. Basic data include names of primary personnel, telephone number, address, as well as names of subsidiaries, various divisions, and imprints. The ISBN prefixes assigned the publisher are indicated as are any acronyms or abbreviations. The service is preferable online where being current is important. Here the information is updated each month.

2. *American Book Trade Directory* lists booksellers, wholesalers, and publishers state by state and city by city, with added information on Canada, United Kingdom, and Ireland. The average edition includes over 28,000 retail book dealers and wholesalers.

3. *The Bowker Annual: Library and Book Trade Almanac* is a related work which includes basic information on publishers and publishing. It is particularly valuable for the statistics on publishing for the previous year. In addition, as the title suggests, there are review articles and summaries of the year's past activities in various types of libraries. Other information includes updates on salaries of librarians, organization reports, product and supply directories, networks and consortia, award winners, and news. Again, statistical data are supplied.

4. *Literary Market Place,* the standard in the field, gives directory-type information on over 12,000 firms directly or indirectly involved with publishing in the United States (about 4250 publisher are listed). It furnishes an answer to a frequently heard question at the reference desk: "Where can I get my novel [poem, biography, or other work] published?" Also, it is of considerable help to acquisition librarians, as it gives fuller information on publishers than do bibliographies such as *Books in Print*. Approximately 500 major, small-press publishers are included, that is, those who issue no more than three titles a year. Standard data, from address and fax number to names of primary personnel, are given for each publisher. It also has sections on marketing and publicity, book manufacturing, and sales and distribution.

The *Literary Market Place* includes names of agents whom the writer might wish to contact. However, it presupposes some knowledge of the publisher and fails to answer directly the question: "Does this publishing house publish fiction or poetry, or other things?" For this, the beginner should turn to *Publishers Trade List Annual*,[11] or several much-used allied titles such as *Writer's Market* (Cincinnati, OH: Writer's Digest, 1929 to date, annual), with a section on book publishers includes not only directory-type information but paragraphs on types of materials wanted, royalties paid, and the manner in which copy is to be submitted. The remainder of the nearly 1000-page directory gives similar information for thousands of periodical publishers to whom freelance writers may submit material. *The Writer's Handbook* (Boston, MA: The Writer, Inc., 1936 to date, annual) gives some of the same information, but at least one-half of each annual volume is devoted to articles on how to write, and its listings are not as complete as those in *Writer's Market*. Writers who wish information on small presses should consult the *International Directory of Little Magazines and Small Presses* (Paradise, CA: Dustbooks, 1965 to date, annual).

5. *The International Literary Market Place* is, as the title suggests, a simple broadening of the scope of the original *LMP*. Here one finds over 10,000 publishers listed from 170 countries, as well as another 18,000 distributors, suppliers, and so forth. Two indexes—subject and types of publications—knit the work together. Short informative essays cover such things as copyright, literary prizes, and the ISBN.

6. The *American Library Directory* is included here to indicate that there are directories for virtually every profession. Published since 1923, it provides basic information on 36,000 public, academic, and special libraries in the United States, Canada, and Mexico. Arranged by state and city or town, the listings include names of personnel, library address and phone number, book budgets, number of volumes, special collections, salaries, subject interests, and so on. It has many uses, from seeking addresses for a survey or for potential book purchasers to providing necessary data for those seeking positions in a given library.

---

[11]At one time the *Publisher's Trade List Annual* (New York: R. R. Bowker, 1973 to date, annual) offered complete publisher's catalogs and could be employed to find additional information about a publisher and the company's books. No more. Due to a change in policy and procedure, fewer and fewer catalogs are now part of the three-volume set. In fact, several major publishers no longer bother sending catalogs.

(Information, for example, on the size of collections and salaries will sometimes tell the job seekers more than can be found in an advertisement.) Unfortunately, all versions are updated only once each year. Which format should the library buy? Again, it depends primarily on the amount of use. If there is little call for the work, online is most economical. If there is much need for printout, for locating odd bits of data, then CD-ROM (and, again online) will be useful. The print version has the decided advantage of libraries.

The World Guide to Libraries lists 40,000 libraries in 167 countries, including many school institutions. Arranged by continent, country, city, and type of library, the directory includes basic information, but not as much as in its American counterpart.

The CD-ROM *Publishing Market Place* (which includes most of the above titles) follows the same search pattern as the earlier discussed *Books in Print Plus*— a real plus if the library is likely to have both systems. One may search for a specific bit of information across the whole CD-ROM or in a specific title. There are some additions not found in the individual print versions: (1) Some 100,000 addresses for school and service organizations allow mailing-label capabilities. This is a plus for marketing people, but of little real value to librarians. (2) A "U.S. and international services and supplies" directory which gives 16,000 records for publishers and related corporations. The only problem with the system is that it is updated only once each year.

Special libraries receive much more detailed treatment in the *Directory of Special Libraries and Information Centers* (Detroit, MI: Gale Research Incorporated, annual. CD-ROM. Price varies. *Print:* 1963 to date, biennial, 3 vols. $360 to $435 per vol.). This work lists over 22,000 units which are either special libraries or ones with special collections, including a number of public and university libraries. Arrangement is alphabetical by name, with a not-very-satisfactory subject index. (Subject headings are furnished by the libraries, and as there is no one standard listing, it tends to be erratic.) The second volume is the geographical-personnel index, and the third is a periodic supplement covering new material between editions. A spin-off of the basic set is the *Subject Directory of Special Libraries*, a three-volume work which simply rearranges the material in the basic set by subject area.

Many special libraries which do not appear in the two basic directories will be found in the print *Directory of Federal Libraries* (Phoenix, AZ: Oryx Press, 1987 to date, irregular). In the second edition (1993) there are over 2500 listings, not only in the United States, but throughout the world. Indexes cover location, subject, and type of library.

As a running record of what is going on in publishing, *Publishers Weekly* (New York: R. R. Bowker Company, 1872 to date) is required reading for reference librarians. This is the trade magazine of American publishers and, in addition, often contains articles, features, and news items of value to librarians. It is difficult to imagine an involved reference librarian not at least thumbing through the weekly issues, if only for the *"PW* Forecasts." Here the critical annotations on approximately 50 to 100 titles give the reader a notion of what to expect in the popular fiction and nonfiction to be published in the next month or so.

BIBLIOGRAPHIES: PERIODICALS AND NEWSPAPERS

CD: Ulrich's Plus. New York: R. R. Bowker, 1994 to date, quarterly. $595.
> *Print: Ulrich's International Periodical Directory,* 1932 to date, annual, 5 vols. $415.
> *Online:* 1991 to date, monthly. DIALOG file 480, $60 per hour.

CD: The Serials Directory. Birmingham, AL: EBSCO Industries Inc., 1988 to date, quarterly. $525.
> *Print:* 1986 to date, 3 vols. $349.

CD: Magazines for Libraries in Ulrich's Plus. New York: R. R. Bowker, 1995 to date, quarterly. $595.
> *Print:* Katz, Bill and Linda Sternberg Katz, eds., *Magazines for Libraries,* 8th ed. New York: R. R. Bowker, 1995, 1200 pp. $155.

When librarians talk about magazines, they usually refer to them as part of a larger family of serials. A *serial* may be defined in numerous ways, but at its most basic it is a publication issued in parts (e.g., a magazine that comes out weekly) over an indefinite period (i.e., the magazines will be published as long as possible; there is no cutoff date). Serials may be divided in several ways, for example: (1) Irregular serials: There are many types of these, such as proceedings of meetings which may come out only every third or fourth year. "Irregular" refers to the fact there is no fixed publishing date. (2) Periodicals: journals, from the scholarly and scientific to the professional; magazines, such as those found on most newsstands; and newspapers. Some would not subdivide journals and magazines, while others would offer more esoteric subdivisions.

Ulrich's International Periodical Directory is a guide to periodicals from the United States and all global points. It comes in five volumes and includes about 155,000 titles, including 7400 daily and weekly newspapers (in the fifth volume) published in the United States. Periodicals are arranged under approximately 600 broad subject headings, and there is a title index. "International" is a true indication of content in that the 70,000 publishers are from 200 countries.

It is extremely easy to use. Say for instance, one looks up a periodical under the subject of architecture. One finds the title and basic bibliographical information from the year it was first published as well as the frequency of publication (monthly, quarterly, etc.) and price. The address of the publisher is given, as is the name of the editor, and there are indications of content in a 10- to 20-word descriptive line for about 12,000 of the more popular titles.

Of particular interest to reference librarians: (1) The primary places where a periodical is indexed are given. (2) There is often a circulation figure which is a rough idea of popularity. (3) Enough bibliographical data are given to allow either the librarian or the layperson to verify and order the periodical from a dealer. (4) Periodicals available online or in CD-ROM are listed.

The CD-ROM, *Ulrich's Plus* consists of the main work, plus related titles with self-explanatory names: *Magazines for Libraries; Irregular Serials and Annuals* (which includes numerous annual reference works), *The Bowker International Serials Database Update,* and *Sources of Serials.* The same data are on the online version and the total includes about 207,000 entries. Online, the service is updated monthly, the CD-ROM, quarterly, while the print volumes come out only once each year. (There is a free supplement issued twice a year, but this is difficult to use and a headache to have to refer back to for information not in the annual set.) The obvious advantage of the electronic formats is frequency and, to be sure, ease of searching. There are 23 points of entry including circulation and editor. And while the print volumes are fine for the average small- to medium-sized library, larger institutions that have considerable work with serials will need the electronic version(s).

Once again the online CD-ROM reference version is preferable where more than routine serials work is involved. Why? Aside from additional entries and titles: (1) The librarian may locate a specific serial when only some of the data arc known about the work, such as a key word in the title. (2) One may quickly verify a publisher's name, find an address, phone number, and so on. (3) The librarian can generate lists of journals, not only by subject, but by publisher, comparative prices, and the like. Refereed journals in a given subject field may be isolated. (4) Document delivery services, where available, are linked to a particular title or titles so the librarian may order them from the UnCover, Faxon, UMI, British Library Document SupplyCentre, and so forth.

The nation's largest vendor of periodicals, EBSCO, publishes *The Serials Directory.* This was developed out of the firm's list of periodicals which it sells, as a vendor, to libraries, bookstores, and corporations. Although not all the titles in the EBSCO *Directory* are available from the firm, most can be ordered from them. How does it differ from *Ulrich's?* The number of titles (170,000) listed is about the same, so there is no real difference. The type of material (from irregular serials to popular magazines) is the same, as is the basic subject approach with a title index. Actually, then, the differences are quite small. The *Directory* indicates major indexing services for each title, but adds dates of coverage of the particular item, although hardly for all entries. It has a listing of 6000 newspapers from around the world, and sometimes the brief descriptions are fuller than in *Ulrich's.*

The CD-ROM version includes the same information as the printed work, plus information about an additional 25,000 serials. There are other pieces of data, too, but essentially they are similar to *Ulrich's* entries.

Given two reference works that are almost identical in purpose and scope, a judgment has to be made about other elements. First and foremost is the matter of accuracy and complete coverage. Here *Ulrich's* is ahead, possibly for no other reason than it has been around a longer and therefore has a considerably more experienced staff. At any rate, the detailed information in *Ulrich's* tends to be more current, more thorough, and more complete in details.

The serial guides are similar to *Books in Print* in that they list what is available, *not* what is best or better. In order to determine that, the librarian should turn to *Magazines for Libraries*. The eighth edition, as those before it, lists and annotates about 7000 magazines considered the best of their type. Selection is made by 150-plus subject experts. The international recommended titles are listed by subject from "advertising" to "women." There is a title index, as well as a separate subject index. What makes this work different is that each title has both a descriptive and an evaluative summary of 100 to 200 words. The result is an invaluable guide for the librarian or layperson who must decide whether to select or drop a magazine. New editions are published every three years. (Note: The CD-ROM version in *Ulrich's Plus* follows the pattern of the print volume in that the information is updated every three years, not quarterly as with other material in the database.

There are now some 6000 small presses and almost as many little magazines published in the United States, Canada and other English language countries. These are dutifully listed in alphabetical order by title in Len Fulton's *International Directory of Little Magazines & Small Presses* (Paradise, CA: Dustbooks, 1963 to date, annual. $30). For each title there is a 50 to 300 word nonevaluative description of the magazine or the press. Basic information is given as to what type of manuscripts are required, subscription prices, frequency of publication, and the like.

A common reference problem concerns the meaning of a particular set of initials or abbreviations used in footnotes for a periodical title. Abbreviations are far from standard, and it just may be that an author has a vital bit of information hidden away under a periodical abbreviation which puzzles everyone. The solution is found, in at least 99 percent of the cases, in *Periodical Title Abbreviations* (Detroit: Gale Research Company, 1976 to date, irregular). This frequently updated guide includes close to 145,000 abbreviations. The first volume lists the abbreviation and the full title. The second volume reverses the process.

Another pressing question these days is "How do you know if X or Y periodical is available online?" This question can be broken down into two parts: (1) "Which magazine is indexed or abstracted online?" (2) "Which magazine is online in full text so that the total contents of the magazine may be printed out at will or the text may be searched for key words which lead one to the article or section of the article of interest?"

There are several guides. *Ulrich's* includes a section on periodicals online in alphabetical order by title. In *Magazines for Libraries* some, although not all, periodicals online are indicated in the individual annotations.

Books and Periodicals Online (New York: Library Alliance, 1988 to date, annual) contains descriptions of more than 60,000 individual publications available in full text by way of about 1800 databases. With each annual issue the number of entries increases from 60 to 90 percent. For each magazine or book, full bibliographical details are given as well as where it appears online, on CD-ROM, or in other electronic format. An appendix includes a listing of document delivery centers.

Listing periodicals *only* available as electronic journals, and *not* in print format, the annual *Directory of Electronic Journals: Newsletters and Academic Discussion Lists* (Washington, D.C.: Association of Research Libraries, 1991 to date, annual) is an invaluable guide for anyone involved in research. The number of titles grows each year, numbering by 1996 well over 700.

In addition, 2500 academic discussion groups and news groups are listed. This list is selective and drawn from a field of over 32,000 possibilities. There is material on online newspapers, the future of electronic services, and the like.

Newspapers, Radio, and Television

Print: Gale Directory of Publications and Broadcast Media. Detroit: Gale Research Company, 1869 to date, annual, 3 vols. $395.
No electronic format.

Newspapers are listed briefly in *Ulrich's* and *The Serials Directory* and are found in the other guides as well. Still, for considerably more complete information, arranged in a standard format, the *Gale Directory* is by far the best. As such, it is a standard item in most reference libraries. Material is arranged by state (and by province in Canada) and then by city and community. Under city, there are three basic subdivisions—newspapers, magazines, and radio and television. Basic data are given about each of 2000 newspapers, whether daily, weekly, or monthly. The data include the paper's name, date of establishment, frequency of publication, political bias, circulation, names of primary staff members, and information on advertising rates. A supplement and an updating service are issued during the year.

In addition to newspapers, the guide includes 11,000 periodicals dutifully listed in the same way as newspapers under place of publication. The information is about the same as that given for the newspapers, but considerably more limited than what is found in *Ulrich's* or the other standard bibliographies.

Therefore, while the *Gale Directory* is useful in spotting, for example, how many magazines are published in Albany, New York, it fails to give the detailed information required by most librarians. Thus, under most circumstances, one may discount the reference value of the periodicals listings.

Maps are presented in the third volume with one map of each of the states and Canadian provinces, as well as one for Puerto Rico. This section is followed by telephone numbers and addresses for feature editors. The bulk of the third volume consists of a number of indexes to material found in the first two volumes.

The basic information for television and radio stations, as well as cable systems, is similar to the newspaper data. But there are vital additions such as call letters, channel numbers, network affiliations, wattages, areas of influence of the station, operating hours, and the like. Advertising rates are included. It is hard to find more complete coverage of radio and television, at least in a general reference work such as this.

Limited to radio and television, the *Broadcasting & Cable Yearbook* (New York: R. R. Bowker, 1935 to date, annual) gives more in-depth information. There is much here, from industry problems to business solutions, but primarily it is an informative listing of anything and everything involved with radio and television.

Serials: Union Lists

"Which library has X newspapers or Y periodicals?" The question is asked when the librarian or user finds just the right article in a magazine or newspaper, but then discovers that the library does not have the item. Usually it can be ordered on interlibrary loan or faxed. Also, it just may be that the full text of the magazine article is online, too. At any rate, faxing and the online route are expensive methods, and most people use the standard interlibrary approach.

Although there are now numerous printed union lists of serials, most larger libraries depend on what they find online, usually through OCLC, RLIN, and other networks. Here one simply types in the name of the required serial and the standard information is forthcoming, from basic publishing data to, and most important, the location of the title. The publishing data usually refer primarily to the first issue and are as complete or as thorough as that found in the periodical directories.

Online one may find records of at least 55,000 U.S. newspapers. The file continues to grow, and eventually will include almost all American papers, plus selected foreign titles.[12]

---

[12]The heart of the serials' online union list is called *CONSER* (Cooperative Online Serials Program) and operated by the Library of Congress as an extension of the *National Union Catalog*. In the early years the entire emphasis was on North American publications, but by the early 1980s the scope was extended to international publications. CONSER includes the symbols for reporting libraries

Beyond online and the printed bibliographies, one must remember that most state and local libraries maintain records of their own regional and city or town newspapers. These usually become part of the online record, but much of this information is printed in more detail in state or local bibliographies of holdings. The programs to store these data often are federally funded and develop into the base of repository collections.

Pamphlets

Print: Vertical File Index. New York: H. W. Wilson Company, 1935 to date, monthly. $38.

Online: 1985 to date, twice a week. WilsonLine, $25 to $40 per hour.

The pamphlet is an elusive bibliographical item, although it may appear in numerous indexes such as *Public Affairs Information Services.* Where indexed, it usually is identified as a pamphlet so the library has sufficient information to place an order. Conversely, it is not a standard item in any of the equally standard bibliographies which draw the line at anything under 49 pages, which is a convenient definition of the form.

Individual libraries classify pamphlets as important enough to rebind and catalog separately or as ephemeral and warrant no more than placement in a vertical file under an appropriate subject.

The *Vertical File Index* is a subject approach to a select group of pamphlets. Selection is based on their probable use for the general library, not for the special, technical library. Each entry includes the standard bibliographical information and a short descriptive note of content. A title index follows the subject list. The online version permits a much wider field of searching and is valuable particularly for finding difficult subjects otherwise not sorted out in the printed work. There are over 30,000 items listed including those as ephemeral as posters, bulletins, and book lists. Wilson does not recommend any of the works, many of which are distributed by companies and organizations for advertising and propaganda purposes.

One of the headaches of ordering pamphlets is that they must be purchased from the publisher. No general book jobber will bother handling them. A free pamphlet may involve many dollars' worth of paperwork and time on the part of a librarian or clerk.

READER'S ADVISORY SERVICES

Reader's advisory services are common in public libraries and are often a part of reference services. They are defined succinctly by the Free Library of Philadel-

---

and serials may be listed. Between CONSER and MARC (i.e., the online version of the *National Union Catalog* which includes serials) almost all serials may be identified online.

phia as "reading guidance, selection of materials to meet a particular interest or need, aid in identifying the best sources of information for a given purpose, instruction in the use of the library or a particular book, seeking an answer from or referral to other agencies or information sources outside the library."[13] Actually, most libraries are somewhat more limited in their definition, and define "reading guidance" as helping people find books they wish to read, as well as assisting in the purchase of those books.

In one sense, the reference librarian is constantly serving as a guide to readers in the choice of materials, either specific or general. This is particularly true as an adjunct to the search-and-research type of question. Here the librarian may assist the reader in finding a considerable amount of material outside the reference collection.

At an informal stage, particularly in small- and medium-sized libraries with limited staff, the reference librarian may help a patron select a "good read." For example, someone may wander into the reference room looking for a historical novel or a nonfiction work on the siege of Troy. The reference staff member may assist in finding the desired material, usually in the general collection.

Reader's Advisory Aids: Print Format

None is available in electronic format.

Fiction Catalog, 13th ed. New York: H. W. Wilson Company, 1995–1999, with four annual supplements. $80.

Public Library Catalog, 10th ed. New York: H. W. Wilson Company, 1993–1997, with four annual supplements. $180.

The Reader's Adviser, 14th ed. New Providence, NJ: Reed Reference Publishing, 1994, 6 vols., $500.

Of lists there is no end, and one of the more popular types centers on "best" books for a given library situation. The lists, despite certain definite drawbacks, are useful for the following:

1. Evaluating a collection. A normal method of evaluating the relative worth of a library collection is to check the collection at random or in depth by the lists noted here.

2. Building a collection. Where a library begins without a book but with a reasonable budget, many of these lists serve as the key to purchasing the core collection.

3. Helping a patron find a particular work in a subject area. Most of the lists are arranged by some type of subject approach, and as the "best"

[13]The Free Library of Philadelphia, "Policies & Procedures," 40B (rev.), Sept. 15, 1979 (processed), p. 5.

of their kind, they frequently serve to help the user find material on a desired topic.

The advantage of a list is that it is compiled by a group of experts. Usually there is an editor and an authority, or several authorities, assisting in each of the major subject fields. However, one disadvantage of this committee approach is that mediocrity tends to rule, and the book that is exceptional for a daring stand, in either content or style, is not likely to be included.

Used wisely, a "best" bibliography is a guide; it should be no more than that. The librarian has to form the necessary conclusions about what should or should not be included in the collection. If unable to do this, the librarian had better turn in his or her library school degree and call it quits before destroying a library collection. When any group of librarians discuss the pros and cons of best-book lists, the overriding opinion expressed is that such lists are "nice," but highly dubious crutches.

Another obvious flaw is that a list is normally tailored for a particular audience. Finally, despite efforts to keep the lists current (and here Wilson's policy of issuing frequent supplements is a great aid), many of them simply cannot keep up with the rate of book production. No sooner is the list of "best" books in anthropology out when a scholar publishes the definitive work in one area that makes the others historically interesting but not particularly pertinent for current needs.

For a number of years the Wilson Company, with the aid of qualified consultants, has been providing lists of selected books for school and public libraries. The consultants who determine which titles will be included are normally drawn from various divisions of the American Library Association. Consequently, from the point of view of authority and reliability, the Wilson lists are considered basic for most library collection purposes.

There are five titles in what has come to be known as the Wilson Standard Catalog Series. They follow more or less the same organization, differing primarily in scope and evident from the titles, for example, *Children's Catalog, Junior High School Library Catalog, Senior High School Library Catalog*, and *Public Library Catalog*. The *Fiction Catalog* crosses almost all age groups, although it essentially supplements the *Public Library Catalog*, which does not list fiction. All the other catalogs have fiction entries.

Typical of the group, the *Public Library Catalog* begins with a classified arrangement of some 7500 nonfiction works. Each title is listed under the author's name. Complete bibliographical information is given as well as an informative annotation. Except for an occasional few words of description added by the compilers, the majority of the annotations are quotations from one or more reviews. The reviews are noted by name, that is, *Choice, Library Journal*, and so forth, but there is no citation to year, month, or page. Quotations are selected to indicate both content and value, but the latter is anticipated in that only the "best" books are chosen for inclusion.

From the point of view of partial reference needs, the librarian may make a selection of a title by reading the annotation, or may invite the inquisitive reader to glance at the description. Further access is provided by a detailed title, author, and subject index.

In order to keep the service updated, a softcover annual volume of new selections is published each year until the next edition is issued. This method of updating is employed by Wilson in all the standard catalog series.

The *Fiction Catalog* follows the same format as the public library aid. In it there are about 5000 titles with critical annotations. An additional 2000 titles will be included in the supplements. It is particularly useful for the detailed subject index, which lists books under not only one area, but also numerous related subject areas. Furthermore, broad subjects are subdivided by geographical and historical area, and novelettes and composite works are analyzed by each distinctive part. Most of the titles are in print and anyone who has tried to advise a user about the "best," or even any, title in a given subject area will find this work of extreme value.

The Reader's Adviser is a standard among scores of general listings of "best" books. Planned originally for the bookseller seeking to build a basic stock, the six-volume set is now used extensively in libraries. Close to 50,000 titles are listed.

Arrangement in each work follows a set plan. First there is a general introduction to the topic, then an annotated listing of basic reference works for that subject, and, finally, biographies and bibliographies for individual authors within the given area. The five volumes move from "the best in American and British fiction, poetry, essays, literary biography, bibliography and reference" in Volume 1 to "the best in the literature of science, technology and medicine" in the fifth volume. Each section is compiled by a subject expert, and the work is fundamental for anyone seeking basic titles.

Note, too, that the inclusion of reference works for a subject may be useful for reference librarians seeking to expand upon what is available, say, in *Guide to Reference Books*. There is a title, author, and subject index for each volume, but for libraries the essential volume is the sixth, which offers a complete index to the five-volume set.

The obvious problems with *The Reader's Adviser* and the other guides is their expense and bulk. For individuals, nothing quite measures up to *Good Reading*, 23d ed. (New York: R. R. Bowker, 1990). This reading list is familiar to many laypersons as it is limited to 2500 of the "best" books arranged by broad subject. Each is annotated briefly, and the work covers all possible topics, including fiction from the Sumerians to modern times. Selection and notes are by 34 experts. And each section opens with a brief introduction. The style is commendable as are most of the choices. It is an ideal list for the would-be well-read individual. The guide is $44. That's not inexpensive, but it is less costly than the others.

SUGGESTED READING

Balsamo, Luigi, *Bibliography: History of a Tradition,* Post Office Box 5279. Berkeley, CA: Bernard Rosenthal Inc., 1990. In this translation from the Italian, bibliography is traced from its beginning through medieval development to about 1900. The social and scholarly aspects of the form are stressed. Note, too, the reading list which traces the broad framework of bibliography over the ages. An excellent background work for the serious student and anyone involved with the history of books.

Martin, Lynne M., "Evaluating OPACs," *The Reference Librarian,* no. 38, 1992, pp. 201–220. An experienced librarian, author, and editor explains the importance of the catalog as a bibliographical reference aid and, in fact, as a more general reference work for many libraries. Well considered, well documented.

Mason, Marilyn, "More than the Library of Congress," *Library Journal,* November 1, 1993, pp. 40–43. An explanation of why the Library of Congress is at the center of reference and bibliographical developments in the United States and the world. The usual catch is that there is not enough money around for the Library of Congress to become a major factor in the development of the information highway.

Olszewski, Lawrence, "Madonna, Brahms . . . ," *RQ,* Spring 1994, pp. 395–403. The OCLC authority file, while usually equated with cataloging problems, is an excellent source of bibliographical data. The author demonstrates how it is used for everyone from Madonna and Brahms to President Clinton. Searching strategies are considered.

Puccio, Joseph A., *Serials Reference Work.* Englewood, CO: Libraries Unlimited, 1989. A member of the Library of Congress has written the best book on serials for reference librarians. In 16 concise chapters he covers every aspect of the subject from defining a serial to "the future of serials reference work." (It looks bright.) The book is particularly valuable for the numerous annotations of reference works used with serials as well as for the comparisons of similar titles.

Shearer, Kenneth, and Pauletta Brach, "Readers' Advisory Services," *RQ,* Summer 1994, pp. 456–459. The authors examine the role of readers' advisory services, but, more important, point out shortcomings in many aids, particularly in terms of subtle ethnic stereotyping.

CHAPTER FIVE
INDEXING AND ABSTRACTING SERVICES: GENERAL AND COLLECTIONS

An index is synonymous with an electronic format in today's library. Normally this means the index is on a CD-ROM, available online, or on a magnetic tape which is part of the individual library's "online public access catalog," known as OPAC. For example, the Cleveland Public Library makes OCLC's First Search databases available from all of its 250 OPAC terminals, and Columbia University Libraries reports that close to 18 percent of searches are conducted through databases on its OPAC system.

Most libraries in the mid-1990s rely on CD-ROMs to carry indexing information. This is likely to change. Indexes will shift to online, perhaps through Internet or other information highway channels, by the beginning of the next century.

In studying an index and in mastering what it does and does not do, the first major consideration is how it is used. This means an understanding of its scope, purpose, and intended audience. There are generalizations about the content and form of all indexes. An index represents an analysis, usually by name and by subject, of a document. Since most books, magazines, reports, and other sources deal with content that is varied, the indexer must select key terms likely to be of most value to the user. (The noun *index* is derived from the stem of the Latin verb *dicare* which means literally to show.) A good index provides enough access points, from author and title to subject to publisher, to allow the user to find precisely what is needed. The index should be current and should be accessed in such a way that it does not take a four-week course of instruction to discover how to find material.

Print versus Electronic

The traditional printed index, which remains a key reference work in many libraries, has several advantages over CD-ROMs and online. (1) As few electronic indexes contain material that precedes the mid-1980s the user needs the printed version for retrospective searching. In time this will change. Older print indexes will be converted to digital. Yet, for the next several years historical research requires the cumulated print indexes. (2) For a simple quick search, for a fact, the print index may be easier to use because (*a*) it does not require hardware or much thought in searching and (*b*) one can scan a page or two by subject or author and find what is needed. (*c*) The same argument applies where an individual is seeking only one or two citations. (3) There are other factors in favor of print, from cost to frequency of publication. These are discussed throughout the text.

Conversely, the CD-ROM/online/magnetic tape index formats have distinct, major advantages over print. These far outweigh the disadvantages. With a mouse and a click, or a few keystrokes at the computer terminal one can now (1) search a number of indexes and (2) turn from the citations and abstracts to the full text of the articles. (Full text may or may not be available, but it is coming for *all* much used services before the turn of the century.) This virtually eliminates scrambling about the library looking for separate volumes of the index, not to mention trying to locate elusive copies of a periodical or newspaper. (3) One can find more points of access and may locate what is needed by searching key words in the title or text abstract, or by chronology, place of publication, or particular periodical, and so on. For example, the printed version of the well-known *Readers' Guide to Periodical Literature* offers two primary points of entry—author and subject. The same index in electronic form has some 20 different access points for finding information. Anyone searching *Readers' Guide* at a computer terminal has many more chances of finding data than someone using the printed version. Another advantage is its size. The CD-ROM or electronic format takes up minimum space—hardware aside.

In most libraries the popular electronic indexes are grouped around general interest subjects. For example, at SUNY-Albany in 1996 the *Academic Index* was three times as popular as its nearest rivals *PsyLit* (i.e., *Psychological Abstracts*) and *ERIC*. One fourth as popular, although among the top ten: *ABI-INFORM, Newspaper Abstracts, PAIS, Social Sciences Index,* and the *MLA.* Among the least popular: *Statistical Master Index* and its almost complete opposite, *Art Index.* This informal survey supports other studies. Common sense dictates that general indexes will outpull subject indexes and subject indexes with a broad base (such as *ABI-INFORM*) will be used more often than narrow-based services such as *Art Index.*

Searching Indexes

Depending on format and content, people approach indexes in different ways. The typical printed index, because of its limited points of access, usually finds the expert searching for another expert's name (i.e., by author). The layperson or student will use the subject approach. With electronic formats, the beginner will simply type in a few key words. The skilled searcher will use numerous more sophisticated avenues. The better one knows the content and navigational paths of an index, the more likely one's success in finding what is needed.

In the majority of small- to medium-sized libraries, no more than a dozen indexes and abstracting services are in use. The larger libraries rely on from 10 to over 1000 available services—particularly where online searching is employed regularly. In terms of daily work habits, however, most reference librarians rely on a half dozen or so indexes which they thoroughly understand.

One day the user will have access to vast numbers of indexes at home. The problem, as stressed throughout this text, is while home delivery of citations is dandy (along, in the not too distant future, with full text of the articles) it may produce information overkill. Unless the individual is an expert there will be no one about to separate the chaff from the jewels of information. Also, it will remain more expensive than going to a library.

INDEX SCOPE AND CONTENT

In the rush to find the best access ramp to the information highway, it may be forgotten that the essentials never change. From the first indexer to the last computer, content is first and foremost in importance. Today's reference librarian must be able to locate the right entrance ramp and map out the road for the individual user. This requires a sophisticated understanding of specifics regarding content.

Indexes follow patterns of content and scope:

1. *Periodicals*

a. General indexes cover many periodicals in a broad or specific subject field. *The Readers' Guide to Periodical Literature* is the most widely known of this type of index.

b. Subject indexes cover not only several periodicals but also other material found in new books, pamphlets, reports, and government documents. The purpose is to index material in a narrow subject field. Examples of this type of index are the *Applied Science & Technology Index* and *Library Literature*.

2. *Newspapers*

There are numerous newspaper indexes in the United States. The best-known newspaper index is *The New York Times Index*. Today, most services offer several indexes to newspapers. For example, *The National Newspaper Index* includes numerous newspapers.

3. *Serials*

There are indexes to reports, both published and unpublished; government documents; proceedings of conferences and congresses as well as continuations; and other materials defined as serials, that is, any publication issued in parts over an indefinite period of time.

4. *Media*

There are indexes to help the user locate every form of the media from graphics and films to art reproductions.

Abstract Services

An abstract offers an objective analysis of what a given article, book, film, and so forth contain. The informative abstract summarizes enough of the data to give the user an accurate idea of content. An abstract is never evaluative, at least by intent. It is purely descriptive. A typical abstract is from 100 to 300 words, but may be shorter or longer depending on the particular indexing service.

Ten years ago few indexes included abstracts. Today it is much the opposite. Users prefer, even demand indexes that include abstracts, because a well-written abstract allows the user to: (1) Decide whether or not it is worth the effort to locate the article, book, document, or other source. (2) Decide whether to simply use the information in the abstract. A good summary may be more than enough to answer a ready-reference query such as How many people are unemployed in New York State? Why? The abstract normally follows the complete citation to the article. Most services offer the citation abstract in chronological order with the latest coming first.

Normally printed abstracts are arranged under broad subject headings, with appropriate author and subject indexing. The arrangement by subject classification sometimes confuses beginners, but it is a blessing to experts who need only turn to the classification section of interest. The librarian unfamiliar with the subject will save time by turning to the annual cumulated index to discover the classifications under which this or that specific subject is likely to appear in the monthly abstracts. Searching an index or abstracting service online or on a CD-ROM eliminates the problem of arrangement, which can be a major headache in the printed version.

SUBJECT HEADINGS AND THE SEARCH

In searching most printed indexes, one has to match the search subject or concept with the term used by the indexer. This is equally true for electronic searching, particularly where precision is called for, although one may entirely bypass assigned subject headings by seeking out key words in the title, abstract, and so forth.

If the indexer uses the term *dwelling*, the user will find nothing if a search is made for *home*, although in many cases there may be a cross-reference under the listing "Home" which states, "see Dwelling." If there were enough cross-references, there would be no real problem, but there would be a gigantic print index. The solution has been to compromise. The indexer scans the text and then tries to assign subject headings most likely to be used by a majority of users.

Where do the indexers get these terms? They come directly from what is known as "controlled" subject-heading lists. These can be useful to the reference librarian seeking a specific subject term:

1. *The subject-heading list.* Most indexes employ some form of controlled vocabulary. The subject headings are predetermined, and the article is matched against an authoritative list of subject headings. The indexer selects one to three, or even more, terms from the list that best describe the article's contents. The two basic lists of subject headings consulted by reference librarians and catalogers are:

a. *Library of Congress Subject Headings* (Washington, DC: Library of Congress, various dates). This is the familiar, fat three-volume set, usually bound in red (hence, often called the *red books*). The set lists the standard Library of Congress subject headings in alphabetical order. If one wishes to see how they list the history of England, one turns to the entry "England" and finds the reference "see Great Britain—History." That one step gives the user a specific subject heading and saves much time churning about the index looking for nonexistent English history books, at least under that subject heading, and covering all the land area of Great Britain. There are cross-references, synonyms, and other bits of advice and help which assist the user in finding the proper subject heading. (See the explanation of symbols, organization, etc., at the beginning of the first volume.)[1]

The Library of Congress list is updated by new editions and, between editions, by additions and changes in the *Cataloging Service Bulletin.* As more than one critic has observed, the subject headings are a profile of our times, particularly in the past few years as the subject heading experts became more sympathetic with change.

b. *Sears List of Subject Headings* (New York: The H. W. Wilson Company, various dates). This is the rough equivalent of the *Library of Congress Subject Headings* for smaller libraries. There are fewer subject headings. Sears represents a much-abridged edition, with changes suitable for smaller collections than the Library of Congress. The fifteenth edition (1994), as

---

[1]Sandy Berman heads a cataloging consumers network (4400 Morningside Road, Edina, MN 55416) whose purpose is to point out errors and "lack of just plain common sense" in many LC subject headings. The veteran librarian, in books and articles, has written extensively on failures of the LC system.

with previous editions, reflects the interests of the times in that there are added subject headings that cover current social and political issues, as well as forms of entertainment and developments in technology. *Note: The Sears List of Subject Headings: Canadian Companion* includes over 150 pages of subjects of special interest to Canadian public and school librarians. As with the basic set, it is often updated.[2]

An end run around the assigned subject heading is provided with the computer search. Generally most databases have assigned subject headings. In this respect they follow the lead offered by their printed versions. At the same time there are numerous other entry points. Thanks to the ability of the computer to search out key words, the opportunities to find a needed piece of information are vastly increased. The computer search allows rapid access to new terms, to new and different ways of examining a subject.

Using an online or CD-ROM search, one may not be tied to the vagaries of subject headings assigned by someone who may not fully appreciate how people seek information. (Keep in mind that the use of subject headings almost always improves the ease and the accuracy of searches. They should be used where possible.)

2. *The thesaurus.* The thesaurus is similar to the subject heading list in that it is a list of terms used for indexing and for searching. It is a frequent companion for anyone doing an online or CD-ROM search. The terms are drawn from the documents themselves, or from similar documents in the subject area. Typically, then, the thesaurus is used in specific subject fields. A thesaurus for an education index is a great help, but would be of limited value for an index to general topics.

The thesaurus shows relationships between terms. One may look up what amounts to broader and narrower concepts within a hierarchical structure built on one or more basic term categories. A term family in *reference services*, for example, could include terms for different kinds of services. Here one might find the term *reference interview* with the broader term, *information search*, and the narrower term, *verbal cues*. It is desirable to have the thesaurus available in print, on the CD-ROM, and online. Taking time to consult it, no matter in what format, will make the search more precise and usually much faster.

Which Index?

Which index should one turn to for the answer to a particular question?

One turns to the general indexes for typical student and layperson queries; and for more detailed questions, one consults a subject index. Most indexes indicate their scope in the title. It is easy to imagine the contents of *Art Index*. At a

---

[2]For a detailed discussion of subject headings, controlled vocabulary, and so forth, see Denise Beaubien, "Wilson vs. IAC On Tape: A Comparison," *Database*, February 1992, pp. 52–56.

more complex level, the librarian becomes familiar with several subject fields and is able to quickly call up names of highly specialized indexes within the subject area. If memory fails, then turn to *Guide to Reference Books, American Reference Books Annual,* and other similar guides where basic indexes are arranged under subjects.

Today the electronic index is more likely to be used and in this case one would rely on memory, experience, and on the current guides such as *Gale Directory of Databases* which list the databases by subject. Online there are some handy aids. DIALOG, for example, offers: (1) *Dialindex.* One enters key words. The service lists the number of times the key words appear in one to two dozen indexes. Given the number of postings for each search statement in a specific index, it is easy enough to go directly to that reference source. (2) *Target.* Under this system the index name is entered first, and then the search terms. The system ranks the number of times the search term appears in specific articles, books, and so on. In other words, it "targets" the best articles with respect to quantitative terms found in the particular, single index. Other major vendors offer similar services.

Where Is It Indexed?

One wants to know where a particular periodical is indexed or what index covers given subject areas. Both questions can be answered by a grapeshot approach. Simply consult a general index that covers popular periodicals—from the *Readers' Guide* to *Expanded Academic Index*—and you are likely to find your title indexed in that service. Obviously, a popular subject title will be found in an equally popular subject index from *General Science Index* to *ERIC.*

There are times when the periodical is too esoteric. Then it is much quicker to find the same information by consulting one or two sources: (1) *Ulrich's International Periodical Directory,* among other directories of this type, indicates one to a dozen particular places where a particular periodical is indexed. Look up the name of the magazine, and, voilà, there is complete information including indexes that regularly analyze the title. (2) Another basic source of information is *Magazines for Libraries,* 8th ed. (New York: R. R. Bowker Company, 1995). Each of the approximately 7000 basic titles includes information concerning where a title is indexed. Also, the first section is an annotated listing of over 250 basic indexes and abstracting services. Both guides indicate what indexes are available in print, online, on CD-ROM, and in other formats.

FULL-TEXT AVAILABILITY

The primary drawback to an index is that it is a secondary reference aid. It is only one step toward finding the information, usually in a periodical. One then moves to the periodical stacks and hopes to find the precise item. This presupposes that the library has the periodical. If not, the library can order the article on interlibrary loan, through a commercial agency, and so forth.

Document Delivery

If the library has the periodical, the next difficulty becomes: "Yes, but is it available?" "Has it been stolen?" "Has the article been ripped out or mutilated?" "Has the individual issue been lost in the library?" "Is the volume in which it is bound not on the shelves?" And finally, and most often: "Yes, we have it, but it is at the bindery!"

Fortunately for the sanity of both the librarian and the user, these problems do not arise that often, and with average skills and luck one can quickly locate the needed periodical (or book or video).

Many CD-ROM databases, as well as some online services allow the library to use holding notes on each record. The note indicates whether or not the journal (with the article) is available in the library, usually giving the holding dates, that is, 1973 to date, 1973 to 1975, and so on. Also, one may enter a negative note such as "Not available in this library. Ask the reference librarian for assistance."

Where full text is *not* available in a library, the movement is toward quick document delivery. The librarian may order the article at the computer terminal from the publisher or from a representative of the publisher, usually the latter. The publisher can deliver the article usually within 24 hours to two or three days. Full text of the article may be faxed or sent through telefacsimile or other means.

How much easier it would be if the article(s) were readily available with the index. Some indexing services meet the problem by offering the full text of the magazine article on a series of CD-ROMs, online, or microform. Many of these are noted throughout the chapters on indexes. (For a discussion of the present and future full-text online possibilities, see the second volume of this text.)

It should be noted that few electronic indexes allow one to search the accompanying full text by key words. The usual approach is to have a method of calling up the required full text on another CD-ROM. Online one can search the given article or specific chapter, but today this is becoming more and more unusual.

Types of Full Text

"Full text" (online, or in CD-ROM format) is not necessarily the complete contents of a magazine or newspaper page. There are several basic forms of full text: (1) The so-called ASCII (American standard code for information exchange) means *only* the text. (2) "Full image" or "scanned image" includes everything on the page from text to graphics and photographs. (3) A combination of ASCII and scan allows some material, some graphics to be deleted. (4) Finally, and often found as part of popular multimedia reference works, the publisher not only includes the full text and illustrations, but adds sound, moving images, and animation—in other words, offers a multimedia approach.

Full text used in conjunction with and in support of commercial indexing services normally use ASCII, concentrating on the text. This is likely to change as better hardware and software make it more feasible to use the scan approach, bringing the user the full content of a given page.

Individual Periodical Full Text

Full-text online will be profitable on a large scale when it is made available to laypersons who simply wish to scan, for example, *The New York Times* or *Cosmopolitan*, at a computer terminal. *U.S. News & World Report* is on CompuServe, complete with graphics and photographs, and is frequently called up for browsing by individuals. The Electronic Newsstand, with 10 magazines including *The New Yorker, Economist, National Review* and *Eating Well,* offers the same service on Internet. Eventually the Newsstand plans to increase the number of titles by 60 to 100. The next step is to include advertising.

Another approach to full-text periodicals is suggested by Time-Warner who combines all of its popular titles for an online service *(Entertainment Weekly, Fortune, Life, Money, People, Sports Illustrated, Time)* in the DIALOG Time Publication file 746. While all the titles are available online as individual magazines in other databases, the argument is that by putting them together a user can get a quick look at popular topics. It's a fast way, for example, to find background on a current sports star, movie figure, or criminal. Material is updated virtually as soon as it is published, and searches can go back to the mid-1980s. The catch is the cost: $1.60 a minute on DIALOG. While this is likely to be reduced, the matter of speed and convenience versus cost has to be considered.

Print, Online, CD-ROM?

The reference librarian must decide whether it is economically advisable to have periodicals on CD-ROMs alone, on print alone, on online alone, or in a combination of these. An example of the problem is a CD-ROM of one of America's top-10 magazines, and certainly a popular title often used by reference librarians. This is the DIALOG OnDisc *Consumer Reports* (1982 to date, quarterly, $375; $235 for renewal). The disc also contains *Travel Letter* and *On Health,* and two *Consumer Report* newsletters from 1989 to date. The text is included, but *not* the illustrations. They are indicated with precise citations for the user to find in the printed issues. Charts with rating information are included. The disc is updated quarterly. (DIALOG offers a low rate for consulting material from monthly current issues online.) Considering the price (vs. $22 a year, for the monthly print issues) and how the popular magazine is used, it seems questionable to purchase the disc. Or is it? The CD-ROM advantage is twofold: (1) There are numerous points of entrance and one can search the whole file (1982 to date) not month by month. (2) The disc offers considerable space saving. It is an example of what is to come.

The major question, though, is: Who wants to read a magazine at a PC monitor—particularly for entertainment? And from this follows another important consideration, namely what advertisers would support a magazine in electronic format. To date there are no answers to either question, no absolute certainty that the popular magazine will be more than a dream. We must also ask, who is going to pay for what? Novelist Nicholson Baker points out that "The National Writers Union is now [1994] questioning the right of one textpoacher to furnish magazine articles to buyers without the authors' consent. Articles, essays and book excerpts . . . are among the many thousands of offerings available by fax [at $8 per retrieval] or electronically [at $3 per retrieval]."[3] Some system must be devised to give publisher and writer a fair sum for their work.

EVALUATION

Evaluation of print or electronic indexes follows much the same rules. There are technological differences between print and electronic formats, but primarily in terms of ease of retrieval of data.

1. *The content.* First, foremost, and always, content is the principle concern. The audience for the index parallels the content and, in fact, is really part of the same evaluative consideration. There may be a half dozen general indexes. The librarian must ask, "For whom?"

2. *Scope.* What years are covered or not covered by the database? Note that most electronic databases originated in the mid-1980s and early 1990s. They rarely cover more than the past ten or so years. This is a major headache for anyone doing historical research, no matter what the field. There is hope that inexpensive optical scanning will make it possible to bring all years of an index into the electronic family.

How many subjects are covered and what type of periodicals are indexed? Is the number adequate for the field, and do the titles represent the best in the United States and, if necessary, abroad? What other formats are included. In some disciplines it will be necessary to consider not only periodicals but newspapers, reports, books, CD-ROMs, and so forth.

There is a tremendous amount of duplication in indexing. Among the 30 basic indexing and abstracting services in the social and political sciences, approximately 50 percent of the journals are indexed in six or more of the services and five indexes give access to 78 percent of the journals in the field.

---

[3]Nicholson Baker, "Infohighwaymen," *The New York Times*, October 18, 1994, p. A25.

A decade or so ago, users complained of the lack of quality indexes or abstracts. Today the same people are complaining about too many services. Ideally, index and abstract publishers would divide the disciplines in such a way that duplication of titles covered would be limited. They do not. Therefore the librarian must always ask the key evaluative question: How much duplication exists between X and Y service, and is the difference so much (or so little) that X should be chosen over Y?

3. *Cost.* This is a major consideration, particularly in terms of online, CD-ROM, and other electronic forms. One must of course counterbalance the gross price of the service with whatever savings in time and effort may be realized to arrive at the true cost.

Figuring electronic database fees is by and large the most difficult aspect of electronic index reference services. There are as many different variables and pricing options as publishers and vendors. The H. W. Wilson Company databases are offered at a single price for one or a group of databases (with variation depending on number of users). OCLC's First Search permits the library users to search as long as they want and display as many records as needed for a flat fee. Unfortunately, the OCLC fee has numerous footnotes. Government files such as ERIC cost no more than $300 per year for an unlimited number of searches and users. Conversely, it will be $6500 for unlimited access to World Cat, ArticleFirst, and ContentsFirst. Mead Data Central's NEXIS has a flat fee schedule, but it is even more complicated.

Licensing is an important factor in determining cost. Each vendor, publisher, and producer varies in the approach to how much the library is charged for x number of users accessing a database, where they are located, how they are using the system, and so on. There are twists beyond the number and cost of stations. Does, for example, the producer allow the library to keep old CD-ROM discs, or must they be returned? If online searching involves x amount of time is the rate lower than when only y amount of time is used? Is there a different rate for the librarian, the student, the faculty member, the layperson? Flexible pricing for various situations is required.

In addition to the importance of content, scope, and cost, there are four other relative constants in evaluation.

1. The Publisher

The H. W. Wilson Company, EBSCO, UMI (formerly University Microfilms), and Information Access Company publish most of the general indexes used in libraries today. One may disagree with what is or is not included in one of these indexes, but the format and depth of indexing are acceptable to excellent.

There are publishers about whom the librarian may know nothing and who seem to be offering (1) a duplication of another service or (2) a questionable venture into a new area. The librarian should check out the publisher, preferably by talking to subject experts and to other librarians who may have knowledge of the field, and by reading reviews. Any or all of these safety checks will quickly reveal who should or should not be trusted.

One must evaluate not only the initial publisher of the database, but in the electronic form one must consider (a) the reputation of the vendor, or middle person between the librarian and the information, such as DIALOG or America Online; (b) the reputation of the producer of the CD-ROM. This may or may not be the same as the publisher. For example, Silver Platter makes available CD-ROMs from a variety of publishers while The H. W. Wilson Company and Information Access Company issue their own CD-ROMs. Sometimes, too, there may be one, two, or more producers of the same CD-ROM index.

The most important question, after reputation, concerns the type of software, that is, navigational aids the publisher, vendor, and producer provide the user for information retrieval from the electronic databases. Do the publisher and vendor supply documentation, that is, guides and manuals to assist the user with the database(s)? Are these frequently updated? Related questions: Do the publisher and vendor provide training courses and refresher courses, and if so, at what intervals and at what cost? Does the publisher have a "hot line" so that searchers can call for assistance with difficult searches? Does the publisher send out a newsletter or other periodic update to inform users of changes? Does the publisher send out a newsletter or other periodic update to inform users of changes? Does the publisher provide the means for users to suggest changes or to make complaints about features of the databases? It all adds up to a single question: Does the publisher-vendor-producer offer sufficient backup for the product?

2. Depth of Indexing

The thoroughness of indexing varies considerably, and the publisher of a periodicals index should explain (but often does not) how thoroughly a particular periodical is indexed.

The obvious, some would say deceptively obvious, way of recovering a maximum amount of information from a given document is to index it in considerable depth. This means assigning a great number of subject headings to the document (as well, of course, as author and sometimes title labels). The question is: What is the optimal depth of indexing? To put it more precisely: For a given collection of documents and a given population of users of those documents, what is the best number of index terms to assign to those documents on the average and for any single document? Unfortunately, there is no consensus on this, even among experts.

One of the advantages of the electronic search of a database is that depth of indexing is not necessarily a problem. Where the search may involve more than subject headings, for instance key words in the title, abstract, or full text, the ability to find terms overlooked by the indexer is not a major consideration.

By combining terms, one can often turn up material which is otherwise lost. There is a caveat in all of this: One may use key words and end up with not one citation, but rather scores of citations, many of which are not relevant. This is a particular problem for laypersons and students searching a CD-ROM without help. Experienced reference librarians easily overcome the difficulty by using precise entries.

Does the publisher or vendor clearly specify which journals are indexed in depth and which are indexed selectively? Publishers of printed indexes rarely give this information, and database publishers will follow suit unless users insist on receiving it.

The index may state that it regularly covers parts of books or related periodicals in the field, but one should check to see that it follows through on its promises. Columnists may or may not be included, and, if they are, it will usually be without an indication of what the particular column is about. Sometimes, too, a given issue of a magazine on a single topic may be indexed only once instead of article by article.

The solution to apparently nonindexed documents, or indexed trivia, has two parts: (1) With practice the searcher will learn which indexes are guilty of one, or both, of these mistakes. The index will probably be avoided and will be used only as a last resource. (2) If the publishers or producers of the index make an effort to learn more about what users wish, they will drop the trivia, and add the essentials. Although several publishers such as The H. W. Wilson Company are constantly in the process of modification to meet needs of users, others do not survey their users that often.

3. Timeliness of Material

In most situations, the more current the index, the more useful it is. One of the great benefits of the online electronic database is that it can be updated minute by minute. Actually, most services tend to do the updates by the week or by the month. But CD-ROM may do less well here. The typical monthly or quarterly update may be less current than the printed version of the same index.

The majority of printed indexes are issued monthly or quarterly. Only a few are published every week or two weeks. The lag between the time a periodical appears and the time it is picked up in the index is easy to check. Compare a few dates of indexed articles with the date of the index or abstract. How often, if at all, is the printed index cumulated? Is there an annual volume which cumulates the weekly, monthly, or quarterly issues? Are there five-year, ten-year, or other cumulations? For retrospective searching, the necessity for frequent print cumulations is apparent to anyone who has had to search laboriously through, say, the bimonthly issues of *Library Literature* before the annual or the two-year cumulation appears.

4. Format

In the electronic index, the questions about format are twofold: (1) Is there a clear menu-driven system which makes it easy to search for material—particularly for the uninitiated? Is the search screen easy or difficult to master? (2) Is there a standard procedure to follow throughout all of the same publisher's or vendor's or distributor's indexes either online or on CD-ROM? It is difficult enough to shift from one publisher's software to another, but within the "family" there should be standard formats. The alphabetically arranged printed index is easy to follow. However, this may not be true if the printed index is arranged by class, or by citation.

SEARCHING TRENDS

Searching both print and electronic databases is considered in detail throughout this text, but a few general comments are necessary.

Drastic changes in reference searches over the past few years have come about primarily through the availability of CD-ROM, magnetic tape, and online searching.

The wide use of CD-ROMs, as well as other electronic formats, has dramatically reduced the use of printed indexes and mediated online searches, particularly in academic libraries. Reasons are many, but basically the users may work on their own without the help of a librarian. Most clients want only an article or two published in the past month or so. Having found these, they end their search.

The implications for reference librarians are numerous:

1. How good are the results of CD-ROM searches when done by a user independent of help or advice from a librarian? The answer here depends, of course, on the individual user, but in general: (*a*) The average layperson or high school or academic student is satisfied with one or half dozen recent citations from a relevant CD-ROM database. (*b*) Graduate students and professional laypersons seeking specific data are less pleased. They sometimes fail to understand that the majority of CD-ROMs offer only limited retrospective searching. Print indexes must be employed for in-depth research. (This is as true online as with a CD-ROM; but when a librarian does an online search for an individual, the lack of retrospective material is made clear to that person by the librarian.)

2. No matter who is searching on a CD-ROM, it is not always clear that: (*a*) There are other databases to search for more relevant material, or simply more data. (*b*) There are risks in depending completely on chronological order, and simply taking the top one or five citations. (*c*) Although most CD-ROMs are easy enough to search, a complicated quest does require search patterns unknown to either student or most professionals, including teachers.

3. There are times when online searching is a better alternative than the quest for data on a CD-ROM. This seems particularly true when a skilled search is needed, and here the professional reference librarian is absolutely necessary. Other considerations range from the tendency of online sources to be more current than CD-ROMs (although, not always) to the availability of guides that indicate related databases and their part in the total search.

Print indexes must never be forgotten. They are the only indexes available for most retrospective searching, and in smaller- to medium-sized libraries may be the only additional indexes to a single CD-ROM alternative. The problem today is that students and laypersons, used to the computer, go to a library (or through their home PCs) to find electronic indexes. All too often they ignore the print formats of the same indexes.

Conclusion

A considerable amount of time and effort is required to evaluate an index. Consequently, the majority of librarians rely on reviews or the advice of experts, or both, particularly when considering a specialized service. The advantages of learning evaluation techniques are as much to show the librarian how indexes

---

SUMMARY OF NUMBER OF PERIODICALS AND COST OF GENERAL INDEXES

Comparison of Selected CD-ROM General Indexes (1995)

Number of Periodical Titles Indexed	Name	Cost
2000	EBSCO: Academic Search	$6000
1600	UMI: Periodical Abstracts Ondisc	2750
1500	IAC: Expanded Academic Index	7500*
1200	IAC: General Periodicals Index	7500*
780	EBSCO: Academic Abstracts	1800
400	IAC: Magazine Index/Plus	4000*
400	EBSCO: Magazine Article Summaries	1599
240	Wilson: Readers' Guide Abstracts	1095
140	UMI: Resource/One Ondisc	795
125	EBSCO: Middle Search	899
100	IAC: TOM	3420*
90	Primary Search	500

*IAC prices include hardware, software, and so on, and are reduced after initial purchase.
Note: The figures are as of late 1995 and unquestionably will change. They are offered here to indicate the relative differences among the various indexes—differences that, in general, are not likely to change.

or abstracts are (or should be) constructed and searched as to reveal points for acceptance or rejection.

GENERAL PERIODICAL INDEXES

CD: Readers' Guide Abstracts. New York: The H. W. Wilson Company, 1984 to date, monthly. $1095.
   Print: 1988 to date, 10 per year. $229.
   Print: Readers' Guide to Periodical Literature, 1900 to date, 17 per year. $180.
   Online: WilsonLine, 1984 to date, twice each week, $25 to $60 per hour. Also available on OCLC and CDP. Also available on magnetic tape.

Not too many years ago there was only one index for the general reader and student: *The Readers' Guide to Periodical Literature.* It remains a basic reference in small- and medium-sized libraries today, but it has competition. The competitors offer indexes to a wider selection of periodicals and subject areas than found in the *Readers' Guide.*

Today the four major companies in the general index field are: The H. W. Wilson Company, Information Access Company (IAC), UMI (formerly University Microfilms), and EBSCO. Their indexes have several things in common: (1) Most index from 100 to 1500 to 2000 titles through various configurations of the same basic service. The exception is The H. W. Wilson Company where only 240 titles are indexed in one general index, the *Readers' Guide.* (2) They have abstracts to almost all their citations. (3) They are available on CD-ROM, with some, but not all, offered online and on magnetic tape. (4) Only The H. W. Wilson Company publishes print indexes.[4] (5) Prices vary wildly. Some include hardware and software in the cost, some include partial full text, and others have different charges for various numbers of users, stations, magnetic tape, and so forth. (6) Lack of standardization in cost is followed through by lack of a standard searching pattern. Each has its own search software, although through vendors it is possible to standardize at some of the services for searches. (7) Indexing begins for most of these services in the mid-1980s. Only the print version of the *Readers' Guide* allows the user to delve into general periodicals before the 1970s. The Information Access Company has several indexes that allow searching only over the past four current years. (8) Again, except for The H. W. Wilson Company, all services have some full-text support. One may, through online, CD-ROM, microfilm, or microfiche, view the full text of from one-fourth to about one-half the periodicals. Several services allow one to call up individual magazines and browse or search through them page by page.

---

[4]By 1996 Wilson was revamping all of their indexes, raising the number of titles indexed, and adding abstracts. How long the print edition will continue is debatable.

The *Readers' Guide*

Thanks to being such a familiar index in print, many librarians, particularly in smaller- and medium-sized libraries, order the *Readers' Guide*. If a general index is required this is the only choice available. But where a CD-ROM is used, and this is preferable, the *Readers' Guide* has heavy competition from the other three companies who offer more, often for less.

The *Readers' Guide* indexes and abstracts 240 of the most popular magazines in the United States and Canada. Many of these are found on newsstands and can be purchased by subscription. The range is wide, from the *Consumer Reports* to *Foreign Affairs,* and the service delivers a good cross section of public opinion at various reading levels. In print, the *Readers' Guide* goes back to 1900, while the various CD-ROM and online versions are only from 1983. The service is updated every two weeks, compared to twice a week online, but only once a month on CD-ROM.

A decided plus for the CD-ROM *Readers' Guide Abstracts* series is that if one can't find what is needed on the CD-ROM (usually because it is too new an event), one may turn to the online service for *no* added cost. The online service for the *Abstracts* is updated twice each week, compared to the monthly update of the CD-ROM.

Note, too, that if one turns only to the online service, it costs more unless one subscribes to the corresponding Wilson CD-ROM or print version. Also, while the company has its own direct online service (WilsonLine), it offers other access points, most particularly through OCLC's First Search.

Wilson Searching Patterns

Searching CD-ROM general indexes is a relatively simple matter. Particular care has been taken to make them easy to use for the general public. The H. W. Wilson Company searching pattern is typical of many general indexes, although each publisher has specific different commands.

Wilson follows basic searching patterns for its online and CD-ROM services. There are three different search modes: The simple, beginner mode is titled "browse." The user types a subject which brings up an index of headings. One may then browse for the correct related topics, even when the subject heading entered by the user was close, but not precisely the same heading employed by the publisher. One may find the correct spelling, or broader or narrower terms within the onscreen index. A key (F8) brings up "see" references when a phrase or word is preceded by an asterisk. The same key works, too, as a "see also." When the desired subject heading is found, the user highlights it, presses enter, and the citation(s) appear with abstracts in chronological order. Other keys allow the user to skip records (press F5), or print (F4), or to print a series of records (F6).

The second mode is titled "Wilsearch". This is for the individual with some knowledge of the system, as well as of searching CD-ROMs and online. Here a prompter on the screen offers several avenues of search from the author's name, to subject words, title words, key words in the abstracts, and so on. Boolean logic may be used for subject and title searching. This system is quite easy to master, and equally easy to understand. Often it is preferred even by beginners as it is quicker and more precise than the sometimes laborious "browse" mode.

The third level of searching is titled "WilsonLine" and, as the name suggests, is used more often online than with CD-ROMs. Here sophistication and experience is the key to success. Not only is basic boolean logic employed, but subtle qualifications are possible from "nesting" to searching for a physical feature such as a graph or illustration as part of the desired article. There are two problems with WilsonLine and other software systems of this type: (1) While a seasoned user might be able to move ahead with the system, the system requires constant use and a good memory to really master. (2) The alternative to use and memory is to consult the guide, but this often takes more time and is more confusing than simply going with the Wilsearch method.

The third level of searching highlights the problem with much current online/CD-ROM quests for data. The software is more esoteric than a VCR manual and some of the possibilities rival a baroque cathedral in construction. While perfectly suitable, and even ideal for the professional who searches day in and day out on the same, or related system, it is a near impossible method for the casual, once-a-week type of quest for information, either by the professional librarian or the layperson. The solution is, to be sure, simplification and standardization not within one system such as Wilson, but across the whole electronic spectrum, at least within subject disciplines.

The preferred solution, and one now much favored by casual users of such databases, is to call upon the skilled reference librarian. And by "skilled" one means a librarian who uses the database often enough to feel comfortable with even the most elaborate search patterns.

While some space is given over to the H. W. Wilson software and search patterns, two points must be understood:

1. As representative of much software for indexes, the Wilson entry differs just enough from the others, and they from Wilson, to make it impossible to set down specific rules applicable to each and every index. What is more, each year the specifics for a given service are likely to be modified and even drastically changed. Only daily or weekly use of these electronic indexes will make it possible for the average reference librarian to feel confident about searching with success.

2. Almost all indexes, general and subject, have easy-to-follow, easy-to-use search patterns for the computer novice, the student or layperson who only wants a few, current citations. Publishers often allow basic commands by simply pressing one of up to 20 keys. For example, press F1 and instructions are given; F2 for databases—when one wants to change discs; F3 for searching, and so forth. Most of the general databases include abstracts. One can call up the full-citation record abstract, or title only. And there are the normal features from boolean logic to marking and collecting records.

Simple search software becomes easier and easier to master. A click of the mouse, an oral command, a twitch of the neck may make it possible for a near illiterate to search an electronic database. Today, tomorrow, and in the future this type of navigation should not be confused with the considerably more satisfactory and necessary searching of difficult-to-find topics. Here an experienced reference librarian is (and will be) needed.

Information Access Company InfoTrac

CD: Expanded Academic Index. Foster City, CA: Information Access Company, 1985 to date, monthly. $7500.
Online: Academic Index, 1976 to date, monthly. DIALOG file 88, $85 per hour. Also part of IAC's Newsearch, but only for recent two to six weeks. DIALOG file 211, $120 per hour.

CD: General Periodicals Index, 1985 to date, monthly. $7500.
Online: Part of Newsearch, recent two to six weeks only. DIALOG file 211, $120 per hour.

CD: Magazine Index/Plus, 1980 to date, monthly. $4000.
Online: Magazine Index, 1973 to date. weekly. DIALOG file 47, $90 per hour. Also available online: Compuserve, NEXIS.
Full text: Selected full text for 100 titles on CD-ROM is the "plus" in the title.

CD: TOM, 1980 to date, 10 per year. $3420.
Full Text: Includes selected texts from magazines and is part of the service.
NOTE: *All services* may draw upon *Magazine ASAP* which includes 100 to 260 titles on CD-ROMs and on microform, in full text.

The Information Access Company's InfoTrac series works on the principle that the more the better. Essentially, no matter what the name or the format, it comes down to indexing and abstracting a minimum of 140 periodicals *(TOM)* to a maximum of 1500 *(Expanded Academic Index)*, plus *The New York Times, The Wall Street Journal,* and *The Christian Science Monitor* in some, but not all.

The online Newsearch claims it includes material in the CD-ROM indexes, plus references from more than 5000 periodicals, newspapers, wire services, and so forth. The catch is the high cost of searching and the fact that it has material only for the current two to six weeks. Online costs vary with the vendor, but IAC is known to many Americans outside of a library because its *Magazine Index* is available through the consumer online service CompuServe, as well as on the library- and business-oriented DIALOG and NEXIS. The CompuServe price is about $24 an hour, whereas DIALOG is over $120 an hour. There are other variables such as *Magazine Index/Plus,* which on a CD-ROM comes complete with hardware, software, and maintenance for $4000 a year. It takes an accountant to wend his or her way through the massive number of price schedules and plans.

An advantage of the *Expanded Academic Index*—and the similar *General Periodicals* series—is that it covers all titles in The H. W. Wilson Company's *Humanities Index* (348 titles), *Social Sciences Index* (349), and *General Science Index* (117). Note that the *Expanded Academic Index* includes only about 10 percent of the titles found in the much used Wilson *Applied Science and Technology Index,* and about the same proportion for the *Biological & Agricultural Index.*

The *Expanded Academic Index* has six months of *The New York Times* and *The Wall Street Journal.* Here it is worth emphasizing that the *Expanded Academic Index* with all of its 1500 plus titles only goes back to 1989 to 1992. (There is a backfile disc available for 1985 to 1988.) Therefore, while it does cover the current material in three basic Wilson indexes, it is useless for retrospective searching before 1985.

When it comes to abstracts, the *Readers' Guide* is much more complete than the *Expanded Academic Index*—although here one should remember that the latter includes 1500 titles compared to only 240 in the former. The annotations in Wilson are better and longer because they are written by the publisher. (Sometimes one does not find an abstract at all in the *Academic* index.)[5]

In all the IAC indexes there is a built-in consumer feature that makes it possible to quickly locate information about products one might be considering for purchase. Book reviews are coded in the index by the grades A through F. Each grade represents a reviewer's opinion, and it is a simple matter to count the number of A or C grades to ascertain the probable level of acceptance of a given work by the critics.

The *General Periodicals Index* comes in two garden varieties. The public one is more appropriate for public libraries and includes more popular, general titles. The other one is for academic libraries and embraces academic journals, that is, *Expanded Academic Index,* with the only change being, as one might suspect, in the type of magazines indexed. Both seem to include many of the periodicals in *Business Index.* As such, they both have *The New York Times,* again, for only two months.

Today, Information Access Company, like everyone except The H. W. Wilson Company, offers at least some of its indexed magazines in full text on

---

[5]The *Expanded Academic Index,* like the majority of the IAC entries, had only simple descriptive notes in the early years. It was not until the 1990s that abstracts were added, if not for all articles, at least for the more scholarly and more used entries.

CD-ROM (*Magazine Index/Plus:* 100 titles; *TOM:* 60 titles online; *Magazine ASAP:* 100 titles; *Magazine Index:* 100 titles).[6]

Ready access to the text (but not the illustrations, graphics, and the like) on *Magazine Index/Plus* is an incentive; but so is the price, which is about half the cost of the three larger indexes. *TOM*, for schools, comes in at even less, again with full text available. Needless to add, as the cost goes down so also does the number of titles indexed.

Through its InfoTrac Articles system the company offers online access to the majority of its CD-ROM databases stored in the firm's primary headquarters. This is in keeping with numerous services which through Internet and other networks make available the CD-ROMs online rather than simply online itself. The fine difference in technology is less important than the pricing. There is a fixed fee, and it costs much less to access the CD-ROMs online than if one went directly online.

InfoTrac Searching

There is a menu approach to simple InfoTrac searching of CD-ROMs. In this respect it is similar to the H. W. Wilson searching pattern. Also, there are steps to take for more sophisticated, more precise searches. All of these are clearly indicated on the menu(s), and there is little point in going over them as they are subject to both major and minor changes from one year to the next.

While laypersons and students will pay little attention to documentation provided by the publisher, the wise reference librarian will read these manuals (and updates) carefully. They contain much subtle data about searching which is not available through the computer screen.

It's worth stressing that InfoTrac puts an emphasis on integrating their indexes into the local library OPAC system. Numerous libraries have taken advantage of the magnetic tape route suggested by InfoTrac (and other publishers, as well). Here again the search patterns are relatively simple and subject to modification depending upon the individual OPAC.

The librarian should be familiar with the full-text possibilities and how the full text is identified (either on CD-ROM or microfilm) in the index. *Business ASAP Select* with *Business Index Select*, for example, is an integrated system which combines indexing of 240 business journals with the full text of close to one-half those indexed. When any article in the full-text titles is wanted, hit the return key and the full text appears. As with all IAC systems, the two may be leased as a single unit, or separately.

Variations on this are found in all of the company's so-called ASAP full-text services. Articles are coded to either the microfilm full text or CD-ROM,

---

[6]In the early years of the company both the index and the full text of selected periodicals were on microfilm. The microfilm index is history but through *Magazine Collection*, backfiles of selected magazines are still available on microfilm and keyed to the various indexes.

or to the online full text available by ordering from InfoTrac Articles which makes possible delivery of articles with or without illustrations as needed.

UMI (Formerly University Microfilms) ProQuest

CD: Periodical Abstracts Ondisc. UMI, Ann Arbor, MI: 1986 to date, monthly. $2750.

Online: Newspaper & Periodical Abstracts. 1986 to date, daily. DIALOG file 484, $95 per hour. Also available online through OCLC, CARL, RLIN. *Full Text: General Periodicals Research II.* 1986 to date, monthly. $12,525 to $17,625 on CD-ROM. Includes the index *Periodical Abstracts*, plus full-text images of articles in 360 out of 1600 titles indexed.

Full Text: General Periodicals Research I. 1986 to date, monthly. $11,625 to $16,725 on CD-ROM. Only full text, not the index, of 985 titles, 289 in full image if desired. Used in conjunction with *Periodical Abstracts*.

CD: Resource/One Ondisc, 1986 to date, monthly. $795.

Full Text: Magazine Express. 1986 to date, monthly. $3150 (with hardware: $5650). Equivalent to *Resource/One Ondisc,* with full-image text of 100 of the 142 titles indexed. On CD-ROM.

Full Text: Resource/One Select Full Text. 1986 to date, monthly. $1200. A cut-down version of *Magazine Express* with full image of 11 titles and full text of 49 more, that is, 60 on CD-ROM.

Periodical Abstracts, with some 1600 periodicals indexed, has competition only from IAC's *Expanded Academic Index* (1500 titles) and the more ambitious EBSCO's *Academic Search* (and *Magazine Search*) with 2000 titles. Price is a major advantage for the UMI index—one-half to two-thirds less than its competitors. And for this reason alone it is strongly favored by academic and research libraries. Other plus points include an excellent choice of journals, good to excellent abstracts of 30 to 100 words, and a relatively easy search strategy.

A junior service by the same publisher is called *Resource/One Ondisc*. It uses the same searching patterns as *Periodical Abstracts,* but differs in two other important respects: (1) It indexes and abstracts only 140 periodicals; all but 18 are found in *Readers' Guide.* (2) The cost is much lower than the senior service and is therefore an ideal work for libraries with limited budgets.

UMI's Proquest series includes full images of some or most of the periodicals indexed. The plan by UMI is to spend over $50 million to make nearly all of its indexes available with full-text images on CD-ROMs. Among these *General Periodicals* is the full-text accompaniment to *Periodical Abstracts.* One searches the latter index, finds a citation, and then turns to *GP* for the full text of the article. The database contains 500 to close to 1000 titles (some text only, some full image). Number and type of full text varies with the plans and, of course, the costs. At a more reasonable price, with only 100 full-image–full-text titles, *Magazine Express* complements *Resource/One Ondisc.*

UMI links its CD-ROMs for availability online through a system it calls Automated Database Distribution System (ADDS). It provides less information than searching directly online through *Newspaper & Periodical Abstracts.*

Searching Patterns

ProQuest is a software for beginners and somewhat experienced searchers. There are, as in most systems of this type, various levels and types of search patterns. The most direct, easiest to use is the topic/subject search. The user enters a topic and that subject as well as surrounding subjects are shown on the screen with the number of articles for each. One may then highlight what is needed and call up one or two sample citations, usually with abstracts.

The advanced step is the use of boolean logic where the searcher can combine terms for more sophisticated quests. An online thesaurus is useful as a guide to scroll through the terms and related terms.

On several of the more popular ProQuest databases the librarian can ask for generated statistics which show over a period of set time the number of records printed, the number of searches made, the amount of time a database was used, and so forth.

EBSCO

CD: Academic Search or *Magazine Search.* Peabody, MA: EBSCO Publishing, 1993 to date monthly. $6000.
    Online: Magazine Search, 1993 to date, monthly, CARL. Rates vary.

CD: Academic Abstracts, 1984 to date, monthly. $1800. Other versions for less: 10 per year and quarterly.
    Full Text: Academic Abstracts Full Text, 1991 to date, monthly. $3399. Full text of 125 titles on CD-ROM. Another "select" version includes 60 titles for $2599 on CD-ROM.
    CD: Magazine Article Summaries, 1984 to date, monthly. $1599.

Online: 1984 to date, monthly, CARL. Rate varies.
    Full Text: Magazine Article Summaries Full Text, 1991 to date, monthly. Price varies. Includes 350 titles. On CD-ROM.

CD: Primary Search, 1988 to date, monthly. $500.
    Full Text: Primary Search, 1994 to date, monthly. Includes 25 titles on CD-ROM.

EBSCO, better known as a periodical vendor, entered the index field in the late 1980s and by the mid-1990s had an edge over its competitors in two areas: (1) It includes more titles on a CD-ROM (2000) than any competitor. (2) It offers not one, but two services specifically for elementary and for middle and high schools. Prices are competitive and the searching software is among the easiest in the group.

Differences among the various indexes are minimal in that the periodicals, from 2000 titles in *Academic Search* and *Magazine Search* to the 90 titles in *Primary Search*, reflect the needs of the particular audiences. As might be expected the majority of magazines are indexed in the corresponding rival indexes. Again, as with its competitors, there is something for everyone in almost every price category. *The New York Times* from 1989 is included as well as *The Wall Street Journal* and *Magill's* book reviews in most of the indexes.

The full-text features are easy to use and complement the indexes. For example, *Magazine Article Summaries Full Text* offers the same indexing as *Magazine Article Summaries*, but makes it possible at the same time to locate the full text of articles from over 90 magazines and *Magill's* book reviews.

The print version of the index has disappeared, and with that many of the objections to such things as lack of proper subject headings and minimal abstracts.

Despite the titles for the various indexes, the real scope is in the number of titles indexed. *Academic Search* and *Magazine Search* for public libraries are almost identical. The latter's titles are changed a bit to include more popular titles suitable for a public library. *Academic Abstracts* can be used in all types of libraries, not just universities. It has the advantage of a low price and close to 800 titles indexed. *Magazine Article Summaries* is useful in all types and sizes of libraries.

Primary Search, with 65 titles for elementary schools is part of a plan to cover every educational base. EBSCO also has *Middle Search* for the middle schools. Both services are supported with full-text capability on separate CD-ROMs. They not only include magazines, but pamphlets and special materials for teachers.

Searching Patterns

The basic approach to the EBSCO indexes is one of the best for the person who knows absolutely nothing about computer searching. Each step is clearly explained and search moves are equally clear. Easy-to-use search screens literally take the beginner from the idea to the citation(s). And, as always, there are considerably more sophisticated search patterns available for those with experience and in a rush.

Unlike other full-text offerings discussed in this section, EBSCO makes it possible for the user to search the text itself for key words. The entire article can be searched word by word, phrase by phrase. This has its advantages, particularly for experienced searchers, but can be a definite drawback for beginners who may be swamped with material. Also, the entire article or a selected portion—as with the other services—can be printed out.

Which?

Which of the four general indexes, and their various cousins and aunts, are best? None is perfect. A decision must weigh the number of periodicals indexed, and the cost which seems to shift from year to year. At the present (1996) UMI's *Periodical Abstracts* is a winner. The UMI index has a good, if not excellent search system. It would be a first choice in public academic, and well-financed high school libraries. IAC's *Expanded Academic Index,* although it costs more, has a history of being easy to use. Third would come EBSCO's *Academic Search,* even though with over 2000 periodicals, more than any other service, the cost is too high. At the bottom of the list, is The H. W. Wilson Company's *Readers' Guide.* While this is by far the least expensive and offers the best abstracts, it simply can't compete with services that have three to five times as many periodicals indexed. With that, though, it is a consideration for small libraries with limited budgets.

Online, the search patterns for the four indexes differ, as does the cost. Again, the real question is a matter of what is indexed and how easy it is to retrieve the material. All, except The H. W. Wilson Company have the option of full text, usually available on separate CD-ROMs (which except for EBSCO, can't be searched). The real question is twofold: (1) Does the library want the full text of the indexed periodicals available in this format, particularly when many will not include graphs, illustrations, and so on? (2) More important, can the library afford the full text in this format? Ideally, the library would have both the CD-ROM and print versions of a magazine, as well as online access to full text, but choices must be made. Unfortunately, no blank statement can be made and each library must make a decision about full text in electronic form according to need and budget.

Another variable is how much, and what type of full-text support is available. Here UMI, with an investment of over $50 million, leads. The catch is cost, which can be from about $3000 to $18,000 depending on how many titles are available and whether simply text or full image.

Abstracts are important. IAC's *Academic Index* is a close contender with UMI's *Newspaper & Periodical Abstracts.* Some prefer the former, others the latter (including the author of this text), but it is really too close to call.

Finally, for larger libraries and possibly for all libraries in the future, is the question of magnetic tape. Indexes on tape, which may be loaded into the library's computer for wide use, often through the online catalog, offer substantial savings in time and effort.

Most libraries will want only one general index. There is too much overlap and repetition among the four to justify purchasing more than one. Hands-on experience (by both librarians and the laypersons likely to use the systems) is strongly recommended before making a choice.[7] Comparative reviews are of tremendous help, and some of the best reviews are found in the "CD-ROM Review" column of the *Library Journal*.

CANADIAN AND BRITISH GENERAL INDEXES

CD: British Humanities Index Plus. New York: R. R. Bowker, 1985 to date, quarterly. $1500.
> *Print:* 1962 to date, quarterly. $610.

CD: Canadian Business and Current Affairs. Toronto: Micromedia, 1980 to date, monthly. Price varies.
> *Print:* 1975 to date, annual. Price varies.
> *Online:* 1985 to date. DIALOG File 262, $72 per hour. Also available online: CompuServe, CAN/OLE.

The *British Humanities Index* is a serviceable and general guide to about 320 British journals covering such subjects as politics, economics, history, and literature. It is of limited use in the area of current materials because it is published only quarterly with annual cumulations. By the time the *British Humanities Index* and the corresponding periodicals reach North America, the timeliness factor is worthless.

Formed by the merger of the *Canadian Magazine Index, Canadian Business Index,* and the *Canadian News Index,* the *Canadian Business and Current Affairs* includes 400 general Canadian English language magazines as well as 200 business and trade publications and seven major newspapers. While it indexes three separate types of publications, it is Canada's only general index. In fact, it has the advantage of covering all the major publications in Canada, with the exception of highly specialized titles and more esoteric periodicals and newspapers. As such it is a requirement for Canadian libraries, and a near must for many medium to large American libraries. To be stressed is the fact that with some exceptions all the indexed titles are published in Canada and are in English.

The CD-ROM searching patterns for both of these indexes follow the basic approach of key word entry and, for more sophisticated searches, boolean logic, truncation, and so forth. They are relatively easy to master and both have good on-screen instructions.

---

[7]For example, in analyzing the general indexes of the four publishers (*Library Journal*, November 15, 1992, pp. 106–107) Cheryl LaGuardia tried searching for "sea turtles" in all services and compared the number of citations for each as well as their quality.

Information Access Company ran its own evaluation of *Magazine Index/Plus* against its closest competitor EBSCO's *Magazine Article Summaries.* The IAC "discovered" many more articles on given subjects in *Magazine Index/Plus* (see *In Forum,* a house organ of IAC, for October 1994, p. 4).

In American libraries, where neither index is likely to be used that much, it is wise to forego the electronic version and subscribe to the much less costly print format. Some libraries, of course, may not want either one of the Canadian indexes because they can be used online at a reasonable rate.

Dissertations

CD: Dissertation Abstracts. Ann Arbor, MI: UMI, 1861 to date, monthly. $1995. (Backfile edition, three disc set: $7995).
    Print: Dissertation Abstracts International. 1938 to date, monthly. $140 per section. *Print: Comprehensive Dissertation Index.* 1973 to date, annual.[8] Inquire for price.
    Online: Dissertation Abstracts Online. 1861 to date, monthly. DIALOG file 35, $96 per hour, 40 cents per record. Also available online: OCLC, CDP, and so forth.

Dissertations normally are not thought of in terms of general indexes, but since they cover so many fields, they at least deserve a hearing and a place of access when one is searching for detailed information and bibliographies about a subject.

Covering over 1.2 million doctoral dissertations[9] from American universities since the mid-nineteenth century, *Dissertation Abstracts* is an invaluable index to almost any topic. Most subject-oriented abstracting services include dissertations. However, only the *Dissertation Abstracts* concentrates exclusively on the form. The publisher claims that more than 3000 subject areas are covered. In addition, since 1980 the scope has been expanded to include 200 institutions in other countries, primarily Asia and western Europe. With an addition of some 3500 records a month there is a virtual guarantee, whether one is seeking current or retrospective viewpoints on pets or physics, that something of interest will be revealed in a search. Dissertations are important for the reference librarian seeking specific, often unpublished, information about a given subject, place, or person.

Since dissertations contain extensive bibliographies and footnotes, they can be used as unofficial bibliographies for some relatively narrow areas. There is a good chance that a dissertation has the bibliography sought, or at least indicates other major sources.

A problem with dissertations is that some librarians will not lend them. Policy differs, but the excuses for not lending include: (1) There is only one copy and it cannot be replaced. (2) A microfilm copy may be purchased from UMI, who just happens to publish the index. Actually, most libraries obtain copies by interlibrary loan through networks such as OCLC.

---

[8]Publication began in 1938 and 1973, but records go back to 1861.
[9]From 1988 to the present the database includes masters' theses.

How does one trace the dissertation? The answer is threefold. The quickest and easiest approach is to use the electronic *Dissertation Abstracts.* Here one may apply boolean logic as well as other search patterns; this is a case where many institutions will prefer the online search. The service often is not used enough to justify the CD-ROM expense, particularly for the three retrospective discs.

If one is confined to print, the first place to go is *Comprehensive Dissertation Index.* The index set is divided into the sciences, social sciences, and humanities, and each of these broad categories has subdivisions, for example, biological sciences, chemistry, and engineering. One locates the volume(s) likely to cover the subject and then turns to the finer subject heading to find a list of dissertations by full title and name of author. Entry is possible by author too; that is, the final volumes of the main set and the supplement are author-index volumes.

After each entry there is a citation to *Dissertation Abstracts,* where the librarian then turns for the full abstract. The citation refers one to the volume and page number in *Dissertation Abstracts.* For example, in the index one finds "Defining the roles of library/media personnel . . ." the author's name, degree-granting university, number of pages, and then: "43/06A, p. 1733." The reference is to vol. 43, no. 06A of *Dissertation Abstracts,* on page 1733. The number system is easy enough to use and it is understood.

Dissertation Abstracts International is a separate set from the index, but is issued by the same publisher. Like the index, it appears in three parts. Until the annual index is issued, the monthly issues of *Dissertation Abstracts International* must be searched individually. Each of the three sections has its own index. It is published monthly, and the arrangement by broad subject headings and then by narrow subject areas is similar to that of the index. Each entry includes a full abstract.

Obviously, because of multiple volumes and types of searching in print, it is much, much easier to use an electronic version. Also, the bound volumes take an enormous amount of valuable space. There is little justification for maintaining the print format.

CURRENT CONTENTS

Online: ContentsFirst. Dublin, OH: OCLC, 1990 to date, daily. Rates vary.
Online: ArticleFirst. Dublin, OH: OCLC, 1990 to date, daily. Rates vary.
　　No CD-ROM or print format.

A useful method of searching a vast number of periodicals, if only in a cursory fashion, is to turn to current contents. Essentially this offers the user the opportunity to examine the table of contents, hence "current contents," of one to 15,000 or more periodicals. OCLC's First Search couple—ArticleFirst and ContentsFirst—are prime examples of how the system operates.

ContentsFirst contains the table of contents of over 12,000 journals in all the disciplines, from science to the humanities. Each record shows the viewer the contents of one journal issue. Aside from the specific commands, the database is searched by asking for a given journal by name (if no date is indicated, the database will show the record of the latest journal content page).[10] "Let me see the contents of the June 1995 issue of *Library Journal*." This appears on the screen and the user then determines which article(s) to read. Depending on the particular periodical, the journal's contents may appear a month or so behind or ahead of the printed version. A handy added feature: The record shows whether your library has the journal or who has it in the immediate region. This information is not always completely accurate, so it is best to double-check in one's own catalog or regional bibliography.

While interlibrary loan information is given for these services, OCLC also provides: (1) A minimum of two document suppliers, one of which usually is the publisher, for many of (but not all) the articles. Users can order the item directly over First Search and pay with a credit card, or through a library account. Delivery can be by fax or more conventional mail. In addition there is a FastDoc option which will fax articles in an hour or less. (2) Full-text online for certain, but far from all, journals. Eventually almost all full-text online periodicals will be available online, by e-mail, or by fax.

OCLC turns the ContentsFirst database on its head and comes up with a first cousin, ArticleFirst. The same 12,000 or so journals are analyzed primarily by subject. Rather than type in a table of contents (although this is a search possibility), one asks for specific subjects or authors. The database then shows where those key words appear in a brief abstract (if the journal has such a thing) or in title(s) of articles in the database. This is hardly a precision-type search. No subject headings are used, and the success or failure depends on the appearance of the key words in an article title, journal title, or abstract.[11] At the same time one is much more likely to find a number of citations not found by using only *ContentsFirst*.

Other publishers and vendors offer, and will offer in the future, various electronic current contents services. For example: *Current Citations* (Birmingham, AL: EBSCO Publishing, 1993 to date, monthly, rates vary). EBSCO's *Current Citations* is drawn from the database at the British Library Document Supply Centre in England. The first disc covers 10,000 journals and has over 900,000

---

[10]A less precise approach, and one which can be frustrating because of the number of titles, is to search by subject, that is, subject heading assigned to the particular journal or subject obvious in the title of the journal. Conversely, one may narrow the search, make it more specific by requesting a specific date, ISSN or CODEN, or issue number, and so forth. It is *not* searchable by key words in the articles or by subjects—other than the overall subject of the journal. For example, one might turn up *American Libraries* and *Library Journal* by using their overall subject interest, "libraries," *but not* individual articles in those two periodicals.

[11]An experienced searcher can overcome this grapeshot approach by using specific terms, avoiding general subjects, and employing a number of limits such as requesting only an editor, a letter, report, review, cover story article, and so forth.

citations. Approximately 1 million records a year are added. CARL has a system similar to OCLC, and it offers table-of-contents searches to over 17,000 periodical titles. (See various sections in the second volume of this text for more information on CARL and other such networks.)

Current Contents and Selective Dissemination of Information

There is another side to current contents and information. Many reference librarians simply photocopy the contents page of a given number of journals and regularly circulate them among professionals and laypersons who are interested in the subject matter of the journal. The individual checks off the article(s) of interest and these, in turn, are photocopied and sent to the interested party. This falls under the category of "selective dissemination of information" or SDI, which is discussed in more detail in the second volume of this text.

The Institute for Scientific Information, publisher of *Science Citation Index,* offers a number of current contents titles: *Life Sciences: Physical, Social, and Behavioral Sciences;* and so forth. These publications reproduce the title pages of journals, usually at the time of publication or even several weeks ahead of publication. The user can then scan the current contents and indicate to the librarian what might be of particular interest, or the librarian can first check off what he or she thinks will be of value and then send the user either the citations or the hard copy of the article.

The computer makes SDI a much easier and more efficient method of helping the individual keep up with developments in a field. The Institute for Scientific Information, for example, offers Current Contents Search online which covers all of their numerous print current contents works in one database. DIALOG 440 charges $102 an hour with 80 cents for a full record. Savings are possible in that the publisher offers the same material on magnetic tape. An individual library may have arrangements to search weekly, monthly, or quarterly for certain terms in one or more databases for the individual. The printed citations are then sent to the person on a regular basis.

INDEXES TO MATERIALS IN COLLECTIONS

CD: The Columbia Granger's World of Poetry. New York: Columbia University Press, 1991 to date, irregular. $699.

Print: The Columbia Granger's Index of Poetry, 10th ed., 1993, 2078 pp. $199.[12]

---

[12]The CD-ROM *Poem Finder* (Great Neck, NY: Roth Publishing Inc., 1994 to date, semiannual) has information on close to one-half million poems found in some 1800 anthologies and in 2500 single poet collections, as well as those published in over 3000 magazines. In other words, the Net is much wider than *Granger's.* The "catch" comes in the searching techniques, few of which are as sophisticated as its better-known rival. Access is provided by first line, last line, and the author. One may

CD: Essay and General Literature Index. New York: The H. W. Wilson Company, 1985 to date, annual. $695.
Print: 1900 to date, semiannual. $110.
Online: WilsonLine, 1985 to date, semiannual. $34 to $50 per hour.

Print: Short Story Index. New York: The H. W. Wilson Company, 1953 to date, annual. Price varies.
No electronic format.

Anthologies and collections are a peculiar blessing or curse for the reference librarian. Many of them are useless, others are on the borderline, and a few are worthwhile in that they bring the attention of readers to material that otherwise might be missed. Collections serve the reference librarian who is seeking a particular speech, essay, poem, or play; but the usefulness of anthologies is dependent on their adequate indexes.

This type of material is approached by the average user in one of several ways. He or she may know the author and want to identify a play, a poem, or other form by that author. The name of the work may be known, but more than likely it is not. Another approach is to want something about a certain subject in a play, poem, or short story. Consequently, the most useful indexes to items in collections are organized so that they may be approached by author, subject, and title of a specific work. Indexes of this type serve two other valuable purposes. They cover books or other materials that have been analyzed. Since the analysis tends to be selective, the librarian has a built-in buying guide to the better or outstanding books in the field. For example, the *Essay and General Literature Index* picks up selections from most of the outstanding collections of essays.

Another benefit, particularly in these days of close cooperation among libraries, is that the indexes can be used to locate books not in the library. Given a specific request for an essay and lacking the title in which the essay appears, the librarian requests the book or article by giving the specific and precise bibliographical information found in the index.

The indexes tend to favor the humanities, particularly literature. There is little need for such assistance in the social sciences and the sciences. Where the need does exist, it usually is met by an abstracting or indexing service. The indexes discussed in this section are the best known, but others appear each year. They include guides to science fiction, information on handicrafts, costumes, photographs, and such. Once the form is recognized, the only basic change in searching is in the topics covered and the thoroughness, or lack of it, in arrangement and depth of analysis.

The single most useful work a library can have as an entry into miscellaneous collections of articles is the *Essay and General Literature Index.* The analyzed essays cover a wide variety of topics. There are subject entries to the contents of approximately 300 collected works on every subject from art to medicine.

---

search by any word in this group. The service, too, is published twice a year, but costs almost twice as much as *Granger's,* that is, $395 versus $199.

The elusive short story may be tracked down in the *Short Story Index*. Now published annually, the *Index* lists stories in both book collections and periodicals. A single index identifies the story by author, title, and subject. The subject listing is a handy aid for the reference librarian attempting to find a suitable study topic for a student who may not want to read an entire book on the Civil War or about life in Alaska. The names of the books and the magazines analyzed are listed. More than 3000 stories are included each year. A basic volume covers collections published from 1900 to 1949, and there are five-year cumulations, or with the 1984 to 1988 cumulation, a group of nine volumes to search. There is also *Short Story Index: Collections Indexed 1900–1978* which lists the 8400 collections analyzed.

Unless heavily used (which it rarely is in most libraries) the print version of *Granger's* is a cost saver. Granted, the electronic format includes added items, for example, full text of 8500 poems and 3000 poetry quotes, but neither is required for daily reference service, and both are an expensive luxury the library can do without. The familiar index follows the pattern of many previous editions. There is a full index to first lines of some 70,000 poems, a subject index with close to 3500 categories, and the expected author and title indexes. An added feature with the tenth edition is an index to 12,500 *last* lines, which can be invaluable when searching out quotations. All of this is mined from 400 anthologies of poetry. Note, however, it does not index the collected work of individual poets. Hence Geoffrey Hill's *New and Collected Poems* is not indexed, but the *Oxford Book of Modern English Verse* includes Hill as one of the poets, and through that anthology one may locate at least some of the poems found in Hill's more extensive one-person collection.

If *Granger's* is not a required item in electronic format, this is not to deny the pleasure and reward of using it on a CD-ROM. In an instant one may run down an elusive first line, last line, author, subject, title, and most important, key word. It is a great bonus for anyone trying to locate a quotation or a poem when only a garbled version of the title or first line is known. If, for example, only a word in Wallace Stevens's "Sunday Morning" is used, such as "complacencies" and "peignoir" in the first line, or one of the two title words, then, presto, the poem is at hand.

Electronic or Print?

The CD-ROM or online format is preferable because one has the usual numerous entry points, as contrasted with only a subject and author approach in the traditional printed version. And, as always, The H. W. Wilson Company allows one to search the online version at no added cost if an item can't be located on the CD-ROM. Note that the print format is updated only once a year while the electronic version is updated twice a year. Retrospective searches, prior to 1985, are important for much work and here one must rely on the printed version.

The question: Is it really worth all that much more to have an electronic format? Answer: For most libraries, no. Print is preferable *unless* the guide is used for extensive research. Electronically, one may search consecutive years in a moment. The print format of the *Essay and General Literature Index* requires going laboriously through numerous volumes—but only to 1985. If the CD-ROM or online version included material from 1900 there would be no question as to which format would be most useful and, in fact, most economical.

Full Text

Guides to collections are less than perfect. It is frustrating to locate just what is needed in *Granger's* and then discover that the library does not have the particular poetry anthology. The way around the problem is to offer full text of all the poems, essays, short stories, and so on online or on CD-ROM. (*Granger's* on CD-ROM does this, but only for some 8500 poems out of some 100,000 possibilities.)

Ideally, all indexes to materials in collections would follow the pattern of *The English Poetry Full-Text Database* (Cambridge: Chadwyck-Healey, 1994, Four CD-ROMs, approximately $55,000) is the near ultimate example of volume (4500 books of English verse by 1350 English poets from A.D. 600 to 1900.[13] The entire text of the poem is included, and usually it is from an accepted, if not definitive edition of the poet's work. It has obvious advantages: (1) In a small space one may cruise all major English poetry. (2) Entry points not only include the obvious, that is, name of poem, first line, name of poet, but searches may be made by key words, terms, expressions, themes, metaphors, or almost anything within the poem itself and the imagination of the searcher. What once might take months or years to find, can now be done in a matter of seconds or minutes.[14]

The database consists of the 1350 poets listed in the *Cambridge Bibliography of English Literature*. Unfortunately, in an effort to avoid any copyright problems, the publisher used out-of-copyright editions rather than more recent, scholarly texts. This hardly matters for hundreds of minor poets whose work was published only once or twice, but for those in the "canon" who are constantly being examined, this is a major fault. The computer image records stanza form, line indentation, typographical effect, and page breaks, but *not* the poem on the printed page.

---

[13]The initial price of the combined index/full-text service is high, but the $36,000 breaks down to about $8 per volume of poetry. This compares with the average $20 to $25 a volume—the normal price for a book of poetry.

[14]Early in 1995 the same publisher offered on CD-ROM (for about $15,000) English Verse Drama: The Full Text Database. This covers 1500 plays by about one-third as many playwrights—and, again, all are out of copyright.

Searching Patterns

Again, as in most widely used databases, three levels of searching are possible. This is true of all the indexes to collections, and the full-text additions. Wilson, of course, follows its standard pattern, discussed earlier in the chapter. The others use a straightforward "standard" search, or a detailed approach, or simply enter a more esoteric command level for the sophisticated quest. The latter mode allows the development of complex search expressions and data-element searching. This presupposes that the user knows command syntax and data codes.

GENERAL INDEXES: PRINT FORMAT

No electronic formats.

Children's Magazine Guide. New York: R. R. Bowker, 1948 to date, nine issues per year. $45.

Popular Periodical Index. Roslyn, PA: Popular Periodical Index, 1973 to date, quarterly. $40.

Access. Evanston, IL: Access, 1975 to date, three issues per year. $157.50.

Despite the electronic revolution, there are a number of general indexes available only in print. The explanations vary, but the primary reasons are because the work is no longer being updated (e.g., *Poole's Index*) or the publisher believes the user will not have a computer (e.g., *Children's Magazine Guide*). Lack of a CD-ROM or online searching in no way detracts from importance.

The only guide to children's magazines is a good example of how specialized abstracting and indexing printed services are likely to coexist with more sophisticated electronic systems for decades to come. Here, in the *Children's Magazine Guide*, young readers, teachers, and parents are given a reliable subject approach to the contents of close to 50 titles. It is useful for recreational reading as well as for students (ages 5 to 14 or so) for finding material for papers. Teachers use it not only for the index, but for the practical suggestions of how to use children's magazines, and for the short notes on new magazines, workshops, and so forth. There are over 16,000 subscribers.

There are two other print indexes that serve to augment the electronic cousins. They are subscribed to by many libraries for three reasons: (1) the cost is low, (2) they cover popular titles not found in the printed *Readers' Guide,* and (3) they are relatively current and accurate.

The earliest index to include the omissions from the *Readers' Guide* is the *Popular Periodical Index,* which includes about 37 titles not found in the Wilson index. The librarian-publisher, Robert Botorff, includes subject headings for reviews, motion pictures, recordings, and so on. Where a title does not describe the content, the editor often adds a word or a line or two explaining what the article is about. While this is hardly a full abstract, enough information is given to make the index particularly useful.

Access is another general index. It emphasizes works on popular music, travel magazines, science fiction, and arts and crafts titles. It is particularly strong in its coverage of city and regional magazines. Its value to librarians is as a wide net in the indexing of really popular titles not found in other general services. About 140 periodicals are indexed in each issue. The index is divided into two parts. The first section is author and the second is subject. After the paperback issues in June and October there is a cumulative hardback issue in December to round out the year.

While technically one should classify the *Catholic Periodical and Literature Index* (Haverford, PA: Catholic Library Association, 1930 to date, bimonthly, service) as a religious index, actually it is much broader in scope. It indexes by author, subject, and title approximately 160 periodicals, most of which are Catholic but vary widely as to editorial content. In fact, many of the titles could be classified as general magazines. Also, the index includes analyses of books by and about Catholics. There are sections for book reviews, movie reviews, and theater criticism. Although this is of limited value in many libraries, it might be considered for public and college libraries serving a Catholic population.

Alternatives and Minorities Indexes: Print Format

No electronic formats.

Alternative Press Index. Baltimore: Alternative Press Center, 1969 to date, quarterly. $100.

Hispanic American Periodicals Index (HAPI). Los Angeles: University of California, 1970 to date, annual. $240.

Index to Black Periodicals. Boston: G. K. Hall, 1950 to date, annual. $95.

Despite the impressive number of general indexes, only a few deal with magazines from the political left, the social right, and almost any place other than dead center. A library may not have such magazines in days of tight budgets and limited readership, but it is a good idea to have the indexes to indicate that there is more than one view of America.

Minority indexes should be a *first priority* if minorities are a primary or secondary audience served by the library.

The *Alternative Press Index* has been about for over 25 years, and it faithfully indexes some 220 titles. All of these are to the left of center. The right is not represented because of the editors' opinion, right or wrong, that conservatives have a voice in other indexes and other services. Be that as it may, the index serves the splendid purpose of opening new doors on new ways of looking at issues. Arrangement is by subject, and there are book reviews by author and title. Although issued quarterly, the index does tend to lag.

The *Hispanic American Periodicals Index* examines about 250 periodicals, most of which are published in Latin America or by Latin American groups in the United States. While popular magazines are not included, the representative group of other titles does reflect trends and ideas in Latin America and among Hispanics living in the United States.

The 1995 edition of *Index to Black Periodicals* did not come out until 1996. Lack of finance accounts for this delay, as it does for publications which rely on volunteer or poorly paid, part-time indexers. There are 37 popular and scholarly titles indexed in the service.

Retrospective Periodical Index: Print Format

No electronic formats.

Poole's Index to Periodical Literature, 1802–1906, vol. 1: 1802–1881. Boston: Houghton Mifflin Company, 1981; vols. 2–6 (supplements 1 to 5): 1882–1907. Boston: Houghton Mifflin Company, 1888–1908; 6 vols. reprinted in 7 vols. Gloucester, MA: Peter Smith Publisher, 1963.

This was the first general magazine index, and the forerunner of the *Readers' Guide*. It was the imagination of William Frederick Poole, a pioneer in both bibliography and library science, that made the index possible. Recognizing that many older periodicals were not being used for lack of proper indexing, he set out to index 470 American and British periodicals covering the period 1802 to 1881. Having completed this work, he issued five supplements which brought the indexing to the end of 1906.

The modern user is sometimes frustrated by the fact that the cited journals do not have a date, but rather are identified only by the volume in which they appear and by the first-page number. For example, the article "Dress and Its Critics" is from *Nation,* **2**:10. A "Chronological Conspectus" in each volume gives an indication of the year.

There is no author approach. Indexing is entirely by subject. The author index to the 300,000 references in the main set and to the supplements was later supplied by C. Edward Wall, *Cumulative Author Index for Poole's Index* (Ann Arbor, MI: Pierian Press, 1971, 488 pp.). The index is computer-produced and not entirely easy to follow, but it is a great help to anyone seeking an author entry in *Poole.*

With all its fault, Poole's work is still a considerable achievement and an invaluable key to nineteenth-century periodicals. The last decade of the century is better treated in *Nineteenth Century Readers' Guide to Periodical Literature,* 1890–1899, with supplementary indexing from 1900 to 1922 (New York: The H. W. Wilson Company, 1944, 2 vols.). Limited to 51 periodicals (in contrast to Poole's 470), this guide thoroughly indexes magazines by author and subject for the years 1890 to 1899. Fourteen magazines are indexed between 1900 and 1922.

SUGGESTED READING

Broering, Naomi, "Libraries of Tomorrow," *Computers in Libraries*, February 1993, pp. 13–26. A virtual medical library system is explained, and indexes and abstracts are given the role they deserve in this ideal library. Discussion of online CD-ROMs and so forth.

Cremmins, Edward, *The Art of Abstracting*, 2d ed. Arlington, VA: Information Resources Press, 1995. Basic information on the preparation of abstracts is counterpointed with editing advice, the use of author-prepared abstracts, and analysis. A thorough, reliable, and even fascinating book. The first edition (1982) was the winner of the Best Information Science Book Award from the American Society for Information Science.

Eldredge, Jonathan, "Accuracy of Indexing Coverage . . . ," *Bulletin of the Medical Library Association*, October 1993, pp. 364–370. Here the author wants to know precisely how much, or how little, information may be gained by the basic periodical directories about indexing of periodicals. *Ulrich's International Periodicals Directory* is included. Valuable as much for the findings as for the procedures of evaluation.

Gomez, Louis, et al., "All the Right Words," *Journal of the American Society for Information Science*, December 1990, pp. 547–559. Although a somewhat technical article, the result is clear enough. In the words of the authors: "Don't try to pick only the best words, try to harvest all the appropriate ones. . . . For end users doing interactive searches, a controlled vocabulary would probably be strongly counterproductive. . . . In the same situation, full text indexing appears likely to yield very high success rates." The research concerned machine-readable databases, but much of the article is applicable equally to print indexes.

Hurd, Julie, et al, "Information Seeking Behavior of Faculty . . . ," in *Proceedings of the ASIS Annual Meeting*, 1992, pp. 136–143. A thorough analysis of how faculty uses indexes and abstracts. The study is limited to the sciences, but the methodology and the findings have wider application.

Mitchell, Eleanor, and Sheila Walters, *Document Delivery Services*. Medford, NJ: Learned Information, 1995. This provides an overall view of current progress and problems in document delivery. Intended as a handbook for working librarians, it offers answers to frequently asked questions of how the systems function. A valuable, generally easy-to-follow guide.

CHAPTER SIX
INDEXING AND ABSTRACTING SERVICES: SUBJECT AND NEWSPAPER

The progression of indexes is simplicity itself. First one has the general index, for example, the *Readers' Guide*. Next comes the index which covers a broad section from the humanities to the social sciences and sciences. Beyond that the field narrows to areas such as business, law, library science, medicine, and the like. Within each of these specific disciplines are countless subsections and indexes to match. One only has to turn to *Guide to Reference Books* and look up any narrow subject to find an index to periodicals, newspapers, reports, and so forth within that field.

The librarian must match the likely subject index with the query. Yet, it is not quite that simple. A high school student who asks for an article on the American Civil War should be referred to almost any general index discussed in the previous chapter. The same student or, for that matter, the teacher or subject expert who is doing a detailed paper on the Civil War, will require more sophisticated approaches. The searcher might turn to several indexes, but will be successful with the one that concentrates on American history, for example, *America: History and Life*.

Subject Index Scope

Once a user understands the average general index she or he may progress to subject indexes. When considering such indexes, three facts must be kept in mind:

1. Many are broader in coverage than is indicated by such key title words as "Art" or "Education." Related fields are often considered. There-

fore, anyone doing a subject analysis in depth should consult indexes that take in fringe-area topics.

2. Most subject indexes are not confined to magazines. They often include books, monographs, bulletins, and even government documents.

3. A great number are not parochial but, rather, international in scope. True, they may not list many foreign language works, but usually note anything in English, even if issued abroad.

Because of this wider base of coverage, a few libraries are doubtful about including such indexes in their collections. What good is it to learn of a particular article in a specialized journal and then be unable to obtain the journal? However, the library should be in a position either to borrow the journal or to have a copy made of the article. Another possibility—full text on CD-ROM or online. If the cost is lowered, this may be the savior of smaller libraries in the decade ahead. All magazines will then be within easy reach.

There is little point in describing each of the approximate 2500 subject indexes. For the most part, their titles explain their scope and purpose. What follows begins with the basic indexes in the humanities, social sciences, and sciences and goes on to consider examples of specific subject indexes.

HUMANITIES

CD: Arts & Humanities Citation Index. See p. 62.

CD: Humanities Abstracts. New York: The H. W. Wilson Company, 1994 to date, monthly. $2295.[1]
Print: Humanities Index, 1974 to date, quarterly. Service. *Online:* WilsonLine, 1984 to date, twice weekly, $37 to $65 per hour. Also available on OCLC and CDP.

The H. W. Wilson Company issues indexes that bridge general and specific subjects. All use much the same approach. The author and subject entries are in a single alphabet. There are excellent cross-references. (Some indexes, such as the *Applied Science and Technology Index,* have only a subject approach.) Subject headings are frequently revised, and in most services, book reviews are listed in a separate section. Each index has its peculiarities, but a reading of the prefatory material in each will clarify its finer points.

Covering as it does all of the areas of the humanities, there is nothing quite like *Humanities Abstracts.* The index offers the average person a clear path to in-

---

[1]Beginning in 1995 The H. W. Wilson Company added abstracts to various indexes. Whereas the abstract editions only begin in 1994, the CD-ROM, without the abstracts, goes back to 1984 and the printed versions to much earlier.

formation about religion, the arts, literary criticism, philosophy, journalism, and many other areas under the broad umbrella of "humanities." Incidentally, this includes history, which others would put in the social sciences.

Some 350 English language periodicals are analyzed. The print index is by subject and author, with the usual section for book reviews. It has several unique features: (1) Opera and film reviews are listed under appropriate subject headings, that is, "Opera reviews" and "Motion picture reviews." (2) Poems may be located both by the author's name and under the section, "Poems." (3) The same procedure is followed for short stories. (4) There is a section for theater reviews. Given these divisions, the work is valuable for checking current critical thought on a wide variety of subjects in the humanities.

Search Patterns

Humanities Abstracts follows the same 1-2-3 search pattern as all other Wilson indexes on CD-ROM. (See the previous chapter for a discussion of this software.) The user who turns to a subject index is likely to be more informed about the topic than the person who sits down to search a general index. Usually the search should begin at the second or third level, rather than the basic first level. The searcher has the opportunity to enter key words, often known only to a particular field. With boolean logic the results are better defined.

SOCIAL SCIENCES

Social Sciences Citation Index. See, p. 162.

CD: *Social Sciences Abstracts.* New York: The H. W. Wilson Company, 1994 to date, monthly. $2295.
  Print: Social Sciences Index. 1975 to date, quarterly. Service.
  Online: 1983 to date, twice a week. WilsonLine: $34 to $50 per hour.
  Full Text: Social Sciences Index/Full Text. Ann Arbor, MI: UMI, 1989 to date, monthly. $17,500 (includes hardware) on CD-ROM.

CD: *Social Sciences Source.* Peabody, MA: EBSCO, 1988 to date, monthly. $1495. (Forty journals searchable with full text.)

CD: *PAIS International.* New York: Public Affairs Information Service, 1972 to date, quarterly, $1600.
  Print: PAIS International. 1914 to date, monthly. Including cumulations, $495.
  Online: 1972 to date, monthly. DIALOG file 49, $72 per hour. Also available on CompuServe and OCLC.

Although there is an ongoing argument about some of the disciplines included in the social sciences (such as history, which some place in the humanities) the area covers anthropology, economics, environmental studies, geography, law and criminology, public administration, political science, psychology, sociology, and urban studies. Between the *Social Sciences Abstracts,* which touches on all these disciplines, and the more specific indexes (which are named clearly), it is hardly necessary to remember more than in a general way the taxonomy of the social sciences.

The social sciences indexes may be used in conjunction with the general index discussed in the previous chapter. PAIS, for example, indexes periodicals, pamphlets, books and other materials which emphasize current events—events which focus on virtually every interest from the arts to the sciences. Granted, the central interest is political science, but the discipline is an umbrella for as many concerns as there are questions at a reference desk. Still, there are three indexes which concentrate exclusively on the social sciences (*Social Sciences Citation Index, Social Sciences Abstracts,* and *Social Sciences Source*). These are major additions for large research libraries. Smaller libraries will want at least the *Social Sciences Abstracts.*

Social Sciences Abstracts

Social Sciences Abstracts covers about 355 English language periodicals. There are author and subject entries with a separate section for book reviews. *Abstracts,* an addition to the service in 1995, is a vast improvement over the much older *Social Sciences Index,* which is still available at a somewhat lower cost. *Abstracts* is so much better that a library should not simply settle for the *Index.*

Social Sciences Index/Full Text offers a monthly full-text service. The 350 periodicals in *Social Sciences Index* are on a series of discs and follow the precise formation found in the other UMI general periodical full-text resources discussed in the previous chapter. The index is on a separate disc. Actual use is easy enough, despite failure to be able to search the full text, but the cost of $17,500 is prohibitive for most libraries. Still, it is the way the H. W. Wilson indexes and others will go in the years ahead.

Social Sciences Source

The EBSCO rival to The H. W. Wilson Company *Social Sciences Abstracts* is edited for the same general audience in public and high schools as well as undergraduates in colleges. *Social Sciences Source* has more titles (400 compared with Wilson's 355). There are other differences. The EBSCO entry, as part of the price, includes the full text of about 40 of the journals indexed. The Wilson index is supported by the ability of the searcher to seek out more recent items online, at no extra expense.

Sociological Abstracts—Sociofile on CD-ROM (San Diego, CA: 1974 to date, three per year, $2000) is a related social sciences title. While the approximately

2000 journals indexed concentrate on sociology, many of them overlap into the more general social sciences. As such, this file is often used by people seeking material not found in the more general database. In one way or another, the index touches on most of the subjects of interest to any researcher in the general area. The index is available from 1953 in print, and online from 1963. Both formats are updated every two months, and are more up to date than the CD-ROM. (Note: Another version of this is available from EBSCO at the same price, but with slightly different software.)

PAIS International[2]

PAIS International offers a general source of information for both expert and layperson. Many librarians consider it the general index of the political and social sciences. Here one turns for current information on government, legislation, economics, sociology, and political science. Periodicals, government documents, pamphlets, reports, and some books in such areas as government, public administration, international affairs, and economics are indexed. About 1400 journals and approximately 6000 other items (from books to reports) are indexed each year. Coverage is international. Arrangement is alphabetical, primarily by subject. A few of the entries have brief descriptive notes on both contents and purpose.

PAIS on CD-ROM is a good example of the delights and problems of the form. The immediate joy of recognition is dulled by the price, $1600 (1995). This contrasts with $495 for the monthly printed version. The CD-ROM includes material from 1972, although the printed file has existed since 1914. Also, note that the disc is updated only quarterly as compared with the more current monthly offering of the printed version and the online work. By now it is obvious to anyone that in terms of cost and coverage, nothing quite beats the printed version. So why go on? Well, for the usual reasons, but first and foremost, many more contact or search points are available on the CD-ROM than with the printed version.

Search Patterns

Again, the H. W. Wilson index, *Social Sciences Abstracts*, is searched in the same fashion as the publisher's other titles. A notable difference is that in conjunction with UMI there is a separate full-text backup of the 350 titles abstracted. These are on separate disks and cannot be searched by key word. Where the library has the disks there is an indication in the Wilson abstracts of where and how to locate the full text.

---

[2]PAIS incorporates the indexing found previously in two separate indexes, that is, *PAIS Bulletin* and *PAIS Foreign Languages Index*. Valuable additions are a "Key to Periodicals References" and a list of "Publications Analyzed." Both serve as a handy checklist and buying guide for the library.

EBSCO's CD-ROM, *Social Sciences Source* is unique in that 40 full-text journals are built into the system. Each may be searched by key words in the text. This is a decided advantage, made even more so by the easy-to-follow instruction screens. There are two steps in the full-text search. The usual step of searching for the desired citation(s) is necessary. Once an article has been selected—and is in one of the 40 titles—the user calls it up and it can be searched by key words. Ideally, of course, this would be a one-step process with the user simply searching for key words in all 40 periodical texts—a process that will gain popularity in the years ahead.

The CD-ROM PAIS illustrates an important point about who publishes what. Although the index is compiled by the Public Affairs Information Service, it is made available on CD-ROM by at least three distributors—the publisher, Silver Platter, and EBSCO. Despite similarity in updates (quarterly) and text (precisely the same for all three CD-ROMs), each is searched in a slightly different fashion.

While there may be argument over which is the best software, choice by librarians at least is based on a simple and tried factor—that the library accustomed to searching with EBSCO or Silver Platter software employed with other reference works will naturally prefer to maintain the same software for PAIS. A library with neither software, or no preference, may wish to go with the publisher who charges a bit less for the CD-ROM.

Actually, the search patterns for all the services is much the same. Differences arise when EBSCO employs one key number to call up a citation while Silver Platter and the publisher rely on other key numbers. Search limiters, truncation, combining sets, and so forth, are similar with various software; and the basic steps for beginners are almost precisely the same. Online search patterns are again much the same, but do differ from vendor to vendor.

SCIENCE

Science Citation Index. See p. 162.

CD: Applied Science & Technology Abstracts. New York: The H. W. Wilson Company, 1993 to date, monthly. $2495.
   Print: Applied Science and Technology Index. 1958 to date monthly. Service.
   Online: WilsonLine, 1983 to date, twice weekly, $43 to $60 per hour.

There are dramatically more print and online indexes available for the sciences than for the humanities or social sciences. The reason is that there are four to five times as many periodicals in this area as in the humanities or social sciences. A common estimate is 65,000 scientific and technological journals. Government and business tend to be more willing to fund science than the other disciplines. Science online databases appeared earlier than those for the other disciplines primarily because of interest and good funding. At the same time, the cost of scientific indexes and periodicals are exceptionally high compared to other areas. To cite an extreme example, a year's subscription to a nuclear physics journal published in the Netherlands is close to $5000. It has more than 11,000 pages but the price is still steep.

The average library may subscribe only to basic science indexes, most of which are provided by The H. W. Wilson Company. The primary index is the *Applied Science and Technology Abstracts*. This analyzes about 390 English language periodicals by subject. In addition to the sciences, it covers such areas as transportation, food, and a wide variety of engineering titles. It is augmented by the *General Science Abstracts* (1993 to date, monthly, $1995) and available in print as the *General Science Index* (1978 to date, monthly) and online from the same publisher. It is a minimal version of the *Applied Science and Technology Index*. With 140 titles it is appropriate for smaller libraries. An expanded, more specialized cousin of both, from the same publisher, *Biological and Agricultural Index* (1983 to date, quarterly, $1495), is available in print and online.

Which?

Touching as it does on almost every interest, the *PAIS International* is a required item in all libraries where research, even at the most fundamental level, is a consideration. There is nothing like it, and as of now nothing can replace its value.

Beyond that index, which of the others discussed here should be considered by the library? It depends on four factors: (1) If the library has any of the giant general indexes available, for example, UMI's *Periodical Abstracts*, IAC's *Expanded Academic Index*, or EBSCO's *Academic Search* (and their various offshoots) then none of the general subject indexes discussed here is necessary. All the periodicals they index, or nearly all, are found in the general indexes. This means there is no need for *General Science Index, Humanities Index*, or the *Social Sciences Index* and possibly even the *Applied Science and Technology Index, Humanities Source*, and so forth. (2) Conversely, if the library does *not* have a large general index, then the general subject titles may be chosen as selected. (3) Since many of the general subject indexes are by The H. W. Wilson Company, they are superior in terms of indexing and abstracts and this may weigh in their favor.

(4) The fourth factor may be the most important as an argument for subscribing to all of these subject indexes, even when most of the periodicals they index are covered in general indexing services. When the library has the funds and concentrates on building a research collection and the library users are relatively refined in their requirements for specific pieces of information, the subject indexes can't be replaced by the more general works. The basic rationale is that the subject indexes have software that allows for more sophisticated searching. The software is built for the specific subject area and is considerably more precise.

In summary, the general library should probably skip most of the subject indexes. The *PAIS* is the happy exception. The academic or special library, budget permitting, should try to have access to all the indexes. If print or CD-ROM is too costly, consider using the indexes, from time to time as needed, online.

CITATION INDEXING

The following are published by the Institute for Scientific Information in Philadelphia.

CD: Arts & Humanities Citation Index. 1990 to date, three per year. $5,000.
  Print: 1977 to date, three per year. Including annual, $2700.
  Online: Arts & Humanities Search, 1980 to date, weekly. DIALOG file 439, $54 to $120 per hour. Also available online on OCLC.

CD: Social Sciences Citation Index. 1986 to date, quarterly. $5595. With abstracts, 1992 to date. $7550.
  Print: 1973 to date, three issues per year. Including annual, $2,700.
  Online: Social SciSearch, time span varies, weekly. DIALOG file 7, $63 to $120 per hour.

CD: Science Citation Index, 1980 to date, quarterly. $12,650. With abstracts, 1992 to date. $17,000.
  Print: 1961 to date, six issues per year. Including manual, $9000.
  Online: SciSearch, 1980 to date, weekly. DIALOG files 34 and 434, $72 to $142 per hour.

Citation indexes are valuable for many reasons, but the primary one is that they index more periodicals than any other service. The titles indicate the scope of each index. They cover every conceivable topic under the umbrella of humanities, social sciences, and the sciences. No other service comes closer to indexing so many journals in a subject area. *Arts & Humanities:* 1100 journals, as well as "selected" items from more than 5800 journals in science and the social sciences. *Social Sciences:* 1400, plus 3200 select. *Science:* More than 4500 titles.[3]

The major drawback is cost—SciSearch *(Science Citation Index)* can run online from $72 for subscribers to the print version to $142 an hour for nonsubscribers, plus about 50 cents for each record. The CD-ROM is $12,650, and if the subscriber wants abstracts the price jumps to $17,000. The other two services are equally costly.

Citation indexing is unique in that it employs a different approach to searching. The avenue of access is through references cited in articles, hence the

[3]Current content services such as OCLC's ArticleFirst actually lists more titles—up to 15,000—but these are not analytical in any sense of the word. Useful as they are, current content services defy the fine-tuned searching that is possible in most indexes and certainly with the citation indexes.

name of the service. It is easier to understand when one considers the printed volumes. These are organized in a peculiar fashion. In print, each index is in three parts:

1. *The Citation Index*, which lists papers cited alphabetically by author. The title of the article appears under the author's name, and beneath each article is a list of those who have cited the author's work. Most of the material is abbreviated.

2. *The Source Index*, which gives standard bibliographical information for each of the papers in *The Citation Index*.

3. *The Permuterm Subject Index*, which indexes the articles by subject, that is, by significant words in the title.

The system expects that the searcher will be familiar with the name of an author in a particular subject field. This is true for electronic searches as well. For example, someone looking for material on Japanese volcanoes would know that the leading expert on this is Kazuo Iskiguro.

The user would then turn to Iskiguro, Kazuo in *The Citation Index*. Beneath his name appears *seven* names of people *who have cited him* (and his article or book). The fair assumption is that these seven are writing about Japanese volcanoes, too. Furthermore, by citing Iskiguro, they are familiar with both the man and the field.

One then turns to each of the seven names in *The Source Index*, and finds articles or books *by the seven*.

Clearly, the obvious "catch" is that one must know an expert in the field in which one is involved. If not, the only solution is to (1) use another index with subject headings or (2) turn to *The Permuterm Subject Index*.

The Permuterm Subject Index is an alphabetically arranged (key-word-in-context) KWIC-type index. Subjects are derived from words appearing in the titles of the source articles. Each significant word is precoordinated with other terms to produce all possible permutations of terms.

The uniqueness of this system, as opposed to other retrieval schemes, is that it is a network of connections among authors citing the same papers during a current year. In other words, if, in searching for a particular subject matter, one has a key paper or review article in the field, or even an author's name, one consults *The Citation Index* by author. Beneath the author's name will be listed in chronological order *any* publications by that author cited during a particular year, together with the *citing* authors (source items) who have referred to the particular work. If one continues to check the citing authors in *The Citation Index*, a cyclical process takes place, often with mushrooming results. *The Source Index* is then used to establish the full bibliographical reference to the citing author.

A citation index has a major production advantage that makes it particularly suited for automation. Indexers do not have to be subject specialists, and there is no need to read the articles for subject headings. All the compiler must do is (1) enter the author, title, and full citation in machine-readable form and (2) list all the citations used in the primary article in order by author, title, and full citation in machine-readable form. As a consequence, a careful clerk may prepare material for the computer. This speeds up indexing and also makes it possible to index considerably more material quickly.

Disadvantages of the printed volumes are numerous, among which are the reliance on type so small that it makes classified-ad-size type look gigantic by comparison and their confusing abbreviations. The most serious drawback is the lack of controlled vocabulary. This may work well enough in science, but often fails when used in the humanities and the social sciences. The multiple volumes make this a difficult print set to use, which is all the more reason for its value on CD-ROM or as an online database.

Search Patterns

The CD-ROM and online citation indexes feature field searching for beginners. This permits the user to search for an article by title word, author name, cited author and cited reference, address word, abbreviated or full journal title, or a combination of these. The search differs from the simple search key word system (such as InfoTrac). Here one simply enters in a key word or phrase. Field searching offers more options.

The CD-ROM version is easier to use for most laypersons than the online product. At the same time, the online work is much more current. It is updated weekly, as compared to quarterly CD-ROMs.

Very few libraries, except for the largest, can offer all or even a good number of the periodicals indexed in these services. But they can and do use interlibrary loan and rapid document delivery. Also, the publisher will supply tearsheets of one or a thousand articles needed—for a price, to be sure. Eventually librarians will be able to access the full text of many of the titles online.

SPECIFIC SUBJECT INDEXES

What follows are examples of the basic types of narrow subject index that make up the 2500 or more indexes in this category. The ones discussed here are found in most medium to large libraries. Conversely, the indexes are only representative. Each library will have particular titles for the particular needs of the community.

Search Patterns

By now it is obvious that the basic search patterns online and on CD-ROM (or, for that matter in print) are relatively easy at a beginning level. When one seeks only basic, fundamental data almost any key word approach will do. This can be modified by subject headings and boolean logic, but where the layperson or student is searching, most don't even bother. A few key words and a few current citations seem to be enough. More often than not this *is enough*. Sometimes it is not, or the citations are wrong for the question, or the user has employed the wrong index, and so forth. There are other related search problems discussed throughout this text.

Art

CD: Art Abstracts. New York, NY: The H. W. Wilson Company, 1994 to date, monthly. $2495.
   Print: Art Index. 1929 to date, quarterly. Service.
   Online: WilsonLine. 1984 to date, twice weekly, $43 to $60 per hour. Also available on OCLC and CDP.

Art Abstracts indexes 260 domestic and foreign periodicals. Museum bulletins, yearbooks, and reviews are included as is other material that may be of value. The abstracts have been included in the index since 1994. Limited as it is to so few titles, the index is fine for the nonspecialist or for someone seeking material from relatively well-known sources, but for esoteric details another index is needed. Here the preference goes to RILA (Repertoire International de la Litterature de l'Art). The service is published by the Clark Art Institute in Williamstown, MA. While not available on a CD-ROM it is online as *Art Literature International* (DIALOG file 191, $39 per hour) and covers the same time span as the corresponding print work, 1973 to date with quarterly updates. Several thousand periodicals, books, reports, museum bulletins, and so on, are covered in each year's publication. The index boasts excellent abstracts coverage from art in Europe from the fourth century to the present.

   On CD-ROM, as well as online, one may turn to *ARTbibliographies Modern* (Santa Barbara, CA: ABC-CLIO, 1993 to date, annual). Unlike the other two indexes, this is limited to twentieth-century art and indexes about 350 periodicals. At the same time it will index and abstract articles that may cover earlier periods related to the current century.

   It should be emphasized that "art" in all of these indexes takes in a wide variety of subject material from painting and sculpture to photography, architecture, furniture, and interior design. Also, social, scientific, and political aspects of the world are found in citations where art is at the center.

Business

CD: ABI/INFORM, Global Edition. Louisville, KY: UMI, 1987 to date, monthly. Current four years. $5500.
   Online: 1971 to date, weekly. DIALOG file 15, $132 per hour.

Full Text: Business Periodicals Global. 1987 to date, monthly. $15,000–$20,000 on CD-ROM. Scanned full-text images of 550 to 750 titles indexed in ABI/INFORM.

CD: Business Index. Foster City, CA: Information Access Company, 1989 to date, monthly. Current four years. $3500.
Full Text: Business Collection, 1989 to date, monthly. Text of 400 titles indexed in *Business Index,* on microfilm. (*Business ASAP* is much the same, but on CD-ROM.)

CD: Business Abstracts. New York: The H. W. Wilson Company, 1990 to date, monthly. $2495. (The CD-ROM version without the abstracts covers 1982 to date.)
Print: Business Periodicals Index, 1958 to date, monthly. Service.
Online: 1982 to date, twice weekly. WilsonLine, $43 to $60 per hour, 10 to 20 cents per record.

Canadian Business and Current Affairs. See p. 142.

CD: Predicasts F&S Index Plus Text. Foster City, CA: Information Access Company, 1991 to date, monthly. $6000 (U.S. alone: $2500: International alone, $3500).
Print: Predicasts F&S Index United States, 1960 to date, monthly, $850; *International* to date, monthly.
Online: Predicasts Forecasts, 1971 to date, monthly. DIALOG files 81 and 83, $114 per hour, 60 cents per record. Also available online: NEXIS.
Full Text Online: PROMPT, 1972 to date, daily DIALOG file 16, $126 per hour.

Online: Dow Jones News./Retrieval—Dow Jones. Princeton, NJ: Dow Jones & Company, 1986 to date. Current 90 days. $93 to $150 per hour.

Interest in business runs as high in America as in any part of the world. Almost everyone is aware of the ups and downs of economic and political fortunes. Radio, television, online, Internet, and just plain talking over a cup of coffee or a glass of milk will often have something to do with business. Little wonder, then, that it is a specialized area of reference services. Many medium to large libraries have sections devoted exclusively to business, economics, and related areas. And the reference librarian who wishes to specialize in this field should study equally specialized reference sources. Here it is possible only to suggest those reference sources that are basic in most libraries.

It is worth stressing, too, that business indexes may be consulted for information on everything from psychology and art to science and prison life. In fact, for a different, broader view of many subjects, the typical business index is a good secondary source.

Much current business news is available online. The online approach is often favored because it is up to the minute. Beyond the online, general newspaper indexes are highly specialized services such as the *McGraw-Hill News On-line* (DIALOG file 600), which transmits news throughout the business day.[4]

There are numerous guides to business sources, including sections in *Guide to Reference Books, American Reference Books Annual* and so forth. One of the best, and frequently updated, is Michael Lavin's *Business Information* (Phoenix, AZ: Oryx Press, 2d ed., 1992). This annotates and explains the basic reference works in business, and with the 1992 edition there is considerable welcome emphasis on electronic products.[5]

ABI/INFORM

ABI/INFORM is available on close to 25 online vendor systems and is one of the most popular of all databases. It has more than 600,000 citations to material in some 1400 periodicals. Almost all items have detailed abstracts. Coverage is international. Topics move from accounting and auditing to taxation and real estate. Almost any aspect of the business/economic world can be found. It is updated monthly, and in a month adds from 3500 to 4000 new records.

Of the 1400 journals indexed since 1971, about 400 to 450 are considered "core" and are indexed in depth. The others (which touch on business through legal and professional organizations) are indexed selectively. This is a common practice in all subject indexes that cover a wide range of periodical titles.

Searching follows standard UMI patterns. For example, taking advantage of the ABI thesaurus terms is simplicity itself. One types in a keyword (find Kw) or a title word (find TW) and other qualifiers as needed. One can browse the UMI subject terms to retrieve the most relevant terms. For example, one may "Bro Su Automobiles" and the screen will then ask if you want broader, narrower, or related headings and these will be displayed for further searching.

About 500 to 700 titles are available in full text, on *Business Periodicals Global.* This CD-ROM backs up ABI/INFORM and provides full-text article retrieval for some 500 to 700 titles indexed in ABI. Coverage includes business and management journals which are most heavily used. Retrospective titles begin with 1987 material. The page reproduction is full image, that is, it includes photographs, graphs, ads, and so forth. A current year includes about 60 to 70 disks. The total package (ABI/INFORM and the full text) makes up about 140 to 150 disks per year. Disk storage carousels overcome some of the problems of using

---

[4]In 1994 business-to-business information services "were split 35 percent/65 percent between electronic information and print." The electronic information databases for business are growing more rapidly than print reference services. See Maureen Fleming, "Congestion in the Information Transport Business," *Online*, November/December 1994, p. 72.

[5]See Frank Allen's "Essential Business Reference Sources" (*RQ*, Fall, 1993, pp. 77–84) for an overview of the seven basic bibliographical guidebooks and for titles considered essential to business reference.

so many disks, but manual handling remains a problem. Cost: $15,000 for the full text alone, or $20,000 for the full text and ABI/INFORM.

In 1995 it was reported that UMI invested more than $50 million in its full-text and full-image databases. The expansion includes putting more than 4000 business and general interest magazines into electronic format, both full text and full image. Sensing a diverse market, with various levels of money available for periodicals, UMI offers different types of full-text service. These range from the less expensive 130 full-image periodical version *(Business Periodicals Ondisk—New Edition)* to ABI/INFORM—express edition with 350 titles—as well as *Business Dateline* with 300 periodicals, approximately 80 newspapers, and 3 wire services.

Business Index

An impressive service on CD-ROM. *Business Index* covers over 800 periodicals, as well as related items from reports to books and reviews. It includes six months' indexing of *The New York Times* financial section, *The Wall Street Journal,* and *Barrons.* Many are confused by the short time period and look for earlier issues.

The *Business Index* is supported with full microfilm text of about half the titles indexed.[6] Another source of full text, of some, but hardly all the articles, is on a CD-ROM, *Business ASAP.* It has the advantage of being updated once a month and allowing the user to search four years of indexing in one place. The disadvantage is that it goes back only four years, and for retrospective materials one must look elsewhere. There is neither a print nor an online version of this work although, again, the publisher is most likely to switch to online shortly.

Information Access Company has two related CD-ROM databases: (1) Business & Company ProFile (1989 to date, monthly, current four years, $5100 to $14,000) is a combination of *Business Index* and *Company Profile.* The latter contains information on all public and private U.S. companies, including complete text of company activities. (2) *General Business File* is a third expanded version, including all that is in the former index as well as a third section on brokerage reports. An annual subscription to this monthly service is high—close to $12,000. It is not likely to be found in many libraries, but is an important service in financial centers.

Business Abstracts

A print, online, and CD-ROM database, *Business Abstracts* began as a print index in 1958. Approximately 350 business, trade, and industry publications are in-

---

[6]The *Business Collection* is in cartridges, which are mounted in a carousel for easy use. These go back to 1982 and are updated biweekly. The user may quickly, and for a small amount of money, have the needed article in hand.

dexed in depth. Since 1993 the titles include the business section of *The New York Times* and the contents of *The Wall Street Journal*. All records since May 1990 (except book reviews) feature a 50- to 150-word abstract written by librarians or subject experts. This aspect of all the H. W. Wilson abstracting services is worth emphasis. Rather than rely on the sometimes less-than-accurate publisher or author abstracts of so many services, the Wilson Company writes its own.

The index is typical of all the publisher's titles. There are uniform subject headings, which are carefully employed. Where the title is vague, the publisher adds parenthetical descriptive subheadings. SIC (Standard Industrial Classification) codes are included for most articles, as well as the ISSN at the end of the citation.

Subjects are so all-inclusive as to make this almost a general index, and it is used as such by librarians who cannot find enough material in the basic services. For example, one may be looking for an article on the relationship between reading and television, only to find that an analysis of the subject (from the point of view of sales of books and television sets) has been indexed in *Business Abstracts* while hardly considered in the more likely *Library Literature*. Still, the index is customarily used primarily for finance, business technology, and economics.

Although the abstracts begin only in 1990, the earlier CD-ROMs and online go back to 1982. And the print index began in 1958. Eventually all of these will be cumulated and one will be able to search online and on CD-ROM for the retrospective items.

Predicasts F&S Index Plus Text

Predicasts is really a collection of several databases, each of which serves a specific purpose. The various services index over 3000 domestic and foreign trade journals, business periodicals, government documents, reports, statistical publications, bank letters, long-range forecasts, and a variety of other materials. Although the focus is on business, the subject matter covers millions of records in related areas, from agriculture to education and the social sciences. The databases are searched by using well-defined thesauruses for products, organizations, events, and geographical locations. Some files are used for both retrieval and computation; that is, it is possible to perform algebraic, statistical, and forecasting routines, as well as to enter data. Both controlled and free searching are possible, but most of the files use the Standard Industrial Classification (SIC) System. This is a numerical hierarchical system established by the United States government to classify the total economy into different industrial segments. Using specific numbers one may retrieve a "needle" from millions of records.

Each printed volume is arranged in a similar fashion and covers the same basic type of data. The first section, "Industries and Products," is a subject-heading approach to a wide variety of topics, from energy to population. Group-ings are in a hierarchical system, and automotive brakes, for example, is a sub-group of "Motor vehicles parts." Fortunately, the major subject divisions are given in alphabetical order in the cumulative alphabetical guide, and each issue has an "Alphabetical Guide to the SIC Code," which allows ready access to the "Industries and Products" section. Also, there is a "User's Guide" which clearly explains the arrangement. The second part of the index is alphabetical by the name of the company and, where the company is vast, there are subheadings.

Predicasts Overview, normally referred to by librarians simply as PROMPT, offers a worldwide view of business and individual companies. Over 1200 periodicals, books, and reports are searched for material. The online ver-sion has about 3 million citations. (Daily coverage is offered by a special online service, otherwise the update is weekly.) Numerous publications, and particu-larly ephemeral newsletters, reports, statistics, and so on are available in full-text online. The emphasis on current data is stressed, and is typical of the rea-soning behind almost all business services, particularly those online. The service keeps the reader on top of competitor activities, new-product development, li-cense agreements, manufacturing methods, and similar categories—all of which mean financial gain or loss.

Dow Jones News/Retrieval

The Dow Jones Company, as the publisher's name suggests, is primarily involved with up-to-date information from and about the financial markets of the world. The material is updated as often as every 30 seconds, *but* available material is retained for only 90 days. The price is high, but it has up-to-the-minute infor-mation on stock, mutual funds, and bond prices as well as finance from through-out the world. Given this, many consider it inexpensive. With the added MCI Mail service—at an extra cost—it offers first-rate electronic messages, includ-ing the ubiquitous e-mail.

Dow Jones, like several online vendors, both produces and networks its financial services. All databases are available only through the company's own vendor system Dow Jones News/Retrieval. *Dow Jones News*, for example, reports on current news about business and finance. The publisher claims that anything of importance is on the line within 30 seconds after its release. Full text of much of the material is available online. The service averages about $1.55 a connect minute or about $90 an hour. There is neither a CD-ROM nor a print equiv-alent of this or other Dow Jones databases.

The real plus of the Dow Jones service is the Database Text Library. The searcher may retrieve part or full text from over 1400 publications, including major newspapers from *The Wall Street Journal* to *The Washington Post* and *The New York times*. (One can only receive abstracts of articles from *The New York Times*, not the full articles themselves. Indexing here is only from 1990.) The time covered from other newspapers is primarily from 1985. The full text is updated each hour and day. Cost runs from $85 to $120 an hour. Cutting the number of available texts by about one-third the company offers DowQuest. The 500 or so titles may be scanned and printed out in part or in full for about $25 to $35 an hour. At equivalent rates, Dow Jones has similar online services, for example, *International News,* updated daily and covering over 6000 companies; *Business and Finance Reports;* and a series of services with financial quotes.

Education

CD: ERIC: U.S. Educational Resources Information Center. Washington, DC: Government Printing Office, 1966 to date, quarterly. $650. (Retrospective disk with current disk: $1200.)
    Print: 1966 to date, monthly. $56.
    Online: DIALOG file 1, 1966 to date, monthly, $30 per hour. Also available online: CDP, OCLC, CompuServe, CARL, and so on.[7]

CD: Current Index to Journals in Education (CIJE on Disc). Phoenix, AZ: Oryx Press, 1969 to date, quarterly. $199. Also available on CD-ROM as part of ERIC, above.
    Print: 1969 to date, monthly. $207.
    Online: See ERIC above, which includes this database.

CD: Education Abstracts. New York: The H. W. Wilson Company, 1994 to date, monthly. $2295.
    Print: 1929 to date, monthly. Service.
    Online: 1983 to date, twice a week. WilsonLine, $25 to $40 per hour.

ERIC/IR [Educational Resources Information Center/(Clearinghouse for) Information Resources] may be consulted for both original and secondary material on education, as well as related fields from library science to numerous social science topics. The system includes (1) an index to unpublished reports *(Resources in Education)* and an index to journals *(Current Index to Journals in Education)* (both are included in a single unit in the electronic version, with each issued as a separate printed index); (2) an ongoing subject vocabulary, represented in the frequently updated *Thesaurus of ERIC Descriptors,* (3) a dissemination system which depends primarily on reproducing the material indexed on microfiche and distributing that microfiche to libraries; and (4) a decentralized organizational structure for acquiring and processing the documents that are indexed and abstracted.

The first part of ERIC is *Resources in Education* which lists unpublished reports and associated items. Each entry has a narrative abstract of 200 or so

---

[7]As a government database, ERIC is not copyrighted and like many government reference works is reprinted and put online and on CD-ROM by various companies. ERIC, for example, is available on CD-ROM from Silver Platter for $650, and EBSCO for $695, to name two of several.

words. The abstracts are written by the authors. Reports are submitted to ERIC each month, but at least 50 percent are rejected, often as much for lack of typing skills as for content. Selection is made at one of 16 clearinghouses, each of which considers a particular subject. Experts evaluate the submitted material.

About 15,000 items are included and indexed each year. The reports are divided nearly equally among three categories: research and technical reports; proceedings, dissertations, preprints, and papers presented at a conference; and curriculum guides, educational legislation, and lesson plans prepared for the classroom.

As indicated, most of the indexed material is rarely published. This means several things for the user: (1) The reports are an excellent source of coverage of some rather esoteric areas. The studies represent a unique point of view as well as sometimes imaginative methods of research. ERIC is an excellent point to begin to discover what is on the fringe of the subject. And some subjects are not found elsewhere. (2) The reports usually are complete with bibliographies, readings, and suggestions for further research. They are an excellent beginning for many longer reports. (3) The research techniques are so varied, so imaginative, that many of them may be used for other types of similar, related studies. In a word, this is a vast source of original thought. Yes, of course, some of it is valueless. The fishing trip will land some fine specimens, if not always a whale.

The first part of the printed *CIJE* index is much like *Resources in Education* in form. Items are abstracted and arranged numerically by the accession number. The second part is the subject index, which, again, follows the style of *Resources in Education*. There is also an author index and a fourth section in which the indexed journals are arranged alphabetically by title. The table of contents for each is given.

Current Index to Journals in Education, is a separate printed work, but is an integral part of the CD-ROM and online formats. It indexes about 775 periodicals in education. Although published by a commercial firm, the indexing is provided by the 16 ERIC clearinghouses. *CIJE* is searched in the same fashion as *Resources in Education* on a single CD-ROM. However, by indicating that one wants only journal articles, or unpublished reports, the two indexes may be searched as separate units. Unless requested, the search results represent a single sweep of the whole ERIC. For those who wish to search the journals only, then the *CIJE On Disc* is preferable. While this costs $199 from the publisher, it may be purchased by individuals for only $99.

An outstanding feature of ERIC, although a usual one among similar documentation systems such as that developed by the National Aeronautics and Space Administration, is that approximately 80 percent of the documents abstracted in *Resources in Education* are available on microfiche. In 350 to 400 libraries, the user finds the required citation on *Resources in Education* and then, instead of having to laboriously look for the item abstracted, simply turns to the microfiche collection. The items are arranged by accession number. This is a total information system and not the normal two-step bibliographical reference quest in which one finds the abstract or the indexed item and then must try to find the document, journal, or book which the library may not have available.

Ideally, the total information system would be offered with the second ERIC finding tool, *Current Index to Journals in Education (CIJE),* included on microfiche. It is not. Why? Because here the index and abstracts are for journal articles. The cost of putting each article on a microfiche card, not to mention copyright problems with publishers, makes the price of a total information service prohibitive, at least for now. This will change. At the same time, the publishers state "that reprints of articles included in approximately 65 percent of the journals covered in CIJE are available from University Microfilms." One knows whether a reprint is available, because "Reprint: UMI" is stated after each citation where the service is available. Ordering information is given in the front of each issue.

ERIC, too, is offered on CD-ROM by several companies. Each of the publishers offers separate software, separate paths to getting the information out of the CD-ROM disk. The obvious difficulty is that no user is going to learn different systems in order to tap the CD-ROM variations. As many libraries build collections of CD-ROM databases, the importance of common search software will carry increasingly significant weight.

Education Abstracts

Comparatively, The H. W. Wilson Company *Education Abstracts* is a poor second to the combined strengths of *ERIC,* with 800 titles analyzed as compared to only 400 in *Education Abstracts.* Still, it has proved useful as an additional approach, a possible secondary search source if ERIC fails. Furthermore, because the printed version (*Educational Index*) has been available since 1929 it has come to be almost an institution in some libraries. Be that as it may, the CD-ROM format, as usual, may be easier to search but it costs $2295 as compared to "service" or several hundred dollars (depending on the budget of the library) for the printed version. If the library can afford both ERIC and *Education Abstracts* on CD-ROM, fine; but in most cases the latter, particularly when used as a backup, is a better buy in print. And, of course, for retrospective searching, the print version is required.

History

CD: America: History and Life. Santa Barbara, CA: American Bibliographical
    Center—Clio Press, 1982 to date, three per year. $3000.
    Print: 1964 to date, seven per year. Service.

Online: 1964 to date, quarterly. DIALOG file 38, $72 per hour. Also available online: CompuServe.

CD: History Source. Peabody, MA: EBSCO, 1988 to date, three per year. $495.

The purpose of *America: History and Life* is to cover complete aspects of American and Canadian history. The publisher indexes over 2100 journals, including many from countries outside Canada and the United States. Films, videos, books, dissertations, and other forms of communication are considered. A search of a span of years will cover every major, and not a few minor, sources about the topic being searched. Again, the recurrent problem is that the CD-ROM goes back only to 1982 while the print version begins in 1964. Here, however, there is a solution to the laborious effort of searching the print volumes. One may turn to an online search where files begin with the first issue in 1964.

Where the print version is searched, the user must be aware of the typical abstract service organization. Material is gathered under broad topics of interest, with a subject and author index. The *Subject Profile Index* expands the subject approach to the classified abstracts in four areas: subject, geography, biography, and chronology. An article on Cornwall's campaign for Virginia, for example, would be listed as follows: subject: "Revolutionary War; biography: Cornwall's; geography: Virginia; chronology: 1781." Under these and other headings, the article analyzed appears in the subject index an average of four or five times, providing insurance against a user's not finding a work. Part B is *Index to Book Reviews* (covering over 130 scholarly U.S. and Canadian journals of history); part C is *American History Bibliography (Books, Articles, and Dissertations);* part D is *Annual Index.* This whole series is simply called *America: History and Life.*

The same publisher covers the history of the world, outside Canada and the United States in *Historical Abstracts On Disc* (1982 to date, three issues per year). Approximately 2200 journals are searched for material; books, dissertations, and related material are indexed as well. Coverage of world history is from 1450 to the present. The beginning date is worth remembering. Anyone, for example, working in Greek or Roman history will be at a loss using this index. The print version goes back to 1955, the CD-ROM to 1982, and the online approach to 1973. A thorough search will require consultation of the two parts of the print volumes: part A, *Modern History Abstracts,* covers material from 1775 to 1914; part B, *Twentieth Century Abstracts,* moves from 1914 to the present.

The publisher has a typical price structure for its services. The printed indexes are priced according to the size of the budget of the library, so the higher the budget the more costly the index. The basic CD-ROM price is only for subscribers of the printed version. Nonprint subscribers must pay more for the CD-ROM. For example, *America: History and Life on Disc* is $3000 for subscribers, but $4250 for nonsubscribers. In addition, prices vary for network use of the databases. It is worth emphasizing that the publisher is following standard 1995–1996 price patterns which, to say the least, are confusing.

History Source

Turning to the popular aspects of history, EBSCO's covers every area of the globe from the first person out of the cave to the present. The only boundary, and it is a major one, concerns the number of periodicals indexed. In *History Source* only 50 periodicals are indexed, compared with over 2000 for *America: History and Life*. And the 50, wisely enough, are limited to more popular magazines and journals appropriate for high school and college students as well as laypersons. Another plus, at least for smaller libraries, is the cost, which is about one-quarter that of its senior competitor. Should the library purchase *History Source?* If it has access to one of the major general indexes, which covers at least 400 to 2000 titles, the answer is no. Most of the titles in *History Source* will be indexed in the general index. Where such an exhaustive index is not at hand, then, and only then, should one consider the *History Source*.[8]

Law

Online: LEXIS. New Providence, NJ: Reed-Elsevier. Beginning date, frequency, cost: varies by files.

Online: WESTLAW. Eagan, MN: West Publishing Corporation. Beginning date, frequency, cost: varies by files.

CD: Index to Legal Periodicals. New York: The H. W. Wilson Company, 1981 to date, monthly. $1495.
Print: 1908 to date, monthly. $165.
Online: 1981 to date, twice weekly. WilsonLine, $43 to $60 per hour. Also available online: OCLC, CDP, LEXIS, WESTLAW.

CD: LegalTrac. Foster City, CA: Information Access Company, 1980 to date, monthly. $5000 (includes hardware).
Online: Legal Resource Index, 1980 to date, monthly. DIALOG file 150, $120 per hour, 35 cents a record. Also available online: LEXIS, WESTLAW, CARL.

Many legal questions may be answered using the particular federal or state laws, or city codes, but this requires specialized searching knowledge. Here LEXIS and WESTLAW are of great help. In between are more general legal

---

[8]EBSCO publishes a series of subject indexes of this type. The others have a select number of titles—out of all those indexed—in full text. (Full text for some of the *History Source* titles is likely to follow.) *Health Source,* for example, indexes 200 periodicals of interest to laypersons, and of these 35 are in full text. There is full text, too, for some 500 health-related pamphlets. Others in the series follow much the same pattern, for example, *Humanities Source* (400 titles, 21 full text with full-text *Magill Book Reviews*), *Social Science Source, Business Source,* and *General Science Source.* These are monthly and range in price from $1500 to $2000 a year.

queries, which can often be fielded using *PAIS* or even *Readers' Guide* or *Maga-zine Index*.

The two major legal indexes are available only online, that is, LEXIS and WESTLAW. Both are made up of separate, distinct databases such as *Westlaw Admiralty Database* to *Westlaw Tax Base*. In between are over a dozen databases. The same is true of LEXIS. Both contain individual parts which are found in print. For example, LEXIS includes The H. W. Wilson Company's *Index to Legal Periodicals*. The services tend to be limited to large law libraries and medium to large law firms.

Both services are supplied directly by the publisher and not through a vendor. They have complex charges that depend on which is used and how often it is employed.

LEXIS has a word-for-word duplication of cases found in print, for example, federal and state court opinions, statutes of the United States Code, or decisions of the Supreme Court. Coverage dates vary, and the whole file is continuously updated. The arrangement is "by library"; hence the New York Public Library would have *New York Reports* and *Consolidated Laws* among others. The Federal Tax Library would have the *Internal Revenue Code*, tax cases, and so forth. Searches follow the normal pattern, and the full text may be searched entirely, that is, not only by title and author, but by words found in the text of the legal material. One must limit the terminology employed, or end up with hundreds of citations to less-than-relevant data. Another difficulty with the full-text search is that in earlier days the recorders were not very careful about how names were spelled, and searches may be incomplete because of an improper spelling.

WESTLAW is similar to LEXIS in that it offers the full text of various federal statutes, decisions of federal courts, and the like. In addition it covers, as does LEXIS, the various state laws.

The two services are obvious competitors, and although they include much of the same material, there is a decided difference in the programs. Some claim WESTLAW is easier to use; others assert that this is the case with LEXIS. Also, of course, there are subtle differences in the types of materials updated which may make one more suitable than the other for certain situations. It is primarily a matter of (1) deciding which is more convenient to use and (2) establishing the cost.

Turning to less technical resources, there are two indexes of law material in many academic and public libraries. Where cost is a consideration, the Wilson entry is best. Where coverage is more important, the IAC resource is better.

The Information Access Company uses a microfilm system with the *Legal Resource Index*. The user receives a monthly reel with a six-year cumulation built in. Approximately 800 journals and law reviews are indexed, and there is partial indexing of 1000 related publications. The law index may be searched online and is available, too, in the publisher's familiar CD-ROM format, *Legal-Trac*.

Wilson's *Index to Legal Periodicals* is available in print, online, and on CD-ROM. It covers only 500 journals and legal publications. It differs from any of the other indexes in that it analyzes books, yearbooks, publications of various law-related institutions, and the like. It has the standard subject and author indexes but adds an index for law cases, and case notes are found at the end of many subject headings. While a good deal of this is technical, the careful librarian will find material which is equally suitable for the informed layperson. It can be of considerable help in almost any field remotely connected with the law or a legal decision.

Electronic formats have meant more indexing companies. For example, in 1992 there were only 62 firms supplying legal data. By early 1996 the number had grown to over 200. Whereas before 1990 WESTLAW and LEXIS dominated the field, today they are challenged on every front. For example, while they may charge hundreds of dollars for online court decisions, Timeline Publishing (Bellevue, WA) charges $6.25 to $10 an hour. Still, lawyers prefer LEXIS or WESTLAW because of familiarity and ease of use, even though the services may cost up to $200 an hour. Single person firms cannot afford such prices and revert to companies such as Timeline.

The developments in legal databases are followed in other subject areas. The day is long past when only a handful of large corporations had a virtual monopoly on print and electronic indexing and abstracting services. The real questions now are just how the new publishers, as well as Internet and World Wide Web, will be able to overcome copyright problems, lower and lower pricing, software updates, and a host of other difficulties and promises.

Library and Information Science

CD: Library Literature. New York: The H. W. Wilson Company, 1984 to date, quarterly. $1095.
   Print: 1934 to date, bimonthly. Service.
   Online: 1984 to date, twice weekly, WilsonLine, $25 to $40 per hour.

CD: Library and Information Science Abstracts. (LISA). East Grinstead, England: Bowker-Saur, 1969 to date, monthly. Price varies.
   Print: 1969 to date, monthly. $500.
   Online: 1969 to date, monthly. DIALOG file 61, $66 per hour.

CD: Information Science Abstracts Plus. Alexander, VA: IFI/Plenum, 1966 to date, quarterly. $1095.
   Print: 1966 to date, monthly. $515.
   Online: 1966 to date, monthly. DIALOG file 202, $132 per hour.

Library Literature offers subject and author entries to articles that have appeared in about 220 library-oriented periodicals. Almost one-third of the entries represent publications outside the United States. (About 30 are non-English language). Books and library school dissertations and theses are included.

As with other specialized Wilson indexes, the contents of books are analyzed as are reports and pamphlets that relate to information science. The index gives the librarian a fairly complete view of the subject field, but it has a poor publication schedule. *Library Literature* is available both online and on CD-ROM. But in both, material is included only from 1984, and hardly begins to tap sources that go back to 1934. Still, for current searching either electronic format is more than adequate.

Library and Information Science Abstracts (LISA) is of added help, although rarely any more current. Major journals are indexed and the service abstracts selected reports, theses, and other monographs. The number of abstracts now runs to well over 4000 each year. There is excellent coverage of U.S. government reports, primarily because the U.S. National Technical Information Service allows LISA to reprint its abstracts. There are similar arrangements with other groups. Whereas the print *Library Literature* is in the traditional alphabetical subject-author arrangement, LISA depends on a classification system for the arrangement of material. Again, of course, the order hardly matters when the service is searched online or on a CD-ROM.

An even-more-sophisticated approach is offered in *Information Science Abstracts Plus*. The emphasis is on about 400 technical periodicals, books, reports, proceedings, and similar materials. And of the some 11,000 abstracts issued each year, a vast proportion deal with aspects of automation, communication, computers, mathematics, artificial intelligence, and so on. It is a service particularly suited to the needs of the information science researcher and the librarian in a large system. The abstracts are well written and complete. Each printed issue has an author index, and there is an annual subject index.

Understandably, librarians find all these services relatively easy to search in electronic formats. The librarians, after all, know the technical language involved and can use precise key words and subject headings. It should be added that anyone in communication and information-related sciences will find the services valuable.

Literature

CD: MLA International Bibliography. New York: Modern Language Association of America. 1963 to date, quarterly. $1495.[9]
   Print: 1922 to date, annual. $750.
   Online: 1963 to date, monthly. OCLC, $50 to $60 per hour.
   Also available on magnetic tape from the publisher.

Providing as it does information on literature in virtually every corner of the globe, the *MLA International Bibliography* is a general index for the imagina-

---

[9]Although published by Modern Language Association of America, the CD-ROM is available through a private vendor. This type of arrangement, where one small institution contracts with a larger vendor or publisher to distribute its reference work, is usual.

tive searcher. As literature is concerned with every aspect of human life, the index can be employed for more than trying to find X material about an author, book, or theoretical formula. For example, anyone searching for data on the history of scientific journals will find more than enough here as well as in specific scientific sources such as *Science Citation Index.*

There are over 1 million citations from some 3000 periodicals. One simply types in a subject or an author to get a complete or partial run of citations. By checking the "Subjects Covered," which comes at the end of each citation, one gets leads for additional related subjects and authors. A more specific approach is to use the thesaurus which is built into the electronic databases. Unfortunately, there are no abstracts.

The printed volumes are a nightmare to use. They are divided into five separate subvolumes with additional subheadings. The organization is so complicated that it requires an expert in the field of a given section of literature to make a search. Fortunately, with the 1981 edition, things became much easier. A subject index was added. This covers all the categories and the some 3500 journals (as well as selected books) which are indexed.

Medicine, Chemistry, and Biology

CD: MEDLINE. Bethesda, MD: U.S. National Library of Medicine. 1984 to date, monthly. $3500.[10]
> *Print: Index Medicus.* 1960 to date, monthly. $250. Annual cumulations, $275.
> *Online:* DIALOG files 152 to 155, 1964 to date, twice a month, $33 per hour. Also available online on many services from CDP (updated weekly) to OCLC.

CD: Biological Abstracts. Philadelphia, PA: BIOSIS, 1985 to date, quarterly. $9700.
> *Print:* 1926 to date, semimonthly. $3650.
> *Online:* BIOSIS Previews, DIALOG files 5 and 55, 1969 to date, weekly, $93 per hour. Also available online on many services from CDP to OCLC.

Online: CA Search. Columbus, OH: Chemical Abstracts Service, 1967 to date, biweekly. CDP Online, $106 per hour. Also available online through many other services.
> *Note:* No CD-ROM version.[11]
> *Print: Chemical Abstracts.* 1907 to date, weekly. $9200.

---

[10]As this is a government publication, there are close to a dozen vendors of MEDLINE on CD-ROM and online, as well as from the publisher. CD versions of MEDLINE, too, are numerous, for example, MEDLINE/clinical collection, MEDLINE/collection, MEDLINE/professional, MEDLINE/standard, and so forth. Each focuses on a particular need or professional aspect of medicine.

[11]There is no current CD-ROM version, but there are retrospective CD-ROM discs, (twelfth collective index, covering 1987 to 1991 from $16,000 to $25,000).

MEDLINE *(Index Medicus)*

Index Medicus is the world's most comprehensive and, probably, best-known medical index. Produced by the National Library of Medicine, and sold through the Government Printing Office, it represents government at its best. Approximately 4000 English and foreign language journals are meticulously indexed. There is, as well, a selective indexing of reports, letters, editorials, and the like. The monthly printed issues are arranged by subject and author. This, along with two other databases (Index to Dental Literature and International Nursing) comprise MEDLINE. The database contains citations, with abstracts, to articles published in the United States and some 70 other countries.

The subject headings are of utmost importance for the medical profession. They are drawn from a special list: *Medical Subject Headings*. This usually is cited as MeSH.

One of the four or five most heavily used databases in all disciplines, MEDLINE offers users a wide variety of searching options. More important, because of the subject matter, it tends to embrace, literally, the world. It has a broad potential beyond medical literature. Thanks to a file of some 7 million citations, MEDLINE may be used to find data on such related fields as psychology, education, anthropology, sociology, technology, agriculture, and almost any other area—including politics—connected in any way with medicine.

The National Library of Medicine backs up MEDLINE with an efficient article and interlibrary loan procedure. About 2000 requests for materials are received each day. Before requests reach the NLM they are filtered through three other possible sources of supply. The librarian may send the request to a local library (one which is large or has medical journals); to a resource library, usually at a medical school; or to one of 11 regional medical libraries that cover well-defined geographical regions. Finally, if none of these are possible sources, to the National Library of Medicine. In other words, the NLM serves as the final resource after requests are unsatisfied at three previous levels of processing.

The NLM library can fill from 80 to 85 percent of the requests received. The unfilled requests are transmitted by computer to the British Lending Library in Boston Spa, England, and quickly accessed by the British Lending Library, thus often making it possible to receive material more quickly from England than from another part of the United States or Canada.

While most scientific databases are complex, at least for the average layperson or librarian, MEDLINE offers numerous relatively easy paths of access. The searcher can browse by key words in the abstracts, and the title, or, more likely will turn to the aforementioned MeSH (Medical Subject Headings) for assistance. Although it does require some experience, one can browse MeSH using a built-in tree hierarchy. This allows immediate access to extremely specific areas of interest. There are numerous other entry points from author to countries and ISSN or gene numbers. There is excellent documentation for the electronic and print databases and this is updated quarterly by the NLM.

Depending on the vendor, the price for the databases varies. There are numerous options (from the beginning date of the file to the number of journals searched) that can lower, or raise, the price. At any rate, it is worth careful study of the various offerings before a decision is made both as to cost and to the best software.

BIOSIS (*Biological Abstracts*)

BIOSIS and *Chemical Abstracts,* which follows, are highly specialized technical services that require equally specialized training to use. They are found only in large or scientific subject area libraries. Here they are little more than mentioned, not for lack of importance but for lack of space in this text.

Aspects of medicine are an important part of the well-known *Biological Abstracts.* Here abstracts from over 9000 journals are included, and among these are biomedicine as well as all the biological and life sciences. As a major indexing and abstracting service, this is as well-known in science-oriented libraries as *Index Medicus* and *Chemical Abstracts.* Often the three are worked as a unit, particularly online.

Because of its wide scope, BIOSIS is employed to answer many scientific and even social science queries. A subject index uses key words in context. Topics may be searched as well by broad subject concepts; genus, species, and organism names; broad taxonomic categories; and author.

As useful as it is specialized, BIOSIS is the ideal service for online searching. It is more frequently updated online and the cost of the CD-ROM version is so high, and so out of date that the online approach is preferable. This is true, too, of almost all expensive CD-ROM versions of indexes. Unless they are used often, online searching, particularly by an expert, will be less costly and more satisfactory than either the CD-ROM or standard print approach.

CA Search (Chemical Abstracts)

CA Search, as it is called online, or *Chemical Abstracts,* as it is titled in the print version, is one of the largest abstracting services in the world. It abstracts over 15,000 scientific and technical periodicals from over 150 countries. Of the many sections, the one devoted to patents is the one that is used most.

As in all print services, the abstracts are arranged by subject, but here over 80 subject sections are consolidated into five broad groups. Each print issue includes indexes for author, patent, and key word catch phrases from the abstract and the title. It also contains a most useful "Index Guide" in addition to the numerous other aids and sections.

The service is available online, but not on CD-ROM. The system is so complicated and is divided into so many different parts that a successful search can be made only by a subject expert or by a librarian who is thoroughly familiar with the literature of chemistry and related areas.

Psychology

CD: PsyLit (Psychological Abstracts). Washington, DC: American Psychology Association, 1974 to date, quarterly. $4495.
   Print: Psychological Abstracts, 1927 to date, monthly.
   Online: PsycINFO, 1967 to date, monthly. DIALOG file 11, $55 per hour.
   Also available online: CDP, Data Star, OCLC, and so on.

Psychological Abstracts is familiar to many people primarily because, as with a few other subject abstracting services (such as ERIC), it can be used in so many related areas. For example, an important section concerns communication which, in turn, includes abstracts on language, speech, literature, and even art. Anyone involved with, say, the personality of an engineer or an artist would turn to this source. The better-educated person seeking information on anything from why a companion talks in his or her sleep to why people can or cannot read will use this index.

The service analyzes over 1400 periodicals from about 50 countries, although 90 percent of the material is in English. In addition it analyzes the contents of from 400 to 500 books each year (1987 to the present). There are about 3000 abstracts in each monthly issue. As in other services of this type there is a cumulative index, but the abstracts themselves are not cumulated.

The printed abstracts are arranged under 16 broad subject categories from physiological intervention to personality. This allows the busy user to glance quickly at a subject area of interest without being bothered by unrelated topics. As a guide for those with less experience, there is an author index and a brief subject index in each issue. The subject approach is expanded and modified in the cumulative indexes published twice a year. (When in doubt about a subject, turn first to the cumulation, not the individual issues.)

Psychological Abstracts (online: PsycINFO) is available from the major vendors. It covers the years from 1967 and is updated monthly. In addition to the basic features it offers the user several advantages. First and foremost one searching for foreign language materials will find them *only* in the database, not in the printed version. Second, dissertations can be found *only* online. The result is that today the online service offers from 25 to 30 percent more material than the printed version.

In an effort to be as current as possible, the same publisher offers PsycALERT. Here the indexing is the same, but there is no abstract, only the citation. The service is updated weekly, as contrasted with only a monthly update for PsycINFO. When the indexing is complete and the abstract added, the file is moved into the main service.

A useful aid is the *Thesaurus of Psychological Index Terms*. As with any really first-rate system, this provides the necessary terminology to aid searching either online or through CD-ROM. Considering the high price of the service on CD-ROM *(PsyLit)* one might be better off using online only.

CURRENT EVENTS AND NEWSPAPER INDEXES

CD: Facts on File NewsDigest. New York: Facts on File, Inc., 1980 to date, quarterly. $795.
Print: 1940 to date, weekly. $496.
Online: 1975 to date, weekly. NEXIS. Price varies.

CD: National Newspaper Index. Foster City, CA: Information Access Company, 1982 to date, monthly. Current four years, $4000.
Online: NewSearch, current two to six weeks only. DIALOG file 211, $120 per hour. Also available on CompuServe.

CD. Newspaper Abstracts on Disc. Ann Arbor, MI: UMI, 1985 to date, monthly. $2950.
Full Text: Proquest Newspapers. Various newspapers, various prices.

Canadian Business and Current Affairs. See p. 142.

CD: The New York Times Index. Ann Arbor, MI: UMI, 1992 to date, monthly. $2450.
Print: The New York Times Index. New York: The New York Times, 1851 to date, semimonthly with quarterly and annual cumulations. $565.
Online: 1980 to date, daily. NEXIS. Pricing varies.
Online: The New York Times Abstracts. Ann Arbor, MI: UMI, 1990 to date, daily. Pricing varies.

CD: CD NewsBank. New Canaan, CT: Newsbank/Readex, 1991 to date, monthly. $1800–$3100.

There are two approaches to indexing current events in libraries. The traditional solution to a question dealing with yesterday's or last week's event is to (1) turn to a newspaper and go through it page by page, (2) turn to a weekly news magazine such as *Newsweek* and thumb through it, or (3) turn to a weekly service such as *Facts on File* (discussed below). Even when the event is only a month or so old, it may prove difficult to find printed material, particularly if an index is needed. Why? The indexes are inevitably late, and even those which come out every two weeks are three to six weeks behind.

The modern solution is to turn to an online database such as *The New York Times* which has yesterday's events online and is searchable by key words; or the *Dow Jones News/Retrieval* which includes the *Times* and other publications, and is updated, literally, minute by minute. The problem, as always, is cost. Still, if someone is in a rush and does not have the patience to go through a paper or a magazine page by page, the online search is the answer. News sources on Internet and the World Wide Web are free, or cost much less, but the precise item required is difficult to find and, as such, neither is suitable for most reference questions.

Facts on File

The print or online *Facts on File* offers a quick route to locating precisely the time and place an event took place. Additionally the service supports the "fact" with a few words of explanation. Essentially, the print loose-leaf service gives the librarian objective summaries of the events of the past week, month, or, in the cumulation, the year. Emphasis is on news events in the United States, with international coverage related, for the most part, to American affairs. Material is gathered mainly from 50 major newspapers and magazines, and condensed into objective, short, factual reports.

Here is a case where the print format is absolutely required unless the library can afford online charges, which is unlikely. Why print, when so many other services are much better on a CD-ROM? Answer: the CD-ROM version comes out only quarterly. It is of limited value for immediate facts. The irony is that the whole purpose of the service is to offer relatively immediate data.

The twice-monthly, blue-colored print index is arranged under four primary headings: "U.S. Affairs," "International Affairs," "World News," and "Miscellaneous." Then, under these one finds broad subject headings, such as "Finance," "Economics," and so on. Every two weeks, each month, and then quarterly and annually, a detailed index is issued which covers previous issues. There is also a *Five-Year Master News Index*, published since 1950.

The subject index (which includes numerous names of people in the news) features the brief tag line name of the item, then gives reference to the date of the event, the page in the issue of *Facts on File*, as well as the margin letter and column number. For example, under Yugoslavia, one might find, "Austerity measures Ok'd 5-15" (date, May 15, 1996) "367 page number G3" (the letter on the margin of page 367 and the third column).

The publisher notes a "few ways" the service may be used: Check dates in the index, skim the weekly issues to prepare for current affairs tests, read Supreme Court decisions in the digest, or scan the "U.S. and World Affairs" column for ideas for short papers. There are countless other uses, although the most frequent call is for specific current data.

At the end of the index is a "Corrections" section. This gives the correct information by page and column, for example: "148A1 chairman (not president)" and "358D2 Symms (not Simms)." This feature is found in every issue.

The disk service, *Facts on File News Digest* is not the weekly *Facts on File*, but the quarterly compilation. This offers text, with line drawings of 200 to 300 maps. It may be searched with the standard boolean logic and offers a valuable overview of the news. The initial disk covers the period 1980 to 1991. The updates are cumulative. Subscribers to the printed version are given a price cut of about 15 percent on the regular price of $795.

Many Western countries have similar services, although the one most used in American libraries is Keesing's On CD-ROM (London: Longman Group Ltd., *Keesing's Contemporary Archives*, 1993 to date, monthly, price varies). It is available in print from 1931 to date, and comes out monthly as well. The emphasis differs from *Facts on File* in two important respects: (1) It covers primarily the United Kingdom, Europe, and the British Commonwealth. (2) Detailed subject reports in certain areas are frequently included (the reports are by experts and may delay the weekly publication by several days). Also, there are full texts of important speeches and documents. However, *Keesing's* does not cover in any detail many events the publisher considers "less important," such as sports, art exhibitions, and movies (all of these subjects are included in *Facts on File*). Arrangement is by country, territory, or continent, with some broad subject subheadings, such as "Religion," "Aviation," and "Fine Arts." An index is issued which is cumulated quarterly and annually.

Newspapers

The New York Times, Washington Post, The Wall Street Journal, Boston Globe, Chicago Tribune, St. Louis Post Dispatch, San Francisco Chronicle, The Los Angeles Times—and about 175 lesser-known daily American newspapers are available in full text online through DIALOG, *Dow Jones News/Retrieval*, NEXIS, *Data Times*, Internet, and many of the consumer online services such as America Online.[12]

Some online services offer only selected full text; for example, *Dow Jones News/Retrieval* concentrates on financial matters and does not offer other sections of the paper. Consumer networks may pick and choose only certain stories they believe of interest to customers. Most of the online full-text newspapers are updated daily, that is, within 24 hours after publication. Few include photographs, advertising, and so forth. The majority are simply the text of the news.[13] Most may be searched using standard Boolean logic. Many have less than adequate indexing.

It is important to determine which online database is best for the individual library. The cost is variable, but high (from $75 to $150 per hour). The usual advice is to turn to the printed version before searching the online format.

One path to economic savings is offered by UMI and its numerous newspapers on CD-ROM. DIALOG on Disc and several other vendors offer similar CD-ROMs. These, like microfilm, tend to be a month or more late and not useful for current searches.

None of the services includes all of the major or minor newspapers. What service offers what newspapers online or on CD-ROM will be found in several directories; for example, *Newspaper Online* (Needham Heights, MA: Bibliodata, 1990 to date, three per year), gives complete information on national, regional, and a few international newspapers available in full text online. The loose-leaf

---

[12]Rosalind Resnick, "Newspaper on the Net," *Internet World,* July/August 1994, pp. 69–73. The author believes an increasing number of "newspaper and magazine publishers will come to see the Internet as a viable alternative to commercial online services." That is debateable as much because of economics as ease of use through the commercial service.

[13]The online newspapers start dates are usually the late 1980s or early 1990s. Another question concerns how long the files are maintained online. Some are for 24 hours to a week. Others are for several years.

format, allows two updates each year. There is complete information on everything from online search tips to the publisher, editor, and so forth. See also *Full Text Sources Online* (by the same publisher) or *Gale Directory of Databases.*

Computer Newspaper Delivery

Full-text and index coverage should not be confused with another aspect of newspapers and the electronic age. For years one has heard of being able to read the morning or evening paper at a friendly computer. This would eliminate any need for a paperboy. Still, the notion of browsing a computer screen while eating breakfast or dinner has had limited appeal. Even traditional hackers pause when offered the alternative. The closest to a substitute for the printed newspaper is on the consumer networks, such as America Online, which carries lead stories from *The Chicago Tribune.* Beginning in early 1996, UMI's online service, ProQuest Direct, provides 90 days of *The New York Times* online, with daily updates. It is searchable by the full page or by individual articles. Another approach to a substitute for the daily paper is suggested by Access Atlanta. This offers illustrations and news for $6.95 a month over the Prodigy network. While national and international news are covered, the selling point is concentration on local, neighborhood information of interest to those in the Atlanta area. Similar local services, from a combination of newspaper chains and consumer networks, are available. CompuServe has newspaper services for about $10 a month—on top of the basic monthly fee of $9 to $15. NewsPage, a computer service offered by Individual, Inc., covers news in 450 newspapers and categorizes it under numerous topics and industries. The online service offers daily updates. A type of *Facts on File* summary is offered and then "if you have the time and inclination drill down to get the whole story." The company advertisements stress how the service "filters over 15,000 stories."

The rate structures are certain to change as are the number of newspapers available in this format. The problem is that the electronic version simply does not pay the publisher, particularly as advertisements are curbed. "In other words, while the electronic newspaper is maturing, it is too soon to tell whether it will grow up to be a bruiser or a wimp."[14]

Meanwhile, the reference librarian does have numerous indexes to newspapers. These do quite nicely for most reference questions.

National Newspaper Index

The *National Newspaper Index* indexes the country's five major newspapers: *The New York Times, The Wall Street Journal, The Christian Science Monitor, Washington Post,* and *The Los Angeles Times.* Only the most current four years are found on the CD-

---

[14]"Press Notes," *The New York Times,* October 10, 1994, p. D5.

ROM. Each month's update, means deleting a month from four years previously. The *National Newspaper Index* does not include abstracts, but much of the time it has comprehensive notes. Where the title of the article is not self-explanatory, a few words of description are added.

The searching patterns are helped by the publisher's addition of subject headings, but one cannot use boolean logic or other typical electronic search patterns. Online the same database includes other services and, particularly, adds *Magazine Index*. The online service is called NewsSearch and is as sophisticated as the CD-ROM is simple. The newspapers online are indexed daily, not monthly as on CD-ROM. Periodicals are indexed as published, and take from one to four days after publication date to be available online. The online service allows one to search not only newspapers, but some 5000 periodicals as well.

There is no full-text service of the newspapers online, but the publisher (Information Access Co.) go in through the back door with Newswire ASAP. This includes the full text of three basic wire services which supply many of the business stories to the papers. As DIALOG file 649, one may search these services, which are updated daily. Most go back only to 1985. The three wire services include Reuters Financial Report, Kyodo's Japan Economic Newswire, and PR Newswire. The emphasis is on business news and so, while useful, the service is of limited value to someone hunting for typical human-interest stories.

Newspaper Abstracts

Appearing once each month, *Newspaper Abstracts On Disc* provides indexing for the eleven major American newspapers, including *The New York Times, The Wall Street Journal,* and *Washington Post.* The CD-ROM version, which is issued monthly, may be subdivided by newspaper. For example, one can get the index to *The New York Times* on CD-ROM for $1500. Additional titles, from the *Atlanta Constitution* to the *Washington Post* and *The Wall Street Journal* vary in price from $150 to $795 each. Retrospective searching is limited to 1985 and the years following, although some begin only in 1989. Searching is relatively simple, and boolean logic may be employed as well as simply searching for subjects and by key words. One may search one or all the newspapers for a given subject.

There are other versions, at various prices, from an index to four newspapers to nine. The real plus for this service is that it supplies, unlike most of the others, 30- to 40-word abstracts of all stories. An interesting feature is the exceptionally well-written set of instructions. They are easy to follow and meet the challenge of the individual who knows little or nothing about the index. Also, reading the first two pages of the thesaurus is a good way for new users to learn how to do quick and dirty searches.

ProQuest Newspapers offers the full text of all the papers indexed by *Newspaper Abstracts.* Again, one may purchase the whole set on CD-ROM, or the text of a single newspaper. The basic CD-ROM provides three years of print. Back-files for different papers are available.

The New York Times

No matter what its form, the best-known newspaper index in the United States is the one published by The New York Times. A distinct advantage of *The New York Times Index* is its wide scope and relative completeness. The *Times* makes an effort to cover major news events, both national and international. The morning edition of the *Times* is available in all major cities. It is printed not only in New York, but in Seattle, San Francisco, Los Angeles, Chicago, Dallas, and several northeastern cities.

The New York Times Index provides a wealth of information and frequently is used even without reference to the individual paper of the date cited. Each entry includes a brief abstract of the news story. Consequently, someone seeking a single fact, such as the name of an official, the date of an event, or the title of a play, may often find all that is needed in the index. Also, since all material is dated, *The New York Times Index* serves as an entry into other, unindexed newspapers and magazines. For example, if the user is uncertain of the day a certain ship sank and wishes to see how the disaster was covered in another newspaper or in a magazine, *The New York Times Index* will narrow the search by providing the date of the event.

The print version of *The New York Times Index* is arranged in dictionary form with sufficient cross-references to names and related topics. Events under each of the main headings are arranged chronologically. Book and theater reviews are listed under those respective headings. Some libraries subscribe only to the annual printed cumulated *Index*. This volume serves as an index and guide to the activities of the previous year. Thanks to the rather full abstracts, maps, and charts, one may use the cumulated volume as a reference source in itself. The annual cumulation is fine, but it appears late; normally it is published from six to seven months after the end of the year.[15]

While full text of *The New York Times* is available on NEXIS, the other services modify the daily newspaper's content.

The New York Times offers a typical example of how the daily paper is presented to the public on Internet, World Wide Web, and so forth. On Internet, it is most of the paper. On America Online the emphasis is on features. Focus is on parts, from arts and leisure and restaurants to theater, book, music, and film reviews. One can browse through a year or more of the reviews, as well as

---

[15]The modern index dates only from about 1913 to the present. The earlier indexes, which begin on September 18, 1851, present problems in terms of alphabetizing and location of the issue (date not given) by issue number. There is also great variation in the method of listing other material.

yesterday's comments. Only one small part of the daily update is given over to news. The "news summary" involves only the "top stories," that is, the day's main events, business and sports articles, along with editorials.

Early in 1996 *The New York Times* introduced a web site which does contain most of the news and features of the daily paper—including classified advertisements. Pictures and limited video and sound are offered in addition to text. There is some advertising. The subscription fee (as of early 1996) has not been set, but there is a $1.95 charge for each article downloaded. Also, there is a customized clipping service.

Variations on *The New York Times* online are offered throughout the United States, and on various consumer services, as well as Internet's World Wide Web. The service, called New Century Network, enables an individual to call up news articles and other information, including advertisements for employment from participating newspapers. (In this case "participating" means the *Times,* plus eight other major papers. The goal, though, is to include 75 or so papers.)

Local newspapers are called up in much the same fashion as *The New York Times.* Again, while this may fascinate some individuals, at least in this form it is of limited use to libraries.

On the *Dow Jones News / Retrieval* the full text of *The New York Times* is stored in the system for only 24 hours. Today's copy of the paper is available, but not yesterday's or last year's. (Similar lack of backfiles are common on the commercial networks such as America Online and Prodigy where papers such as the *Chicago Tribune* or *USA Today* are available only for current issues.)

Beginning in mid-1995, NEXIS offers *The New York Times* online the same day it is published. Until then, articles were available only through the previous day's issue. The paper is updated each day at 5:00 A.M., Eastern time, with articles from that day's issue. UMI provides copies of the *Times* online for 90 days— in both standard text form, and if needed, in full-page form, including pictures, advertisements, and so forth.

Filtering out only what is of interest to individual groups of customers such services as Dow Jones DowVision offer newswire stories and newspaper articles from *The New York Times* and *The Wall Street Journal* to the user at his or her computer workstation. Current material comes in each day, but archives going back several months are available to the user searching for a particular topic. Back issues are rarely available after three months.

The best way to evaluate the various format approaches to *The New York Times* is by time. The printed index is published every two weeks, but is at least two to three months behind. This means that a mid-June issue will not arrive until sometime in August. Further up the scale is the monthly index on CD-ROM, plus the full text of the newspaper for the current year, as well as two back years. If only the index is wanted each month then the CD-ROM service available through *Newspaper Abstracts* is preferable, although, again, it is a month later.

The online service offers the most current news and indexing. Updated daily, one has access to the paper almost instantly after publication on the Internet. NEXIS offers this at various rates, as does Dow Jones News/Retrieval and the consumer service, America Online. A less expensive service, *The New York Times Abstracts* is available daily, but does not have the complete text.

CD NewsBank

Selecting key stories, often of interest to the local community, *CD NewsBank* indexes each month some 60,000 to 65,000 articles from American and Canadian newspapers, liberally salted with newstories from wire services. Depending on the price paid, the disk covers five topics (low price) or eleven topics (high price). Anything outside the broad topics cannot be located.[16] About two dozen papers are included from the *Boston Globe* to the *Seattle Times*. The much indexed *New York Times* and *Wall Street Journal* are not included, but the *Washington Post* and *The Christian Science Monitor* are analyzed. Unfortunately, each monthly update includes only one year.

This same service, but covering 450 newspapers, is available on microfiche. There is a printed index which covers eleven major topics. One may, as with the CD-ROM, search A or Y topic and see how it was handled in a newspaper on the East or West coast.

The *Newsbank CD-News* is the publisher's full-text service of about two dozen individual, national newspapers. Each newspaper on a disc is around $1000 for a year, with backfiles available to about 1991.

Which?

Given the price, ease of searching, brief abstracts, and supporting element of full-text availability of the indexed newspapers, the UMI *Newspaper Abstracts on Disc* is a best buy for most libraries. *Facts on File,* which is not really an index to newspapers but a current reviewing service, is equally important. After that, the field is wide open to the particular needs of a library, for example, the *CD News-Bank* is useful for finding data on given subjects across a wide variety of regional newspapers.

No matter which service is selected, the library should have an index to (1) the local and regional newspapers, (2) *The New York Times* and the *Washing-*

---

[16]The high price of $3100 covers arts and literature, economics, education, environment, health, international, law, people and government, social issues, and sports. At the low $1800 level the number of topics is reduced to environment, health, and international and social issues.

ton Post, (3) *The Wall Street Journal,* and (4) whatever newspaper is required for a particular need.

At one time, the library may have indexed the local paper. These days doing so is hardly required, as most newspapers have their own indexes. At any rate, one should certainly inquire.

SUGGESTED READING

Eldredge, Jonathan, "Accuracy of Indexing Coverage Information as Reported by Serials Sources," *Bulletin of the Medical Library Association,* October 1993, pp. 364–370. A study of just how accurate the entries are in Ulrich's, *The Serials Directory,* and an online service, Serline. All are quite high in accuracy, but none gives complete index coverage. The study is as interesting for the methodology as for the results.

Katz, Jon, "Online or Not, Newspapers Suck," WIRED September 28, 1994, pp. 20–21. This is a two-pronged attack (fittingly enough online) against newspapers in general and newspapers online in particular. The author (no relation to the author of this text) points out "that reading a newspaper online is difficult, cumbersome, and time consuming. There is none of the feeling of scanning a story. . . ."

Kinyon, W. R., and K. E. Clark, "Producing In-House Indexes," *RQ,* 1990, vol. 30, pp. 51–59. While introducing the reader to one index project (at Texas A&M) the authors consider the process of indexing itself. Emphasis is on the PC electronic index.

McClamroch, Jo, et al., "MLA on CD-ROM: End-Users Respond," *Reference Services Review,* Spring 1991, pp. 81–86. The measure of success of the *MLA International Bibliography* on CD-ROM is how well it is used by the average individual. It is quite satisfactory, although there are points of difficulty. The short article is not so much a study of one index as it is a method of studying other CD-ROM indexes. See, particularly, the questionnaire.

Moline, Sandra, "Campuswide Access to OCLC's First Search," *Reference Services Review,* 1994, vol. 22, no. 1, pp. 21–28. Who uses the indexing and other services provided by OCLC? How well is it used? A study at the University of Minnesota attempts a response. The article is good both for the methodology and for what it tells about online searching.

Sasse, Margo, "Electronic Journals" in *Advances in Librarianship.* New York: Academic Press, 1993, vol. 17, pp. 149–173. An excellent overview of the present and future of electronic journals. See, too, the current bibliography. A useful consideration of both the pros and cons of the new format and its likely future in libraries.

Stein, Jonathan, "LISA's Move . . . ," *Electronic Library,* February 1994, pp. 5–11. Compares LISA (Library and Information Science Abstracts) in various software offerings. Along the way the author shows the difference (for better, usually) from the new R. R. Bowker software. A good review, which can be applied to other specialized indexes.

Walker, Geraldene, "Searching and Humanities," *Database,* October 1990, pp. 37–46. Many indexes (in print or in electronic form) are much broader than their title employs, and they may be used for numerous types of searches. The author looks at about a dozen of the databases in the humanities and explains their content, search patterns, and, most important, overlap between one and the other. An extremely useful overview for both beginner and expert. Note, too, the references.

Weinberg, Bella Hassed, *Indexing.* Medford, NJ: Learned Information, 1989. Here are 10 essays from the annual (1988) meeting of the American Society of Indexers. The contributors concentrate on the practical aspects of indexing, not on theory. The essays represent a landmark for the individual who wants to know the basics of indexing. A must for anyone who would understand the subject.

Weller, Carolyn, *ERIC Clearinghouse Publications*, Rockville, MD: ERIC, 1994. A 111-page summary (actually an annotated bibliography) of documents produced by ERIC—primarily from 1968 to 1993. The summary offers a history and an explanation of ERIC activities.

PART III
SOURCES OF
INFORMATION

CHAPTER SEVEN
ENCYCLOPEDIAS:
GENERAL AND SUBJECT

A nd now for something entirely different.

Bibliographies and indexes are paths to information found in magazines, books, films, and other communication forms. The librarian turns to an index to find a citation. Then it is necessary to locate the article in the periodical. It is, at a minimum, a two-step process.

An encyclopedia, and similar sources short-circuit the method. Looking up an article or a two-sentence entry in an encyclopedia is usually sufficient to answer a question abut the population of Cuba or the European Community. Given a one-volume source along with a multiple-volume set of encyclopedias—in traditional print or on CD-ROM—and the average reference librarian can successfully field a majority of ready-reference or search questions.

THE CD-ROM ENCYCLOPEDIA

As an enthusiast puts it: "CD-ROM is the biggest thing to hit the computer world since the invention of the mouse . . . I can not only read anything in the 29 volume *Funk & Wagnalls Encyclopedia* [i.e., *Encarta*] but I can almost make it play national anthems, watch a slow motion video of how cats always land on their feet, and see an animated map demonstrate how, by a flanking movement, Napoleon lost the battle of Waterloo."[1]

The CD-ROM has revolutionized the format, sale, and publication of gen-

---

[1]"Honey, I Shrunk the Encyclopedia," *The Globe and Mail*, March 19, 1994, p. 10.

eral encyclopedias. In the 1980s the average number of printed sets sold each year, usually door to door by salespeople, averaged about 1 million. Today the familiar salesperson is almost a thing of the past. Sales of print sets are down to half what they were before, but an estimated 4 million CD-ROMs have been sold since the early 1990s. Hardly a week goes by that a CD-ROM encyclopedia is not on the best-selling CD-ROM list. Over 2.1 million of *Compton's Interactive Encyclopedia* were purchased in 1995 alone, at least double the number of *all* print sets sold each year in the past. By the next century predictions are that the general multivolume print encyclopedia will be a thing of the past. CD-ROMs (or their equivalent, possibly online) will be the format.

Why are the CD-ROM encyclopedias such a hit? Several responses are evident. Young people enjoy the bells and whistles (from animation to music) they can call up at a computer terminal. Second, it is easy to search by typing in a word or phrase. Most CD-ROMs allow boolean searching and have simple approaches to accessing information. Furthermore, one can search a complete set without reaching for separate volumes—a plus and a minus in a nation of overweight people. When one operates a word processor, it is a simple matter to shift a quote or a paragraph from the encyclopedia into a written report. Finally, given a CD-ROM player, which is now a usual part of almost any consumer computer sold, the electronic work costs from one-quarter to one-tenth the price of a printed volume. And, of course, there are no bookshelves required.

Both the print and electronic sets have their places. In a library, and in many homes, it is much faster simply to consult the alphabetically arranged articles in a printed volume. It is easier to scan the index for data, and it is more satisfying to read and examine illustrations in the standard printed sets. A library should (1) have at least two electronic versions—adult and young people; and (2) maintain, for the next few years, the standard print sets recommended here.

CD-ROM Drawbacks

There is some concern that CD-ROM encyclopedias, and similar reference works, put too much emphasis on entertainment, and to little on content, particularly in children's and young people's sets.[2] It is one thing to link text on baseball with Babe Ruth and 9 seconds of "Let's go out to the ballgame." It's quite another to trace the importance of the Homeric epics on a CD-ROM. All of this sparks the eternal debate, the eternal question: "Does education mean hard work, or should it be fun?" A combination will do nicely, and that's what the

[2]"Family Encyclopedias on CD-ROM," *U.S. News & World Report*, April 4, 1994, p. 66. "My major nitpick has to do with those multimedia special effects, too many of which are in the one-trick-pony group. Once you've oohed at Babe Ruth hitting a homer, why watch again? And some of them simply fall short. A nice color photo of the Alamo in *Compton's* is accompanied by a 'Remember the Alamo!' yell that's anything but inspiring, and nine seconds from the *Nutcracker Suite* hardly conveys Tchaikovsky's style. I'll take *Grolier's* word that a small, dim movie of a spider spinning a web was what I saw."

more serious publishers attempt. If they falter on the side of sometime faint animation, bad music, and even worse film tracks, it is because the technology is new. With time all will improve, or so one hopes.

There are other CD-ROM drawbacks, not the least of which is text that is often less in depth than in the printed sets. Needing storage space for sound and animation, publishers of CD-ROMs may cut back on the number of illustrations found in the printed volumes. They may reduce the length of articles and word count, although in some cases the actual amount of text will increase.

Looking to the future, these same publishers predict more pictures, and (1) additional hypertext to link animation, sound, and articles in one easy-to-understand sweep; (2) innovative 3-D animation and menus that will make the works easier to access; (3) added and better color (a weak point in some CD-ROMs); and (4) full-screen full-motion video. The ultimate will be voice commands that will eliminate the need to type instructions.

Online

Many of the sets, particularly the ubiquitous *New Grolier Interactive Encyclopedia* (in print: *Academic American Encyclopedia*), are available online. They are accessed through one of the commercial online services such as America Online or CompuServe. Internet and World Wide Web also include the basic online sets and some peculiar works such as *Encyclopedia Mystica*, about mystery and magic. Cost is computed on the basis of how much and how often the work is used. Depending upon the sophistication of the online service, illustrations, animation, and even sound may be part of the encyclopedia packages. Beginning in 1995–1996, at least three of the sets *(Grolier, Compton's, Encarta)* will offer CD-ROMs which will allow the user to log on to an online service for up-to-date information from the encyclopedia publisher. If this functions properly, it will solve the problem of both CD-ROM and print encyclopedias rapidly becoming dated.

Conclusion

When discussing electronic versions of encyclopedias, which in a decade or two may totally replace the printed volumes, it is worth stressing: (1) They are less expensive than the print sets and are likely to become even less costly when used online through a commercial online service. (2) Often the material in the CD-ROM or online version has more current data and articles than the print set, but it tends to lack the well defined and numerous illustrations. In time, of course, the illustrations will be there with sound and who knows what.

Best Sets

In selecting the best printed sets, the choices are limited to: (1) adults: *New Encyclopaedia Britannica, The Americana;* (2) young people: *The Academic American, Col-*

liers, and *Funk & Wagnalls;* (3) children: *The World Book; Compton's.* This is a total of seven. Give or take a title, this is the same number given the highest rank by the American Library Association and Kenneth Kister, the world's leading authority on the subject. Turning to electronic formats, six of the seven are available for consideration. (Only *Collier's* is not in electronic format.)

Since choice is limited, why, one might ask, should an entire chapter be devoted to an apparently easily resolved question? There are three answers: First and foremost the encyclopedia, in print or as an electronic database, is among the most frequently used reference works, particularly in school and public libraries. There may not be that much difference in quality between, say, the *Americana* and the *Britannica,* but there are subtle differences of content which every working librarian should appreciate in order to answer questions more efficiently. Second, as one of the world's oldest and most pervasive reference works, the encyclopedia established early on the patterns so often repeated in other reference works. To understand an encyclopedia is to understand a whole universe of reference and information sources. If one is able to evaluate an encyclopedia, one is usually able to judge other reference books (as well as electronic databases) from dictionaries to biographical and government sources. Third, while the general encyclopedia sets are well-known, the equally useful subject works, one-volume titles, and foreign encyclopedias are not. They must be a part of every professional librarian's knowledge.

Definition and Background

An encyclopedia is an effort to gather information either from all branches of knowledge or from a single subject area and arrange it, usually in alphabetical order, for ready reference. The desire to understand, to describe, to encompass all known things goes back to the earliest effort of a Sumerian or an Egyptian to comprehend the world.

The word *encyclopedia* from the Greek "instruction in the circle of knowledge" was first applied to what we conceive of as an encyclopedia by Pliny the Elder (A.D. 23–79). Pliny, who had a remarkable capacity for work, wrote *Natural History,* of which 31 books survive. This vast encyclopedia is shapeless, but in it the Roman deals with everything from the universe and zoology to the fine arts. Most of the material was taken from other works, and Pliny estimated he had gathered about 20,000 facts from 100 authors.

Other men and women followed in Pliny's ambitious footsteps. One classical example is Isidore of Seville (A.D. 560–636), who wrote a history of the Visigoths and composed the *Etymologies,* an effort to gather all human knowledge in 20 volumes. Drawing primarily from Greek and Latin authors, he composed what was to be the basic encyclopedia of the Middle Ages. Isidore derived his title for the set from the fact that he gave the origins of names and words he wrote about. In about 1360 the English monk Bartholomew de Glanville repeated the process in 19 books written in Latin. John Harris of England (1667–1719) was the first to produce an English language work.

The eighteenth century was the Age of Enlightenment, when Diderot, the eternal optimist, believed it was possible to capture all knowledge in his great *Encyclopédie*. The Enlightenment, although a landmark in the history of knowledge, remains, as Hugh Kenner has put it, "a mystical experience through which the minds of Europe passed." Kenner then goes on to cleverly summarize the content and purpose of an encyclopedia:

> We carry with us still one piece of baggage from those far off days, and that is the book which nobody wrote and nobody is expected to read, and which is marketed as The Encyclopaedia: Britannica, Americana, Antarctica or other. The Encyclopaedia . . . takes all that we know apart into little pieces, and then arranges those pieces so that they can be found one at a time. It is produced by a feat of organizing, not a feat of understanding. . . . If the Encyclopaedia means anything as a whole, no one connected with the enterprise can be assumed to know what that meaning is.[3]

The complaint is common, although in some ways it misses the point of the modern encyclopedia. Today the general set serves a variety of purposes, but its essential objective is to capsulize and organize the world's accumulated knowledge, or at least that part of it which is of interest to readers. Through detailed articles and brief facts an effort is made to include a wide variety of information from all fields.[4]

The revolutionary electronic format began in 1985 with Grolier's first effort. It was followed four years later by Compton. Today every major publisher of encyclopedias offers one or more versions of their works on CD-ROM and/or online. Although these feature everything from animation to sound, the basic content is much the same as the printed set. An exception is that in some CD-ROMs there are fewer illustrations than in the printed work.

Electronic databases aside, encyclopedias may be divided into two or three categories of organization: (1) *by format*—there are the general and subject sets of 4 to 32 volumes (such as the *World Book*) and the smaller works of 1, 2, or 3 volumes (such as the one-volume *New Columbia Encyclopedia*); (2) *by scope*—here the division is either general (the *World Book*) or by subject (*International Encyclopedia of the Social Sciences*); (3) *by audience*—the general work may be for a child, teenager, or layperson. If a subject set, it is likely that its intention is to appeal to an expert or near-expert in that subject field. There are other methods of dividing and subdividing encyclopedias, some of which will be explained as the reader progresses through this chapter.

---

[3]Hugh Kenner, *The Stoic Comedians* (Berkeley, CA: University of California Press, 1974), pp. 1 and 2.

[4]The best short history of the encyclopedia will be found in Kenneth Kister's *Kistner's Best Encyclopedias*, 2d ed. (Phoenix, AZ: Oryx Press, 1994). See, too, the history of the work in any set of encyclopedias, and particularly the latest *Britannica*.

Purpose

Any encyclopedia will usually include detailed survey articles, often with bibliographies, in certain fields or areas; explanatory material that is normally shorter; and brief informational data such as the birth and death dates of famous people, geographical locations, and historical events. This scope makes the encyclopedia ideal for reference work, and the general set is often the first place the librarian will turn to answer questions. One obvious exception is when one is seeking an answer to a question involving an event that has taken place since the last edition of the work.

When an overview of a topic is wanted, one will consult the *Britannica*'s main articles in the *Macropedia* (usually through the index) or, at another level, the well-illustrated background pieces in *World Book*. The librarian soon learns which set is best. "Best" is determined by the type of user and the depth of information needed.

The bibliographies at the end of articles may help the reader find additional material in a given subject area. Several encyclopedias offer a variety of study guides which indicate related articles, so a student may put together a truly creative paper rather than a carbon copy of an encyclopedia article.

It is a common misunderstanding that a general encyclopedia is a proper source of research. An encyclopedia is only a springboard. Furthermore, in presenting material with almost no differentiation, the general encyclopedia is not completely accurate or up to date. Important facts must be double-checked in another source, if only in a second encyclopedia.

At the child's level, there's another misconception: an encyclopedia, no matter how good, is not a substitute for additional reading or for a collection of supporting reference books. In their enthusiasm, some salespeople and advertising copywriters are carried away with the proposition that an encyclopedia-oriented child is an educated child.

CD-ROM

With the exception of *Collier's*, which is in a drift mode, all the aforementioned publishers offer CD-ROM versions of their various, if not all, sets.

Britannica made an economic error in 1993 by selling their profitable children's set, *Compton's*, to the publishers of the *Chicago Tribune* newspaper.[5] Furthermore, the understanding was that Britannica would not produce a competing CD-ROM or electronic version until late 1994.

Compton's tops the sales of CD-ROM encyclopedias. As of 1995 it had an estimated 18 to 22 percent of the market share. Behind is Grolier with about 10

---

[5]Gary Samuels, "CD-ROM's First Big Victim," *Forbes,* February 28, 1994, pp. 42–44. A short explanation, as well as a bit of history, concerning the financial woes of Britannica. In the early 1990s the firm earned an estimated $40 million after tax on sales of $650 million. According to *The New York Times* (December 19, 1995, p. D2) a Swiss-based firm is set to buy the Britannica.

percent and then Microsoft, which became a major publisher of CD-ROM encyclopedias and related full-text works in 1993. It has two encyclopedias, *Encarta* (a version of the *Funk & Wagnalls* set) and *Microsoft Bookshelf,* which is a bundle of seven reference works, including the *Concise Columbia Encyclopedia.*

EVALUATING ENCYCLOPEDIAS

Most librarians and, for that matter, laypersons will turn to one or two sources for objective evaluations of encyclopedias. These are trusted, tried, and true.

The first choice is Kenneth Kister's *Kister's Best Encyclopedias,* 2d ed. (Phoenix, AZ: Oryx Press, 1994. 464 pp.; $39.50. No electronic format). An introduction considers basic questions concerning the evaluation and purchase of an encyclopedia. There are excellent encyclopedia comparison charts that, at a glance, allow one to see the difference in price, number of volumes, illustrations, and so on. Each set is considered in terms of history and authority, purpose, reliability, recency, objectivity, and all of the major points one would wish to consider in an evaluation of any type of reference work. Also, there are brief reviews of 800 subject and specialized works.

Kister affords numerous insights into objective evaluation of not only an encyclopedia, but also most reference works. He employs a methodical approach to all sets by checking the same dozen or so subjects in each work. These range from Galileo and Philip Glass to Panda Bears and Uzbekistan. He then rates the set in terms of what each entry has covered, and its accuracy, recency, and clarity. The "report card" is used for each of the general encyclopedias. A similar report card system may be applied to other reference book comparisons.

In *Encyclopedias Atlases & Dictionaries* (published by R. R. Bowker in 1995) one finds authoritative, lengthy reviews of the basic sets with an eye to the needs of the level of readers. As might be expected the evaluation follows the pattern accepted by almost everyone, and except for this or that point, the reviews are in line with the standard comments.

Another basic source of reviews is the well-known "Reference Books Bulletin" in *The Booklist,* which is discussed earlier in this text. Almost every, or every other, issue has a lengthy review either of a general set or, more likely, of a subject encyclopedia. These are detailed, objective, and meticulously documented. The most useful current check for the standard sets is offered by the same service in the September 15 issue. "Encyclopedia Update" includes material previously published about the basic 10 to 12 general sets. There is a succinct summary of the primary points of each print and electronic title.[6]

---

[6]This is republished with additional points on the evaluation of encyclopedias, both print and electronic, as *Purchasing an Encyclopedia: 12 Points to Consider* (Chicago: American Library Association, 1990 to date, annual). The $8 paperback is edited by Sandy Whiteley.

Evaluation Points[7]

Librarians tend to make up their own minds about which are the better encyclopedias. Their decision is based primarily on daily use, but there are specific points to consider in a systematic evaluation: (1) *scope,* or subject coverage, emphasis, and the intended audience; (2) *authority,* which includes accuracy and reliability; (3) *writing style;* (4) *recency,* including revision plans, if any, of the publisher; (5) *viewpoint* and objectivity; (6) *arrangement and entry;* (7) *index* with reference to how one gains access to information in the set; (8) *format,* including the physical format and illustrations; (9) *cost;* and (10) the presence of *bibliographies.*

Scope

The scope of the specialized encyclopedia is evident in its name, and becomes even more obvious with use. The scope of the general encyclopedia is dictated primarily by two considerations, age level and emphasis.

Age Level. The children's encyclopedias, such as the *World Book,* are tied to curriculum. Consequently, they include more in-depth material on subjects of general interest to grade school and high school students than does an adult encyclopedia such as the *Britannica.* Most encyclopedia publishers aim their strongest advertising at adults with children. All the standard sets claim that an audience ranging from grades 6 to 12 can understand and use their respective works. This may be true of the exceptionally bright child, but the librarian is advised to check the real age compatibility of the material before purchase, not merely advertised age level.

There are two consequences of attempting to be all things to all age levels: (1) In many adult-level encyclopedias, when the material is shortened for easier comprehension by a child, the adult loses; and (2) the effort to clarify for the lower age level frequently results in an oversimplified approach to complex issues.

Who is the encyclopedia really for, that is, who is the salesperson trying to reach? If one believes the advertisements, the answer is everyone. The problem is evident: Can a single set be equally useful for children and adults? Of course not, but you'd never know that from the ads. For example, an advertisement for *Britannica* shows middle-aged adults saying about the set, "The only thing it can't tell you is the time." Another ad shows children and the lines: "Curiosity withers in frustration. That can easily happen with school-age children." The emphasis on children is understandable. Most sets are purchased for the children in the family. Single persons and the elderly do not usually buy encyclopedias.

[7]These are points used to evaluate a print set, but the content (aside from hypertext) in electronic format is much the same. Hence, the same points are applicable to sets in other formats.

Emphasis. If age level dictates one approach to scope, the emphasis of the editor accounts for the other. At one time, there were greater variations in emphasis than there are today; one set may have been especially good for science, another for literature. Today, the emphasis is essentially a matter of deciding what compromise will be made between scholarship and popularity. Why, for example, is as much space given to the subject of advertising as to democracy in most adult encyclopedias? This is not to argue the merit of any particular topic, but to point out that examining emphasis is a method of determining scope.

Authority

A major question to ask about any reference book has to do with its authority. If it is authoritative, it usually follows that it will be up to date, accurate, and relatively objective.

Authority is evident in the names of the scholars and experts who sign the articles or who are listed as contributors somewhere in the set. It is also associated with the names of the publishers who distribute the sets. There are three quick tests for authority: (1) recognition of a prominent name, particularly the author of the best, most recent book on the subject; (2) a quick check of a field known to the reader to see whether leaders in that field are represented in the contributor list; and (3) finally, determination of whether a contributor's qualifications (as noted by position, degrees, occupation, and so on) relate to the article(s).

A reader gains an indication of the encyclopedia's revision policy and age from knowledge about the authors. Some contributors may literally be dead, and although a certain number of deceased authorities is perfectly acceptable, too many in this category would indicate either overabundant plagiarism from older sets or lack of any meaningful revision.

Any encyclopedia unfortunately will contain some errors and some omissions. Most are quickly corrected when brought to the attention of a publisher. The real test, of course, is the number of such mistakes. The sets considered here, while not perfect, can rarely be faulted for more than a few errors.

Writing Style

When one considers the writing style of today's encyclopedia, one notices that none of the general sets is aimed at the expert. Recognizing that laypeople considerably outnumber scholars and therefore purchase considerably more volumes, encyclopedia firms tend to cater to their market in a relatively standard fashion: Contributors are given certain topics and outlines of what is needed and expected. Their manuscripts are then submitted to the encyclopedia's editors (editorial staffs of the larger encyclopedias range from 100 to 200 full-time persons), who revise, cut, and query—all to make the contributions understandable to the average reader. The extent of editing varies depending on each encyclopedia's audience. It can be extensive for children's works (where word difficulty and length of sentence are almost as important as content), or it can be limited for major contributors to an adult volume.

Serving as a bridge between contributor and reader, the editor strives for readability by reducing complicated vocabulary and jargon to terms understandable to the lay reader or young person. The purpose is to rephrase specialized thought into common language without diminishing the thought—or insulting an eminent contributor. In the humanities and the social sciences, this usually works. The contributing scholars must be willing to have their initials appended to a more accessible version of their work.

Recency: Continuous Revision

As most large encyclopedia companies issue new printings of their sets, or revised individual volumes each year, they also incorporate updated changes. Electronic databases make this process considerably easier; editors can enter new materials, delete, and correct without completely resetting the whole article or section.

No matter what the technological procedures employed for updating, the librarian should know: (1) Few general encyclopedias use the "edition" as an indication of the relative currency of the work. For example, the *Britannica*'s fourteenth edition was just that from 1929 until the fifteenth edition in 1974. (2) The relative date of the printing will be found on the verso of the title page, but this in itself means little because there is no accurate measure of how much of any given encyclopedia is revised or how often it is done. Most large publishers claim to revise about 5 to 10 percent of the material each year. The claim to continuous revision is a major selling point for publishers involved with selling sets to libraries. They reason that no library is going to buy a new set of the same encyclopedia (loss or damage aside) unless there has been substantial revision. (3) Most encyclopedias do revise material with each printing or electronic update. A printing normally is done at least once or twice a year. Electronic updates may be even more often.

Viewpoint and Objectivity

Since general encyclopedias are published as profit ventures, they aim to attract the widest audience and to insult or injure no one. Despite their sometimes pious claims of objectivity on grounds of justice for all, they are motivated by commercial reasons. Only after many years of active prodding by women did encyclopedia publishers respond to this segment of the market and make a conscious effort to curb sexual bias.

Blatant sexual and racial bias have been eliminated from standard, acceptable encyclopedias, but the slate is not completely clean or neutral. One way to check this particular area is to look up names of prominent women, and particularly from African American and Hispanic backgrounds, to see how well (if at all) they are represented. Check, too, such obvious articles as sexual harassment, homosexuality, and abortion. A similar investigation may be carried on for other controversial areas from hypnosis to euthanasia.

Another way to consider the question of viewpoints is to see what the editor chooses to include or to exclude, to emphasize or to deemphasize. Nothing can date an encyclopedia faster than antiquated articles about issues and ideas either no longer acceptable or of limited interest. An encyclopedia directed at the Western reader can scarcely be expected to give as much coverage to, let us say, Egypt as to New York State. Yet, to include only a passing mention of Egypt would not be suitable either, particularly in view of ancient history and the emergence of Africa as a new world force.

The problem of assigning the size of one article as opposed to another plagues any conscientious encyclopedia editor. There is no entirely satisfactory solution. With worldwide audiences, the major sets never quite hit the right balance. *World Book* is used widely in England, as it is in many English speaking countries. Generally the British school child finds it satisfactory, but there are moments of doubt. A thirteen-year-old "had to write an essay on the Great Fire of London and found only a short paragraph on the subject under a more general title of 'Fires in London.' He found the entry inadequate and simplistic for such a popular subject among school children."[8]

International conflicts reported in encyclopedias pleases no partisan. The Middle East has advocates on a number of sides. Each advocate claims to have the "truth" about not only current affairs, but also history. A critic observes that the *Britannica* editor "has failed to address the question of why the encyclopedia should have delineated a picture so biased both in myriad particulars and in cumulative effect as to seem designed for Arab political purposes."[9] In another study, it is reported that *Collier's* "joins the *Britannica* in allowing its pages to be filled with spurious Middle East history."[10] There is no Arab response. One can be certain it would take another viewpoint.

---

[8]"Something Wrong for All the Family," *The Spectator*, January 9, 1993, p. 25. The reviewer adds that the same student "thought the entries for fish and electricity were more impressive."

[9]Andrea Levin, "The Encyclopedias," *Commentary*, July 1993, p. 51. The author is a partisan of Israel. She documents her contention in the article, pp. 47–51.

[10]*Camera Media Report*, Winter 1994, p. 3. This is another response by Ms. Levin on the same subject. Given this unresolved situation for numerous areas, the wise librarian will invest in subject sets to supplement the larger works. Here, for example, a response might be *The Middle East*, 8th ed. (Washington, DC: Congressional Quarterly Books, 1995). Updated frequently this one-volume encyclopedia treatment is objective and comprehensive.

Arrangement and Entry

The traditional arrangement of a printed encyclopedia follows the familiar alphabetical approach to material, with numerous cross-references and an index. Average users are accustomed to the alphabetical order of information, or the *specific entry*. Here, the information is broken down into small, specific parts, but the data are arranged alphabetically.

Index

Some publishers have concluded that, with suitable *see* and *see also* references, the alphabetical arrangement should serve to eliminate the index. The strong argument for an index is simply that a single article may contain dozens of names and events which cannot be located unless there is a detailed, separate index volume. A detailed index is an absolute necessity.

Format

A good format covers such points as appropriate type sizes, typefaces, illustrations, binding, and total arrangement. When considering format, evaluate the following:

Illustrations (Photographs, Diagrams, Charts, and Maps). Nothing will tip off the evaluator faster as to how current the encyclopedia is than a cursory glance at the illustrations. But just because the illustrations are current, they are not necessarily suitable unless they relate directly to the text and to the interests of the reader. The librarian might ask: Do the illustrations consider the age of the user, or do they consist of figures or drawings totally foreign to, say, a twelve-year-old? Do they emphasize important matters, or are they too general? Are they functional, or simply attractive? Are the captions adequate?

Maps are an important part of any encyclopedia and vary in number. Many of the maps are prepared by Rand McNally or C. S. Hammond and are generally good to excellent. In the adult sets, the major maps appear frequently in a separate volume, often with the index. The young adults' and children's encyclopedias usually have the maps in the text, and if this is the case, there should be reference to them in the index and cross-references as needed. The librarian should check to see how many and what types of maps are employed to show major cities of the world, historical development, political changes, land use, weather, and so on. The actual evaluation of the maps is discussed in the chapter on geography.

Size of Type.   The type size is important, as is the spacing between lines and the width of the columns. All these factors affect the readability of the work.

Binding.   Encyclopedias should be bound in a fashion that is suitable for rough use, particularly in a library. Conversely, buyers should be warned that a frequent method of raising the price of an encyclopedia is to charge the user for a so-called deluxe binding which is often no better, and in fact may be less durable, than the standard library binding.

Volume Size.   Finally, consideration should be given to the physical size of the volume. Is it comfortable to hold? Equally important, can it be opened without strain on the binding?

Cost

Not only do prices vary dramatically from set to set, but they can range from under $1000 to several multiples of that figure for precisely the same work. One can buy the *Britannica* alone, but this is not easy. The salesperson will try to have the sale include other Britannica items from *Great Books of the Western World* to junior encyclopedias. The end result is that one can pay from $1500 to $8000 for the *Britannica*, depending on what else is purchased along with the basic set as well as what kind of binding was chosen.

Realizing the public relations aspect of sales to libraries, publishers of general sets usually give relatively good discounts. For example, and this is true of all major sets considered here, *The Encyclopedia Americana* is about $1000 for libraries and schools. Retail, it is priced at $1400. The *World Book*'s retail price is from $560 to $679. For libraries it is $550.

Libraries buy only about 5 to 6 percent of all print encyclopedias sold, and only about 1 percent of electronic versions. Still, the value to a publisher is not so much in the sales as in the seal of approval. If the library has it, it must be good—and with that the individual rushes out to buy a copy of the library encyclopedia or encyclopedias.

The same green light encourages laypersons to purchase subject sets. Here, though, the library is often a key factor in the financial success or failure of a work. The more esoteric and expensive subject sets may be sold almost exclusively to libraries. Without those sales the publisher shows a loss.

CD-ROMs have no built-in library discounts, but may be purchased for considerably less than advertised from dealers and often from book jobbers. Publishers hope to make up the loss of profit on the initial purchase of an electronic encyclopedia by selling the buyer an annual update. This proves to be good business. For example, the update of the *Grolier Multimedia Encyclopedia* is $49.95 to

$100. Each updated CD-ROM contains numerous new features, illustrations, text and so on.[11]

Sales Practices

Even a cursory glance at newspaper, magazine, or television advertisements for encyclopedias will demonstrate the power of parental guilt. The desire to help the child, the sense of guilt "is a big reason for surging sales of . . . electronic encyclopedias on CD-ROMs."[12] At one time a salesperson pressed home the anxiety. Today, though, this is left pretty much up to advertisements. The familiar door-to-door salesperson has virtually disappeared.

Of the seven major print sets considered here, only two are still sold door to door and by "authorized sales representatives": *New Encyclopedia Britannica* and *World Book*. Available from salespeople as well as in bookstores, or by mail, or wherever one finds books are *Academic American, Collier's, Compton's*, and *Encyclopedia Americana*. *Funk & Wagnalls New Encyclopedia* is available only in supermarkets. CD-ROMs are sold in countless stores, and not by individual salespersons.

All of this leads many to ask: "Whatever happened to the encyclopedia sellers?" Up until the late 1980s they dominated the sale of sets and, in fact, few multivolume works could be purchased any other way. Given a hammerlock on sales, the representatives, the door-to-door pitch men and women racked up a generally terrible press for overcharging, selling more than the encyclopedia, and offering the sky as well as the set. The Federal Trade Commission seemed to be constantly calling a halt to the shady practices, but never quite succeeded. Technology did what the government could not accomplish. With CD-ROMs came the dawn. Publishers realized that they would have to have as many sales points as possible to survive. The salesperson became a thing pretty much of the past. Bookstores, and particularly large chains, took over with massive mail campaigns. Computer centers also grabbed the lead. The salesperson was killed off, too, by sales wars between the publishers. Television advertisements urged the buyer to go directly to the bookseller or the publisher. A shadow of past glories remains in the diligent work of *World Book* and *Britannica* representatives, but they are fast becoming a soon to be forgotten page in encyclopedia history.[13]

---

[11]One of the tremendous appeals of CD-ROM encyclopedias is their low cost—often under $100. As the producer-publisher may spend over $1 million to publish the CD-ROM, costs must be recovered from massive initial sales, as well as from annual updates which may be no more than $50 to $100 a year.

[12]Walter Mossberg, "Parental Guilt Sells Encyclopedias on CD-ROM, too," *The Wall Street Journal*, April 28, 1993, p. 30.

[13]Samuels, op. cit., p. 43. "The Britannica's sales force has collapsed. Two years ago [i.e., 1992] it included 2300 active sales representatives in the U.S. and Canada. . . . The count has since shriveled to fewer than 1,100."

Replacement

The library with a basic work on a CD-ROM may update it each year for a modest price. Therefore the wise move is to update CD-ROM titles every year and, as long as there is demand, the printed version on alternative years.

In practical terms this usually means that one of the most used print sets (*World Book, Americana, Britannica,* or *Collier's*) is replaced with a revised set every two years, the next most used every three years, the next every four years, and so on. Depending on whether the library is medium or large, the two-to-four-year-old sets are sent to the branches, put in the general reading room, or duplicated in heavily used parts of the library, such as the young adult's area. When a print set is more than five years old, it should be discarded.

Consumer Advice

The librarian can meet the request for information about a given set in several ways:

1. *Give no advice.* Several major public libraries, fearful of repercussions from publishers, adamantly refuse to allow their personnel to advise on the purchase of one or another set. This author believes that such a refusal is unprofessional and highly questionable.

2. *Give limited advice.* The librarian can give the inquirer several reviews of the set or sets under question, and leave the final decision to the user.

3. *Go all out with an endorsement or a condemnation.* Privately, of course, many librarians do just this. Such opinionated statements may have some nasty repercussions, particularly when the concern is among sets that are approved by the ALA and are more or less even in quality.

Of the three, the second option is best. If the set is not readily recognized either by publisher or by reputation, the librarian should not hesitate to point out that the chances are that it is a poor buy from the standpoint of both cost and quality. The librarian should be prepared to support this statement with reviews; or lacking reviews (either because the set is too new or such a "dog" as not to have been noticed), the librarian should not hesitate to stand on her or his own professional evaluation of the set.

Used Sets

What follows is advice librarians might give patrons who are worried about the cost of print encyclopedias.

Take any of the seven major print sets listed here and money may be saved by buying them secondhand. An encyclopedia which is two to three years old will go for one-half to one-third the price of the new work. True, they will not offer current information. On the other hand, they serve as superior reference works when one is seeking background information on events, persons, and places. Purchase a current almanac, and much of the problem with capturing the latest material will be solved.

Warning. Limit the age of the secondhand set to five or six years. Beyond that it is dangerous, particularly in terms of interpretation and explanation. A good example of the difficulty is reported by an English writer examining a much older *Oxford Junior Encyclopedia:* "I turned to the entry on the Irish. . . . 'The peasants in the west live for the most part in little white-washed, one story cottages, generally of only two rooms. . . . Pigs and chicks are apt to get very mixed with the family, and all live mainly on potatoes.' " The critic adds: "It's enough to make anyone blanch."[14]

With that, the ultimate economical move is to purchase a good one-volume encyclopedia or a CD-ROM version. These cost many hundreds of dollars less than the printed sets, and some are even less costly than secondhand works.

ENCYCLOPEDIA COMPARISONS

The following table gives comparisons of cost, number of illustrations, and number of words and articles for various encyclopedias on CD-ROM and in print.

Cost/Illustrations. These begin with the lowest and move to the highest Figures.

CD-ROM/Print. The first name is the title of the CD-ROM version and, in the next column, is the print title. Thus, *Encarta* is the CD-ROM version and *Funk & Wagnalls* is the title for the print version.

ADULT ENCYCLOPEDIAS

CD: Britannica CD. Chicago: Encyclopedia Britannica Inc., 1993 to date. $995. School and library advertised price, approximately $300.
   Print: The New Encyclopaedia Britannica, 15th ed. 1771 to date, 32 vols. $1600.
   Online: Britannica Online, Internet, 1990 to date. $5000 to $25,000.

---

[14]"Look and Learn," *The (London) Observer,* March 13, 1993, p. 10. See Kister's *Best Encyclopedias,* pp. 14–15, for excellent advice on secondhand sets and where they may be purchased. Of course, some may wish to purchase much older sets, such as the ninth or eleventh edition of the *Britannica,* for historical research. This would hold as true for libraries as for individuals.

CD-ROM	Print	Cost (1995–1996)
Encarta		($45–$100)
	Funk & Wagnalls	($164–$250)
Compton's Interactive		($70–$100)
	Compton's	($395–$500)
Grolier		($75–$100)
	Academic American	($719–$1150)
World Book Multimedia Encyclopedia		($179)
	World Book	($560–$679)
Collier's (No CD-ROM)	*Collier's*	($1000)
Britannica		($995)
	Britannica	($1,299–$1600)
Americana		($600)
	Americana	($1000–$1400)

		Illustrations
World Book Multimedia Encyclopedia		(5,000)
	World Book	(28,000)
Encarta		(7800)
	Funk & Wagnalls	(9500)
Grolier		(8000)
	Academic American	(18,000)
Comptons Interactive		(8000)
	Compton's	(22,500)
(No CD-ROM)	*Colliers*	(14,000)
Americana		(Limited Number)
	Americana	(22,000)
Britannica		(Limited number)
	Britannica	(12,000)

		Words (in millions) /Articles
Compton's Interactive		(9 M/34,000)
	Compton's (26 vols.)	(9 M/34,000)
Encarta		(9.5 M/26,000)
	Funk & Wagnalls (29 vols.)	(9 M/25,000)
Grolier		(10 M/33,000)
	Academic Americana (21 vols.)	(9.1 M/29,000)
World Book Multimedia Encyclopedia		(10 M/17,000)
	World Book (22 vols.)	(10 M/18,000)
Americana		(31 M/52,000)
	Americana (30 vols.)	(31 M/52,000)
Britannica		(44 M/65,000)
	Britannica (32 vols.)	(44 M/65,000)

CD: The Encyclopedia Americana on CD-ROM. Danbury, CT: Grolier Incorporated, 1994 to date. $600.
Print: Encyclopedia Americana. 1833 to date. $1000–$1400.

The Britannica

NOTE: The following discussion is based on the 1995 fifteenth edition, and does not take into consideration the possible sale or change of the set in 1996. The historical data remain valid as do comments on the text of the fifteenth edition. A new owner is likely to overhaul and reprice the whole set's format.

The best-known encyclopedia in the Western world is the *Britannica.* First published in 1768, it underwent many revisions and changes until the triumphant ninth edition in 1889. This was the "scholar's edition," with long articles from such contributors as Arnold, Swinburne, Huxley, and other major British minds of the nineteenth century.

In 1974 the entire set was completely revised and the format was changed. In 1985 the set was again revised and additions made, including a two-volume index.

CD-ROM Online

Late off the mark, Britannica lost millions for their failure to produce a CD-ROM of their set. They feared electronic formats would cut into profits from the printed set. The estimate was a disaster. They lost out to the new electronic encyclopedias and witnessed drops in the print sale. Lesson learned, finally in 1994 the first electronic version appeared, but with text only. No pictures. No sound. By mid-1995 a revised edition (version no. 2) was published with a limited number of graphics, but nowhere near the number of illustrations found in the printed set. Again, though, no multimedia features. Another problem was the price. Advertised at $995, it is available to schools for $300.

Drawing from their experience with *Compton's* (a cousin of the major set), the publisher allows the user to seek out information in natural language. One types in "Chinese calligraphy" and the screen shows, in order of importance, the title of articles and bits of text that can be found on the subject. The rating system is one of the best features in that it accurately tells the user the relevance of the data. A question about the dramatist Ionesco will bring up 81 entries, each with a given score representing its likely value as an information source.

There are two other approaches: boolean logic and the ability to simply scroll through the index. Unfortunately the 32-page manual is of little real assistance in navigating the electronic encyclopedia. And if the user asks for on-screen help the computer tends to reproduce what is in the manual. The CD-ROM version includes *Merriam-Webster's Collegiate Dictionary*, tenth edition (1993), with some 160,000 words and the same firm's *Collegiate Thesaurus.* They are updated regularly with the encyclopedia text. One simply double keys a word within an article or index term and the dictionary gives up a definition.

The 1995–1996 edition examined is only a beginning. There is no doubt that in the years ahead the set will add its much missed illustrations and maps as well as vastly improve the searching techniques. Meanwhile, no matter what the form, the *Britannica* represents the best general set about.

Britannica Online, as it is called by the publisher, is available on the Internet. A student, or anyone with access to a library that has *Britannica Online* may mine the text at $150 a year. The institution, of course, pays for the online costs ($1 per student per year, up to $25,000 maximum). Searching online follows the CD-ROM pattern, but adds a few nice touches such as linking various articles. One may, for example, check out "horses" and at the end of the piece find what amounts to cross-references to other material buried in various places in the online text. The publisher says the online is updated quarterly as compared to annual updates in the other formats. In 1995–1996 the publisher made available close to 3000 illustrations on the Internet/Web and claims to provide 2900 links to other related sites on the Internet. Precisely how well this will work depends on the needs and sophisticated search abilities of the user.

Thrashing about for a method of redefining the *Britannica* in an electronic format, the company came up with an online version in 1994. In itself this is a step forward in that online the publisher can update the material regularly, instead of waiting for a new CD-ROM or print version. Grolier's *Academic American* online has proven a success. The catch to the *Britannica* effort—and it is a major one in the opening of their campaign—is the cost. Because of legal constraints they can offer it only in a certain way. In this case it is to universities. A minimum cost is $5000, while if the university has a large enrollment, the cost can shoot up to $25,000 a year. The price is based on use; the more it is used by the greatest number of students the more it costs. As the print edition is available for much less (around $1300), one wonders what hard-pressed university can afford the luxury of a $25,000 set, even if it is online. Catch no. 2, of course, is that the online version has no illustrations.

In time the company will offer the set for much less to public libraries, school libraries, and individuals directly. The key to success will be, ultimately, adding the illustrations (which will be done through the World Wide Web) and lowering the cost considerably. Meanwhile, the *Britannica* online is more of an experiment than a working reality for the average user or, for that matter, the university.

Print

The text found in the printed volumes is identical, except for updates, to what is found in the electronic version. The major difference is that the print set has illustrations. The printed set consists of:

1. A 12-volume *Micropaedia* which has short, factual ready-reference-type material arranged in alphabetical order. This is an imitation of the specific entry found in many European works. There are approximately 65,000 separate entries and close to half that number of cross-references. The average length of an entry is about 300 words. (A few—covering countries, outstanding personalities, and ideas—go as high as 3000 words, but these are the exception.) Each serves to summarize and outline the topic. Often, too, more detail is found in the companion set or part, the *Macropaedia*.

2. The second part of the set, which like the *Micropaedia* may be used independently, is the *Macropaedia*. The 17 volumes follow the nineteenth-century tradition of offering long (20- to 100-page) detailed articles, again in alphabetical order. Each volume has about 40 articles, for a total in the full 17 volumes of only 681. In effect, the reader is offered an overview of a person, field, or idea in each of the essays.

The guide to the detailed examinations is a table of contents at the head of each essay. For example, in the survey of the West Indies, instead of breaking up the various islands alphabetically (as is done in most sets) they are treated as a single unit in the *Macropaedia*. A score of individual parts treat as many of the individual countries and islands, but always within the context of the main article. Thus the major entries have a coherence not usually found in encyclopedias.

3. The two sets are held together by a detailed two-volume index[15] and the *Propaedia*, which is a guide to related items within the two works. Referred to in advertisements as an "outline of knowledge," this single volume is arranged by broad subjects. The idea is to outline human knowledge, to show relationships among ideas, persons, and events. The *Propaedia* is a commendable failure because the complexity of knowledge simply does not allow such a simplistic approach. The index, on the other hand, is one of the best for any set and has about 232,000 entries and over 720,000 cross-references.

Weak Points. Similar to many sets, the *Britannica* has a distinct failing. It updates material likely to be in the news or the classroom, for example, computers and President Clinton, but it fails to do very much with "standard" entries from the history of painting to the life of President Grant. This is particularly evident in the much dated bibliographies for the "basic" articles, primarily in the *Macropaedia*. (The *Micropedia* has few bibliographies.) The publisher's claim of about 12 percent revision each year is correct, although there are still too many articles in need of revision.

[15]A CD-ROM version of the index is available. This is fine in that it may be searched by boolean logic. Still, the printed index is equally easy to use. A distinct drawback to the CD-ROM index, is that one must search each part of the set *(Macropedia* and *Micropedia)* separately. Given this, one actually is better off to simply search the print index.

The division of the set into two major parts is confusing, and although the format has some benefit for ready-reference work, it is decidedly confusing for laypersons. Another real difficulty is that many of the detailed articles in the *Macropaedia* are highly technical (e.g., see "Mathematics") and beyond the comprehension of all but experts. At the same time, the very challenge makes this a refreshing counterpoint to the sometimes too easy other sets.

The small illustrations in the *Micropaedia* are fine, but the plates, while numerous enough, are not always tied to the articles. This seems particularly true in work of specific artists, architects, and others in the graphic arts. The primary article will include two or three illustrations, but others pertaining to the creators may be scattered through numerous volumes. Also, color is used sparingly.

The Americana

The Encyclopedia Americana is based on the seventh edition of the German encyclopedia *Brockhaus Koversations Lexikon*. In fact, the first published set (1829 to 1833) consisted of little more than pirated, translated articles from the German work. It was asserted in 1903 that the *Americana* was a wholly new work, but still many of the articles were carried over from *Brockhaus*. The set was reissued in 1918 with changes and additions, although still with material from *Brockhaus*. It claims to be the oldest "all-American" encyclopedia in existence.

As the title implies, the strength of this work is its emphasis on American history, geography, and biography. The *Americana* unquestionably places greater emphasis on these areas than any of the other sets, and it is particularly useful for finding out-of-the-way, little-known material about the United States. However, general coverage of the United States is matched in other major encyclopedias.

CD-ROM

An unfortunate aspect of the Americana on CD-ROM is the high cost. The publisher has attempted to justify the high price, by claiming: (1) that the CD-ROM allows rapid access to facts for ready-reference purpose, and since the database is 50,000 to 150,000 words greater than most of its rivals, the work is ideal for quick reference; (2) that the search is faster and "cleaner." The sophisticated search software, which allows entry to natural language questions, ranks responses according to likely relevance of material to the query. Actually, in daily use the Britannica system is much the same. Granted much more data are available, but the process of extracting it is not that much different than from any CD-ROM. (3) There are at least 4000 revised or totally new articles in the CD-ROM version not found in the print volumes. This is the major selling point of the CD-ROM. For example, one finds "compact disc" as an article in the CD-ROM but not in the print. The publisher says, too, that there are close to 4000 minor revisions in the electronic format. Much of this is welcome, particularly as the print set is often out-of-date, but even the CD-ROM is not totally revised.

A definite minus for the CD-ROM is the lack of illustrations. There are charts and graphs, but essentially none of the 20,000 plus illustrations in the print set are found in the electronic work. In time this is likely to change, but for 1995–1996 it is a drawback.

Print

A major plus for the set is that it is fairly current. Each year all the primary articles are updated, and new or revised illustrations are considered. Bibliographies are frequently updated.

The writing style is clear, the arrangement admirable, the index good, and the general format (including illustrations and type size) adequate. A helpful feature is the insertion of summaries, resembling a table of contents, at the beginning of multiple-page articles. The set is edited for the adult with a high school education. It is not suitable (despite the zealous efforts of copywriters) for grade school children.

The illustrations are closely associated with the text. The maps are detailed and easy to follow, although those of detailed city plans are not always the best.

The emphasis is on short, specific, ready-reference entries and is, therefore, ideal for reference work. However, it sometimes contains much longer articles, particularly those which cover states, countries, and historical events. The *Americana* is excellent for *both* the concise articles and the fewer in-depth pieces. Use is made even more effective thanks to a detailed index of 354,000 entries.

Weak Points. Although its performance in revising items and personalities likely to be in the news is fairly good, the same is not true in continuous revision of the basic articles. This lack of timeliness in certain sections can be a major drawback, particularly in schools where curriculum is tied to basic knowledge and not the passing scene.

Art work remains mediocre to poor. A preponderance of illustrations are in black and white and the color pictures are far from ideal. The general layout follows this rather dismal attitude toward the graphic. All and all, one of the less interesting of the group in terms of appearances.

Which Is Best

Most libraries will want both of these standard adult encyclopedias. The sensible approach is to have one on CD-ROM (in this case the *Americana*) and the other in print. If funds allow, one might alternate print and CD-ROM each year so the library has both in both basic formats.

Where a choice must be made, the *Britannica* wins without hardly a contest. It has more in-depth information than any of the sets, including the *Americana*, and the prices are about the same. It is by far the "best buy" among the two adult contestants.

POPULAR ADULT AND HIGH SCHOOL

CD: New Grolier Multimedia Encyclopedia. Danbury, CT: Grolier Incorporated, 1985 to date. $99.95–$395. Annual upgrade, $49.95.
Print: Academic American Encyclopedia. 1980 to date, 21 vols. $1150.
Online: 1983 to date. Dow Jones News/Retrieval, Prodigy, CompuServe. Various rates per hour.

Print: Collier's Encyclopedia. New York: P. F. Collier, 1951 to date. 24 vols. $1000. No electronic format.

CD: Microsoft Encarta Multimedia Encyclopedia (Encarta). Redmond, WA: Microsoft Corporation, 1993 to date. $90 to $140.
Print: Funk & Wagnalls New Encyclopedia. Mahwah, NJ: Funk & Wagnalls, 1912 to date, 29 vols. $164.

There are at least three sets that claim to be of equal value to adults and to young people. The reading level is suitable for those from twelve to eighteen years of age, as well as for older adults. *Collier's* and *Academic American* are better suited to adults than *Funk & Wagnall's* but all may be used by teenagers.

All three differ from the *Americana* and *Britannica* in that they have particular emphasis on popular, concise writing. They are deliberately edited for the person with a high school education or for the high school or beginning college student. All claim, too, that they are suitable for upper elementary school students, but this is questionable. All are relatively accurate, but vary in their practices of keeping material up to date.

Academic American/New Grolier Multimedia Encyclopedia

First published in 1980 by a Dutch firm, and then sold to Grolier, the *Academic American Encyclopedia* is prepared expressly for high school students and for less sophisticated adults. The 21 volumes feature brief articles, numerous illustrations, and a relaxed writing style that offers few challenges in terms of vocabulary or complex ideas. The printed set as well as the electronic version are updated regularly with about 10 percent of the material changed or added each year. With that, the editors carefully keep up with current events and it is among the better sets for finding what major new legislation passed Congress or who won this or that literary or sports prize during the past year. Bibliographies are updated regularly, too.

CD-ROM/The New Grolier Multimedia Encyclopedia[16]

An early leader in the development of the popular CD-ROM encyclopedia, *Grolier* now has one of the best adult–young people's electronic works available. The "multimedia" serve to allow the user many delights. The student may call up Genghis Khan and read about the man and his terror, as well as see a picture of him and his hoards. A more modern version, Hitler, calls up clips of the Second World War. At the touch of a mouse one can read about a humming-bird and see it move as well as hear its song.

On the plus side: (1) It contains almost 1 million more, not less, words than the printed set. (2) There are close to 100 video clips with about six hours of sound, animation, and maps. Combined with visuals, the videos offer short essays on a broad range of topics. (3) It may be searched using boolean logic, and there are specific keys to equally specific sections from bibliographies to lists of facts and illustrations. (4) "Pathmakers" are video interviews with well-known people, which are, in turn, linked to the text. (5) The maps include limited animation and sound, particularly valuable for tracing historical events and shifts.

On the minus side: (1) There are less than half the number of pictures found in the printed set, that is, 8000 versus 18,000. (2) The audio "knowledge explorers" discuss subjects from painting to space but are too brief to be of any real value. The sounds are less than high-fidelity quality and sometimes it is difficult to make out a non-American's speech or the true sound of classical music. (3) The animations are generally good, but some are a trifle pedestrian and of little real value.

Online

Keeping up with technological advances, the online version of the set is favored by most of the consumer online vendors. Without pictures or sound, the text is available for comparatively low rates on systems from Prodigy, CompuServe, Delphi, and Genie among others. It is available, too, on magnetic tape.

The online version is updated quarterly, as compared with annual revisions for the CD-ROM and print. As such it is more current than either the print or CD-ROM formats. It also has more text. There are more than 10 million words compared to 9.1 million in the other two formats. A hypertext version, with pictures, sound, and animation is likely to appear shortly online. And, as with other encyclopedias, it is equally likely that the online version will eventually replace both the print and the CD-ROM versions.

Print

An outstanding feature of the printed set is that the illustrations are bright, well selected, and appealing. They dot almost every page and include photographs,

[16]Also sold as *Software Toolwork Illustrated Encyclopedia*.

line drawings, charts, maps, and even "exploded" illustrations which show, for example, the interior of a ship or airplane. The 17,600 illustrations, according to the publisher, make up 20 percent of the space. Almost one-half of these are in color. In the revision process, the editors add new, color photographs each year and the general level of the illustrations is improving. The page makeup and general layout are among the best among the sets.

The set manages to eliminate any overt bias in the biographical entries and in the articles. But there could be still better coverage of prominent modern women. The coverage of minorities is not all it might be, either.

The index of over 400,000 citations is one of the best available, and extremely easy to use. Unfortunately, the publisher does not follow through with enough adequate cross-reference within the set itself—a pity because many students tend to avoid the index and rely on such references. A bibliography of over 200 pages winds up the index volume and offers approximately 12,500 titles under broad-to-narrow subject headings.

Weak Points. While most of the material is under continuous revision, and the "news" items are current, there is evidence that some basic articles are not. Although the quality of the illustrations has been improved, some are still a bit muddy and not related to the subject matter. On the whole, though, it is difficult to fault the set on any of the major criteria.

Never let a good database go! Grolier uses the *Academic American Encyclopedia* as the springboard in terms of text and illustrations for numerous other licensed or smaller titles: (1) *Barnes & Noble American Encyclopedia* is a familiar item in the national bookstore advertisements, and sells from $199 to $299 as compared to *Academic American*'s $720 to $1150. This, however, is a 1992 printing of the other set, and lacks a twenty-first volume. (2) *Grolier Encyclopedia of Knowledge* is an abridged version of the *Academic* and sells for $120, primarily in competition with the more current, more desirable *Funk & Wagnalls*. It's no contest. F&W remains king of the supermarket trade. (3) Using variations on a theme, Grolier is behind the *Macmillan Family Encyclopedia,* the *Lexicon Universal,* as well as the *Global International.* None is recommended. The *Academic American* is the one to buy.

Grolier, too, is among the first to extensively advertise the benefits of "update." The key to keeping the encyclopedia current is simplicity itself; subscribe to the annual update disc "for only $49.95, plus $5 shipping and handling."

Collier's[17]

Collier's is good to excellent in almost all areas of evaluation. It contains contributions of close to 5000 authorities, and most of the articles are signed. The pub-

---

[17]With the fall of Macmillan in the early 1990s, *Collier's* was purchased from that company by Editorial Planeta–De Agostini, a European conglomerate.

lisher claims a balance in coverage, that is, about 30 percent in the humanities, 15 percent in science, 35 percent in geography and regional studies, with 20 percent given over to the social sciences.

CD-ROM

There is no CD-ROM version of this set.

Print

Collier's has a revision program that makes most of the material current. For example, in the 1995 set there is an extensive rewrite of European countries which brings them into the age of the European Community.

The writing style may be too bland for some, but it has the advantage of clarity. The articles are extremely well organized and the set is unusual because it stresses long, rather than short, articles that are often accompanied by biographical sketches and glossaries of terms. The longer articles often include subject glossaries, a welcome feature for many users.

Some complain that the articles in *Collier's* are too long. In fact, they can run over 40 or even 70 pages for a particular country. At the same time, there is a fine index which has over 400,000 entries—almost double those found in rival sets. Another plus for the final volume is the section on bibliographies. About 12,000 titles are arranged under 31 broad subjects and are subdivided. Most entries are current, and the reading lists offer adults and students a satisfactory choice of supplements to material found in the set.

The 14,500 illustrations, according to the publisher, make up 20 percent of the space. Almost one-half are in color. In the revision process, the editors add new, color photographs each year and the general level of the illustrations has improved. The page makeup and general layout are among the best among the sets. The set manages to eliminate any overt bias in the biographical entries and in the articles.

Weak Points. While most of the material is under continuous revision, and the "news" items are current, there is evidence that some basic articles are not. Although the quality of the illustrations has improved, some are still a bit muddy and not related to the subject matter. On the whole, though, it is difficult to fault the set on any of the major criteria.

Funk & Wagnalls/Encarta

A familiar sight in many supermarkets, *Funk & Wagnalls New Encyclopedia* is an example of a good-to-superior set, sometimes downgraded because of the company it keeps. One of the few works approved by the American Library Association, its frequent revision, serviceable format, and low, low price makes it a bargain for almost anyone. It is the least costly of all printed multivolume encyclopedias. It is a buy among the cut-rate CD-ROMs where its electronic cousin, *Encarta,* is sometimes under $100.

CD-ROM *Encarta*

Thanks as much to Microsoft's marketing position concerning the quality of the CD-ROM, *Encarta* is a leader among general encyclopedias suitable for high school and adults. It has more bells and whistles than its competitors, including a full eight hours of sound as contrasted with the average of an hour or so in other CD-ROMs. Add about 8000 illustrations, some 100 video and animation clips, close to 1000 bits of music, 60 language samples, and a relatively easy search pattern and the explanation for success is even clearer.

By using a new name, *Encarta* nicely sidesteps the unjustified supermarket reputation of *Funk & Wagnalls.* At the same time it draws most of its articles and illustrations from the printed set. About 1000 articles are added by Microsoft staff, which actually increases the amount of coverage. At the same time, the electronic version is about 1500 illustrations short of what is found in the printed set. On balance, though, the CD-ROM is an even better buy.

In searching one may use boolean logic. There are numerous other approaches from key words to topics. The latter approach, however, is weak in that the divisions are limited to nine broad subject areas from sports to history. Still, numerous other points of entry overcome this somewhat awkward approach.

Searches are explained in two guides—one for the beginner and the second for the more seasoned searcher and for the student who wants to know how to do such things as cite sources. The first thing the user sees on the monitor is the Encarta Highlights, which shows clearly an overview of the major topics for searching. This is followed by other screens that demonstrate different approaches to accessing material. One may enter key words, such as "Space exploration," and be led through the main article to photographs, maps, and related items.

There are handy extras such as an adequate dictionary and a thesaurus. A "time line" of world history gives the viewer an accurate notion of historical developments. There is even a game. In fact, the structure of the database is such that many younger people think they are playing a game, for example, music, footage of hurricanes, and over 100 animation and video clips give it a distinctive tone which may or may not be appreciated by all.

Print

Aside from the point of sale, *Funk & Wagnalls* confuses many by its deceptive, almost casual appearance. The two columns to a page format is no more inviting than the unappealing binding. The articles are short—averaging no more than a quarter to a half page—and the illustrations are numerous, if somewhat less than exciting. Is this the stuff of a traditional encyclopedia? Yes, in that the articles are well written, authoritative (there are close to 1000 outside consultants), current, and often illustrated. One can go to the set for almost any item and be sure to find it offered in almost a *Readers' Digest* fashion. In this respect it is ideal for the high school student or adult who rarely uses a set. Ease of use is helped by an excellent 135,000 entry index in the last volume. Add to this a well-chosen bibliography section in the next to the final volume and one has a most useful set. While not always current, most of the choices are at least suitable for the set's target audience.

Funk & Wagnalls has almost the same number of words as the much better designed *Academic American*. They are relatively close to covering about the same amount of material, and they are both quite good in their different ways.

Weak Points. Perhaps the greatest fault, although built into the set by the audience scope, is the uneven treatment of material. The popular and current are often stressed at the expense of standard, historical items. Understandably, the set with the fewest words cannot hope to brag about in-depth articles—and that can be a major weakness. On the other hand, for its intended audience the short entries are possibly even more useful for a quick, easy-to-understand overview.

The thin-ice area is in the humanities and the arts. Here, for some odd reason, many of the articles are unaware of either progress in literature or development in, say, painting. Editors, from time to time, say these sections are to be improved. Illustrations are not indexed, and some relatively common controversial topics such as gun control and oil spills are not covered adequately.

Another Print Set

New Standard Encyclopedia (Chicago: Standard Educational Corporation, 1910 to date, 20 vols., $550) is continually recommended by the American Library Association as a suitable set for middle and high school students, as well as adults. This is neither good nor bad. Falling as it does between the better-known, better-edited sets for this audience, it serves real little purpose in home or library. On the plus side are the short, easy-to-understand articles. On the minus side is that most are written by staff with few outside contributors. Illustrations are current, and about 40 percent are in color. Bibliographies, which are directed at both children and adults, are dated. Biographical material, on the other hand, is quite current. (There is no electronic format.)

Which Is Best

In the CD-ROM contest, which is best—*Grolier* or *Encarta*? Both are edited for the midrange young person and adult, and both are excellent in terms of content and presentation. *Encarta*, though, is a bit brighter, a bit more imaginative, and would win by a click. At the same time *Grolier* has more in-depth articles and certainly is up to and surpasses the *Encarta* in coverage. Again, the advice for the adult sets stands—where possible simply update each year and alternate between *Encarta* and *Grolier*.

The print race between *Academic American* and *Collier's* is not even a race. *Collier's*, by its massive amount of information and presentation, is so far ahead of *Academic American* that it is a first choice without question.

CHILDREN AND YOUNG ADULTS

CD: World Book Multimedia Encyclopedia. Chicago: World Book, 1989 to date. $179.
   Print: World Book Encyclopedia, 1971 to date, 22 vols. $560.

CD: Compton's Interactive Encyclopedia. Carlsbad, CA: Compton's New Media, 1989 to date. $70 to $100.
   Print: Compton's Encyclopedia. Chicago: Compton's Learning Company, 1922 to date, 26 vols. $395 to $500.
   Online: Compton's Encyclopedia, America Online, 1992 to date. Rates vary.

CD-ROM: *Compton's Interactive Encyclopedia*[18]

In 1989 Compton's introduced the *Compton's MultiMedia Encyclopedia* which is the printed work on CD-ROM. It also contains a 60-minute token amount of sound. Today's updated version has more than 14 hours of sound and some 100 videos and animation. There are even 3-D animations. As such it is "top of the line" in the CD-ROM encyclopedia world, and a steady best seller even though the price is higher than the less ambitious, but impressive *Encarta*. There are about 8000 illustrations, or no more than half those found in the printed set.

In addition, the disc features the 65,000-word *Merriam-Webster Intermediate Dictionary*. Given this, the user may click on a word from the set for a handy definition. There is an audio glossary with 1500 words that are pronounced and accompanied by a simple definition.

There are numerous ways to look for other types of information from a capability for scanning the 5000 titles and subjects used in the set to searching for basic ideas. For example, one types in key words and the screen shows a series of indicators down one side. These indicate various types of searches ("Idea search," "Picture tour," "Atlas," etc.). These descriptors are not always clear,

---

[18]There are several versions: Schools and libraries are still sold the original *Compton's Multimedia Encyclopedia*, although updated and with some features not found in the newer CD-ROM: price $150–$400. *The Compton's Family Encyclopedia*, as part of the Sony Laser Library, is the most expensive: $400–$700. These vary in the amount of video, audio, and so forth, For details, see Kister, op. cit., p. 298.

for example, "InfoPilot," but are generally easy enough to understand. "InfoPilot," a new feature in 1995, shows articles related to the user's topic. Unfortunately, the number of paths to relationships are so vast, so complex that this requires considerable experience before really being useful. The manual, although it lacks an index in the 1994 edition, is easy to follow and answers most questions likely to arise over operations.

The "Idea search" allows the user to type in a key word (or words). The screen then shows a list of articles that have the key words. To cut it down to size, the major articles with the key words are starred. Other features: (1) A title finder allows the user to scroll through and choose an article. (2) A topic tree breaks down all the articles under 19 broad classifications and into subtopics. One may then broaden or narrow the search by selecting one of the topics. (3) The picture explorer allows one to type in a broad description of what is wanted, and up comes the picture(s). (4) A note system allows one to type in notes and then, or later, have them printed. The disk is priced at $75 to $100, while the printed set is $395.

Not all critics are pleased with the electronic shift in encyclopedias. Children's CD-ROM encyclopedias, in particular, offer "high class window shopping with no access to the department store of knowledge behind a (print encyclopedia)." The CD-ROM offering "will confirm children in their belief that a picture is worth a thousand words."[19]

Online

Online the *Compton's Encyclopedia* typically includes all of the text of the printed set, but none of the pictures. Available through the consumer America Online, it is accessed by way of a mouse and an array of symbols, menus, and other user-friendly devices. It is easy to search, but so slow that it is of limited value to anyone but a dedicated young adult. Also, it lacks any sophistication, including boolean logic. A poor, poor choice for more than a few checks for ready-reference facts each year. NOTE: Hypertext, the World Wide Web, and other technological advances are likely to improve the online version by mid-1996.

Print

Compton's is unique for its "Fact Index" in the final volume. The feature serves both as an index to each volume and as a source of ready-reference data for basic queries. The publisher claims that there are over 28,500 short, up-to-date articles in the "Fact Index." These ready-reference-type entries cover a wide variety of topics, as well as people and places. There are also useful "Reading Guides," which are edited to suit current curriculum-oriented subjects and give the young reader related materials to consider.

[19]"Look and Learn," *The (London) Observer*, March 13, 1993, p. 10.

The writing style is passable, and while far from sparkling, it is clear enough. The articles are generally short, although major topics may cover several pages. Controversial topics are handled, but gingerly. There are some 15,000 illustrations of which about two-thirds are in color.

The set is extremely well organized for easy use. Among encyclopedias it is one of the easiest to use, particularly for the audience of upper elementary grade students and high school students. It can also be recommended for general family use.

Weak Points. Sensitive subjects are often overlooked or simply skated over. The reader may have no idea that the topic is controversial. The article on abortion includes only a few words on why someone is for or against abortion. There was nothing in the 1995 edition on homosexuality as such, although it is considered under "Sexuality." Nothing concerning the political-social-economic aspects of the subject is discussed. Arrangement, for example, with the index part of the "Fact Index," can be confusing as can the letter-by-letter rather than word-by-word arrangement in the main volumes.

One can recommend the set for most children, although there is little reason to consider it over *World Book.* The excellent and numerous illustrations make it a good buy for some, but only as a second set in the library.

World Book

The triumph of *World Book* is that it is a planned, careful combination of many elements, not the least of which is a nice balance between timely illustrations and text. The clarity of style and the massive number of excellent illustrations put it so far ahead of the other sets that it really has no competitors. Inevitably, critics rank it highly and librarians regularly repurchase. Its popularity makes it the best-selling single set in America. Its target audience is the student, ages ten to sixteen, give or take a year or so.

CD-ROM: *Multimedia Encyclopedia*

On CD-ROM the full title is *The World Book Multimedia Encyclopedia.* The "multimedia" is to separate out this version from an earlier one which had few of the astonishing illustrations which made up the printed set. Needless to say, the first edition was less than a success. The new CD-ROM is somewhat better in that it has about 5000 of the 28,000 illustrations in the print version—which is still far short of the desirable number. (There are some 8000 in their rival, *Compton's*). Lacking as it does the illustrations, it might have made up some of the differences with animation, audio, and the other standard features of the CD-ROM encyclopedias for young people and children. At least in 1995, this was not the case.

On the plus side, the searching techniques are better than most. The user can type in natural language commands. The software compensates when the key words differ from the natural order found in the printed set's subject headings. A split screen shows the needed material, plus a useful outline of the entire article—at least where applicable. Advertisements stress the quality of the search software, but, naturally, fail to point out the lack of illustrations.

Without the sound, without the animation, without many of the basic illustrations, this is a poor buy for individual or for library. True, the searching patterns are good, if not excellent. True, the text is all that is found in the print set, and equally excellent. But with that, why bother? The answer is one should not consider it, at least until the CD-ROM is much, much improved. Until then rely on the still superior printed set.

Note: Originally *Multimedia Encyclopedia* was called *Information Finder* on CD-ROM, and an all-text version minus illustrations is still available with that name. It is not recommended.

Print

Among the children's and young adults' encyclopedias, there is one clear print favorite. The *World Book* really has no competitors.

Not only does the *World Book* stand alone, but it has the advantage of price. At $560 it is a bargain.

The *World Book* follows a pattern of initial ease to progressive difficulty in longer articles, which is sometimes a policy of adult encyclopedias and other reference works. For example, a detailed piece on energy begins with not only an easy vocabulary, but also careful attention to definition and explanation of unusual words and phrases. As one progresses, say past the first one or two columns, the material becomes more sophisticated, that is, more difficult. For the most part, though, the policy of short, specific entries makes this usual only for the detailed, lengthy articles. All of the brief pieces, which are the background of the set, may be easily understood by the average grade school student. The editors follow a much heralded reading-level test pattern based on curricula across the United States.

The twenty-second and last volume contains an excellent index of approximately 15,000 entries. Because the set has numerous cross-references, the index may not be needed for most students, and rarely for ready-reference work.

The most dramatic aspect of the set are the illustrations on each and every page. It has more illustrations than any set, adults' or children's, and the 31,000 plates include 24,000 in color. Illustrations take up over one-third of the total space.

While all children's sets are kept current, the degree of revision varies considerably. *World Book* is by far the best in this respect, particularly in that careful attention is given to current events, and biographical data are updated regularly. In the 1994 set, for example, the publisher claims 97 new articles, in-depth revision of 290 articles, and partial revision of 2300 articles. Comparatively, there are some 18,000 articles in the set.

Weak Points. Few of the sets are likely to win applause for challenging the reader to consider controversial issues. Here the publisher is more concerned with not shocking the parents than with the children. The article on human reproduction, for example, seems to avoid sexual intercourse as a necessary part of the formula. The editors, wisely or not, leave the vital act up to parents to explain.

World Book, closely tied to the curricula of the nation's schools, assiduously avoids appearing to endorse anything that may be controversial. At the same time, it is quite objective in handling national arguments from abortion to the place of religion in education. It often fails to indicate that foreign affairs affect American policy. The advertising for *World Book* may be faulted for indicating that it is for younger children. Actually it is for someone at least nine years of age, but probably closer to ten or twelve years old up through high school.

Childcraft

World Book publishes a 15-volume set, *Childcraft,* for preschool children, which is really a luxury for both parents and a library. Perfectly suitable, and extremely well illustrated and cleverly laid out, the 750,000 words and 4600 illustrations cost $170. Many volumes give pronunciation for new words and sentences to show how the words are used properly. Articles are arranged by topic, but each volume has its own index, with a general index in the last volume.

The topic arrangement by science, children's literature, social studies, and so forth, is reminiscent of a shelf in the library trying to appeal to all interests of young readers. Is it really an encyclopedia or a collection of nicely presented fiction, nonfiction, and activities? The latter is the real answer and as such it is of more real value to families than to libraries.

Other Sets: Print Format

The New Book of Knowledge (Danbury, CT: Grolier Incorporated, 1908 to date, 21 vols., $679), edited for children from about seven to thirteen years of age, is a full-fledged set and not, as it was for many decades, a simple collection of reading materials. It puts almost as much emphasis on leisurely reading as facts and background. For example, there are numerous pieces about how to build this or that, questions such as "Was Mother Goose a real person?" (with the answer), and numerous articles on children's hobbies. The real plus—excerpts from the classics, as well as complete short stories. Close to 100,000 entries are in the index.

A definite plus are the 25,000 illustrations and maps. This is close to the number in the more elaborate *World Book* and ahead of all other children's sets except the *World Book*. Within many of the longer articles are charts, graphs, and summaries, such as "quick-reference" materials.

The articles are well written and, in fact, the writing style is better than that found in many of the pieces in *Compton's*. An effort toward clarity is made and most of the articles are short with precise definitions and explanations, usually punctuated with illustrations.

Weak Points. Considering the age group for which this is designed, and the careful attention to their interests, there is little to fault. It is *not* appropriate, though, as some have suggested for older children with reading problems. The coverage of countries other than the United States is rather simplistic. As of 1995 there was no version of this on CD-ROM or in any electronic format. Likely, this will change and Grolier will publisher a CD-ROM equivalent.

There are no electronic formats. *Children's Britannica* (Chicago: Encyclopedia Britannica, 1960 to date, 20 vols., $369) is a nondescript set which has about 4000 articles written for children ages eight to fourteen. It is edited and published in England, but is sold here as an American set. Except for minor changes for Americans, it is directed to English school children. The 6000 illustrations, primarily in black and white, are as inviting as the dismal layout. Although recommended by the American Library Association, it is not recommended by this author. The money is better spent on a CD-ROM or a secondhand set of the *World Book* which may be purchased for less than the new *Children's Britannica*.

There are no electronic formats.

Other Sets: CD-ROM

First Connections: The Golden Book Encyclopedia (East Lansing, MI: Hartley Courseware, 1993 to date, $90 to $150) is the familiar Golden Book set on CD-ROM format. Given a child from ages five to ten who can function at a computer terminal, this is a possible purchase. The audio (about 60 minutes) is imaginative. The animations appeal to children from pregrade through about the sixth or seventh grade. The more than 3000 maps and illustrations are adequate. The text is easy enough to understand.

The catch is that this is edited primarily for entertainment. Few articles go into any depth. Some basic entries are skipped over. Material is relatively current, but not always that up to date. As a tool to draw young children into the world of information it is a success, and as such can be used in many schools. At the same time it is not the place to turn for up-to-date answers to reference questions put by children. Considering the appealing features of the set, as well as its low price, it might be purchased for reading and browsing. It is not up to passable encyclopedia criteria.

Which To Buy?

Choices of children's and young adults' encyclopedias are quite easy. First and foremost, the printed version of *World Book* should be in every grade school, high school, and public library. It is so far superior to others that it has no real competitors.

    With that, though, the CD-ROM format winner is equally clear—*Compton's Interactive Encyclopedia.* Where older children and young adults are a consideration, then CD-ROMs should be in this order: *The New Grolier Multimedia Encyclopedia* and then *Encarta.* In the not-too-distance future the CD-ROM *World Book* will be improved, and when that happens it will be a contender. As of now, though, it is out of the electronic running.

ENCYCLOPEDIA SUPPLEMENTS: YEARBOOKS

Encyclopedia yearbooks are published annually to (1) keep the basic set up to date and (2) present a summary of the year's major events. A third, less obvious, purpose is to increase sales: It is comforting for the buyer to hear that the set will never be outdated (a questionable assumption, but the claim is used by almost every encyclopedia salesperson).

    The future of the traditional encyclopedia yearbook is in question. CD-ROMs will update the set. Each year the replacement disc is mailed out at a minimal cost. Updated quarterly or more often, the online encyclopedia eventually will replace both the print and CD-ROM. The electronic format not only is more economical, but also solves the problem of tying the update to the main set itself—a problem never resolved by the printed yearbooks.

    Meanwhile, the standard yearbook continues to be published, continues to be part of the sales pitch and, in its way, serves a useful purpose in the library, if rarely in most homes. The supplements are not related to the complete set except by name. The arrangements are broad, with emphasis on large, current topics. Most of the material is not incorporated into the later revised basic sets.

    The *Britannica World Data* annual is typical of the type. It has excellent, current articles on the passing world scene. It devotes about 450 to 500 pages to "The Year in Review." Here the data are arranged by subject from agriculture to world affairs. Subsections include biographies, obituaries, and special features such as the presidential election. These are followed by 250 to 300 pages of world data—a useful comparison of language, religion, health services, and the like among major nations. There are 200 or so pages given over to standard national information, country by country. The statistics and other data are relatively current. There is little or no connection with the primary set. Sometimes even the main headings differ from the subject headings in the *Micropedia*.

Yearbook Variations

Aside from the age of the audience for which each is prepared, significant differences among the various yearbooks are difficult to discover. In this respect, they resemble the daily newspaper. One reader may prefer the slant or emphasis of one newspaper over another, but both papers are drawing from the same general materials. The analogy is not as far-fetched as it may seem. In the annuals particularly, the predominantly newspaper-trained staffs of the larger encyclopedia firms have free reign. Format, content, and the ever-important emphasis on up-to-date, often exciting events reflect newspaper rather than scholarly influence behind the final book; they reveal an emphasis on what makes the daily newspaper sell, at least from the standpoint of the ex-newspaper writer.

If a single adults' or children's yearbook is to be purchased, the nod will go to the work preferred by the librarian and the patrons of the library. As long as the preference is within the standards set for encyclopedias, it is a matter more of taste than of objective judgment, and any one of the accepted publishers will serve as well as another.

ONE-VOLUME ENCYCLOPEDIAS

Print: The New Columbia Encyclopedia, 5th ed. New York: Columbia University Press, 1994, 3050 pp. $125. (Distributed by Houghton Mifflin Company). No electronic format.

CD: The Concise Columbia Encyclopedia in Microsoft Bookshelf. Redmond, WA: Microsoft Corporation, 1987 to date. $99–$195.
Print: Concise Columbia Encyclopedia, 3rd ed. New York: Columbia University Press (distributed by Houghton Mifflin Company), 1994, 975 pp. $49.95.
Online: The Concise Columbia Electronic Encyclopedia. 1993 to date. OCLC First Search, rates vary.

Print: The Random House Encyclopedia, 3rd ed. New York: Random House, 1990, 3000 pp. $95–$130.
No electronic format.

One-volume encyclopedias meet the needs of people interested in a single fact, date, person, or place, who may consult a reference work no more than once or twice a year. It is economical to invest in a relatively inexpensive encyclopedia, which, for little added expense, can be replaced in home and library as it becomes dated.

Currently the best, *The Columbia Encyclopedia*, is not available either online or on CD-ROM. This will change. Yet, the real question is whether it makes much sense to invest in a CD-ROM limited to a single, cutback encyclopedia. The answer is a flat no. If nothing else, the print version is easier to use and, for once, really less expensive than its electronic cousin. An exception may be where the encyclopedia is part of a package, as in the *Microsoft Bookshelf*.

Returning to the excellent *Columbia*, this is the best of a group that embraces close to 18 various titles. Only three or four can be recommended. The fifth edition of the *Columbia* follows the pattern of the early editions. It has over 6.6 million words, or about 3 to 4 million words less than the multiple sets from *Compton's* to *Funk & Wagnalls*. Over 3000 pages claim 50,000 articles and 750 illustrations. It is priced at $125, although it sells for as little as $75 in numerous bookstores and chains.

The oversized, close to 12-pound volume is equally in the top-weight quality ring. Thanks to its long history, academic publisher, and numerous advisers and contributors *The Columbia Encyclopedia* easily shoves all competitors to one side. While written for adults, the majority of high school students can cope with the relatively easy-to-follow, brief entries. Longer articles include impressive, current bibliographies. The black-and-white drawings dot the three-column pages. They lend an air of scholarship to the work, but hardly excite either the imagination or the eye.[20]

Much the same praise and mild criticism hold for the set's junior partner, the *Concise Columbia Encyclopedia*. Here "concise" is translated into a *Reader's Digest* approach. There are 1 million words versus 6.6 million in the larger volume, and one-third the number of pages. The 150 illustrations hardly count. The smaller book has the advantage of a low, low price ($39.95, often discounted) and, for many, the delight of weighing only one-third as much. The minimal attitude is not reflected in the equally excellent text. There simply is less of it and, of course, many fewer entries. Still, for all but the most esoteric ready-reference questions, it more than meets the average need of a reader. Good as it is, it is not recommended for libraries, which should stay with the senior member.

One-Volume Encyclopedias: CD-ROM

On a CD-ROM by its lonely self, the *Concise Columbia Encyclopedia* would not be worth a notice. Aware of this, the ubiquitous Microsoft Corporation puts on a low-priced disc along with six other equally valuable reference titles. In typical Microsoft fashion, the encyclopedia section includes most of the illustrations, as

---

[20]"There's Always an Explanation," *The New York Times Book Review*, October 31, 1993, p. 38. One of numerous reviews, but this is recommended for its background data and careful analysis, which are applicable to other one-volume sets.

well as enhanced animation, sounds, and music. Often sold for about $99 the *Bookshelf* is a best buy. The package not only includes the $50 encyclopedia, but close to $150 more in reference books, often, again, with enhanced pictures, pronunciation, and so forth. These include *The American Heritage Dictionary, Roget's Thesaurus, Bartlett's Familiar Quotations, Hammond Atlas, The World Almanac,* and the *Concise Columbia Dictionary of Quotations*.[21] Thanks to well-worked-out search software, a simple point and click will usually find the precise information required. There are numerous integrated cross-references. Given all of the features and the five other basic reference works, the *Microsoft Bookshelf* is a best buy for library and individual.

A "thumbs down" electronic version of the concise encyclopedia is found in the handheld *Franklin's Concise Columbia Encyclopedia*. Selling for $160 to $250, and sometimes less on sale, the 12-ounce, 8-line "electronic book" is a toy, but no more. The keyboard requires someone with fingers the size of toothpicks to operate and the screen is so limited that it might take a lifetime to scroll through all of the text. It is a sterling argument for rushing to buy the print volume, or the CD-ROM package.

The Random House Encyclopedia

The print version of *The Random House Encyclopedia* has a distinguished history. It has 3 million words and is only about one-half the size of the *New Columbia*. Unlike the *Columbia* it stresses illustrations. In fact, the primary draw, particularly among shoppers, is the stunning, usually full-color drawings, photographs, charts, and other graphics. It has no competitors in terms of appearance. It is a better buy for younger adult. It should be found in all libraries next to the *Columbia*.

As with the previous two editions, it is in two sections. The first is called the "Alphapedia" and has short, useful entries. This is the most updated part of the new edition and may be of value for ready-reference queries concerning recent news events and personalities. ("May" because most of the data are just as readily available, at less cost, in standard works from the *World Almanac* to a basic encyclopedia yearbook.)

The second part (the "Colorpedia") is where one finds the majority of illustrations, usually in color, and longer topical essays on everything from the nature of things to world history. It is a visual delight and of some interest to younger readers and adults who enjoy *The National Geographic*. All and all it is a delightful set.

Not known for its strength of text, the one-volume work is imaginatively designed and packaged. Edited for all markets, not just English-speaking nations,

---

[21]The content is from 1996, but each year the Microsoft people tend to update, change, and otherwise improve on the *Bookshelf*. It probably will have a different content in the years to come.

the work compromises and cuts to satisfy everyone. Children seem to enjoy the colorful MTV-like format and if the information does not run deep, it runs with style. Parents and libraries would be better off with a CD-ROM encyclopedia, but if a relatively inexpensive print version in one volume is needed, this is the answer.

As with the *Columbia,* the *Random House* is available in a handheld disc model produced by Sony. This is called *The Random House Electronic Desk Reference.* It is a terrible buy. It costs $70, has no illustrations, and has all the disadvantages of a handheld reference reader. The plus side is that it does include the Random House reference titles: *The Random House Webster's Electronic Dictionary* and *Thesaurus College Edition.*

A children's *Random House* one-volume work becomes *The Random House Children's Encyclopedia* (New York: Random House, 1991, 664 pp., $50). This is *not* a revised edition of the adult *Random House Encyclopedia.* Rather it is a slightly modified version of the English *Children's Illustrated Encyclopedia,* which, like its adult counterpart, has been translated into numerous languages. It is a rare item, in that few children's encyclopedias are limited to a single volume. Also, it is the largest of its kind, with more than 3500 attractive illustrations. Most of the 400 entries are broad in scope and limited to one to four pages, with some going to six pages.

Other One-Volume Titles

Hardly six months goes by that some firm does not offer a general one-volume encyclopedia for adults and young people. (As noted, the single volume for children is a bit rare.) In 1996, *Books in Print* lists some 21 titles, although several might be called subject works. Be that as it may, how many are worth considering? None. Where only a one-volume encyclopedia is needed the *Columbia* will suffice. Another obvious choice is to annually update one of the electronic versions for current data and, particularly, the Microsoft entry.

Individuals who wish to keep up with current material, are advised to explore other print one-volume encyclopedias as they are published. For example:

1. *Webster's New World College Encyclopedia* (New York: Prentice-Hall, 1993, 1156 pp., $35) has 1.5 million words, or about one-half million more than the *Concise Columbia,* which was published a year later. It is mentioned here because, when its new edition is published in 1996, it becomes suitable update for the *Concise Columbia.* The problem is lack of focus, and a mishmash of definitions with sometime minimal data on people and places. It will do, but just. (No electronic format.)

2. *The Cambridge Encyclopedia* (New York: Cambridge University Press, 1990 to date, 1488 pp., $49.95), is a good general work, produced in England.

It is updated every two or three years. There are about 30,000 articles and approximately 1.5 million words, or double the number of articles and about 500,000 more words than the *Concise Columbia*. A 130-page supplement at the end of the volume, printed on yellow paper, features statistical data on everything from baseball to politics. Unfortunately, this is not closely tied to the data in the main work. There is a color section with maps and a number of scientific illustrations. In fact, the numerous pictures set this off as a most useful work for younger people as well as adults. It is arranged logically with 75,000 cross-references. A minor difficulty with the *Cambridge* and the other English works is the close tie to British terminology and culture. Sometimes the British spellings are different. More disturbing is the inclusion of data on such things as how to address a member of the House of Lords, but nothing on how to address a member of the United States Congress. (No electronic format.)

The *Concise Columbia* is preferred because it is more suitable for American libraries. Other than that, though, it is pretty much of a toss-up and the *Cambridge* is a good extra one-volume title where needed.

3. Actually, a better buy is *The Barnes & Noble Encyclopedia* (New York: Barnes & Noble, 1990 to date, 1488 pp., $19.98). It is precisely the same work as the *Cambridge,* but with a different title, binding, and publisher. At $19.98 one gets the *Cambridge* at about $30 less. That is difficult to beat. (No electronic format.)

FOREIGN-PUBLISHED MULTIVOLUME ENCYCLOPEDIAS: PRINT FORMAT[22]

For Americans, most reference questions can be quickly and properly answered by an American encyclopedia. There are occasions when a foreign language work is more suitable. Obviously, a foreign encyclopedia will cover its country of origin in greater depth than an American work, including biographies of nationals, statistics, places, and events.

Even for users with the most elementary knowledge of the language, several of the foreign works are useful for their fine illustrations and maps. For example, the *Enciclopedia Italiana* boasts some of the best illustrations of any encyclopedia, particularly in the area of the fine arts. A foreign encyclopedia is equally useful for point of view: Some American readers may be surprised at the manner in which the Civil War, for example, is treated in the French and the German encyclopedias. Further, the evaluation of American writers and national heroes in these works is sometimes equally revealing about the way Eu-

---

[22]Ken Kister, "Foreign Language Encyclopedias," in his *Kisters Best Encyclopedias,* op cit., pp. 443–451. Here one finds the basic sets arranged by country and language with brief annotations. See, too, his section "Geography and Area Studies," where many foreign language works are listed, but published in English.

ropeans judge the United States. More specifically, the foreign encyclopedia is helpful for information on less-well-known figures not found in American or British works, foreign language bibliographies, detailed maps of cities and regions, and other information ranging from plots of lesser-known novels and musicals to identification of place names.

In Europe, as in America, there are only two or three major publishers (including, incidentally the *Encyclopaedia Britannica*, which has arrangements for copublishing with the firms). The giants include (1) Brockhaus and Herder in Germany, (2) Larousse in France, and (3) Garzanti in Italy. When the librarian finds one of these names on a new or revised set, the odds are about 99 to 1 that the work will be of high quality.

Note: All of these sets are print. No electronic formats.

French

Print: Grand Dictionnaire Encyclopédique Larousse. Paris: Larousse, 1982–1989, 10 vols. $1250. (Distributed in the United States by French and European Publications, Inc.)

The name Larousse is as familiar in France as the *Encyclopaedia Britannica* is in the United States. Pierre Larousse was the founder of a publishing house which continues to flourish and is responsible for the basic French encyclopedias. In fact, *Larousse* in French is often used as a synonym for *encyclopedia.*

Larousse continues with the policy of short, specific entries, but it does give some rather extensive treatment of major subjects. For example, the length of articles for countries and leading personalities often equals that found in American works. Returning to an older concept of encyclopedias, the *Grand Dictionnaire* is precisely what the title suggests in that it not only includes specific encyclopedia entries, but definitions of words as well. These is a strong emphasis on brilliant illustrations, usually in full color. Each page includes photographs, charts, maps, diagrams, and the like. Regardless of one's command of French, everyone will enjoy the illustrations.

Another major set is often found in American libraries: *Encyclopaedia Universalis*, 2d ed. (available in the United States from Encyclopaedia Britannica, 1993, 30 vols., plus a 2-vol. supplement, $1600). This work is in the fashion of the *Macropaedia*, in that the articles are long, detailed, and scholarly and are extremely well illustrated. The 23 to 24 volumes are a type of ready-reference work with brief entries. The next two volumes called the *Symposium* consist of 180 essays, with a particular emphasis on current political and social trends. This is supplemented in two volumes. The index, with short fact-finding entries as well, is in volumes 27 to 30.

German

Print: Brockhaus Enzyklopadie, rev. 19th ed. Wiesbaden: Brockhaus, 1986, 24 vols. $4000. Plus irregular supplements.

First issued as *Frauenzimmer Lexikon* (between 1796 and 1808), this was an encyclopedia whose content, as the title indicates, was focused primarily on the interests of women of the period. The original publisher, possibly because of his limited sales, gave up the financial ghost; in 1808, Friedrich Brockhaus purchased the set and issued the last volume. A wise man, Brockhaus continued to offer his volumes not as scholarly works, but as books guaranteed to give the average man (or woman) a solid education. By doing so, he was years ahead of the times, in fact, he was so far ahead of his American and British counterparts that they freely borrowed his text, if not his sales techniques. As noted earlier, the Brockhaus works were the basis for the early *Americana* and *Chambers*'s.

Brockhaus developed the idea of short, easy-to-read entries. Some articles were little more than a few sentences or paragraphs in length. Consequently, all the Brockhaus encyclopedias—and there is a family of them—are an admixture of dictionary and encyclopedia. (The family includes the basic 24-volume set, the revised 12-volume set, and a 1-volume work, among others.)

As might be expected, the longer articles, some of them over 100 pages, focus on European countries. In many respects, the *Brockhaus* encyclopedia is considerably more nationalistic than the *Larousse,* and while it is an excellent source of material on German history and personalities, it can be passed by for other items.

Because of its scope, the *Brockhaus* is useful in large research libraries or where there is a German-speaking populace, but it is probably near the bottom among choices of all the foreign language encyclopedias, if for no other reason than the outrageous price of $4000, plus the cost of supplements.

Italian

Print: Enciclopedia Europea. Milan: Garzanti, 1976–1984, 12 vols. $3600.

This is the most modern of the Italian sets, and is updated from time to time. It is important for three reasons: (1) It has brief, specific entries that afford a marvelous overview of Italian and European history, culture, and science. (2) There are longer companion articles of considerable substance, particularly in terms of coverage of the sciences and social sciences. (3) There are excellent illustrations.

One of the major European records of the arts is the famous *Enciclopedia Italiana* (Rome: Istituto della Enciclopedia Italiana, 1929–1936, 35 vols., plus supplements 1958 to date; price varies, but in 1995 was $17,500). The basic pre-World War II set is found in almost all large libraries because of its superb illustrations and its scholarly and well-documented articles. Although the articles on the government are far from impartial, the general coverage is excellent and the set is one of the best prewar works to come out of Europe.

Japanese

Print: Kodansha Encyclopedia of Japan. New York: Kodansha International, 1983, 9 vols. and supplements. $900.

This is an unusual and superior encyclopedia which analyzes, explains, and even critically assesses Japan, past and present. The all English-Japanese encyclopedia represents the work of 1300 scholars from 27 countries, including Japan and the United States. The text was written with the average layperson in mind, although much of the material will interest the subject specialist. The style is much above average. There are about 10,000 entries and 4 million words. The largest single category of entries concerns Japanese history, followed by geography and art. These are slightly over 1000 articles covering Japanese economics and business. The articles are quite objective, and considerable effort was made to ensure that nothing about Japan's past was glossed over or ignored.

The same publisher, in 1993, issued the widely acclaimed *Japan: An Illustrated Encyclopedia* (2 vols., 1924 pp., $250). A shorter version of the larger work, this has the advantage of superior illustrations (the main set is weak in this respect) and current data on Japanese politics and culture. Here one will find practical advice on making sushi as well as philosophical meditations. The price is as reasonable as the set is superior.

Russian

Print: The Great Soviet Encyclopedia, 3d ed. New York: Macmillan, 1973–1983, 32 vols. $2500. (Published in Russia from 1970 to 1980 as *Bol'shaia Sovetskaia Entisklopediia,* or *BSE.*)

With the chill of the Cold War past, this set is now primarily of value for its historical material and the static information on such things as geography, music, and the arts. Beyond that, it offers some striking examples of bias.

The *BSE* is somewhat equivalent in scholarship to the older version of the *Britannica.* The entire set has more than 21 million words and over 100,000 articles. Including both the specific-entry and the broad-entry forms, the set is a combination of routine dictionary and gazetteer items, with detailed, lengthy articles covering every aspect of Soviet interest.

Since most American readers will use the English translation, two points are worth making: (1) The index is necessary because of the unusual alphabetical arrangement of each volume, caused by differences between the Russian and Latin alphabets. For example, the first translated volume "A to Z" contains entries for "Aalen Stage" and the "Zulu War of 1879." (2) The quality of the translation is good. The American version differs from the Russian in that cost considerations made it necessary to delete the fine maps in the original Russian version.

There are numerous current books on today's Russia, and these should be turned to first for the average query. Among the best: *The Cambridge Encyclopedia of Russia and the Former Soviet Union* (New York: Cambridge University Press, 2d ed., 1993).

Spanish

Print: Enciclopedia universal ilustrada Europeo-Americana (Espasa). Barcelona: Espasa, 1907 to 1933, 108 vols., including annual supplements, 1934 to date. $8995. (Distributed in the United States by French and European Publications, Inc.)

Hispanics are fortunate in that there are a number of excellent, relatively inexpensive encyclopedias in Spanish. These are listed and annotated by Kenneth Kister in his *Kister's Best Encyclopedias*.

Even a cursory glance at his selection indicates a problem for younger American students; except for one, all are published abroad.[23] The language is the same, but the cultural, political, and social differences are tremendous say, between Arizona and Barcelona. Therefore, while many of these sets can be recommended, as Kister does, it is questionable how suitable they really are for youngsters in Spanish-speaking American communities.

Beyond that there is the scholarly aspect of the encyclopedia, and here the clear leader is the famous *Espasa*. Usually cited simply as *Espasa,* the *Enciclopedia* is a remarkable work. First, it never seems to end. Forgoing continuous revision or new editions, the publishers continue to augment the 80 volumes (actually 70 basic volumes with 10 appendixes) with annual supplements, which are arranged in large subject categories and include an index. (The term *annual* must be taken advisedly, as the supplements generally are not issued until three to five years after the period covered. For example, the 1981–1982 volume came out in 1985.)

Second, *Espasa* has the largest number of entries—the publishers claim over 1 million. Since they evidently do not count on "authority," no articles are signed, although they are signed in the supplements after 1953. Again, as in the German and French encyclopedias, the emphasis is on short entries of the dictionary type. Still, there are a number of rather long articles, particularly those dealing with Spain, Latin America, prominent writers, and so forth.

---

[23]The exception is the *Diccionario Enciclopedico,* published by the Encyclopaedia Britannica in 1988 (15 vols., $199). Although designed for elementary grades, the fact is that most of the set remains as it was when first issued in Barcelona.

One problem, as with most European encyclopedias, is the alphabetical arrangement. Any student who has had a brush with a foreign language realizes that although the Latin alphabet is employed, there are variations in letters; Spanish, for example, has two letters not found in English, "ch" and "ll." There are also marked differences in common names. In other languages, *John* turns up as Giovanni, Jan, Juan, Johannes, or Jehan. Consequently, before abandoning a foreign encyclopedia for lack of an entry, the user should be certain to look for the entry in terms of the language employed.

SUBJECT ENCYCLOPEDIAS

In a world of increasing specialization, it is understandable that for every general encyclopedia available there are a dozen or more subject works. A cursory glance at reference book reviews in *Library Journal, Choice,* or *Booklist* will show that each and every month a dozen or so new titles, or revisions of older works, are published. In English alone there are close to 1000 subject encyclopedias. Few at this stage are online, but a growing number are available on CD-ROMs.

In *Kister's Best Encyclopedias,* Ken Kister annotates "more than 800 of the best or most useful titles published in English in recent years." Grouped under approximately 30 subject headings, over 100 pages open with *American Shelter: An Encyclopedia of the American Home* and end on wings of praise for the *World Encyclopedia of Civil Aircraft.* From another point of view the American Library Association's list of outstanding reference sources includes among the 40 to 50 titles listed a dozen or more subject encyclopedias. For example, the 1994 selection includes, among others, *The Cambridge Encyclopedia of Human Evolution* with the suitable *Encyclopedia of Child Bearing,* followed by the *Illustrated Encyclopedia of Fly Fishing.*

The reasoning of publishers and producers is that it is no longer possible or profitable to reach out to everyone. The best approach is to prepare a work for a select group, normally a group with both a high interest in the subject and a medium-to-high income to purchase the book. A near perfect example of this is *The Encyclopedia of New York City.* New Haven: Yale University Press, 1995. Published for the New York Historical Society for $60, the 1350 pages appeal primarily, if not exclusively, to New York City residents. It appears to be the only encyclopedia dedicated to a single city.

Publishers of subject encyclopedias follow the special-audience philosophy. Generally, the result is encouraging for reference librarians, particularly when (1) a ready-reference question is so specialized or esoteric that it cannot be answered in a general encyclopedia, or (2) a user needs a more detailed overview of a subject than that found in a single article in a general encyclopedia. The more limited the library budget for both reference work and general titles, the more reason to turn to subject encyclopedias. The librarian may have a small amount of material on, for example, dreams, but finds all that is needed in *The Encyclopedia of Dreams* (New York: Crossroad Publishing, 1993). In dictionary order it explains over 60 varied common dreams.[24]

Encyclopedias and Handbooks

Such key descriptors as "companion," "handbook," or "dictionary" may indicate a subject one- to three-volume encyclopedia. For example, Oxford University Press is known for companion series such as *The Oxford Companion to American Theatre* and, in a narrower field, *The Oxford Companion to Chess*. There are dozens of these reputable works edited by well-known experts. Inevitably they are alphabetically arranged by subject. The price may range from $30 to $75. The number of entries can be from 2000 to 6000.

One may argue that these are not encyclopedias, but another form of information package. No matter, the point is that the arrangement, scope, and audience for each is such that it fits the encyclopedia pattern. More important, they often serve as reference sources for quick, often in-depth answers to common questions.

Evaluation

Use the same evaluative techniques for subject sets as those used for general encyclopedias. Even with limited knowledge of the field covered, librarians may judge a set. Using reviews or subject experts for evaluation of the expensive works is useful. Subject sets often are evaluated in scholarly periodicals, which discuss them at greater length than in standard reviews.

Examples

Space does not permit a full discussion of the numerous, many quite superior, subject encyclopedias. The focus here is on works that are best known and likely to be found in many medium to large libraries. Most, although not all, have been published relatively recently. This rather arbitrary approach gives at least a cursory glance at the direction of subject encyclopedia publishing.

[24]Should a library, then, purchase a reference work that is entertaining, but hardly scientific or even based on social or humanistic research? James Rettig, the expert on such matters, gives a fine judgment about this and other books of the same type. *The Encyclopedia of Dreams* "is the sort of source whose authority and usefulness derive not from itself so much as from the user's willingness to invest it with authority and utility. . . . Sometimes a cigar is just a cigar, and other times it can signify something more" (*Wilson Library Bulletin*, December 1993, p. 78). In its annual selection of outstanding reference sources, the American Library Association gave the work a pass, but did recommend *Encyclopedia of Sleep and Dreaming*, which is a trifle more scientific.

Another purpose, particularly in the "Anthropology," "Art," and "Science" sections that follow is to indicate the pros and cons of subject encyclopedias on CD-ROMs.

Anthropology

CD: The American Indian: A Multimedia Encyclopedia. New York: Facts on File, 1993. $295.

Print: Carl Waldman. *Encyclopedia of Native American Tribes.* New York: Facts on File, 1988. $29.95.

Based on Carl Waldman's popular *Encyclopedia of Native American Tribes,* the CD-ROM version adds material and comes up with coverage of more than 150 tribes of native peoples in what is now the United States. The standard illustrations (250 out of 900 in color) are coupled with the full text of documents relating to the government and the tribes. Maps, charts, time lines, and related material round out the reading matter. It boasts the usual features such as cross-references to related material and the possibility (equipment being suitable) to print out the illustrations. An added voice-over of sound bites of Native American songs is pleasant. With that, though, one wonders why the CD-ROM is considered much better than the main work by Waldman. The answer is hard to find, although would not be so if the price were under $100.

The librarian here is wise to (1) purchase the Waldman print version (for under $30) and (2) invest in *Handbook of North American Indians* (Washington, DC: Smithsonian Institution, 1978 to date). Individual volumes are from $25 to $50 and eventually 20 will be published. As of 1995 about one-half the volumes were available. Thanks to the clear writing style, the marvelous illustrations, and the careful indexing these are both scholarly and popular. Together they may cost a bit more than the CD-ROM, but together they represent the best there is on the subject.

All of this is to illustrate the point that while electronic databases for reference works are a blessing, there are times, particularly in certain subject encyclopedias, when the librarian is wiser to consider the print version.

Art

CD: Microsoft Art Gallery. Redmond, WA: Microsoft Corporation, 1994. $80.

Print: Encyclopedia of World Art. New York: McGraw-Hill Book Company, 1959–1968, 15 vols. $1500. Two supplements, 1983 and 1987. $100 each. No electronic format.

Depending on hypertext, rather than simply straight text with illustrations, the popular CD-ROM subject encyclopedias have a bright future. The Microsoft entry is an example of what to expect. The *Art Gallery* allows the user to view the complete holdings of The National Gallery in London. At a simple command one may call up one of more than 2000 pictures. Navigation is by title of the painting, artist's name, or more general topics such as artists' lives, which brings on the screen an alphabetical listing from Aachen Master to Zurbarán. The latter is activated with a thumbnail biography and images of Zurbarán's works in the National Gallery. Key an image and the screen is filled with the particular work in glorious color. A brief explanatory text accompanies each painting. Key words in the explanation can be used to link the artist to Spain, fellow artists in the seventeenth century, and so on.[25]

Three points: (1) The expert, the scholar, or the advanced student of the subject will continue to rely on text and necessary art. (2) CD-ROM subject works tend to stress entertainment. This is fine for amateurs, but not for experts. (3) There is no reason the needs of both expert and amateur cannot be met in a single disk, particularly where art and sound are important aspects of the subject, but this is unlikely.

Using this, and similar systems, is like shuffling through postcards or a large book of reproductions which, incidentally, tend to be visually sharper than on a computer monitor. It can be instructive and entertaining at the same time, but Microsoft is not likely to find a large audience for its work among art experts. They will turn to the *Encyclopedia of World Art* and related titles, of which Kister, for example, lists a good current dozen.

The *Encyclopedia of World Art* is the finest set available among encyclopedias devoted entirely to art. It includes art of all periods and has exhaustive studies of art forms, history, artists, and allied subject interests. Arranged alphabetically, it contains many shorter articles that answer almost every conceivable question in the field. The fifteenth volume is a detailed index.

An outstanding feature is the illustrations. At the end of each volume, there are 400 to 600 black-and-white and color reproductions. They, as well as some color plates in the main volumes, are nicely tied to the articles by suitable cross-references and identification numbers and letters.

The supplements are chronologically arranged. They trace new findings in art from prehistory to the present. Extensive bibliographies end each chapter. There is a subject, artist, and title index. Each volume ends with color and black-and-white reproductions.

---

[25]For a review that points out the good and bad points of this particular disk as well as those that attempt the same thing, either on a CD-ROM or online, see Bernard Sharratt's review "Please Touch the Paintings" in *The New York Times Book Review*, March 6, 1994, pp. 3–100, and Cheryl LaGuardia's *Library Journal* column (September 1, 1995, pp. 215–216) on art discs. The combination of print and graphic material, particularly on CD-ROMs and through the Internet Web, is most obvious in titles dealing with art. There are scores of CD-ROMs that center on art. Some are concerned with specific collections (Tate Gallery, Attica Cybernetics Ltd.) or with artists (Great Artists, Attica Cybernetics), or in a broader sense with architecture (The Ultimate Frank Lloyd Wright, Microsoft) and related art subjects. Typical museum collections on CD-ROMs are discussed by David Noack in "Visiting Museums Virtually" (*Internet World*, October 1995, pp. 86–91).

What should the librarian do? The choice is simple. In a smaller library the prohibitive cost of the larger art set eliminated it as a consideration. The lower cost of several excellent one- and two-volume art encyclopedias solves the problem. And for those who enjoy art at a computer, the low-priced Microsoft entry is a second, good choice. Larger libraries should have them both as well. The real problem will arise when there are dozens, rather than one or two art encyclopedias on CD-ROM. As of now it is a clear field for Microsoft.

History

Print: Civilization of the Ancient Mediterranean: Greece and Rome. New York: Charles Scribner's Sons, 1988, 3 vols. $259.
No electronic format.

Print: Dictionary of the Middle Ages. New York: Charles Scribner's Sons, 1983–1990, 13 vols. $940.
No electronic format.

Greece and Rome occupy considerable space in any multiple-volume general encyclopedia, but neither is treated in the depth desirable for either the expert, or the would-be expert, who needs to know, for example, how women fared in one or both of the societies during a certain time frame. It is for that type of query that one turns to a subject set such as this, or the numerous other works in the field, for example, the excellent one-volume *Oxford History of the Classical World* (New York: Oxford University Press, 1988).

The three-volume Scribner's work covers the sciences, social sciences, and of course the humanities in the two civilizations, but taking a somewhat different approach. Rather than a chronological system, there are 95 individual essays by as many experts. Organized under broad subject headings, each article considers the topic in some depth. Illustrations accompany some of the pieces, and there is a detailed index in the final volume.

History attracts many publishers but, as indicated, the leader in historical sets is Scribner's. For example, between 1983 and 1990 they published the first edition of the *Dictionary of the Middle Ages.* The 13-volume work (including a detailed index) moves from A.D. 500 through to the end of the period A.D. 1500. There are over 5000 articles by some of the world's leading historians in this area.

A fascinating point about the coverage is the emphasis on daily life of average people. One moves from the monastery to the farm, not just from the castle to the king. In addition, there are biographical pieces on both famous and minor figures. There are some black-and-white and a few color illustrations, but the strength of the set is the text, not the illustrations. The articles are by 1300 scholars from approximately 30 countries. It can be read as a history book as well as used for a reference work—an almost ideal situation.

Library Science

Print: Encyclopedia of Library and Information Science. New York: Marcel Dekker, 1968 to date, 35 vols., plus supplements. $115 each.

No electronic format.

Even though it is controversial, the *Encyclopedia of Library and Information Science* cannot be faulted for its wide coverage and its ambitious effort. Some think there is too much material; others, that areas are not always covered as well as they might be, particularly by the contributors involved. The set is quite uneven. Sections of the writing are excellent, but they tend to be superficial and dated. The supplements, issued approximately yearly, are an effort to keep the complete set current. Actually, the lengthy articles in the supplements tend to be better than those in the primary set, and are a good source of information on major trends in library and information work.

Ironically, this is a major subject set that is not available in electronic format. Still, it makes the point that limited readership, limited interest, and limited funding is not conducive to CD-ROM or online versions of subject encyclopedias—even when dealing with library and information science.

Less ambitious, but more current and certainly better written, the *Encyclopedic Dictionary of Library and Information Science* (London: Routledge Reference, 1966, 700 pp.) is a one-volume approach to the subject. Edited by John Feather and Paul Sturges this book includes over 1000 alphabetical entries which provide information on all aspects of information science. While published in England, the contributions represent most European countries as well as the United States and Canada. The result is a truly international work. Note, too, that there are separate biographical entries. Numerous bibliographies are part of the individual discussions. At $150 this is a relatively inexpensive aid.

Parenthetically, even a cursory glance at the English publisher's catalog will indicate the extent to which encyclopedias cover every conceivable subject. The 1995 catalog, for example, includes over 100 titles from *Encyclopedia of Arabic Literature* to *The World Encyclopedia of Contemporary Theatre*. And this is only from *one* reference publisher.

Literature[26]

Print: Benet's Readers' Encyclopedia, 3d ed. New York: HarperCollins, 1987, 1091 pp. $45.

---

[26]It is hardly surprising that among all subject areas, literature has the greatest number of subject encyclopedias. And the number grows. The publisher of Benet's *The Readers' Encyclopedia of American Literature* (1991) produced *Readers' Encyclopedia of Eastern European Literature* two years later. More titles of this type are planned. Oxford University Press publishes numerous literature titles from *The Short Oxford History of English Literature* (1994) to the *Oxford Companion to Classical Literature,* 2d ed. (1989). At least as of 1995, the publisher has no plans to update the CD-ROM any faster than the printed set, that is, every five years. This will likely change, particularly as a strong advantage of an electronic database is the ease of update—in this case overlooked.

No electronic format.

There are scores of one- and two-volume guides to literature, most of which are particularly suited for the ready-reference questions: "When was R. R. Boyd born?" "When did she die?" "What did she write?" "How important is her *Tale of Three Horses* among her other works? And on and on. One finds answers in these guides.

There is no better-known one-volume literature reference than *Benet's Readers' Encyclopedia*. Named after its first compiler, William Rose Benet, this is an alphabetically arranged, short-entry format of the world's literature and arts. The close to 9500 entries move from biblical personalities to best-selling authors, right up through and including most of 1987. Much of the data are in handy chart or outline form. Mentioned are not only literature, but also the other arts, from painting and opera to the military. The explanations are usually short, clear, and well written.

Benet, as it is called by librarians, deserves a place on the ready-reference shelf right next to *Bartlett* and *World Almanac*. It is a most valuable aid, and one, by the way, which can be recommended to almost anyone as the ideal birthday or holiday gift.

Music

Print: The New Grove Dictionary of Music and Musicians, 6th ed. New York: Macmillan Company, 1980, 20 vols. $2300, paperback, $500.
No electronic format.

The 20-volume *New Grove* is unquestionably the standard set in the field of music. Like earlier editions it is extremely reliable, drawing on the experience and skills of over 2500 contributors. While of value to reference librarians, primarily for the detailed articles on pre-twentieth-century music and musicians, the latest edition now includes detailed information on modern musical life, covering not only the contemporary classical composers and performers, but also those from popular music, including the vast area of folk music.

There are some 22,500 articles with over 3000 illustrations which, according to the publisher, occupy about 7 percent of the page space. In addition, there are several thousand musical examples. Of particular interest, in addition to the detailed material on music and the long biographical sketches, are the many bibliographies. Not only are these found at the end of articles but in numerous cases they are separate entries, for example, "Germany and Austria: Bibliography of Music to 1600." There is equal emphasis on lists of works by various composers. Still, there appears to be a consensus in many reviews of the set that the high points are the biographies. These are the best of their type to be found in any reference source, and a first choice for reference libraries. NOTE: In 1995 a paperback edition of the complete set was published. This is, by the way, a "best buy," particularly for individuals and for libraries with budget problems.

The New Grove Dictionary of American Music (1986, 4 vols., $695) is primarily an original work. One may find entries in *The New Grove Dictionary of American Music and Musicians* for the same material but nowhere in such depth as in this new work. For example, "Popular Music" is in the basic set, but here it is expanded to almost 22 pages. When the ads claim that 70 percent of the material is original to this set, they are right. Its primary contribution is the stamp of approval (often in elegantly written essays) given to American music in its many forms from the classical and jazz to folk and rock. It is exceptionally useful for biographical sketches and thoughtful pieces on regional contributions. A related, equally excellent work, again by the same publisher is *The New Grove Dictionary of Jazz* (1988, 2 vols., $350).

Psychology

Print: Encyclopedia of Psychology, 2d ed. New York: Wiley Interscience, 1994, 4 vols. $475.
No electronic format.

An award-winning set, this encyclopedia has a basic approach to psychology and related areas. It is found in most medium to large libraries. Coverage is broad from excellent history and background articles to specific material, and articles on therapy and research, which vary from region to region, country to country. All the disagreements among the experts are found here, as is the occasional broadside from the lay press.

As psychology touches so many human areas, one will find numerous articles on music, sociology, art, science, business, law, and so on. Whenever there is a call for a profile of the people involved in the human comedy/tragedy something is to be found in the four volumes. The quest for bits and pieces is helped tremendously by an excellent name and subject index. (Also, the fourth volume has an up-to-date bibliography, as well as biographical sketches of leading psychologists.)

About 400 contributors who sign their work, account for the approximate 2500 articles. Many of these boast charts, graphs, and other helpful illustrations. The purpose is to cover the subject in depth and there is little or no effort to simplify sometimes dense material. Jargon is limited, though, and a careful reading (sometimes with a good dictionary) will be worth the work.

The publisher offers a one-volume abridgement of the set, the *Concise Encyclopedia of Psychology*, for $100. The catch is that this is based on the first edition and is dated. Apparently a new edition is planned in the next year or so.

Religion

Print: The Encyclopedia of Religion. New York: Macmillan Company, 1986, 16 vols. $1400. (In 1993 the set was reissued in 8 volumes for $600.)

No electronic format.

Entries are current and arranged in alphabetical order with cross-references and an excellent index. There are superior bibliographies. Coverage is international and the authorities move with ease and clarity from Jewish and Muslim history and rites to the beliefs of the Hindus. There are superior entries for related areas from the occult and alchemy to atheism. Particularly noteworthy is the fine style of writing and editing which opens up the set not only to students of religion, but also to casual readers.

The field study of religion, as literature, has spawned many one-volume to multivolume encyclopedias. For example, consider the *New 20th Century Encyclopedia of Religious Knowledge* (New York: Baker Book House, 1991, 896 pp.), which is an evangelical Protestant view of the world and has a definite bias that appeals to many Americans. *The New Age Encyclopedia* (Detroit: Gale Research Inc., 1990, 586 pp.) is at the other extreme. The subtitle fairly well embraces the scope of the work: "a guide to the beliefs, concepts, terms, people, and organizations that make up the new global movement toward spiritual development, health and healing, higher consciousness and related subjects." An ideal work for the alternative side of the library collection.

Science

CD: McGraw-Hill Multimedia Encyclopedia of Science and Technology. New York: McGraw-Hill, Inc., 1995 to date. $1300 (discounted to $495 or less).
Print: McGraw-Hill Encyclopedia of Science and Technology, 7th ed. New York: McGraw-Hill, Inc., 1992, 20 vols. $1900.

Print: McGraw-Hill Concise Encyclopedia of Science and Technology. 1995, 1200 pp. $115.
No electronic format.

CD: Mammals: A Multimedia Encyclopedia. Washington, DC: National Geographic Society, 1990 to date. $99–$150.
Print: Book of Mammals. National Geographic Society, 2 vols. Various dates, prices.

Thanks to its frequent revision (about every five years), the *McGraw-Hill Encyclopedia of Science and Technology* is considered a basic set for library or home. The 1992 edition has approximately 7700 articles of varying length, and over 14,000 illustrations. There are numerous charts, graphs, and summaries that make even the most detailed articles exceptionally easy to follow. Written with the layperson in mind, the encyclopedia can be read with ease even by the most scientifically naive individual. The writing style is directed to teenagers and adults.

The set is ideal for an overview of a given topic, whether it be tube worms or artificial intelligence, and it has an excellent index, which makes it suitable for ready-reference purposes. Also, one part of the index is called the "Topical Index." It groups all the articles under major subject headings for the person who wants to see relationships among various subjects. There are numerous cross-references for ease of use and current bibliographies.

Published on a five-year schedule, the next edition of the 20-volume *McGraw-Hill Encyclopedia of Science and Technology* is slated for 1997. Meanwhile, issued each fall, the volume *Technology* acts as an update for the basic set. Unlike many yearbooks, it has references from its pages to the encyclopedia, and it can be used in conjunction with the main encyclopedia.

The CD-ROM format of the *Multimedia Encyclopedia of Science and Technology* includes the printed set (1992), as well as the *McGraw-Hill Dictionary of Scientific and Technical Terms* (5th ed., 1994). Almost everything found in the well-established printed set is available in the electronic format. The usual plus features are included: (1) boolean logic, (2) hypertext linking, (3) 39 animation sequences, (4) 45 minutes of audio demonstrations, and (5) 550 of the over 14,000 illustrations from the printed work. There is the rub, as in so many encyclopedias that turn from print to an electronic format. In an effort to contain the set in one disk, in an effort to save valuable space, there is a need to cut back. And that cutback inevitably comes with the illustrations. The rational is that the high-powered capacity for searching and the added features more than make up for the loss of illustrations—and, not incidentally, a lower price than the printed set, even with the addition of a valuable dictionary.

Which is best—print or CD-ROM? That depends on use. For younger people and for laypersons the CD-ROM is a best buy. On the other hand, where experts or semiexperts are concerned the print set is preferable. Actually here, as in many cases, it's pretty much of a draw. The final decision is up to the particular need of the library.

The print *McGraw-Hill Concise Encyclopedia of Science and Technology* has more than 7300 articles which cover close to 80 major subject and technological areas. The numerous illustrations include photographs, charts, diagrams, and other graphic devices to clarify sometimes difficult points of explanation. The dictionary, often updated, contains about 100,000 terms.

Produced by the National Geographic Society for children from about ten to sixteen years of age *Mammals: A Multimedia Encyclopedia* has the familiar full-screen photograph with brief captions. But that, of course, is only the beginning. The user can call up the animal information and then (1) see 45 full-motion clips of the mammals in action, (2) listen to 155 digitized vocalizations, (3) play a game, (4) locate definitions, (5) hear a narrator pronounce animal names, and so forth. Many of the film clips are from the well-known television features from the Society. The children control the presentation by using graphical icons. The CD-ROM is taken from the Society's two-volume set, *Book of Mammals*.

On the same topic, yet at another extreme is the CD-ROM *McGraw-Hill Multimedia Encyclopedia of Mammalian Biology* (1992, $495). Based on the almost legendary set, Grimzek's *Encyclopedia of Mammals*, the electronic version has the entire text of that work, as well as its numerous illustrations. The reason for purchase is the addition of hypertext features from sound and video clips to graphics. This work is primarily for advanced high school students and adults.

Science seems particularly suited to hypertext and there are scores of other possibilities for adults, children, and a mix of the audiences. For example: *Multimedia Audubon's Birds* (Portland, OR: CMC Research, $49.95) and the same company's *Multimedia Audubon's Mammals* ($49.95). All have sound, motion, and delights for the user, no matter what age.

SUGGESTED READING

Andrasick, Kathleen, "Multimedia Encyclopedias Come of Age," *English Journal*, December 1993, pp. 77–78. A short analysis of three encyclopedias with notes on evaluation.

Beckman, David, "The Evolution of Encarta," *CD-ROM World*, July 1993, pp. 26–34. While somewhat dated, this is an excellent overview of the technology required to produce a CD-ROM encyclopedia. From testing to the marketplace, the author covers all relevant points in easy-to-understand language.

Gross, John, "The Book of Books, The Columbia Encyclopedia," *The New York Review of Books*, June 9, 1994, pp. 25–28. A famous critic and author takes a close look at America's best one-volume encyclopedia and decides it could be much better. Along the way he points out the various steps necessary to properly evaluate this work, as well as almost any reference title.

Jasco, Peter, "Encyclopedias on CD-ROM," *Link-up*, September–November 1994, pp. 24, 27. A two-part series that offers a thorough, objective view of the general sets available on CD-ROM. Along the way the author points to the good and bad points of the format itself for such sets.

"Pseudonym or Hoax?," *Chronicle of Higher Education*, May 26, 1995, pp. 1–26. In this exposé article, the *Chronicle* reveals a number of articles in the *Encyclopedia of Homosexuality* (Garland, 1990) that are attributed to Evelyn Gettone, while actually the work of the encyclopedia's editor. Highly acclaimed by the library press, the encyclopedia offers a fine example of how even the best critics may be fooled. See the library world response in *Library Journal*, June 15, 1995, p. 58, "In Reference We Trust?"

Salpeter, Judy, "The Multimedia Encyclopedias Face Off," *Technology and Learning*, September 1993, pp. 30–36. Comparison of three titles *(Compton's, Encarta, Grolier)* in the young people's encyclopedia set. The comparison points to the various methods of evaluating electronic encyclopedias, as well as other electronic resources.

Shoemaker, Joel, "The Bottom Line: Are CD-ROM Encyclopedias Worth the Cost?" *School Library Journal*, February 1995, pp. 28–31. The answer to the article query: "Buy both . . . I advocate the use of both CD-ROM and print encyclopedias." To reach this conclusion the author compares price and other features of the basic children's works from *Encarta* to *Compton's*. By the end of the year, interestingly enough, most of the CD-ROM prices had been cut by as much as one-half.

Thomas, Gillian, "A Position to Command Respect," *Women and the 11th Britannica*. Metuchen, NJ: Scarecrow Press, 1992. The author traces the development of an editorial policy which, for the first time in the history of encyclopedias, encouraged women contributors.

Valauskas, Edward, "Britannica Online," *Database*, February/March 1995, pp. 14–20. A laudatory article, without comments about earlier failures of Britannica to realize the importance of an electronic format, this is interesting in that it outlines the possibilities of an encyclopedia online—particularly through the Internet. The high cost of the set online is considered, but brushed aside.

Wertsman, Vladimir, "Reference Sources and American Ethnic Groups," *The Acquisitions Librarian*, 1993, no. 9/10. Part of this discussion concerns encyclopedias and their problems in terms of ethnic groups served or not served.

CHAPTER EIGHT
READY-REFERENCE SOURCES: ALMANACS, YEARBOOKS, HANDBOOKS, DIRECTORIES

The reference desk is at the center of a daily quiz show. A puzzled student wants to know who said "I am not what I am." (Answer: Iago in Shakespeare's *Othello*. Source: Any book of quotations.) A woman asks: "How do I know whether my pain threshold is low or high?" (Answer: The body makes its own pain killer, endorphin. Depending on the number of pain sites and the endorphin response, the pain will be slight or high. It varies with individuals. Source: CD-ROM: *Mayo Clinic Family Health Book*, 1992.) A child questions, "What's the largest volcano explosion in history?" (Answer: Debatable, but probably Mt. Krakatau in Indonesia in 1883. Source: *World Almanac*.) And a traveler wonders, "What is the most remote city on earth?" (Answer: Perth, Western Australia. Source: *Guinness Book of Records*.) Actually, most ready-reference queries are more prosaic. They tend to center around names and addresses, with answers found in directories.

Grace Anne DeCandido, editor and critic, calls it "the back fence, the neighborhood bar, the lunch counter of the profession."[1]

Correct answers to ready-reference questions, which can be plucked from a dozen or so books near the reference desk, will resolve instantly any heated argument or the idle curiosity of a child. When standard sources (many of which are discussed in this chapter) fail, then there are emergency escapes: (1) Call a library near you, particularly where you have a friend. (2) Put the query to an expert—or do it directly by Internet calling, faxing, and so forth if you know the expert's name and address. Countless directories help you find the names

[1] *American Libraries*, October 1994, p. 831.

of experts, organizations, and havens where the ready-reference query can be put to rest, for example, *The Encyclopedia of Associations,* to name only one.

Where time is no problem, try "The Exchange," a regular feature in *RQ,* the reference librarian's own journal from the American Library Association. Here, each quarter, difficult questions are asked and often answered in subsequent issues. Then there is the Internet, which may be a bit quicker. There are numerous Listservs on the Net, including probably the most used, Stumpers-L Listserv. In 1994 a Stumpers archive was created at Rosary College's Graduate School of Library and Information Service in River Forest, Illinois. This is employed for questions and answers. In either form, the advantage is twofold: First, one may consult with fellow librarians who have a question or an answer. Second, resource sharing on a grand scale is offered by Stumpers in that hundreds of various library collections are linked.

The Internet Whois directory sometimes provides the required address, phone number, and e-mail entry. A more thorough search is offered by Knowbot information service which searches the Net for other systems including MCI Mail. It takes familiarity with the Net and its many possibilities to zero in on specific answers to equally specific questions. Normally it is faster to consult a printed source or its equivalent electronic format. Still, when an expert is needed, when a question simply can't be answered by standard sources, the Internet is an amazing resource.

The ready-reference question usually requires no more than a minute or two to answer. But it may develop into an involved question when (1) one cannot immediately locate the source of the answer and must spend much time and effort seeking it out, or (2) the question becomes a search or research topic because the person asking it is really in need of more data than the query implies. For example, someone who wants the address of a corporation may actually want not only that address, but also information on how to apply for a position with that firm, lodge a complaint, find data to prepare a paper, or make an investment. The ready-reference question may be only an opening gambit for the person who uses it to start the interview dialogue.

It is this latter development—the possibility that a ready-reference question may become more complex—which supports the view that professional librarians should be on duty at the reference desk. Although it is true that someone with a minimum of training is able to find a book to answer a question about a title or an address, it requires an expert to know when the query is really an opener for a complex series of other questions on the same or a related topic.

Much of ready reference might be dismissed as trivia, as beneath the dignity of the librarian. Nevertheless, the librarian is urged to treat each question seriously—unless in residence at the Vatican Library, where the guide carries a warning that any reader who asks more than three "senseless" questions will be expelled. (Just who evaluates what is *senseless* is not explained.)

One person's trivia is another's major concern. Looking up a fact about business may help someone decide on the course of an investment or the future of a career. Checking a trend in climate or the amount spent for arms may trigger or settle an argument. The entire course of a meeting or courtship may depend on the turn of a rule of order or the interpretation of a rule of etiquette.

There are several periodicals which focus on odd facts and particularly on the work of the American, Charles Fort (1874–1932). Fort wrote a number of books which were a combination of data from encyclopedias and strange facts gathered in, say, any of the *Guinness* titles. Out of these works, out of his propensity for finding peculiar facts, grew the flourishing Fortean Society and a term associated with the strange, "forteanism." Actually, Fort is said to have denied the truth of most of his "facts," but they make entertaining reading, for example, see a copy of the *Fortean Times* (Box 2409, London, England NW5 4NP).

Only the Facts

Ready reference is about facts, as Mr. Gradgrind of Dickens' *Hard Times* knew: "Now what I want is, facts. . . . Facts alone are wanted in life." An experienced librarian can field ready-reference questions with the grace and speed of an expert ballplayer. The queries range from the meaning of *lucent* to the meaning of a sign pointing to the reference section. The importance of ready reference is seen by a regular advertisement in *Library Journal* for Gale Research Inc. It is called "Ready Reference" and is a "page of tips, techniques, and rules of thumb contributed by our readers for librarians."

Publishers of books, magazines, CD-ROMs, newsletters, and other forms of communication often have a specific department devoted to fact-checking. It is essential to be certain the printed, written, or spoken word is an accurate word. The fact checkers use the tools familiar to any good reference librarian— telephones, CD-ROMs, networks, and shelves of ready-reference books from handbooks to encyclopedias and maps.

EVALUATION

The general rules for evaluating a reference work, from audience to cost, are applicable to ready-reference titles. Some works have specific points to evaluate, and these will be considered as the chapter moves along.

Outside the scientific community, there are very few "facts" per se. In the humanities and social sciences, almost everything is up for interpretation, debate, and reevaluation. Often the so-called facts allow us to behold ourselves and make sense of the world in a way that is comfortable. A case in point is almost any political debate where each side seems to be discussing an entirely different set of conditions, with almost as many solutions.

To some extent we all rely on what reference works say a fact is, but these should be tested regularly. Is it a fact, or an opinion? Is the fact no longer true, that is, has it been bypassed by new findings? For example, what is one to make of the book which states categorically that "babies should be handled as little as possible." A common notion (or fact) in the nineteenth century, this belief has been canceled out by experiment and common sense in the twentieth.

An invaluable way to quickly check a fact is to see its original source. *World Almanac,* like most ready-reference works, clearly indicates where information is obtained. If a reference work does not show a fact source, one should be doubly cautious.

Points of Evaluation

Particular points of evaluation for ready-reference works should include:

1. *Arrangement.* Is the work easy to consult for quick facts? An index is an absolute necessity. The only exception is if dictionary order with brief entries is used, as in the classic *Brewer's Dictionary of Phrase & Fable* (London: Cassell, 1870 to date). This work has gone through numerous editions and is a core item for checking out odd facts, particularly of a literary nature. When in an electronic database and arrangement is of no importance, one should ask equivalent questions, that is, Can boolean logic be employed? Are there subject terms? Can key words be used?

2. *Current information.* This problem is overcome by almanacs, yearbooks, and titles that are updated once each year. Others have semiannual or more frequent additions, as for example, *The Gale Directory of Databases.* This has regular twice-each-year updates. Where data must be minute by minute and up to date, there is nothing to compare with the online databases.

3. *Illustrations.* Whereas most ready-reference queries are verbal and can be answered the same way, there does come a time when one illustration is well worth the proverbial thousand words. Therefore, where appropriate, one should test the ready-reference work for adequate illustrations.

GENERAL FACT BOOKS

The titles discussed are considered "basic" by reference librarians, although any given library, librarian, or situation may have a different list. Scores of fact books are published throughout the world each year. When one goes out of print two more rush in. All of these, or at least those published by a reliable firm, can be used in a library. As with books of quotations, there can't be too many about. There is always an odd query, a peculiar fact that can be dug out of one of these less-well-known titles.

The obvious problem of looking for a fact in a haystack of various titles, on shelf after shelf of books, can be resolved by an electronic database. A dozen, a hundred, a thousand or more print titles in full-text online (or on a CD-ROM) should allow one to seek the fact throughout the ready-reference landscape in a matter of seconds, instead of sometimes hours. As of now there is no such single work about, but it will come shortly.

Meanwhile, there are the standard titles, such as the *Guinness Book of Records*, as well as numerous lesser-known works. Just to give a notion of what is available, here are a few of the fact books published since 1990. They are representative, and only begin to indicate what is available. (Note: All are given in print format.)

1. The *Encyclopedia of World Facts and Dates* (New York: HarperCollins, 1993) is compiled by Gordon Carruth and complements approximately 10 editions of the same editor's *The Encyclopedia of American Facts and Dates*, also published by HarperCollins. The titles are self-explanatory of scope. The world net pulls in about 50,000 facts, arranged chronologically under broad subject headings. A detailed index helps. One can fish here not only for dates, but also for a few brief words about each place, event, person, and so forth.

2. Henry Petroski's *The Evolution of Useful Things* (London: Pavilion, 1993) explains how practical objects came to be part of the daily currency. Here the author has short essays, paragraphs, and explanations about the earliest zipper, fork, paper clip, ring-top can, and other useful objects. Related titles from Gale include: *World of Invention* (1993) and *World of Scientific Discovery* (1993).

3. *Science and Technology Desk Reference* (Detroit: Gale Research Inc., 1993) is based on questions often put to librarians at the Carnegie Library of Pittsburgh Science and Technology. Fifteen hundred topics are answered in a question and answer format with full citations to close to 900 books used to find the answers.

4. *The New York Public Library Desk Reference* [Englewood Cliffs, NJ: Webster's New World (Prentice-Hall) 1989][2] is divided into 26 basic subject areas (including "Dates" and the "Animal World" to "Etiquette" and "Religion"). The book covers a wide area, although there are too many errors to make it entirely reliable. Where a fact counts, it might best be double-checked in another source.

5. *The Cambridge Fact Finder* (New York: Cambridge University Press, 1994) is a British-born guide to fact that, in the usual fashion, divides the world into broad subject sections, adds a good index, and compiles thousands of bits

---

[2]Although the title gives the impression that it is the work of The New York Public Library (NYPL), it is actually the brainchild of the publisher and a group of writers and editors. They put it together and, aside from the fact that it has the endorsement of the NYPL, it has little to do with the real questions put to that library. The NYPL did supervise the answers, however, and receives unspecified royalties from the publisher. The fact book is followed by related titles, *NYPL Encyclopedia of Chronology* and the *NYPL Book on Where & How to Look It Up*, by the same publisher. New titles with the NYPL signature appear once or twice each year.

of data. Cricket scores to varieties of common grapes vie for attention with endangered species and computers.

In short, there are hundreds of ready-reference works. Librarians more or less agree on a few that are essential. Beyond that, the specific choices depend on specific needs.

Although there are numerous specialized ready-reference sources, the librarian should not forget the general places to turn for answers, which are first and foremost, any of the good encyclopedias. Encyclopedias, particularly, are good for isolating ready-reference facts. One immediately thinks of the *Micropaedia* of the *Britannica* or the short, fact entries in the *World Book* described in detail in Chapter 7. All too often the librarian may be so anxious to match the specific answer to the specific question that the obvious encyclopedia is overlooked.

Then, too, for current data, there are no better places to turn than the numerous newspaper indexes, and particularly *The New York Times Index* or *Newspaper Abstracts*. The *Abstracts* alone may provide the needed answer. *Facts on File* is another excellent source. These and others are covered in Chapter 6.

The Odd Fact

CD: Guinness Multimedia Disc of Records. London: Guinness Publishing, 1993 to date, annual. $99. (Annual update, $49.)

   Print: Guinness Book of Records, 1955 to date, annual. $16.95.

CD: The Book of Lists. Soquel, CA: VT Productions, 1993, no updates. $30.

   Print: Book of Lists. Various publishers, editions, dates.

Print: Kane, Joseph N., *Famous First Facts*, 4th ed. New York: The H. W. Wilson Company, 1981, 1350 pp. $70.

   No electronic format.

The Guinness Book of Records, *The Guinness Book of Answers*, and *The Guinness Encyclopedia* are but three in a family of a dozen fact giants. Over the years the publisher has eliminated more garish facts, disgusting records by deranged individuals, and diverting horrors. Still, there is enough here to surprise, shock, and stimulate curiosity. There is always more data most people would just as soon never know, or quickly forget. For example, "Which newspaper holds the record for misprints per column inch?" *(The Times of London)*. "What was Heisenberg uncertain about?" (The location of subatomic particles.)

Although the *Guinness Book of Records* needs no introduction—it is among the top-10 best-selling books of all time, and known to almost all readers—it is worth reminding sports and game fans that it is a reliable place to check records. Divided into broad sections, it includes everything from the final scores of soccer and baseball contests to those of football and tennis. There are illustrations, some of them in color. Also, it features much trivia from the fastest wedding to the record speed for pushing a baby carriage. For example, Bozo Miller ate 27 two-pound chickens at one sitting; Alan Peterson holds the record for eating 20 standard hamburgers in 30 minutes. It is a place to find information on almost any winner, and the quest is aided by an excellent index.

The title is updated each year, and past editions are useful for sometimes out-of-the-way facts. A good part of every edition of *Guinness* consists of records set by swimmers, climbers, pilots, runners, and others determined to establish a new test for ultimate endurance and adventure. As there are no physical frontiers this side of space, adventuring today means doing old things in a new way.

The CD-ROM adds data from several Guinness works. The hypertext approach is as much for facts as for fun. There are, in addition to the close to 4000 records, approximately 600 pictures, video clips of record breakers in action, and many, many sounds of grunts, groans, and applause.

The best wines, the tallest, shortest, or fattest people, the Nobel Prize winners, the favored movie stars—well, just about any list is found in the various editions of *The Book of Lists*. (There have been three to four "editions" of the CD-ROM, although each new one tends to carry over data from the previous disk.) The creation of Irving Wallace and family, the book has been about for the past 20 years in various forms. It is likely to continue for another 20 to 100 years. The lists are compiled by the Wallace clan as well as numerous friends, outsiders, and critics. In addition to text, the books and the CD-ROMs include pictures and small bits of audio comments. The search patterns are broad and, in fact so broad, that it takes some clever navigating to find the specific answer. Be that as it may, the CD-ROMs (and print versions) often supply answers to questions that can be found nowhere else. It is a required item in most libraries and, if only for fun, in public and high school libraries.

Famous Fist Facts, simply called "Kane" after the compiler, is primarily concerned with American "firsts" in everything from the first toothbrush to a first major discovery. It is arranged in such a way that one may find an umbrella subject area and either browse or seek out the essential first fact. For example, under "Library" one finds the *first* library catalog (Library of Congress); first library chair endowed in a library school (Columbia University); first library periodical *(Library Journal);* first library building (Philadelphia); and so on. It indexes events by the days of the month, as well as year by year. It also contains personal names and geographical indexes.

ALMANACS AND YEARBOOKS

Although almanacs and yearbooks are distinctive types or forms of reference work, they are closely enough related in both use and scope to be treated here as a single class of ready-reference aids.

Almanac. An almanac is a compendium of useful data and statistics relating to countries, personalities, events, subjects, and the like. It is a type of specific-entry encyclopedia stripped of adjectives and adverbs and limited to a skeleton of information.

When most special-subject almanacs are published on an annual or biannual schedule, they are sometimes called yearbooks and annuals. Historically, the almanac per se was general in nature; the yearbook and the annual were more specific, that is, they were limited to a given area or subject. No more. There are now subject almanacs and encyclopedia yearbooks which are as broad in their coverage as the general almanac.

Yearbook/Annual. A yearbook is an annual compendium of the data and statistics of a given year. An almanac will inevitably cover material of the previous year, too. The essential difference is that the almanac will also include considerable retrospective material, material which may not be in the average yearbook. The yearbook's fundamental purpose is to record the year's activities by country, subject, or specialized area. There are, to be sure, general yearbooks and, most notably, the yearbooks issued by encyclopedia companies. Still, in ready-reference work, the type that is most often used is usually confined to special areas of interest.

Compendium. A compendium is a brief summary of a larger work or of a field of knowledge. For example, the *Statistical Abstract of the United States* is a compendium in the sense that it is a summary of the massive data in the files of the U.S. Bureau of the Census. As almanacs and yearbooks have many common qualities, they are sometimes lumped together as *compendiums*.

Purpose

These types of works serve several definite purposes in the average library. Among the more important:

Recency. Regardless of form and presentation, the user turns to a yearbook or an almanac for relatively recent information on a subject or personality. The purpose of many of these works is to update standard texts which may be issued or totally revised only infrequently. An encyclopedia yearbook, for example, is a compromise—even an excuse—for not rewriting all articles in the encyclopedia each year.

Although most almanacs and yearbooks are dated 1995, 1996, and so forth, the actual coverage is for the previous year. The 1996 almanac or yearbook probably has a cutoff date of late 1995. The built-in time lag must be understood. If, in middle or late 1996, one is looking for current data in a 1996 reference work, it simply will not be there.

Brief Facts. Where a single figure or a fact is required, normally without benefit of explanation, the almanac is useful. A yearbook will be more useful if the reader wishes a limited amount of background information on a recent development or seeks a fact not found in a standard almanac.

Trends. Because of their recency, almanacs and yearbooks, either directly or by implication, indicate trends in the development or, if you will, the regression of civilization. Scientific advances are chronicled, as are the events, persons, and places of importance over the previous year. One reason for maintaining a run of certain almanacs and yearbooks is to indicate such trends. For example, in the 1908 *World Almanac,* there were 22 pages devoted to railroads. The 1995 issue contained about 2 pages, while television performers rated close to 14 pages. The obvious shift in interest of Americans over the past fifty years is reflected in collections of yearbooks and almanacs.

Informal Index. Most of the reliable yearbooks and almanacs cite sources of information, and thus can be used as informal indexes. For example, a patron interested in retail sales will find general information in any good almanac or yearbook. These publications in turn will cite sources such as *Fortune, Business Week,* or *Moody's Industrials,* which will provide additional keys to information. Specific citations to government sources of statistics may quickly guide the reader to primary material otherwise difficult to locate.

Directory and Biographical Information. Many yearbooks and almanacs include material also found in a directory. For example, a yearbook in a special field may well include the names of the principal leaders in that field, along with their addresses and perhaps short biographical sketches. The *World Almanac,* among others, lists associations and societies, with addresses.

Browsing. Crammed into the odd corners of almost any yearbook or almanac are masses of unrelated, frequently fascinating bits of information. The true lover of facts—and the United States is a country of such lovers—delights in merely thumbing through many of these works. From the point of view of the dedicated reference librarian, this purpose may seem inconsequential, but it is fascinating to observers of human behavior.

GENERAL ALMANACS AND YEARBOOKS

CD: World Almanac in *Microsoft Bookshelf.* Redmond, WA: Microsoft Corporation, 1990 to date, annual. $50 to $195.

    Print: World Almanac and Book of Facts. New York: Newspaper Enterprise Association, 1868 to date. $11.95. Paper, $6.95.

Print: Information Please Almanac. Boston: Houghton Mifflin Company, 1974 to date. $21.95; paper, $10.95.

No electronic format.

Print: Whitaker's Almanac. London: J. Whitaker & Sons Ltd., 1869 to date.

$32. (Distributed in the United States by Gale Research Inc.)

No electronic format.

The titles listed here are basic, general almanacs found in most American libraries. For use and importance, they are ranked as follows: (1) *World Almanac,* (2) *Information Please Almanac,* and (3) *Whitaker's Almanac.* The order of preference is based on familiarity. Sales of the *World Almanac* (over 2 million copies) now exceed the combined sales of its two principal competitors.

Except for the *World Almanac* none is available in an electronic format. This will change, but as the printed volumes are so well known, relatively so inexpensive, the publishers see little immediate reason to switch over or offer a parallel electronic version.

With the exception of *Whitaker's,* all are primarily concerned with data of interest to American readers. To varying degrees, they cover the same basic subject matter, and although there is much duplication, their low cost makes it possible to have at least two or three at the reference desk. The best one is the one that answers the specific question of the moment. Today, it may be the *World Almanac,* tomorrow, *Whitaker's.* In terms of searching, though, it is usually preferable to begin with the *World Almanac* and work through the order of preference stated above.

All almanacs have several points in common: (1) They enjoy healthy sales and are found in many homes. (2) They depend heavily on government sources for statistics. Readers will frequently find the same sources (when given) quoted in all the almanacs. (3) Except for updating and revising, much of the same basic material is carried year after year.

Of the three works, *Whitaker's,* the British entry, is the most extensively indexed (10,000 entries), followed by the *World Almanac* (9000 entries). The cousins of the *World Almanac* feature discursive, larger units on such subjects as the lively arts, science, education, and medicine.

World Almanac

The *World Almanac* will tell the reader everything she or he wants to know about efficient driving, the literacy rate in Zimbabwe, and the elevation of Albany, New York. It provides brief, accurate essay pieces on topics of current interest. For example, there are sections on diet and a part devoted to forecasting the future. Still, the real strength of the work is in facts, facts, and more facts. A quick reference index, with 60 to 75 broad subject headings from actors to zip codes, provides access to the work. There is a 16-page section on maps and flags in color.

Microsoft Bookshelf, as noted earlier in the discussion of the *Concise Columbia*

Encyclopedia, is a package of ready reference works. One of these is the *World Almanac.* It is accessed by key words, subjects, and boolean logic. As part of a group of reference works it is in good company, and useful. But as a separate CD-ROM version of the *World Almanac* it has little to recommend it, particularly in view of the price which, for a group, is fine but for a single work hardly worth considering. Nevertheless the CD-ROM version has all the traditional assets of the form, particularly as no other general almanac is available in an electronic format. This, of course, will change and one will soon have all of the titles listed here available on CD-ROM, as well as online. NOTE: The price of the Microsoft package varies widely, and can be lower than $50 or higher than $195.

Information Please

The cousin of the *World Almanac* features discursive, larger units on such subjects as the lively arts, science, education, and medicine. *Information Please Almanac* expanded its contents to include medicine, the economy, and political and world developments. It has several pages of colored maps. *Information Please* gravitates more to the methods of encyclopedia yearbooks than to the standard form set by traditional almanacs. *Yearbook* in the subtitle emphasizes this focus as does the advertising, which stresses that it is the "most complete, up-to-date, easiest-to-use reference book for home, school, and office." While "most" is Houghton Mifflin's claim, it is certainly excellent. Its makeup is considerably more attractive with its larger type and spacing than the *World Almanac.*

Whitaker's

Whitaker's Almanac, as one English reporter puts it, "offers a magisterial guide to the Establishment, to projected high tides, recent sporting records and the pay of Field Marshals."[3] *Whitaker's* is distinctive in that, as might be expected, it places considerable emphasis on Great Britain and on European governments. For example, the edition has an almost complete directory of British royalty and peerage, with another 150 pages devoted to government and public offices. Other features include an education directory, lists of leading newspapers and periodicals, and legislative data. Each year the almanac includes special sections on items in the news, such as the conflict in Ireland, and current exhibitions. Usually from 60 to 75 pages are devoted to this "events of the year section." There are from 250 to 300 pages on Commonwealth nations and their activities, as well as major foreign countries. Other unique features include the only easily accessible list of salaries of the upper civil service, including Church of England stipends for dignitaries. No other almanac offers so much up-to-date, reliable data on Great Britain and Europe.

[3] *The Weekend Telegraph,* November 27, 1983, p. 28.

REPRESENTATIVE YEARBOOKS

There are two types of yearbooks. The first, and probably best known, is the general work that covers, as the title suggests, the past year's activities. The type found in most libraries is the annual encyclopedia yearbook which is used to check names, dates, statistics, events, and almost anything else that might have been noticed in the past year. Newspaper indexes, from the *National Newspaper Index* to *The New York Times Index*, often serve the same purpose, as does the weekly *Facts on File.*

Almost every area of human interest has its own subject compendium, or yearbook. It is beyond the scope of this text to enumerate the literally hundreds of titles. What follows, then, is a representative group and, more particularly, those "basic" or "classic" works that cross many disciplines and are used in some libraries as often as the familiar index, encyclopedia, or general almanac.

Government: International

Print: Europa World Yearbook. London: Europa Publications, Ltd., 1926 to date, 2 vols., annual. $450. (Distributed in the United States by Gale Research Inc.)

No electronic format.

Print: Statesman's Year-Book. New York: St. Martin's Press, Inc., 1864 to date. $65. No electronic format.

It is somewhat arbitrary to separate these yearbooks from the "general" category, particularly as they all relate directly to the type of material found in encyclopedia annuals. The major difference is an emphasis. The government titles stress the standard, statistical, and directory types of information, which change only in part each year. The aforementioned general yearbooks stress the events of the past year.

Published for over a century, the *Statesman's Year-Book* provides current background information on 166 nations. Along with a general encyclopedia and an almanac, it is a cornerstone for reference work in almost any type of library. It has a distinct advantage for ready-reference work: It is up to date and can be relied on for timeliness. It has a superior index. The indexes include a name, place, and product category.

The *Year-Book,* grouping countries alphabetically, begins with comparative statistical tables and information on international organizations. The first section is devoted to international organizations, including the United Nations. This includes useful charts of comparative statistics, such as price levels and wheat production. The quantity of information varies in proportion not so much to the size of the country as to the definite Western slant of the reference work.

The book arranges the information systematically. Typical subheadings for almost every entry concern heads of government, area and population, constitution and government, religion, education, railways, aviation, and weights and measures. There are excellent brief bibliographies for locating further statistical and general information and numerous maps showing such things as time zones and distributions of natural resources.

Europa

The *Europa World Yearbook* covers much of the same territory as its competitor, but it has several advantages. (1) Timeliness is one. Not all the material is updated (an anticipated weakness in yearbooks), but most of it is relatively current, and both volumes begin with a page of late information on election results, cabinet changes, deaths, and the like. The work is almost as timely as the *Statesman's Year-Book*. (2) It leads in the number of words and amount of information. (3) The first volume covers the United Nations and special agencies and international organizations by subject and European countries. (4) The second volume covers non-European countries. There is a uniform format throughout. Each country begins with a short introductory survey, followed by a statistical profile, the constitution, government, political parties, diplomatic representatives, judicial system, religion, the press, publishers, radio and television, trade and industry, transportation, higher education, and miscellaneous facts peculiar to that country. This wider coverage, particularly of the media, gives it a substantial lead for ready-reference queries over the other two works. The balance among countries is good.

Europa is far from perfect; the flaws continue despite its long publishing history. For example, the index in the first volume is only for the UN and international organizations. One must turn to the second-volume index for material on Europe. There is no composite index.

There are scores of titles covering much the same territory, although always in a somewhat different way. Europa, for example, publishes six related titles, which simply expand on the data found in the basic work, for example, *Africa South of the Sahara*, *The Middle East and North Africa*, and *Western Europe*. See, for another example, the data section of *Britannica Yearbook*.

Annual Events and Book of Days

Print: Chase's Annual Events. Chicago: Contemporary Books, 1957 to date, annual, 320 pp. $25.

No electronic format.

Print: American Book of Days. New York: The H. W. Wilson Company, 1978, 1212 pp. $75.

No electronic format.

These are available only in print. There are no electronic formats for the normal reason: They do not lend themselves to being "packaged" with another title and are long enough to warrant a separate CD-ROM or online treatment.

Questions such as "What happened on November 23?" or "I am doing a paper on George Washington. Who else was born on his birthday?" "What are the appropriate ways to celebrate Ground Hog Day?" are answered in numerous sources. Encyclopedias and almanacs, for example, list important events by the day of the year and usually give birth dates of important individuals. Some may offer suggestions on how to celebrate National Totem Pole Week. An easier approach is to look in one of scores of reference works specifically edited to tell the curious what made this or that day memorable.

A good example is *Chase's Annual Events*. Published each fall, it traces the events of the previous year, as well as marks the upcoming year's day-by-day celebrations. For each celebration or event, it gives the name of the sponsor(s). Of special interest is the attention to trivia. For example, January 1 marks a turn in events, but also is the time when there is the "announcement of the ten best puns of the year" and it opens "National Hobby Month." *Chase's* also includes more substantial information, for example, a good, short biography of E. M. Forster and an accurate account of the anniversary of the Emancipation Proclamation.

The American Book of Days is a classic that is updated infrequently. It is among a few ready-reference aids which really need little revision. The basic material—how and why to celebrate holidays—changes little from year to year, generation to generation. Beneath each day of the year the guide lists major and minor events. Most of these are explained in detailed essays which indicate, too, the traditional method of celebration. Particularly useful in schools, it puts most of the emphasis on the major days of celebration.

Numerous titles in this area range from *Anniversaries and Holidays* (Chicago: American Library Association, 1983), which offers succinct data and additional readings; to *Holidays and Anniversaries of the World*, 2d ed. (Detroit, MI: Gale Research Inc., 1990); and the classic *The Book of Days* (London: W. R. Chambers, 1864), which is reissued from time to time. This is the earliest of the genre and of value today as much a curiosity as a profile of Victorian historical and cultural views.

HANDBOOKS AND MANUALS

The next large group of ready-reference sources consists of handbooks, manuals, and directories.

Because it is difficult to distinguish between the average handbook and the average manual, the terms are often used synonymously, or the confused writers solve the definition problems by again using the term *compendium* for either or both.

The primary purpose of handbooks and manuals is as ready-reference sources for given fields of knowledge. Emphasis normally is on established knowledge rather than on recent advances, although in the field of science, handbooks that are more than a few years old may be almost totally useless.

The scientific handbook, in particular, presupposes a basic knowledge of the subject field. A good part of the information is given in shorthand form, freely employing tables, graphs, symbols, equations, formulas, and downright jargon, which only the expert understands. Much the same, to be sure, can be said about the specialized manual.

With some exceptions, most handbooks and manuals have one thing in common—a limited scope. They zero in on a specific area of interest. In fact, their particular value is their depth of information in a narrow field. There are countless manuals and handbooks. New ones appear each year, while some old ones disappear or undergo a name change. It is obviously impossible to remember them all. In practice, based on ease of arrangement, or amount of use, librarians adopt favorites.

Etiquette

Print: Emily Post's Etiquette, 15th ed. New York: HarperCollins, 1992. $30.

No electronic format.

In a country where the class system is denied, but evident to anyone, the etiquette book serves a useful purpose. It helps the stranger navigate through dangerous social situations. Librarians find, for example, the three most common concerns involving manners and form are (1) the arrangement of weddings, funerals, and special events; (2) the proper way to address someone in office, whether it be a politicians or a priest; (3) rules of personal behavior at meals, in conversation, and in the working environment. Obviously, there are numerous other specific problems but as one advertisement for an etiquette book explained: "To move ahead faster . . . survive longer . . . rise above the crowd . . . you need to know what's in this book."

What book?

Actually the answer is twofold. First, the library has the standards from Emily Post to Amy Vanderbilt to Judith Martin (Miss Manners) to Letitia Baldrige. These grande dames of the etiquette court are rarely challenged by a man.[4] The majority of aids to proper behavior, at least in the twentieth century, originate with women. This is equally true of the captains of the familiar newspaper and magazine columns.

[4]An exception: Nigel Rees, *Bloomsbury Guide to Good Manners* (London: Bloomsbury, 1993). However, it was not widely acclaimed, and is not recommended.

While the modern genealogy of etiquette began with Erasmus in the sixteenth century, today its primary ruler, if only a ghost, is Emily Post. She realized that a new, affluent group of middle-class people needed help on where to put the second fork. And in 1922 she brought out the first edition of a major work which is known throughout the world. Her success continues, carried on by her publisher and family. (She died, close to 90 years of age, in 1960.)

Today's etiquette book pretty much follows the Post pattern. It is directed to Mary and Joe average, not to aristocrats or those who head the Fortune 500. As such the guide is a great leveler, a democratic force. Needless to add, generation after generation claim that manners have deteriorated. Perhaps, but the sales of etiquette books increase. Every library should have the standards, and backups when a few are stolen.

There are now numerous basic books of etiquette, but the only traditional rival to Emily Post is the familiar *Amy Vanderbilt Complete Book of Etiquette* (New York: Doubleday, 1995). The author, of course, is dead but each new edition has another compiler. In this 1995 edition (the last was in 1978) the compilers are Nancy Tuckerman and Nancy Dunnan. Be that as it may, this follows the usual pattern of practical advice on everything from cellular phones (it is bad form to pop one out at the dinner table) to tipping, weddings, and funerals.

Interestingly enough, there is no etiquette guide available on CD-ROM or online. Are hackers beyond help?

Literature

CD: Masterplots II CD-ROM. Pasadena, CA: Salem Press, 1991, no updates. $1295.

> *Print* (All Salem Press): *American Fiction Series,* 1986; *Short Story Series,* 1986; *British and Commonwealth Fiction Series,* 1987; *WorldFiction Series,* 1988; *Non-fiction Series,* 1989; *Drama Series,* 1990; *Juvenile and Young Adult Fiction Series,* 1991; *Cyclopedia of World Authors,* 1989; *Cyclopedia of Literary Characters,* 1990. Note: All have various numbers of volumes in a set, and all have supplements.

CD: Monarch Notes. Parsippany, NJ: Bureau of Electronic Publishing, 1992, no updates. $99.

> *Print:* More than 200 separate pamphlets. Various prices.

Online: Barron's Book Notes. Hauppauge, NY: Barron's Educational Series, 1993. No updates. Available on America Online. Price per hour varies.

As far back as the Middle Ages, there were so-called cribs to assist students studying for an examination or working on a paper. There is nothing new about the medium and, in its place, it is a worthwhile form of publishing. A reference librarian may have mixed views about the desirability of such works for students, but that is a problem which students, teachers, and parents must work out together. It is an error to deny a place on the reference shelf to valuable sources, regardless of how they may be used or misused.[5]

Students often request plot summaries and other shortcuts to reading. By far the most famous name in this area is Frank N. Magill's *Masterplots,* a condensation of almost every important classic in the English language. Not only are the main characters well explained, but there is also a critique of the plot's highlights and its good and bad points. Somewhat over 2000 books are considered and there is easy reference to about 12,000 characters. Beyond these basics there are numerous stepchildren, cousins, and aunts to the main volumes of *Masterplots,* which is now out of print, but found in many libraries under various main titles and subtitles. *Masterplots II* covers books from the nineteenth century through to the 1990s. It is similar to the basic set, but adds female and minority authors, a welcome change. Also, it adds books published after the basic work.[6]

Masterplots II, up to 1991, on a CD-ROM is much less expensive than the collected volumes. As it is used often, it is a good purchase for most libraries. Unquestionably, as revisions are made to the printed volumes, as new works are added, the CD-ROM will be revised. Still, the material does not become dated and is valuable with or without revisions. The software allows for the standard type of searching patterns, and it is quite easy to use. Author, title, genre, and subject are the common access points. The directions on the screen can lead the reader to even more sophisticated searches such as "fiction of manners" or "roman à clef."

On CD-ROM the user finds the complete *Monarch Notes* series (at least up to 1996). The print 35- to 80-page pamphlets are familiar to almost any senior high school or college student. As a crib, *Notes* is useful for a summary of plot or content, character analyses, commentary on the text, author background data, and so forth. Searching follows standard paths by author, title, subject, or a combination. And while boolean logic is possible, it is much too involved for most situations where title or author alone is the usual navigational tool. Again, because the price is low the search patterns are rudimentary and sometimes require numerous tries. For example, some entries can be located with punctuation, others cannot. Closely related to senior high school and college English courses, the relatively inexpensive CD-ROM, which includes all the guides, is too useful to pass over. Libraries should consider this, particularly if they have *Masterplots* in print or in electronic format.

---

[5]Some librarians and teachers believe the cribs serve to virtually write a student's paper. For a more sophisticated approach to selling academic research, see "Shopping for Ideas" *The New York Times,* December 12, 1993, p. 7. This is a study of firms who sell finished student papers. By 1996 there was a CD-ROM available with abstracts of papers for sale. An eight-page paper on file is about $50. More advanced works run to $200 plus.

[6]For example, in 1993 *Juvenile and Young Adult Biographies* was added to *Masterplots II.* The four volumes ($365) inevitably will become part of the CD-ROM revision as will other earlier print additions published after the CD-ROM: *Poetry Series* (1992) and *African American Literature Series* (1994), to name but two.

As part of the consumer online service, America Online, *Barron's Book notes* offer the complete text of 100 cribs published by Barrons. Most are the classics from Beowulf to Shakespeare and Hemingway. The approach is similar to *Monarch Notes,* and while not a consideration for libraries, is a useful enough work for students at home.

Cliff Notes (Lincoln, NE: Cliff Notes, 1980 to date) contains even more familiar study aids. The firm was founded by Cliff Hillegass who mastered the art of condensing books into 70 to 90 easy-to-read pages. About 5 million paperback black-and-yellow copies are sold each year. *Notes* is not available in any electronic format, possibly because it does so well in print. The greatest audience for the notes are tenth, eleventh, and twelfth graders. Freshmen and sophomores are heavy users in college, but usually break the habit by their senior year. The 10 best sellers, in no particular order, include *The Odyssey, Hamlet, Great Expectations, The Grapes of Wrath, Huckleberry Finn, The Great Gatsby, Julius Caesar, Macbeth, A Tale of Two Cities,* and *The Scarlet Letter.*

The CD-ROM publisher of *Monarch Notes* and similar services offers the full text of close to 950 "literary classics" assigned in senior high schools, colleges, and universities. This is *CD-ROM: Great Literature* (Parsippany, NJ: Bureau of Electronic Publishing, 1992, no update, $99). In addition, there are a limited number of spoken passages and full-color illustrations. In view of the low price, the searching is rudimentary, that is, limited to title, author, subject. There is *no* key word search of texts. Some of the material is given in full, some in part. A bad choice for libraries, as all of the texts should be available on the shelves.

Great Literature is mentioned here for what it represents, not for what it delivers. No question that in the near future most uncopyrighted works of literature, both fiction and nonfiction, will be available in an electronic format.[7] The good side of this is that a work no longer has to be out of print. Even the most esoteric title may be viewed in any part of the world. The bad, or at least at the present less than favorable, aspect of the matter is that few people want to read for any extended time off a computer screen. This is fine when there is no choice. It is a last resort when for a few pennies or dollars one may pick up the same title in a bookstore.

Occupations

CD: Occupational Outlook in *DISCovering Careers & Jobs.* Detroit: Gale Research Inc., 1994 to date, annual. $495.

> *Print:* U.S. Department of Labor, *Occupational Outlook Handbook.* Washington: Government Printing Office, 1994 to date, biennial. $22.

[7]There are numerous full-text CD-ROMs available, but few are really satisfactory in that searching is primitive. One example: *Library of the Future,* 3d ed. (Irvine, CA: World Library, 1993 to date, price varies.) This has the text of some 1800 classics with illustrations and about a dozen limited video clips from films made from the classics. A questionable purchase.

CD: DISCovering Careers and Jobs. Detroit. Gale Research Inc., 1994 to date, annual. $495.

Although vocational guidance is not usually a part of the reference service in larger libraries, it is very much so in medium-sized and small libraries, and certainly in schools. When occupational and professional advice is given to students by trained counselors, inevitably there is a fallout of young men and women seeking further materials, either for personal reasons or in the preparation of class papers. The rush has grown so that even the smallest library is likely to include a considerable amount of vocational material in the vertical file.

Where a CD-ROM is available, *DISCovering Careers & Jobs* is a winner. It has most of the information people need as well as specific advice on the careers and occupations to which students are drawn. A simple menu allows the user of *DISCovering* to search for a career by subject, that is, "career category"; by employer, with 30,000 firms at the user's fingertips; and by job title, from librarian to mechanic. Current literature offers information from about 1000 articles, with abstracts and full text.

The *Occupational Outlook Handbook* is especially useful. This is a United States government publication, which cannot be copyrighted and therefore is available to Gale as part of their CD-ROM. Close to 700 occupations are discussed in terms that can be understood by anyone. Each of the essays indicates what a job is likely to offer in advancement, employment, location, earnings, and working conditions. Trends and outlook are emphasized to give the reader some notion of the growth possibilities of a given line of work. Unfortunately, the writers are often no more accurate in their predictions than economists and racehorse touts. An effort to update the title is made through the *Occupational Outlook Quarterly* (Washington: Government Printing Office, 1957 to date, quarterly). The periodical contains information on employment trends and opportunities.

Occupational Outlook is in company with other useful print companions. Among these: (1) The *U.S. Dictionary of Occupational Titles* (Washington: Government Printing Office, various dates), which lists all of the legitimate working careers recognized by the government. It is as much a mnemonic device as a reminder that there are thousands of occupations out there in addition to airline pilot and model. (2) Gale's own *Career Advisor Series* (Detroit: Gale Research, various dates) a six-volume set of books which is frequently updated. Each volume features a full description of the work, as well as how to prepare for the occupation. In addition there is good advice on interviewing, résumés, and the like. The series is of equal use to high school graduates and university students in quest of a career. (3) *Professional Careers Sourcebook* (Detroit: Gale Research, various dates) is an annotated bibliography covering 118 professional careers. Directory and background data are given as well.

Online employment services are on the Internet (through Usenet, for example, Help Wanted USA lists professional jobs as does Online Career Center and Federal Job Opportunity Board. The usual problems are evident: The material is out of date; posted résumés may be lost online, or never read; and some services require the applicant and the employer to pay for the services. Online employment services, usually through one of the consumer networks (Prodigy, America Online, etc.) are also available. The World Wide Web offers numerous services such as "CareerPath" which includes want ads from six major American newspapers. The service is frcc at http://www.careerpath.com.

QUOTATIONS

CD: Gale's Quotations: Who Said What. Detroit: Gale Research Inc., 1994, no update. $400.

CD: Bartlett's Familiar Quotations in Microsoft Bookshelf. Redmond, WA: Microsoft Corporation, 1990 to date, annual. $50 to $195.

> *Print:* Bartlett, John, *Familiar Quotations,* 16th ed. Boston: Little, Brown and Company, 1992, 1405 pp. $40.

Disk: The Columbia Electronic Dictionary of Quotations. New York: Columbia University Press, 1994. $89.95. (Note: On three diskettes, *not* CD-ROM.

> *Print: The Columbia Dictionary of Quotations.*

> *Online: Quotations Database.* 1979. No updates. DIALOG file 175, $60 per hour.

Print: The Oxford Dictionary of Quotations, 4th ed. New York: Oxford University Press, 1992, 1061 pp. $35.

> No electronic format.

Quotations are beloved by everyone, and they pop up everywhere. They may salt an after-dinner speaker's delivery, get a laugh on a late television show, or be enshrined in literature. It may be true that the love of the quotation is disappearing with the dominance of television. What is worse, quoting can be dangerous because these days few realize that the speaker or writer is quoting at all. Still, let's quote on.

If one wishes to find the precise source of a quotation, it is necessary to search a book of quotations. The librarian would hope (1) that it was an actual quotation, and not one made up or slightly changed by the seeker; (2) that the wording was approximately, if not precisely, correct; (3) and that the primary actors involved in the quotation were accurately named.

Indexing "who said what" is the role of the book of quotations. There are 250 to 300 in print. Actually, these books are not so much indexes as distinctive forms unto themselves, defying ready classification. Having found the quotation, for example, the average user is satisfied and does not want to go to the source, as he or she might when using the standard index to materials in collections. Be that as it may, the good quotation book will indicate the source, usually a printed work. Lacking a source, one is left in doubt, particularly when there may be a question about when and just who did say "You dirty rat" or "Eternal vigilance is the price of liberty."

How do a phrase or a few sentences become a memorable quotation? There are two or three rules governing compilers. First, if it is well known and memorable the quotation is automatically included. Shakespeare's "What's in a name? That which we call a rose by any other name would smell as sweet" is found in almost all books of quotations. Second, the quotation may reflect current feeling and policy. Third, it may drive home a point about morals, homespun wisdom, and so forth.

While the first two rules are applicable to almost all works, the third should be kept in mind as well. For example, Civil War general John Sedgwick's last words fit nicely into a work of last words or "black" humor but not into a book celebrating the skill of generals. This quotation is supposedly the general's last comment as he raised his head above the parapet in the Battle of the Wilderness: "Nonsense, they couldn't hit an elephant at this dist. . . ."

Electronic Formats

There is a need for quotations in electronic databases. Scores of questions cross the reference desk every week. Most librarians scramble for the standard guides listed here, and failing to find the subject or the specific words of the elusive quotation they begin to search every such book in the library.

A step toward a solution is suggested in *Gale's Quotations*, which the publisher claims has over 117,000 common quotations. This is about the number of quotations found in four to five standard reference works. What is needed, of course, is one which would have a minimum of a million quotations, and to do this properly, an online service is badly needed.

Given the need, why isn't there such a database? Answer: Each copyrighted quotation book is from a different publisher. Each represents the work of a different compiler or team of compilers. Each wishes to be paid. Each believes an electronic wedding with 100 or 1000 other quotation books would cut back substantially on potential income. One might circumvent this by using out-of-copyright titles as Gale has done, but this would eliminate the magic words for the past fifty years. Eventually the copyright problem will be resolved, but until then one has the single CD-ROM filled with at least an impressive beginning.

Gale's Quotations may be searched, as one would expect, by the name of the author or speaker, by a key word or phrase, and by year of origin of the quotation. This latter feature is useful when someone is quoted at length, such as American presidents and celebrities; but as there are few such people it is of little practical value. It is one thing to limit a search for words by John F. Kennedy, and quite another to use it for Shakespeare, the Bible, or for Dr. Johnson when most users have not the faintest notion of years involved. An added feature, of dubious use again, in the context of quotations is short bits of biographical material about some (but hardly all) the people who are authors of the quotations. This is taken from the same publisher's *Almanac of Famous People*. Still, with all its faults, it is a great and useful resource for busy reference librarians. And in time, as more quotations are added, it may develop into the needed single source of quotations so badly needed.

One CD-ROM producer, the National Information Services Corporation of St. Paul, Minnesota, publishes a number of CD-ROMs as sources for quotations. Among these: (1) *25,001 Jokes, Anecdotes and Funny Quotes* ($99) offers the complete text of about a dozen books from *Treasury of Wit and Humor* to *Complete Book of Insults*. The search for quotations is possible by key words and broad subject areas. While hardly a necessity for either library or home, it does provide some out-of-the-way places to pin down an elusive quotation. (2) The same company (for $59) publishes an equally useful CD-ROM: *Proverbs & Quotes for All Occasions*. Here the material is drawn from two titles: *The Prentice-Hall Encyclopedia of World Proverbs* and *What a Piece of Work Is Man*—a collection of unfamiliar quotations collected by Wesley Camp. (3) *Speaker's Lifetime Treasury* on CD-ROM ($129) is drawn from six sources including a handy *Complete Speaker's Almanac*, which offers suitable quotations for each day of the year.

Bartlett's

By far the most famous book of quotations is Bartlett's (as *Familiar Quotations* is often called). A native of Plymouth, Massachusetts, John Bartlett was born in 1820 and at sixteen was employed by the owner of the University Bookstore in Cambridge. By the time he owned the store, he had become famous for his remarkable memory, and the word around Harvard was, "Ask John Bartlett." He began a notebook which expanded into the first edition of his work in 1855. After the Civil War, he joined Little, Brown and Company, and continued to edit his work through nine editions until his death in December 1905.

The work is updated about every ten to twelve years and the sixteenth edition, published in 1992, includes numerous new authors. Justin Kaplan has added 340 new voices from Toni Morrison to Russell Baker in the new edition. Most of these are contemporary and, thanks to a famous word or two, have made their way to fame in the standard work. A few are historical and represent a new look at history; for example, the sixteenth edition has several more representatives of the early women's movement than has the fifteenth. The total is now around 2500 individuals. The number of quotations is claimed to be near 20,000.

The compiler of the sixteenth edition of Bartlett added hundreds of quotations from modern culture, including those found in movies, television, theater, and politics. A few of the easily recognized words indicate that while Shakespeare and the Bible continue to lead in number of quotations, there is nothing lacking in colorful modern summations. "Go ahead, make my day" (Spoken by Clint Eastwood in the film *Sudden Impact*) is alongside the memorable summary of the poor by President Ronald Reagan, "It's difficult to believe that people are starving in this country because food isn't available."

Bartlett's is available as part of the aforementioned *Microsoft Bookshelf.* The quotation may be searched through key words, authors, sources, subjects, and the like. Still, one cannot help but think that it might be even faster to simply look it up in the print source. It certainly would be less expensive.

The Columbia Electronic Dictionary of Quotations (and its print version) features about 18,000 quotations that have been found useful by writers and speakers. Many are familiar. In fact, most will be found in Bartlett's and other standard quotation books. The advantage here, although at a rather high price, is to have a single volume of quotations on three diskettes, rather than mixed in with other reference works.

The Columbia online database has the misleading name of *Quotations Database* with no indication that it is no more than a single quotation book on-line and, at that, not updated since 1979 with fewer quotations (about 14,000) than in the CD-ROM or print formats. At $60 a hour (and 50 cents per print-out) this is a poor buy for libraries and for individuals.

The Oxford Dictionary of Quotations is a popular book found in many libraries. The fourth edition represents substantial revision. According to the admirably written preface, selection is based on what is most familiar to a majority of people and, in this case, while the bias is British, most of the 17,000 quotations represent a considerable international tone and will be equally well known to educated Americans. There is no electronic version.

There are two other recommended sources for quotations: (1) "Another Look at Quotation Books" is an annotated guide to the genre in the *Reference Books Bulletin* (*Booklist,* November 15, 1993). This is updated from time to time. (2) *The Quote Sleuth* (Urbana: University of Illinois Press, 1990) is a detailed "manual for the traces of lost quotations." The author, Anthony Shipps, gives detailed reports on the major dictionaries of quotations and then moves on to specialized quotation titles. Along the way he gives scores of hints and suggestions on how to locate difficult-to-find quotations.

Concordances

There is another form of related quotation index. This is the concordance. A concordance is an alphabetical index of the principal words in a book—or more likely, in the total works of a single author—along with their context. A concordance is used in a library for two basic purposes: (1) to enable students of literature to study the literary style of an author on the basis of the use or nonuse of given words; and (2) more often, to run down elusive quotations. With one or two key words, the librarian may often find the exact quotation in the concordance. This approach presupposes some knowledge of the author. Early concordances were limited to the Bible; a classic of its type, often reprinted, is Alexander Cruden's *Complete Concordance to the Old and New Testament . . .* , first published in 1737. The laborious task of analyzing the Bible word by word, passage by passage, is matched only by the preparation of early concordances of Shakespeare.

The advent of the computer considerably simplified the concordance effort (for both editorial and production purposes). Today there are concordances not only to the Bible and Shakespeare, but to almost every major writer. *Books in Print* lists columns of such reference works from a *Concordance of Ovid* to *Concordances to Conrad's the Rover.*

ADVICE AND INFORMATION

A common question in reference service is when to give information, when to give advice, and when to give neither. Normally, the emphasis is on information, not advice. The distinction is important, because in some librarians' minds, advice and information are confused when medicine, law, or consumer information is sought by the layperson. Most librarians are willing to give consumer data, even advice (as this author believes they should about reference books and related materials), but some hesitate to give out data on medicine and law.

There is no reason not to give information about law or medicine. This does not mean the librarian is offering guidance. The trend today is to welcome legal and medical queries. Still, doubts may arise:

1. "I feel that I am practicing law (medicine) without a license." In no case has a library been named defendant in a legal suit on this ground. Of course, the librarian should not try to diagnose the situation or offer treatment (legal or medical), but simply provide the information required, no matter how much or in what form.

2. "I don't know enough about law (medicine) to find required information." There are now numerous books, articles, pamphlets, and television and radio tapes available for the layperson. These are reviewed in most of the standard reference review media. Furthermore, as with any subject area, the librarian soon becomes familiar with ways to evaluate a title for reliability, currency, or style of writing.

The sections which follow, on medicine, law, and consumer advice, point up specific problems and reference works. It is wise to remember that many basic legal or medical questions may be answered by consulting equally basic periodical indexes. The *Readers' Guide* and *Magazine Index* cover both general and some specialized magazines of interest to laypersons concerning consumer, legal, and medical problems. Newspapers, too, help by use the National Newspaper Index or NEXIS. And, of course, one should never forget excellent overviews offered in encyclopedias.

Medicine

CD: Mayo Clinic Family Health Book. Minneapolis, MN: IVI Publishing Inc., 1993 to date. $69.95–$99.95.

> *Print:* New York: William Morrow, 1990. $34.95.

CD: Scientific American Medicine on CD-ROM. New York: Scientific American, 1990 to date, quarterly. $645. (Individual CDs, $395).

> *Print: Scientific American Medicine.* 1978 to date, monthly. $245.

> *Online:* CDP, 1990 to date, monthly, $49 per hour.

CD: The Family Doctor. Portland, OR: Creative Multimedia Corporation, 1990 to date. $79.99.

CD: The Merck Manual in *Physician's Desk Reference Library on CD-ROM.* Montvale, NJ: Medical Economics Data, 1990 to date, quarterly. $595–$895. (See below.)

> *Print: The Merck Manual of Diagnosis and Therapy.* Rahway, NJ: Merck and Company, 1899 to date. $45.

CD: Physicians; Desk Reference Library on CD-ROM. Montvale, NJ: Medical Economics Data, 1990 to date, quarterly. $595–$895.

> *Print: PDR/Physicians' Desk Reference to Pharmaceutical Specialities and Biologicals.* 1947 to date, annual. $42.

There is consensus that librarians should neither interpret nor analyze medical data. It is equally true that the librarian should be scrupulous about medical reference sources purchased. The user must be able to understand the books concerning consumer health information. This can be ensured by (1) purchasing books written for laypersons; (2) purchasing medical dictionaries which give solid, clear definitions; and (3) purchasing or providing access to technical information which is not beyond the understanding of the better-educated or the more involved layperson.

In addition to the volumes listed at the beginning of this section as being appropriate for a library, there are a number of standard medical dictionaries; among those most often found in libraries is *Dorland's Illustrated Medical Dictionary* (Philadelphia: W. B. Saunders Co., 1900 to date). Frequently revised, this is the work over 80 consultants, who review all entries and the numerous illustrations. *Stedman's Medical Dictionary* (Baltimore: Williams & Wilkins: 1911 to date) is another often-revised work which has some of the more up-to-date entries.[8]

---

[8]Stedman's is available, for $69 to $99, on a diskette from the publisher of the print version. It adds some 85,000 definitions from a Merriam-Websters Tenth New Collegiate Dictionary. It is updated "as needed" but has no particular advantage over the print version.

There is considerably more to health information than simply selecting the best books and having current reference works available. The whole process of the reference interview may be quite different from the usual question-and-answer encounter. The reference interview should ascertain precisely what information is required and at what level of sophistication. Many librarians feel slightly uncomfortable because they think the type of information required is more personal than usual. Then, too, there are other problems that range from offering "bad news" about a particular disease, to the user who wishes to talk at great length about a personal difficulty. Nevertheless, the librarian is morally bound to remain objective, to give the right information, and to refrain from making judgments either about the patron or the advice given in a particular source.

Unquestionably the best guides, the best bibliographies of health books for laypersons, are found in the listing edited by Alan Rees: *The Consumer Health Information Source Book,* 2d ed. (Phoenix, AZ: Oryx Press, 1994). This annotates basic titles. The arrangement is by subject, that is, usually the medical problem. See, too, his *Consumer Health USA* by the same publisher (1995). This reprints 151 government publications that provide answers to many of the most commonly asked questions. Again, arrangement is by subject, in this case body parts and systems. See also, the final section on "National Library of Medicine's Health Hotlines" which gives toll-free numbers for emergencies and added help.

Several other directories and bibliographies assist the librarian and layperson. An annual feature of *Library Journal,* is "Best Lay Medical Books for Public Libraries." About 30 titles are suggested, and each is annotated briefly.[9] "Medical Reference Tools for the Layperson" is an ongoing selective list published by *Reference Books Bulletin.* The annotated work "emphasizes authoritative materials that can be used by the general public." It is updated every two or three years. The librarian might check the current books on health and medicine in any medium to large bookstore to gain an idea of ongoing interests by laypersons.

The librarian should look for current reviews in the *Library Journal, Choice,* and *The Booklist* where particular care is taken to point out flaws and the general reliability of medical books for laypersons. The reviews are important if only to help the librarian keep a current collection.

How else do the librarian and the layperson keep up with the latest medical advice and research? One can always turn to MEDLINE *(Index Medicus),* but this is much more than the average individual needs. There are scores, if not hundreds of volumes dedicated to informing the layperson, not simply the doctor. These can be found on newsstands and in bookstores. Their number

---

[9]See, too, Barbara Bibel, "A Remedy for Women's Health Collections," *Library Journal,* August 1993, pp. 69–72. This is a typical *LJ* annotated guide which offers practical bibliographical information and tips on how to use them. The author is an experienced reference librarian.

and titles change each month, and while many are indifferent, others are at least passable.

Mayo Guide

Under the familiar name of *Mayo* (the editor is a "widely respected Mayo Clinic physician") the CD-ROM offers a full range of information on medical problems likely to involve the average American family. Here one finds reliable answers to queries about exercise and child care to first aid and various diseases. The CD-ROM has added delights such as 500 color illustrations, 45 animations, and close to two hours of audio. Questions may be targeted by using key words and phrases as well as boolean logic. The text is clear and precise. For those with more time there are the usual menus and five large areas of discussion: modern medical care, human disease, life cycles, the world around us, and keeping fit. The medical care section gives diagnosis, care, and treatment tips. Generic and brand name drugs are covered as well as a splendid atlas of the human body. A nice feature is a type of cross-reference in the form of sidebars which refer the user to parallel topics of interest. All and all this is a first-rate CD-ROM for any library and, for that matter, many homes.

The print version of the Mayo title is precisely the same in content as the CD-ROM. While it lacks animation and sound, it makes this up with a low price and ease of use. Also, the illustrations are a trifle more well defined than on a computer screen.[10]

On a CD-ROM, in print, or online the *Scientific American Medicine* service is much the same.[11] The only real difference is the ability to quickly search in the electronic form, although cross-references and indexing in the print version are equally good. While tailored for laypersons, the CD-ROM does require patience and skill to use.

The loose-leaf *Scientific American Medicine* is updated monthly, making it one of the more current ready-reference health services. (The online version is on the same schedule. The CD-ROM comes out only every quarter.) Prepared and written by medical researchers and doctors, the service is divided into 15 sections from dermatology to rheumatology. Within each part one finds illustrations, charts, tables, and other graphics to help explain the sometimes technical details. The writing style is generally easy to follow, although it does presuppose a reader who is a college graduate or equivalent.

[10]The print Mayo guide is a best seller, averaging over one-half million copies sold from 1990 to 1992. It continues to sell, as it is updated frequently.

[11]The CD-ROM differs from the other two formats in that it contains a library of some 50 to 60 problems faced by doctors in managing patients. However, this is for physicians and not for laypersons. It is labeled as DISCOTEST.

Only the Mayo work matches this in depth of coverage and current advice on such matters as drug dosages, developments in treatment of given diseases, and excellent diagnostic hints.

A syndicated columnist, Dr. A. H. Bruckheim, is the compiler of *The Family Doctor*. It is little more than the questions and answers that make up his column by the same name. The publisher claims that there are approximately 2000 queries with short, easy-to-follow responses. In addition, the disk features information in 1600 brand name drugs, the human anatomy, 300 plus illustrations, and definitions of common medical terms. The anatomy chart offers three different approaches, with voice-over of proper pronunciation of 250 anatomical descriptors. Searching assumes the user knows little or nothing about medical terminology and it sometimes can be slow and plodding. What it may lack in sophistication, it makes up for in practical advice and current information. (The disk is updated once each year and, other than the weekly newspaper columns, has no print equivalent.)

The Mayo entry is by far the better, but *The Family Doctor* has enough good points to warrant inclusion in libraries. A similar version is available for $60 on disk for a handheld reader. It is called *The Portable Family Doctor* and while the content is recommended, the necessary access makes it a poor buy.

The Personal Medical Advisor (Los Altos, CA: Medical Data Exchange, 1992) is a CD-ROM that contains the complete text of seven print volumes. The series is the "Complete Guide to . . ." and runs from sports injuries to drugs and medical tests. Updated as needed, the guide sells for $150 to $300. It is a useful, although not necessary acquisition. On the plus side is the relatively low price and the ease of searching.

The Center for Medical Consumers Ultimate Medical Answerbook (New York: Hearst Books, 1995) describes the causes and the probable symptoms, as well as treatments of close to 80 common medical problems from acne to varicose veins. It is a balanced, trustworthy print compilation with frequent references to more extensive readings.

A much-used technical work, although suitable for certain library situations, is the *Merck Manual of Diagnosis and Therapy*. Published for many years as a manual for physicians, it is clear to laypersons with a medical dictionary at hand. Illnesses and diseases are described in relatively nontechnical language, symptoms and signs are indicated, and diagnoses and treatments are suggested. A quarterly CD-ROM update of *Merck* is found as part of the *PDR*, discussed below. But this costs an additional $300, and hardly seems worth it, even in medical libraries where there is instant access to MEDLINE.

PDR

The best-known and most often found pharmacology work in a library is the *Physicians' Desk Reference*. Frequently referred to as the *PDR*, it provides information on close to 3000 drug products. The publisher notes that "the information is supplied by the manufacturers." At the same time, the Food and Drug Administration has approved the material sent by the manufacturer. Brand, generic, and chemical names are given, and so, with a little experience, one can easily check the content of this or that drug. (A generic and chemical name index is a major finding device.) For each item, the composition is given, as well as such data as side effects, dosage, and contradictions. One section pictures over 1000 tablets and capsules, with product identification. The neatly divided six sections are arranged for easy use.

The CD-ROM *Physicians' Desk Reference Library* picks up the printed version. It adds related titles: the *Physicians' Desk Reference for Nonprescription Drugs* and the *Physicians' Desk Reference for Ophthalmology*. The complete text of *The Merck Manual*, is an optional add-on for another $300. It can be searched independently, or one can cross-search all titles. In addition to ease of searching, it has the advantage over the print format in that the CD-ROM is updated each quarter, rather than annually. If being completely up to date is not a major problem, and it is not for most libraries, then one should consider the difference in cost between the print volume ($42) and the augmented CD-ROM ($595–$895).

The *Physicians' Desk Reference for Nonprescription Drugs* on the CD-ROM *PDR* considers some 1000 over-the-counter products. Arrangement and content are much like the basic title, including a section with photographs of actual tablets and packages. It is particularly useful for an objective analysis not only of what the drugs promise, but also of any bad side effects. The printed volume (1980 to date) is issued once a year from the publisher of the *PDR*.

The same people who publish the *Mayo* health book have a useful addition to the *PDR*. This is the *Mayo Clinic Family Pharmacist* (1994 to date, annual, $59.95). The disc has trustworthy information on 7600 prescription and over-the-counter drugs. In addition there is space for a personalized family record and text on first aid. The personal medical record is unusual in that one may set up a record for individuals from when they had a physical checkup to drug allergies, vaccinations, and so forth.

The Pill Book (Carlsbad, CA: Compton's News Media, 1993 to date, annual, $40) is a question and answer format for 1500 drugs that may be suggested by a doctor. This is organized by name of drug, side effects, symptoms, and so on. Of the two, the *Mayo* is by far the easiest to search, but both serve the purpose of clarifying sometimes difficult questions about drugs and their use. Both would be an inexpensive, useful addition to a public library.

There are other CD-ROM products of value to a library, but with the reservation that most are too costly. Three examples:

Health Reference Center (Foster City, CA: Information Access Company, 1987 to date, monthly) is primarily an index to about 165 health care periodicals of interest to laypersons. The full text of some 130 periodicals is included, as well as 500 related pamphlets, and a half dozen popular books. Among the books is the *Columbia University . . . Home Medical Guide* and *The People's Book of Medical Tests.* This is, by and large, the best of all the index services in that it offers full text of numerous types of reference sources and concentrates on relatively easy-to-understand articles, pamphlets, and books. True, there may be too much in any given quest, but one is able to weed out what is not required. An excellent guide. Useful as this may be, the $5000 price tag makes it a questionable purchase. Eventually, the price will drop, and then it should be considered.[12]

Health for All (New York: CD Resources, 1982 to date, annual, $250–$350) is a CD-ROM that contains the text of some 140 books and documents relating to health administration and education. While not precisely a guide for laypersons, it can be used effectively in libraries to field queries about primary health care legislation, consumer health care problems, and anything that deals with the politics and problems of education. Here the price is right, particularly for larger libraries.

The CD-ROM *MDX Health Digest* (Los Altos, CA: Medical Data Exchange, 1992 to date, quarterly) covers a broad range of health news in popular and technical journals, newspapers, and newsletters. Abstracts may give down-home advice on back problems or provide a technical approach to disks which only a doctor would understand. A poor mix and a high price: $1900. It is included here to indicate that not all electronic databases are worth either the price or the text.

Law[13]

Legal questions are similar to medical queries in that they require more than an average knowledge of the field. This side of a professional law library, most librarians consult general works as well as specific laws of the state, city, and region. The section on law—in the discussion of indexes earlier in this text—indicates the basic places (such as LEXIS) to turn for current data, both specific and general.

Who asks what? In one survey of public libraries it was found that the people asking legal questions are primarily students and business people. Others want to know about divorce, wills, tax laws, and immigration procedures in up-to-date reference works. For an ongoing list of helpful legal books for layper-

---

[12]IAC, in its usual fashion, offers numerous prices that become lower as one goes from monthly updates to other frequencies and/or subscribes to other IAC indexes. A ridiculous, confusing system which, in time, will go.

A competitor is the *Health Source* (Peabody, MA: EBSCO Publishing, 1992 to date, monthly) which indexes 160 periodicals, many of which are in the IAC index. It includes the full text of 15 journals. The price, again, is prohibitive—$2000.

[13]Kathleen Lance, "Basic Legal Resources . . . ," *Reference Services Review,* Summer 1993, pp. 91–96. A useful, quick guide to the basics for medium to large libraries. Only print sources are included, but several of these are now available in an electronic format.

sons see the mid-year issue of *Library Journal* (usually June or July) where there is a roundup of suitable law guides. Three points should be kept in mind in purchasing a legal guide: (1) Is it current? (2) Is it written for nonlawyers? At the same time it should not be oversimplified. (3) Do the works clearly indicate when a lawyer should be consulted?

There are several much-used guides to legal research, but they are for the librarian. The average layperson wants the information, not a book on how to find it. The best guide for nonlawyers is Stephen Elias's *Legal Research* (Berkeley, CA: Nolo Press, various editions and dates). It gives step-by-step instructions, is frequently updated, and is reliable. Robert Schachner's *How and When to Be Your Own Lawyer* (New York: Avery, 1993) is a detailed guide that gives clear signals about when to hire or avoid a lawyer.

Consumer Aids

CD: Consumers Index in *Consumers Reference Disc.* Baltimore, MD: National Information Services Corporation, 1985 to date, quarterly. $695. *Print:* Ann Arbor, MI: Pierian Press, 1973 to date, quarterly with annual cumulations. $180.

Online: OCLC 1985 to date, annual. Rate per hour varies.

CD: Dialog Ondisc: Consumer Reports. Palo Alto, CA: DIALOG Information Systems, 1982 to date, quarterly. $375. Annual updates, $235.

Print: Consumer Reports. Boulder, CO: Consumer Reports, 1936 to date, monthly. $22. (*Consumer Reports on Health,* monthly, $24; *Consumer Reports Travel Letter,* monthly, $39).

Online: Consumer Reports Full Text. DIALOG file 646, $60 per hour. Also available on CompuServe.

Print: Brands & Their Companies. Detroit: Gale Research Inc., 1984 to date, annual, 2 vols. $395; supplement, $281.

Online: 1990 to date, semiannual. DIALOG file 116, $90 per hour.

The reference librarian is usually asked one of three questions about products and consumer protection: (1) "What is the best product for my needs?" (2) "To whom can I complain, or to whom can I turn for information about a product or service?" (3) "How can I protect myself from poor-quality products or services?" No one reference source answers all queries, although several are of particular value in locating possible sources. The best product answer may be found in numerous places, including articles indexed in *Readers' Guide* and *Magazine Index.*

Given the popularity of consumer-type information, and the various reference works it crosses and recrosses, many public and school libraries meet the problem by establishing special consumer collections or sections. These may include the whole range of Dewey numbers, and everything from books to magazines and video. The collection is used both for reference and for circulation, particularly when there is more than enough material to cover popular topics.

Current Consumer Material

The Consumers Reference Disc is in two parts, which may be searched together, or separately. *The Consumers Index*, covers reports in some 100 periodicals. Excerpts are included from the reviews and enough information is given to indicate a "buy" or "no buy" decision. The problem is that many of the indexed magazines offer consumer information that is biased in favor of the manufacturer. Rarely are the articles objective. On the other hand most, at a minimum, describe the product and this is often enough for many consumers.

The second part of the *Disc, Consumers Health & Nutrition Index*, indexes some 80 popular health magazines and is of limited assistance to those seeking data on nonhealth products. Still, as far as it goes, it can be useful. The problem is price. The *Disc* is useful, easy to search, and current. Still, at close to $700 is it worth that much more than the printed version, *Consumers Index*, at $180, which is also updated quarterly? The answer must be no. Granted, the print *Consumers Index* does not have the added *Consumer Health & Nutrition Index*, but the two have little in common. Otherwise, the printed version of the consumer guide is the same as what is found on the disc, but at a considerably lower cost. Still, no matter which format is selected, the work is valuable, particularly in public libraries where anxious consumers have anxious questions.

A practical, more reliable source of information on products is found in the well-known *Consumer Reports*. The electronic version goes back to 1983, which is sufficient for ever-changing goods. The only catch is that it is published quarterly, while the magazine comes out monthly. On the CD-ROM plus side is the addition of two good publications: *Consumer Reports Travel Letter* and *Consumer Reports on Health*. Complete text is included for all articles.

Again, the problem is cost. The initial disc is $375. Annual updates are $235. A subscription to the magazine, without the two added services, is $22 a year. A case might be made for the disc in that the magazine is so heavily used, but it is not really a close call. One might simply subscribe to several copies of the same issue for much less.

An equally good, but not as well-known, monthly is *Consumers' Research Magazine*, formerly *Consumers Bulletin* (Washington, NJ: Consumers' Research Inc., 1931 to date, monthly) with reports of the same type. Both magazines issue annual summaries in paperback, which should be kept near the reference desk. The best known of these is *Consumer Reports Buying Guide*, issued by Consumer Reports since 1936.

The question "To whom can I complain?" may be answered in many ways. At the local level, a call to the Better Business Bureau may serve the purpose. When one is trying to contact the manufacturer of the product, often a careful look at the container will give the address. If this fails, or if more information is needed, then the guide to brands is helpful.

Although there is no CD-ROM version of *Brands & Their Companies* (formerly: *Trade Names Dictionary*), it is available online. The print version, like the electronic format, lists close to 50,000 firms and for each gives trade names, trademarks, and brand names. There is a separate yellow-page section. Annual and semiannual supplements are issued. And the same update schedule is employed online. Unless it is heavily used, the online version is considerably less expensive.

In an age of catalogs flooding the mails, it is sometimes helpful to be selective. The reader may want to depend on personal choice rather than bombardment by mail-order houses. There are numerous directories to catalogs. A representative choice: *Catalog of Catalogs* (Kensington, MD: Woodbine House, 1987 to date). Updated about every three years this includes close to 13,000 catalogs under various brand subject headings from computers and baby care to games and high fidelity. The inexpensive paper reference work gives full data on where to get, usually, a free catalog.

How to Do Practically Everything

Hundreds of other types of how-to-do-it information books can be found in *Books in Print* and on many library shelves. "How-to . . ." books, magazines, newsletters, and online services are favored among many library users. These range from the car manual on repairing an automobile, to newsletter on how to become rich, to scores of books on home repair, to some rather unique services. Among the latter is the famous Dr. Ruth's advice on sex to a lesser-known expert Frank Sweeny. His organization tells the curious what "to expect and how to survive in jail. Our consultants are graduates of the Federal prison system."[14]

DIRECTORIES

Directory information is among the most called for in libraries, particularly public libraries. People often try to locate other people, experts, and organizations through addresses, phone numbers, zip codes, titles, names, and so on.

Staff-produced directories are found in almost all libraries. They augment the standard reference works, from the city and telephone directories to the zip code directory. The directory made by the local library includes such items as frequently requested phone numbers, the names of individuals and agencies in

---

[14]"Prison Graduate Sells . . . Words to Live (or Do Time) By," *The New York Times,* January 23, 1994, p. E8. A prison insider, the expert tells all.

the community, sources of help for difficult questions, often-requested names of state and federal officials, and a wealth of other miscellany. The Chicago Public Library reference staff, for example, lists the staff-produced files as the most useful source of data for daily reference work, matched only by the *World Book Encyclopedia* and the *World Almanac*.

Definitions

The *ALA Glossary of Library Terms* defines a directory as "a list of persons or organizations, systematically arranged, usually in alphabetical or classed order, giving addresses, affiliations, and so forth, for individuals, and address, officers, functions, and similar data for organizations." The definition is clear enough for a directory in its "pure" form; but it should be reiterated that, aside from the directory type of information found in biographical sources, many other ready-reference tools have sections devoted to directory information. Yearbooks and almanacs inevitably include abundant amounts of directory-type material.

Purpose

The purpose of directories is implicit in the definition, but among the most frequent uses is to find out (1) an individual's or a firm's address or telephone number; (2) the full name of an individual, a firm, or an organization; (3) a description of a particular manufacturer's product or a service; or (4) the name of the president of a particular firm, or the head of a school, or the person responsible for, say, advertising or buying manuscripts.

Less obvious uses of directories include obtaining (1) limited, but up-to-date, biographical information on an individual, whether still president, chairperson, or with this or that company or organization; (2) historical and current data about an institution, a firm, or a political group, such as when it was founded, how many members it had; (3) data for commercial use, such as selecting a list of individuals, companies, or organizations for a mailing in a particular area, for example, a directory of doctors and dentists serves as the basic list for a medical supply house or a dealer in medical books; and (4) random or selective samplings in a social or commercial survey, for which they are basic sources. Directories are frequently employed by social scientists to isolate certain desired groups for study. Because directories are intimately concerned with human beings and their organizations, they serve almost as many uses as the imagination can bring to bear on the data.

Scope

Directories are easier to use than any other reference tool, chiefly because the scope is normally indicated in the title and the type of information is limited and usually presented in an orderly, clear fashion. There are many ways to categorize directories, but they can be broadly divided as follows:

Local Directories. There are primarily two types: telephone books and city directories. However, also included in this category may be all other types issued for a particular locality, for example, directories of local schools, garden clubs, department stores, theaters, and social groups.

Governmental Directories. This group includes guides to post offices, army and navy posts, and the thousand and one different services offered by federal, state, and city governments. These directories may also include guides to international agencies.

Institutional Directories. These are lists of schools, foundations, libraries, hospitals, museums, and similar organizations.

Investment Services. Closely related to trade and business directories, these services give detailed reports on public and private corporations and companies.

Professional Directories. These are largely lists of professional organizations such as those relating to law, medicine, and librarianship.

Trade and Business Directories. These are mainly lists of manufacturers' information about companies, industries, and services.

The electronic format is suited to directories that need to be updated monthly or once a quarter or once a year. Numerous directories are available online and on CD-ROMs.

Additional Directory-Type Sources

The almanac and the yearbook often include directory-type information, as do numerous other sources of directory information:

1. Encyclopedias frequently identify various organizations, particularly the more general ones that deal with political or fraternal activities.

2. Gazetteers, guidebooks, and atlases often give information on principal industries, historical sites, museums, and the like.

3. A wide variety of government publications either are entirely devoted to or include directory-type information. Also, some works are directories in name (*Ulrich's International Periodical Directory*, for example) but are so closely associated with other forms (periodicals and newspapers) that they are usually thought of as guides rather than as directories.

Directory of Directories

Print: Directories in Print. Detroit, MI: Gale Research Inc., 1977 to date, annual, 2 vols. $315. Supplement, $185.

Online: In *Gale Database of Publications and Broadcast Media,* 1990 to date, semi-annual. DIALOG file 469, $84 per hour.[15]

The basic listing of directories is the *Directories in Print.* The annual publication (augmented by a semiannual supplement) lists more than 16,000 new or revised titles under about 26 broad subject categories from business to professional and scientific. There are a detailed subject index and a title index. Information for each entry includes the name of the directory, the publisher, address and phone number, and full description of the work. A separate section lists over 8000 publishers of directories with necessary information from address to telephone number. There is a geographical approach to states, and there are other helpful indexes. An "alternative format index" primarily lists those directories available in electronic versions. Also, it includes mailing-list information. The supplement adds about 1000 new and revised titles each half year. Note: Beginning in 1993 *Gale's City and State Directories in Print* was incorporated into the main work.

City Directories

The two most obvious, and probably the most-used, local directories are the telephone book and the city directory. Although separate printed works, they are more and more being combined on CD-ROMs and online.[16] The city directory is particularly valuable for locating information about an individual when only the street name or the approximate street address is known. Part of the city directory includes an alphabetical list of streets and roads in the area, giving names of residents (except for an apartment building, when names may or may not be included). The resident is usually identified by occupation and whether she or he owns the home. Some city directories, but not all, have reverse telephone number services, that is, a "Numerical Telephone Directory." If you know the phone number, you can trace the name and address of the person who has the phone.

[15]*Directories in Print* is one of the three main works in the online version. The content follows the print edition and it is updated as regularly. If the library has only infrequent calls for this type of information, the online approach is preferable. The other two guides in this online database include *Gale Directory of Publications and Broadcast Media,* discussed earlier in the text, and *Newsletter in Print,* which is the electronic format of the one-volume print edition. There are about 12,000 items listed under seven broad subject headings.

[16]Douglas Ernest et al., "Telephone Directory Use in an Academic Library," *Reference Services Review,* Spring 1992, pp. 49–56. An excellent overall view of the type of questions that turn the librarian to a phone book.

The classified section of the directory is a complete list of businesses and professions, differing from the yellow pages of the telephone book in that the latter is a paid service which may not include all firms. Like the telephone book, city directories are usually issued yearly or twice yearly.

Most city directories are published by the R. L. Polk Company of Detroit, founded in 1870, which issues over 800 publications. In addition to its city directories, it publishes a directory for banks and direct-mail concerns.

A number of ethical questions arise regarding the compilation and use of the city directories. For example, bill collectors frequently call large public libraries for information which can be found only in the city directory, such as reverse phone numbers and addresses and names of "nearbys," that is, the telephone numbers of people living next door to the collector's target. Some librarians believe such information should not be given over the telephone. They argue that this helps the collectors in an antisocial activity and promotes invasion of privacy.

This policy may be commendable in spirit, although questionable in practice, as it simply makes it more difficult, but not impossible, to use the directories. The author of this text would say that the librarian is there to supply information, not to question how or by whom it is used. Several large urban libraries are currently examining their policy in this regard, and most now do give the information over the phone.

City and Telephone Directories: CD-ROM[17]

All of the below are on *CD-ROM only*.

Direct Phone. Marblehead, MD: ProCD Incorporated, 1994 to date, quarterly. $149. Includes 72 million white-page listings, plus 7.5 million business white-page listings.

PhoneDisc. Bethesda, MD: Digital Directory Assistance Incorporated, 1993 to date, quarterly. $249. Five disks: Western, Central, Middlewest, Northeast, Southeast states. Includes 90 million residential and business listings.

Online. All of the below are online only.

Electronic White Pages. Atlanta, GA: Directory Net Incorporated, $25 monthly fee. Includes: 120 million listings, residential and business.

[17]Few city directories are available by themselves online or on CD-ROM, but much the same information, with sometimes even more, is available through telephone city-directory-type electronic services such as *People Finder* discussed in this section.

AT&T 800 Toll-Free Directories. 1992 to date, irregular. Includes all AT&T listed toll-free numbers for both residential and business. This is on CompuServe, free to customers.

People Finder. Atlanta, GA: Information America, $25 to $95 per hour, depending on information required. Includes 61 million phone numbers.

The day when libraries might have shelf after shelf of telephone books is past. Today the average library will have a CD-ROM or online service that can pick a single number or series of names and numbers from almost any part of the United States and Canada. To be sure the local phone book, as well as phone books of major cities in the area are retained as much for ease of use as for constant demand for information. A telephone book will give the address of a friend, business contact, hotel, and so on, in almost any community. Using the familiar yellow pages to find the location of potential customers or services is a frequent purpose. And from the point of view of a historian or genealogist, a long run of telephone books is a magic key to finding data on elusive individuals.

Thanks to a 1991 Supreme Court ruling, the various telephone companies can no longer copyright phone number information. This led to a small deluge of CD-ROM compilations of regional and national phone numbers. Each year more are added to the group. The ones listed here are considered among the best. The librarian should look for the lowest price with the most detailed searching patterns. Most of those online and the CD-ROMs are updated quarterly.

Depending on the sophistication of the software, the various CD-ROM approaches to phone numbers generally have much in common. The CD-ROMs are used much like a regular phone book. If the user knows a name, this is typed in and the phone number and address appear. But unlike the printed version, the searchers have numerous paths: (1) They can look up the known phone number and find (in reverse) the name of the person or business and address. (2) If they know the address, then up pops the phone number and name. They can narrow the quest by zip code, area code, city, state, or a combination. All the people who live on a given street can be traced, as well as businesses. The business section may be searched, too, by Standard Industrial Classification, again for the nation, or by zip code, and so forth.

Generally, the CD-ROM is accurate, but from time to time one finds the wrong phone number, the wrong name, the wrong zip code, and so on. This seems to be more as much the fault of the phone companies as the CD-ROM disc producers.

A tremendous advantage of these systems is that they are updated quarterly and one subscribes, usually at reduced rates, for the various updates. Many of the services offer variations on a theme at different prices. Thanks to the competition, most prices are reasonable.

The people who publish *PhoneDisc* offer half a dozen other versions from *PhoneDisc QuickRef* (with 100,000 of the most frequently dialed business, educational, government, etc., numbers for $69) to *PhoneDisc California*. The *DirectPhone* people bring up *SelectPhone*, a $300 four-disc package covering various sections of the United States.

The least expensive discs (under $300) are easiest to use because they have less information and fewer access points. Normally one simply types in the required name and the number appears. Problems arise when there are hundreds of John Smiths without proper indication of location, or when a name pops up without a phone number. Comparatively, if the library has the $9500 plus NYNEX system, there is a manual of over 100 pages that makes it possible to find even a lost cousin in the wilds of Arizona.

A few of the better-known other services would include: (1) *11 Million Business Phone Directory* (Omaha, NE: American Business Information, 1992 to date, annual, $79) which covers the whole of the United States; (2) *LocatorPlus* (Denver, CO: U.S. West Communications, various dates/updates, but monthly updates are $14,500) includes 12 million business and residential numbers. The high price is due to the frequent updates to software, which can be used for many things including mailing labels and lists. (3) Much the same explanation holds for the $9500 price tag for the 10 million listing in the *NYNEX Fast Track Digital Directory* (New York: NYNEX).

Online there are not as many services as on CD-ROM, but those that are available are impressive. The *Electronic White Pages* covers virtually every home in America as well as numerous business and government numbers. The fee of $25 is low, but the user must put down a $250 user fee as well as some 65 cents per minute and screen time.

Information America offers a more complex service in its *People Finder* which lists 61 million numbers. There are profiles, the company claims, of 111 million people in 92 million households with the 61 million phones. Rates vary for searches depending on how much is wanted on each individual or household unit. This information on American households makes the system virtually a city directory, for example, for most phone listings the user can find date of birth of the resident, residence type of home, length of residence, number of family members and their dates of birth, and (by a special search) up to 10 neighbors with addresses and phone numbers.

The same company has an allied *Business Finder* with city-directory-type information on 17 million companies, including 2 million in Canada. It can act as a directory, too, of business officials. Rates vary from $15 to $39 per hour.

Consumer online services such as CompuServe wish to offer as many "free" services as possible, and one of these is the AT&T 800 listings. This includes some 80 million telephone listings of individuals, with some business numbers. Still the focus is on the household and the user can locate a number not only by name, but also through numerous other channels such as address.

Where available, the directory indicates the length of time an individual or family has lived at a given location.

Still another, which may be used alone or in conjunction with the telephone book collection, is the annual print *National Directory of Addresses and Telephone Numbers* (Detroit, MI: Omnigraphics, Inc., 1985 to date, biannual). This has over 115,000 numbers of businesses and government agencies across the United States. Fax numbers, addresses, and zip codes are given. It includes, too, all four-year American universities and colleges, toll-free numbers, and 1200 leading foreign corporations. It is available on CD-ROM from the publisher for $195, but the printed version at a modest $50 is a best buy.

There are special print guides to fax numbers alone. *The National Fax Directory* (Detroit, MI: Gale Research Inc., 1989 to date) is a good example. This has 80,000 major business and organizational fax numbers under approximately 150 subject headings. The 160,000 fax listings are arranged alphabetically by name and by area.

Associations and Foundations

CD: Encyclopedia of Associations: U.S. Association. Detroit: Gale Research Inc. 1995 to date, annual. $725.

> *Print:* 1956 to date, annual, 3 vols.. $295 to $375 each.

> *Online:* 1986 to date, semiannual. DIALOG file 114, $102 per hour. Also available on OCLC.

Print: The Foundation Directory. New York: Foundation Center, 1960 to date, annual, 3 vols. $435.

> *Online: Foundation Directory.* New York: Foundation Center, 1987 to date, annual. DIALOG file 26, $60 per hour.

CD: Prospector's Choice. Rockville, MD: The Taft Group, 1994 to date, annual. $795.

Directory searching is not the most scintillating reference work. Still, given a bit of imagination, it has promise. Consider the print version of the *Encyclopedia of Associations* which lists and dutifully describes over 23,000 groups. Divided by broad subjects, with detailed indexes, this is a profile of American realities and dreams. It goes from the "American Association of Aardvark Aficionados" (600 members who love the animals) to the "Zippy Collectors Club" ("philatelists interested in the collecting of zip code and other marginally marked material"). This catalog of organizations brings the often arid landscape of American commerce to multifarious life. The same inventory that includes the Financial Accounting Federation also yields up the Electrical Women's Round Table and the Pressure Sensitive Tape Council.

A typical print entry covers 15 to 20 basic points about the organization, whether it has a half dozen members or many thousand, whether it be deadly serious or just deadly, for example, see "The Flying Funeral Directors of America" (who "create and further a common interest in flying and funeral service"). Information for each entry includes the group's name, address, chief executive, phone number, purpose and activities, membership, and publications (which are often directories issued by the individual associations). There is a key word alphabetical index, but the second volume is really an index to the first in that it lists all the executives mentioned in the basic volume, again with complete addresses and phone numbers. A second section rearranges the associations by geographical location. The third volume is issued between editions and keeps the main set up to date by reporting, in two issues a year, on approximately 3000 changes in the primary set. One other volume, while useful, is not essential to the main set. *International Organizations* covers groups outside the United States not found in the first volume.

A habit of directory publishers is to develop "spin-offs." A case in point: *Encyclopedia of Associations: Regional, State and Local* (Detroit, MI: Gale Research Inc., 1988 to date). First published in 1988, with promises of frequent updates, this follows the pattern of the major set, but is limited to 53,000 local, state, and regional associations. There are five volumes (at $470). If there is humor and pathos in the directory of national organizations, one can only imagine what can be found in the entries arranged here alphabetically: first by state, then by city and town, and finally by the association name. The subject index is little more than a key word approach, that is, it lifts the key words from the title, and if these are not explanatory of subject matter, one is lost. True, the editors do add subjects, but not enough.

There are countless methods of searching the CD-ROM from subject and name of a group to address and geographical location. One may use one or all of the services in a database sweep. Through boolean logic, for example, the quest might limit hits to Oklahoma associations with a membership of more than 3000 and with budgets in excess of $4000. It is helpful too when the patron knows only a few key words such as "bowling" and "restaurants." A search may turn up organizations that deal with bowling alley food requirements.

In the online format the same text is included, but there are additions which include (1) the aforementioned regional, state, and local directories; and (2) *International Organizations*, with coverage of over 14,000 organizations. The total comes to close to 100,000 organizations in various fields. The online version has the advantage of being more current than the print work in that it is updated semiannually.

If one adds up the cost of all the electronic services, the total cost—particularly online for infrequent searches—is actually less, for a change, than the print volumes. The directories show the tremendous advantage of electronic databases over print.

Foundations

Updated each year, the *Foundation Directory* online includes added works by the same publisher, such as the National Directory of Corporate Giving. The database describes some 12,000 sources of potential grant funds. Private as well as business and community organizations are included. Full information is given regarding the amount of money involved, and there is considerable detail available on what must be filed by whom. Most important: addresses, phone numbers, names of personnel, and so on, make it possible to gain further information where and when needed. If it is not consulted often the hourly rate is low enough to warrant the online format. (It is not available on a CD-ROM.)

The initial printed volume includes only foundations with assets of at least $2 million. There are close to 7000 listings. The second volume includes another 4000 "mid-sized foundations." The third volume is a supplement issued about six months after the initial two volumes.

A more descriptive title, but with the same purpose, the CD-ROM *Prospector's Choice* lists 8000 private foundations, corporate groups, and related sources of funding by philanthropic organizations. Complete information is given, including a helpful biography of major officials. The file is easy to search, and can be purchased in five subdivisions for considerably less than the national disk. While this is a poor choice for most libraries, primarily because of the high cost, it is a marvelous aid for individuals and groups seeking funding.

Business

CD: Business America on CD-ROM. Omaha, NE: American Business Information, 1991 to date, semiannual. $7500.

Online: U.S. Business, 1991 to date, monthly. $60 per hour. Also available DIALOG file 531 and 532.

Business America on CD-ROM is representative of scores of similar directories. It gives current information on close to 11 million business organizations in the United States and Canada. The listings include phone numbers, names, addresses (including zip codes), number of employees, annual sales volume, and similar information. The facts may be located by a variety of search patterns that are relatively easy to master. The high price of the CD-ROM puts it beyond most libraries, but the online cost is reasonable and it is a worthwhile quick guide to specific data.

The same publisher has a similar directory service in *U.S. Manufacturers,* at much the same online rates. Here one locates information similar to that in *U.S. Businesses* on 551,000 manufacturers in United States.

Education

CD: Peterson's College Database. Princeton, NJ: Peterson's, 1987 to date, annual. $595.

Print: Peterson's Annual Guides to Undergraduate Study. Various dates, prices.

Online: 1987 to date, annual. DIALOG file 214, $45 per hour. Also available numerous online services, including CompuServe.

CD: Lovejoy's College Counselor. Philadelphia: Intermedia Active Software, 1994 to date, annual. $99. Professional/profile edition: $199.

Print: Lovejoy's College Guide. New York: Monarch Press, 1949 to date, semiannual. Paper, $14.95.

Detailed information on colleges, universities, trade schools, graduate degrees, and other aspects of advanced education are found in scores of directories. The majority are in various electronic formats as well as in print. One envisions the time when scores of numerous and varied print guides to education will find a home in a single electronic database.

The most thorough and extensive listing of universities and colleges is found in the Peterson series, both on a CD-ROM and online. All the nation's institutions of higher education (some 3400) are in the printed *Guide to Two Year Colleges* and *Guide to Four Year Colleges* which make up the electronic databases. Searches may be made with boolean logic and one can limit the quest to a given institution, subject, area, cost estimate, and the like. Full and current data are given from graduate requirements to special programs and number of students and teachers.

A similar service called Peterson's GRADLINE (available online and on CD-ROM) offers detailed descriptions of the more than 30,000 graduate and professional programs in about 1500 accredited colleges and universities. Updated annually, the CD-ROM is $695 and the online search on DIALOG file 273 is $60 per hour. Most libraries will want the first of these services. Universities will want both.

On Internet, the Peterson's Education Center is accessible over the World Wide Web. The Center carries "searchable data and narrative on educational institutions at all levels and provides communication and transaction services, such as e-mail and college applications. All institutions listed in Peterson's printed guide have a home page at the Center to offer admissions information, online applications, and financial aid guidance etc."[18]

A more modest, certainly less expensive approach to the same type of information is found in the familiar *Lovejoy's College Counselor.* For under $100 the library has access to data on 1600 four-year colleges and universities as well some 4000 two-year community institutions, trade schools, technical schools, and business schools. While the amount of information given is considerably less than in Peterson's, it does cover many one- and two-year programs not found in the other guide. More important are the hypertext features: (1) A clever method of entering words and phrases which will indicate the type of education or the type

---

[18]"Peterson's Launches Education Center," *Library Journal,* March 1, 1995, p. 14. The dozen or more Peterson print guides range from *Peterson's Guide to Colleges in New York* (1984 to date, annual, $12.95) to the mentioned *Peterson's Guide to Two Year Colleges* (1960 to date, annual, $15.95).

of college an individual should attend. The system can store up to 1000 personal profiles that require a password to find. (2) Videos and pictures of about 500 of the most popular universities are also included. This is fairly simple, but gives at least a broad idea of what to expect.

There are several CD-ROM services which usually correspond to the printed editions. For example, *The College Handbook* (New York: College Board, various dates) is a standard print work which has a CD-ROM equivalent for $40. Both the print and electronic versions have data on 2700 United States colleges, but no universities, as in *Lovejoy's*. The same publisher offers a CD-ROM *College Explorer Plus* for $125, which adds 1200 graduate and professional schools as well as more details. Both titles are updated annually.

The frequently revised printed *Comparative Guide to American Colleges* (New York: HarperCollins) explains the best school for the person looking for the best in social activities or academic excellence, or both. Everything from admission requirements and the racial composition of the student body to the amount of social life is considered in a standard form for each institution. It answers such questions as how many full-time men and women are on the campus or what percentage of students go on to graduate work. Many students have found it to be remarkably accurate over the years. The listings are by the name of the academic center, and at the end of the book there is an index by subject from accounting to library science and zoology.

A standard work in the field, *American Universities and Colleges*, 14th ed. (New York: Walter deGruyter, 1993, 1991 pp., $150) gives detailed information on over 1900 institutions. One finds answers to questions ranging from what is taught by whom, to the number of students, to the shape of various graduate and professional education programs. Schools are listed by state and by city, and there are a detailed index and several appendixes which list ROTC schools, dress codes, and so forth. Among hundreds of such single-volume printed guides, it provides the details most students and parents are seeking. Consider, for example, the faculty, shown here by number as well as by sex and rank. But there is a drawback. Usually the statistical data are three to four years behind the date of the latest edition, and editions come out only every four or five years.[19]

LIBRARIES

See Chapter 4, Bibliographies.

---

[19]Another aspect of educational guides: the test preparation books that give hints on how to do well on the SAT (Scholastic Aptitude Test), the LSAT (Law School Admission Test), and civil service exams. Most of these are issued by Arco, Barron's, HarperCollins, and the College Board. For an annotated guide, see Linda Carroll's "Examining Your Test Preparation Books," *Library Journal*, August 1994, pp. 51–53. See, too, the detailed bibliography of resources found in Peter Olevnik, *American Higher Education: A Guide to Reference Sources* (Westport, CT: Greenwood Publishing, 1993). This lists and annotates more than 800 titles by form, that is, bibliographies, almanacs, indexes, and so forth.

STATISTICS

CD: Statistical Masterfile. Bethesda, MD: Congressional Information Service, Incorporated, mid-1960s to date, quarterly. Prices vary.

Print: American Statistics Index. 1973 to date, monthly. *Statistical Reference Index.* 1980 to date, monthly. *Index to International Statistics.* 1983 to date, monthly. *Note:* prices vary, but about $2000 per year for each.

Online: American Statistics Index. 1973 to date, monthly. DIALOG file 102, $125 per hour.

CD: Statistical Abstract of the United States, 1993 to date, annual. Washington, DC: Bureau of the Census, 1993 to date, annual. $50.

Print: Washington, DC: Government Printing Office, 1879 to date, annual, 980 pp. $30. Paperback, $25.

Statistics are concerned with the collection, classification, analysis, and interpretation of numerical facts or data. Statistical questions begin with "How much?" or "How many?" Depending on whether the query is motivated by simple curiosity or by a serious research problem, the reference librarian can go to the hundreds of reference works dealing peripherally or exclusively with statistical data as sources of possible answers.

The reference librarian's most difficult problem remains one of identifying a source for an answer to the esoteric, specialized statistical query; almost as hard is translating the query into the terminology of the statistical source. Given the numerous sources it is no wonder that in larger libraries the expert in statistics is as important as the subject bibliographer. Normally, this librarian is located in the government documents or the business section.

A statistical reference work is highly specialized, this text indicates only the basic general sources with which the beginner should be familiar. The federal government, followed by state and local governments, provide the greatest number of statistical documents. A number of agencies issue them regularly, and they are an important source of forecasting in the private sector.

Statistics Sources (Detroit, MI: Gale Research Inc., 1962 to date, annual) in the 1994 edition lists more than 2000 sources of statistics under 20,000 subject headings. To be sure, not all of these are issued by the government, but the major American government sources are listed, as are sources for 200 nations of the world.

How reliable are the statistical data? If they come from standard federal and major state agencies, they are likely to be quite reliable, although there are always exceptions. Most errors are caught, but international data are likely to be more error-prone because, among other things, there are legal constraints imposed on the collection agencies. The parent organizations of the agencies that collect and disseminate international statistics heavily influence the accuracy and validity of the data presented for consumption. They may be less than ideal because of political constraints or because the governments simply do not have the funds for extensive statistical data.

It is one thing to gather statistics, quite another to understand and interpret them. Is there anyone who has not heard the saying, "Statistics lie"? Statistics are as much an art as a science. Numbers mean little unless they are interpreted properly. And that is precisely what makes many of the statistical works published by the government so baffling. Rarely is proper guidance given to help interpret what they mean.[20]

Indexes

Anyone who feels uncomfortable with statistics will bless the three indexes published by the Congressional Information Service. Available both in print and on a single CD-ROM, they are easy to use and equally reliable. Almost any question dealing with statistical data can be answered using this service. If the answer is not found, there usually is an indication of where to turn next. Thanks to the excellent abstracts one rarely has to go to the complete document, at least for most ready-reference queries.

Searching the CD-ROM *Masterfile* is a delight. The librarian may search all the indexes, or as is normally the case, a single index. One may find the information by countless paths. Still, the most common is by subject and or by name of a particular statistical report. To get a better notion of content, consider the print versions.

The print indexes, as well as the CD-ROM cousins, follow a basic pattern: (1) Issued monthly, they have a quarterly index and are cumulated, with an index, annually. When searching the print volumes one should begin with the annual index to get a sense of subject headings and general arrangement. (2) The index, a separate section or volume, refers the user to the document in the main work. Material is indexed by subject, title, issuing agency, primary individuals involved with the document, and so forth. Each document or series is abstracted, and there is complete information about the issuing agency and the necessary background about the statistics. The entries in the main section are arranged by accession number. Each document is within a particular issuing agency.

Almost all the documents are available, as with ERIC and similar services, in microfiche. Each abstract is keyed to the proper microfiche item. In addition there is a Superintendent of Documents classification number to help locate the hard copy. Given this type of detailed support system, the librarian has a marvelous set of tools for answering almost any statistical question.

[20]Cynthia Crossen, *Tainted Truth: The Manipulation of Fact in America* (New York: Simon & Schuster, 1994). A documented, yet popular examination of statistics and how they are manipulated to support an argument. The purity of data, such as the census, can be tremendously important. Advertisements to political jabs use the same numbers for some very poor conclusions.

The indexes are extremely easy to use, particularly as they have such detailed abstracts. There is no problem in locating the documents themselves. Actually, the abstracts are often sufficient to answer many research questions other than the most involved.

The three cover distinct areas. The *American Statistics Index* indexes and abstracts almost every statistical source issued by the federal government. This includes the contents of over 800 periodicals. It provides entry to close to 10,000 different reports, studies, articles, and the like. Note: It is the only one of the three available online, and is part of the *Statistical Masterfile*.

Its twin, *Statistical Reference Index,* indexes and abstracts state documents. It does *not* include federal materials. It *does* include many nongovernmental statistics as well. These range from those issued by private concerns and businesses to nonprofit organizations and associations.

The *Index to International Statistics* includes major governmental statistics from around the world. There is particular emphasis on western European countries, including the European Community. It is an excellent source of United Nations statistical data. As in the other indexes, periodicals are analyzed (in this case about 100). Almost all the publications are in English, albeit there are some in Spanish and other languages when there is no English equivalent.

Statistical Masterfile has the same microfiche backup, and offers sophisticated boolean search patterns. The disc has the tremendous advantage of allowing the user to search three services at once. Then, too, there is an invaluable "category" index that analyzes the data in terms of age, income, states, type of legislation, and so forth. All and all, the CD-ROM version is superior to the printed format and much easier for the layperson to master. The drawback is the same as for many CD-ROMs: It is quarterly instead of monthly, and the cost is high. Price is based on the size and budget of the library, but the annual CD-ROM, goes from $1020 to $4275. The rate is lower when the library already subscribes to the print version. The two-disc retrospective set (covering 1973–1988) is $7000.

Yearbook

Statistical Abstract of the United States is the basic source of American statistical data in any library. Filled with 1500 tables and charts, the work serves to summarize social and economic trends. The guide is divided into 34 major sections—from education and population to public lands—with a detailed 40- to 50-page index that takes the reader from abortion to zoology. Despite the good index, the over 500,000 statistics are not always easy to understand. There is, for example, need for clearer explanations of the figures. Reference librarians should study each edition with care.

As a profile of America, the *Statistical Abstract* attracts much journalistic attention. Each annual volume brings a group of stories in magazines and newspapers about the many strange facts and statistical data. In the 1994 edition, for example, "one learns that the average American now eats 12 pounds more chicken in a year than in 1980 . . . that 48 percent of America's math and engineering doctoral students are foreigners . . . the American crime rate over the last decade has declined."[21] Within the average 1000 pages of charts and tables a reader will find a true reflection of America. True, that is, if one cares to believe the implication of the numerous statistical tables.

In 1994 the first CD-ROM format of the *Statistical Abstract* became available, and at quite a reasonable price. All the information in the print volume is included, but it has some drawbacks in searching—problems which are likely to be solved with future editions of the CD-ROM. There are the typical menu screens, but the steps are not easy to follow. Some menus take the user around the electronic barn. Table headings are another typical difficulty. Instead of maintaining them on the screen, as one scrolls down, they disappear. Halfway through a table, or set of tables, one may have no idea where it all began. Still, these are minor problems. Most libraries will want both the CD-ROM and print version. If a choice must be made, the nod goes to print, at least until the CD-ROM format is improved.

The majority of Western nations follow the pattern established by the American government in issuing equivalents of the *Statistical Abstract* and specialized statistical information. For example, England has *Annual Abstracts of Statistics* (London: Her Majesty's Stationery Office, 1854 to date). On an international level the best-known equivalent is the United Nations *Statistical Yearbook* (New York: The United Nations Publications, 1949 to date, annual) which covers basic data from over 150 areas of the world. The information is broken down under broad subject headings.

Relatively current international statistics are not easy to locate, and that is why basic reference works in this area are welcome. A good exmaple is the *Statistical Abstracts of the World* (Detroit, MI: Gale Research, 1994). This is a compilation of data for 185 United Nations and nonmember nations. Arranged by country, it offers easy-to-understand figures. The topics, which are the same for all countries, include population, health, crime, government, finance, and so forth. Data are primarily from the early 1990s, with projections to 2020. Note the appendix which is a listing of sources—sources useful in themselves for larger collections. This is an addition, not a replacement, for the standard United Nations *Statistical Yearbook*.

Statistical information is hardly limited to these indexes. Other valuable data will be found in the basic indexes such as *Public Affairs Information Service Bulletin*, ABI/INFORM, *Business Periodicals Index*, and any service which regularly reports on the activities of government and business such as Predicasts. *Facts on File* contains statistics, and as explained previously, is a good launching pad to

---

[21]"The Home of the Brave . . . ," *The Spectator*, January 16, 1993, p. 22.

find more about a particular matter. A related work, available online as well as in print is *A Matter of Fact* (Ann Arbor, MI: Pierian Press, 1984 to date, annual). This draws facts and statistical data from approximately 300 newspapers and periodicals, and various government documents. OCLC offers it online under the name of Fact Search.

Two valuable titles cover American historical statistics. They are *Historical Statistics of States of the United States* (Westport, CT: Greenwood Press, 1994, 478 pp.) and *Historical Statistics of the United States* (Washington: Government Printing Office, 1975 and 1979, 2 vols.). The first has 18 data items, for each decade from 1790 to 1990, for each of the then existing states. Territories are considered as well. The latter two volumes consider historical data from 1790 to 1979, but this time for the nation as a whole. Here one finds comparative figures for wages, production, agriculture, and the like.

SUGGESTED READING

Anderson, Byron, ed., "Library Services for Career Planning, Job Searching, and Employment Opportunities," *The Reference Librarian*, 1992, no. 36. How can the reference librarian help the student find a career path? How can the same librarian assist someone seeking a new path of employment or, for that matter, a desperately needed job? Answers are given by experienced reference librarians who are dealing with this type of query each and every day.

Boettcher, Jennifer, "Telephone Directories . . . ," *The Reference Services Review*, Summer 1994, pp. 54–61. A survey of the great step toward electronic formats for all telephone directories. The pros and cons of the move are explored, but the author generally favors the new formats. A good overview, too, of what is available.

Clark, Juleigh, and Karen Carey, "An Approach to the Evaluation of Ready Reference Collections," *Reference Services Review*, Spring 1995, pp. 39–44. What constitutes a good ready-reference collection? College librarians indicate how to ascertain the answer to this for individual situations.

Dewdney, Patricia, et al., "A Comparison of Legal and Health Information Services in Public Libraries," *RQ*, Winter 1991, pp. 185–196. A Canadian study that finds, as might be expected, that most librarians have difficulties in answering health or legal questions. Most of the study is applicable to U.S. libraries and the findings, sadly, are still true.

Havener, W. M., "The Use of Print versus Online Sources to Answer Ready Reference Questions in the Social Sciences," *Library & Information Science Research*, 1990, no. 4, p. 425. A review of the problems and the solutions to online ready-reference work. Most of the comments about the social sciences are applicable to other parts of the library.

"The Man Historians Hate," *Library of Congress Information Bulletin*, November 13, 1995, pp. 463–464. In 1995, Joseph Kane, the fact man, was 95 years old. In that year he donated a collection of 78 rpm records of his 1938–1939 radio show to the Library of Congress. The short article talks about Mr. Kane and his contribution to facts and ready-reference works.

"Never Sleeps, and Never Runs out of Questions," *The New York Times*, March 20, 1993, p. 25. This is the story of a typical day "in the telephone research room at the Brooklyn Public Library." The story has numerous examples of the types of questions (and responses) likely to flood a library with a staff willing to answer ready-reference queries over the telephone.

Paris, Marion, "Making Medical Reference Accountable," *American Libraries,* 1994, no. 8, pp. 772–776. A discussion of the references interview and other matters associated with the use of medical literature in the library. The pros and cons of certain information procedures are explained.

Paterson, Ellen, "Sharing Skills," *School Library Media Activities,* October 1992 (monthly), pp. 35–37. The author spells out a game that can be used to teach ready-reference skills to students. While a trifle elementary, the author's imaginative approach will help even experienced reference librarians and certainly library school students.

Rettig, Hillary, "The King of Quant," *Wired,* March 1995, pp. 86–91. Using historical demography, a University of Minnesota professor indicates a new trend in the employment of statistical data. "The secret of historical demography is that it uses modern information technology to bridge two scholarly disciplines."

Thomas, Joy, et al., "Automating Your Ready Reference File," *Reference Services Review,* 1994, no. 1, pp. 89–93. A description of the automation of an in-house ready-reference card file. Much of the technical data are applicable to others who may wish to automate.

Tomaiuolo, Nicholas, "An Overview of General Health Science Compact Discs for Libraries," *CD-ROM World,* January 1993, pp. 38–49. While an overview of this type becomes dated quickly, the basic information and the basic titles remain much the same from year to year. The author gives an excellent overview.

CHAPTER NINE
BIOGRAPHICAL SOURCES

What does the Sunday newspaper supplement *Parade* have in common with *Who's Who in America*, *The Dictionary of National Biography*, and *Stipple, Wink & Gusset: Men and Women Who Gave Their Names to History*?[1] The answer—they tell the reader what the "folks" have done and are doing. They are constant sources of gossip, fact, and pictures of everyday life. They are gems of biographical information.

In a library, bookstore, and home the biographical sketch or book is extremely popular. The ephemeral *Parade* explains the status of the Beatles in the mid-1990s. The *Stipple* book reports that Alessandro Fiasco (1792–1869) lent his name to the dictionary because he was an impresario whose productions were dogged by collapsing stages and crashing sets. *Who's Who in America* lists the activities of eminent men and women as well as the address where Madonna may be contacted. And the *Dictionary of National Biography*, whose major requirement for entry is that the person be dead, will afford hours of leisurely reading about such people as Guy Burgess, Soviet spy, multimurderer John Christie, as well as Queen Victoria and painter Gwen John.

Entertainment aside, in reference work the primary use of biography is: (1) to locate information on a person, which can be done through an index, encyclopedia, directory or one of the many sources in this chapter; (2) to locate people who are famous in a given occupation, career, or profession; (3) to locate supporting material about an individual for any number of reasons from a paper on the fall of Rome to a study of the modern automobile's brake system;

---

[1]The *Stipple* reference work was published by Century of London in 1992. For a review see the *Guardian Weekly*, December 20, 1992, p. 24.

and, not the least (4) to locate a possible name for the baby. This is not discussed here, but there are countless entries, for example, *The Perfect Name of the Perfect Baby* (New York: Ballentine, 1993) to *Dictionary of First Names* (New York: Oxford, 1990).[2]

SEARCHING BIOGRAPHICAL SOURCES

In determining which biographical sources to search, the librarian will work from two basic beginning queries: How much of the history of an individual life does the user require and what type of data are required? The data type of question is by far the most common in the ready-reference situation. Typical queries: "What is the address and phone number of X?" "How does one spell Y's name?" "What is the age of R?" "When did Beethoven die?" Answers will be found in the familiar who's who directory-biographical dictionary sources. Approach varies with each title, but all are consistent in listing names alphabetically and, at a minimum, in giving the profession and position (with or without claim-to-fame attributes) of the individual. At a maximum, these sources will give full background on the entry from birth and death dates to publications, names of children, and so on. The information is usually, although not necessarily, in outline form. It is rarely discursive or critical.

At what depth and sophistication should the answer be to a more involved biographical question? This can be determined by the education and needs of the individual user.

The second major type of biographical question comes from the person who wants partial or relatively complete information on an individual. The questioner may be writing a paper, preparing a speech, or seeking critical background material. Typical queries: "How can I write a paper on Herman Melville?" "What do you have on [X], a prominent American scientist?" "Is there a book about George Washington and the cherry tree?" Answers will be found in reference sources with an emphasis on essays (i.e., entries of 300 words to several pages in length).

A standard bibliography such as *American Reference Books Annual* will indicate the wide variety of reference works in biography published each year. An impressive reminder of just how much is involved is found in *Biographical Dictionaries and Related Works* (Detroit, MI: Gale Research Inc., 1986). Here are some 16,000 entries, and then only of biography compilations which have at least 100 entries.

How many biographical reference works would one find in the average medium to large public or academic library? There will be a half dozen CD-

[2]Biography and biographical reference titles may be used in countless ways, and those listed here are only the basic approaches. For example, the person with a query about the actress Maria Montez and the roles she played might turn to *The Name Is Familiar* (New York: Neal Schuman, 1992).

ROM or online indexes, and 200 to 500 print or electronic sources. Actually, many small- to medium-sized libraries might get along with even fewer biographical reference sources.

Discussion here is limited to reference books. If the librarian moves from the reference section to the reading area, there may be many thousands of individual biographies and autobiographies. If the individual biography was included—since biography is at least as popular as fiction in many libraries—the number of different volumes would be considerably greater. The person who wants biographical information will use the general collection as well as the reference section. And the primary avenue to find the material, of course, is the catalog.

EVALUATION

The quest for information about the living and the dead has made numerous publishers, compilers, and biographers (not to mention living celebrities penning their autobiographies) richer. Whether the massive numbers of biographies issued each year has made the reader or the librarian richer is another question.

How does the librarian know if a biographical reference printed source or electronic database is truly legitimate, that is, authoritative and based on relatively accurate material? A rule of thumb will do in most cases: If the title is not listed (or minimally praised) in any of the basic bibliographies such as Sheehy and Walford, *American Reference Books Annual,* or the current reviewing services, there is the possibility it is worthless.

The publisher's name is another indication of authority. Five publishers are responsible for a large number of available biography reference titles. They are Gale Research Inc., The H. W. Wilson Company, St. Martin's Press, Marquis Who's Who Inc., and R. R. Bowker Company. It is no surprise that most of these are major publishers of other standard reference works. If the librarian does not recognize the publisher, and particularly if it is not one of the major five, then the warning flag should be out to do further checking. (Trade publishers, from Random House to Harper & Row, publish popular biographical sources, but namely reference titles.)

Beware

Dealing as much with individual ego and pride as with accomplishment and fact, biographical reference sources can be great sources of income for what some call the "tin cup" brigades. These are people who literally move into a community, establish a biographical book of that community, and then charge individuals for an entry. These "mug books" are a far cry from the legitimate works. Yet, ironically enough, historians are grateful for the information they provide of Americans, particularly in the nineteenth and the early twentieth century.

Another example of questionable reference value are the thousands of directories of high school and college students. A few are sound, but the majority are not. Numerous publishing companies, or tin cup artists, dupe parents and students by asking them to pay from $50 to $150 per entry (1995 prices).

A typical example of a biography directory scam was reported in the early 1990s. A Chicago-based publishing company began work on *American Artists*. The reference work was to give who's who information on about 3000 artists. A person contacted to be included was told: "If you want a color plate of your painting in the book, you must pay $695." The painter submitted the money and, a year later another $295. It is estimated the phony publisher received about $1.7 million. The reference work was never published.[3]

Bells and red lights should flash when the publisher insists the honored person buy the book(s) before an entry is possible. This is a sure signal of a rip-off. Of course, even the most legitimate source will often suggest that the individual buy the book; but there is a great difference between "suggest" and "insist." For example, the honorable *Who's Who in America* will include a name without requiring that the individual purchase anything. At the same time a series of letters will suggest purchase of one of "several distinctive items especially for you." These represent the "lasting symbol of your achievements," and range from a $65 paper weight to a $150 mantel clock. Well, all of this is perfectly legitimate, and may please those being included, but, again, the purchase of the book or wall plaque has nothing to do with acceptance or rejection in *Who's Who in America*.

Other Evaluative Points

Beyond the publisher, how does the librarian know whether a biographical source is reliable? The key questions are as valid for print sources as for electronic databases. There are a number of tests.

---

[3]This is a report from a friend of the author's who asked that his name not be used. The realization that nothing was to be published, that he was out close to $1000 came in October of 1991. The game never ends. *The New York Times* (March 31, 1995, p. B2) reported that on that day "26 people were under arrest . . . with what . . . the United States Attorney in Brooklyn said was a bogus *Who's Who* publishing company that operated out of Lake Success, LI and Manhattan." For $1400 a person could be listed in *Who's Who*, "right along with Boris Yeltsin and Barbara Walters. You'd be invited to international conferences to network with the movers and shakers." The criminal charge was making false claims for a work which probably never would be published. (Any reference librarian, of course, would be warned off when the boiler room employees guaranteed a place in what is essentially an English biographical source. A poor choice of titles, at least for anyone in the know.)

Selection. Why is a name selected (or rejected) for the various biographical reference aids? The method for the several who's who entries is discussed later, but the process is relatively easy to describe for biographical aids limited to a given subject or profession: The compiler includes all the names that qualify for the scope of the work, as in *American Men and Women of Science* or *World Authors*. In both cases, the widest net is cast to include figures and authors likely to be of interest. There are limitations, but they are so broad as to cause little difficulty for the compiler.

A publisher may apply automatic standards of selection or rejection in a biographical source. Briefly, (1) the person must be living or dead; (2) the individual must be a citizen of a given country, region, or city; (3) the person must be employed in a specific profession or type of work; (4) the individual must be a given sex. One or more of these measurements may be employed in any given reference work.

Editors of reputable works establish some objective guidelines for inclusion; for example, *Who's Who in America* features many people "arbitrarily on account of official position." This means that a member of Congress, a governor, an admiral, a general, or a Nobel Prize winner, is automatically included; and people in numerous other categories as well, are assured of a place in the volume because of the positions they hold. The *International Who's Who* is certain to give data on members of all reigning royal families. The *Dictionary of American Biography* takes a more restrictive approach: One must first be dead to be included; after that requirement is met, the editor begins making selections.

There are levels of exclusiveness; it may be somewhat more difficult to get into *Who's Who in America* than *Who's Who in American Art*. For the former listing, it is a matter of "Don't call us, we'll call you," and inclusion depends on some public achievement. Being listed in other reference sources may depend only on membership in a group or profession. It is difficult to stay out of such titles as *Who's Who in the United Nations* if one happens to work there, or *Who's Who in Golf* should one be a professional or a well-known amateur.

A listing in a given biographical title depends on whether one responds to the publisher's request to fill out an entry form. Failure to answer may mean failure to be included unless one is such a famous UN employee or golfer that the editor digs out the information without the help of the person to be listed.

Then, too, there are some automatic exclusions. In the case of subject biographical reference works, the exclusion is usually evident in the title: One does not look for poets in *Who's Who in American Art* or *American Men and Women of Science*. Although the *Dictionary of American Biography* now includes a few outstanding criminals, some biographical sources restrict selections of everyone from popular entertainers to sports figures. Some counter that any person of importance, acceptable, respectable or not, should be included. In the past, admission to a biographical reference book was seen as a sign of moral approval, and this is still true for a few works today. A more mature editorial policy would include everyone the broad public wants to know about—a policy now followed by *The New York Times Biographical Services* as well as *Current Biography*.

Audience. The majority of reference works in biography are published for adults, although there are some (particularly concerning books and writers) for younger people. For the adult searcher, works can then be divided by purpose, education level of the user, and so forth. Obviously, the lines here are not all that clear, and an adult may well refer to a child's reference work (such as the *World Book* biographies).

Length of Entry. Once a name is selected, a question is: How much space does the figure warrant, five or six lines a page? The purpose and scope of the work may dictate a partial answer. The who's who data calls for a relatively brief outline or collection of facts. The biographical dictionary may be more discursive; the essay type of work will approach the same entry in a way particular to its form. Regardless of approach, the editor still has to make decisions about balance and length.

Authority. Biography began as an accepted form of approbation, for example, *Ecclesiasticus* (44:1) has the famous line, "Let us now praise famous men"; and this was the purpose of biography until well into the seventeenth century. After a period of relative candor, including Boswell's famous *Life of Johnson* and Johnson's own *Lives of the Poets*, the form returned to uniform panegyric in Victorian nineteenth century. With the Freudian influence in the twentieth century, unabashed praise once more gave way to reality. The fashion today is for truth in biography, at least of historical figures. Living people who are more in the publicity spotlight than in the realm of fact often will hire a professional writer to doctor their biographical source—particularly if it is an essay, or a book. Still, it hardly takes a trained librarian to determine glitter from fact.

Sources of Information

Today the question about authority must begin with another question: Who wrote the biographical entry—an editor, the subject, an authority in the field, a secretary? In preparing almost any material except statistical information, the person who penned the entry will have had either conscious or subconscious biases. Even in a straightforward presentation of data, if the biographical subject supplied the information (the usual case with most current biographies), there may be slight understatements or exaggerations concerning age (men more often than women lie about this), education, or experience. Biographical sources relying almost entirely on individual honesty cannot be completely trusted. This leads to the next query: Have sources of information other than the subjects' own questionnaires been cited? The preface should make these two points clear.

Some think the directory approach is critically flawed in that the subject supplies the material. She or he is asked to fill out the publishers' standard form and return it to the publisher. Questions range from age and education to accomplishments and address. Accuracy of the entry, then, depends almost entirely on the thoroughness, the honesty of the individual who filled out the form. *Who's Who* (for example) is not so much a biographical reference work as an autobiographical one—a crucial distinction. This may not automatically lead to the telling of outright untruths, but it does promote the suppression of facts embarrassing to the author.

It is useful to know whether the biography was prepared completely by the publisher's editorial staff, whether it was simply slightly edited by that same staff from the form received from the subject, and whether it includes sketches written by outside experts. The last is the usual procedure for essay-length biographies.

When the biographical reference work is questionable, it should be verified in one or more other titles. If a serious conflict remains that cannot be resolved, what should be done? The only solution is to attempt to trace the information through primary source material, such as newspapers, contemporary biographies, or articles about the individual, or through his or her family or friends. This undertaking involves historical research. An excellent example can be found in the recurrent arguments concerning the details of Shakespeare's life and times or the famous attempt to straighten out the facts in the life of Sir Thomas Malory, author of the stories of King Arthur and his knights.

Frequency. Most biographical reference sources are on a regular publishing schedule. Some are issued each year, or even every month, while others are regularly updated every three or four years. With celebrities coming and going rapidly, it is obviously important to know the range of time covered by the parent work and its supplements. Many (although not all) biographical reference books are less than satisfactory because of no regular updated procedure. This problem is solved, if only in part, by electronic databases.

Other Points. Are there photographs? Are there bibliographies containing material both by and about the subject? Is the work adequately indexed or furnished with sufficient cross-references? (This is important when seeking individuals connected with a major figure who may be mentioned only as part of a larger biographical sketch.) Is the work arranged logically? The alphabetical approach is usual, although some works may be arranged chronically by events, birth dates, historical periods, or areas of subject interest.

Actually, in practice, few of these evaluative tests are employed. If a person is well known, the problem is not so much one of a source but of screening out the many sources for pertinent details. If the individual is obscure, usually any source is welcome.

ELECTRONIC DATABASES

Electronic databases now make it considerably easier to find information on any individual from a 2500 B.C. early ruler of Mesopotamia to a modern-day pop star. An index to the ranks of saints and sinners will bring up well over 3 million names. Another index reveals secrets about some 200,000 artists, scientists, and politicians. It is no longer a problem to find personal data. It is a problem to determine what is essential for a particular question. Generally there is too much, not too little, whether it be the baseball player Hank Aaron or the Byzantine empress Zoe.

An important point to remember about biographical electronic databases is that the majority are indexes. They do not include the text itself. There are exceptions such as *Who's Who in America* which is available in print, on a CD-ROM, and online. Still for every directory source of this type there are still scores of standard biographical works only available in print. Again, as with so much reference work, this is going to change. The day is not too far off when one may simply locate a given name and with a computer key or a click of a mouse bring up the complete biography or biographical bits as needed.

By now it is redundant to point out that, where available, the search on an electronic database is usually more thorough than a print source. In many of the services available online or on a CD-ROM one may broaden or narrow the search with boolean logic. In addition, depending upon the software, one may seek an individual by profession or occupation, in a certain time period, and in a given country or state or even city.

Still, the primary benefit of the electronic database, as when one searches for a telephone number or a quotation of a magazine citation, is the ability to scan thousands of possibilities in a matter of seconds. Rather than laboriously search individual biographical indexes and sources, one simply types in the name, profession, and so on, and up comes a likely response.

Online Services

Any of the subject databases on DIALOG or other online services are good places to look for a name. Most databases on vendor files include a named person field. For example, to search the name field on DIALOG, for any of the databases, use the inverted name format (?S=Kennedy, William). The "Expand" Command should be used when one is not quite sure of the exact form of the name (?E=Kennedy). Unfortunately each system has a different approach, that is, NEXIS would use name (William w/3 Kennedy).

INDEXES TO BIOGRAPHY

CD: Biography and Genealogy Master Index. Detroit, MI: Gale Research Inc., 1993 to date, annual. $1250. Annual update, $375.

Print: Biography and Genealogy Master Index, 2d ed. Detroit, MI: Gale Research Inc., 1980, 8 vols., out of print; 1981–1985 cumulation, 5 vols. 1986–1990 cumulation, 3 vols. $810; 1991–1995 cumulation, 3 vols. $900. Annual supplements, 1996 to date. $299 each.

Print: Abridged Biography and Genealogy Master Index. 1988, 3 vols. $475.

Print: Almanac of Famous People, 5th ed. 1994. $99.
Online: Biography Master Index. 1991 to date, annual. DIALOG file 287, $30 per hour.

CD: Biography Index. New York: The H. W. Wilson Company, 1994 to date, quarterly. $1095.
Print: Biography Index. 1947 to date, quarterly with annual cumulations. $135.
Online: 1984 to date, semiweekly. WilsonLine, $25 to $40 per hour. Also available on OCLC and CDP.

There are two types of indexes to biography. The first, represented by *Biography and Genealogy Master Index,* is a key to 9 million entries found in more than 700 biographical dictionaries and directories such as *Who's Who in America.* The purpose is to reduce tedious searching of basic, generally current guides.

The second type of index, represented by *Biography Index* includes citations to biographies appearing in periodicals and selected books. The purpose is to offer a key to biographical information about persons living and dead from a wide variety of general sources.

The first type would be employed for ready reference when the data type of information is required. The second would more likely be used to seek detailed information for a paper, research project, speech, or other presentation.

For example, a user who wishes to find the address of Mary Doe would turn to the *Biography and Genealogy Master Index* for sources of short data entries in the various biographical dictionaries indexed. The user who wishes to write a paper on the achievements of Doe would need a fuller entry and would turn to biographical information in periodicals as indicated in *Biography Index.*

In an opening search, where not much is known about an individual, the *Master Index* would be preferred. If the person is well known to the searcher and the essential facts are in hand, one would go first to *Biography Index.* All of this is to say that the two basic reference works may be used separately or together, but they are the first steps in any biographical search.

Since 1985, the publisher of *Biography and Genealogy Master Index* has issued a new volume each year, and cumulates the annual volumes every five years. (The CD-ROM is updated once a year.) The work is arranged in a single alphabet by the last name of the individual. After the name, are the birth and death dates, and then a key to one or more sources in which there is a short entry or essay about the individual. Famous people may have up to a dozen or more citations, but for the most part the citations usually number no more than two to three. So, while there are some 9 million citations, only about one-third of that number represent individuals. Still, 3.3 or so million names are usually sufficient for most reference situations.

Among the 700 biographical works indexed are both data type (*Who's Who* variety) and essay type (*Dictionary of American Biography*). In the early years the focus was almost entirely on the data variety, but this changed as the publisher indexed more and more biographical sources. Most of the standard works published by the five largest biographical reference publishers are indexed in the *Master Index*.

As useful as all of this may be for the librarian, the index is far from perfect. The publisher simply prints names as found in the sources. If, for example, Joe Doaks cites his name in this form in *Who's Who in America,* but prefers Joe Vincent Doaks in *Who's Who in American Rat Catchers* and Joseph V. P. Doaks in *American Businesspersons,* his name will be alphabetically arranged in three different ways. Of course, it could be three different Doaks, but the date of birth indicates that it is probably the same person. Just to make things confusing, the date of birth for the same person may vary, depending on which source was indexed. Also, there may be a simple listing of the same name, albeit with reference to four or five different sources.

Aside from the obvious advantages of searching for names on the CD-ROM version (or online) there are several arguments for an electronic database search: (1) A search may be done by birth or death year. This will bring up all people who died or were born within the given time frame. (2) A search may be by the source year, that is, a librarian may ask for a listing of all the biographical dictionaries published in a specified year. (3) The search may be limited to entries with a portrait. There is a slight catch, at least for the CD-ROM format. The disc, which covers the complete print volume collection up to 1996, is two, not one disc. The first is used to conduct a name search. But if one wants to go beyond that to birth and death years, and so forth, one must turn to the second disc. Another more serious problem, at least for now, is that the searcher cannot use true boolean logic.

There are several versions of the *Master Index:*

1. *Abridged Biography and Genealogy Master Index.* This includes the basic set, plus the supplementary volumes from 1980 through 1987, cut from 6 million to about 1.6 million entries. Some 115 current and much-used basic sources are analyzed. According to the publisher, the selection of biographical source material is based upon a nationwide survey of holdings of small- and medium-sized libraries, for example, only standard biographical sources are indexed. Updates are planned every five years.

2. *Almanac of Famous People.* In an effort to bring the set within the financial means of libraries, this work is only $99 for data on about 25,000 people.

At times, even the *Biography and Genealogy Mastery Index* fails—the name cannot be found. There may be many reasons to explain the omission. One may not be so obvious; that is, the name may be of a literary character, and such names are not found in standard biographical guides of real people. (An exception, although limited to major characters based on real people, are listings in *Biography Index*.) If one suspects this to be the situation, numerous literary guides, as well as general encyclopedias, carry entries for everyone from Simon Legree to Holden Caulfield. Two examples: *Dictionary of American Literary Characters* (New York: Facts on File, 1990) has brief notes on over 11,000 personalities from American novels published between 1789 and 1980. *Characters in 20th Century Literature* (Detroit, MI: Gale Research Inc., 1990) is another source that considers characters from 250 novels. *Masterplots*, and its numerous spin-offs, is a third good place to seek a literary character.

Biographies in Periodicals

Where information from periodical articles is required, *Biography Index* is the first choice. More than 3000 different magazines and newspaper obituaries are analyzed for biographical material. This gives the user an extremely wide range of sources, which move from the popular to the esoteric. The end result is rarely disappointing. When searched over several years, inevitably something turns up, and often that "something" may be quite detailed. Arrangement is by name of the person. An added bonus is that birth and death dates, nationality, profession, and of course, the citation to the periodical are given.

Another useful feature is the index by profession or occupation. Someone looking for material on an architect simply turns here, as would another individual looking for biographical data about dentists or zookeepers.

The index also covers some books, and makes particular note of individual biographies and autobiographies, as well as collections. A nice touch is the inclusion of some, but certainly not all, fiction that has a well-known real figure at the center of the novel. The same is true of poetry, drama, and so forth. Obituaries are indexed, including those from *The New York Times*.

UNIVERSAL AND CURRENT BIOGRAPHICAL SOURCES

Universal biographical sources include entries from all parts of the world, or at least those parts selected by the editors. Normally they list both living and dead personalities. The result is a compendium of relatively well-known individuals from all periods and places.

Biographical Dictionaries

Print: Webster's New Biographical Dictionary. Springfield, MA: G. & C. Merriam Company, 1985. $21.95.
No electronic format.

Before the advent of the *Biography and Genealogy Master Index*, the biographical dictionary was a first place to turn to identify, qualify, and generally discover basic facts about an individual. With that, one might go on to other works, or if nothing more than a birth or death date, occupation, claim to fame, and so on, was needed the biographical dictionary might be quite enough. Today, in order to quickly find information about an individual, it is much faster to consult the *Master Index* first. Lacking that reference work, one might return to the dictionary, and it can still be used for ready-reference facts about famous people.

By far the best known and most used of the biographical dictionaries, *Webster's* gives brief biographies for about 40,000 people from the beginning of history through the early 1970s. The individual's primary contribution is noted, along with nationality, birth (and death) dates, and pronunciation of names. The majority, well over 80 percent of the listings, are deceased, and its primary, if not almost exclusive value, is for checking on persons who are dead. American and British subjects receive the most space, with appropriate attention given to major international and historical figures.

Other reference works of this type are found in larger ready-reference sections, such as *Chamber's Biographical Dictionary*, rev. ed. (London: Chambers, 1986), which lists 15,000 prominent people, with particular emphasis on British and American personalities. *the New Century Cyclopedia of Names* (New York: Appleton-Century-Crofts, 1954) is a three-volume work of some 100,000 names, including fictional and mythological characters.

Pseudonyms

Print: Pseudonyms and Nicknames Dictionary, 3d ed. Detroit, MI: Gale Research Inc., 1987, 2 vols. $143.
No electronic format.

Covering all periods and most of the world, this is a listing of about 55,000 pseudonyms and nicknames from Johnny Appleseed (John Chapman) to Mark Twain (Samuel Clemens). Information includes birth and death dates, nationality, and occupation. When one looks up the pseudonym or nickname, there is a reference to the original name and the primary information. Cited sources are included, and these amount to over 200 basic biographical works. Arranged in a single alphabet, the guide is extremely easy to use. It is updated by two supplements which are issued between editions of the primary work.

Directory: The Who's Who Form

CD: The Complete Marquis Who's Who Plus. New Providence: NJ: Reed Reference Publishing, 1992 to date, quarterly. Price varies.[4]

---

[4]Published by the Marquis family of Chicago until 1991, the series was then sold to Reed Reference Publishing Company. Reed retains the "Marquis" as an indicator of the official status of the works. In addition to *Who's Who in America* the publisher by 1996 published 20 other related works, all identified with Marquis, a registered trademark.

Print: Who's Who in America. 1889 to date, annual, 3 vols. $475.
Online: Marquis Who's Who. 1991 to date, biennial. DIALOG file 234, $162 per hour. Also available on CompuServe.

Print: Who's Who. London: Black, 1849 to date, annual. Price varies. (Distributed in the United States by St. Martin's Press, Inc.)
No electronic format.

Print: International Who's Who. London: Europa Publications Ltd., 1935 to date, anual $280. (Distributed in the United States by Gale Research Inc.
No electronic format.

The "who's who" hieratic structure began with a single *Who's Who* in England, spread to a single similar title in America, and then to points east and west. By the end of the Second World War it became apparent to publishers that everyone wants, or appears to want, a part of the fame bestowed when listed in a biographical source. From this developed the geographical series of who's who from *Who's Who in the West* to *Who's Who in California.* Next came the who's who professions explosion with self-explanatory titles such as *Who's Who Among Artists.*

The who's who aids may be classified by scope as international, national, local, professional or business, religious, racial, and so on, and is usually indicated in the title.

Information is normally compiled by sending a questionnaire to the candidate, who is then free to provide as much or as little of the requested information as he or she wishes. The better publishers check the returns for flaws or downright lies. Other publishers may be content to rely on the honesty of the individual, who normally has little reason not to tell the truth, although—and this is a large "although"—some candidates for inclusion may construct complete fabrications.

The directories are among the most frequently used of the biographical sources. Common questions they answer: (1) Where does X live, or receive his or her mail? (2) What is X's age and position? (3) What has X written? (4) What honors does X claim? These are just a few of the typical queries.[5] The who's who directory forms list only the living and, for that matter, only those in some outstanding position. Again, most of the who's who are indexed in the *Biography and Genealogy Master Index.*

The ultimate who's who was published in 1993 by Companion Books (Durham, NC). For a mere $32 the library can now purchase *Who's Who of Animals: Biographies of Great Animal Companions.* This contains "pithy profiles of more than 1,200 dogs, cats and other so called animal companions."[6]

---

[5]Data on most who's who subjects include date and place of birth; names of parents, spouse and children; education; current and past political, governmental, and business positions; military service; honors and awards; publications; memberships; religion; legal (voting) residence; and current mailing address.

[6]"Who's Who of Animals," *The New York Times,* April 25, 1993, p. 11.

The who's who directories vary in scope, and often in accuracy and timeliness, but their essential purpose is the same: to present objective, usually noncontroversial facts about an individual. The approach and style are monotonous. Most are arranged alphabetically by the name of the person. The paragraph of vital statistics normally concludes with the person's address and phone number.

The American *Who's Who in America* has a long history of reliability. It is a source of about 80,000 names of prominent American men and women, as well as a few foreigners with some influence in the United States. As the nation's current population is close to 270 million, how do the editors determine who is, or who is not, to be included? The answer is complex, usually based on the person's outstanding achievement or perceived excellence.

The inclusion-exclusion process is of more interest when the reputation and fame of a work, such as *Who's Who in America,* is purposely built upon selectivity of a high order. The natural question is one of legitimacy. Is the selection of Y based on Y's desire to be included (supported by willingness to buy the volume in question or, in a few cases, literally to pay for a place in the volume), or is it based on the editor's notion of eminence, where no amount of persuasion of cash will ensure selection? All works listed here are indeed legitimate; in them, one's way to fame cannot be bought. This is not to say there is no room for criticism. No one will entirely agree on all names selected or rejected in, say *Who's Who in America.*

On balance, the selection is adequate, if not brilliant. The data for entrants varies in length but not in style, as each fills out a standard form requesting basic information, including date of birth, education, achievements, and address. The form is used to compose the entry, and a proof of the entry is sent to the individual for double-checking.

The set also includes a list of those who died and those who retired since the last edition, and a feature "Thoughts on My Life" is included in some entries. Here the notable figures are asked to reflect on principles and philosophies that have guided them through life. This can be inspirational, or downright disturbing, but it is an always-fascinating facet to otherwise straight directory-type information.

Searching the printed volumes is a matter of simply looking up the name(s), which are arranged in alphabetical order. A third printed volume allows searching by geographical area and professional interests. Subject headings in the latter category are too broad, but the solution is to use, where available, the CD-ROM or online version.

Electronic Formats

Who's Who in America is part of the CD-ROM called The Complete Marquis Who's Who Plus. Here, as usual in electronic formats, the searcher may have over 40 different points of entry, from the person's name to his or her address, company, or other affiliation. The geographical possibilities are even more rewarding; for example, the number of prominent Americans who are women living in Chicago or the ratio of successful attorneys in Los Angeles and San Francisco compared to the total number in the guide or those not found in the guide. Another advantage is that new names may be added each quarter.

The online service is limited to what is found in the three-volume *Who's Who in America*. The CD-ROM, following the tradition of "plus" employed by Reed and by its subsidiary R. R. Bowker, includes numerous other related titles originally initiated by Marquis as part of the "who's who" cycle, including *Who Was Who in America*. Many of these individual print titles are found in libraries. The regional titles: *Who's Who in the East*, *Who's Who in the Midwest*, *Who's Who in the South and Southeast*, and *Who's Who in the West*. Topical titles: *Who's Who in the World*, *Who's Who of American Women*, *Who's Who in Finance and Industry*, *Who's Who in American Law*, *Who's Who in Entertainment*, *Who's Who in Advertising*. The databases may be searched collectively or individually.

England's *Who's Who*

Who's Who was first published in Britain on January 15, 1849, fifty years before there were enough prominent Americans to make a volume possible here. During its first forty-seven years, *Who's Who* was a slim book of about 250 pages which listed members of the titled and official classes. In 1897, it became a biographical dictionary, and the 1995 edition is close to 4500 pages. Selection is no longer based on nobility but on "personal achievement or prominence." Most entries are British, but the volume does include some notables from other countries. And in the past decade, it has put more and more emphasis on prominent scholars and professional people as well as political and industrial leaders among approximately 30,000 entries.

The British *Who's Who* is the only one that does not have a qualifier, that is, Who's Who in *Siberia*, Who's Who in *America,* and so forth. Why? The not too subtle point is that there is no need to go beyond *Who's Who*. It must be a select group of British, or it would not be the genuine thing.

International

Depending on size and type of audience served, most American public, university, and college libraries will have *Who's Who in America* and possibly *Who's Who*—"possibly" because the better-known figures apt to be objects of inquiry in *Who's Who* are covered in the *International Who's Who,* which opens with a section of names of "reigning royal families," then moves to the alphabetic listing of some 20,000 brief biographies of the outstanding men and women of our time. The range is wide and takes in those who are prominent in international affairs, government, administration, diplomacy, science, medicine, law, finance, business, education, religion, literature, music, art, and entertainment.

Marquis issues *Who's Who in the World* (1970 to date, biennial; and in *The Complete* CD-ROM) which lists about 31,000 names, or about 10,000 more than the *International*. Interestingly enough, duplication is minimal, although the form and type of information is much the same in both.

Almost every country in the world has a similar set of who's who directories, that is, a basic work for the living famous and a set for the famous who have died. Most of these are published by reputable firms listed in the standard bibliographies such as *Guide to Reference Books* and *Guide to Reference Materials*. For example, there is *Canadian Who's Who* (Toronto: University of Toronto Press, 1910 to date, every three years). This includes a wide variety of biographical sketches form all walks of life, including businesspeople, authors, performers, and teachers.

Who's Who of American Women (Chicago: Marquis Who's Who, Inc., 1959 to date biennial, again, in *The Complete* CD-ROM) is a dictionary of notable living American women. It follows the same general pattern of all the Marquis works. The average edition includes 30,000 women's names. The editors' breakdown of 1000 sketches indicates that, according to occupation, a woman's chances to earn an entry are best if she is a club, civic, or religious leader (9.6 percent of all biographies).

There are separate multicultural directories. One example is *Who's Who among Black Americans* (Detroit, MI: Gale Research Inc., 1976 to date, about every two years). This lists 20,000 people from all fields of endeavor. Entries include the standard type of material, and there are cross-references when needed. The "Occupational Index" lists most, although not all, of the names under 150 categories. There is a "Geographical Index" which needs to be improved.[7]

Unquestionably, biographical dictionaries that focus on occupations and professions are valuable reference aids and, as such, serve a real purpose. (Some of these are considered later in this chapter). Turn from the professional and subject titles to the multicultural and women's listings and the territory becomes foggy. A serious case might be made in opposition to multicultural separate titles as well as those for women. If people in these groups are truly a success they belong first and foremost in the who's who where it all began. At best they might be in a geographical who's who or by subject and professional interest. But to

---

[7]Gale publishes a number of related titles: *Notable Black American Women* (1992 to date, annual); *Notable Asian Americans* (1994 to date, annual); *Notable Hispanic American Women* (1993 to date, annual). Gale also publishes: *Who's Who Among Hispanic Americans* (1990 to date, every two years); *Who's Who Among Asian Americans* (1994 to date, every two years).

The publisher of the *International Who's Who*, beginning in 1992, brought out *The International Who's Who of Women*. It makes the point that the more than 3300 entries are important, but why not add them to the main volume?

divide these books by culture and by sex is at least questionable, and in some ways insulting.[8]

ESSAY FORM OF BIOGRAPHICAL SOURCES

CD: Current Biography. New York: The H. W. Wilson Company, 1983 to date, annual, $189.

Print: Current Biography, 1940 to date, monthly except August, $58.

Print: The New York Times Biographical Service. New York: The New York Times, 1970 to date, monthly. Loose-leaf $120.
Online: The New York Times Biographical File. Parsippany, NJ: The New York Times, 1980 to date, weekly. NEXIS, rate varies per hour.

Current Biography is the single most popular essay-length biographical aid in all types of libraries. Issued monthly, it is cumulated, often with revised sketches, into annual volumes with excellent cumulative indexing. Thanks to the format and rather "catchy" photographs on the cover, *Current Biography* resembles a magazine which, literally, can be read cover to cover.

Annual emphasis is on around 200 international personalities, primarily those in some way influencing the American scene. Articles are long enough to include all vital information about the person. They usually are objective. The sketches are prepared by a special staff which draws information from other biographical sources and from the person covered in the article. Subjects are given the opportunity to check the copy before it is published and, presumably, to approve the photograph which accompanies each sketch. Source references are cited. Obituary notices, with due reference to *The New York Times Obituaries Index*, are listed for those who at one time have appeared in the work. Each issue includes a cumulative index to past issues of the year, and with the twelfth number, the title is published as a hardbound yearbook. The yearbook adds a subject index by profession, useful for looking for leaders in various fields.

The CD-ROM edition (first made available in 1995) includes articles on 3500 people who have appeared in the print version since 1983. It includes, too, a complete index to the sketches found in the print magazine from 1940 to date. The catch is that it comes out only once a year and is three times the cost of the magazine.

The New York Times Biographical Service serves the same purpose, and usually the same audience, as *Current Biography*. The essential difference is that *Current Biography* is staff-written with source references. *The New York Times* biogra-

---

[8] The opinion is hardly unique to the author. See "Who Cares Who's Who?" *The Times* (London) November 8, 1992, p. 4. "It's all the more insulting to women who have managed to smash the glass ceiling, that instead of giving them their rightful position alongside their male peers in the existing . . . *Who's Who*, Europa has chosen to shunt them up a separatist, and arguably, sexist siding," in a who's who for women.

phies are usually written by reporters who do not cite sources. Published online and each month in loose-leaf form, it is a first choice for any medium-sized or large library. It includes obituaries, the "man in the news," and features stories from the drama, book, sports, and Sunday magazine sections. Each sheet is a reprint of biographical material that has appeared in *The New York Times*. The monthly section has its own index, cumulated every six months and annually.

The lack of current indexing is a real headache, and one must search through up to five or six months of individual issues to find persons recently in the news. One might locate persons through the regular *New York Times Index*, but this, other than online, is late as well. The efficient way is to search for names where *The New York Times* is indexed on CD-ROM, such as Newspaper Index or Newspaper Abstracts Ondisc. The sketches are often reports on controversial, less-than-admirable, individuals. Most of the reporting is objective.

A better solution to the haphazard indexing of *The New York Times Biographical Service* is to use it online. Although available only through NEXIS, this is likely to change as more networks became available to laypersons and libraries. At any rate, online the librarian has access to biographies of from 15,000 to 20,000 people. About 50 records a week are added and, as in the printed source, all are taken from the daily newspaper. The deceased are dutifully listed under "Deaths" in the annual and online and CD-ROM versions of *The New York Times Index*. Usually, too, there are appropriate cross-references in the main index.

No matter how large the cast of characters in these various biographical sources, someone is always missing. Counting on that, as well as introducing a new approach to the famous found in all sources, Gale Research Inc. *Newsmakers* (1985 to date, annual) considers about 200 people in each issue. All are presented in a uniform style, including numerous photographs. Emphasis is on Americans, but there is a fair amount of international coverage.

The correct use of these national, retrospective biographical aids depends on the librarian's or patron's recognizing (1) the nationality of the figure in question; and (2) the fact that all entrants are deceased. When the nationality is not known, it will save time to first check the *Biography and Genealogy Master Index*. Where this is not available, one might turn first to a biographical dictionary, to an encyclopedia, or to the *Biography Index*. The latter may prove particularly productive when the name cannot be found in any of the sources noted.

Retrospective Essay: Print Form Only

No electronic formats.

Dictionary of American Biography. New York: Charles Scribner's Sons, 1974, 10 vols., eight supplements, 1977 to date, irregular. The set, $1,400.

Stephen, Leslie, and Sidney Less, eds. *Dictionary of National Biography*. 1885 to 1901; reissue, London: Oxford University Press, 1938, 22 vols. with supplements. $2,250 including supplements.

James, Edward T., ed. *Notable American Women 1607–1950: A Biographical Dictionary.* Cambridge, MA: Harvard University Press, 1971, 3 vols.; Paperback. Price varies. Supplements 1980, 1983, paperback, $25, $50.

The listing in either the *DAB* or *DNB* is a way of making certain that a person's reputation lives forever. Usually a candidate for inclusion has been dead at least 10 to 20 years before his or her name is considered for the honor. The judgment of the work is the yardstick whereby everyone from historians to politicians measure the importance of an individual. Posthumous celebrity is the final accolade, although it is often bestowed on the somewhat obscure, the dimly remembered.

The *Dictionary of American Biography* (or the *DAB*, as it is usually called), with its supplements, covers 18,000 figures who have made a major contribution to American life. Almost all are Americans, but there are a few foreigners who significantly contributed to our history. (In this case, they had to have lived in the United States for some considerable length of time.) Furthermore, no British officers "serving in America after the colonies declared their independence" are included.

About 3000 scholarly contributors add their distinctive styles and viewpoints to the compilation. As a consequence, most of the entries, which vary from several paragraphs to several pages, can be read as essays rather than as a list of connected, but dry, facts.

The original set and the supplements are indexed in a single volume and published in 1990 as *Dictionary of American Biography: Comprehensive Index.* The index is in six sections: subjects of the biographies, their birthplaces, schools and colleges attended, occupations, topics discussed within the biographical entry, and names of contributors to the biographical essays. There are numerous cross-references in each section, which makes the index easy to use. It is a required item for any library with the basic set and supplements.

The National Portrait Gallery in Washington, DC, offers a complimentary CD-ROM. This is called *The National Portrait Gallery: Permanent Collection of Notable Americans* (1991 to date, update irregular, $100). It contains high-resolution reproductions of portraits of some 3100 famous Americans. The paintings, drawings, and photographs are found, of course, in the National Gallery. Each picture has a limited, although useful caption with background information on the individual. One can search for a particular person by name and by artist, date of the portrait, time, and other elements.

The *DNB*

The *Dictionary of National Biography* (or *DNB*) is the model for the *DAB*. Having learned how to use one set, the librarian can handle the other without difficulty. The *DNB*, approximately twice the size of the *DAB*, includes entries on over 37,000 deceased "men and women of British or Irish race who have achieved any reasonable measure of distinction in any walk of life." It also includes early settlers in America and "persons of foreign birth who have gained eminence in this country." The 1981 to 1985 supplement, was published in 1990 and another supplement is expected in 1996 or 1997.[9]

A *Chronological and Occupational Index to the Dictionary of National Biography* (New York: Oxford University Press, 1985) is primarily an index that divides the entries into 20 basic professional and occupational categories. There is a separate chronological listing for each category. This is a massive index (close to 1000 pages) to both the basic set and the supplements.

An unusual out-of-phase supplemental volume was published in 1993 with the subtitle *Missing Persons*. Oxford University Press had experts go back over the *DNB* volumes and suggest who should be added in the "missing persons" category. The suggestions resulted in 1086 entries from Thomas Tuberville (d. 1295), the first person in England to be executed for spying, to Julian Maclaren-Ross (1912–1964), a bohemian writer on a heroic scale.[10]

The Concise Dictionary of National Biography (New York: Oxford University Press, 1992, 3 vols., 3334 pp. $195) is a substitute title for libraries that do not have the funds, or the space, for the primary set. The *Concise* covers every major entry in the main set up until 1981. The problem is that most of the biographical sketches have been cut back so drastically that little is left of the wit and intellectual challenge of the full entries. Shakespeare receives five columns (as compared to 49 pages in the main set) while Jane Austen is limited to nine lines. On the whole the *Concise* is dependable for essential facts, but not for critical comments.

Notable American Women includes 1359 biographies of subjects who died prior to 1950, and the supplements add around 900 who died between 1951 and 1980. Inclusion is based on their "lives and careers (having) had significant impact on American life in all fields of though and action." The long, signed biographies are similar to those in the *DAB* and *DNB*, and the author of each entry has special knowledge of the subject. In explaining who was included or excluded, the editors noted that the usual test of inclusion—being the wife of a famous man—was not considered. (The only exception is the inclusion of the wives of American presidents.) Once more, the domestic skills of a woman were seldom a point, and no moral judgments as to a woman's being a criminal or an adventurer were used to exclude a name. There is an excellent 33-page introduction, which gives a historical survey of the role of women in American life; there is also an index of individuals groups by occupations.

[9]Beginning in 1994 the publisher started work on an entirely new edition of the set. The present 37,000 entries will be expanded to about 50,000 revised and rewritten. The set is to be published in about 2004. More than likely it will be available in electronic format as well.

[10]There were scores of witty reviews of the "missing persons" volume, but one of the best, and still worth reading: Israel Shenker, "Let Us Now Praise Famous Women and Pugilists," *The New York Times Book Review*, May 27, 1993, p. 1, 23.

The biographical form that honors the dead and the worthy is found in almost all countries. A single example close to home is the *Dictionary of Canadian Biography* (Toronto: University of Toronto Press, 1966–1990, 12 vols.). About every five or six years, a new volume that covers a particular time period is issued. For example, the twelfth came out in 1990 and features people from 1891 to 1900. The set has biographical sketches of educators, military figures, craftspeople, and so forth. Published in French as well as English, this is considered a definitive source of biography in Canada. A cumulative index to the first part of the series was published in 1991, which solved the problem of multiple indexing. Note, especially, the useful bibliographies. Subsequent volumes are in progress.[11]

Newspaper indexes offer an excellent key to retrospective biography of both the famous and the infamous. Some newspaper obituary columns, such as *The Times* of London and to a lesser extent *The New York Times*, have distinctive points of view about people who may not quite make the *DAB* or the *DNB*.

PROFESSIONAL AND SUBJECT BIOGRAPHIES

The interest in biography to almost everyone from the researcher to the layperson has not escaped publishers. Consequently, almost every publisher's list will include biographical works, from individual biographies to collective works to special listings for individuals engaged in a profession. The increase in the number of professions (almost every American claims to be a professional of sorts), coupled with the growth in education, has resulted in a proliferation of specialized biographical sources.

What was stated before applies here: The reliability of some works is questionable, primarily because almost all (and sometimes all) the information is supplied directly to the editor or publisher by the subject. Little or no checking is involved except when there is a definite question or the biographical sketch is evaluative. Entries tend to be brief, normally giving the name, birth date, place of birth, education, particular "claim to fame," and address. There are rare exceptions to this brief form. The H. W. Wilson Company series on authors features long, discursive essays. Most biographical works devoted to a subject or profession have mercifully short entries, however.

The primary value of the specialized biographical work is as a

1. Source of address

2. Source of correct spelling of names and titles

3. Source of miscellaneous information for those considering the person for employment or as an employer or as a guest speaker

[11]Claire England, "The Dictionary of Canadian Biography . . . ," *Reference Services Review*, Summer 1993, pp. 71–76. This is a clear, fascinating history of the set.

4. Valuable aid to the historian or genealogist seeking retrospective information (if the work has been maintained for a number of years)

Following are only *representative examples* of professional and subject sources. There are hundreds more. When conducting a search for a specific individual, it is usually much faster to begin with the *Biography and Genealogy Master Index* or one of its spin-offs. The exception is when the profession of the individual is known and it is obvious that he or she will be listed in one of the basic professional and subject biographical sources.

Art-Politics-Science

Online: Bowker Biographical Directory. New York: R. R. Bowker, 1993 to date, updates vary. DIALOG file 236, $96 per hour.
   Print: Who's Who in American Art. New York: R. R. Bowker, 1950 to date, every two years. $176.

   Print: Who's Who in American Politics. New York: R. R. Bowker, 1970 to date, every two years. $223.

   Print: American Men and Women of Science. New York: R. R. Bowker, 1906 to date, every three years, 8 vols. $850.

Combining three of their biographical dictionaries, the R. R. Bowker Company comes up with the online *Bowker Biographical Directory.* The listings contain the standard who's who type of information and are primarily used for addresses, titles, and brief background data on an individual. Quantitatively, there are 11,500 biographies in *Who's Who in American Art;* 26,000 in *Who's Who in American Politics;* and 126,000 in *American Men and Women of Science.* (Despite the title, contents of the arts and sciences services include Canadians as well as Americans.) Updated every two to three years, the numbers change, but content primarily remains much the same. Few new people enter or leave the fields.

The print volumes are in alphabetical order. There are discipline indexes from librarians and critics in art to engineers and research scientists in science. The online service allows the same type of access, as well as by gender, date and place of birth, research interests, and the like.

Except for special situations, such as an art museum library, most of the services are used only infrequently. In view of their print cost, it is much more economical to rely on the online approach.

Literature

CD: Contemporary Authors on CD. Detroit: Gale Research Inc., 1960 to date, semiannual. $4197, plus $914 for annual and semiannual updates.
   Print: 1960 to date, approximately 100 volumes, annual update. $119 per vol.

CD: DISCovering Authors. Detroit: Gale Research Inc., 1992 to date, updated every
3 years. $500.

CD: Gale's Literary Index. Detroit: Gale Research Inc., 1993 to date, semiannual.
$175.

Print: World Authors, 1980–1985. New York: The H. W. Wilson Company, 1990,
1000 pp. $80. Supplements: *World Authors 1975–1980,* 1985, 831 pp.,
$68; *World Authors 1970–1975,* 1979, 893 pp., $73; *World Authors
1950–1970,* 1975, 1340 pp., $90.
No electronic format.

There are biographical essay collections for many subject areas, but those
consulted most often concern writers and writing. Students use the library for
information on specific authors for class reports. When the author is well known,
there is little difficulty. A good encyclopedia will give information, which can
be supplemented by literature handbooks and periodical articles.

Almost any published American writer is included in the *Contemporary Authors* volumes; the qualifications according to a publicity release by the publisher
are that "The author must have had at least one book published by a commercial, risk publisher, or a university press within the last three or four years. . . .
Novelists, poets, dramatists, juvenile writers, writers of nonfiction in the social
sciences or the humanities are all covered." In fact, just about anyone who has
published anything (this side of a vanity or a technical book) is listed. Newspaper and television reporters, columnists, editors, syndicated cartoonists, and
screenwriters are included.

The information is gathered from questionnaires sent to the authors and
arranged in data form—personal facts; career data; writings; and "sidelights,"
which includes discursive remarks about the author and his or her work. As of
1996, the over 100 volumes included about 100,000 contemporary writers.
This makes *Contemporary Authors* the most comprehensive biographical source of
its type. Each volume has a cumulative index to the whole set.

Since the work has been published in annual volumes, plus additions, since
1960 it has undergone numerous revisions. These, including changes in title and
scope, are reflected in the printed volumes, which can be extremely difficult to
use. The problem is solved by the CD-ROM.[12] Then, too, it solves several other
problems. It is less expensive than the printed volumes. It certainly takes up less

[12]This includes: *Contemporary Authors,* Volumes 1–140; *Contemporary Authors, New Revision Series,* Volumes 1–41; and *Contemporary Authors Permanent Series,* Volumes 1–2. (Note: The volumes are not necessarily separate printed volumes, i.e., Vol. 1–3, may be physically only in one volume.) Confusion
is the name—particularly as the CD-ROM does *not* include all the print material. According to "The
Reference Books Bulletin" (*The Booklist,* July 1994, p. 1970) the full text of the entire series is not on
the disc. "Public and academic libraries will find CA on CD a valuable reference book, though they
should hold off tossing the printed set until Gale reconciles the differences between the two."

space. And, most important, all of the over 100 print volumes can be searched in seconds, sometimes volume by volume, series by series. The CD-ROM is searchable by the author's name, title of works, and often by genre. In addition there are numerous other access points from geographical location of the writer to education, religion, politics, and even the writer's military service.

Moving rapidly toward putting many of their reference publications on CD-ROMs (and online), Gale Research Inc. offers a group of author biographical titles available *only* on CD-ROM. These are identified by the common opening part of the title, DISC. . . . Among those in the CD-ROM series: *DISCovering Authors* and *Junior DISCovering Authors*. At the same time the publisher maintains, if only in transition, printed as well as CD-ROM versions of its popular *Contemporary Authors*.

While *Contemporary Authors* is directory in style, the DISC . . . CD-ROM series go into essay-length discourses and comments about writers. The *DISCovering Authors* is limited to about 300 authors most likely to be studied in high schools and colleges. Updated every three years, it adds and deletes writers as the curriculum changes. As *Contemporary Authors* on CD-ROM it can be searched by well over 20 access points and is easy to use, even for beginners. The main menu opens up five possible avenues of information: biographical, personal and career information, bibliography of writings, and media adaptations. Sources for further reading and criticism are included as entrance points.

With an addition of 47 authors, *DISCovering Authors: Canadian Edition* is available from the same publisher for $50 more, or $550. This includes all the material on the original disc plus the 47 Canadian writers. Still another version with a self-explanatory title: *Junior DISCovering Authors* (1994 to date, $325). This provides biographical and related material on 300 authors who write for children and young people.

Gale's Literary Index combines the indexes from 32 of their different series on writers. The result is a gateway to the contents of over 675 volumes where the user may find ready reference to in-depth information on writers, literary criticism, reviews, and related material.[13] The publisher claims the index directs readers to material on over 11,000 authors and 120,000 titles. While easy to use, it presents problems: (1) The library must have access to the series indexed, which is rarely the case except in larger institutions. (2) The titles of books and the names of authors may be presented in different ways, often with equally different citations. In other words no one apparently has screened the CD-ROM for

---

[13]Material is drawn from *Contemporary Authors* plus two other Gale publications—the *Literary Criticism* series and the *Dictionary of Literary Biography*. Gale has a massive number of related literary biographical reference works that range from *Twentieth Century Romance* and *Historical Writers* to *Twentieth Century Western Writers*. Most are available only in print. These are listed and annotated in frequently updated catalogs involved only in literature, for example, in 1995 to 1996 the Gale *Literary and Biographical References* catalog.

inconsistencies and duplications. This is more irritating than not, but the librarian should expect more.

World Authors is one of the best-known series on authors, and includes not only essential biographical information but also bibliographies of works by and about the author. The source of much of the material is the author, if living; or careful research by consultants, if the author is deceased. Some of the entries are printed almost verbatim as written by the author and are entertaining reading in their own right.

An example of the series is *World Authors 1950–1970*, edited by John Wakeman, with Stanley Kunitz as a consultant. International in scope, the alphabetically arranged volume includes material on 959 authors, most of whom came to prominence between 1950 and 1970 or, for one reason or another, were not included in previous volumes. Entries run from 800 to 1600 words, with a picture of the writer and a listing of published works, as well as major biobibliographies. The style is informative, and about half the biographies include autobiographical essays. The work is periodically updated.[14]

Genealogy

Print: Raymond Wright. *The Genealogist's Handbook.* Chicago: American Library Association, 1995, 280 pp. $40.
No electronic format.

A major interest of many library clients is genealogy. The quest for family history fascinates and confuses. As a result it tends to be the province of experts, but there are numerous basic handbooks and guides that may be used by the librarian (and layperson) to launch and complete a genealogical project.

Both for the beginner and the experienced reference librarian *The Genealogist's Handbook* spells out the steps necessary to fill out the family tree. The author explains the basics and then indicates the various paths, highways, and accidents that may help or hinder along the way. There is even a chapter on how to write about ancestors. A useful guide for almost any library.

From time to time *Library Journal* publishes annotated lists of current genealogy books. See, for example, "Branching Out into Genealogy" by Judith Reid in the November 1, 1992 issue.

---

[14]Related titles in the H. W. Wilson series are *Twentieth Century Authors,* 1942, and the *Supplement,* 1955. Until publication of *World Authors,* these two titles were the basic sources of "current" information on writers. They now may be used to supplement *World Authors.* For deceased writers, Wilson has five author titles: *Greek and Latin Authors, 800 B.C.–A.D. 1000,* 1980; *American Authors, 1600–1900,* 1938; *European Authors, 1000–1900,* 1967; *British Authors before 1800,* 1952; *British Authors of the Nineteenth Century,* 1936. All these follow the style of *World Authors.* Also, note that The H. W. Wilson Company publishes a series of related works from *Current Biography* (which often includes writers) to *World Artists 1950–1980* and *Junior Authors and Illustrators.*

SUGGESTED READING

Ambrose, Stephen, "Thoughts on Biography," *Humanities,* July/August 1993, pp. 4–8. The author makes the point that when the average layperson reads history, he or she would prefer to approach it through biography. Also includes tips on writing biography.

Brown, Craig, "Reading between the Lines," *The Spectator,* February 4, 1995, pp. 27–28. In this review of the 1995 edition of *Who's Who,* a case is made for the enjoyment of the reference form as good reading. Also, the author explores the biases of the editors. "But these are quibbles. *Who's Who* is a book of unrivalled interest and amusement on all sorts of different levels."

Hannabuss, Stuart, and Rita Marcella, et al., *Biography and Children.* London: Library Association Publishing, 1993. An English approach to "a study of biography for children and childhood in biography." The work concludes with a useful "core collection of children's biography" and chapters on "provision of biographical materials in children's and school libraries" and "sources of biographical information."

Homberger, Eric, ed., *The Troubled Face of Biography.* New York: The Macmillan Company, 1989. Biographers are "asked to reflect upon their own practice and upon the state of biography today." The 11 contributors vary in content from the genuinely informative to the egotistical, but it is good reading.

Piternick, Anne, "Author, Author," *Scholarly Publishing,* January 1992, pp. 77–93. A library school professor writes an entertaining and informative essay on "what's in a name." Sometimes, even otherwise reliable guides such as *Contemporary Authors* may be deceptive or, at least, entertaining in their presentation of author information.

Robinson, William C., "Adult Biographies Reviewed by *Library Journal* in the 1960s and 1980s." *RQ,* Summer 1990, pp. 540–553. Just how sexist are biographies? How well are various occupations and professions explained? What nationalities are favored, if any? In an effort to answer these and related questions, the library and information science professor examines "all biographies reviewed in *LJ* in 1962 through 1965 and 1981 through 1985." The methodology would be suitable for similar projects. Need one add that a good three-quarters of the biographies are about men and fully over 94 percent concern the lives of whites?

CHAPTER TEN
DICTIONARIES

There is the story of a man who bought a dictionary to read cover to cover. He found the story hard to follow, but at least every word was explained as he went along. Definition of words and spelling are the primary use of the dictionary, particularly among Americans who, on the average, consult this reference work once each week.

If nothing else, the dictionary indicates the reader's own, sometimes deplorable, knowledge of his or her native language. Dictionaries are far more effective instruments for inculcating linguistic humility than prayer books are for inculcating the spiritual variety. One may turn to the dictionary for the last word on spelling, pronunciation, meaning, syllabication (word division), and definitions. Hardly a day goes by that the average person does not have need of a dictionary, if only to check the meaning of this or that word or to assist (on the sly) with a crossword puzzle.

People turn to dictionaries because they expect to be told what is true, what is right. They look to the dictionary, as to the Bible, as the ultimate authority. A related misunderstanding is the nonappearance of a word. Many think this means there is *no* such word. In a fast-changing world this is as sad a commentary on education as on the temerity of lexicographers to drop words they believe are too esoteric, racially insulting, sexually vulgar, and so forth. Another error is to assume that the order of a definition or spelling or pronunciation represents preference. An earlier spelling may be seen as preferable to a later one. Finally, most do not understand labels such as "colloquial." (College students usually think this means regional or sloppy rather than the true meaning of "conversational.")

Scope[1]

The public is apt to think of dictionaries as representing only one type or category. They cover almost every interest. Eight generally accepted categories are: (1) General English language dictionaries, which include unabridged titles (i.e., those with over 265,000 entries) and desk or collegiate dictionaries (from 139,000 to 180,000 entries). These are for both adults and children. (2) Paperback dictionaries which may have no more than 30,000 to 55,000 words and are often used because they are inexpensive and convenient to carry. (3) Historical dictionaries which show the history of a word from date of introduction to the present. (4) Period or scholarly specialized titles which focus on a given time period or place, such as a dictionary of Old English. (5) Etymological dictionaries which are like historical dictionaries, but tend to put more emphasis on analysis of components and cognates in other languages. (6) Foreign language titles, which are bilingual in that they give the meanings of the words of one language in another language. (7) Subject works which concentrate on the definition of words in a given area, such as science and technology. (8) "Other" dictionaries which include almost everything from abbreviations to slang and proper usage.

Compilation

How is a dictionary compiled from the written and spoken words that are its source? Today the larger publishers, from Houghton Mifflin to Merriam-Webster, Prentice-Hall, and Random House, have substantial staffs and free-lance lexicographers.

The process differs from firm to firm, but essentially it is in two stages. Freelance readers send in new or unusual uses of words taken from magazines, newspapers, and other sources. The newly coined words, or the variations on an older word (as for example the use of "hardware" in relationship to computers) are dutifully recorded on 3- by 5-inch cards, or, these days, entered in a computer's memory. At a later stage they are considered for inclusion based on their probable "lasting" power.

Electronic Dictionaries

The doyen of dictionaries, Ken Kister, puts the rhetorical question, "Won't computers replace dictionaries?" After several pages of exploration, he concludes with a proper response: "Just as radio has withstood the advent of television, we

[1]Annie Brewer, *Dictionaries, Encyclopedias, and Other Word Related Books,* 4th ed. (Detroit, MI: Gale Research Inc., 1988, 2 vols.) includes more than 35,000 titles. The compilation indicates the number of both English and non-English language dictionaries and related titles. (This has not been revised since 1988.)

can expect dictionaries in print form to survive the electronic revolution, at least for the short term. Beyond that, it's anyone's guess."[2]

Here, then, is one guess. The average home will retain the print college or desk dictionary, as will the library. It is easier to use, easier to read, easier to reach than the computer version, whether that be online, on a CD-ROM or on handheld reader. Furthermore, the print version tends to be less expensive.

Conversely: (1) Major, large sets, such as the *Oxford English Dictionary* and little-used subject dictionaries, such as *Harrod's Librarians' Glossary*, 8th edition (Aldershot: Gower, 1995) will be available only in electronic formats. As such they are easier to publish, easier to store (taking little or no space), unlikely to be damaged, and, where an involved search is needed, much easier to use. (2) The dictionary is now a part of almost every computer's word-processing software. It is, at a minimum, a spelling check. In more sophisticated systems the electronic dictionary gives definitions and synonyms, catches grammatical errors, and can be called upon for other useful dictionary roles. None of this is perfect, but it improves. (3) Often, as in the popular CD-ROM, *Microsoft Bookshelf*, the dictionary is built into a complete system of reference works used in writing letters or a novel. This is not only handy, but saves much time and effort. Meanwhile, as will be noted in this chapter, the primary dictionary publishers are covering all bases by offering most of their dictionaries on CD-ROM as well as in print. Few are online, although this is to come and will, in the future, probably surpass the popularity of the CD-ROM.[3]

Where a dictionary is available on CD-ROM the librarian must ask all the usual questions about its relative value to the printed version. Each situation is different. Answers are suggested in the discussion of a particular dictionary.

The small disc-loaded dictionaries are difficult to use because of the limited screen space and the impossibly small keys. More important, they tend to be four to five times more costly than the much easier to use printed version, or, for that matter, CD-ROM with other reference tools aboard. They are not recommended, particularly as the same content is available in a practical format such as a CD-ROM or diskette.[4]

---

[2]Kenneth Kister, *Best Dictionaries* . . . (Phoenix, AZ: Oryx Press 1992), pp. 53, 60.

[3]Ideally the stand-alone online dictionary should be used at a most accessible point for all, that is, as part of a network. The dictionary should be instantly accessible at a computer terminal.

[4]A single example: *The Random House Electronic Desk Reference* (New York: Random House, 1993; no update, $70). This includes an abbreviated Random House encyclopedia and *The Random House Webster's Electronic Dictionary* and *Thesaurus College Edition.* The former is based on the large Random House dictionary and the latter on the firm's standard thesaurus, and both are available in print from $18 to $20. The handheld operation, at $70, is a poor buy as well as an impossible tool to use unless the purchaser has thin fingers and patience to match. A similar summary holds for all such handheld dictionaries.

EVALUATION

For those who seek to evaluate dictionaries, the first rule is not to expect any dictionary to be perfect. Dr. Johnson said, "Dictionaries are like watches: the worst is better than none, and the best cannot be expected to go quite true." There is no perfect dictionary, and there never will be one until such time as the language of a country has become completely static—an event as unlikely as the discovery of a perpetual-motion mechanism. Language is always evolving because of the coining of new words and the change in meaning of older words. No single dictionary is sufficient. Each has its good points, each its defects.

This is true of the CD-ROM version, which normally is no more than the print text in an electronic format. Sometimes additions like pronunciation of words are added. Still, the technological aspects of the disc aside, the evaluation of a CD-ROM is much the same for the print version.

The first evaluation rule should be self-evident, but is rarely followed: Consult the preface and explanatory notes at the beginning of a dictionary. The art of successfully using a dictionary, or any other reference book, requires an understanding of how it is put together. This is important because of the dictionary's constant use of shortcuts in the form of abbreviations, various methods of indicating pronunciation, and grammatical notations.

In dictionaries and other commonly used reference works, it is particularly important to read the preface and introductory material. Here one finds the rules employed for everything from determination of pronunciation to proper usage and spelling. Because dictionaries vary, the preface is a necessary introduction to those differences that may cause confusion.

Guide to Dictionaries: Print

None is available in electronic formats.

Kister, Kenneth. *Kister's Best Dictionaries for Adults & Young People: A Comparative Guide.* Phoenix, AZ: Oryx Press, 1992, 448 pp. $39.50.

Loughridge, Brendan. *Which Dictionary?* London: Library Association Publishing, 1990, 177 pp. $26.

Kabdebo, Thomas. *Dictionary of Dictionaries.* London: Bowker-Saur, 1992, 253 pp. $100.

Kister's *Best Dictionaries,* is the leading guide to English language dictionaries. There are over 132 entries for general adult works, from the *Oxford English Dictionary* to inexpensive paperbacks. Some 168 children's dictionaries are evaluated. An excellent preface sets the stage on how to evaluate a dictionary. Necessary background information is given about publishers, publishing, and the electronic dictionary.

For each of the titles there is a thorough analysis, often over several pages. Helpful charts and graphs with forthright grading of A to failure, are extremely useful. No library can afford to be without this guide. It is revised every three or four years.

Published by the equivalent of the American Library Association in England, Loughridge's *Which Dictionary?* is an approach similar to that employed by Kister. Here there are seven divisions of dictionaries from standard to pocket to a group of works that defy categorization. Unlike Kister, Loughridge includes many "odd" titles from those covering crossword puzzles to subject dictionaries. Not as thorough as its American cousin, but casting a wider web, the Library Association publication is a nice addition for larger libraries. It in no way replaces Kister.

Kabdebo has an impressive descriptive-evaluative annotated grouping of dictionaries under suitable subject headings. There are about 4500 titles categorized from "abbreviations" to "Zulu." As a practical and more detailed reference guide, it augments general bibliographical aids such as *Guide to Reference Books*. The librarian or layperson will turn to the compilation for information on an appropriate dictionary in a field of interest. All entries give basic bibliographical data, and there is a combined author-title index. Annotations vary from little more than title to a full column or more on each two-column page. The latter part of the guide is devoted to subject dictionaries from art and architecture to transportation, as well as foreign language titles.

The best review of current dictionaries will be found in the "Reference Books Bulletin" of *The Booklist*.

Points of Evaluation

In evaluating dictionaries, the same general approach is used as in the evaluation of all reference works. Still, there are differences. Briefly these are the points to check in deciding whether to purchase or avoid a dictionary.

Authority. There are only a limited number of publishers of dictionaries. The reputable ones include Merriam-Webster; Oxford University Press; Random House; Scott, Foresman; Doubleday; Macmillan; Simon & Schuster; and Houghton Mifflin—to name the larger, better-known publishers. Among these the clear leader is Merriam-Webster. Their college dictionary goes through five or six printings each year and sells over a million copies annually. In specialized fields and other areas where dictionaries are employed, there are additional reputable publishers.

The reason that there are comparatively few general dictionary publishers is the same as that used to explain why there are so few working on general encyclopedias—cost. A dictionary is an expensive matter. For example, Simon & Schuster's *Webster's New World Dictionary* took seven years to complete and a basic investment of well over $2 million. Over $9 million was spent on revising *The Random House Dictionary*.

"Webster" in the title of a dictionary may be a sign of reassurance, and it is frequently found as the principal name of a number of dictionaries. G. & C. Merriam Company, which bought out the unsold copies of Noah Webster's dictionary at the time of his death in the nineteenth century, had the original claim to the name. For years the use of Webster's name was the subject of litigation. Merriam-Webster finally lost its case when the copyright on the name lapsed. It is now common property and may be used by any publisher. Hence the name "Webster's" in the title may or may not have anything to do with the original work which bore the name. Unless the publisher's name is recognized, "Webster" per se means nothing.[5]

Vocabulary. Vocabulary can be evaluated in terms of the period of the language covered, as well as in the number of words or entries. Other special vocabulary features may include slang, dialect, obsolete forms, and scientific or technical terms.

In the United States the field is divided between the *unabridged* (over 265,000 words) and the *abridged* (from 130,000 to 265,000 words) type of dictionary. Most dictionaries are abridged or limited to a given subject or topic. The two unabridged dictionaries vary from about 460,000 entries for *Webster's* to 315,000 for *Random House*.[6] The *Oxford English Dictionary* has 500,000 words but is not considered a general dictionary.

Most desk dictionaries, such as the much-used *Merriam-Webster's Collegiate Dictionary*, tenth edition, or the *American Heritage*, have about 150,000 to 170,000 words, and are considered more than sufficient for average use. There are many paperback dictionaries of from 50,000 to 85,000 words which serve the purpose of millions of people.

[5]The battle over "Webster" in a title continues to break out from time to time. In 1991 a federal jury in Manhattan awarded more than $2 million to Merriam-Webster after finding that Random House intentionally copied the jacket design of the Merriam-Webster dictionary. Random House used the name "Webster" in its competing desk dictionary, the *Random House Webster's College Dictionary*. In late 1994 a federal appeals court reversed the decision, allowing Random House to insert "Webster's" in the title of its dictionaries. The ruling noted there "was no testimony by any consumer, retail or wholesale, who intended to buy a Merriam-Webster dictionary but mistakenly bought a Random House dictionary because of confusion between the two product's trade dresses." "In a Word . . . ," *The New York Times*, September 14, 1994, p. B3.

[6]As no dictionary can meet the ultimate requirement of "unabridged," that is, contain all the words in the language, the descriptor is open to interpretation. *Webster's* claims the honor in its own definition of "unabridged," that is, "being the most complete of its class." It certainly is more complete than the *Random House*, which avoids this definition in favor of "a dictionary which has not been reduced in size by omission of terms or definitions; the most comprehensive edition of a given dictionary." The "given," of course, wraps up the case for Random House.

Up to Date. Dictionary revision is a never-ending affair. New editions are usually issued every seven to ten years, but hundreds of changes are usually made in each reprinting. These include adding new words, revising definitions of older words which have taken on new meaning, and dropping a few technical terms that are no longer used. A quick check of a desk or unabridged dictionary that claims to be up to date should include the common, sometimes much overused words, introduced into the language by television, radio, and film.

Again, the obvious advantage of a dictionary on a CD-ROM is that it can be updated rapidly by simply adding words and definitions. Still, someone has to make the additions. Simply because a dictionary is in an electronic format does not necessarily mean it is any more current than its print equivalent.

Format. A major consideration of format is the binding of the dictionary. Both individuals and libraries should purchase hardcover editions because the hard binding will withstand frequent use.

Another consideration is how the words are arranged. Most dictionaries now divide the words among a great number of separate headwords. If a dictionary does not do this, and crams many items under a single entry such as *lay,* one must look for *lay* to find such words as *layout* or *lay by.*

Other important factors to be evaluated are print size and how readability is affected by spacing between words and lines of type, the use of boldface type, and the differences in type families.

With the exception of some colored plates, most dictionary illustrations are black-and-white line drawings. The average desk dictionary has from 600 to 1500 illustrations, the unabridged from 7000 to 12,000.

Encyclopedia Material. Some dictionaries are a combination of facts found in an encyclopedia and a dictionary. To a certain extent all have some of these features in that they include sections, or work into the text, biographical and geographical data. A typical example of the encyclopedia wrapped with a dictionary is *The Oxford Encyclopedic English Dictionary* (New York: Oxford University Press, 1992, 1740 pp., $35). It is made up of material, slightly revised, from two separate works by the same publisher: *The Oxford Reference Dictionary* (1986, 992 pp., $29.95) and the *Concise Oxford Dictionary* (1990, 1493 pp., $25). The two are wedded in an awkward way throughout the text. In addition an appendix consists of world history and chronologies as well as charts and maps. Now while this may be suitable enough for home use, and many believe it and similar titles are now de rigeur for the individual, it would be a foolish choice for a library. The library would have the two works it compresses, as well as considerably better and more complete dictionaries and encyclopedias.

An exception to the rule against buying a combination of reference works with an encyclopedia is when one turns to a CD-ROM. Here it is perfectly acceptable. The CD-ROMs fill a need for numerous reference aids in one place.

A high-quality dictionary for a layperson, combined with a thesaurus, illustrations, and spelling guides as well as sound of pronunciation is a welcome addition.

Spelling. Where there are several forms of spelling, they should be clearly indicated. *Webster's* identifies the British spelling by the label "Brit."; other dictionaries normally indicate this variant by simply giving the American spelling first, for example, *analyze, analyse* or *theater, theatre.* Frequently two different spellings are given, either of which is acceptable. The user must determine the form to use. For example, *addable* or *addible, lollipop* or *lollypop.* (It is worth reminding both librarians and laypersons that explanations of such refinements are found in the preface. Always examine the preface.)

Etymologies. All large dictionaries indicate the etymology of a word by a shorthand system in brackets. The normal procedure is to show the root word in Latin, Greek, French, German, Old English, or some other language. Useful as this feature is, the student of etymology will be satisfied only with historical studies, such as Mencken's *The American Language,* to trace properly the history of a word and how it developed.

Definitions. Dictionaries usually give the modern meaning of words first. Exceptions include most older British-based dictionaries as well as the Merriam-Webster publications and *Webster's New World.* Without understanding the definition ladder, an unsuspecting reader (who has not read the preface) will leave the dictionary with an antiquated meaning. Also, the meaning may be precise, but it can lead to "circularity" in which words of similar difficulty and meaning are employed to define one another.

The quality of the definition depends on several factors. Separate and distinct meanings of words should be indicated clearly, and this usually is done by numbering the various definitions. The perfect definition is precise and clear, but in more technical, more abstract situations this is not always possible. What, for example, is the true definition of *love?*

Pronunciation. There are several different methods of indicating pronunciation, but most American publishers employ the diacritical one. In *Merriam-Webster's Collegiate Dictionary,* tenth edition, the pronunciation system tends to be quite detailed and, except for the expert, quite confusing. In the *American Heritage Dictionary* the process is much easier to understand. Again, look in the preface when in doubt.

All dictionaries employ the simple phonetic use of the familiar, that is, a person looking up *lark* finds the "r" is pronounced as in *park.* Regardless of what the person's accent may be, the transferred sound will be the same as that in *park.* Regional accents do make a difference in that *park* may be pronounced as "pock," "pawk," or even "pack." At the same time, the phoneticists consider variations such as the pronunciation of *tomato, potato,* and *economics* which differs from region to region, even person to person. In these cases, more than one pronunciation is noted as correct.

Anyone who listens to the British Broadcasting Corporation (BBC) news programs or their international World Service on shortwave is struck by the ease with which difficult personal and place names are pronounced. This is due to clever announcers and the BBC Pronunciation Research Unit which tells the newscaster how to say "Izetbegovic" or "Gventsadze" or whether General Colin Powell is pronounced as "pole" or "Powell."[7] A great advantage of electronic dictionaries is that many have pronunciation built in, and one may hear how the word should sound.

Syllabication. All dictionaries indicate, usually by a centered period or hyphen, how a word is to be divided into syllables. The information is mainly to help writers, editors, and secretaries, divide words at the ends of lines. There are special, short desk dictionaries which simply indicate syllabication of more common words without benefit of definition or pronunciation.

Synonyms. The average user does not turn to a general dictionary for synonyms, but their inclusion helps to differentiate among similar words. Some desk dictionaries indicate the differentiation and shades of meaning by short essays at the conclusion of many definitions.

Grammatical Information. The most generally useful grammatical help a dictionary renders is to indicate parts of speech. All single entries are classified as nouns, adjectives, verbs, and so on. Aside from this major division, dictionaries vary in method of showing adverbs, adjectives, plurals, and principal parts of a verb, particularly the past tense of irregular verbs. Usually the method is clearly ascertainable; but, again, the prefatory remarks should be studied in order to understand any particular presentation.

Bias. Most dictionaries are quick to point out that certain terms or words are not socially acceptable because they are vulgar or have insulting ethnic overtones. Cultural prejudices took many years to overcome in dictionaries. Although this is changing, at least in part, dictionaries may continue to err.

Usage. The most controversial aspect of evaluation concerns how proper usage is or is not indicated. Today there is division between those who wish a dictionary to be *prescriptive* (i.e., to clearly and categorically indicate what is or is not good, approved usage) or *descriptive* (i.e., to simply describe the language

---

[7]"How the BBC Learns to Say It Right," *The New York Times,* August 27, 1992, p. C20.

as it is spoken and written without any judgment as to whether it is acceptable by the common culture).

Dictionaries vary on how they handle usage. At one extreme is the work which says almost anything goes as long as it is popular (e.g., most of the Merriam-Webster dictionaries). At the other is the dictionary which is critical and gives rules of good usage (e.g., *Webster's New World Dictionary* from Simon & Schuster). In between is the "it depends" school which is more pragmatic than prescriptive or descriptive (e.g., *The American Heritage Dictionary*).

Most people believe that dictionaries should be prescriptive, setting rules about right and wrong usage. No one would deny that rules exist, as for example that verbs and subjects must agree in number. Bound up with belief in traditional grammar is a conviction that modern English is worse than that of previous generations because of a failure to teach grammar. Such apprehension was felt as early as the seventeenth century. Since then few can confidently claim many rules as absolute. Usage has become the foundation of not only descriptive linguistics, but also much grammar. The study of spoken English has become more important than written English.

> Nowadays there are newspaper stories at regular intervals lamenting the inability of students to write correct English sentences. . . . Most people . . . have a vague belief that grammar should be prescriptive, laying down rules about right and wrong. . . . (Unfortunately) few of the rules urged by prescriptive grammarians can confidently be declared absolute . . . (because) of the constantly changing nature of linguistic conventions. . . . One revolutionary consequence . . . has been a displacement of the study of the grammar of written English by the study of spoken English.[8]

The ultimate modern example of prescriptive dictionaries stems from a ruling of the Académie française in 1994. Established in 1635 to define and keep the rules of the French language, the Académie in the spring of 1994 promoted a law requiring that 3000 English words widely used in France be replaced by newly created French equivalents. Hence "prime time," used as part of everyday French, becomes "heure de grande écoute." The effort to protect French failed when the country's Constitutional Council ruled the Académie was in violation of laws governing freedom of expression.[9]

What makes anyone's English "correct"? Some say an answer is impossible. There are too many variables from a definition of correctness to the mean-

[8]Dean, Paul, "More Grammatical than Thou," *The Times Literary Supplement*, April 22, 1994, p. 8. Even Noam Chomsky now agrees that innate linguistic capacities, which enable children to generate language structures independently, are subject to speech displacement.

[9]"Mr. All-Good of France . . . ," *The New York Times*, August 7, 1994, p. 6. The British countered the French proposal by calling for the expulsion of all French words from the English language. Half in fun the member of Parliament urged England "forget words like baguette or croissant; they would be out. No one could visit a café or brasserie. There would be no aperitifs or hors d'oeuvres." "Why Don't They All Just Talk . . . ," *The Wall Street Journal*, August 18, 1994, p. B1.

ing of semantic competence. Different social and cultural situations offer their own rules.

UNABRIDGED DICTIONARIES

CD: Random House Unabridged Electronic Dictionary, 2d ed. New York: Random House, 1993, irregular update. $79.
Print: 1993, 2510 pp. $89.95.[10]

Print: Webster's Third New International Dictionary. Springfield, MA; Merriam-Webster, Inc., 1961, 2752 pp. $89.95. Supplements, 1976 to 1988, various paging, each $10.95.
No electronic format.

In 1988 it was called *The Random House Dictionary of the English Language*. By the early 1990s the marketing department saw the advantage of a switch to "unabridged." The question is then, Is it truly unabridged? The answer is yes, in that it has well over the average 130,000 to 265,000 words found in smaller works. The answer is no if it is compared with its competitor. *Webster's* claims 450,000 entries or some 145,000 more than in *Random House*.

Today there is only one unabridged dictionary of the English language. This is *Webster's Third New International*.[11] One may count *The Oxford English Dictionary* (*OED*) in this category, but it really is more concerned with etymology than definitions, and is not meant to be an everyday working dictionary.

Essentially, then, "unabridged" is what the publisher cares to define. As long as it is within reason, which the *Random House* is, few will argue, or for that matter, care. Where does this leave libraries? Most libraries should have the *Webster's* (which does have more words) *and* the *Random House* (which is more current).

The *Random House* dictionary, no matter what the publisher wishes to call it, has a solid reputation. There is no argument that this is one of the best "big" dictionaries. The publisher claims 315,000 entries and 2500 illustrations. There are added features, such as concise, yet quite practical, bilingual dictionaries in French, German, Spanish, and Italian; almost 30 pages of full-color maps; and the usual style manual.

Although not as large as *Webster's*, the new *Random House* has the distinct advantage of being relatively current. Approximately 50,000 new words were

---

[10]While the print and CD-ROM versions are priced separately, in most situations the user may buy the two for $100 total.

[11]Many libraries still have the now out-of-print *Funk & Wagnalls New Standard Dictionary of the English Language* (New York: Funk & Wagnalls, 1964.) This contains close to 460,000 words, even more than in *Webster's Third New International*. Unfortunately, the publisher (now HarperCollins) has no plans to revise. In its time it was a competitor to *Webster's*. Most libraries had both.

added or revised for the second edition, such as carjacker. Expletives are in more common use, and many four-letter words were added. These are normally identified as "vulgar."

The dictionary is descriptive. One looks, without much help, for some guidance in the use of the word *hope* as a modifier. Disputes about *hopefully* are noted, and other embattled terms are described as such. It accepts the word, *infer* in its accepted meaning to draw a conclusion and also as a synonym "to imply" or "to suggest," but adds that the distinction between the two words is "widely observed."

Definitions are clear, and uses words likely to be understood by the average person. Many entries conclude with helpful synonyms and antonyms.

The CD-ROM version of the *Random House Unabridged Dictionary* consists of the second edition of the printed version, first published in 1988, with about 1000 new entries. There are some 1500 revisions of the initial work. So while the 1993 CD-ROM is improved it remains primarily the 1988 work with its 315,000 entries.

There is no equivalent CD-ROM for *Webster's*. The *Random House* CD-ROM has all the usual advantages. First and foremost one may search for related words, quotations, synonyms, and the like by a click or a key. Second, in a library it is available for everyone as a supplementary aid to searching at a computer. And, finally, it has the usual plus of taking up little or no space.

Webster's

Despite the publishing date (1961), *Webster's* is essential. Each new printing includes some new words, or variations on definitions of older words. See, for example, recent computer, political, and sociological terms. Most will be included, if not in the main work, at least in the two supplements which add about 22,000 words to the basic 450,000 in the primary volume.

Noah Webster had been involved with publishing dictionaries through the early nineteenth century. It is important to stress that 1909 was the date of the first current series of *unabridged* titles. A second edition came out in 1934 and a third in 1961. A 1996 dictionary has several copyright dates: 1961, the date of the original revision, and later dates—usually every five years—which imply some revisions since 1961. However, the work is primarily the original 1961 work. The publisher has given no indication when the next edition will be available, although this is expected toward the end of the century. Until then the library must have *Webster's* as the only true unabridged dictionary, along with the much more current *Random House*.

Since it is a recognized authority, many claim *Webster's* should be prescriptive and lay down the verbal law. It does not. It is descriptive, and sometimes it is difficult, despite labels, to pinpoint the good, the bad, or the indifferent use of a word. Also, it has such an involved scheme of indicating pronunciation that most people are helpless to understand how to pronounce anything.

DESK (COLLEGE) DICTIONARIES

CD: Merriam-Webster's Collegiate Dictionary and Thesaurus. Springfield, MA: Merriam-Webster, Inc., 1995. $199.
Print: Merriam-Webster's Collegiate Dictionary, 10th ed. 1993, 1559 pp. $20.95.

CD: The American Heritage Talking Dictionary. Boston: Houghton Mifflin Company, 1995. $40. (Note: Also a part of the *Microsoft Bookshelf,* discussed elsewhere in this text.)
Print: The American Heritage Dictionary of the English Language, 3d ed. 1992, 1664 pp. $35.
Online: 1993 to date, not updated. CompuServe, rates vary.

CD: The Random House Webster's Dictionary and Thesaurus College Edition. New York: Random House, 1995. $99.
Print: The Random House Webster's College Dictionary, 1984, 1600 pp. $17.95. Paperback, 1994. $20.

CD: Webster's New World Dictionary of the American Language, in *The Software Toolworks Reference.* Novato, CA: Software Toolworks, Inc., 1991 to date, annual. $99.
Print: Webster's New World Dictionary of the American Language, 3d ed. Englewood Cliffs, NJ: Prentice Hall General Reference, 1994. 1574 pp. $18.1600 pp. $1795.

The four dictionaries listed are the four best, and the four most often found in libraries and, for that matter, in the home.[12] While most are available in electronic format, only one or two need to be purchased by a library on a CD-ROM. On the other hand, all four of the print versions are necessary, except in the smallest library. A careful watch should be kept for new editions, for updates of the four. The standard publishers' dictionaries are periodically revised, and all are authoritative.

The core of the dictionary publishing business is the familiar desk or college version. It normally includes from about 150,000 to 175,000 words, has the familiar illustrations, and offers added material such as short biographical and geographical notes. The definitions are written for those with a college education, although they can be used by almost all age groups and by anyone who has basic literacy.

---

[12]The library should purchase these four, but laypersons have numerous acceptable alternatives. Each firm publishes variations on the basic dictionary, often for less money. Houghton Mifflin publishes several versions of the primary dictionary, for example, see *The American Heritage Concise Dictionary,* 3d ed. (1994, 960 pp., $10.95). This has an excellent format and is in paperback.

These four primary college or desk dictionaries by these four publishers meet accepted standards. Any dictionary of this type by another publisher is highly suspect. The four account for sales of about 2.5 million hardcover copies each and every year. Shorter paperback versions of some are available, but are not all that popular.

Differences are essentially those of format, arrangement, systems of indicating pronunciation, and length of definitions. All include synonyms, antonyms, etymologies, and limited biographical and gazetteer information. Price variations are minimal. The natural question is which is best, and the answer depends primarily on personal need. All have about the same number of words, and all meet the evaluative tests of excellence.

The CD-ROM versions are not as popular, although they are gaining ground as part of networks in libraries. In the home and in the office they usually are part of a larger reference system, such as *Microsoft Bookshelf.* It remains to be seen whether the dictionary by itself on a CD-ROM will ever do as well as the familiar printed volumes.

Webster's Collegiate

On CD-ROM the *Merriam-Webster's Collegiate Dictionary* picks up all the material from the printed work. But, in addition, it includes the same company's *Collegiate Thesaurus.* The menu screen allows the user to call up the dictionary or the thesaurus. After one types in the main word, there is a standard chart which gives part of speech, date of its appearance in the language, the usage label, pronunciation, and etymology. The full definition is given. Full boolean searches are possible. A nice touch is that if one misspells the word, the screen shows a question, as well as a list of words which may offer the correct spelling. Cross-references may be checked from the definitions and examples. *Webster's* is typical of many CD-ROMs at this level. While the primary word may be searched, one cannot, as in more sophisticated systems, search for etymologies, parts of speech, usage, and the like.

Merriam-Webster's Collegiate Dictionary, tenth edition, is based on the unabridged *Third.* It has about 160,000 words and 600 illustrations. It reflects the philosophy of the larger work and places considerable emphasis on contemporary pronunciation and definitions. As in the primary dictionary, the philosophy is descriptive, although with the tenth edition there is more emphasis on usage notes (fully explained in the explanatory preface). "Nonstandard" is the warning for the use of *ain't,* and this is followed by a short paragraph that discusses the current use of the word. In this case it is noted that "although widely disapproved as nonstandard and more common in the habitual speech of the less educated, *ain't* . . . is flourishing in American English." When the four-letter words are explained, and major ones are included, the usage note is "considered obscene" or "considered vulgar."

There are passable line drawings, although in number they do not come close to those found in the *American Heritage Dictionary*. The history of words is usually shown, along with a date when the word first appeared in the language. The pronunciation system remains a problem. The symbols employed are listed in full inside the back cover, and a shorter version appears at the bottom of each right-hand page. The whole is extremely complicated and it takes a special section, "Guide to Pronunciation," to try to explain the process to readers. The overall result is less than satisfactory.

Although the maze of pronunciation symbols may be puzzling, the definitions are improved. Derived from the unabridged version, the definitions are considerably more lucid and simplified. They are still given in chronological order, with the modern meaning last. For example, *explode* begins with the labeled archaic definition "to drive from the stage by noisy disapproval."

The 12,000 geographical and 6500 personal names are not included in the main alphabet, but are separate features in the appendixes, a habit now followed by other dictionaries. The appendixes also include foreign words and phrases.

American Heritage

The famous *American Heritage Dictionary* is transformed only in part on its CD-ROM.[13] The CD-ROM contains all the information in the print volume, with a distinct plus. The 1995 version, with "talking" in the title, reveals a strong selling point. Many of the words are pronounced for the viewer. Other than that, it adds *Roget's II: The New Thesaurus*. The search patterns are clear and one may move from the simple definition of a single word to matching it with synonyms, parts of speech, correct or incorrect usage, and the like. The linkages are good to excellent and the disc may be used as much for a history of the language as for a definition of a single word. (Note, too, this is part of the *Microsoft Bookshelf*, but without the verbal cues.)

It is the only desk dictionary (1995) available on online through CompuServe. This is a smaller work with only 116,000 of the 200,000 words found on the CD-ROM and in print.

American Heritage stresses prescriptive entries. The usage notes are useful to help guide the average person seeking to find whether this or that word may be used in polite society. This is determined by a panel, and the collective result is a valuable guide for laypersons. The notes summarize the sometimes differing views of the panel and are well worth reading.

[13]Numerous versions of this CD-ROM came out before 1994. Some are drawn from an abridged version of the dictionary, others from the *American Heritage Illustrated Encyclopedic Dictionary* (with 80,000 words), a less than successful wedding of encyclopedia and dictionary. None is recommended.

On the middle ground between the standard desk or college dictionary and the unabridged dictionary, the *American Heritage* weighs in at a hefty 7 pounds (vs. about 4 pounds for the desk version) and at $40 or about twice as much as its competitors. How can a publisher manage to compete? The answer is: First, there are more words, about 200,000 versus some 160,000 entries in the nearest competitor. There are, or so the publisher claims, over 16,000 new words in the 1995 edition from computer terms such as "laptop" and "pixel" to socially new expressions from "birthparent" to "slam dunk." Second, the third edition carries on the tradition of a superior format. The entries are in boldface. The illustrations, typography, and general layout are quite superior to those of competitors. Third, it has the famous "usage panel" (now almost 175 members) who determine what is good or bad usage and say so in over 500 usage notes.

In a perceptive review of the *American Heritage*, English scholar Noel Perrin points out the importance of the usage notes. He deplores "to author," and winces when he runs across phrases like "she has authored four best sellers." It should be "she has written." In *Webster's*, "author" is simply defined as to be the author of. In the *Random House* the definition is much the same. But in the *American Heritage* there is a 22-line note, after and separate from the definition. Among other points the note makes is that "one can write, but not author."[14]

Fourth, there are 30,000 or so illustrations of how the words are properly used. These are made up by the staff, and sometimes the examples are silly. On the other hand, they are easy to understand and fortified with some 4000 quotations. The *American Heritage* is the best single desk dictionary for etymology and gives details on the linguistic sources of most words. By contrast *Webster's* (both titles) are incomplete and much briefer.

Webster's New World Dictionary

As part of a larger unit, *Webster's New World Dictionary* is on a CD-ROM with numerous reference publications by Simon & Schuster, for example, *Webster's New World Thesaurus*, *Webster's New World Guide to Concise Writing*, and five other related titles. It is searched in the usual fashion, although, because the disc has so many other units, it is employed primarily for spelling and definition of words. This hardly discounts the value of the CD-ROM, particularly as the annual updates do include new materials and are one-half the price of the original disc.

Again, though, one would be better off simply using the printed work for most questions, and the print version is quite superior. *Webster's New World Dictionary of the American Language* is not from Merriam-Webster, and the two works

[14]Noel Perrin, "Two Tomes Four Our Times," *The New York Times Book Review*, August 23, 1992, p. 3.

are often confused. This Prentice Hall *Webster's* is not a Merriam-Webster product, but it is equally reliable.

A total revision of the desk dictionary was made in 1988, about seventeen years after the previous edition. Since then partial revision has been made biennially. The publisher claims that there are now 170,000 entries, and about 800 black-and-white illustrations. The *New World* is aptly named because its primary focus is on American English as it is spoken and written. There are particularly good definitions which are closely related to current speech. The definitions are in historical order, not by the most common current understanding of the word.

A star preceding an entry indicates an American word or expression. There are some 11,000 of these. Meaning is illustrated with made-up sentences and phrases. Pronunciation is clear, and a key is found in the lower corner of every right-hand page. There are only a few—about 800—illustrations, but these are at least adequate.

Of the three, it is by now the most prescriptive, even more so than the *American Heritage*. It is favored by *The New York Times*, as well as by various press services. Given this type of recommendation, it has won many readers.

Random House

The Random House Webster's Dictionary and Thesaurus College Edition CD-ROM includes the text from the printed version with 180,000 words and includes biographical and geographical data. The thesaurus has the total text of the *Random House Thesaurus* with more than 275,000 synonyms and antonyms. The CD-ROM version has many advantages, most of which are found in other CD-ROM dictionaries. Among these: (1) The ability to move back and forth from the words in the dictionary to needed synonyms in the thesaurus. If, for example, the user needs another word for "sarcastic," a key will bring up "acerbic," "caustic," and so forth. If one is not sure of the meanings, another key defines "acerbic." And so it goes for words as needed. (2) Boolean logic allows one to find the word or phrase for an uncertain phrase.

The print *Random House* is, like *Merriam-Webster's*, modeled after the parent company's larger work, that is, *The Random House Unabridged Dictionary*. It is much the same, only it is less costly and has fewer words, that is, $18 versus $89.95 and 180,000 entries versus 315,000. It is also smaller in physical size and a good addition to any personal library. It has a fine "User's Guide" in the introduction, and one librarians might consult for general information on dictionaries. Unfortunately, not one person in a thousand is likely to read the introductory material.

The entries are the same as in the larger volume. As with the parent work, the dictionary can be considered "best" in several areas: its commonsense treatment of slang; the concise, clear definitions; and a descriptive approach to words.

The *Random House Webster's College Dictionary* was both applauded and hissed for its deference to politically correct spellings and synonyms. It includes entries such as "womyn" (as an alternative for women), "herstory" for (history), and a primer on avoiding sexist language. Other substitutes suggested: firefighter for fireman; ancestor for forefather; homemaker for housewife; housecleaner for cleaning woman; and human being, or human or person or individual for man.[15]

Reduced-Word Dictionaries

There are many dictionaries limited to under 60,000 words. Some of these are available in paperback and from the same publishers of the standard desk works. Others are from equally reliable firms. For example, the *Oxford American Dictionary* (New York and London: Oxford University Press, 1986) has only 30,000 words. *The Concise Oxford Dictionary of Current English* from the same publisher has 50,000 words, and there are other versions from Oxford.

An expensive, although satisfactory CD-ROM dictionary which falls out of the usual category is *The Find It Webster* (North York, ON, Canada: Quality Learning, 1991, to date, annual, $99). This includes 85,000 entries with short definitions and examples of usage. Also, (1) there are subentries of words grouped to show relationships, and (2) audio pronunciation is available for about one-third of the words defined. The peculiar thing here is that the dictionary is based on *The New York Times* newspaper citations and not on a standard dictionary publisher's file. Nevertheless the result is passable. (Note: Earlier editions of this were called *The New York Times Dictionary* and *The New York Times Everyday Dictionary*.

CHILDREN'S DICTIONARIES

CD: Macmillan Dictionary for Children. New York: The Macmillan Company, 1991 to date, irregular update. $60.
   Print: 1994, 900 pp. $15.

CD: The World Book Dictionary in The World Book Multimedia Encyclopedia. Chicago, IL: World Book Publishing, 1992 to date, annual. $395.
   Print: 1983, 2 vols. $79.
   Print: Scott, Foresman Beginning Dictionary. Glenview, IL: Scott, Foresman,

---

[15]See, too, *Official Politically Correct Dictionary and Handbook* (New York: Villard Books, 1992). The latter is a listing of language manglers such as "accidental delivery of ordinance equipment" (translated: "bombing something other than the intended target"); or "follicularly challenged" (tr: "bald"), "horizontally challenged" (fat), and "temptron" ("temptress or tempter." See "waitron.")

1988, 832 pp. $17.95.

No electronic format.

CD: Merriam-Webster's Dictionary for Kids. Springfield, MA: Merriam-Webster, Inc., 1995. $59.95

Print: Webster's Elementary Dictionary, 1990, 607 pp. $12.95

There are as many, if not more, dictionaries for children as for adults. The reason is easy to see: There are many school libraries and all of them require not just one dictionary, but different ones to fit different grade levels. It is, in a word, a lucrative market for publishers.

Are they of equal worth? It is the same story as for adult works. A few publishers are responsible for the accepted titles. And these few are generally the same publishers who issue the adult dictionaries. World Book; Scott, Foresman; and Macmillan are exceptions in that they concentrate on children and young people's dictionaries rather than adult titles.

Oddly enough, there are a minimum of CD-ROM versions for children. It is strange because this is one area where animation and sound would be appreciated. A CD-ROM dictionary for children seems more appropriate than for adults. Unquestionably all of this will change.

The works are usually graded for preschool through elementary grades, for junior high school or equivalent, and for high school. The rub is that by junior high school, students should be able to use adult desk dictionaries and not need special works for their age group. Obviously, some teachers (and librarians) do not agree. If they did, there would not be the specialized dictionaries for younger people. A case can be made for elementary grades, and most would agree that at this level at least, the younger dictionary is preferable to the adult work.

The four listed here are the ones most often found in school and public libraries along with the standard adult works for beyond elementary grades. They are four out of almost 50 possibilities. Many of the 50 are spin-offs of the basic four titles from the publishers. For example, Macmillan has about 10 related works. On the other hand, World Book has only the single title.

The CD-ROM *Macmillan Dictionary* is typical of what is likely to be a developing group. It has the complete text of the printed volume (i.e., 12,000 words and approximately 1000 illustrations) plus the necessary animation and sound effects to make looking up words much fun. There are several word games as well. In addition to the careful, easy-to-understand definitions, the dictionary offers word histories and language notes. The animated character "Zac" provides a guided tour showing the beginner how to get started. From time to time Zac pops up with comments about this or that word. The whole is for the reader who is from seven to twelve years old, although it may be used by younger and older children. While a bit crude, it is at least a beginning.

Librarians often favor the print *Macmillan Dictionary* over all the others because: (1) It has 35,000 entries for grades 2 through 6, although it may be used by younger or older students. (2) It has 1000 illustrations in color. (3) It uses simple easy-to-understand definitions with numerous illustrative phrases and sentences. (4) Its pronunciations, given at the end of the definition, are clear. (5) It contains added materials such as maps, lists of presidents, and so forth.

All this adds up to a work a trifle too elementary for some, and it lags in including new words which may be used regularly on, say, MTV. Nevertheless, because it is so easy to use and so easy to understand, librarians have found many children prefer it.

The *World Book Dictionary* has 225,000 entries. It has from 125,000 to 200,000 more words than its rivals. This makes it the "unabridged" dictionary for children and young people. The dictionary follows the familiar Thorndike-Barnhart system of using definition words that are within the grasp of the reader. One does not have to turn to other entries to find the meaning of words used in a definition. The definitions are models of clarity, although a sophisticated adult is likely to find many of them much too simple. The format is good, and the illustrations, although not up to the number in the *American Heritage*, are at least clear and placed properly.

The problem is the price. One may buy an excellent desk dictionary that contains about 150,000 to 175,000 words for about $18 to $20, and *Webster's Third New International*, with about twice as many words is only $79.95, the same price as the *World Book* entry. Nevertheless, if a dictionary must be purchased for children and young adults, it is a first choice.

The *World Book Dictionary* is available on CD-ROM, but only as part of the less than satisfactory CD-ROM version of the fine encyclopedia. As part of *The World Book Multimedia Encyclopedia*, the dictionary has the advantage of being closely tied to the information work. Words can be called up for definition and explanation as found in the text of the encyclopedia, or separately. Unfortunately, the dictionary cannot be purchased without taking on the encyclopedia. So, for all intents and purposes, it really is not a separate CD-ROM dictionary.

Scott, Foresman publishes a series of dictionaries that include titles for the elementary grades through high school. The beginning version for elementary grades 1 to 5 is typical, and is based on the Thorndike-Barnhart system, which relies heavily on illustrations. About 75 percent of the pictures are in color. Some words have histories set off in a different-colored ink. The whole is in a pleasing format, but is as much for instruction as for definitions.

Equally an opinion winner among librarians is *Webster's Elementary Dictionary*. It is somewhat similar to the Macmillan entry in terms of number of entries (33,000), care of definitions used, and so forth. On the other hand, and this is a major difference, the publisher relies on quality rather than appeal to a special age group. The result is a true junior type of adult work rather than a specialized dictionary for children.

The CD-ROM version, based on the printed work, has a new name *Merriam-Webster's Dictionary for Kids* and is distributed in the United States by Mindscape. It appeared first in 1994 and contains the same number of words and definitions as the printed work. Is it worth the difference between the price of the printed volume and the higher priced CD-ROM? The added $45 or so will buy the user phonetic pronunciations for 20,000 of the 33,000 entries, 200 animations, 500 color illustrations, word games, and approximately 200 sound effects. Is it worth the extra money? Possibly, but the other dictionaries seem to do better in the CD-ROM area.

Which is best among the numerous children's dictionaries? To reach a consensus much depends on whether the work is used in a classroom, in a home, or in a library. Among the titles listed here one could not go wrong in selecting any depending on purpose and age of the prospective user. Considering the basic works for preschool through high school, and the numerous spin-offs (for grade levels), any of the dictionaries by the firms listed will be good to excellent. Beyond that, and for a definitive appraisal of scores of such titles see Kister's *Dictionaries*, pp. 255–339. This is by way of a definitive listing, with grades for each title.

SUPPLEMENTARY DICTIONARIES

There are a group of works, primarily synonyms and guides to good usage which supplement the regular dictionaries. All of these, in one form or another, should be found in libraries, and many are useful in the home.

Synonyms and Antonyms

Print: Roget's International Thesaurus. New York: HarperCollins, 5th ed. 1992, 1280 pp. $19.
>   No electronic format.
Print: Roget A to Z. New York: HarperCollins, 1994, 765 pp. $17.
>   No electronic format.
Print: Roget's II: The New Thesaurus. 1993, 800 pp. $13.50.
>   No electronic format.
CD: Roget's II: Electronic Thesaurus. Boston: Houghton Mifflin, 1991, in *American Heritage Dictionary* and in *Microsoft Bookshelf.*
CD: *Merriam-Webster's Collegiate Thesaurus.* Springfield, MA: Merriam-Webster, Inc., 1994 to date. (Note: The *Merriam-Webster's Collegiate Thesaurus* is also included in the CD-ROM electronic edition of *Merriam-Webster's Collegiate Dictionary* discussed earlier.)
>   *Print:* 1976, 944 pp. $14.95.

A book of synonyms is often among the most popular books in the private or public library. It offers a key to crossword puzzles, and it serves almost everyone who wishes to increase his or her command of English. There are some

50 dictionaries giving both synonyms and antonyms in English, but the titles listed above appear more often in libraries. Certainly, the best known is the work of Peter Mark Roget (1779–1869), a doctor in an English mental asylum. He began the work at age 71 and by his ninetieth birthday had seen it through 20 editions. (The term *thesaurus* means a "treasury," a "store," a "hoard"; and *Roget's* is precisely that.)

His optimistic aim was to classify all human thought under a series of verbal categories, and his book is so arranged. There are approximately 1000 classifications. Within each section, headed by a key word, are listed, by parts of speech, the words and phrases from which the reader may select the proper synonym. Antonyms are usually placed immediately after the main listing; thus, "possibility/impossibility," "pride/humility."

The advantage of *Roget's* is that like ideas are placed together. An American professor and writer explains the practical use of *Roget's:* "When I began to write I learned never to repeat a word, but to vary the term or phrase so as to avoid the dead hand of repetition."[16] The distinct disadvantage is that *Roget's* offers no guidance or annotations; and an overzealous user may select a synonym or an antonym which looks and sounds good but is far from expressing what is meant. Sean O'Faolain, the Irish short story writer, recalls giving a copy of *Roget's* to a Dutch-born journalist to improve his English, but the effect was appalling. For example, the journalist might have wished to know the synonym for *sad*. He would have consulted the index and found four or five alternatives, such as "painful," "gray," "bad," "dejected," and, surprisingly, "great." When he turned to the proper section, he would have found 200 or 300 synonyms. Unless the user has a clear understanding of the language, *Roget's* can be a difficult work.

There are at least a dozen titles which freely use Roget's name. Like Webster's, the name Roget cannot be copyrighted and is free to any publisher. Many of the dozen titles are little more than poor, dated copies of the master's original work.

The genuine *Roget's* (from the master's original work) was published first in the United States by Thomas Crowell in 1911. Longman began work on a new edition in the late 1980s, but with each printing, minor additions and changes have been made. HarperCollins *Roget's* is organized in the original way, that is, by concept. The work sells about 175,000 copies each year in hardcover and close to 45,000 in paperback. This is the most popular thesaurus on the market. The 1992 fifth edition, which has no CD-ROM version, includes 140,000 basic words under 15 broad classifications—from body to place—which are further subdivided into about 1100 categories such as pleasure, space, and the like. The logically connected series of idea groupings, for example, move from "attraction" to "repulsion" to "ejection."

[16]Daniel Bell, "Referred Pleasures," *The Times Literary Supplement,* April 22, 1994, p. 12.

The fifth edition of *Roget's* was edited by Robert Chapman, familiar as the editor of the *New Dictionary of American Slang* and the *Thesaurus of American Slang.* Chapman not only arranged *Roget's* in a fashion that is easy to follow, but also included new categories and numerous slang words. (The latter are usually labeled as "nonformal.") He expects another edition will not be published for ten to fifteen years. Chapman is editor, too, of the same publisher's *Roget A to Z* which is an alphabetical arrangement of terms.

Most versions of *Roget's* are in alphabetical order, not arranged by concept like, for example, *Roget A to Z* and *The Oxford Thesaurus: American Edition* (Oxford University Press, 1992, 1005 pp. paperback. $19.95). This is a "reverse dictionary," that is, it allows one to ask and find the answer to such a question as "What is the synonym for *sloppy?*" or "What is the precise word to describe a *kindly person?*" The catch is that one may suffer a mental block and be unable to look up a related word.

As the advertisement for *Roget A to Z* claims, there are more than "300,000 up-to-date words" which open with "abandon" and closes with "zoom." Several helpful features make this the best of its kind: (1) Most frequently used synonyms are printed in boldface. (2) Quotations, which illustrate usage, are from literature. (3) Slang is included, and dutifully labeled as "nonformal." This latter feature literally creates a useful thesaurus of slang.

As part of two CD-ROM packages, *Roget's II: The New Thesaurus* offers more than 100,000 synonyms and antonyms for about 75,000 terms. The search process allows one to switch from a definition in the *American Heritage Dictionary* to a synonym, or to search for a synonym of any given word. Easy to use and inexpensive, it is a useful addition to these all-purpose dictionary and writer's guides. On the other hand, it is often faster to simply employ the printed version, at least when looking up only one or two synonyms.

Aside from *Roget's International,* the most popular book of synonyms is *Merriam-Webster's Collegiate Thesaurus.* Here the 100,000 entries are arranged alphabetically. After each main entry there is a definition (a useful device) and then a list of synonyms. This is followed by related words and, finally, by a list of antonyms. Sometimes quotations are employed to make it clear how words should be used.

Webster's is updated with each edition, and the work is as current as almost any now in print. However its primary claim to popularity is its ease of use. Some would say it is too easy and totally ignores the purpose of the original *Roget's* but nevertheless *Webster's* should be found in libraries.

The *Merriam-Webster's Collegiate Thesaurus* stands alone as a single CD-ROM or as part of a package. It has about 35,000 headwords with 100,000 or so synonyms and antonyms. Whether the separate CD-ROM is an advantage is questionable in that it is easier to use the printed version or the combination with the *Merriam-Webster's Collegiate Dictionary* on a single CD-ROM.

Webster's New Dictionary of Synonyms (1980, 942 pp.) is another version of the *Collegiate*. It has fewer words, but the arrangement and the approach are much the same. The work is particularly helpful in discriminating between what, at first sight, appear to be similar words.

As noted in the discussion of desk dictionaries, Random House offers a combination of thesaurus and dictionary in its CD-ROM *Random House Webster's Dictionary and Thesaurus College Edition*. This functions like the other CD-ROM combinations, for example, *Merriam-Webster's Collegiate Dictionary and Thesaurus*. There is a print version, *Random House Thesaurus, College Edition* (1992, 812 pp., $16.95).

Usage and Manuscript Style

CD: The Chicago Manual of Style, 14th ed. Chicago: University of Chicago Press, 1993, in *Microsoft Bookshelf.*
Print: 936 pp. $40.

Print: Turabian, Kate. *A Manual for Writers of Term Papers, Theses, and Dissertations,* 4th ed. Chicago: University of Chicago Press, 1987, 300 pp. $20. Paperback, $7.95.
No electronic format.

Print: Wilson, Kenneth. *The Columbia Guide to Standard American English.* New York: Columbia University Press, 1993, 482 pp. $24.95.
No electronic format.

Print: Webster's Dictionary of English Usage. Springfield, MA: Merriam-Webster, Inc., 1989, 980 pp. $18.95.
No electronic format.

As few standard dictionaries are prescriptive, that is, establish rules of good and poor language usage, many people require outside help. This comes in a number of guides. Also, others may need suggestions about how to use more than one word, for example, to describe delight or the sensation after eating too much.

As one of the eight members of the *Microsoft Bookshelf, The Chicago Manual of Style* can be turned to on a CD-ROM. It appears to be the only one of several standard guides to good English, available in an electronic format. Be that as it may, the purpose, the content, and the scope of the work are the same as in the printed volume.

First and foremost, the *Manual* is a guide for preparation of papers, either for publication or for a class. Second, these days it shows how to employ electronic databases for everything from indexing to footnotes. Third, it has significant, accepted advice on nitty-gritty matters from the proper use of authors' initials to arrangement of citations as references, footnotes, additional readings, and the like. There are sections, too, with definitions of book and paper terms, copyright information, and related areas. It is a standard for all libraries and for many individuals.

Turabian, as *A Manual For Writers* is often called, is an even more specific work for students. It is updated regularly and is, in a real sense, a shorter version of the *Chicago Manual*. Here one finds specific rules for everything from grammar and footnotes to the type of paper to employ. It also discusses rules concerning punctuation, spacing, and indexing. There are discussions of how to cite computer sources, nonprint material, the meaning of cataloging in publications, and even how an author should phrase a letter when sending a publisher a manuscript.

Another favored guide to composition is the *MLA Handbook for Writers of Research Papers*, 4th edition (New York: Modern Language Association, 199.5). This covers much the same ground as Turabian, but it is more detailed in such areas as how to choose a topic, how to use the library, and how to write the paper. The new edition is particularly useful in explaining how to cite electronic publications from the Internet to CD-ROMs.

There are at least a dozen guides to good English, and new ones come out each year. Still, among the standards are the two listed here. The *Columbia Guide* offers the obvious rules for spelling, grammatical twists and turns, and appropriate speech for various situations. The dictionary form, with numerous cross-references, makes it easy to follow. A novel, some would say democratic, approach not found in other guides of this type includes recommendations for various levels of speech and writing. If, for example, "hopefully" is acceptable at the lower part of the five levels analyzed, it is not the best expression for a formal paper at the high level. This allows the author, Kenneth Wilson, to be both prescriptive and descriptive. This can become confusing and in most cases *Webster's* is preferable, at least for amateurs.

Webster's Dictionary of English Usage offers direct advice and clear instructions about proper usage. It is highly recommended for all libraries as an up-to-date, easy-to-follow guide. It will answer the vexing problems of usage. Arranged alphabetically from "a, an" to "zoom" it is extremely easy to use. The editors tend to follow the prescriptive school, as does the publisher, but there is a discussion of different points of view. See, for example, the ubiquitous "ain't" and some 10 columns of discourse with scores of illustrative quotes. (There are 20,000 such quotations used throughout to emphasize this or that point of usage.)

Another fascinating aspect of usage concerns English as spoken by sections of minority groups in America. For example, students whose language is BEV (black English vernacular) find that standard English can be a barrier. The problem is that what is acceptable in one's own particular culture may be different from what is acceptable in the working world. At one extreme are those who view BEV as a civil right, so much so that a study of it may be part of the curriculum. At the other extreme are those who attack it for being little more than poorly mastered English.

HISTORICAL DICTIONARY

CD: The Oxford English Dictionary (OED) 2nd Edition on CD-ROM. New York: Oxford University Press, 1992 to date. Not updated, $895.[17]
Print: 1989, 20 vols. $2500.[18] Additional series: Vol. 1 (234 pp.) and Vol. 2 (234 pp.), 1995, $35 each.

Print: The New Shorter Oxford English Dictionary. New York: Oxford University Press, 1993, 2 vols., 3776 pp. $100.
No electronic format.

Of all the dictionaries of the English language, the *Oxford English Dictionary* (begun as the *New English Dictionary on Historical Principles*) is the most magnificent, and it is with some justification that H. L. Mencken called it "the emperor of dictionaries." The purpose of the dictionary is to trace the history of the English language. This is done through definitions and quotations which illustrate the variations in the meaning and use of words. The entry on "set" alone is 60,000 words long; *Paradise Lost* has just under 80,000 words in total.

Author and critic Hugh Kenner ranks the *OED* as the single "epic" of reference works, or, for that matter, the one epic of the nineteenth century. If *Paradise Lost* is the epic of the seventeenth century, Gibbon's *Decline and Fall* of the eighteenth, and Joyce's *Ulysses* of the twentieth, then the *OED* is the nineteenth-century's "unparalleled achievement, more multi-authorized even than Homer."[19] The *OED*'s first fascicle was published when the Irish author of *Ulysses* was two years old, and the last when *Ulysses* itself was six. Work on the great dictionary began about the middle of Victoria's and Tennyson's century.

[17]A CD-ROM version appeared first in 1988, but contained only the contents of the 1933 edition without the supplements. It is no longer being published, and should be removed from most libraries.

[18]By 1995 the publisher was offering the printed set for "sale price $1500." The second edition is a combination of the older work, plus four supplements. The original 13-volume printed set was completed in 1933, and from 1972 through 1986 a 4-volume supplement was published which, among other things, updated material in the original work and added new words, including the four-letter variety. With the publication of the second edition, the editors added only another 5000 words and meanings. The four supplementary volumes, incorporated into the 1989 second edition, are available in a single one-volume "compact edition" for under $100 from numerous used-book and remainder dealers. Also, the original 20-volume set in a 1-volume compact version, but lacking the supplementary volumes, can be had for $49.95. Note: a "compact" edition means reducing the print so that about nine pages of the original can be set on one 9 by 12 page of the compact. A magnifying glass is required.

[19]Hugh Kenner, "Pound and Eliot in Academe," *The Times Literary Supplement*, November 5, 1993, p. 13.

The dictionary defines 616,500 words and supports the definitions and usages with some 2.5 million quotations. In *Webster's New World Dictionary* the etymology of *black* takes 5 lines, whereas in the *OED* it takes 23 lines. The word *point* in the *OED* consumes 18 columns and *put* accounts for 30 columns. (This is an observation of fact, not a criticism. After all *Webster's* is in one volume, while the *OED* is in 20.)[20]

The *OED* on a CD-ROM is a "best buy" in every sense. It is more compact than the printed set, it costs less ($850 vs. $1500 to $2500), and, most important, it gives the user access points impossible to find in print. Just what can one do with the CD-ROM besides checking out the history, definition, spelling, and so forth, of a single word? Many things: (1) Search for quotes with key words from among the 2.5 million possibilities in the work. Quotations may be isolated by date, author, title of work, and the text. One can, for example, find every quotation with the word "football." (2) Find words from the definitions, that is, if one only knows "conspicuously bad" the computer will turn up "egregious" as one possible word. (3) Filter headwords by part of speech or date. (4) Follow the close to 600,000 cross-references to pursue a given word or idea in its multiple forms. (5) List all the words that have entered the language from French, German, and so forth. (6) List every word ending in "q" and identify every adverb that does not end in "ly." (7) Select entries according to the earliest quotation cited. And much, much more.[21]

The *OED* CD-ROM is the ideal, sophisticated system for dictionaries. Many of the less ambitious CD-ROMs, particularly for desk or college dictionaries, have the basic search patterns, although none offers so many possibilities. As one critic put it, the *OED* CD-ROM is to all other dictionaries as a Formula I race car is to a Model T. "It exposes the wealth, history, power and versatility of the world's leading language in ways that could not be imagined in the nineteenth century, astounds the twentieth, and we will take for granted in the twenty-first."[22]

A basic problem with the *OED* on CD-ROM is that it is difficult, if sometimes impossible, to print out the results. The software will be improved, but meanwhile the system is more creaky than some would like. It will show the reader all, but ever so slowly.

---

[20]Other facts about the *OED:* the first word is "a" the last word is "zyxt." There are a total of 60 million words. The greatest number of citations and quotations are from Shakespeare (33,150). The *OED* does not employ usage labels, but it does indicate whether a word or a phrase is "slang," or "coarse." Both labels are found because the decision was made in 1970 to, at long last, print, define, and explore the history of four-letter Anglo-Saxon words.

[21]The "much more" is explained in detail in the 71-page CD-ROM user's guide and the 123-page user's manual. Fortunately, most of the material is well written and easy to follow. Also, there is a good index to the manual.

[22]Andrew Rosenheim, quoted in *CD-ROM Librarian*, September 1992, p. 16. Mr. Rosenheim was then an Oxford Press executive.

Work on the third edition began in the early 1990s, and by 1995 the publisher had issued, in print, two volumes of the third that will become part of the proposed revision, that is, identified as *Oxford English Dictionary Additional Series, Volumes I and II.* (Eventually these will be part of a revised CD-ROM.) Each of the first two volumes contains about 3000 words, meanings, or earlier citations for words. Actually, these serve as supplements to the main set until a third edition is published. And when will that be? According to Oxford University Press, it will be late in this, or early in the next century. Today thousands of volunteers are helping gather revisions, new items, new etymological and bibliographical information from the ever-growing body of scholarly literature as well as popular material. All of this will be part of the new edition.

The *OED* is not entirely the last word on the history of English. There are other supplementary titles. Published in 1995 by the University of Michigan *The Middle English Dictionary* has some 80,000 words, and is one of several examples. The number of listed words is not so impressive as the length of an entry which can run to 28 pages, as it does for one verb—*setten* (*to set*). The dictionary complements the *OED* in that it spans the time from the Norman Conquest to A.D. 1500 and the dawn of modern English.

The *New Shorter*

Published in late 1993, the *New Shorter Oxford English Dictionary* has a tremendous advantage over its senior, as well as many other dictionaries. It is more current than most, and the quotations used to support the history of words are more up to date. It is an excellent place to turn for etymologies and fine points of history. Note, though, that the *Shorter* takes up the history of words only since 1700, while the *OED* goes back to the beginnings of English around 1066. It is a specialist work and not to be confused with an everyday dictionary.

There are over 500,000 words but only about 170,000 entries and under 100,000 headwords. Actually, one will find more definitions in the average desk dictionary, but the reader will not find better history, better examples, and, often, more current words.

There are 83,000 quotations. These are quite superior and, unlike many other competitors, really do support an understanding of the history and the use of a given word or phrase.

The two volumes belong in most libraries, if only to update the *OED*. They are, on the other hand, a questionable purchase for individuals who will get more words per dollar in either the unabridged *Webster's* or *Random House,* and will do equally well with a $20 recommended desk dictionary. The *Shorter Oxford* is a delight for the scholar, for the individual in love with words. It is too much for the average person interested in a quick definition or spelling tip.

American Regional Dictionaries

Print: Dictionary of American Regional English (DARE). Cambridge, MA: Harvard
University Press, 5 vols.; vol. 1, 1985, vol. 2, 1991; vols. 3 to 5, in progress.
Price varies.
No electronic format.

While the *OED* remains the "Bible" of the linguist or the layperson tracing the history and various meanings of a word, it is not the best place to go for
correct usage, at least for Americans. English-speaking Americans and English-
speaking Britons actually come close to using two different languages, the latter, of course, being recorded in the *OED*. A decision was made that in the *OED*
supplements more attention would be paid to American words, particularly as
most of these are now familiar to Europeans or to viewers of American television and films and readers of American magazines. In fact, since 1970, the *OED*
is better than many American dictionaries at providing careful definitions and
the history of new and slang American words.

In any discussion of the history of the American language, there is one
outstanding work many have enjoyed reading, literally from cover to cover. This
is Henry Mencken's *The American Language* (New York: Alfred A. Knopf, Inc.,
1919 to 1948). In three volumes, the sage of Baltimore examines a very large
proportion of American words in a style and manner that are extremely pleasing and always entertaining and informative. The initial one-volume work of
1919 was supplemented with two additional volumes. All are easy to use as each
volume has a detailed index.

Planned for completion in the mid-1990s, the *Dictionary of American Regional
English* assembles colloquial expressions and their meanings from all 50 states.
The monumental project began in 1965, and specially trained workers spent five
years interviewing nearly 3000 Native Americans in over 1000 communities. In
addition to the interviews, material for the *Dictionary of American Regional English*,
often referred to as *DARE*, has been gathered from countless printed sources including regional novels, folklore journals, newspapers, and diaries.

SPECIALIZED DICTIONARIES

There are hundreds of specialized and subject dictionaries. Almost every discipline from economics and law to sociology and zoology has its own specialized
work. A cursory check of the *American Reference Books Annual,* as well as *The Guide
to Reference Books,* will clearly indicate the scope of the subject dictionary. The
most common specialized dictionaries, which cross every subject field and are
found in most libraries, include slang, abbreviations, and foreign language.

Abbreviations and Acronyms

Print: Acronyms, Initialisms, and Abbreviations Dictionary, 14th ed. Detroit, MI: Gale
Research Inc., 1995, 3 vols. $250 to $310 each.
Diskette format.[23]

The basic guide in this field is the Gale publication. It is in three volumes.
The first volume has over 520,000 entries for acronyms, initialisms, and related
matters. These are listed alphabetically, and the full meaning of the term is then
given. Most of the focus is on the United States, but acronyms from western Europe are included. The second volume is really two softbound supplements issued between editions. They provide about 15,000 new acronyms in two sequences, by acronym and by meaning. The third volume is a "backward," or
"reverse," companion to the first volume, that is, one looks up one of the 520,000
entries to find the acronym. For example, one would turn here to find the
acronym for the *Dictionary of American Regional English—DARE.*

A smaller version is DeSola's *Abbreviations Dictionary* (New York: Elsevier,
various editions) has 180,000 entries and is about $65.

Crossword

CD: Webster's Official Crossword Puzzle Dictionary. Springfield, MA: Merriam-Webster, Inc., 1992. Irregular update, $29.95.
Print: 1992. Paperback. $4.99.

The CD-ROM version of the typical crossword puzzle dictionary allows
entry by either (1) the phrase or definition that is used in the puzzle or (2) the
individual words. Actually, given the power of the CD-ROM it seems almost
pointless to do a crossword puzzle. In fact, crossword purists say it is not fair to
consult a dictionary. Still, when one is stuck and frustrated, the crossword puzzle can be solved by turning to dictionaries for synonyms and antonyms, or to
this guide. The clues, that is, the typical entries, are listed in alphabetical order
in print works with the key words to fill in the boxes. Little is left to chance, and
an experiment indicates that from 50 to 70 percent of the queries put to the
reader in a typical crossword puzzle can be answered here.

Foreign Language Dictionaries (Bilingual)

CD: Languages of the World. Lincolnwood, IL: NTC Publishing Group, 1991 to
date, updated periodically. $129.95.
Print: Various titles, publishers, dates, prices.

---

[23]Although there is no CD-ROM version, Gale makes the dictionary available on a diskette which
is updated annually. Price varies. In a short time the format is likely to be changed to a CD-ROM
and made available online as well.

Print: The HarperCollins Series, all published by HarperCollins of New York and
London. Different editions, different dates, various pagination, and so
forth. *HarperCollins-Robert French Dictionary, HarperCollins Spanish Dictionary,
HarperCollins German Dictionary,* and so on. Price range: $4.99 paperback
to $21.95 hardbound.
No electronic formats.

The foreign language dictionary is now available on CD-ROMs. Still, the
more conventional print dictionary should be considered first. Most readers are
familiar with the typical bilingual print dictionary which offers the foreign word
and the equivalent English word. The process is then reversed with the English
word first, followed by the equivalent foreign word. For other than large public, academic, and special libraries, the print bilingual dictionary is quite enough.
The HarperCollins entries are standard, familiar desk dictionaries. Most have
gone through numerous editions and revisions by many editors. Pronunciation
is given clearly enough for even the amateur to follow, and the equivalent words
are accurate. All the dictionaries usually include slang words, colloquialisms, idioms, and more common terms from various subject areas. The number of main
entries varies from 40,000 in paper to 120,000 to 130,000 in hardback.

There are several other reputable publishers of basic print foreign language dictionaries. Cassell (by Sterling Publishing in the United States), Charles
Scribner's Sons, Simon & Schuster, and Oxford University Press, as well as
Cambridge University Press, are only a few of the better-known, reliable publishers of works that range from Arabic to Swahili.

The person who simply seeks a common foreign word or phrase is likely
to find the answer in almost any desk dictionary as either part of the main dictionary or set off in a special section. When it comes to more sophisticated, specialized words, the choice is to turn to a bilingual dictionary.

Larger and specialized libraries will have dictionaries of other countries.
Larousse is the venerable French publisher of dictionaries (and encyclopedias).
University libraries are likely to have several of the Larousse dictionaries such
as *Larousse French Dictionary* (New York: Macmillan, 1994) or the *Petit Larousse en
Couleurs,* a common title found in most French homes. Equally basic dictionar-
ies from other countries will be purchased.

Even those who have no idea of mastering Spanish, for example, turn to
a Spanish dictionary for more detailed entries than those found in the standard
bilingual edition. And this type of person is increasing in numbers as travel increases. This same individual is more likely than not to wonder about slang and
street terms rarely found in the bilingual work. Here HarperCollins, for one,
marks such words with little stars. In the *HarperCollins Spanish Dictionary* (3d ed.,
1992) the user finds one star means "the expression, while not forming part of
standard language, is used by all educated speakers in a relaxed situation."
Three stars, though, indicates "words liable to offend in any situation."

CD-ROM

There are numerous bilingual and foreign language CD-ROMs. The CD-ROM is useful in two situations: (1) When one wants to compare or find words in more than a single language, and (2) when the user wants to retrieve simple translations of a specified word in business, technology, science, and so on. These and other translation programs are available for as little as $60.

Languages of the World is a relatively inexpensive approach to translation, and, as such, is by way of an ideal CD-ROM in the library where there is only an occasional call for translations of individual words or small pieces of text, such as a letter. Within the disc are 18 dictionaries in 12 languages. Again, they follow the two-way path of, say, French-English and English-French. What is different here is the inclusion of synonyms as well as scientific terminology. There are, according to the publisher, about 7 million words. While the focus is on western European languages, the disc contains Chinese, Japanese, and Finnish.

One of the largest publishers of electronic translations, Globalink Inc. of Fairfax, VA, offers: Power Translator for business (about $129); and Power Translator Professional for larger corporations (about $600). Each program is specific to one foreign language with a bilingual directional. A French CD-ROM, for example, translates English documents into French or French documents into English. The more powerful the program the better the translation capacities, but even the most expensive produces translations which must still be edited by expert translators.

Professional translators have little real competition from CD-ROMs, or online services. Even the best CD-ROM (up to $20,000) does not match the expert who often will turn a bewildering electronic translation into one of common sense. Electronic translations are rough. The computer systems have trouble choosing the correct definition when a word has more than one meaning. For example, the expression "out of sight, out of mind" will be translated from English into Japanese as "invisible, insane."

Other types of CD-ROMs promise the user the ability to master a language, for example, the Learn to Speak series by HyperGlot Software Company of Knoxville, Tennessee. The discs (at an average price of between $200 and $250) have standard language lessons with interactive exercises and a built-in French, Spanish, and so on, dictionary.

Slang

Print: Random House Historical Dictionary of American Slang. New York: Random House, 1994 to date, 3 vols. Vol. 1: A–G, 1994. $50. Vols. 2 and 3 to be published.
No electronic format.

Print: The Oxford Dictionary of Modern Slang. New York: Oxford University Press, 1992, 299 pp. $22.50.
No electronic format.

In the past most of the vulgar, four-letter words were simply not included in dictionaries. Today even the desk dictionary includes the common words and expressions. Most are labeled, usually, as "offensive."

The common desk dictionaries also list and define words that describe people who are physically or mentally lacking *(loony, fatty);* slang terms for religious or ethnic groups (from *WASP* to *wop*); designations for women *(doll, tomato);* slang terms for homosexuals, and so forth. All these terms should be clearly labeled to show that they are far from acceptable. Today the committee of the "Reference Books Bulletin" considers a dictionary remiss if it refuses to include such words—carefully labeled, to be sure—as "vulgarisms" or "unacceptable." Other reviewers, aside from those evaluating children's works, take much the same attitude.

Still, the library needs dictionaries of slang because: (1) Most dictionaries do not indicate the variations of meaning given slang terms or words. Few trace their history, which is a part of the history of a nation's popular culture. (2) Readers come across expressions that are not well defined in an ordinary dictionary. (3) Authors look for words to convey background, class, or occupation of a given character, and the slang dictionary is a fine place to double check such words. (4) Readers indicate just plain curiosity and interest in the language.

A fascinating aspect of slang is that as a concept it appears to be relatively recent. Chaucer and Shakespeare used ribald language, but there is no indication either author, or their audience, considered the words in a special category. The point is obvious that before you can have slang you must have a public awareness of standard language from which deviants spring. Only with mass education in the nineteenth century did the awareness of slang become widespread.

The first volume of the *Random House Historical Dictionary of American Slang* appeared in 1994 and the third and final volume is to be published in late 1997 or 1998. The over 300,000 entries are the work of J. E. Lighter, an English instructor at the University of Tennessee who spent more than two decades tracking down the history of unusual words. When complete, the dictionary will record lexicographic information on all major slang words and phrases coined in the United States from Colonial times to the present. As with the larger historical dictionaries, the word is defined and then its development in chronological order of first use is shown. Quotations are used as supporting evidence. In fact, this "has to be the only guide to the English language ever published to quote 'Public Enemy' and 'The Valley Girl Handbook' more often than Henry James or the Bible."[24]

[24]"In Other Words . . . ," *The New York Times,* June 5, 1994, p. V8.

In terms of coverage the "f" words occupy over a dozen pages and even the innocuous "biscuit" takes up the equivalent of one page. Biscuit is not only food but can mean a watch, a head, a bomb or a pistol, the buttocks, narcotics, or a young woman. The work will include an extensive bibliography which features all of the important dictionaries of slang.

The *Oxford Dictionary of Modern Slang* is an excellent, short version. It includes over 5000 terms, most of which have been introduced into the language since the beginning of this century. Each entry contains the headword, part of speech, and definition. The majority have at least one illustrative example of the term in context usually drawn from prominent writers.

Other standard, but somewhat dated works include Harold Wentworth and Stuart Flexner's *Dictionary of American Slang*, 2d supplemental ed. (New York: Thomas Y. Crowell Company, 1975, 766 pp.). While the three-volume Random House work will date this basic guide, it is still useful for its broad general approach to all aspects of slang.

Among other standard titles: Robert Chapman's *New Dictionary of American Slang* (New York: HarperCollins, 1986) and the revised edition of *The Thesaurus of Slang* (New York: Facts on File, 1983). This latter dictionary has some 165,000 alphabetically arranged standard words followed by lists of slang words and phrases: a cadaver, for example, is "cold meat."[25]

Subject Dictionaries

Subject dictionaries explain particular meanings of particular words in terms of professions, occupations, or areas of subject interest. Otherwise, of course, most of the material might be found in the unabridged dictionary, or desk dictionaries which are regularly updated and show an interest in adding new terms.

While all evaluative checks for the other dictionaries apply, there are also some special points to watch. The major question to ask when determining subject dictionary selection is: Does this title offer anything which cannot be found in a standard work now in the library? It is surprising, particularly in the humanities and social sciences, how much of the needed information is readily available in a general English dictionary. Also:

1. Are the illustrations pertinent and helpful to either the specialist or the layperson? Where a technical work is directed to a lay audience, there should be a number of diagrams, photographs, or other forms of graphic art, which will make it easier for the uninitiated to understand the terms.

[25]There is a handheld slang dictionary. It is not recommended. It is difficult to use and a printed work is considerably more useful and current. At any rate, the handheld version is *NTC's Dictionary of American Idioms, Slang and Colloquial Expressions* (Lincolnwood, IL: NTC Publishing, 1991, not updated, $29.95).

2. Are the definitions simply brief word equivalents, or is some effort made to give a real explanation of the word in the context of the subject?

3. Is the dictionary international in scope or limited chiefly to an American audience? This is a particularly valuable question for the sciences. Several publishers have met this need by offering bilingual scientific dictionaries.

4. Are the terms up to date? Again, this is a necessity in a scientific work, somewhat less in a social science dictionary, and perhaps of relatively little importance in a humanistic study.

Many of the subject dictionaries are virtually encyclopedic in terms of information and presentation. They use the specific-entry form, but the entry may run to much more than a simple definition.

Some 1990s examples of print subject dictionaries include: *McGraw-Hill Electronics Dictionary* (New York: McGraw-Hill, 1994, 596 pp., $49.50), a fifth edition of a standard guide with 14,000 easy-to-understand entries. *The Oxford Dictionary for the Business World* (New York: Oxford University Press, 1993, 996 pp., $24) has a strong British slant, but marvelous definitions for such phrases as "Lady Macbeth strategy."

An unusual approach to dictionaries, or more precisely to linguistics can be found in the *Atlas of the World's Languages* (London: Routledge, 1994, 322 pp., $600). The high cost is accounted for by the fact that it is a specialized work which attempts to map the location of every single living tongue on earth, no matter how small the number of its speakers. The eight sections, each with an introductory essay of explanation about language in the particular area covered, often highlight languages with fewer than 100 speakers. Helpful "time of contact" maps indicate how the settlement of outsiders influenced on native languages.

SUGGESTED READING

Anthony, Carolyn, "Words to the Wise," *Publishers Weekly*, April 25, 1994, pp. 39–41. A wide range of lexicography, on both page and disc, is discussed. Examples are given showing the numerous possibilities opened with a dictionary in an electronic format.

Aust, Ronald, et al., "The User of Hyper-Reference and Conventional Dictionaries," *Educational Technology Research Development*, 1993, no. 4, pp. 63–73. Hyperreference dictionaries incorporated into basic learning tools for undergraduate foreign language learners are considered. Bilingual and monolingual dictionary use is compared. Note the bibliography.

Cmiel, Kenneth, *Democratic Eloquence*. New York: William Morrow, 1990. In this study of popular language from 1776 to 1900, the author explores the arguments for and against prescriptive and descriptive approaches to speech. The way a gentleperson is supposed to talk and write has changed drastically. Dictionaries first were prescriptive, but by the turn of the century leaned in the direction of sanctioning new styles of popular speech. The book is based on wide reading and is fully documented.

Davies, P., and S. Karavis, "Choosing and Using Dictionaries," *Language & Learning*, 1994, no. 9/10, pp. 36–39. Some tips on evaluation, particularly of younger people's dictionaries, are given. A useful guide for beginners.

Finneran, John, "The Tale of Two Dictionaries," *The Freeman*, December 1992, pp. 483–485. This is a short, witty history of Dr. Johnson's dictionary and the French Academy effort of the same period.

Gray, Richard, "The American Heritage Dictionary . . . ," *Reference Services Review*, Winter 1993, pp. 91–96. In this review of the third edition, an editor points out its strengths and weaknesses (and prefers the first edition). At any rate, it is a model of analysis for any dictionary.

Morton, Herbert, *The Story of Webster's Third*. New York: Cambridge University Press, 1995. While this is a discussion of one dictionary, the real point is that the author gives an account of the battle between partisans of description and prescription. The battle still rumbles on, Morton claims. The author concludes that there are better things, these days, to argue about.

Mosely, Shelley, et al., "Lexicons for Linguists: The Basics," *Library Journal*, July 1995, pp. 43–46. An annotated list of the best in foreign language dictionaries. It is prefaced by an excellent section on how to select and evaluate such titles. "Basic" for selection of dictionaries in reference work.

Rulon-Miller, Robert, "A Brief History of English Language Dictionaries," *A Bookman's Weekly*, January 3, 1994, pp. 4–6. A bibliographical essay on the history of the dictionary. Although brief, the highlights are covered and the author has the imagination to point up what is truly of value, and of equal interest. Well written and informative.

Willinsky, John, *Empire of Words: The Reign of the O.E.D.* Princeton, NJ: Princeton University Press, 1995. The thesis of this fascinating history of the *OED* is that it was more than a catalog of the English language. It was part of a whole nation-building process. "It appeared in the age of empire, a period in which Great Britain was having all sorts of impacts on the world."

CHAPTER ELEVEN
GEOGRAPHICAL SOURCES

"Maps are a combination of purposeful representation and pure abstraction. . . . Maps are symbols of power, politics and expressive imaginings. . . . From the beginning of history, man has made maps to match his expanding knowledge of his surroundings. . . . Man must continue to re-draw his world."[1] These quotations, celebrating an exhibit at the New York Museum of Modern Art, emphasize the peculiar quality of maps and geographical resources. Many maps are works of art. They provide a type of satisfaction rarely found in the purely textual approach to knowledge.

Geographical sources may be used at the mundane level (Where is it?), or in a more sophisticated way to help clarify linkages among human societies. Reference librarians are familiar with both approaches. The first, and the more common, is the typical question about where this or that town is located, the distance between points X and Y, and what type of clothing will be needed to travel in Italy in December. Moving away from the ready-reference query, one becomes involved with relationships concerning climate, environment, commodities, political boundaries, history, and everything with which geographers are deeply interested.

When she is asked to quickly identify a city or a country, the reference librarian has little difficulty matching the question with a source. Usually, the correct answer is in an atlas, an individual map, or a compilation of geographical

---

[1] *MoMA Magazine,* Fall-Winter 1994, p. 12, 35. Raven Maps of Medford, Oregon, have established a reputation for apparent three-dimensional maps. (Actually, they are masters of trompe l'oeil). The large wall maps are as accurate as they are things of beauty. See "An Artist's Precise Hand," *The New York Times,* November 15, 1992, p. 14, travel section.

data, which may be readily available on a CD-ROM or in an online database. Asked to establish the elements common to the Philippines and Ethiopia, the librarian must turn to both geographical sources and related works which, in this case, might range from the *Statesman's Yearbook* and an encyclopedia to the periodical and newspaper indexes for current events. Then, too, the librarian would wish to search the geographical texts and individual economic and political historical studies.

If the reference librarian thinks of the typical atlas or map as the center of a pool with ripples that may wash over scores of reference works, then geographical sources assume their true importance. Granted this type of use is limited to larger libraries, to a smaller group of people than those asking for help on finding a hotel in Paris or Peoria, but its importance and scope are likely to increase as the world shrinks, as trade and travel become increasingly widespread.

Computers and Maps

Since the late 1980s modern mapmaking has become dominated by the computer. The reasons are not hard to find. First, the computer permits one to make a projection from a standard Mercator to a heart-shaped map. Computers can virtually eliminate distorted projections and give the viewer a true world viewpoint. Second, there is now an exhaustive database that allows cartographers to make historical, economical, demographical, and you name it, maps with as much detail and overlap as needed. Third, revisions that used to take months can be done in minutes. Maps can be updated, revised, and changed in format and type of details as often as necessary.

Until late 1995 71 percent of the Earth was not as well mapped as the surface of Venus. Most of that 71 percent was the ocean floor. In late 1995 the National Oceanic and Atmospheric Administration corrected the situation with a map 12 feet wide and 8 feet high of the portion of the Earth under the oceans. Scientists charted the map from 500-mile-high satellites. (A color copy of the map, ideal as much for decoration and for information, is available from the Scripps Geological Data Center in California by phoning (619) 534-2752. Cost: $40.)

Using electronic databases to plot and eventually print an atlas or a single map, cartographers have seen the benefit of other formats. On CD-ROMs, and to a lesser extent online, more and more electronic maps are becoming a regular part of library reference services. These range from an expensive researcher's tool to the child's hypertext mixture of maps, bird songs, and animation. At the same time, the well-known printed atlases hold their own in almost all libraries and homes. For quick reference purposes they remain easy to use, inexpensive, and relatively current. Whether or not the electronic database will replace the print atlas is a question to be decided. More likely the two formats will go on together, one complementing the other.

GEOGRAPHICAL SOURCES

No matter what format, geographical sources come in several content packages. Geographical titles used in ready reference may be subdivided into three large categories: maps and atlases, gazetteers, and guidebooks.

Maps and Atlases. A map is, among other things, a representation of certain boundaries of the earth (or the moon and planet as well) and we generally think of them as on a flat surface. Maps may be divided into flat maps, charts, collections of maps in atlas form, globes, and so forth. Cartographers refer to these as *general* maps, that is, for general reference purposes.

A physical map traces the various features of the land, from the rivers and valleys to the mountains and hills. A route map shows roads, railroads, bridges, and the like. A political map normally limits itself to political boundaries (e.g., towns, cities, counties, states) but may include topographical and route features. Either separately or together, these three types make up a large number of maps found in general atlases.

Cartography is the art of mapmaking, and a major headache of cartographers is achieving an accurate representation of the features of the earth. This task has resulted in various projections, that is, the methods used to display the surface of a sphere upon a plane without undue distortion. Mercator and his forerunners devised a system, still the best known today, based on parallel lines; that is, latitude (the lines measuring the "width" of the globe, or angular distance north or south from the equator) and longitude (the lines measuring the "length" of the globe, or angular distance east or west on the earth's surface). This system works well enough except at the polar regions, where it distorts the facts. Hence, on any Mercator projection, Greenland is completely out of proportion to the United States. Since Mercator, hundreds of projections have been designed; but distortion is always evident—if not in one section, in another. For example, the much-praised azimuthal equidistant projection, with the north pole at the center of the map, indicates directions and distances more accurately, but in other respects it gives a peculiar stretched and pulled appearance to much of the globe.

The only relatively accurate graphical representation of the earth is a globe. The need for a globe in a reference situation is probably questionable. The reference librarian who has had occasion to use a globe instead of a map to answer particular reference questions is rare indeed.

The average general map gives an enormous amount of information for the area(s) covered. Cities, roads, railroads, political boundaries, and other cultural elements are indicated. The physical features, from mountain ranges to lakes, are depicted. Relief is usually indicated by shading and contrast or color.

Libraries will primarily purchase *atlases,* or collections of maps. Libraries with larger holdings will include flat or sheet maps such as those distributed by the National Geographic Society or the traditional state and regional road maps.

Another large group of maps are termed *thematic,* in that they usually focus on a particular aspect of geographical interest. Reference here is usually to historical, economic, political, and related matters which may be shown graphically on a map. An example: *The Times Atlas of World History.*

Note: When speaking of flat maps, atlases, relief maps, and even globes it is assumed the reader appreciates that many, if not most of these are available in electronic format. Still, the content, no matter what the format, remains much the same.

Gazetteers. Gazetteers are geographical dictionaries, usually of place names. Here one turns to find out where a city, mountain, river, or other physical feature is located. Detailed gazetteers will give additional information on population and possibly leading economic characteristics of the area.

Guidebooks. Guidebooks hardly need a definition or introduction; they furnish information on everything from the price of a motel room in Paris or Kansas to the primary sights of interest in New York or London.

There is no equivalent *Books In Print* for maps, but *The World Map Directory* (Santa Barbara, CA: Map Link, 1988 to date, irregular) comes close. The directory indicates maps available from the publisher, who is also a map vendor. Over 46,000 are listed. David Cobb's *Guide to U.S. Map Resources,* 2d ed. (Chicago: American Library Association, 1990, 495 pp.) is updated every few years. It is a state-city-institutional listing of what library has what in the way of geographical resources. There are close to 1000 entries and it gives an excellent overview of American map resources.

Why bother with more than a token number of geographical resources in the reference section? "As much as 80 percent of all information held by business and government may be geographically referenced," is the short persuasive answer.[2] Everything from census data and land-use information to transportation may be related to geographical sources.

How many maps, atlases, CD-ROM titles, and the like should the library have in a reference section? The possibilities are limitless. The Library of Congress, with one of the largest holdings in the world, claims 53,000 atlases, 4 million maps, and 300 globes. Still, for the more modest collection, a standard figure is from 10 to 15 atlases, along with two or three hypertext CD-ROMs.

[2]Carl Franklin, "An Introduction to Geographic Information Systems . . . ," *Database,* April 1992, p. 12.

GEOGRAPHICAL INFORMATION MANAGEMENT

Structured electronic databases are employed by cartographers to do everything from fixing projections to determining the size of a dot that indicates a town or city. As with most reference works, electronic formats for geographical sources are developing rapidly. "What we're looking at here is all first generation. We're seeing just the beginning of what's possible: getting up-to-date, thorough travel information that's individually tailored (via online services)."[3]

Geographical information programs, primarily based on the 1990–1991 census, are now relatively common. Software allows one to analyze data and link it to a specific location. This permits someone to find the right neighborhood to open a pizza outlet or an opera house.

The information in machine-readable form gives unprecedented access to information about customers and citizens. The government sells its data, and that census information, plugged into a geographical information program, helps companies determine sales opportunities. Census software allows one to zoom in on a continent, country, state, city, and small section of a city right down to a particular block or point. It can be used to keep track of everything from population trends to the number of manhole covers.

The formal and informal collaboration between cartographers and the world of data has introduced a new type of librarian, the one in charge of the "geographical information management" center. Both policy and technology involve this librarian. She has the ability to give current, firsthand information on everything from a complete list of recorded plants in the San Francisco area to suggestions for easing traffic problems in New York City. All of this requires specific software, but the number of databases increases each year, both in number and sophistication.

Consider a single database: American Profile (Stamford, CT: Strategic Mapping Inc., 1980 to date; updated regularly, $9000).[4] Used by a manager (i.e., librarian) it is so expensive as to be found in only highly specialized libraries. In time, though, cost will come down and this type of data will be available to those outside the aforementioned geographical information management center—whether that be in a government agency or a Madison Avenue advertising agency. The Profile contains U.S. Census current data as well as five-year projects of much-used demographic characteristics such as retail sales, home ownership, automobile sales, socioeconomic status of residents, and the like. The primary users of this type of information are salespersons, as well as investors and anyone involved with the local and national economy.

The CD-ROM (and online version) of Profile offers geographical files with pinpoint information up to 250 to 300 individual bits of data. One can create

---

[3]"Star Trek Tech," *Publishers Weekly*, May 23, 1994, p. 58.

[4]Another less dramatic version of this is available online from the same publisher. It is called Donnelly Demographics, DIALOG file 575. It is $60 per hour, but the full record displays are $10 each.

a map to show, for example, potential sales of shoes or cars within a given area of a city. At the same time the map will indicate, if the user wishes, the age and economic and educational status of the residents of the area. The bundled geographical and demographical information require subtle employment of the software, but at $9000 for an annual package it is assumed the average user (librarian or expert layperson) will have some notion of how it is employed.

The ability to both create maps at a computer terminal as well as target, for example, high-income groups within a city or region who might be interested in purchasing X or Y goods gives a new dimension to the graph, written report, and map. Data diving, one may also map out educational, medical, and occupational needs for an area, city, or complete region. This technology combines aspects of hypertext and database management software in a unique and highly useful form.

EVALUATION

Geographical CD-ROMs and online maps have their own individual evaluative problems, although content, as always, remains most important and this is covered in the general evaluation below. There are several major points to consider in map evaluation that differ from book evaluation. Because maps and atlases depend on graphic arts and mathematics for presentation and compilation, a librarian is called on to judge them with a type of knowledge not usually important in book evaluation. From time to time, the "Reference Books Bulletin" in *The Booklist* offers reviews of just-published atlases. The Geography and Map Division, Special Libraries Association, issues a bulletin which frequently has articles of interest to librarians. Contributors cover new atlases, books, and related material in each issue.[5]

Publisher

As with dictionaries and encyclopedias, there are no more than a half dozen competent cartographic firms. In the United States, the leading publishers are Rand McNally & Company, C. S. Hammond & Company, and the National Geographic Society. In Great Britain, the leaders are John G. Bartholomew (Edinburgh) and the cartographic department of the Oxford University Press.

When the cartographic publisher's reputation is not known, it is advisable to check through other works it may have issued, or in a buying guide. The mapmaker may differ from the publisher, and in the case of an atlas both should be checked. All of this is particularly true of electronic maps where the vendor or even the publisher may differ from the standard companies of print atlases.

---

[5]See *Special Libraries Association Geography and Map Division Bulletin.* (Topton, PA: Special Libraries Association, Business Manager, 406 E. Smith St. 19562.) The quarterly has been published since 1947 and is free to members. Others: $25 per year.

Scope and Audience

As with all reference works, the library geography section must represent a wide variety of titles for many purposes and, in a public or school library, for the appropriate age groups. Essentially, it is a matter of scope. Some atlases are universal; others are limited to a single country, or even a region. Other maps, even within a general work, may be unevenly distributed so that 50 percent or more of the work may give undue attention to the United States or Canada, ignoring the weight of the rest of the world.

Scale

Maps are often classed according to scale. One unit on a map equals a certain number of units on the ground, that is 1 inch on the map may equal 10 or 100 miles on the ground. The detailed map will have a larger scale. The scale is indicated, usually at the bottom of the map, by a line or bar that shows distances in kilometers or miles, or both.

Geographers use map scale to refer to the size of the representation on the map. A scale of 1:63,360 is 1 inch to the mile (63,360 inches). The larger the second figure (scale denominator), the smaller the scale of the map. For example, on a map that shows the entire United States, the scale may be 1:16 million (1 inch being equal to about 250 miles). This is a small-scale map. A large-scale map of a section of the United States, say of the Northwest, would have a scale of 1:4 million. In the same atlas, the scale for Europe (and part of Russia) is 1:16 million; but for France (and the Alps) it is 1:4 million.

The scale from map to map in a given atlas may vary considerably, although better atlases attempt to standardize their work. The standardization is determined both by the size of the page on which the map appears as well as the effort of the publisher to use the same basic scales throughout.

Currency

World tension, as for example in the former Yugoslavia, results in a plus for map publishers. New maps are required almost every week or month, if only for consumption by newspapers, television, and other visual forms of communication. New maps, of course are necessary for libraries and for travelers. Virtually every library must update its world map collection at least once each year. The task has been made considerably easier (and less expensive) thanks to digital maps.

As it is not practical to make a new atlas every time a place changes name or a border shifts, publishers have reached two solutions. The first, as Rand McNally offers with some of its more expensive atlases (such as *Atlas of Today's World*), is to provide a free world map showing changes since the atlas was published. A second, more favored approach is to use a computer program which is considerably easier to edit than the printed work. Hammond, for example has its own Digital Cartographic Database which contains constantly updated information on the state of the world. The database allows the publisher to transform the new or revised data into new maps almost within seconds. With that one can then print a map quickly.

It should be noted that the date of publication for almost all geographical maps and atlases is the latest year on the calendar. At the same time, it may not be a new edition (i.e., an atlas with 1995 on the title page may not have been thoroughly revised since 1991). It is more likely to be a revision, and particularly of new geographical points and names. A new edition, that is, when the title is completely overhauled and developed from possibly another point of view, normally takes place every 10 years. Why 10 years? This is obvious. That is the time span between the American census.

The Index

A comprehensive index is as important in an atlas as the maps themselves. On-line or on a CD-ROM the software should make it easy to find a name, place, or by-product, say, of mining. A good index clearly lists all place names that appear on the map. In addition, there should be a reference to the exact map, and latitude, longitude, and grid information. A page number alone is never enough, as anyone who has sought an elusive town or city on a map lacking such information will testify. The index in many atlases is really an excellent gazetteer; that is, in addition to basic information, each entry includes data on population and country.

A check: Try to find four or five names listed in the index on the maps. How long did it take, and how difficult was the task? Reverse this test by finding names on the maps and trying to locate them in the index. Difficulty at either test spells trouble.

Format

When one considers print format, the basic question is simply: Can I find what I want easily on the map, and is it as clear as it is legible? The obvious problem is to print a map in such a way that it is easy to read a mass of names that cover a densely populated area. It is one thing to clearly print maps of the north and south polar regions, and quite another to be able to arrange type and symbols so that one can find a path from point to point on a map of the areas around New York City, Paris, and London. Maps with fewer items of information will be clearer and easier to read. The actual number of points represented on the map is a major editorial decision.

CD-ROMs are not the best source of clear, easy-to-read maps. The resolution on a computer screen is normally much less satisfactory than in a printed book. Still, the advantages, particularly of being able to zoom in on a given section, more than make up for the loss of color sharpness.

Internet grows increasingly important as an online access point to sources of geographical information. Thanks to the World Wide Web and software, such as Mosiac, the maps themselves become increasingly sharp on a computer screen and may, in time, replace the CD-ROMs. There are scores of geographical sources on the Internet, but three will serve as examples: (1) Estuaries are coastline maps from the government's National Estuary Program. (2) Xerox PARC World Map Viewer allows the user to zoom in on a map of any part of the earth. (3) Take The Subway is a series of maps of all the world's major subway systems.

WORLD ATLASES: PRINT FORMAT[6]

Note: Throughout this chapter *the electronic and print formats are presented separately.* The electronic format rarely, as in other reference works, is matched by the print. In fact, the CD-ROM, online, and print versions of atlases and maps tend to be individual units with little in common other than the publisher and the general map or maps.

Times Atlas of the World: Comprehensive Edition, 9th ed. London: Times Newspapers Limited, 1992, 345 pp. $175. (Distributed in United States by Times Books: Random House.)

The New York Times Atlas of the World, 3d rev. ed. New York: Times Books, 1992. 288 pp. $75.

The New International Atlas. Chicago: Rand McNally & Company, 1995, 568 pp. $150.

Libraries, and to a great extent individuals, seem to prefer the traditional atlas in print. This may explain why few of the standard atlases are available in digital form. This will change, although it is most likely that print and digital will go on together for many decades. Be that as it may, the maps discussed in this section are entirely print formats.

The *Times Atlas of the World* is the best single-volume atlas available. That it happens to be the most expensive is chiefly because such meticulous care has been taken, with emphasis on large-scale, multiple maps for several countries, and with attention to detail and color rarely rivaled by other American atlases.

The volume consists of three basic parts. The first section is a conspectus of world minerals, sources of energy and food, and a variety of diagrams and

[6]None of the atlases in this section are available in electronic format (1996). Although, as shown later in this chapter, some of the publishers and cartographic firms do have electronic versions of some of their maps and atlases.

star charts. The atlas proper comprises 123 double-page eight-color maps, the work of the Edinburgh house of Bartholomew.[7] This is the vital part, and it is perfect in both typography and color. The clear typeface enables the reader to easily make out each of the enormous number of names. A variety of colors is used with skill and taste to show physical features, railways, rivers, political boundaries, and so on. A remarkable thing about this atlas is that it shows almost every noteworthy geographical feature from lighthouses and tunnels to mangrove swamps—all by the use of carefully explained symbols.

The *Times Atlas* is suited for American libraries because, unlike many other atlases, it gives a large amount of space to non-European countries. No other atlas matches it for the detailed coverage of the Soviet Union, China, Africa, and Southeast Asia, lands not overlooked in other atlases, but usually covered in much less detail. A uniform scale of 1:2,500,000 is employed for most maps, but is changed to 1:850,000 for the United Kingdom. Maps of the larger land masses are supplemented with smaller, detailed maps which range from maps of urban centers to maps of the environs of Mt. Everest.

The final section is an index of over 210,000 place names, which, for most purposes, serves as an excellent gazetteer. After each name, the country is given with an exact reference to a map.

About half the size and about half the price of the *Times Atlas of the World*, *The New York Times Atlas* is a close cousin of the larger work. While the format is a bit smaller, the maps are much the same, and all are from the firm of John C. Bartholomew & Son in Edinburgh. The atlas scales are in keeping with the reduced format. There is a well-balanced coverage of the world. The index is smaller (100,000 entries) and the introductory matter more concise, but essentially this is a moderately priced version of the larger title and an excellent choice for library or home where the original atlas is not found.

The New International has 160,000 entries in the index and 300 good to excellent maps. A team effort of international cartographers, the atlas strikes a good balance between the needs of American readers and those in other countries. The scales are large with most countries at 1:6 million to 1:3 million. The maps tend to be double-paged and are models of legibility. The atlas' "birthday-cake-icing" material (from essays on the climate to thematic maps) is mercifully missing. The main focus is on maps of extraordinary quality.

Larger libraries will want all these atlases. If a choice has to be made, *The Times Atlas* (or *The New York Times Atlas of the World*) would be first; although the *International* would be a close second. *The Times* has the reputation and is expected to be found in major libraries.

---

[7]Bartholomew maps appear in many different grades of atlases, from the highest *(The Times Atlas of the World)* to the average *(Reader's Digest/Bartholomew Illustrated Atlas of the World*, rev. ed. Pleasantville, NY: *Reader's Digest*, 1992, $22). The latter is a typical inexpensive work with 78 small-scale color maps. The Edinburgh firm's contribution, as always, is the detail and the excellent color.

Medium-Sized Atlases: Print Format

The New Cosmopolitan World Atlas. Chicago: Rand McNally & Company, 1995, 340 pp. $60.

Hammond Atlas of the World. Maplewood, NJ: Hammond Incorporated, 1995, 304 pp. $65.

Oxford Atlas of the World. New York: Oxford University Press, 1995, 288 pp. $65.

National Geographic Atlas of the World, rev. 6th ed. Washington, DC: National Geographic Society, 1995. 403 pp., paperback. $65.

The 350- to 550-page, $50 to $75 atlas, is typical of the one found in most small- to medium-sized libraries, along with, to be sure, less costly items. The atlases listed here have three to four things in common, besides price and relative size. They are by reputable publishers and the text can be trusted. They are well designed and the maps are of high graphical quality. All offer additional information from population and climate data to profiles of cities, states, and so forth. And, finally, all have adequate to excellent indexes, varying from 70,000 to 150,000 entries. (Generally, the size is in direct ratio to the price.)

Given the similarity among reputable publishers of atlases, the question is which one(s) to pick? The answer: desired scope. Which covers what in most depth, and the "what" is of greatest interest to people using the library. For example, one would turn to the Hammond entry for a greater coverage of North American countries, cities, and places. A close contender for the same area of the world, and equally good in other areas, the *Rand McNally Cosmopolitan* would be a Hammond rival. Oxford would be the choice for in-depth European treatment. Both pretty much treat the remainder of the world in similar fashion.

Thematic maps are the added strength, the added reason for purchasing the *National Geographic* atlas. These are particularly useful in secondary schools and universities and colleges. Here one finds excellent graphics to bring home the importance of such things as food, energy, overpopulation (or underpopulation). At a glance one may see where the primary oil-producing areas of the world are to be found. It is also a winner in terms of vivid comparisons between places of the world, that is, Would you really like to live in X or in Y?

The Rand McNally Cosmopolitan differs from the others in three respects: (1) It is the smallest of the group; (2) it has more textual material than normal; and (3) it concentrates on North America, although the rest of the globe is covered adequately.

The *Cosmopolitan* has approximately 300 maps on a scale of from 1:3 million (1 inch equals about 4.75 miles) to 1:16 million (1 inch equals about 250 miles). The 12 largest metropolitan areas in the United States benefit from the larger scale. Heaviest emphasis, as might be expected, is on American maps. About 70,000 entries are in the general index, and these help locate political names and physical features. The facts and text material found in the nonmap sections are in another index.

Hammond maps and atlases are among the most reliable in the world, and the firm has numerous individual atlases.[8] One of the standards is the *Atlas of the World*. This has 160 pages of oversized maps, with slightly under one-half on double pages. The average scale is 1:3 million, with particular emphasis on North America. Thanks to imaginative use of the computer, the maps follow a new projection which is good in showing relative size of areas. There are five pages of eight U.S. urban centers (at 1.1 million) along with numerous smaller insert, blowup maps. Thematic maps showing global relationships are well designed and there are several text sections on such things as the environment and the development of cartography. There is a 115,000-entry name index.

A computer and a satellite survey of the earth help Hammond cartographers make three-dimensional relief map models for a number of their atlases. The models depict the earth's curved surface better than most projections. While this process is excellent for large areas, the cartographers resort to standard projections for smaller sections, and as one critic observes, "for all its technology, Hammond still nods to the old master, Mercator."[9]

Maps by the firm of George Philip & Son set the *Oxford Atlas of the World* apart. The 160 pages of maps are quite up to those of the better-known Bartholomew. Topographic maps usually have five to eight shades of color. Here there are 14 shades. Scales along the edge of the page clearly indicate what heights the shades represent. The atlas emphasizes the world rather than Europe or North America. It is one of the few atlases that gives a relative balance to the nations of the globe. There are the usual introductory material and beautiful illustrations with photographs, charts, and other forms of graphics. There is a separate 11,000-entry name index for a section of city maps and another 62,000-entry index for the names in the atlas as a whole.

The *National Geographic Atlas* has much in addition to maps. It is quite attractive, at least to many people and school children. Here one finds numerous thematic maps and discussions of world resources. Divided by continent, the 172 maps are introduced in each section by an encyclopedic) like article on the various countries. The maps, while clear and easy enough to read, fail to indicate more than rudimentary aspects of relief. Another negative aspect is found in the 100,000-entry index where there are no coordinates of latitude and longitude. Finally, there is too much emphasis on American interests, sometimes to the neglect of proper attention to third-world countries. The atlas does have its strong

---

[8]In 1996, for example, Hammond offered *The Hammond Odyssey Map of the World*, the *Hammond Odyssey Atlas of North America*, and the *Hammond Explorer Atlas of the World*, to name but three of dozens of atlases and maps which range in price from a low of $6.95 to a high of $100. Rand McNally has an even larger group of related maps and atlases.

[9]*The Observer*, May 16, 1993, p. 12.

points, including large scales, good-sized pages, and the aforementioned extensive index. It is favored by many who want something more than just an atlas.

Desk/School Atlases: Print Format

Goode's World Atlas. Chicago: Rand McNally & Company, 1995, 368 pp. Price varies.

Low price ($9.95 to $20), reasonable size, and ease of use are the three basic reasons many people prefer a school or desk-type atlas at home. And they are used in numerous elementary school geography classes. The problems are threefold: the format requires small-scale maps which result in tremendous distortions; the gazetteer or index, when it exists, is limited to 20,000 to 36,000 names; and the maps while adequate lack the refinement of larger works.

The inexpensive atlas found in most libraries, and particularly small public and almost all school libraries, is the familiar *Goode's*. This is revised every other year, and is as much a part of most people's memory of geography as any other single item in elementary schools. It is typical of the small, inexpensive works. It has a serviceable index (36,000 entries) and close to 400 (sometimes less than astonishing) maps. As it is a part of the curriculum, it is updated frequently. And at under $25, it is the best buy for smaller libraries.

There are countless variations of intermediate to small atlases. Take, for example, the *Desk Reference World Atlas* (Chicago: Rand McNally, 1995). This sells for a modest $20, it has 350 pages of good maps and an index of some 30,000 place names. Between these two sections is a modest encyclopedia of 200 pages filled with tables and facts pertaining to geographical queries.

Check, too, the large bookstores for atlas bargains. Barnes & Noble, for example, lists the $50 *Rand McNally New Universal World Atlas* for $20. This is a current edition with 11- by 14-inch maps. Particular focus is on Canada and the United States. There is a modest, but useful 39,000 entry index/gazetteer.

Rand McNally publishes a series of atlases for children from *Rand McNally Children's Atlas* (7 vols.) and *Rand McNally Picture Atlas of Prehistoric Life* to *The Rand McNally Children's World Atlas*. Hammond offers *Discovering Maps: A Children's World Atlas*.

Geographical Encyclopedias

Print: World Geographical Encyclopedia. New York: The McGraw-Hill Companies, Inc., 1995, 5 vols. Translated from the Italian edition. $500.
No electronic format.

An expansion of political yearbooks, a series of atlases, and a number of subject encyclopedias, the *World Geographical Encyclopedia* casts a wide geographical net. The five volumes, translated from the Italian edition, include the expected maps, and add statistics, history, and cultural background for continents and individual countries. The advertisement claims that the ambitious work "creates a living tapestry out of the accurate and up-to-date geographic facts." No one can argue with that claim. Each of the five well-documented volumes include over 1000 illustrations, the majority in color. The text is geared for the average high school student and adult. The volumes cover Africa, the Americas, Asia, Europe, and Oceania. There is a detailed index.

WORLD ATLASES: CD-ROM FORMAT

Rand McNally's America: Family United States Atlas. Chicago: Rand McNally & Company, 1991. $49.50.

Picture Atlas of the World. Washington, DC: National Geographic Society, 1992 to date, updated regularly. $99.95.

Software Toolworks World Atlas. Novato, CA: Software Toolworks, 1990 to date, biannual. $60.

The Small Blue Planet. San Francisco, CA: Now What Software, 1992 to date, annual. $60.

America Alive GUIDisc. Sunnyvale, CA: MediAlive, 1992 to date, updated regularly. $99.

USA GeoGraph II—The Multimedia Edition. Minneapolis, MN: MECC, 1993, updated regularly. $69.

There are few CD-ROMs, at least of a popular nature, that are exclusively maps. Most are hypertext affairs with everything from background material on birds and mountains to the videotape of someone swimming in the Red Sea. Those listed here (a few out of dozens available) are the types most likely to last. They exemplify the future of maps and atlases in electronic format.

The multimedia/hypertext map or atlas represents the world in text, images, or sound. Overlay data, from the average salary of a citizen of Cleveland to the cost of the Gulf War may be shown. Press a button and the red-backed shrike will appear at the center of a computerized map of a London park and will warble. It is this ability to show relationships and predict consequences that makes a new generation of electronic maps so useful. The same projection of a London park will indicate what will happen to the same red-backed shrike if certain types of trees are removed or the park is opened to a given number of visitors over x number of years.

Rand McNally's CD-ROM serves two or three typical CD-ROM format purposes. First, it is fun. Second, it helps children and young people plot papers and talks for school. Third, it gives the kind of information a family might need before deciding on a trip or a permanent home in a given part of the United States.

Based on each census, the Rand McNally entry is a true multimedia offering. It offers, in sound, pictures, and text, a relatively complete summary of American demographic information. The large unit is the state. And for each state there are audio narration (which can be cut off), pictures, charts, graphs, and other audiovisual technologies to bring up everything from who lives where to how much water is used in an upscale income area.

As the title implies, the *Picture Atlas of the World*, published by the National Geographic Society, features more than 800 maps, 1200 photographs, and some 50 video clips as well as music and even phrases pronounced in foreign languages. Each country, of course, has its own maps, as well as text which gives vital statistics and background history. Full-screen photographs, when available, are indicated as is animation, video, diagrams, and the like. There are maps, as in a standard printed atlas, for larger and smaller sections of the world and country.

One calls up Germany, for example, from the menu of 190 countries and a map and basic statistics appear on the screen. A picture file has over a dozen choices of what one assumes are typical German events and scenes. The captions give simple information about the site or events. One can click to get language clips, hear spoken phrases and some national music, and videos for some other 49 countries. The German entry shows Bavarian cows wearing wreaths and walking down the screen to the sound of music. In addition, there are narrations on the skills of making maps and indicating time zones as well as other items useful for school papers.

Combining text and graphics, the Software . . . Atlas is typical of many of its type which share low cost and relatively easy-to-follow paths for displaying a map or a section of a map. The database combines statistical and almanac text with 300 high-resolution maps of countries. In addition there are from 50 to 60 smaller maps of cities and regions. Add 150 or so video clips, some 1000 photographs, voice pronunciations of selected geographical points, and even bits of national anthems and this is the true, by now not uncommon multimedia/hypertext CD-ROM.

Typically, the user selects a city. The name appears in red and then a window gives information on everything from the telephone code to temperature and precipitation, as well as distance from a previously selected city or place on the map. In addition there are up to 11 full pages of text about the selected place. These cover crime, agriculture, travel, the economy, education, geography, people, education, health, government, and communication. As with numerous inexpensive atlases on CD-ROM it has several drawbacks, not the least of which is lack of state and province maps as well as details necessary for more sophisticated searching. Still, it is a useful buy for libraries with undemanding users, particularly of the younger variety.

The *Small Blue Planet*, so named after the appearance of planet earth in space, consists of three primary parts: the standard maps, satellite images, and a world political map along with historical and statistical data. Edited for the young adult to interested adult, it is as much fun to use as it is easy to bring up information. (One nice feature tells the time of day throughout the world.) There are excellent photographs and illustrations which can be used with the maps. The software makes it easy to target all of Europe or London. And with one button the screen tells you immediately what one should know about London or the swamps of Angola, depending on what cue is on the screen.

Video, maps, photographs, music, and text are combined in *America Alive GUIDisc*. The CD-ROM allows the user to call up any of the states, major cities, and specific attractions from national parks to historical homes. The 75 maps pinpoint the desired place and then the hypertext can be called upon to show specific features, as well as offer a sound track.

USA Geograph II covers all 50 states at two distinct levels. The first furnishes information on social, environmental, economic, and related data for each of the states, including the territories. The 60 maps have 25 thematic overlays and there are 125 categories of data which one may call up on the computer. The user, interested in California, asks to see the map. A window of information about the state is produced from water use per capita to postal abbreviations. This may be reproduced in graph form and linked to the map in countless ways. There are so many ways to manipulate the maps and information that it requires close to a 300-page manual to explain the entry points.

Remember, too, that electronic encyclopedias have maps that are part of the hypertext search. Electronic encyclopedias allow one to focus on a map and then call up articles related to the country, area, city, or community. The screen automatically shows information about X or Y point from government and history to natural resources and agriculture.

Gazetteers

CD: Omni Gazetteer. Detroit, MI: Omnigraphics, 1992 to date, updated irregularly. $2200.

Print: Omni Gazetteer of the United States of America, 1992 to date, updated irregularly, 11 vols. Price varies.

In one sense, the index in any atlas is a gazetteer, that is, it is a geographical dictionary for finding lists of cities, mountains, rivers, population, and the features in the atlas. A separate gazetteer has precisely the same information, but usually without maps. Why, then, bother with a separate volume? There are three reasons: (1) Gazetteers tend to list more names; (2) the information is usually more detailed; and (3) a single, easily managed volume is often welcomed. Having made these points, one can argue with some justification that many atlas indexes often have more entries, that they are more up to date, and that they contain a larger amount of information than one finds in a gazetteer. The wise librarian will first consider what is to be found in atlases before purchasing any gazetteer.

The expensive *Omni Gazetteer* is limited to place names in the United States and its territories. Still, it contains considerably more information than simply 1.5 million names. Its primary users are researchers and marketing types. The database includes information on features, coordinates, longitude and latitude, zip codes, population figures, elevation data, and even variant forms of spelling. One can find the name of a city, state, country, or small town, and it is possible to isolate and locate battlefields, shopping malls, hospitals, places of worship, and even caves. In fact, almost anything with a name is here.

The 200-page user manual covers the various possibilities in use of the CD-ROM. A series of menus allow one to search the various names and subjects. A nice feature allows one to narrow down the search, for example, if one types in "Albany," some 52 hits are registered. One can scroll through the list until the proper Albany is located. Although this is an expensive item, it has so many possible uses that it should find a place in larger research libraries.

Internet

Geographic Name Server is an easy-to-use gazeteer database on Internet. One of many, it permits the user to enter a geographical location, name of a city, state, and so on, and receive information about population and elevation to zip code. The World Wide Web, too, offers scores of atlases, small gazeteers, and the like online.

In Print

There are three reasonably priced print American gazetteers found in almost every reference section. The most used is *Webster's New Geographical Dictionary* (Springfield, MA: Merriam-Webster, Inc., various dates). This has 47,000 entries and over 200 maps. The work is easy to consult, and the information, while quite basic, gives specifics on where a given place is located. It can be used for many other purposes, including checking the spelling and pronunciation of place names. More detailed information is given here than in atlases on states, such as date of entry into the United States, motto, chief products, and so forth. The entries for countries follow the same detailed presentation, but for most place names, the entry is short and primarily useful for location.

Unfortunately, the second work is now so far out of date that it is of limited use. This is the *Columbia Lippincott Gazetteer of the World* (New York: Columbia University Press, 1952, 1962). The initial work and the 1962 supplement have over 130,000 entries, or almost seven times the number found in *Webster's*. Where the latter has constantly revised their dictionary, Columbia has chosen not to do so, and it must be used with that in mind. *Chambers World Gazetteer* (New York: Cambridge University Press, 1988, 845 pp.) is the most current, but it has only about 20,000 entries as compared to more than double the amount in *Webster's*. The obvious advantage is that the entries are more lengthy.

GOVERNMENT AND LOCAL MAPS

Conservatively, at least 90 percent of maps published each year originate from government sources. They provide details of almost every area of the world, with particular emphasis on the United States. Many are available to the public and are found in libraries.

The U.S. Geological Survey (USGS) has a continuing publishing program whereby many librarians routinely receive maps as issued. The maps are detailed, covering elevation, vegetation, and cultural features. The National Mapping Division of the USGS provides mapping information to the library as does the National Cartographic Information Center for the USGS. Libraries may learn about these various publications through the USGS's *New Publications of the Geological Survey* and *A Guide to Obtaining Information from the USGS. The Monthly Catalog of United States Government Publications* is another source, and, from time to time, maps appear in *U.S. Government Books,* a quarterly listing of more popular publications.

Of all the USGS series, the topographic maps are the best known, the most often used. The maps show in detail the physical features of an area, from streams and mountains to the various works of humankind, and are of particular value to the growing number of hikers and others who enjoy outdoor activities. Libraries have a separate collection of these maps and take particular pride in offering them to the public. They are sold by map dealers throughout the United States and are available directly from the USGS, National Mapping Program at Reston, Virginia.

Local and Regional Maps

In evaluating a local map, the requirements are usually threefold. First, the map should be truly local and should show the area in detail. Second, it should be large-scale. Third, it should be recent. Although all these requirements may be difficult to meet, an effort should at least be made to keep the local collection as current and as thorough as possible.

The United States Geological Survey topographic maps, mentioned in the previous section, are ideal local maps. Thousands of these are issued covering every region and area in the United States. One will inevitably find the detailed map needed for either an urban or rural area among those in this series.

Local state and city government departments are good sources of maps. State and provincial offices issue them, usually to encourage tourism. Chambers of commerce usually have detailed city maps as well as considerable information on the city itself. The most direct way for a library to get such material is to send a request to the chamber of commerce in the desired city or town.

STREET MAPS: CD-ROM FORMAT

Street Atlas USA. Freeport, ME: DeLorme Mapping, 1992 to date, updated regularly. $125–$170.

Street Reference Files. Stamford, CT: Strategic Mapping Inc., 1980 to date, annual. $425.

Rand McNally TripMaker. Skokie, IL: Rand McNally & Company, 1994 to date, annual. $60.

The hypertext CD-ROM series tend to have all the bells and whistles to enthrall and educate the user. Not so the street map. Here utility is the primary goal. Simplicity and clarity are important. There are many CD-ROM street maps about. The ones listed here tend to be among the best.

With *Street Atlas USA* the user has a chance to investigate literally every marked street in the United States. The user can view the whole country on a screen and then zoom down to his or her own city street or road. The publisher says the CD-ROM has more than 5 million streets and 1.1 million geographical and man-made features. In addition to the street name, the projected map will give data on physical features and prominent crossroads and buildings. By zooming in and out of Y town, for example, the user can find the necessary street or streets by name, or even by the zip code for the area or an individual phone number. One can make up maps as needed. Simple to use and relatively inexpensive, this is a sure winner in many school and public libraries.

Street Reference Files does two things. First it locates the necessary street(s) by name, zip code, and a variety of approaches. Second, and this is what makes it expensive, it offers additional data, where needed, on demography drawn from the larger database. All major streets and roads are found here, including some without names or numbers.

The triptik approach to maps for drivers has become a cottage industry among computer software producers. There are now at least a dozen such possibilities. These include, among others: *Map'N'Go* (Freeport, ME: DeLorme, 1992 to date, $30) with major roads and streets as well as data on hotels, campgrounds, points of interest, and the like. Each CD-ROM, from the *AAA Trip Planner* to *Expert Travel Planner,* has the same basic approach with added features, various prices, and always easy-to-follow navigational paths on the computer.

One of the best is produced by Rand McNally and has some 650,000 miles of road and 125,000 cities in its database. The driver seeking the shortest route from Seattle to Washington, DC, simply turns to the *Rand McNally TripMaker.* By typing in the point of origin and the point of destination, the route is drawn on the map. One may qualify this with cities, parks, historical sites, and so on that one wishes to visit along the way. It can be manipulated to show how much distance is covered in day 1, day 2, and so forth. And for each community there is a fine breakdown of streets and major sites. When the routing preference is worked out the driver may then print out the map or, more likely, a series of maps with driving directions, added features, and the like. The work is updated each year for $30.

A problem with printing out maps, as with any graphics, is that unless the computer is fast the process is quite slow. A good deal of computing power is required, particularly for color and for more intensive graphs and maps. Also a top-rate printer is a necessary partner. Of course, the assumption is that the software is free of wrinkles.

Most, if not all, of these street maps and triptiks may be eliminated by automobile technology. Major firms are building road maps, or navigational guides, into their new cars. In one system, for example, the driver enters a destination (from a street address to a national park). The computer calculates the most efficient route and displays a map in the car.[10] By 1995 to 1996, Hertz rental, among others, offered automobile navigation systems whereby a driver gets turn-by-turn directions from a small video screen mounted under the dashboard. An automated voice gives the necessary instructions.

THEMATIC MAPS AND ATLASES: PRINT FORMAT

The Times Atlas of World History. New York: HarperCollins, 1993, 380 pp. $65.

Rand McNally Commercial Atlas Marketing Guide. Chicago: Rand McNally & Company, 1976 to date, annual. $295.

The thematic or subject map is usually limited to a specific topic or related topics. Almost anything with a geographical focus may be the subject of such a map. Those listed here are representative of a much larger number which can be located by consulting the *Guide to Reference Books*, *American Reference Books Annual,* and, of course, geographical bibliographies.

Historical maps may settle more than one argument. In *The Two Gentlemen of Verona,* Shakespeare has Proteus travel from Verona to Milan by boat. A modern-day map indicates that this is impossible. But a map of the 1483 to 1499 period shows a series of canals, once designed by Leonardo da Vinci. Even though the two Italian cities are not connected by water, the canals come quite close—within 40 miles of each other—so a substantial part of the trip could have been by boat as Shakespeare claims.

Updated every five to six years, *The Times Atlas of World History* shows parallel historical events, cultural activities, and social movements in parallel development in Europe, Asia, Africa, and the Americas. The maps are large, easy

[10]One system is described in detail in *The New York Times,* November 27, 1994, p. 27A, with the promise that the whole of the United States will have the satellite navigational aid for cars by 1997 to 1998.

to read, and placed in such a way that one may trace the history of an event, individual, or, more likely, a movement that is developing. The atlas has an excellent index and a useful glossary of unusual historical terms. A $40 companion by the same publisher, *The Times Atlas of European History* (1994), covers Europe from about 900 B.C. to 1994. A brief text accompanies the maps.

The value of the *Rand McNally Commercial Atlas* is that it is revised every year. The library that can afford to subscribe to the *Atlas* solves the problem of adequate United States and Canadian coverage. The *Commercial Atlas* accurately records changes on a year-by-year basis. All information is the most up to date of any single atlas or, for that matter, any print reference work of this type. It is an excellent source for current statistical data. The first 120 pages or so offer (1) regional and metropolitan area maps, (2) transportation and communication data, (3) economic data, and (4) population data. Most of this is listed by state and then by major cities with codes that clearly indicate the figures.

The largest single section is devoted to "state maps and United States index of statistics and places by states." Here one finds the large-scale state maps. Statistical data, arranged by state, follow. These include such details as principal cities and towns in order of population, counties, basic business data, transportation, banks, and post offices by town, and are followed by briefer data for Canada and the world. The approximately 128,000 locations are analyzed with easy-to-use tables that summarize such things as population, economic data, and 1998 to 2000 projections. One can quickly find data on the per capita, median household as well as help patrons find a hard-to-locate place. The details and maps make this a necessity in almost any library.

Reference questions reflect the link between maps and almost every human activity. For example, there is a *Sports Atlas* (New York: Gousha/Macmillan, various dates) and the same firm's *The Official Baseball Atlas*. All of these help the traveler spot destinations of interest. Hammond has a *Vietnam Conflict* wall map which chronicles the dates, places, and events of the Vietnamese war. This is for both historians and ex-servicemen returning for the first time to Vietnam.

TRAVEL GUIDES: PRINT FORMAT[11]

Travel Books: Guide to the Travel Guides, 2d ed. Metuchen, NJ: Scarecrow Press, 1993, 350 pp. $42.50.

The purpose of the general guidebook is to inform the traveler about what to see, where to stay, where to dine, and how to get there. A book best carried in one's pocket or in the car. Librarians frequently find the works useful because

[11]No guide of any consequence is available either on CD-ROM or online. (Prodigy, CompuServe, and so on, do have limited data on hotels, and so forth, but no real effort is made to include the contents of an average travel guide.) There are a half dozen guides such as *Frommer's Guide to America's Most Traveled Cities* available on a SONY Data Discman, but these are of little real value for either a library or an individual.

of details about places. Atlases and gazetteers are specific enough about pinpointing locations, yet rarely deal with the down-to-earth facts travelers require.

Travel guidebooks are a popular item in libraries—and bookstores. Many bookstores have large sections of current guides which, particularly in the spring and summer, attract browsers. One of those browsers might be the librarian in quest of new editions and new approaches to current travel tips. The library collection should have a nice blend of the standard guides along with popular works on geography and picture travelogues. Picture books are a particularly useful mix with the guides.

Two questions must be answered by the reference librarian. The first concerns the countries that are popular among library users. Inevitably the first choices are books about the United States and Canada. Next come the Caribbean for East Coast residents, and the Pacific regions for those on the Pacific Rim. Turning to Europe, as might be expected, England is the most popular European country, followed by western Europe. Of course, none of this is pertinent when an individual wants a particular title on some unexpected section of the world. On the other hand, the consensus on points of interest does help shape the collection.

The second question concerns which guides are best. Given that the points of travel are more or less settled, then the reference librarian turns to well-known publishers and ongoing reviews of new titles. Usually only prices change from year to year, so one can get along on a series for three to four years without much updating. Provided, that is, that another series or two purchased in alternative years, does have the latest information. An ordering schedule which assures that this year's updated guides are available, if only from one or two standard publishers, is desirable.

Publisher series tend to emphasize the same basic data such as location and price of hotels, hours of opening of museums and points of interest, and background information on places and people. Beyond that each specializes. For example, the *Fodor* series focuses more than most on shopping; *Frommer's* on culture; and *Michelin* on a star rating system which informs the reader about the best hotels, sights, museums, and the like. In addition, there are specialized guides such as the *Let's Go* which offers suggestions for out-of-the-way, often inexpensive, methods of travel.

There are several bibliographies to travel guides, and most of these are updated every two to four years. Among the best is *The Travel Book* by Jon Heise and Julia Rinehart, which gives critical comments on the basic guides. Its particular strength is referral to lesser-known publishers, lesser-known books for equally odd parts of the globe.[12]

---

[12]See, too, *Going Places: The Guide to Travel Guides* (Cambridge, MA: Harvard Common Press, 1989 to date, irregular), which evaluates over 3000 guides. After an introduction to the genre, it divides the guides by geographical areas. The short annotations are descriptive and evaluative. An appendix lists travel magazines and newsletters. Ann Cohen, "Travel Reference Sources," *The Booklist*, April 15, 1994, pp. 1554–1556; Marguerite Mroz, "How to Select Travel Guides," *Library Journal*, May 1, 1991, pp. 51–55.

Where to Live

While most people believe that the best place to live is where they are (prison, hospital, and terrible job aside), others long for greener hills. Whether on the move to improve education, income, or the chances of living well after retirement there is a book out there to help. Two titles from Universal Reference Publications of Boca Raton, Florida, are *America's Top Rated Cities* (5 vols.) and *America's Top Rated Smaller Cities*. Each is updated regularly, and while the first statistical analysis is much more than most people require, one has the satisfaction of knowing that much of the supporting data for considerably shorter books and magazine articles draw upon the five volumes.

SUGGESTED READING

Barkow, Tim, "Ground Truth," *Wired*, December, 1995, pp. 96–105. A discussion of present and future plans for the "smart car" with a built-in computer to give the driver basic geographic information. This "will change the way we drive, the way we think on the road." Much of the dicussion concerns the firm NavTech.

Behroozi, Cy, "Children's Atlases," *Western Association of Map Libraries / Information Bulletin*, November 1993, pp. 23–27. This is an informative bibliography of basic works that, in either print or electronic format, will be of great assistance to younger children. Although the names of the atlases change, the publishers tend to remain the same and the compiler's comments are equally valid for new editions.

Buttimer, Anne, *Geography and the Human Spirit*. Baltimore, MD: Johns Hopkins University Press, 1995. This is a philosophical history of geography and cartography. The author is superior in her chronological treatment of geography's history. An excellent guide.

Feigenbaum, Mitchell, "Maps, Molecules, Computers, and Chaos," *Grand Street*, 1994, no. 50, pp. 223–230. A discussion of the modern Hammond Atlas Company and the production of maps. Well written and informative.

Gregory, Derek, *Geographical Imaginations*. Oxford: Blackwell, 1995. This is a subtle and absorbing meditation on the role of geography in the construction of society and political practice. Links are traced to anthropology, sociology, and economics. Urban geographical points are considered. "Cartographic anxiety" over change is covered.

Harley, J. B., and David Woodward, eds., *The History of Cartography*. Chicago: University of Chicago Press, 1987 to date. This definitive history has seen the death of one of the coeditors, J. B. Harley, and by 1995 only three volumes had been published. The first covers ancient and medieval Europe (1987), while three more (two have been issued) discuss cartography in non-Western countries. An infinitely valuable source for any medium to large library. Eventually there will be 7 to 10 volumes.

Hitt, Jack, "Atlas Shrugged: The New Face of Maps," *Lingua Franca*, August 1995, pp. 24–33. Until recently, cartographers worked with paper, ink, and a list of coordinates to construct maps. No more. The new breed has "massively parallel computers crunching ever-expanding lodes of information." The new maps, usually computer originated, are three dimensional, organic "and Mandelbrotian, akin to a moment of video." The explanation of how all this came about is clear and nicely illustrated.

"The Message in the Map," *The Chronicle of Higher Education*, May 19, 1995, p. A12–00. The author of a manual to decipher what is wrong and what is right with maps, Mark Monmonier, explains how to determine whether a map is correct. His *Drawing the Line* (New York: Henry Holt, 1995) is a cartographer's method of exposing poor maps.

Monmonier, Mark, *How to Lie with Maps*. Chicago: University of Chicago Press, 1991. The author demonstrates how, from newspapers to textbooks, it is possible to turn data into eye-catching diagrams which may or may not be accurate representations of the data.

Novell, Joan, "It's a Whole New World," *Instructor*, February 1994, pp. 51–54. The author explores the various electronic formats one may use with children. Online field trips as well as hypertext links show the universality of maps and geography. The short article shows, too, the value of networking.

Pack, Thomas, "The Online Reference Shelf," *Database*, October/November 1994, pp. 67–72. One of three articles about online reference sources, this covers "basic information on places" and briefly explores databases from those issued by the Census Bureau to online dictionaries and encyclopedias.

Watts, Anne, and Charles Kofron, "The St. Louis Public Library's Electronic Atlas," *Illinois Libraries*, April 1993, pp. 173–175. A practical explanation of an equally practical electronic map system. Much of the data will be of value to any librarian in other types of libraries.

Weide, Janice, "Electromap World Atlas," *CD-ROM Librarian*, July/August 1990, pp. 27–32. In this discussion of a CD-ROM map system, the author not only evaluates the particular work, but also explains other points which anyone interested in CD-ROM geographical source evaluation will find of value.

CHAPTER TWELVE
GOVERNMENT DOCUMENTS

Government documents come in many different forms. They do have one thing in common, and that is numbers: In 1996, the Superintendent of Documents sold over 100 million copies of its publications. In the mid-1990s the federal government was spending from $5 to $6 billion each year on information sources. These range from congressional bills to advice on growing tomatoes.

A *government document* is any publication that is printed at government expense or published by authority of a governmental body. While the United States Government Printing Office is responsible for the publication of documents, by the mid-1990s more than 70 percent of all government printing was actually contracted out to private firms. Most of the contracts are based on the lowest, suitable bid.

Documents may be considered in terms of issuing agencies: the congressional, judiciary, and executive branches, which include many departments and agencies. In terms of use, the documents may be classified as: (1) records of government administrations; (2) research documents for specialists, including a considerable number of statistics and data of value to science and business; and (3) popular sources of information. The physical form may be a book, pamphlet, magazine, report monograph, or may be electronic, particularly CD-ROMs.

While this discussion mainly concerns federal documents, state, county, and municipal governing bodies issue publications. Space and scope permit only mention of local documents here, but they are of importance in all libraries.

Some of the mystery surrounding government documents will be dispelled if one compares the government with the average private publisher. The publishing process is much the same for both, although normally the commercial publication will be expressed in somewhat more felicitous prose.

Bibliographical control and daily use of documents in reference work are often difficult and require expertise beyond the average experience of the reference librarian. Nevertheless, there are certain basic guides and approaches to government documents that should be familiar to all librarians.

ORGANIZATION AND SELECTION

The organization and selection of government documents in all but the largest of libraries is relatively simple. Librarians purchase a limited number of documents, usually in terms of subjects of interest to users or standard titles, such as the *Statistical Abstract of the United States*. If they are pamphlets, they usually are deposited by subject in a vertical file. If books, they are cataloged and shelved as such. In electronic format, they become part of the CD-ROM and online reference services.

Normally, the reference librarian will be responsible for the acquisition of documents. Confusion is minimal because government documents are rightly treated like any other information source and shelved, filed, or clipped like other media.

When one moves to the large or specialized libraries, the organizational pattern is either a separate government documents collection or, as in the smaller libraries, an integration of the documents into the general collection. Even the large libraries tend to partially integrate government documents with the general collection, although complete integration is rare. About one-third of large libraries have totally separate collections.

The justification for separate collections is that the volume of publications swamps the library and necessitates special considerations of organization and classification. There are other reasons, but on the whole, the decision is the librarian's in seeking the simplest and best method of making the documents available. The separate documents collection isolates the materials from the main reference collection. The reference librarians are inclined to think of it as a thing apart and may answer questions with materials at hand rather than attempt to fathom the depths of the documents department. The wide use of CD-ROMs and online reference services (including Internet, which is a highway for many government documents and pronouncements) has brought the documents collection closer to the daily life of the average reference librarian. Still, when it comes down to actually locating the needed material it is often left up to a specialist.

Evaluation

There are no problems with evaluation of government documents; there are no choices. One either accepts or rejects, say, *The Statistical Abstract of the United States*.

The government has no competitors, and evaluating such a document in terms of acquisitions is as fruitless as commanding the seas to dry up. Many government documents are unique and no one, but no one, is going to challenge them with another publication. The *Congressional Record* more or less dutifully records the words and actions of Congress each day. There is no possibility of (and no gain to) anyone's publishing another version.

These days evaluation is more in terms of how the information is delivered rather than the information itself. What, for example, is the best CD-ROM or online service for the text of the *Congressional Record?*

Depository Libraries

In order to ensure that the documents are freely available, the government established places where they might be examined. These are called depository libraries. The purpose is to have centers with relatively complete runs of government documents located throughout the country. In 1995 the Federal Depository Library Program (DLP) celebrated its hundredth birthday. There are some 1400 depository libraries in the United States, with at least one in every congressional district.

Federal agencies are not mandated to disseminate material through the program and as a result much information has been and is lost. A central system to ensure deposits of all, not just select, government information sources is needed.

The depositories are entitled to receive publications free of charge from the Superintendent of Documents. In each of the 50 states there is one depository library which accepts *every* unclassified government publication. Few other libraries take all the government documents (the average is about 54 percent of what is published). About two-thirds of the depository libraries are academic, whereas public libraries account for about 20 percent of the total. The remaining (less than 14 percent) consist of federal, state agency, court law, historical society, medical, and private membership libraries.

The basic problem faced by all but the largest of the depository libraries is the volume of material. Much of it is of limited use, and a good deal is nothing but raw data and statistics employed to support arguments or gathered more for the sake of gathering than for any specific purpose. The volume problem may be solved by putting most, if not all, of the documents in electronic format.[1]

---

[1] In late 1988 the Federal Depository Library Program joined the electronic revolution by making depository documents available on CD-ROM, magnetic tape, and online. As part of an earlier program, many depository documents are only on microfiche. By the end of 1995, about one third of the depository libraries offer a direct channel to federal documents online through a program titled "GPO Access." Developed by the Government Printing Office, the service allows library users to search several basic federal databases. Among these are the *Congressional Record,* the *Federal Register,* *Congressional Bills,* and the *General Accounting Office Reports Service.* More sources are to be added. The

ONLINE AND ON CD-ROM

The federal government, as well as state and local governments, have embraced the new digital technologies. Masses of paperwork are ideally suited to the CD-ROM and online formats. Many, if not most, of the basic works in this chapter are available on CD-ROM and online. They represent only a sampling of the overwhelming number of titles which range from Toxic Release Inventory from the Superintendent of Documents to the National Economic-Social and Environmental Database from the U.S. Department of Commerce. Gradually the U.S. Government Printing Office is switching over to electronic databases, although maintaining the print format as well for popular, general titles. The trend is becoming international. The North Atlantic Treaty Organization in Belgium, for example, offers citations to close to 45,000 papers in its NATO-PCO Database, published each year since 1973.

CD-ROM

The scores of federal documents now available on CD-ROM are entered in the *Monthly Catalog* as well as listed by broad title in the *Gale Directory of Databases*. One, much-used example is CD/ER: Compact Disc Federal Register (Cambridge, MA: Counterpoint Publishing, 1990 to date, weekly and annual, $1200). This contains the complete text of the daily *Register*. There is an online version.[2] As is often typical, both are made available in electronic form by a private publisher-vendor. Widely distributed, popular government documents on CD-ROMs and online may be offered by a number of different private concerns at sometimes various rates, primarily because of differences in software.

The U.S. Government Printing Office distributes some basic government documents on CD-ROM and online. For example, the aforementioned *Federal Register,* from 1980 to date, is a product of the GPO; and available online daily from DIALOG (file 669 at $90 per hour). A great success, *The National Trade Data Bank,* from the U.S. Department of Commerce, is a monthly CD-ROM for only $360. The disc covers every conceivable aspect of U.S. and international trade.

A growing number of private CD-ROM producers are offering government documents, often augmented by the vendor with hypertext. This is possible because government documents cannot be copyrighted and can be reprinted,

---

service is free to libraries and to laypersons seeking information in the library. "Federal Deposit Libs. Online via GPO Access Program," *Library Journal,* October 15, 1995, p. 19.

[2]The *Federal Register* and its cousin the *Code of Federal Regulations* is a running bibliographical record of action taken by Congress and various government agencies each day. Every topic is covered from agriculture and art to meeting and hearing notices about the plight of zebras. Approximately 400,000 to 450,000 documents are published each year in the *Register* and *Code.* See Joe Morehead, *Introduction to United States Government Information Sources,* 4th ed. (Englewood, CO: Libraries Unlimited, 1992), Chapter 7, Administrative Law. . . .

republished by anyone. An example of privately published documents is the *U.S. Civics* (Minneapolis, MN: Quanta Press, Inc., 1990 to date, annual, $49.95). This is a total guide for people seeking U.S. citizenship. Included, and available in print form as well are two titles from the U.S. Immigration and Naturalization Service: *A Reference Manual for Citizenship Instructors* and *Citizenship Education and Naturalization Information*. Both of these are available in print from the government, precisely as they are found on the commercial disc. The producer "salts" the two government documents in a typical fashion, often using illustrations, animation, and even sound to provide major aids for the user. In this case it is data on American history and civics which are likely to be part of the expected answers to questions put to would-be citizens. There are illustrations of individuals and various historical points, as well. This wedding of government data with private, often imaginative additions, is becoming more and more common in various electronic formats.

Database Searching

On a CD-ROM or online, the searching of government information differs from document to document, publisher to publisher, vendor to vendor. With that, though, the basic search process is much the same. Selection of specific data may be made by date, by entering search terms, and by boolean logic. Depending on the system, one may enter the Superintendent Document number or the corporate author, or the place(s) involved with the particular title, or . . . well, the possibilities are the same as they are on much online and CD-ROM navigating.

　　Because of their extensive coverage and often complete full text online or on a CD-ROM, many digital databases with government information add such things as an index of terms or a table of contents.

Acquisition

Once a document has been selected for purchase (in print, as a CD-ROM, or the now-common microfiche for many congressional publications), its acquisition is no more difficult—indeed, often somewhat easier—than that of a book or periodical. Depository libraries have a peculiar set of problems, but for the average library, the acquisitions process may be as follows:

1. Full information is given in the *Monthly Catalog* and *U.S. Government Books* on methods of purchase from the Superintendent of Documents. Payment may be made in advance by purchase of coupons from the Superintendent of Documents. In the case of extensive purchases, deposit accounts may be established.

2. Some documents may be obtained free from members of Congress. However, as the supply of documents is limited, the member of Con-

gress should be notified of need in advance. It is particularly advisable to get on the regular mailing list of one's representative or senator to receive publications.

Issuing agencies often have a stock of publications which must be ordered directly from the agency. These are noted by a plus sign in the *Monthly Catalog* and frequently include valuable specialized materials, from ERIC documents to scientific reports.

3. There are government bookstores that sell documents. In addition, some larger private bookstores sell the documents, or at least the books dealing with the popular subjects from space to gardening.

FEDERAL INFORMATION SERVICE

Offering direct answers to questions, the United States government, through a private firm, operates its own ready-reference telephone service in Washington, DC. The government's ready-reference service functions as follows:

1. Anyone can call 1-800-347-1997. (Note: This is as of 1996 and the number can change.) The usual message comes through to push a button for information on federal employment, immigration, Social Security, or income tax. Several of these have a taped response that gives you another number to call.

2. Actually the best ploy is to wait for "5." Here the response is not limited to the four topics above, and covers any subject. One may gather information on everything from a new Chinese language typewriter to what to do about a violent crime. The people responding are likely to accept queries under a large umbrella. For example, the *Washington Post* decided to test the service with six "off-the-wall questions picked at random from the garbage cluttering up one reporter's mind." In 30 minutes the center responded with five answers to questions about the number of National Western Service satellites (10) to the number of endangered species, animal and plants (760).[3]

The service began in 1966, and in 1990 the General Services Administration turned it over to Biospherics, Inc. The company is paid about $19 million over five years for the service which employs 90 information specialists. The General Services Administration operates its own 72 Federal Information Centers in 35 states, but none gives the complete service of the Washington center.

---

[3]Guy Gugliotta, "Capital Notebook: The Government's Answer Man," *The Washington Post,* October 4, 1994, p. 15. The U.S. General Services Administration issues a free pamphlet, "Federal Information Center" with current phone numbers.

GUIDES

Print: Morehead, Joe. *Introduction to United States Public Documents,* 5th ed. Englewood, CO: Libraries Unlimited, Inc., 1996, paperback. To be announced.
No electronic format.

Print: Schwarzkopf, Leroy. *Government Reference Books.* Englewood, CO: Libraries Unlimited, Inc., 1972 to date, biennial. $67.50.
No electronic format.

The basic textbook in the field is the Morehead-Fetzer volume, which is revised about every four years. It is a nice combination of facts about individual reference works and a clear, concise explanation of how the government manages to publish documents. Thanks to the superior organization and fine writing style, the textbook is easy to read. Both the beginner and the expert will find considerable assistance here. It is the first place to turn when puzzled about some mysterious aspect of the acquisition, organization, and selection of government documents. It should be noted that the author is a frequent contributor to periodicals and for a number of years has been the editor of the government documents column in *The Serials Librarian.*

Government Reference Books is published every two years and is a roundup of basic reference books, many of which are not familiar to either the layperson or the expert. Here they are arranged by broad subject, that is, general, social sciences, science and technology, and humanities. The documents are then indexed by author, title, and subject. Each is fully described. About 1200 titles are annotated every two years. Carefully edited and easy to use, the Schwarzkopf bibliography augments the standard sources. Libraries Unlimited also publishes a more general *Guide to Popular U.S. Government Publications.* The 1993 third edition moves from "accidents" to "wildlife." It is a good source of material for the whole library collection as well as for reference.

The best, selective list of government documents for small- to medium-sized libraries is published each year by the American Library Association's Government Documents Round Table or GODORT. The annotated list of 50 to 75 publications includes federal, state, and local efforts as well as those published by international groups. Usually the list appears each April or May in the standard library periodical from *Library Journal* to *American Libraries.* It is a splendid guide.

GOVERNMENT ORGANIZATION

CD: U.S. Government Organization Manual. Alexandria, VA: Government Counseling, Ltd., 1993 to date, annual. $99.[4]

---

[4]The CD-ROM Organizational Manual (which uses the older title, and is published by TAURUS Sondisc, a trademark) is precisely the same as the print version. It is approached in the standard

Print: United States Government Manual. Washington, DC: U.S. Government Printing Office, 1935 to date, annual, 904 pp., paperback. $30.

Print: U.S. Congress Joint Committee on Printing. *Official Congressional Directory.* Washington, DC: U.S. Government Printing Office, 1809 to date, biennial, 1625 pp., paperback. $15.
No electronic format.

All federal, state, and local governments issue documents. The nature of those publications depends upon the particular organizational patterns of the issuing body. There are various guides and textbooks that explain the activities of these groups, but the best overall guide to the federal government is the *United States Government Manual.*

The basic purpose of the *Manual* is to give in detail the organization, activities, and chief officers of all government agencies within the legislative, judicial, and executive branches. Each of the agencies is discussed separately, and the units within each organizational pattern are clearly defined. Occasionally, charts and diagrams are employed. The style is factual, yet discursive enough to hold the interest of anyone remotely involved with such matters.

Directory data are given for each agency, and list the telephone numbers, addresses, names of officials, and addresses of regional offices for the major departments. There are several indexes, including one by subject. A useful feature of each year's issue is the list of agencies transferred, terminated, or abolished. Full particulars are given. This, by the way, is a justification for holding several years of the *Manual* on the shelves. All too often, someone will want information on a certain agency which can be found only in earlier editions.

Congress

Issued every two years, *The Congressional Directory* includes biographies of members of Congress. The sections include data, too, on Supreme Court justices, names of foreign representatives and consular offices in the United States, and the chief officers of departments and independent agencies. It is a type of "who's who" of government, along with the essential addresses, phone numbers, and even maps of congressional districts. The drawback: Matters change quickly in Washington and the *Directory* comes out biennially. It cannot be trusted, for example, to have the latest information on committee assignments or members of the press corps, both of which are included. One might think it would be cur-

---

CD-ROM search patterns and offers little or no difficulty. The question, once again, is Is this necessary, at three times the price on a CD-ROM? The answer is no. There is really little or no advantage to the digital version.

rent when first issued, but it can be up to six months behind official publication date.

There are numerous more current directories. An example is *Staff Directories* (Mt. Vernon, VA: Staff Directories, 1990 to date, semiannual, $395) which is on CD-ROM and includes three directory files covering the congressional staff, the judicial staff, and the federal staff (about 30,000 executives and military people). All three have a limited number of short biographies, as well as the standard data from telephone numbers and titles to addresses. The bulk of the volume is an alphabetically arranged entry of members of Congress, as well as resident commissioners, delegates, and vice presidents. A short "who's-who" type of entry is used for each name.

Among the most-used directories and biographical sources for members of government, at both the national and local levels, is *Who's Who in American Politics* (New York: R. R. Bowker Company, 1967 to date, biennial). This work gives information on 25,000 individuals at the federal, state, and local level. The "who's-who" data include office held and current address as well as basic biographical facts.

Where does one find information on former members of Congress no longer listed in the *Congressional Directory?* They will be listed in such sources as the *Dictionary of American Biography* (if deceased) or in a good encyclopedia. But for short, objectives sketches of all senators and representatives who served from 1774 to the present, the best single source is *Biographical Directory of the American Congress, 1774–19–* (Washington, DC: U.S. Government Printing Office, various dates, prices). There is a handy first section which includes officers of the executive branch.

The Encyclopedia of the United States Congress (New York: Simon & Schuster, 1995, 4 vols.) is the most current, definitive general reference work on Congress. Everything from history to biography and landmark decisions are explored in the over 1000 articles. The illustrations, index, and modest bibliographies add to the value of the set, particularly for students working on papers and laypeople seeking easy-to-understand background information.

Executive and Judiciary

CD: U.S. Presidents. Minneapolis, MN: Quanta Press, Inc., 1990 to date, updated as needed. $69.95.

Print: Kane, Joseph. *Facts About the Presidents*, 5th ed. New York: The H. W. Wilson Company, 1989, 419 pp. $55.
No electronic format.

Print: Encyclopedia of the American Presidency. New York: Simon & Schuster, 1994, 4 vols. $355.
No electronic format.

Questions concerning the presidents are answered in considerable detail in almost any encyclopedia as well as in the basic guides to government discussed in this chapter. The two titles listed here are easier to use because they offer facts in a consistent, well-organized fashion. Also, of course, they are both limited to the presidents.

Everything, and then some, that anyone wants to know about a president will be found on the CD-ROM *U.S. Presidents.* The disc even includes pictures of the gentlemen, from the first to the immediate occupant of the White House. While most of the data are available in any good encyclopedia, it has the advantage of having supporting statistical comparisons as well as historical sketches of the first ladies.

The first section of Kane has a chapter on each of the presidents, including family life. A bibliography is included. Possibly of more use, at least for ready-reference purposes, is the second part, which is a comparative guide of all the presidents. Here one finds everything from the number of children each had to their last words. Also, there are facts on the office itself from legal problems to the cabinet officials.

The definitive work on the subject is the four-volume *Encyclopedia of the American Presidency.* It is a scholar's dream. There is little that is not covered, from the dentistry of George Washington to the romances of some of the other gentlemen who filled the office. Thanks to an excellent index one might add that it is a place of last resort for puzzled reference librarians unable to find, for example, a clue to the fate of President Cleveland's home after he left office. And there are other gems.

There are similar directories and sources of background information for the executive and judiciary branches. Many are from private publishers and are listed in Morehead's guide, *Introduction to United States Public Documents,* and other places.

Background

While any good encyclopedia will give the necessary framework of American government, both federal and state, there are some specialized sources which can give the details not often found in a general encyclopedia. The most obvious for specific data is the aforementioned *United States Government Organization Manual* and *Official Congressional Directory.* In addition there is the excellent *Encyclopedia of the American Legislative System,* 3d ed. (New York: Scribner, 1994, 3 vols., $320). This consists of close to 100 signed articles by political scientists and historians. The experts cover everything from the history to the present problems of the government. Fortunately, the scope includes state, federal, and local governments. There is an adequate index, although it sometimes fails to point out specific areas of interest.

CATALOGS

CD: GPO (Monthly Catalog). Washington, DC: U.S. Government Printing Office, 1976 to date, monthly. $600.[5]
>   *Print: Monthly Catalog of the United States Government Publications.* 1895 to date, monthly. $199.
>   *Online: GPO Monthly Catalog.* 1976 to date, monthly. DIALOG file 66, $35 per hour. Also available on OCLC and RLIN. Rates vary.

As with the majority of government-sponsored databases, the *Monthly Catalog,* online and on CD-ROM, offers a relatively inexpensive way of searching and is familiar to almost every reference librarian. No matter its time limitations (the electronic version goes back only to 1976) the electronic form of the *Monthly Catalog* is found in almost every medium or large library. The latter, particularly where there is a significant collection of separately filed documents, tends to rely on the *Catalog* both as a finding device and catalog, as well as a source of information for purchase.

Arrangement in the print *Catalog* is by the classification number of the Superintendent of Documents. This amounts to arrangement by issuing agency; that is, most documents issued by the Library of Congress will be listed under that agency name—most, but not all. Special classification situations arise when documents are arranged under a main entry other than the organization that issued the document. Hence, it is always wise to check the indexes and not assume that the document will be under the likely agency, department, and so on.

There are four major indexes: author, title, subject, and series and reports. For reference, the subject and title indexes are the most useful. The subject and title indexes list the documents by their full title.

With that, the print version has rapidly fallen out of favor because of the searching problems. In electronic form, and particularly with boolean logic, the experienced librarian can normally find what is wanted, if only by searching by key words.

Estimates vary, but only about 2 or 3 out of every 10 documents now come from the U.S. Government Printing Office. The remainder, therefore, are not in the *Catalog.* It also does not index periodicals and the material therein. Documents are not included in the *Monthly Catalog* for a number of reasons, although the most common one is that they are issued outside the U.S. Government Printing Office and printed or otherwise made available somewhere besides the GPO. Other reasons for nonentry include secrecy or failure of a given section, office, or department to use the GPO or otherwise send a copy of a document for cataloging.

---

[5]As with all government publications, the *Monthly Catalog* is available to any publisher. Consequently there are various versions (and prices) on CD-ROM. Online possibilities, too, are numerous.

There is another approach to government documents from the U.S. Government Printing Office. It is *GPO Sales Publications Reference File,* a type of *Books in Print* for government documents. Here one finds, on average, about 27,000 public documents currently for sale, as well as forthcoming titles. This is available in print and online as DIALOG file 166, and on CompuServe.

Other governments follow much the same bibliographical control. For example, Canada publishes *Government of Canada Publications Catalogue* (Ottawa, CN: Canadian Government Publishing Center, 1953 to date, weekly and quarterly). This is a listing of Canadian departmental and parliamentary documents, which range from the esoteric to the popular.

Online

GPO Online is the U.S. Government Printing Office full-text service which offers a number of services. Among the more important are: (1) *The Monthly Catalog of United States Government Publications;* (2) *BillText,* which contains the complete text and synopsis of current bills introduced in Congress, as well as an objective analysis for many of the bills regarding changes they may bring about in particular areas of law, business, social life, and the like; (3) *U.S. Government Publications,* in full text, for areas from health and energy to food preparation and automobiles. Most popular and semipopular government documents are made available in this way. There are a half dozen other services online from the GPO and from various online services from DIALOG to CompuServe. Rates vary.

Catalogs for Smaller Libraries: Print Only

No electronic format.

U.S. Superintendent of Documents. *U.S. Government Books.* Washington, DC: U.S. Government Printing Office, 1982 to date, quarterly. Free.

————. *New Books.* 1982 to date, bimonthly. Free.

————. *Subject Bibliographies.* 1975 to date, irregular. Free.

Turning to a more manageable type of bibliography, *U.S. Government Books* is an annotated listing of about 1000 popular and semipopular documents for laypersons and professionals. The bibliography starts out with "Recent Releases" and then is broken down under 20 broad subjects. The approximately 60 pages are presented in magazine format and almost every one of the entries includes a picture. It is a persuasive sales tool as well as a source of information. For small- to medium-sized libraries, it is an ideal buying guide. Also, thanks to its pleasing format, it will be of interest to many laypersons, and it should be made available for easy inspection.

New Books is a drab 25-page listing of new publications listed under 20 broad subject headings (agriculture to transportation). It simply lists the title, date of publication, number of pages, Superintendent of Documents number, and price. There are no annotations, although often the title is descriptive enough. It is useful as a checklist. One major help is the highlighting of two or three documents on the cover, for example, "Conditions of education . . . page 6," "Desktop publishing guide . . . page 16," and so forth.

Subject Bibliographies, as the title indicates, stresses documents in a specific area. There are now close to 300 topics, and they cover material on everything from air pollution to zoology. Many of the entries are annotated.

For the library seeking information on government periodicals, the best single source is *Price List 36: Government Periodicals and Subscription Services,* (Washington, DC: U.S. Government Printing Office, 1974 to date, quarterly, free). This is an annotated listing of over 500 publications, the majority of which are classified as periodicals.

Popular Guides

New layperson guides to basic government documents appear each year, as do new editions of older titles. Most are outlined in Morehead's guide and *American Reference Book Annual.* One example, typical of the group, will suffice: William Bailey's *Guide to Popular U.S. Government Publications,* 2d ed. (Englewood CO: Libraries Unlimited, 1990) divides much-used documents into 75 broad subject areas. Full bibliographical data are given for each item and there are brief descriptive notes, as well as a title index and a superior subject index.

An extremely useful, selective list of from 100 to 150 government documents is chosen each year by the Notable Documents Panel of the American Library Association. Basic federal, state, and even international documents are selected. These are likely to be most used in answering topical reference questions. The annotated list appears in numerous journals including *Library Journal* for May 15 of each year.

Almost all the periodicals that carry reviews of books from time to time consider government periodicals. *The Booklist,* for example, has a regular annotated selection section. *Library Journal* and *Choice,* as well as *American Libraries* feature articles and reviews. Joe Morehead has a regular column on documents in *Serials Librarian,* and *RQ* has different experts.

GOVERNMENT IN ACTION[6]

CD: Congressional Masterfile. Bethesda, MD: Congressional Information Service, 1989 to date, quarterly. Price varies.

---

[6]There are several indexes to government documents. Only the basic ones are considered here. For those who wish additional information on these and other indexes, see John Ross's *How to Use the Major Indexes to U.S. Government Publications* (Chicago: American Library Association, 1989), as well as Morehead's text.

Print: CIS/Index to Publications of the U.S. Congress, 1970 to date, monthly service. $800 to $2500 per year.

Online: CIS. 1970 to date, monthly. DIALOG file 101, $90 per hour.

Print: CQ Weekly Report. Washington, DC: Congressional Quarterly Inc., 1945 to date, weekly. Library rates on request.[7]

Online: CQ Washington Alert Service, 1983 to date, weekly. $65 to $156 per hour.

Turning to the indexes, one of the most frequently used is the *Index to Publications of the United States Congress,* usually called the *CIS/Index.* The *Monthly Catalog* lists only complete congressional documents; the *CIS/Index* analyzes what is *in* those documents, covering over 900,000 pages of special studies, bills, hearings, and so on each year. All congressional publications, with abstracts, are indexed. Online and in print it is updated monthly (at about 1000 records each month).

The *CIS/Index* is one of the single best sources of information concerning ongoing activities of government. As one of the most comprehensive of document indexes, although limited to the activities of Congress, the *CIS/Index* is a blessing for the reference librarian seeking information on the progress of a bill through Congress. Popular names of bills, laws, and reports are given, as well as the subject matter of those materials. In addition, an index covers the same material by bill number, report number, and so on. Hearings are covered as well as the names of the witnesses, committees, and the like, and so the librarian can easily keep up with the development of legislation. The comprehensive nature of the *CIS/Index* is such that, with a little practice, the reference librarian will feel fully capable of tracking down even the most elusive material. Searching patterns follow the publisher's CD-ROM methods, as discussed in the following section.

Masterfile

The CD-ROM version, as is often the case, considerably eases the difficulty of searching. Called *Congressional Masterfile,* it is divided into two sections. The first is an invaluable retrospective guide covering documents from 1789 to 1969.[8] Depending on type of library, subscription to printed version, and so forth, the price is from a low of $9092 to a high of $32,000. The basic Masterfile is updated by Masterfile 2, which carries material from 1969 to date. Again the prices vary.

---

[7] *Congressional Quarterly* publishes useful reference works that can be used with or without a large government documents collection. *Guide to Congress,* updated every few years, covers the history of Congress as well as its day-to-day operations and government printing that comes out of congressional sessions.

[8] Historically, the CD-ROM is extremely valuable in that it is a key to U.S. congressional committee hearings, journals, and all congressional publications from the earliest Congress.

The searching is made easy through a clear menu system which leads the user through various paths to the documents. The user may search by standard index terms, congressional session and data, the name of a witness, the title of a hearing, committee print, serial set, and so on. A considerable amount of information—as in the printed work—is given on the screen. Often this is more than enough information so the user does not have to turn to the actual documents. Valuable as it is, the CD-ROM is only updated quarterly.

There is a complete system for the library that can afford to purchase all the indexed materials. CIS/Congressional Bills, Resolutions and Laws on Microfiche offers the full-text collection in one place. The user locates the desired item in the index and, through a simple key system, finds the microfiche copy.

The print *Index* averages between 150 and 200 pages a month in looseleaf form. It is in two parts: (1) The index section offers access by subject, author, and title. This section is cumulated quarterly, and there is an annual. (2) The summary section gives the full title of the document and includes an abstract of most of the items indexed.

CQ Weekly Report

The *CQ Weekly Report* is by another private publisher and it supplements its rival, the *CIS/Index*. It too focuses primarily on congressional activity, but on a weekly rather than a monthly or quarterly basis. The *Report*, a much-used reference aid, is similar in some ways to a congressional version of *Facts on File*. It is *not* an index but a summary of the week's past events, a summary which is often sufficient to either (1) identify a government document to be later found in a specialized work, or (2) answer, in one step, a reference query.

Each issue analyzes in detail both congressional and general political activity of the week. The major bills are followed from the time they are introduced until they are passed and enacted into law (or killed along the way). A handy table of legislation shows at a glance where the bills are in the Congress. Cross-references to previous weekly reports allow easy access to material until the quarterly index is issued and cumulated throughout the year.

Trying to keep track of a piece of legislation, from its formation to its final passage (or death) is difficult. The process is made relatively easy through a series of online services offered by the publisher of *CQ Weekly Report* under the umbrella term CQ Washington Alert Service. (This is carried, at various rates, on the publisher's own SprintNet network.) The base of the system is the *CQ Bill Tracking* (1983 to date, daily) which chronicles all bills and resolutions introduced into Congress since the 98th Congress. There are cross-references to the *CQ Weekly Report* and *Congressional Record*. The full bibliographical information helps find the piece of legislation. Also the online system has summaries of the bills and resolutions beginning with the 101st Congress. The user may find background on members of Congress, research current issues, and so on. The service offers, too, the full text of bills and major documents. The main menu lists all of the databases that may be searched individually or across as required.

Related databases under the same umbrella, that is, CQ Washington Alert Services include many with self-explanatory titles: CQ Committee Action Votes . . . , CQ Committee Reports, CQ Text of Bills, and the like. The result is complete and total coverage of Congress and legislation. As most of these are updated online daily there are, again, no print or CD-ROM versions.

The *Congressional Quarterly Almanac*, by the same publisher (1945 to date, annual, $195) is a handy reference work for almost all libraries. The annual divides the work of Congress into 11 subject areas (from environment and health to transportation and law). Summaries are given of each bill in the various subject categories. Most of the material is analyzed objectively. In addition, there is a handy summary of Supreme Court decisions and data on presidential messages. Thanks to a splendid index, it is the ideal reference work in the area it covers.

Online Full-Text Documents

Today the majority of legislative government documents are available in full text online. Most are made available through essentially legal services, or an online service specifically for legislative matters. WESTLAW and LEXIS are legal research systems, discussed in an earlier chapter, which, among other things, make it possible to access the full text of primary and secondary sources of United States government documents. They are particularly useful for data on U.S. laws. Incidentally, both perform much the same service for state legal documents. The online user may use LEXIS to locate text of articles from over 300 law reviews and bar journals, many of which are involved with federal regulations.

LEGI-SLATE (Washington, DC: Legi-Slate, 1979 to date) is a much-used online service with various rates for the complete text of numerous legislative documents, from the *Federal Register* to the *Congressional Record*. It is much used because in addition to government documents it includes the full text of *The Washington Post* as well as daily press briefings from various branches of the government. A transcript service offers verbatim online transcriptions of interviews, committee hearings, press briefings, and related matters. Morehead points out that this is an outstanding online service and, unfortunately, a very expensive one. It has tremendous advantages in that bill tracking can be accomplished daily. Digests prepared by the Congressional Research Service of the Library of Congress are provided online, and all parliamentary versions of all bills introduced.

The two largest bibliographical utilities in the world OCLC and RLIN offer access to government documents, although not often the full text found in such services as LEXIS. Both give the library the *Monthly Catalog* and, as such, serve as a broad index to government documents. More important, at least for the average library, is that the two services make it possible to borrow documents on interlibrary loan. Both are useful for cataloging and verification of documents as well. And RLIN, to be sure, is the place to turn first when there is a question of locating a government document from another country, another part of the world. Both, too, draw upon the records of the Library of Congress and its MARC tapes, discussed elsewhere in this text.

In the mid-1990s the U.S. Government Printing Office opened the Columbia Online Information Network or COIN. By dialing 314-884-7000 (or by telnet 128.206.1.3.) users may search a number of government databases without charge. The major databases are The Congressional Record, Federal Register, and Congressional Bills with the latter offering the full text of documents on the day of publication. The plan is to open up all government documents, in full text, for users who may not be able to go to a depository library, but do have access through Internet or gateways such as the Seattle Public Library's Quest System. (Information on current Internet availability of documents may be had by e-mail or by calling 202-512-1530.)

Technical Reports

CD: NTIS. Washington, DC: U.S. National Technical Information Service, 1980 to date, quarterly. $2300–$2900.
  Print: Government Reports Announcements & Index, 1946 to date, semimonthly. *Government Report Annual Index,* 1965 to date, semimonthly. Price varies.
  Online: NTIS Bibliographic Data Base, 1964 to date, biweekly. DIALOG file 6, $84 per hour. Numerous other services offer this online from CDP (after dark at $20 per hour) to ORBIT, $81 per hour.

Librarians familiar with the reports on ERIC, may not be as well acquainted with studies available through the U.S. National Technical Information Service. While ERIC is concerned primarily with education, NTIS turns to technical reports from U.S. and non-U.S. government sponsored research. As of the mid-1990s there were some 2.5 million such reports available and accessed through CD-ROM, print, or online. For a detailed analysis of the hundred or more publications from the NTIS see the 1995–1996 catalog which is available free from the U.S. Department of Commerce, NTIS, Springfield, VA 22161.

In print there are two distinct services, the *Government Reports Announcement* and the *Government Reports Annual Index.* Both are joined in digital formats, and become one. The announcement section includes abstracts of about 70,000 reports each year. They are divided into 26 major subject areas and then subdivided. Produced by local, state, and federal government agencies, as well as by individuals and private and for-profit groups, the reports cover a wide spectrum of interests, including much material in the social sciences. In fact, NTIS and ERIC interchange some report information and there is a limited amount of duplication. The *Index* includes subject, personal and corporate author, contact number, and access/report number. Annual cumulations may be purchased separately.

NTIS is backed up by documents on microfiche, which may be on standing order selectively through the Selected Research in Microfiche program (SRIM). Standing orders are for subject, category, agency, or descriptor. The library may also order individual documents on microfiche or in printed form as needed.

LEGISLATIVE QUESTIONS AND ANSWERS

Typical questions concerning government documents may be answered in most of the aforementioned reference works. In addition, there are other approaches, other reference works. Still, the basic steps employed will proceed something like this:

1. "I am looking for information about a congressional hearing."[9] Turn to the *Congressional Masterfile* CD-ROM or the print or online *CIS/Index* which covers subjects and titles as well as other points of access such as the name of the committee.

a. Lacking the *Index,* or for hearings of several years ago, turn to the *Monthly Catalog* where the subject, title, and committee involved offer access.

b. *PAIS (Public Affairs Information Service)* offers a subject approach to most major hearings, but not all, and it is highly selective. Note, too, that *PAIS* will index periodicals and some books and reports *about* the hearings, and so for background information this is most useful.

c. Other sources include current newspapers (usually online) such as *The New York Times Index* or online periodicals in the subject area.

2. "What is happening to the bill which guarantees three little pigs for every family in America?" Here one might turn to the *CIS/Index.* A more current, somewhat easier-to-follow approach is offered by the *CQ Weekly Report.* This traces the development of the bill into a law. See sections "On the Floor" and "In Committee." See, too, the excellent status tables of important legislation

---

[9]When someone desires a new law, normally a "hearing" is held before Congress (either/or both House and Senate) to determine the wisdom of the proposed law. Expert testimony is given. Also, hearings are heard to clarify a public issue such as the budget hearings; examine the appointment of officials; and so forth. Hearings are familiar to an estimated 30 million people who watch C-Span (the cable television network). This channel often gives full television coverage of Senate and House hearings about a given issue and debates about new proposed laws.

A *report* is the result of the hearing and the recommendations of the legislative body. This accompanies the proposed new law, that is, the *bill* as it goes to the full House and/or Senate.

which include the votes as well, and the entries in (1) above for additional information, particularly as the progressing bill is viewed by the public and by officials outside Congress.

3. "Where can I find a current law?[10] It just became law." Laws are cumulated at the end of each session of Congress in volumes called *Statutes at Large* (1789 to date). Later the laws are organized in a more detailed fashion and become part of the *U.S. Code*. Current laws are in the *Statutes* and those of some standing are in the *Code*. While the full law may not be given, the content is reported, often with its implications, in the *CIS/Index, CQ Weekly Report,* and the other reference works listed in (1) above.[11]

These steps will result in finding 90 to 95 percent of the answers to questions put to the reference librarian about ongoing federal legislative activities.

INDEXES AND THE CENSUS

CD: U.S. Government Periodicals Index. Washington, DC: Congressional Information Service, 1994 to date, quarterly. $795.

Print: 1994 to date, quarterly. $795. (This replaces the 1970 to 1993 *Index to U.S. Government Periodicals.*)

An expensive index, it costs the same on CD-ROM or in print. It gives access to 180 government published periodicals.[12] The index follows the usual place, subject, corporate name, and the like, as entry points. Although expensive, the index has a definite place in large research libraries. Much of the information found in the federal journals and magazines is found nowhere else. Subjects range from economics and business to satellites and ethics. And while it is true that most of the emphasis is on science and technology, there is a great deal of information on social sciences and politics.

---

[10]When the bill is passed either by both houses of Congress or by one (as procedure dictates), it becomes a "law." Of course, many hearings do not result in either a report or a bill or a law; and numerous bills are killed or vetoed by the President before they become law. Actually, if it really did "just" become law, it probably would appear only in what is called "slip law" form, that is, an unbound pamphlet which has not been cumulated and bound as part of the *Statutes at Large.* These are normally identified by public law number and filed as such according to their reference government document section.

[11]*The Congressional Record,* the daily record of the proceedings of Congress, has a section on the "history of bills and resolutions." This is too difficult to use because of poor indexing, and most librarians rely on other sources such as the *CIS/Index.* The *Record* is another major government document that includes and excludes material dictated by members of Congress.

[12]There are about 2000 periodicals and serials currently available from the federal government and probably several times that number from agencies and sections not found in Washington. The smaller number of titles indexed is not a drawback, in that many of the 2000-plus government periodicals and serials are so specialized as to be of little use to more than a few people locally and, except in a depository library, not likely to be readily available.

U.S. Census

CD: TIGER/Line Files. Washington, DC: U.S. Bureau of the Census, 1922 to date, irregular update. Price varies.

Print: Current Population Reports. Washington, DC: U.S. Bureau of the Census, various dates, prices. See also related print reports such as *Current Business Reports.*

Online: CENDATA, 1980 to date, daily. DIALOG file 580, $36 per hour. Also available on CompuServe. Rates vary.

Data collected by the U.S. Bureau of the Census are the statistical backbone of many of the statistical works considered in this text. Often the secondary statistical sources (such as *Statistical Abstract of the United States*) are enough, but where primary material is required the librarian turns to the U.S. Bureau of the Census. Before discussing the basic sources, consider other excellent places to go for both statistical data and for Census Bureau information. First, one should turn to *American Statistics Index.* Second, other business and related indexes (from *Predicasts* to the *CIS/Index*) will analyze census material.

Third, for a detailed description of the various files and reports there is the *Bureau of the Census Catalog* (Washington, DC: U.S. Government Printing Office, 1946 to date, annual). Although this has changed in form and format, essentially it arranges news and information about statistical data by subject, from agriculture to trade. There is a detailed index that allows one to locate material by a specific area. Most of the statistical data found in reference works, including those considered in this chapter, are based on the last *Census of Population.* The 10-year overview is the single best and most expansive source of information of its type in the world.

The online CENDATA is divided into 14 main subject sections which include both economic and population data. Most of the file parts are updated regularly by ongoing census and Bureau of Labor figures. Among categories are standard demographical reports; statistics on over 200 basic countries; and data on the latest durable goods manufactured, housing starts, building permits, and related data employed to chart the status of the national economy. There is a mine of information on almost every human activity which comes under the scrutiny of the statistician.

Online files are relatively easy to search, using the standard methods from boolean logic to easy-to-follow menus. Interestingly enough this is one of the few statistical services offered on a consumer's network, that is, CompuServe. Note, too, that many of the reports that make up the online databases are available in print, for example, *Current Population Reports, Current Housing Reports,* and *Construction Reports.*

On a CD-ROM, but not online, the famous TIGER/Line Files are used by a wide variety of professionals. Essentially the primary database is made up of maps covering all of the United States—including territories and protectorates, counties or equivalent entities—from the 1990 census. (With the next census the figures, of course, will be revised. Also they are revised regularly with new reports from the Bureau and other agencies.) The disc follows the standard patterns for searching, and is relatively easy to navigate.

Stressing as it does the geographical and economic facets of the United States, TIGER may be searched by itself or in conjunction with CENDATA and other Bureau publications, in print or online. At any rate, the medium- to large-sized libraries with these two databases available will be able to respond to most questions concerning the census and statistical matters.

THE INTERNET

Adding to the hurricane of data coming out of Washington, the Internet is a major factor in bringing even more information to the people. The Clinton administration made it possible to receive everything at a computer from news about the planet Jupiter to presidential press releases. Telecommunications is a major concern of both Republicans and Democrats.

There are government information sources available through the Internet. The basic ones, some of which are discussed in this section, include the following few e-mail addresses and site directories. (Note: These are only representative of hundreds of addresses. Also, they are subject to change.)

Site Directories

FedWorld (NTIS BBS): http://www.fedworld.gov

Thomas: http://thomas.loc.gov

The White House: http://www.whitehouse.gov

E-Mail

Directory of Congressional E-Mail Addresses:
gopher://una.hh.lib.umich.edu/0/socsci/poliscilaw/uslegi/conemail

House Committee on Science Space and Technology:
housesst@hr.house.gov

House Committee on Natural Resources: natres@hr.house.gov

Vice President Al Gore: vice.president@whitehouse.gov

Speaker Newt Gingrich: georgia6@hr.house.gov

Senator Edward M. Kennedy: senator@kennedy.senate.gov

Thomas, in honor of Thomas Jefferson is representative of many of these sources. It is an Internet service inaugurated by the Republicans in 1995. It is repetitious of several other services, but over the World Wide Web allows free access to: (1) the full text of any bill introduced in Congress since 1992; (2) *The Congressional Record;* and (3) other pieces and bits of legislation, hearings, and so on. All the texts may be searched by key words, subjects, and names.

A common problem, aside from that of having the money to buy the hardware and software to access Thomas, is speed. Set up in the Library of Congress, Thomas, comes in over the standard modem of 14,400 bits per second. This takes minutes to hours to gain access to the full text of a bill or other material.

Thomas also encourages the citizen to contact members of Congress by way of e-mail. As of 1996, only a few of the lawmakers had e-mail addresses, and most had to be reached by phone or by mail.

Bulletin Board Systems[13]

The federal government increasingly employs electronic bulletin board systems (BBS) to provide government-generated information. The BBS is a dial-up computer service that offers e-mail, various forms of message exchanges, and access to both retrospective and current data. About 35 to 40 federal agencies have open BBS. In the mid-1990s there were some 200 services, of which about 40 to 50 have limited access because of secret documents or their intention of serving only a limited, special audience.

All of the open services are free to the public and offer a wide variety of data from the latest government reports and economic indicators to federal and state regulations. Current information includes such things as consumer tips (from buying a home to a tomato), economic statistics, bibliographies, full text of publications and documents, and background data on a wide variety of topics. The cost is minimal—the price of connecting the computer to a Washington agency. A few boards have toll-free numbers. Those who have access to Internet usually pay nothing.

The NTIS FedWorld bulletin board is by and far the most popular of all the federal BBS because of its gateway feature. In addition to the gateway, FedWorld offers numerous full-text documents from presidential speeches to federal budget items. A unique feature—the GIF images coming from the Hubble space telescope. Most of the boards are public, but a few are private, for example, the one operated by the Defense Department. The government takes a dim view of anyone trying to crack the private boards.

---

[13]John Bertot and Charles McClure, "Assessing U.S. Government Bulletin Boards . . . ," *Internet Research,* Spring 1994, p. 46. This is a superior article on the BBS. See, too, Bruce Maxwell, "The 10 Best Federal Government BBSs," *Database,* December 1994, pp. 30–34. The author gives brief directions on how to access and use the databases, including FedWorld.

Simple e-mail exchange forums are available as are technical data on scientific problems and breakthroughs. In a word, almost any topic can be found on one or more BBS. All of the open services are free to the public, but "federal BBS are not truly publicly accessible due to the overall lack of citizen awareness of their existences, user-incurred phone charges, technology requirements, and user skill requirements." Other than the National Technical Information Service's FedWorld there is no governmentwide information locator system to organize access to the information in these BBS. There is a definite need for organization and improved access. "Otherwise BBS will abound without rhyme or reason—and may hamper, rather than assist, successful access to government information."[14]

Usenet, the shared network of thousands of bulletin boards, has a more informal approach to political issues. Here one can discuss everything from President Clinton (alt.politics.clinton) to the proposal changes in medical services (talk.politics.medicine).

Some of the consumer networks, such as CompuServe, offer political access. One types in "Go Congress" for the latest information on congressional movement. America Online even has a handy guide to political debates with background information.

A Yawn

Electronic democracy depends on everyone having free access to the various channels on a computer. Computers in the mid-1990s are limited to households that are predominantly white, male, well educated, and well to do. But for those few there are countless resources available online.

When in 1995 Thomas was introduced as a quick, efficient way for citizens to keep in contact with government, *The New York Times* commented: "Washington has long been infamous for producing mountains of paper. . . . Now the Internet is transforming all of that into billions of bytes of data, an electronic swamp where even the most determined electronic citizen can be bogged down."[15] The White House online system, which started its own service years before Thomas, has no more than 550,000 to 600,000 users a year. This may change as the Internet develops, but most government officials are inclined to greet the whole with a yawn. Once more, Thomas illustrates the point that it takes more than easy electronic access to information to encourage people to

---

[14]Ibid., p. 61. It is unlikely that the federal government or its agencies with BBS will do much about accessing. All the more reason, then, as with the confusing electronically based information, that a reference librarian is necessary as a vital part of the search process.

[15]"Mr. Smith Goes to Cyberspace," *The New York Times,* January 6, 1995, p. A22.

venture into cyberspace staked out by government or anyone else they are not excited about.[16]

STATE AND LOCAL DOCUMENTS

CD: The *USA State Factbook.* Minneapolis, MN: Quanta Press, Inc., 1990 to date, annual. $49.95.

Print: Book of the States. Chicago: Council of State Governments, 1935 to date, biennial, 500 pp. $79.
No electronic format.

CD: County-City Plus. Washington, DC: Slater Hall Information Products, 1990 to date, annual. $195.
Print: County and City Data Book. Washington, DC: U.S. Bureau of the Census, 1952 to date, updated irregularly. Price varies.

Print: U.S. Library of Congress, *Monthly Checklist of State Publications,* 1910 to date, monthly. $26.
No electronic format.

Built on material from the U.S. Bureau of the Census, *The USA State Factbook,* is updated each year and allows the user to search a single CD-ROM for masses of information on the individual states. Territories are included, back to 1776 when the statistical data begin. Still, most of the information relates to current rather than historical situations. Here one may check, for example, the size of major cities in Nevada, who is governor of Oregon, or how much is manufactured in Maine. There is little of a political, geographical, or economic interest not covered in this single, easy-to-search source. As a virtual almanac of the states, this includes, too, numerous maps, state seals, and helpful graphs and illustrations.

The aptly named *Book of the States* is valuable on three counts. First, there are standard articles on issues such as reapportionment, consumer protection, rights for women, and the like. These are updated with each new volume. Second, there are reviews of trends, statistics, and developments at both the local and federal levels which have, or will have, a strong influence on state government. Third, it has relatively current information on names of principal state officers. The wealth of data make it an invaluable print reference work for almost any type or size of library.

---

[16]Conversely, the Internet, CD-ROMs and print offer invaluable help to experts and specialists seeking specific bits of information. And it is to these people most Internet value is apparent. For example, in late 1995 the U.S. Patent and Trademark Office made available, free of cost on the Internet, abstracts of the nation's vast patent data base. See "Patent Office Plans to Supply Abstracts Free on the Internet," *The New York Times,* September 27, 1995, p. D8.

Demographical data on all United States counties, as well as statistical data on cities of more than 10,000, are offered in the *County-City Plus* CD-ROM. With an easy-to-use menu system, the comparisons, say, between housing costs in one major city and/or county and another can be made in seconds. In fact, the primary use of this database is for comparative purposes and, of course, to answer specific questions about any area of the country as well. Based in part, but with additions, on the *U.S. County and City Data Book*. Unlike the print book from the government, the CD-ROM is updated each year and the information on everything from banking and crime to education and health care is relatively current.

At the state level, there is no entirely satisfactory bibliographical tool that lists the majority of publications of all states. Individual states tend to have their own bibliographies and listings. The *Monthly Checklist of State Publications*, prepared by the Library of Congress, represents only those state publications received by the Library. Arrangement is alphabetical by state and then, as in the *Monthly Catalog*, by issuing agency. Entries are usually complete enough for ordering, although prices are not always given. There is an annual, but not a monthly, subject and author index. The indexes are not cumulative. Periodicals are listed in the June and December issues.

Various library periodicals feature bibliographies and articles on state and local publications, for example, *Library Journal's* "What's Good from Government" (May 15, 1994, pp. 42–49); "State Publications" from the always useful *Government Publications Review* (November/December 1993, pp. 615–633); and related guides in *Journal of Government Information*.

SUGGESTED READING

Balas, Janet, "At the U.S. Postal Service," *Computers in Libraries*, February 1995, pp. 42–44. A brief examination of how the post office has joined the technological age from bulletin boards to conferencing. It is a useful overview of one section of government, and much of the material is applicable to other services.

Government CD-ROMs. Westport, CT: Mecklermedia, 1994. Subtitled, "a practical guide to searching electronic documents databases," this publication describes some of the most frequently used U.S. government databases and methods of retrieval of information. Much of the material in the 13 chapters on searching is applicable to other CD-ROMs. The Villanova Center for Information Law and Policy has available its Federal Web Locator (1995). This allows a user with access to the World Wide Web the ability to access close to 200 different federal government information sources as well as signposts to other federal sites.

Kinder, Robin, ed., "Government Documents and Reference Services," *The Reference Librarian*, 1991, no. 32. All topics of interest to reference librarians and in the use of government documents are considered. There is an emphasis on the daily activities of the government documents librarian. The "electronic document" is considered in the last section.

Love, James, "A Window on the Politics of the Government Printing Office Electronic Information Access Enhancement Act of 1993," *Journal of Government Information*, January/February 1994, pp. 3–13. The politics of information and the use of government publications are discussed. The role of libraries in this important act is considered as is the hope to be able to limit paperwork in government.

Maxwell, Bruce. *Washington Online: How to Access the Federal Government on the Internet.* Washington: Congressional Quarterly, 1995. This 400 plus page guide, to be updated each year, is organized by broad subjects from agriculture to science. Each of the listings includes a description of the database(s), sites, and so forth, as well as comparisons with similar sites. Precise information is given on how to reach a site.

Morehead, Joe, "Into the Hopper," *The Serials Librarian.* This is a regular column on some aspect of government documents and one which should be read just as regularly by reference librarians. The columns are witty, informative, and, rare among writers in this field, bristling with style. See, for example, "Voluble Siblings: The Federal Register and the Code of Federal Regulations," *The Serials Librarian,* 1993, vol. 24, no. 1, pp. 34–54.

"Recent Literature on Government Information," *Government Publications Review,* March/April 1990 to date. This annual feature offers current material (usually no more than one year old) on all aspects of government documents and information policy. The citations (without annotations) are arranged under broad subject headings. This is an excellent place to turn for current articles, as well as a limited number of books, on government publishing.

Skeers, Timothy, and Sherry McCowan, "Social Science Reference and U.S. Government Information on CD-ROM," *Behavioral & Social Sciences Librarian,* 1993, no. 2, pp. 23–36. The Federal Depository Library Program offers numerous CD-ROMs. These are discussed in this informative article. While limited to the social sciences, the approach is suitable for other disciplines.

"Star Spangled Net," *Internet,* August 1995. A special issue of the popular magazine considers major ways "citizens can tap into more government info than ever before." The dozen articles cover both federal and state government documents and services. Helpful hints are given on how to best use these various resources.

INDEX

Note: Page numbers in *italic* refer to tables. Page numbers in **boldface** refer to the main listing and/or discussion of a specific reference work, where publication or electronic source information and, usually, cost are given; often, the main discussion of a work follows the main listing after a gap of one or two pages. References to notes are indicated by an *n* appended to the page number (e.g., 175*n*).

For the archives of the
Director's Office in the British
Museum, with much gratitude
from the author.
10 June 1979.

PRINTED MUSIC
IN THE
BRITISH
MUSEUM

THE LARGE ROOM.

Frontispiece: *The Large Room of the British Museum, which contained the presses used for music, 557 and 558. The westernmost Reading Room can be seen through the far doorway.*

PRINTED MUSIC

IN THE

BRITISH
MUSEUM

AN ACCOUNT OF THE
COLLECTIONS, THE CATALOGUES,
AND THEIR FORMATION,
UP TO 1920

Alec Hyatt King

CLIVE BINGLEY LONDON

K G SAUR   MUNICH · NEW YORK · PARIS

3107

First published 1979 by Clive Bingley Ltd
Set in 12 on 14 point Aldine Roman by Allset
Printed and bound in the UK by
Redwood Burn Ltd Trowbridge and Esher
Copyright © Alec Hyatt King
All rights reserved
ISBN 0-85157-287-1

Clive Bingley Ltd
Commonwealth House
New Oxford Street, London WC1

K G Saur Verlag
Postfach 711009
D-8000 Munich 71

K G Saur Publishing Inc
175 Fifth Avenue
New York, NY 10010

K G Saur Editeur
38 Rue de Bassano
F-75008 Paris

British Library Cataloguing in Publication Data

King, Alexander Hyatt
    Printed music in the British Museum.
    1. British Museum. Music Room — History
    I. Title
    026'.78   ML111

    ISBN 0-85157-287-1

To all my former colleagues,
both
in the Music Room of the British Museum
and
in the Music Library of the British Library

Contents

Illustrations

9

The frontispiece and Plate 1 are reproduced by courtesy of the Trustees of the British Museum, Plates 2–7 and the plan by courtesy of the British Library Board.

Preface

THIS BOOK has its origin in research undertaken by Cecil Bernard Oldman (1894-1969), who was Principal Keeper of Printed Books in the British Museum from 1948 to 1959. He had long studied the history of his department, and from his remarkable knowledge contributed much to Arundell Esdaile's book *The British Museum Library*. Oldman was particularly interested in the growth of the collections of printed music and its catalogues, and during the 1950s began to abstract information on these topics from the Panizzi[1] Papers which form part of the department's archives. In June 1959, at the fifth International Congress of the International Association of Music Libraries, held at Cambridge in conjunction with the Galpin Society, Oldman read a short paper, 'Panizzi and the music collections of the British Museum'.[2] This was based on only part of the material relating to music in the Panizzi Papers. It dealt largely with Panizzi's rules for cataloguing music, and gave a summary account of the work done by Thomas Oliphant from 1841 to 1850.

After his retirement, Oldman replaced his abstracts by complete transcriptions in fair copy, and carried them right up to the end of 1855, the last full year of Panizzi's Keepership of Printed Books. In addition, he extracted other details about music from Panizzi's Register of Payments, which John Laurence Wood, a Keeper of Printed Books from 1966 to 1976, had discovered among the departmental archives. Oldman also made transcripts of purchases of music from invoices of the 1840s. But unfortunately,

11

ill-health and other work prevented him from making any further use of this material. A year or so before his death, Oldman gave me all his files, knowing that I had previously read a paper on other aspects of the subject to the Royal Musical Association,[3] and that, while Superintendent of the Music Room, I had accumulated from other sources notes on the history of the collections which were complementary to his. The early part of the present book is therefore indebted to Oldman's transcripts, and the whole may serve as a belated tribute to the memory and researches of a distinguished Principal Keeper of Printed Books.

* * *

It seems certain that before the end of the present century, the former library departments of the British Museum will have been moved away from Bloomsbury and out of the museum, to join other components of the British Library in its projected new buildings adjacent to St Pancras Railway Station. Within a few decades of that event, the details of the work of a small section of the Department of Printed Books within the British Museum—methods of cataloguing, location of the collections, systems of pressmarking, general usage and the like—may well have become part of an unreal, vanished world. In the hope that such details from the past will interest anyone who has a feeling for the history of a great library, I have set them down here.

NOTES
   1 Antonio (Anthony) Panizzi (1797-1879) left his native Italy as a political refugee in 1822 and reached England in May 1823. After considerable hardship, he was appointed Professor of Italian language and Literature in the University of London in 1828, but it proved a frustrating post.

In 1831, he secured an appointment as an Extra-Assistant Librarian in the Department of Printed Books, and was promoted to Keeper of Printed Books in 1837. He was appointed Principal Librarian in 1856 and retired ten years later. He received a knighthood in 1870. See also note 10 to chapter 1.

2 Subsequently published in *Music, libraries and instruments, papers read at the joint Congress* . . . Editors: Unity Sherrington and Guy Oldham. Hinrichsen Edition, 1961. A good photograph of Oldman was used as part of the frontispiece to this volume. Details of his numerous services to musical bibliography are given in my obituary notice 'C B Oldman: a tribute', *Brio*, vol 7, no 1, spring 1970. A list of Oldman's writings, complete up to 1964, appeared in *The music review*, May 1964, vol 25, no 2, pp154-157.

3 'The Music Room of the British Museum 1753-1953', *Proceedings*, session 59, 1952-53, pp65-79.

Acknowledgements

I WISH TO thank Her Majesty the Queen for gracious permission to quote two letters written by Lord Stamfordham, Private Secretary to King George V.

My thanks are also due to the Trustees of the British Museum for permission to quote various documents in their archives, and to the British Library Board for permission to quote from the archives of the Department of Printed Books —minutes, reports, drafts, letters and other documents— which passed into the board's possession under the British Library Act, 1972, Section 3.1.b.

Miss Doris Pepita Chappell has kindly allowed me to quote the 'Memorial' submitted by William Chappell to the Trustees of the British Museum in 1841. While I have made every effort to trace the copyright-holders of other manuscript documents quoted in this book, I have been unable to do so, and would welcome any information which would enable me to repair such omissions in a future edition.

For permission to quote published copyright material my thanks are due to: Messrs A & C Black, from *A Handelian's notebook* by William C Smith; the Oxford University Press, from *R.V.W.*, by Ursula Vaughan Williams.

I owe a special debt to Mr Edward Miller, Honorary Archivist of the Department of Printed Books in the Reference Division of the British Library. He helped me to trace the numerous volumes I needed to consult among the archives in his care, and generously gave me much useful help. He drew my attention to the Registers ('Daily statistics') of the Copyright Office (1856-1922) on which appendix 5 is largely based. Mrs Ann Hopley, Archivist of the British Museum, supplied me with transcripts of passages from various minutes and reports. She also made available to me early staff records, and answered my innumerable questions with exemplary patience. I am most grateful to her.

I also owe thanks to Miss B M Rimmer, of the Industrial Property Section in the Science Reference Library of the British Library, who kindly traced for me the two patents of Ralph Wedgwood, and sent me photocopies of them.

Mr O W Neighbour and Mr Malcolm Turner both kindly read the book in typescript, and made valuable criticisms. For information of various kinds I am glad to record my thanks to: Mr Bentley Bridgewater, the late Mr Charles Humphries, Mr David McKenna, Mr Peter Ward Jones, Dr Harold Watkins Shaw, Miss Pamela Willetts. Not my least debt is to my wife, who read the book in manuscript, clarified it here and there, and typed it.

Introduction

THIS IS, as far as I am aware, the first attempt to write a full account of a great music library in its historical context. It has three principal, closely interwoven themes—the origin and growth of the collections and the policy of acquisition followed at various times; the planning and control of the catalogues and their publication, both intended and achieved; the technical procedures adopted by a succession of dedicated men to carry out their work. Primitive as these procedures may seem today, they were the best of their kind then available, and were designed to maintain a high degree of accuracy and consistency. I have also given as many details as I could discover about the staff who worked on music, but most of those who were active before the 1880s can only be seen now as rather shadowy figures.

I have also traced, as far as possible, the successive locations of the collections of printed music within the several parts of the museum buildings occupied by the Department of Printed Books. I believe this to be relevant because, as Churchill said, 'We shape our buildings and afterwards our buildings shape us',[1] and this is certainly true of a library which formed a living part of a world-famous museum. I hope that the reproduction of the few extant illustrations that are germane to the collections of music may help to bring the past to life.

These collections were not developed in isolation, but as part of the work of the Department of Printed Books as a whole. From time to time, therefore, I have alluded briefly to the larger affairs of the department and to some of the

17

great issues that it had to face during the nineteenth century, in order to set the music in its proper context and explain what may seem an apparently parsimonious official attitude —in terms rather of staff than of money—to the needs of music. But it was clearly undesirable to overload a specialised narrative with extraneous detail, especially as there exist admirably comprehensive histories of the museum and of its library by Edward Miller, and by the late Arundell Esdaile, as specified in the List of Sources. For a similar reason, I have relegated to appendixes an account of the management of the department and the grades and functions of its staff, a description of the technical processes of maintaining its catalogues, with special reference to music, and some statistical information.

The raw material for the history of any department in the Museum is found in various official sources—the annual returns to Parliament, the vast two-volume *Report of the Royal Commissioners appointed to inquire into the constitution and management of the British Museum* (1850), the Keepers' reports, on a great variety of matters, to the Trustees, and the latter's minutes on these reports. For the Department of Printed Books in particular there exists a long series of papers, drafts, letters, estimates and other documents, which constitute its archives. There are also extant the invoices of purchases of which the complete, dated sequence begins in 1837. All these are complemented, especially for the earlier period, by the archives of the Trustees of the British Museum.

Something must be said about the method of reference to these sources. For the early period, a document can be found by its date and the type of trustees' committee or report from which it originated. For the period from 1835 to 1856, the Panizzi Papers are the chief source: they are bound by years, and are foliated, which simplifies consistent reference. For some thirty years after 1857, however, the volumes of minutes and reports are not foliated, although after about 1875 they are grouped consistently under seven or eight headings, each arranged chronologically. Whenever I have quoted or referred to any document from this period, I have given its full date, from which the original should be traceable without much difficulty.

Until about the middle of the nineteenth century, the Department of Printed Books was relatively small. Its senior staff (ie Assistants and Transcribers) could deal personally with the Keeper in a way which became quite impossible later, as their numbers increased and as the business of the department grew more complex and was conducted under greater pressure. After about 1860 it was most unusual for an Assistant to write at length to the Keeper, in order to report progress, explain his difficulties and ask for advice. Such letters from the earlier years are a mine of information, and I have not hesitated to quote them in full. If today their tone seems rather formal or deferential, it should be remembered that they merely reflect the manners of an age when respect for authority was an accepted part of the social order. These documents have a unique flavour, as have also the letters occasionally written by the Keeper to the Principal Librarian, which likewise are most informative.

The term 'printed music' in the title of this book has been used in the traditional sense of music intended for performance, and it is this aspect of the subject which predominates. In the early years of the museum, however, it was regularly linked with works of musical theory, and this link was not entirely broken even in the early twentieth century. For this reason I have made occasional mention of theoretical works. By far the largest source for the growth of the collections has always been the music received by deposit under successive Copyright Acts. In general, though very important, it was, by its nature, unspectacular. (It did, however, secure for the collections some useful first and early editions of French and German music while the International Copyright Acts were in force; see appendix 5.) A considerable quantity of contemporary foreign music was acquired by purchase, but again, apart from a number of first editions, it was not very remarkable. Far more so was the astonishing wealth of rare early music thus added by each generation. As it would have been quite impracticable to mention this with any degree of completeness, I have treated it selectively, in order to show changing aspects of a purchasing policy. For reasons stated in appendix 5, it is not possible to give a precise, overall figure for the total of printed music in the collections. A fairly explicit total can, however, be compiled for the number of entries written for the catalogues, and I have given this in appendix 4. I have mentioned music in the Department of Manuscripts only when it became temporarily or incidentally the responsibility of a member of the Department of Printed Books, or when it was a joint matter of public or official concern.

For several reasons I decided that my narrative should terminate in 1920. In that year Barclay Squire retired, and this event, which coincided with the post-war reconstruction of the Department of Printed Books, marked the end of the old order in the Music Room. A new era began under Squire's successor William Charles Smith,[2] who retired in 1944 and lived until 1972. In this period I was myself ultimately involved, from December 1944 to May 1976, and it therefore seemed best that I should not extend my narrative to cover the developments of the inter-war years and those of the next generation. I have, however, written about a few events that took place after 1920, principally in order to record the completion of important projects which were planned or begun well before that date, but were mostly delayed by the first world war.

NOTES

1 *The Prime Minister's speech on the House of Commons rebuilding*, Cambridge, 1944, p1.

2 Smith himself gave an account of these events in *A Handelian's notebook*, but it is not altogether objective.

1

THE YEARS OF APATHY AND PROTEST:
FROM THE FOUNDATION TO 1840

WHEN THE British Museum was founded in 1753, and for well over half a century afterwards, music was not a matter of much concern to the Trustees. There were various reasons for this. Throughout the eighteenth century their staff was very small, and there was no specialist on it who could advise them of opportunities to acquire items at important sales, and in any case funds would have been hard to find. There were no booksellers specialising in old music, and there was no idea of the need to purchase what was then being published abroad. More important, perhaps, was the fact that no demand for the materials of research came from the universities, where the study of the historical aspects of music was practically unknown.

The scholar of those days engaged in musical research was largely self-taught. He was likely to have his own library of music, printed and manuscript, which he could try to supplement by consulting musical sources—if he could find them—in the British Museum's foundation collections, in the Bodleian and elsewhere in England, or even abroad. Such was the case with Burney and Hawkins, whose monumental works, *A general history of music* (4 vol) and *A general history of the science and practice of music* (5 vol) were published respectively in 1776-89 and 1776. But despite the fairly large sales of both these books, their influence was limited, and the growth of historical awareness among members of the musical profession remained very slow.

There was thus no general demand for music during what was, broadly speaking, a time of consolidation in the

23

Department of Printed Books. The Trustees were deeply preoccupied with the difficulties of arranging their multifarious collections within the constricted apartments of Montagu House. As the skills of cataloguing and handling books in quantity were then rudimentary, the staff had a formidable task in dealing with the printed volumes comprised in the foundation collections, augmented by the Old Royal Library which was given to the Trustees by George II in 1757. Both these contained some very important early printed music—the sixteenth century part books in the Arundel Library,[1] for instance, and the copy of Sir William Leighton's anthology *Teares or lamentacions of a sorrowful soule* (1615), which had belonged to Charles I as Prince of Wales. There were also the Mozart sonatas op 1 and op 2, bound with the autograph of his motet 'God is our Refuge',[2] which Leopold Mozart presented in July 1765 when he visited the museum with his children, and the early music and works of musical theory presented by Hawkins on 23 October 1778. In 1815 the museum purchased from Burney's library, for £253, a collection of books on music, of which unfortunately no list is extant. Besides such rarities, the collections were augmented from the mid-1780s onwards by a small but steady accumulation of English music received through Stationers' Hall. It is true that this was a mere fraction of the vast quantity then being published, but though it was to slumber virtually uncatalogued until 1841, it was to prove of great historical value in the course of time.

This state of affairs continued throughout the first three decades of the nineteenth century. Even for the purchase of foreign literature, the Trustees still had no clear policy, and none at all for foreign music, old or new. Nor did they purchase any early English music during this period. It was the all-round inadequacy of the musical collections which gradually gave rise to outside concern, from the mid-1820s

Plate 1: *The second, westernmost Reading Room of the British Museum, c1845; later it became the first Music Room.*

onwards. The earliest expression of it that survived is found
in a remarkable letter written by Vincent Novello[3] on 24 May
1824, to an MP addressed as 'J Banks'.[4] It deserves quotation almost in its entirety.

Sir,
I have ventured on the liberty of addressing you relative to a department of the British Museum which
appears to me susceptible of improvement; and as a
bill is to be brought into Parliament in this session for
the amendment of the former acts relative to that
establishment, I have thought the opportunity an
appropriate one for presenting the subject for your
consideration.

The particular department to which I allude is the
musical library. This branch, having so direct a reference
to one of the most tasteful of the fine arts, will, I am
sure, meet with an advocate in Mr Banks, for being
placed on an equally honourable footing with the rest of
the library: and the collection of standard compositions
to which the musical students should have access, ought
to be of a nature, both as to extent and excellence,
commensurate with the literary treasures preserved for
the improvement and gratification of the British public
in this magnificent national establishment.

According to the present system, I understand that
the care of the musical department is left merely as a
part of the duties to be performed by one of the Assistant Librarians, but the utter inadequacy of such an
arrangement must be evident, when it is considered that
in order to do justice to the department in question,
it is necessary (in addition to the regular classification,
&c of the collection already belonging to the establishment) that the person upon whom the charge devolves,

should have continually in view the extension of the
library by the constant accession of additional and
valuable works—that he should ascertain and attend the
sales of curious and rare musical collections—selecting
the most sterling and scarce compositions of the best
masters, both ancient and modern, especially in MS—
that he should daily examine what modern publications
are brought out by the various music sellers both in
England and on the continent . . . He will afterwards
have to arrange the whole by assigning each work to
its proper class for facility of reference and make the
requisite catalogues.

Novello went on to point out, at some length, that these
were whole-time duties requiring specialist knowledge, urged
the appointment of a musical professor, and emphasised the
need for the rigorous enforcement of the Copyright Act.
He concluded with an offer, couched in suitably diffident
terms, of his own services. Novello sent a copy of this letter
to Canning, then Foreign Secretary and *ex officio* a Trustee
of the Museum (though he never attended a meeting), with a
covering note in which he wrote: 'A word, sir, from you in
my favour . . . would, I am certain, at once secure me the
preference over any other candidate'. The reply, sent on
27 May, was curt: 'As Mr Canning's occupations do not allow
him to take any part in the general business of the Trustees
of the British Museum, he cannot possibly interfere on a particular occasion'.

Novello's ideals speak for themselves. They were very far
ahead of their time, and we may doubt whether, had he been
appointed, he would have found congenial the incessant work
of cataloguing, with little or no assistance. It seems unlikely
that the Trustees heard, officially at least, of his proposals,
but if they had been carried into effect, the benefit to the

collections and the public service would have been immense. It was not long, however, before the Trustees learned of the gross deficiencies of the music in their charge. On 24 March 1835 they received a memorial[5] from George Herbert Bonaparte Rodwell.[6] This document puts a point of view which is radically different from that expressed in Novello's proposals, but is equally valid. It reads thus:

> To the Trustees of the British Museum.
> The Memorial of George Herbert Rodwell, Musical Composer, Sheweth,
> That Music is a science deemed by almost every European nation, excepting England, of sufficient importance to be protected by various laws, and to be engrafted upon the system of national education as one of those liberal arts which tend to civilise, adorn and dignify a nation.
> That this being the case, your memorialist imagines it to be his duty, as a member of the musical profession, and a lover of his country, to point out to your honorable notice any circumstance that might by elevating the one add an honor to the other.
> Your memorialist in common with his musical brethren has felt the almost insurmountable barrier to his studies in the want of a national library of Musical Works—a library to which students might obtain easy access, and over which a Professor might preside, who should be capable of directing the student to such works as might be most likely to point out the shortest road to eminence, and thus by placing before him some of the brightest and most powerful examples, greatly diminish his labour and stimulate him to increased exertion.
> That a Library founded upon these principles, and possessing the best works in score, must to the young student become of inestimable value. There he might

study from, and compare the best foreign with the best English works and by thus comparing a variety of styles be enabled to form an original one of his own, and not become an imitator, as is generally the case where, from want of pecuniary means, the student is unable to study from more than one or two works. This library would become as useful to the young musician as the Sculpture Gallery of the British Museum is now to the rising generation of Sculptors and Painters.

Your memorialist humbly trusts your honorable body will take into your favourable consideration the subject of this Memorial, and by establishing a Musical Library in the British Museum, encourage and elevate the English School of Music—and your memorialist as in duty bound, will ever pray &c &c.

GEORGE HERBERT RODWELL.

23 Brompton Row,
March 24th 1835.

In the Trustees' Committee Minutes, vol XXIV, c3964, it is recorded that Rodwell's memorial was read, but apparently no decision was taken. Unlike Novello, who was interested in the music library for purposes of research, Rodwell was concerned to foster it in order to improve British standards of composition.

His appeal to patriotic sentiment was subtle, but it did nothing to affect the Trustees' attitude. Esdaile records that in this same year, 1835, one H S Peacock made a complaint about the lack of a catalogue, but it is not known whether it ever reached the Trustees.[7] Another instance of their lack of interest occurred a year later, when on 15 April 1836 W E Shuckard, of 31 Robert Street, Chelsea, offered for £70 a 'large collection of portraits of musical individuals made at considerable expense in Germany'. Even at the subsequently reduced price of £45, the collection was declined by the Trustees.[8]   Although this offer was not the concern of the Department of Printed Books but was referred to the Department of Prints and Drawings, the refusal characterises the official attitude, and shows what great need there was for new ideas such as those aired by Novello and Rodwell.

Protest was still very much alive, and very soon some forcible views began to be expressed in *The musical world*, a London journal edited by Cowden Clarke (an uncle of Novello by marriage) and noted for its outspokenness.   A leading article of 9 February 1838 pointed out that the needs of the musical researcher were sadly neglected in the British Museum. 'In his department', wrote the leader, 'there is still a *hiatus maxime deflendus* in the catalogue.   Treasures there are: but the individual in search of them is in the situation of Tantalus, hearing the gurgling, ever-living springs, but doomed never to slake his thirst.   Your attendant affirms that there are piles, folios, sheets innumerable of music: but they are admitted to the bewildered enquirer to be in most admired confusion.'   Another leader, of 16 August, referred to a proposal by Edward Taylor, Gresham Professor of Music, for founding a 'Metropolitan Library of Music', and summarised it on pp264, 265 of this issue.[9] Very sensibly, however, *The musical world* thought that this should not be, as Taylor suggested, a new library, but rather an expanded department of the British Museum.   It went on to mention the sad case of the ten famous private music libraries at the recent dispersals of which the museum had failed to bid.

Again, on 6 September, another leader continued the attack on the museum.   This issue also printed a long letter from the eminent antiquary Joseph Warren, about the musical defects of the library, especially its arrears.   'I was informed', he wrote, 'that there was a large collection of musical works in a lower apartment, not yet catalogued'. The issue of 8 November printed a letter from Taylor about his own address (to which the editor added lengthy comments), still pressing the case for a national collection. The commentary alludes to an earlier proposal of an 'individual' to Canning—a clear allusion to Novello's letter of 1824. This suggests that Novello may have prompted Cowden Clarke to give the whole matter an airing in his journal.

Meanwhile, all unknown to *The musical world*, the Trustees had acted, partly perhaps with Rodwell's memorial still in mind, and partly, it seems, because of Panizzi's initiative. Panizzi had been appointed Keeper of Printed Books on 19 July 1837, and quickly began to rouse the Trustees and the staff to a proper sense of their responsibilities.[10] His long general report to the Trustees of 12 October 1837 included the following recommendation: 'For which purpose [ie the cataloguing of maps] as well as for that of cataloguing the collection of music daily added to by virtue of the copy-right act, and of which Mr Panizzi is not aware that there is any catalogue whatever, a person should be temporarily engaged.'[11] There had in fact been a summary entry for printed music in the *List of additions made to the collections of the British Museum in the year MDCCCXXXI (—MDCCCXXXV)*, in which, under the heading MUSIC and the description 'miscellaneous pieces of vocal and instrumental music by various composers', the totals for the respective years were 159, 200, 272, 173, 152. Such treatment may at least have served to remind authority of the need for something better.

On 14 October 1837 Panizzi's suggestion was referred to the Subcommittee on the department, which met on 18 November but postponed further consideration until 25 November, without, however, any action then being taken. Three years elapsed, during which, as we have seen, the agitation from *The musical world* added fuel to the smouldering flame. Panizzi returned to the charge on 10 November 1840, and reminded the Trustees of the continuing lack of a music catalogue. At a Committee on 28 November 1840 they took a cautious step forward and ordered 'that Mr Panizzi lay before the Trustees a plan for cataloguing in a brief and economical manner the Collections of music in his Department. That Mr Panizzi lay before the Trustees a statement of the assistance necessary for this purpose and of its expense.'

Within a week Panizzi had completed his report, a momentous document, which was to shape the whole future of the catalogue of printed music. It reads as follows:[12]

5 December 1840.

Mr Panizzi has the honor to propose the following plan for cataloguing in a brief and economical manner the collections of music in the Department.

1 All works having the name of a composer to be catalogued under such names, as is done for printed books.

2 Works or any parts of them originally composed by one person and then adapted or arranged for any particular purpose by another person to be still catalogued under the name of the former with a cross-reference from that of the latter.

3 Cross-references to be given from the names of the authors of words or works set to music to the name of the musical composer under whose name the music is to be entered.

4 Anonymous vocal music to be entered under the first word of the poetry set to music, of which the first line should be given.

5 The above rule to be observed even when the author of the poetry be known, whose name, however, should be used as a cross-reference.

6 Any piece of music, more especially songs, known by any particular name or designation, whether anonymous or otherwise, to have a cross-reference from this name or designation.

7 Anonymous music which cannot be otherwise designated to be entered under the generic name of the piece, and to identify each piece the first three bars of each piece to be given as well as the name of the publisher when it occurs.

8 The titles of each composition, as well as each cross-reference and their respective press-marks, to be written on separate slips of paper, and afterwards transcribed with their press-marks in two copies of a catalogue in alphabetical order.

Practically it may happen that this outline may require some modification, which might be left to the consideration of the person to whom the work may be entrusted and whose opinion would no doubt carry great weight.

Mr Panizzi thinks that the entry of the titles from the slips into the two copies of the catalogue ought not to begin till a large proportion if [not] the whole of the collection is catalogued on slips, and arranged, which cannot be before the end of 1841. At present, it would, in his opinion, be sufficient to engage a competent person for twelve months for the purpose of carrying this plan into execution. Towards the end of this period the Keeper of the Printed Books on reporting what has been done would have to make what suggestions he might deem necessary on the subject for the further determination of the Trustees. Mr Panizzi thinks the remuneration of a temporary assistant for this purpose ought to be on the normal rate of £2.12.6 per week.

The expense now proposed would not therefore exceed
£137.

Now Panizzi was apparently quite unmusical, and he was
also an exceedingly busy man. Although he had a thorough
grasp of the complex principles of all kinds of cataloguing,
it was remarkable to have drafted such comprehensive rules
in such a short time, even if, as he admitted some eight years
later, he did so 'with the advice of a gentleman who understood the subject'.[13]   One general point is Panizzi's wisdom
in insisting on the accummulation of the titles, in order presumably to gauge as well as possible the amount of space to
be allowed for the various headings. (In the event, the
physical form of the catalogue turned out to be very different from what he had in mind—entries were written by
hand on large folio sheets, in the style of the titles for accessions added to the catalogue of printed books. See appendix 2.)
The rules which Panizzi devised have served with modifications ever since, and are fundamental to most systems of
music cataloguing. The only rule not put wholly into effect
was no 7, undoubtedly because of the extra time and expense
that would have been involved. (So far as is known, Panizzi's
rules were the earliest ever devised in any country to include
incipits for any type of music.)   Rule 4 was, it seems, so
strictly applied that for many years the article, definite or
indefinite, was taken as the heading if it was the first word
of a song title.[14]   Rule 6 was only observed in part: references have seldom been made from the titles of instrumental
works, however well known.   The weakness of Panizzi's
rules was that they were not based on knowledge of a wide
enough range of music to accommodate all the variety of
forms in which it has been printed. There is, for instance,
no rule to cover anonymous collections, such as chansons

and motets, which were often issued without an editor. We may suspect that owing to lack of time and precedent, Panizzi and his adviser based their thinking on such of the famous Ninety-One Rules (completed in 1839) for cataloguing printed books, as were relevant to music, and made additional ones to suit its peculiar character.

On 12 December 1840 the Trustees referred Panizzi's plan to the Sub-Committee on the Department of Printed Books, 'for their consideration as soon as the necessary funds should be appropriated by the Trustees for its execution'. But it did not meet until 31 May 1841. By a coincidence, on that very day the noted music antiquarian William Chappell wrote to Sir Henry Ellis, the Principal Librarian, as follows:

> 31 May 1841
> Mr Chappell presents his Compliments to Sir Henry Ellis and will feel much indebted if, at the next meeting of the Trustees of the British Museum, he will favour him by allowing the enclosed Letter to be read. He has already spoken to the Earl of Cawdor who showed him Sir Henry Ellis's Letter in reply, and has promised to advocate the formation of a Catalogue on presentation of the enclosed.[15]
>
> 14 George St.
> Hanover Square
> To Sir Henry Ellis, K H etc etc.

The memorial addressed to the Trustees is short:

> To the Trustees of the British Museum.
> My Lords & Gentlemen
> Feeling considerable Interest & Anxiety in the Enquiry if any Measures are likely to be soon adopted for facilitating reference to the large and valuable Stores of Music in the British Museum, which, up to this time

remain without Classification, Arrangement or Catalogue, we beg most respectfully to submit to your Consideration the great advantage that would accrue to Musical Students, Professors and all engaged in Musical and Literary Research, from the formation of a Catalogue of the Music & Musical Manuscripts (especially of such as are of an early date); & which would be of tenfold value if entirely separate from that of the Books.

The ninety-odd signatories included many of the most famous musicians of the day – Crotch and Walmisley, Professors of Music at Oxford and Cambridge respectively, Edward Taylor (Gresham Professor, and author of the *Address* already mentioned), Bishop, Macfarren, Sterndale Bennett, Potter and Moscheles. The Philharmonic Society, founded in 1813, is well represented. The names of Warren, Rodwell and Novello round off a distinguished company. Clearly this was the culmination of attempts going back over the previous seventeen years to rouse the Trustees to action. As the date at the foot of all the signatures is 14 December 1840, it seems likely that they would have got wind of this document in the five months that elapsed before Chappell wrote to Ellis.

The memorial was read at a committee on 12 June 1841, and was referred to Ellis, 'to report to the Trustees as to the extent and nature of the Collections of Music in the Museum, both Manuscript and Printed, the Catalogues existing of them, and the plan which it seems to him should be taken, if the Trustees resolve on complying with the prayer of the Memorial'. Ellis asked Panizzi for information, which the latter supplied on 17 June,[16] including the interesting statement that 'works of old English masters as Purcell, Ravenscroft &c' had been bought at his recommendation. He also reminded Ellis of his reports of 10 November and 5 December 1840.

Ellis also consulted Sir Frederic Madden, the Keeper of Manuscripts, and then combined his reply with Panizzi's in a long report to the Trustees, which is a document of primary importance, giving as it does a full account of the state of music in both departments.

The Principal Librarian's Report on the Collections of Music in the Museum.

July 10.1841

In obedience to the Order of the Trustees of June 12th, that Sir Henry Ellis should report as to the extent and nature of the Collections of Music; the Catalogues existing of them; and the Plan to be taken if the Trustees resolve on complying with the prayer of the Memorial presented to them from certain Composers and Professors of Music, He begs to submit the following details

I As relates to the Manuscript Department:

There are Ninety four Volumes of Music of which every separate piece is catalogued, amounting to 1524 in number. These include the Service-Books of Henry the Eighth's Chapel, and a large Collection of Italian Music, chiefly in the Harleian and Additional Collections.

Dr Tudway's Collections in the Harleian Library (Harl 7337-7343) have not every piece catalogued: but there is a separate full Index in each of the Seven Volumes.

Matthias's Collections (Addit 5036-5039) have, for the most part, Indexes to each Volume, and in the Catalogue every author whose name occurs is mentioned. Many of them are copied from printed Works.

The Collection of Purcell's Works presented by Mr Novello is that which served as the basis for his Edition of them.

Dr Burney's Extracts in eleven volumes (11581-11591) have not been catalogued. Many of these Extracts are from printed sources, or were made to be used in his History.

In King George the Third's Library are Eight Volumes, and in the Egerton Library four Volumes of French Satirical Songs and Ballads with the Airs attached: there are many hundred in number, and it may possibly be thought not necessary to particularise them.

There are Twelve other Miscellaneous Volumes, shortly described, but of which the particulars are not given. They are chiefly mentioned in the Lists of Additions.

Beside these there are numerous Treatises on the History and Science of Music: some, of the Middle Ages, by Guittone d'Arezzo, Franco, Boethius, Berno, Aristides, St Bernard, St Augustine, &c. and some of a later date. All of them are described in their various places in the respective Catalogues. The number of this description of Articles may be about 180.

A general Index, such as shall comprize all the Music and Musical Treatises (exclusive of the French Satirical Songs) will occupy about Two Thousand Titles. This Calculation, however, does not embrace the Common Service Books, Antiphoners, Graduals, Missals, &c.

Although Sir Henry Ellis has here included the Works on the History and Theory of Music, he takes it for granted that the Trustees intend their own Enquiry to extend to composed Music only. He has referred to the Treatises, only that the Trustees may have the complete view of the subject before them as concerns Music generally.

Whatever Catalogue the Trustees may order to be made of the Music among the Manuscripts in the Museum, the same can be prepared as one of the ordinary labours of the Manuscript Department. It will not require a large space of time, and certainly need not form any part of the employ of the person whom they may engage to catalogue the printed Music.

2 Of the Music in the Department of Printed Books.

In the Department of Printed Books, the Music amounts to about seven hundred Volumes or Bundles, large and small: a third of which is of old Music, printed before 1700. The remainder consists of Music published since; the greater part of which was received under the several Copy-right Acts; which, however scanty in their deliveries to the Museum (in former days) of other Works, were always productive of Music in score. The first of these portions is almost wholly catalogued with the general Collection of the Library; but of the latter portion no Catalogue whatever exists.

As to the Plan to be pursued in forming a Catalogue, Sir Henry Ellis has no hesitation in stating that that which Mr Panizzi proposed to the Trustees on Dec. 5th 1840, of which he annexes a Copy, is in his opinion the best which can be devised.

The Trustees are, no doubt, aware that the Old Library of Printed Books in the Museum contains not only numerous Treatises on Music (like the MS. Department) but also the Collections in mass on its Theory and Science which were made by Sir John Hawkins and Dr Burney, when they were preparing their respective Histories of Music. These books are all severally entered under the names of their Authors in the General Catalogue of the Library, and Sir H Ellis presumes are not included in the Scheme entertained by the Trustees. He still thinks it right to mention them here, as he has already noticed the Treatises in the MS Department.

In preparing a Catalogue of Composed Music of the Printed Library, the quantity of worthless Compositions which such an Accumulation must contain naturally presents itself to the mind: but what may or not be useful in particular researches (however in itself contemptible) it is impossible for any one to say; and Sir Henry Ellis doubts whether any thing but a full and entire Catalogue will satisfy all the Memorialists.

Henry Ellis.

The section dealing with printed music goes into more detail—for instance, about the working of copyright deposit—than did Panizzi's letter to Ellis. The final sentence shows clearly that whether it was Chappell himself or another who had collected all the signatures to the memorial, he had not laboured in vain.

At a Committee on 10 July 1841 the Trustees decided:[17]
Upon Sir H Ellis's report respecting the collections of Music in the Museum.

It was resolved

That a Catalogue be forthwith made of the Music both printed and MS. in the Museum.

That the principle of Mr Panizzi's report of 5 Dec. 1840 be adopted for this Catalogue, and

That the Secretary apply to the Principal Trustees to nominate a proper person to make this Catalogue, his engagement in the first instance to be limited to a year, and his pay to be at the rate of £2.12.6 a week

[signed] J Forshall,
Secretary

On 25 November Thomas Oliphant was appointed a Supernumerary Assistant.[18] No letters survive supporting his application for the post, but however eminent their writers may have been, he was decidedly not *persona grata* with *The musical world*. For on 9 December that journal, announcing his appointment as the result of Chappell's memorial, went on: 'We must most earnestly censure the appointment of T Oliphant, Esqre or of any other amateur, to one of the few government offices . . . which it falls within the province of a musician to fill . . . T Oliphant, Esq, interferes too much already with the interests and pursuits of his profession by his dabbling in madrigalian resuscitations, textual new versification, and vapid Germanic naturalisation, without intercepting the very easy and dignified bread and butter which it is in the power of the government to rain into the mouth of a musician.' The next issue printed a letter from a correspondent signing himself 'C O': 'Having been asked by many British musical friends who were the candidates for the office of librarian to the British Museum; and not obtaining the information, you, Sir, will confer a favour on myself and other [sic] of your numerous readers, by furnishing their names.' To which the editor appended this note: 'The appointment of T Oliphant Esq, to the best of our knowledge was not settled by election, but was entirely an affair of private interest. This gentleman is so completely an amateur, even in his antiquarian researches, that his qualifications are as questionable as we think his appointment unjust.' For some obscure reason Oliphant does not seem to have been popular with another section of the musical press. In connection with his translation of Schubert's 'Erl König', *The musical examiner* alluded to him as 'Mr Elephant'.

Even the best researcher does not necessarily become a good cataloguer and librarian. 'Amateur' though Oliphant may have been in his 'researches' compared perhaps with someone like Chappell or Rimbault, his speed, accuracy and thoroughness, combined with a quick mind, show him to have been a good choice: He seems to have had an instinctive grasp of his work. (We may wonder whether he was the 'gentleman' whom Panizzi consulted when drafting the rules.) The little that is recorded of Oliphant's life, apart from his work in the British Museum, is mostly found in the article written by William Hayman Cummings for the *Dictionary of national biography*.

Born in 1799 at Condie, in Perthshire, of a distinguished Scottish lineage,[19] he was educated at Winchester, and was for a short time a member of the Stock Exchange. He became secretary to the Madrigal Society and did research into the history of madrigals. In 1837 he published *La musa madrigalesca*, an anthology of the text of some 400 madrigals, which anticipated E H Fellowes's *English madrigal verse* (1920). Oliphant sang in the chorus of the great Handel festival of 1834, of which, under the pseudonym of 'Solomon Sackbut', he wrote a slightly whimsical account, *Comments of a chorus singer*. He also translated parts of *Lohengrin* for a performance given in London at a Philharmonic Society's concert in 1855 under Wagner himself. He published well over 180 arrangements of madrigals, glees, old English songs and the like. Apart from this, little is known of his musical interests, or of his life beyond the period he spent in the British Museum.

The various documents quoted up to this point give a rather vague, general idea of the state of the collections of printed music in the Department of Printed Books before Oliphant's time. He was faced with a great challenge. Its nature and extent will be better understood if they can be brought into sharper focus by a more detailed account of their history and bibliographical background. For this the evidence is scattered: it lies partly in the classification of the books in Montagu House, partly in the books themselves and in the early catalogues and other documents in the departmental archives.

The earliest separate mention of music in the collections is found in the 'analytical syllabus' appended to the first edition of the *Synopsis of the contents of the British Museum* (1808). (It was based on the 'synthetical arrangement' of the printed books devised in about 1790 by the Rev Samuel Ayscough, who worked in both that department and in Manuscripts, and was put into effect in the next decade or so.) In this 'syllabus', music is located in rooms 7 and 13 of the sequence of apartments on the ground floor, which contained the printed books. The music presses were those marked AA in Room VII and T and V in Room XIII.[20] The shelves were denoted by a lower case letter or by a single arabic figure. The position of music in the 'syllabus' is instructive, for it forms a sub-division of mathematics within which it is preceded by 'astronomy, astrology, ephemerides', and is followed by 'navigation and naval architecture'. As a matter of theoretical interest, this grouping may be compared with that in the Rev Thomas Hartwell Horne's *Outline for the classification of a library*, privately printed for the Trustees in 1825. In this scheme music is placed in subsection VIII of section IV, which comprises mathematical philosophy. The sequence of this subsection is:

VI Perspective
VII Acoustics
VIII Music
IX Navigation

Music is subdivided thus:

i) Antient writers on music and their interpreters
ii) Modern writers on music
(1) Dictionaries and elementary treatises on the theory and practice of music
(2) Works of musical composers
(3) Treatises on vocal and instrumental music

Although Horne's scheme for the British Museum Library was never used as a whole, the ideas which underlie the section on music have some curious affinities with the classification of the subject devised by his successors of the mid-nineteenth century. His placing of music in the main group of 'Mathematical philosophy' also faintly echoes the concepts of far earlier times, during which it was often linked with the study of mathematics and philosophy.[21] But those who put Ayscough's 'synthetical arrangement' into effect had occasional difficulties with music. For instance, while most of the early part-books were comfortably assigned to 7AA, such a volume as Leighton's *Teares* was one of the odd men out, so to speak. Presumably because its contents consist partly of settings of the psalms, it was placed with theology at 11.x.h ('Commentators on the Old and New Testament').

Small though the quantity of printed music and musical literature still was, it needed rational treatment, but this was quite impossible within the cramped and overcrowded rooms of Montagu House. Most of the North Wing of the new building was completed to Smirke's designs late in 1837 and the transfer of the books began in January 1838. The whole of its ground floor was allotted to Printed Books: two presses, numbered 557 and 558, were given to music.

Their position can be deduced from the sequence of press numbers marked, at intervals of five, on the plan of the ground floor of the North Wing reproduced overleaf. (See the caption for the identification of the first five rooms listed below.) Some thirty years later, another of the rooms in this wing was to be allocated, almost in its entirety, to music. Since their nomenclature became rather confusing in course of time, it may be helpful at this point to describe briefly the layout and use of the North Wing as a whole. It comprised six rooms, which, from east to west, were:

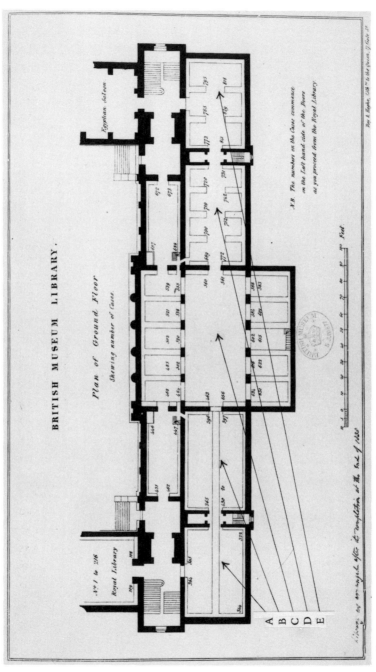

A plan, c1838, of the ground floor of the North Wing of the British Museum, showing the numerical sequence of the presses in the Department of Printed Books (see p43). The letters added to the plan identify the rooms as follows: A, first Reading Room; B, second Reading Room; C, Large Room; D, first supplementary Room; E, second supplementary Room.

The first Reading Room (originally for Manuscripts)[22]
The second Reading Room (for Printed Books)
The Large Room (completed in 1840)
First supplementary room
Second supplementary room
Third supplementary room (the Arch, or Arched) Room,
completed in 1841)

The second Reading Room is shown on plate 1, in which the first also can be glimpsed through the open door at the far end. (This later became the Catalogue Room.) In the later 1860s the second Reading Room became the Music Room, and continued in this use up to 1922. The Large Room (frontispiece), besides being used for book storage, was originally open to the public at certain times and was fitted with some cases for the display of choice volumes. Subsequently it was entirely closed to the public, and became a reading room for rare books. (The name 'Large Room' persisted until very late in the nineteenth century.) After it was rebuilt and extended to the north, from 1909 onwards, it was called the 'North Library', the term originally applied to Smirke's North Wing as a whole. (It was again rebuilt in 1936-8;) It was in the Large Room, at its south west corner, just out of sight on the right of the frontispiece, that music presses 557 and 558 were situated. The shelving ran from top to bottom of the tall room, broken only by the narrow gallery.[23]

The transfer of the music seems to have been a protracted business. In April 1841 Joseph Warren again complained to *The musical world*. He was told, he said, that the books 'were being moved', and objected that his tickets were returned with the words 'moving' written across them. When warned that he could not have these books unless he supplied the new press-marks, he complained that he could not provide them because they were mostly not in the catalogue. It may be mentioned here that presses 557 and 558 remained in limited use right up to the later 1850s for placing musical literature and some early music acquired by presentation or purchase.   The early musical literature including much of Hawkins's gift, has remained at those presses ever since, and the music remained too, for the time being.   By about 1860 almost all of it had been transferred to the main music collection.   The following table (p47) shows seven characteristic examples of music whose pressmarks provide the evidence for the sequence of locations.

The coordination of the books of music was only one aspect of the beginning of a huge task.   The other, as we have seen, was due to the fact that there was no separate catalogue of them.   They were scattered under various headings throughout the general catalogue.   The difficulties and contradictions were similar to those which bedevilled the cataloguing of the printed books as a whole.   At the heart of the matter lay the lack of any code of rules.   A straightforward title such as Bataille's *Airs mis en tablature de luth* was correctly entered under his name in the 1787 catalogue,[26] the pressmark being later added, as throughout, by hand. But several collections of sixteenth century motets, some even by only one composer, were entered under the generic heading MUSICA.[27]   In the much enlarged edition of the catalogue, 1813-19, similar principles were observed, but this heading was expanded to serve as a sort of happy dumping-ground for anonyma and for books of musical theory in which the name of the author seems not to have been obvious. Here, sensibly enough, we find Eisel's anonymous *Musicus* αὐτοδίδακτός (1738).   But under this same heading is Lossius's *Erotemata musicae practicae* (1570), although his name is printed large and clear on the title page.   Other oddities can readily be seen in those parts of this heading reproduced as plate 2a and plate 2b.

Composer and short title	Date of acquisition, or source	Montagu House pressmark	North Wing pressmark	Music collections pressmark
Bataille, *Airs*,[24] 1608	Hawkins, 23 October 1778	7AAd	557.d.10.	K.3.g.9.
Bataille, *Airs*,[24] 1612-18	Hawkins, 23 October 1778	7AAe	557.*d.12.	K.3.g.10.
Muffat, *Componimenti*, 1727	J Groombridge, 1828	13Tf	557.e.21.	e.461.
T Kelly, *Hymns*, [n.d.]	probably by copyright, c1824	13Tf	558.c.33.	E.1414.
Willaert, *Musica nova*, 1559	Arundel	7AAe	558.c.15.	E.1495.—then, c1860, to K.3. m.14. (Title page initialled in pencil 'T.O.', ie Thomas Oliphant.)
Liber primus (—quartus) sacrarum cantionum, 1546	Arundel	7AAe	558.c.4.	E.1439.—then, c1860, to K.8.k.1. (Title page initialled, in pencil, 'T.O.', ie Thomas Oliphant, and with his 'K' mark in pencil, 'Motetti'.)
Vocal music, [1771]	Musgrave, 23 July 1790	3Ga[25]	1078.c.22.	A.889.

It is interesting to discover in the interleaved copy of the 1813-19 catalogue[28] that the heading MUSICA included accessions up to 1846, which consisted mostly of works of musical theory and periodicals, the titles of which were entered by hand in chronological order of imprint date. This implies that the title-slips were accumulated for quite a long time before the transcription was done, which must have caused much frustration to the reader—unless information was provided for him from the title-slips. Nothing is known about the early cataloguers of music. The assistants worked on it as best they could as part of their general duties. We have, however, one piece of information about the copyright music. In his evidence to the Royal Commission of 1847-50, Panizzi said: 'There was a large quantity of this music which had come in by copyright, but which had never been catalogued or a list made of it since it came into the museum. A gentleman of the name of Bean, I think, took care of it formerly; afterwards it was left to accumulate unarranged.'[29]   The 'gentleman' referred to by Panizzi was the Reverend James Bean, Curate of Carshalton, Surrey, who died on 26 May 1826, having worked in the Department of Printed Books since 1812 as Assistant Keeper.[30] No titles in Bean's hand can now be identified, and the precise dates of such responsibility as he had for the music (among his other duties) are unknown, with one exception. In a report of 11 February 1815 Bean said he had found 52 duplicates in the 257 works recently purchased from Burney's library.

Panizzi's allusion to the music being 'unarranged' is most interesting, but seems to be true only if taken to mean 'not in alphabetical order of composers'. For there is good evidence that for many years this copyright intake, practically none of which bears a date of imprint, was in fact 'arranged' in that it was accumulated in piles or 'bundles'[31] marked by the year of receipt. The most cogent evidence for the

MUSGRAVE (WILL.) De Arthritide symptomatica Dissertatio. 8° *Exon.* 1703.
―――― De Arthritide anomala Dissertatio. 8° *Exon.* 1707.
―――― Julii Vitalis Epitaphium, cum Notis criticis, Explanationeque, H. Dodwelli, et Comm. Guil. Musgrave Editore. 8° *Isca Dunm.* 1711.
―――― De Geta Britannico, accedit Domus Severianae Synopsis chronologica, et de Icuncula quondam Regis Ælfredi Dissertatio. 8° *Isca Dunm.* 1715.
―――― Belgium Britannicum. Præfixa est Dissertatio, de Britannia quondam pene insula. 8° *Isca Dunm.* 1719.
MUSGRAVE (WM.) Life of Robt. Earl of Orford. 8° *Lond.* 1745.
MUSGRAVE (Sir W.) T. GRANGER. MEYRICK.
MUSHARD (CHR. GUY.) Dissert. de purgatione per Alvum. 4° *Helm.* 1721.
MUSHARD (FRANC.) Dissert. de morbis fibrarum in genere. 4° *Lug. Bat.* 1716.
MUSHET (ROB.) An enquiry into the effects produced on the national currency and rates of exchange by the Bank restriction bill : explaining the cause of the high price of Bullion. 8° *Lond.* 1811.
MUSICA. Treatise on the transposition of Music. 12° *Lond.*
―――― Account of the origin and Improvement of the Diatonic scale or system of Music. 8° *Lond.*
―――― A poetick descant on a private Musick Meeting. fol.
―――― Il teatro alla moda o sia Metodo sicuro, e facile per ben comporre, et esequir l'Opere Italiane in Musica all' uso moderno. 8°
―――― Difesa della Musica moderna contro la falsa opinione del Vescovo Cirillo Franco, tradotta di Spagnuolo. 4°
―――― 4° *Alt. edit.*
―――― Musices figuræ, seu Notæ novæ. 4°
―――― The By-Laws of the Musical Society at the Castle Tavern in Pater Noster Row. 8°
―――― Letter to the Author concerning the Music of the Ancients. 8°
―――― Moteta quinque Vocum. 5 Partes. 4° *Ant.* 1546-7.
―――― XIV Livres de Chansons a 4, 5, & 6 Parties, composées par divers Aucteurs. 4 vol. 4° *Ant.* 1543-55.
―――― VI Livres de Chansons. 4 Partes. 4° *Lovan.* 1554-9.
―――― Chansons a 5 & 6 Partes. 4° *Lov.* 1556.
―――― Mottetti da diversi Autori. 5 Partes. 4° *Mediol.* 1542.
―――― 5 Partes. 4° *Ven.* 1538.
―――― Musica Quatuor Libris demonstrata. 4° *Par.* 1551.
―――― Practica Musicæ Præcepta. 12° *Duisseld.* 1557.
―――― Thesaurus Musicus. Cant. 2. 4° *Norib.* 1564.

MUSICA.

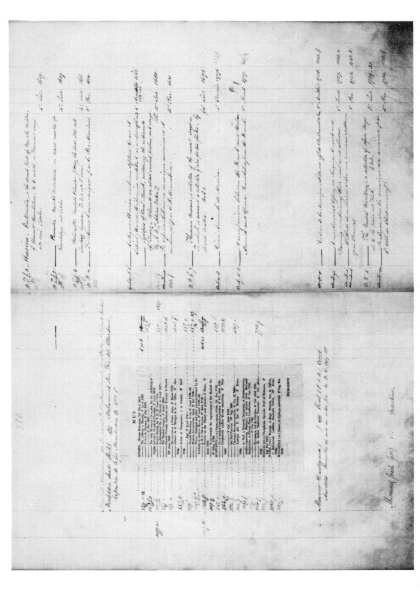

Plate 2b: Two pages of the inlaid, interleaved copy of the catalogue of printed books (1813-19), showing the continuation of the heading MUSICA.

earlier and continued use of this system is inferential. It is based on facts that have come to light during a comparison of dates given in the catalogue for numerous pieces of early nineteenth century music with the relevant entries in the Stationers Hall Register. In many cases the date supplied in square brackets on the original title agrees with that in that Register. But many other entries are incorrect, often by some years. This must be due to the fact that the music was originally stored in 'bundles' by years. Some of the pre-1840 bundles were disturbed, and their contents reassigned to the bundle of an adjacent year. This probably happened during the removal of the uncatalogued music from Montagu House, at some time between the end of 1837, when most of the North Wing was completed, and the end of 1841, when Oliphant began work.[32]

Such then were the antecedents of the rather confused situation which faced Oliphant—no separate catalogue of music; the music in the foundation collections and in the extensive additions of the later eighteenth century entered haphazardly in the General Catalogue, and on no very clear principles; the music in the King's Library (presented by George IV in 1823) entirely ignored; recently purchased or donated items only catalogued in part and probably not easily available to readers; some antiquated and inconsistent classification; and a growing accumulation of uncatalogued copyright music (probably unshelved and partly disarranged), going back to 1790 or a little earlier. In a department which was rapidly expanding under a dynamic Keeper, it was certainly an advantage that, at forty-two, Oliphant could bring to his daunting task a fresh mind, untrammelled by earlier tradition.

NOTES

1 This music is itemised by Sears Jayne and Francis R Johnson, *The Lumley Library. The catalogue of 1609*, London, 1956, pp284-286, 312.

2 Where this volume, which bears no early pressmark, was preserved, remains a mystery. The two printed pieces were apparently first catalogued by Squire, at some date after 1885.

3 Vincent Novello (1781-1861) was famous as organist, teacher and musical editor. He was also a prolific if unoriginal composer. In 1811 he founded the music publishing firm which still bears his name. His home was a centre of hospitality to a wide and distinguished circle of musicians and men of letters. He generously presented both printed and manuscript music from his library to the British Museum.

4 An error for Henry Bankes, MP for Corfe Castle, and a Trustee of the British Museum 1816 to 1834. Canning's pencilled endorsement on Novello's letter refers to 'Bankes'. (The letters are now in the Music Library of the British Library, pressmark K.5.b.8.) See Esdaile, p70 and p324, and Violet Bankes, *A Dorset heritage*, London, 1953, p107.

5 Original Letters and Papers, vol XII. Oct 1834—June 1835.

6 Rodwell (1800-1852) was a prolific composer of operettas, and a professor of harmony and composition at the Royal Academy of Music. In 1836, he became director of music at Covent Garden, and persistently advocated the establishment of a national opera. In the context of his memorial, it is worth remarking that he was a pupil of Novello, and that he published, in 1833, *A letter to the musicians of Great Britain*, containing proposals to encourage native talent.

7 Esdaile, p210, and p371, note 21, apparently a defective reference, as no source is given.

8 Original Letters and Papers vol XIV. Letter from Henry Josi, Keeper of Prints and Drawings, 9 May 1836, vol XV. Letters from Shuckard, 13 May 1836, and Josiah Forshall, Secretary of the Museum, 18 May 1836, Letter Book 8.

9 Taylor had just published the proposal as *An address from the Gresham Professor of Music to the patrons and lovers of the art.* The British Museum's copy was destroyed in 1941, and no other can now be traced.

10 For an account of Panizzi's appointment, and of the state of the department before it and in the subsequent years, see Edward Miller, *That noble cabinet*, 1973, p130 onwards, and Arundell Esdaile, *The British Museum Library*, 1946, p90 onwards. Panizzi's remarkable dynamic character is well delineated in Miller's *Prince of librarians. The life and times of Antonio Panizzi of the British Museum*, 1967.

11 Panizzi Papers, 31 July 1837–23 Jan 1839, f11.

12 Panizzi Papers, 3 Sept 1840–30 June 1841, ff107, 108.

13 *Report of the Royal Commission*, 1850, Q.4040.

14 See Thomas Nichols, *A handbook for readers at the British Museum*, 1866, p63, for an example. In the catalogue of printed music, the practice seems to have been modified in the later 1860s, so that thenceforth the first word other than the article was used for the heading. The articles govern the order of titles in the indexes to Augustus Hughes-Hughes's *Catalogue of manuscript music in the British Museum*, 1906-1909.

15 Original Letters and Papers, vol XXIV. Jan-Aug 1841.

16 Panizzi Papers, 3 Sept 1840–30 June 1841, f329.

17 Panizzi Papers, 1 July 1841–24 Dec 1842, f31.

18 One holding his situation without any written appointment from the Principal Trustees (Report of the Royal Commission, 1850, vol 2, p420).

19 BL Add MS 25073, f44b, contains a harpsichord piece, c1800, entitled 'The Oliphant of Condie's welcome home'.

20 If the room numbers used in Montagu House correspond to the letters of the rooms–'a' to 'n', without a 'j'–as
printed on the plan of the lower floor in *London and its
environs described* (anon), 1761, vol 2, between p32, 33,
then Room VII was Room g and Room XIII was Room n.
If this correspondence is correct, the latter was just above the
basement room, in the south west corner of Montagu House,
which was used as the first Reading Room. See Esdaile, p40.

21 See Nan Cooke Carpenter, *Music in the mediaeval
universities*, Norman, 1958.

22 See Crook, p154.

23 Of all the six rooms in the North Wing, through which
in their pristine state there was a splendid unbroken vista,
only the Arch Room now (1979) survives in something like
its original form. See the view of it reproduced in Crook,
plate 63, p137.

24 Both the volumes of *Airs* by Bataille have '2BBL'
pencilled on the lower part of the title page. As this is not a
museum pressmark, it may be the original mark of Hawkins's
own library.

25 According to the 'Syllabus' of 1808, this was the
shelf-mark either for English poetry or 'miscellanies'.

26 *Librorum impressorum, qui in Museo Britannico adservantur, catalogus*, 2 vol.

27 The identical principle is found in *Catalogus librorum
impressorum bibliothecae bodleianae*, Oxford, 1843. Here
the heading for various works of musical theory and anonymous collections is MUSICES, the feminine genitive of the
Greek adjective μουσικός, the noun τέχνης being understood,
ie 'of the musical art'. (Cf the title of Petrucci's anthology
of 1501, *Harmonice musices odhecaton*.) The catalogue of
the Douce collection in the Bodleian includes a similar heading
for music.

28 Pressmark L.R.419.b.1. For both this and the readers' copy—now no longer extant—the octavo sheets were inlaid onto, and interleaved with, folio sheets.

29 Q.4040. Bean was probably 'the gentleman who at present fills the office' mentioned in a part of Novello's letter not quoted on p26.

30 In the minutes of the General Meeting, 11 Feb 1815, p1133, Bean and Baber were authorised 'to demand such works as the Museum may be entitled to under the new Copy Right Act'. Before appointment to the staff of the museum 8 February 1812, Bean had been employed as a temporary worker from 1810 to 1812 'on the Revisal of Ascough's [*sic*] catalogue of manuscripts'. (Officers' Reports 1805-1810, no 285, 12 May 1810.) This revision came to nothing: see T C Skeat, *The catalogues of the manuscript collections in the British Museum*, 1951, p4, no2. Bean's death is recorded in the *Times*.

31 Panizzi used the word 'bundles' in his letter of 17 June 1841 to Ellis which the latter incorporated in his report to the Trustees quoted on p38. A yearly accumulation is also suggested by the separate totals in the *List of additions* etc quoted on p30.

32 I am indebted to O W Neighbour, Music Librarian in the Reference Division of the British Library, for the facts about the disturbance of the 'bundles' and the evidence for it. The incorrect dating only occurs for music received by copyright prior to 1833. See O W Neighbour and Alan Tyson, *English music publishers' plate numbers of the first half of the nineteenth century*, London, 1965, p13.

2

OLIPHANT, PANIZZI AND THE CATALOGUE: 1841 TO 1850

OLIPHANT set to work at once. On 9 December 1841 Panizzi reported:[1]

> Many imperfections have been discovered by Mr Oliphant, owing to the copies sent being partly merely proofs, some of them unfinished, partly title-pages only or incomplete portions of works entered as complete. It is for the Trustees to decide what steps ought to be taken both for making more perfect the collection as to the past, and insuring a better delivery for the future.
>
> Mr Panizzi begs to be authorised to have some of the Manuscript Music catalogued, as he should wish to see whether his plan, intended for printed music only, answers in practice for cataloguing the MS music likewise, as ordered by the Trustees.[2]

On 11 May 1842 Oliphant wrote a long letter[3] to Panizzi, which begins thus:

> Sir,
>
> 1 I have the honour to inform you that I have carefully inspected the whole of the unbound Music at present in the Museum, and have arranged the same in alphabetical order of composers' names, in two grand divisions, viz vocal and instrumental.
>
> 2 What I next propose to do is to make a selection of all that I consider worth binding of those composers

55

whose works will make one or more volumes, and afterwards classifying the less voluminous writers in each way as may seem most suitable. In using the word <u>worth</u> I allude of course only to the condition of the music.

He went on to re-emphasise the imperfections, and Panizzi laid the letter before the Trustees, who gave the proposals their approval, especially regarding the cheapest possible way of listing the imperfect copies. Oliphant made steady progress with the labour of cataloguing. From various reports and letters, the following can be summarised (the annual totals of entries written are given in appendix 4):

By Christmas 1842—4,631 titles written

By 20 June 1844—19,500 titles written

By 24 Dec 1846—about 24,000 titles written

In 1847, 1,500 separate pieces dealt with and made up in to 200 volumes.

Cataloguing was only a part of Oliphant's duties. Working single-handed, he also wrote the pressmarks on the music and on the title-slips, and—as indicated above—made the volumes up into a suitable size for binding; he probably wrote the binding orders himself. He likewise placed the music on the shelves and entered it in hand-lists, by means of which he provided the collection with a flexible framework for future growth. Although these hand-lists are not mentioned in any letters or reports, they are still preserved in the Music Library today. Some account of them and the system which they embody is essential to an understanding of his achievement. All entries for music entered up to 1850 are in his writing, as seen in those forming a page of the instrumental list, reproduced as plate 3.[4]

The lists themselves were written on ruled foolscap sheets, the quires of which were ultimately made up into two substantial volumes. We find a hint of Oliphant's system in the first paragraph of his letter of 11 May 1842, quoted above, which refers to the 'two grand divisions, viz vocal and instrumental'. It seems safe to assume that all the details of the system as a whole were devised by Oliphant himself, though he would naturally have sought his Keeper's approval. The two 'divisions', each of which had its own hand-list, accorded with the fundamental nature of music, and the same principles of shelving and pressmarking were applied to each. In order to economise space, Oliphant placed the music on the shelves entirely by format, and used the first eight letters of the alphabet in succession to denote this criterion, and as the first component of the pressmark. For vocal music he used capital letters, 'A' to 'H', and lower case for instrumental, 'a' to 'h'. 'A' and 'a' comprised volumes whose height corresponded roughly to that of sexto-decimo in book-format. 'H' and 'h' were for folios. ('I' and 'i', for outsize folios, were added in the later 1850s.) The second component of the pressmark was a number, which denoted either a composer or a category. This system meant that a prolific or popular composer, or a popular type of music, would be allotted pressmarks in perhaps two or three sizes. But the space thus saved was enormous compared to the waste of it that would have occurred if, for example, small octavo scores of music by Haydn had rubbed shoulders with his tall folios.[5]

This system proved easily capable of expansion. Some years after Oliphant's time a third component was added, a lower case letter which denotes the sequence of the volume on the shelf. By about 1860 a fourth component appears, a number, used only for volumes in which two or more pieces were bound together. This denotes the place of any piece within the volume. When Oliphant did this, he simply continued his main numbering right through the volume.

On the titles after his time, this number was originally written under a dash, and below the 'third-mark', thus G.116.$\frac{a}{2}$. After the introduction of printing for the accessions, in 1884, the pressmark continued to be so written on the title—and still is—but was printed with the fourth component in round brackets, thus: G.116.a.(2). This system of letters and numbers had the great merit of making it easy to keep the volumes in the right place on the shelves, with the minimal risk of being misplaced. It has also proved almost infinitely expandable, and with some modification is still in use today.

Oliphant completed most of his task, including the arrears, by about the middle of 1844: this is the date that was put on the spine of both hand-lists—each comprising several hundred folio sheets—when they were first bound. He must have devised his system very soon after he took office, perhaps early in 1842. He used it not only for single works currently received, but also retrospectively for periodicals that were in progress before his appointment. It is instructive to see how the system worked in the case of an annual album named *The musical bijou*. This began in 1829, in quarto, and right up to the issue of 1837 (the issue for 1838 was purchased later, as were also some earlier volumes) was placed at 13 T*c, one of the Montagu House pressmarks for music, then still in use. (Obviously, not all the books had been transferred to the North Wing by 1839). In 1839, the format changed to folio and this and subsequent issues up to 1843 were placed, by someone unaware that the earlier volumes were in Montagu House, at 767.m.5 (see the position of this press on the plan on page 44). Then in 1844, when the issue for that year had come in by copyright, Oliphant retrieved both sets and, as his pressmarking shows, replaced them in the music collection, the quarto volumes at F.149, and the folio volumes at H.2330.

There is no record of where in the North Wing Oliphant did his work, assembling the music according to its carefully graded sizes and allowing space for growth. The sequence of presses in the ground floor of the North Wing was fully allocated to books, as is shown on the plan reproduced on page 44, and on another contemporary plan of its galleries (not reproduced). The same was true of the presses in the Arch Room, which was added to the west end of the North Wing in 1841. Consequently, it seems likely that Oliphant had to work in the basement of the North Wing, and that the music was scattered among two or three of its numerous rooms. (This is borne out by the words Panizzi used a little later, 'whenever there was a room provided to place the music in'.) In the early days of this basement, conditions were probably not quite so bad as they became later, when, for example Gosse (who entered the department in 1867) described them as 'ill-lighted . . . with a smell of dry rot'.[6] Once he had agreed the principles of his work with Panizzi, Oliphant was probably allowed to pursue it undisturbed in what was a peaceful backwater of the department. For in the 1840s the museum in general and Printed Books in particular were the focus of fierce public and internal controversy. The great debate about printing or not printing the General Catalogue, the public controversy about its rules, and public allegations of maladministration were only a few of the elements in the storm that raged far above Oliphant's head during the years of turmoil. Just how little music was affected by these events is shown by the very small number of the questions that were asked about it when the Royal Commission heard evidence from 1847 to 1849.

What Oliphant had achieved so far is all the more remarkable when it is realised that the printed music had not occupied all his time. His other work merits a brief digression. Quite soon after his appointment, his services were requested by the Department of Manuscripts, whose Keeper, Sir Frederic Madden, was aware that the cataloguing of music was in arrears.   On 7 July 1841 John Holmes, one of his assistants and later an Arabic specialist, had reported to Madden that 'he has been engaged in making a rough index to the Music contained in the Department of MSS, [and] in revising sheets B.C.D. of the list of Additions for 1840'.   Holmes was also working on the description of topographical plans and drawings: clearly, he had too much to do.   It is worth repeating here the optimistic statement found in Ellis's long report to the Trustees of 10 July 1841 (already quoted on pp37, 38):

> Whatever Catalogue the Trustees may order to be made of the Music among the Manuscripts in the Museum, the same can be prepared as one of the ordinary labours of the Manuscript Department.   It will not require a large space of time, and certainly need not form any part of the employ of the person whom they may engage to catalogue the printed Music.

But this hope proved vain.   For on 20 December, Ellis, replying to a report of Panizzi's about the possible trial cataloguing of manuscript music already mentioned (p55) wrote thus:

> My Dear Sir,
> I have always been accustomed to consider a written Minute from the Trustees as final in its Direction.
> I expect Mr Oliphant will proceed without delay to catalogue the manuscript music.   Sir Frederic Madden is ready to receive him, and is prepared to offer him every assistance.[7]

The Trustees' Minutes of 11 June 1842 record that Madden reported:

> that the Catalogue of MS Music had been revised by Mr Oliphant and had been sent to the printer.
>
> Upon Sir F Madden's report the Principal Librarian was requested to give instructions that Mr Oliphant, while employed in the Department of Printed Books, should give up so much time as might be requisite for the correction and revision of the printed sheets of the Catalogue of the Manuscript Music . . .

Oliphant's work was duly acknowledged in Madden's preface to the catalogue, dated 8 December 1842, but its exact nature is unclear. He himself, in a later letter to Panizzi—undated, but probably written in April 1848—said that this 'catalogue has been made and printed under my superintendence', which contradicts Panizzi's evidence to the Royal Commission. For there he recorded that Oliphant 'catalogued all the manuscript music': but perhaps he was speaking loosely. At any rate, even if the work was partly revision and partly cataloguing, it must have taken up a lot of time.

The need for his services did not end there. On 21 December 1844, the Trustees requested Ellis to instruct him 'to catalogue the large Collection of Music presented by the Marquis of Northampton, and a few other Musical MSS'.[8] Again, on 11 July 1846, Madden asked for Oliphant's assistance in cataloguing the '202 volumes of MS Music bequeathed to the Museum by the late Mr D Dragonetti', and the Trustees asked Panizzi to 'transfer Mr Oliphant's services to the MS Department for this special service'.[9] All this must have reduced considerably the time which Oliphant could give to printed music. It makes the speed and extent of his work all the more meritorious, and his subsequent treatment by the authorities quite deplorable.

Oliphant was not content merely to overtake the arrears of copyright and other cataloguing. He found and catalogued most of the music in the King's Library. He also traced in Montagu House (at 13 V a) the large collection of English eighteenth-century sheet songs once owned by Charles Burney (purchased in 1838: see note 7 to appendix 5), replaced it at G.304 to G.313, and catalogued and pressmarked them all. He searched the General Library for music wrongly placed in it. (For example, besides the older items shown in the table on p47, he found the Musgrave copy of *Vocal music* (1771) at 1078.c.22, and replaced it at C. 373.) He was also responsible for the beginning of a sensible policy for purchasing earlier music.   On 27 March 1846 there was issued by the House of Commons a paper entitled *Copy of a representation from the Trustees of the British Museum to the Treasury, on the subject of an enlarged scale of expenditure for the supply of printed books*, of which Section 4(a) deals with music. It points out that, while the library had a good collection of musical theory, 'no foreign music was ever purchased . . . the works of Handel and Mozart are equally wanting with those of Beethoven and Rossini'. A footnote adds that Arnold's edition of Handel (1787-97) and Alfieri's selected edition of Palestrina (1841-46) had recently been acquired; both are referred to as 'modern books'.

Oliphant, as secretary of the Madrigal Society, was specially interested in English composers of the sixteenth and seventeenth centuries. Between 1844 and 1848, there are records, either in Panizzi's own Register of Payments (which ends in 1845) or in the invoices, of over thirty important batches of purchases from such dealers as Addison & Hodson, Cramer, Calkin & Budd, Thomas Rodd, and Leader & Cook. All the great English names are here—Dowland, Byrd, East,

Morley, Hilton, Rosseter, Daniel, Robinson (Cithara Lessons), Locke, Ford, Greaves, Purcell, and so on. We also find the 1655 edition of *Parthenia*, purchased from Calkin & Budd with other items all on offer prior to the issue of their splendid catalogue of antiquarian music of 1844, 'feeling it to be our duty', as they wrote on the invoice, 'as it is our pleasure, to offer every work of rarity and value to the British Museum'. Early psalm books arc well represented. These purchases also included such foreign masters as Marenzio, Mazzocchi, Legrenzi, Giansetti, Monte, Wert, Lully, Corelli and Marcello. The total spent in five years was just under £500, including the cost of Arnold's Handel. Panizzi would have authorised the expenditure himself, but Oliphant was the mainspring of this splendid achievement, as indeed he had occasion to remind the Trustees in his memorandum of 1850 (sec p70). There were also some useful presentations. Novello generously gave some early Purcell and Avison's Concertos of 1758, and one C F Barnwell, a Fellow of the Royal Society, presented over thirty eighteenth century Italian editions, including Galuppi, Porpora, Terradellas and Lampugnani.

Moreover, Oliphant looked ahead in planning the expansion of the collections, and in laying the wider foundations of the new catalogue. He devised such special headings as Motets, Chansons, and Liturgies (which was abandoned some sixty years later). What he envisaged was a sort of 'dictionary' catalogue, including headings for composers and editors, for works of musical theory, dictionaries and periodicals, but excluding bibliography. To this end he traced many liturgies and theoretical works in the General Library, and added new entries for them to the growing accumulation of titles. Among the works of theory were all those still (1979) placed at 557* and 558, including Hawkins's valuable donation: every title page bears a neat 'T.O.' in pencil as a record of his work.

In all this, Oliphant clearly had the support of Panizzi. Indeed, from the autumn of 1845 onwards, the latter exchanged with the Trustees some most interesting ideas on the future of the music collections.[10] On 8 October Panizzi reported '. . . It is for the Trustees to determine now the principle whether a collection of Music on a scale worthy of the rest of the library is or is not to be formed'. If it was, Oliphant's services should be retained and £400 a year granted for purchases. The Trustees then asked Panizzi on 29 November for information about other national collections of music. On 11 December he replied,[11] saying *inter alia*: 'It is still more important to give the public the means of consulting rare and important works of all countries not so easily accessible as the modern English ones', and went on to provide some details about those in Vienna and Berlin. He pointed out that the latter had just spent £1200 on buying the famous Pölchau collection of J S Bach. On 13 December the Trustees decided in committee to maintain and increase their collection, and gradually acquire 'the works of the more eminent and valued composers, whether foreign or British'; and on 24 January 1846 they sanctioned £200 a year for buying music. Admittedly, this was only half the amount requested, and the duration was not mentioned, but it was nevertheless a substantial sum and surely amounted to an endorsement of Oliphant's policy.

All this must have delighted him. But soon his relationship with Panizzi began to deteriorate, and the latter's attitude to the development of the collections of printed music became—to say the least—ambiguous. The reasons are complex, and seem to lie partly in the difference between the characters of the two men, and partly in circumstances which can be explained by the sequence of events. Although Oliphant undoubtedly got through a lot of work in his first four years or so, the view he took of his duties clearly diverged from that of Panizzi, who was a disciplinarian and a martinet, with strong views about lax time-keeping. On one occasion he even rebuked one of his most valued assistants, Thomas Watts, (later to become successively Superintendent of the Reading Room and Keeper of the department) for unpunctuality.[12]

It is not then surprising that Panizzi took a very stern line with Oliphant, and on 5 March 1846 sent him a written reprimand for late arrival.[13] On 19 November 1847 he drafted a letter, probably to Ellis, about Oliphant's poor time-keeping.[14] This second letter probably marks a different occasion from that related to another draft letter to Ellis, written on 14 January 1848:[15]

January 14th 1848

To Sir H Ellis
Dear Sir,

I have signed Mr Oliphant's memorandum for his attendance during the last four weeks and have done so with great reluctance, but if that gentleman does not alter his conduct very much I shall not sign any more and tell the Trustees my reasons.

Mr Oliphant as I have informed you before takes vacations when he pleases, comes when he likes, and goes when he likes; the effect of this is shown by the return of the work which he has done during 1847. That return is very unsatisfactory.

I have remonstrated with him in a friendly tone and have begged of you to do the same. As he has taken no notice of either communication and has gone on just the same I beg now that you will officially and as Principal Librarian let him know what I mean to do the very first time he gives me any cause of dissatisfaction.

Believe me . . .

Panizzi must have told Oliphant of his displeasure, for the latter replied on 15 January:[16]

Dear Sir,

I am sorry that you should apparently so misunderstand me, as to suppose that the irregularities of which you have complained to Sir H Ellis proceed from carelessness or inattention to my duties in the Museum.

I have so many other things to do, that it is not always possible for me to be as punctual as I could wish, but I beg to assure you that several of the days for which I have not charged my attendance are put down in lieu of those single hours when I have been unavoidably absent, and I would also add that during the six years I have been here, I have been away on 36 days (exclusive of the holidays allowed) being an average of six days per annum.

As you seem to view the matter in so serious a light as to example &c I will endeavour to make such arrangements in regard to my other occupations as will enable me to conform more to your wishes, but I much fear that unless I can stop away occasionally for a day at a time, without giving notice, when accidental circumstances occur (which I certainly understood at the commencement from Mr Forshall that I might do, deducting the pay for the same) I shall have no alternative but to withdraw myself from the service of the Museum.

Believe me to be
Yours very truly
Tho: Oliphant

On 1 March Oliphant developed gout, and pleaded a few days absence. A little later, he excused himself from duty for two or three days because he had 'business of some importance'.[17]

Nothing more affecting Oliphant or the music seems to have happened for over a year. But on 25 October 1849 Panizzi made a very significant report:[18]

> Mr Panizzi has the honor to inform the Trustees that as Mr Oliphant reports the whole of the collection of Music to be now catalogued and arranged, it would be desirable to have the titles transcribed three times over— by Wedgwood's manifold writer[19]—and then arranged in volumes for the use of the Library and the Reading Room. Owing to the pecularity of the work the transcript ought to be made by Mr Oliphant himself who would apply to it all the spare time he has from cataloguing the accessions . . .

Then follows, on 7 Dec 1849, an unusual passage in a letter from Ellis to Panizzi:[20]

> . . . In preparing my Precis of the duties and services performed in the Museum since July, I find no mention in any of your Reports respecting the pains taken in the Arrangement of two very important branches of your Department, one of great importance, the Geography. The other is Music. I wonder that you do not enumerate these services, and think it right to mention them to you.

May this not be taken as the first hint that Panizzi's attitude to music was changing? It was quite out of character for Panizzi to have to be reminded of his duty. Admittedly he had also omitted to report on the map collection, but this had been a matter of far less concern to him in the previous four or five years.

Meanwhile, Oliphant had been worrying about the implications for himself of 'Wedgwood's manifold writer', and on 18 December he wrote to Panizzi:[21]

> Dear Sir,
>   The operation of writing on the manifold plan would be to me so unpleasant, that I hope you will not press it; and if another were to do it, so much of my time would be consumed in overlooking that I think there would be little saving in that respect.
>   I feel convinced that by my writing out a fair copy (which, after a certain amount was finished, might be transcribed by another), two copies of a Catalogue may be completed with scarcely any loss of time, or addition of expence; and to my thinking, in a more satisfactory manner.
>
> I remain
Dr Sir
Yours faithfully
Tho. Oliphant

Panizzi professed himself unable to decide, and referred the matter to the Trustees. They sent a curt reply on 12 January 1850: 'The Trustees left it to Mr Panizzi to give the Directions he thought fit'.

But Oliphant had had enough, rightly seeing that he could have little future in a post, where, besides being on bad terms with the Keeper, much of his time might have to be spent merely copying out all the titles he had already written. In the spring of 1850, he submitted to the Trustees a lengthy, undated document, headed 'Memorandum respecting the Music in the British Museum'.[22] It is so important that it must be quoted in full.

In the year 1841 the Trustees of the British Museum determined that a Catalogue should be made of the music contained in that establishment, and they did me the honour to appoint me as Assistant in the Library for the purpose of making the same. When I undertook the task, I had no idea that it would occupy me more than 4 or 5 years; but my anxiety to see the completion of my labours, combined with the wish that no detriment should occur to the progress of the work in case of my sudden resignation, have induced me to remain to the present period.

The Catalogue being now finished as far as practicable, and in course of rapid transcription, a few months more will show the result of nine years of uninterrupted and I may say of painful toil, which however I shall not regret, if it should lead to the formation of a collection of music valuable in an artistic point of view.

The cultivation of music has of late years made such rapid strides in this country, that if it be thought proper to include musical works amongst the requisites of a National library, such works should be for the most part first rate. I do not pretend to set myself up as an arbiter of what is good or bad in original compositions, which to a certain extent may be a matter of opinion; but I do maintain without fear of contradiction, that a great proportion of the music which is annually deposited in the Museum in compliance with the Copyright Act, neither is or ever can be of the slightest use for reference or any other purpose, being chiefly composed of Polkas and other dance tunes, trumpery songs &c, merely manufactured to satisfy the craving for novelties during the London Season, or else second hand arrangements of works which ought to be, but are not in the Library. What would be thought of an Act of Parliament [that] compelled the Trustees to receive and place by the side of the Townley and Elgin Marbles all the plaster casts which are hawked thro' the streets by the Italian boys.[?]

In forming such a musical library (I am here partly using the language of Dr Burney) as would assist the student, gratify the curious, inform the historian, and afford a comparative view of the state of the art at every period of its existence, a collection should be made of the Masses, Motetts, Madrigals, Chansons and such like, published in Venice, Antwerp, &c from the infancy of printing, to the middle of the 17th century, when such compositions fell into disuse, and thenceforward from that period to the present, full scores (when they can be procured) of Church Music, Operas &c by the greatest masters of every country.

Of the first named portion I believe there is small chance of ever being overloaded with copies, even if all that exist in the present day could be procured, from the difficulty of getting perfect sets of the works, they being for the most part printed in separate parts, many of which are lost. Since the year 1841 it is true a considerable number of perfect books of this description have been acquired, chiefly thro' my instrumentality, but much is still wanting, especially amongst the Italian and Flemish masters. A fine copy of the works of Handel with some full scores by Mozart, Haydn and other more modern composers have also been added, but until some more consistent plan be adopted, the collection will be but an irregular mixture of odds and ends as they may be from time to time offered for sale from different quarters.

It cannot, I think, be denied that in the present day the study of music takes a most prominent position amongst the lighter pursuits of mankind, and whether considered as one of the highest intellectual enjoyments (which it certainly is) to the cultivated mind, or as an innocent amusement to the less gifted, its great moral influence on society is unquestionable.

If for the above considerations it should be the wish of the Trustees to elevate still further the Musical library of the British Museum above being a mere receptacle for the works published in this country, and deposited in accordance with the Copyright Act, it will afford me much pleasure to devote my best energies to their service, on such terms as may be considered somewhat of a remuneration for having worked for 9 years at an average of about 9s/3d per diem.

I may also remark that during this time, a Catalogue of the Manuscript music up to the year 1841 has been made and printed under my superintendence, and to the entire satisfaction of Sir F Madden.

[signed] Tho Oliphant

This memorandum was laid before the Board by HRH the Duke of Cambridge on 13 April, and was then referred to the Sub-Committee on the Library, which simply referred it back to Panizzi, asking him to state 'in what manner the Collection of Music in the Museum may henceforth be arranged and completed'. His reply, dated 28 May, was extraordinary:[33]

> With reference to Mr Oliphant's memorandum Mr Panizzi has the honor to report that it would be unadvisable to adopt the suggestions therein contained. In Mr Panizzi's opinion as soon as the present transcript of the Catalogue of Music is completed the place of extra-assistant for that branch of the service ought to be abolished; no step could be taken more advantageous to this department.

With respect to the arrangement of the ordinary additions to the Musical collection in future Mr Panizzi thinks he can manage without any additional expense; as to its future increase, whenever a fund is provided for that object as well as room prepared wherein what will be added may be placed, Mr Panizzi will suggest what he may think best under the <u>then</u> circumstances; he feels that past experience will be of great use to him.

The Trustees clearly felt rather unhappy, and on 12 June asked Panizzi 'to explain to the Committee what his plan is . . . for the Improvement of the Collection of Music'. Panizzi replied on 20 June:[24]

Mr Panizzi did not intend to convey the impression that he had any plan in contemplation for the improvement of the Collection of Music. He merely stated that whenever there was room provided to place the Music in & a fund granted for that object, he would do himself the honor of suggesting what he might think best under the <u>then</u> circumstances. Mr Panizzi has learned from experience that even then there would not be occupation enough for an assistant in that branch only. At present, when the transcript of the catalogue now in hand is completed, there will be hardly anything to do—certainly nothing of any importance. Much of the Music which Mr Oliphant thinks it would be desirable to procure—even supposing there was space & funds for it—is only to be procured when opportunities offer, and it would be a waste of money to employ a person to watch opportunities that may never offer themselves & which the Trustees will see from their accounts have not been neglected when offered for [*sic*] the past by Mr Panizzi. Whenever the Trustees have space & funds there are other branches of the collections which have a much higher claim to attention than Music.

Mr Panizzi begs in conclusion to observe that Mr Oliphant's engagement in 1841 was for one year & that in Mr Panizzi's opinion it ought to terminate. Mr Panizzi willingly refrains from submitting other reasons in support of his opinion, but he is ready to lay them verbally before the Trustees if they deem it necessary.

Panizzi's untruthfulness and the Trustees' ambivalence are astounding. To say that there was 'certainly nothing of importance' to do was grotesque. The Annual Returns for the early 1850s (see appendix 5) show that the intake of copyright material remained steady. Several thousand titles had to be written, revised and incorporated each year: old ones had to undergo consequential alterations. As for 'opportunities that may never offer themselves', Panizzi knew perfectly well that in the 1840s important collections of all kinds,[25] including music, had regularly appeared at auction in London: there were to be over thirty more music sales in the 1850s alone. Moreover, important editions of older music were beginning to pour from the presses of the great German music publishers, and the arrears of the purchase of living European composers were gigantic. By then London was not lacking in dealers and importers competent to have helped.

How different all this was from the tone and intention of Panizzi's report of 11 December 1845 and the Trustees' speedy decision taken two days later! Now they simply wanted to get rid of Oliphant. At a committee on 22 June 1850, 'the Principal Librarian was directed to inform Mr Oliphant that the Trustees do not intend to renew his engagement after the present year'. But Oliphant did not wait. At another committee, on 6 July:[26]

A note from Mr Oliphant to the Principal Librarian dated 5th inst was read, acknowledging the receipt of the Trustees Minute of 22 June, and intimating his intention not to remain longer in the service of the Museum than for the purpose of completing the transcription of the Catalogue of Music, and leaving the unbound music in order, and catalogued, up to the present time, as far as practicable; this, Mr Oliphant conceived would occupy the remainder of the present month.'

In the circumstances, this was indeed 'turning the other cheek'.

When Oliphant resigned, he was still under fifty-two. With rather more sensible behaviour on his part, and more tolerance on Panizzi's, he could have given the Trustees at least another eight years' service, much to the benefit of the Museum's repute and the scope of its collections. He had certainly not fallen far short of that one of its statutes[27] which enjoined the staff to 'conduct themselves as becomes men of honour, integrity, and liberality, in the conscientious discharge of the respective duties of their stations, and as men who have the credit and utility of this Institution truly at heart'.

Oliphant bore the museum no ill-will. In 1853 he sold to it twenty-one musical rarities, mainly of the seventeenth century, including such things as Anerio's madrigals book I, all for the low price of £41 (an invoice, in his hand, dated 16 April, is extant). Another small lot followed on 1 August 1859, including the very rare 1722 edition of Hotteterre's *Principes de la flûte* for one shilling. On 8 October 1861, the Trustees purchased another score of choice items for the modest price of £15.4.0. They included books 1 to 4 of Kapsberger's *Villanelle* (1610-23) and books 1 and 2 of

Borchgrewinck's *Giardino novo* (1605, 06)—all now exceedingly rare. Two years later Oliphant wrote in a friendly tone to Winter Jones (Panizzi's successor) as follows:[28]

36 Gt Marlbro St

30 Nov^r /63

My dear Jones,

In the sale of Professor Taylor's Music on Thursday there is a work which I think you have not got. It is very scarce.

No 78 Batesons 2^d set of Madrigals—I am almost certain you have the first set, which is an additional reason for having this. I am laid up with rheumatiz otherwise would have called myself.

Yours very truly

Tho Oliphant

The book will likely fetch a high price, say £5.

These madrigals were purchased for the Museum at the sale, by Boone, for £7.10.0. Shortly before his death in 1873, Oliphant offered the whole of his own very valuable library for sale to the Trustees. When however it was found to contain a good many duplicates, he consented to a reduction being made, and this was in progress when he died, on 9 March.[29] In retirement, Oliphant had undertaken a rather unusual type of business, having become 'caterer to the musical visitors to the Crystal Palace'.[30] He also continued his work as secretary of the Madrigal Society, of which he was elected president in 1871.

The enduring monument to his selfless public service was the 57 bound volumes of the catalogue of printed music (45 of music, 12 of the authors of words), comprising in all 31,083 entries, of which one copy was placed along the north wall of the easternmost of the two Reading Rooms in

January 1851.[31]   For nearly sixty years Oliphant's work served intact[32] as the basis for the continuous and rapid expansion of the music catalogue. (See appendix 3.) Although its structure was radically altered by the ultimate extraction and publication (in 1912) of all the entries for pre-1801 music, as described in chapter 4, substantial traces of Oliphant's work still remain in the catalogue today. Combined with his ideas, and with our knowledge of his achievement in initiating the purchase of early rareties, these traces are enough to show that he was one of the great pioneers of librarianship in music, to whom posterity owes an incalculable debt of gratitude.

NOTES

1 Panizzi Papers, 1 July 1841–24 Dec 1842, f108.

2 The idea that rules suitable for cataloguing printed music might possibly also be used for manuscript music shows that Panizzi knew nothing of the fundamental differences between the two.

3 Panizzi Papers, 1 July 1841–24 Dec 1842, ff181, 182.

4 Oliphant's entries are 123, 124, 128, 129, etc. This plate also shows the hands of four of his successors—Johann F von Bach (140-143), E A Roy (125-127, 134), C J Evans (130, 131, 135, 146-152) and Barclay Squire (153, very faint, in pencil).

5 One factor that may have influenced Oliphant to devise a system with letters rather than numbers as its first component was the certain confusion that would have arisen between such numbers and their counterparts in the General Library. Admittedly some such confusion did arise in later years, between music letters and such general library group pressmarks for various tracts, such as 'E' for Thomason, and 'F' for French Revolution and the 'G' used for the Grenville library. But it is relatively small, and Oliphant could hardly have been expected to foresee it in principle.

6 Esdaile, p364, 365.

7 Panizzi Papers, 1 July 1841—24 Dec 1842, f114a.

8 Panizzi Papers, 1 Jan 1843—29 Dec 1844, f260.

9 Panizzi Papers, 1845, 46, f305.

10 Panizzi Papers, 1845, 46, ff116v, 147, 151, 155.

11 Panizzi Papers, 1845, 46, f151.

12 Esdaile, p123.

13 Panizzi Papers, 1845, 46, f199.

14 Panizzi Papers, 1857, no fol number.

15 Panizzi Papers, 1848, f22.

16 Panizzi Papers, 1848, f28.

17 Absence without pay seems at this time by no means to have been confined to Oliphant. Some years later, when daily pay had been replaced by an annual salary, the Trustees sent a stern memorandum to all staff, reminding them of their obligation to regular attendance (bound at the front of the volume of departmental minutes, 1856-60).

18 Panizzi Papers, 1849, f442.

19 See p172.

20 Panizzi Papers, 16 Nov 1849—31 Dec 1850, f34.

21 Panizzi Papers, 16 Nov 1849—31 Dec 1850, f53.

22 Panizzi Papers, 1849-50, f294-295.

23 Panizzi Papers, 1849-50, f296. The mention of the lack of a room for additions is suggestive.

24 Panizzi Papers, 1849-50, f325.

25 That Panizzi was aware of the importance of bidding at auctions is shown by his purchases of incunables from this source. See C B Oldman, 'Panizzi's acquisition of incunables', in *Essays in honour of Victor Scholderer*, ed D E Rhodes, Mainz, 1970, pp284-291.

26 Panizzi Papers, 1849-50, f344.

27 *Acts and Votes of Parliament relating to the British Museum, with the Statutes and Rules thereof*, etc, 1828, chap II, 20, p140.

28 Letter in British Library Archives, discovered by Edward Miller.

29 Letter from Bullen to Winter Jones, 14 June 1878. Bullen states that 152 rare works were obtained at the subsequent auction, held on 24 April, by Puttick & Simpson (copy of catalogue in British Library, S.C.P.155 (8)).

30 Robert Cowtan, *Memories of the British Museum*, 1872 [1871], p422, 423, who also mentions Oliphant's gifts as a raconteur.

31 The exact date is given by Richard Sims, *Handbook to the Library of the British Museum*, 1854, p164, where he also mentions the number of volumes, which is confirmed by the Annual Return for 1850. The latter records the number of titles in each of the two bound copies of the catalogue. Though the location of the staff copy is not known, Sims, p292, gives a plan of the Reading Rooms, which shows the exact place of the readers' copy. After the opening of the circular Reading Room in 1857, the former easternmost reading room became known as the 'old catalogue room', a designation which lasted nearly a century.

32 The Words Catalogue was discontinued in 1886. See also p148, and plate 4.

3

INTERREGNUM:
BACH, ROY, CLARKE AND EVANS
1851 to 1884

TO ONE MEMBER of the staff at least, Oliphant's resignation offered a welcome opportunity. This was Eugene Armand Roy, who was born in Soho in 1820, the son of parents from Dijon. He was educated at 'Mr Chambers' Academy, Castle Street, Leicester Square',[1] and started his career in the service of a bookseller named Rolandi.[2] Though apparently lacking in formal education, Roy had an excellent knowledge of French and Italian, and was appointed a Supernumerary Attendant on 3 April 1841. Five years later, he was promoted to Transcriber, and, with A S Neustein and Edward M Bellamy, two other Transcribers, was still working on the music when he wrote to the Archbishop of Canterbury, William Howley, and asked to be given charge of it. Although the letter[3] is undated, it must have been written in the autumn of 1850, not long after Oliphant resigned. It runs thus:

> My Lord
> A vacancy occurring among the assistants of the Printed Book Department of the British Museum thro' the resignation of Mr Oliphant, I beg most respectfully to offer myself as a candidate for the situation.
> Besides the qualifications which I had the honor of submitting to your Grace on a former occasion, when recommended by Mr Panizzi to apply for promotion, I may add that I consider myself specially competent to take charge of the musical collection thro' having made music one of the recreations of my leisure hours

for several years and being consequently acquainted with much vocal and instrumental music of various kinds—and, thro' being already conversant with the manner in which the music is arranged and catalogued in the British Museum, in consequence of having, since the month of January last, been engaged in transcribing that collection under the superintendence of Mr Oliphant himself.

Should your Grace be pleased to nominate me to the situation it will be my aim to serve your Grace's patronage by the strict discharge of my duties and the pursuit of such studies as will prove most serviceable to me in my new capacity.

I have the honor to be My Lord Your Grace's most humble & obedient Servt.

[E Roy]

What his grace replied to Roy is not known. But we may guess that Panizzi did not recommend him, being perhaps reluctant to give such a responsible post to a Transcriber. There was another applicant, from outside the department. He was Matthew Cooke, a chorister of the Chapel Royal, St James's; in his letter to Panizzi, dated 12 September 1850,[4] he emphasised the need to keep the music publishers up to the mark on copyright deliveries, urged the necessity of expanding the collection of foreign publications, and commended his own knowledge 'of the early masters of English and continental reputation'. Nevertheless, he was unsuccessful.

Panizzi, despite the bland assurance he gave to the Trustees on 20 June 1850 (p72), that 'when the transcript of the catalogue now in hand is completed there will be hardly anything to do—certainly nothing of importance', knew that he had to maintain the work on music. In fact, within six months, at the most, of Oliphant's resignation in July 1850, Panizzi had filled the vacancy by transferring Johann F von Bach, who had joined the department in 1847 as a Supernumerary Assistant, and was therefore senior in grade to Roy.

Bach's succession to Oliphant is officially known solely because he was a self-assertive person who did not underestimate his own merits, and consequently had a brush with Panizzi and the Trustees. Otherwise, because internal transfers were not usually the subject of a report, Bach's work on music might well have gone unrecorded. Early in 1853 he submitted two memorials to the Trustees, stating that he was dissatisfied with his pay. He had the temerity to ask that the second memorial should be widely circulated in lithographed copies, which the Trustees rightly deemed 'contrary to the good order of the British Museum'.[5] In the first memorial, of 1 February, Bach reminded the Trustees that he had originally been engaged to catalogue 'large accessions of books in the Russian, Polish and other languages of Europe rarely studied', and that, two and a half years prior to the memorial, he had been selected, on account of his musical qualifications, to replace Oliphant 'temporarily'.[6] (This not only supplies the approximate date when Panizzi transferred Bach, but also lends colour to the idea that the former may have been waiting for Roy to gain promotion before he gave him charge of the music.) Bach may have been of some stature musically, for there survive two letters from George (afterwards Sir George) Grove to Panizzi[7] which deal with the department's deficiencies in the works of Johann Sebastian Bach, and which mention some correspondence on the subject between Grove and Johann F von Bach.[8] Nevertheless, Panizzi reported curtly and sarcastically on Bach's memorial: 'The services of Mr von Bach are not such as to entitle him to any distinction, and he is utterly mistaken in assuming that those of other Assistants, who are satisfied with their remuneration, are not even of more value than his own'.[9] Bach resigned in July, and ultimately returned to Germany.[10] Roy, who had been promoted to Extra Assistant on 3 May 1851, replaced him with little delay.

Although Roy had worked as a Transcriber under Oliphant, and therefore knew something of the work, he was confronted by various difficulties which he explained in a series of letters to Panizzi. The first, written from his home at 7a Orchard Street on 23 October 1853, runs thus:

> Dear Sir,
>   As you have done me the honor to confide the collection of music to my care, I think it my duty to give you some idea of what appears to be the work before me.
>   There are at present, as well as I can judge, more than 5000 pieces of music, unavailable to the readers viz
>
> | | about |
> |-------------------------------|-------|
> | Uncatalogued— | 3100 |
> | Catalogued, but not transcribed | 2000 |
>
> all of which require binding.
>   At the last incorporation of titles were found differences and omissions of Christian names, involving questions of identity &c which, after the requisite investigation, will necessitate the retranscription of from 600 to 700 titles. As this is probably but a small portion of the whole amount of such differences, it would be well, when time can be spared, to give the entire catalogue a careful revision.
>   The 3100 uncatalogued pieces will require, at a low estimation, 1000 cross-references, so that about 4100 titles and cross-references will have to be written; the pieces must then be arranged for binding, entered in the hand catalogue, and have press-marks affixed to them.

At the rate of 35 titles a day, my present average working only 3 hours, it would take more than 4 months to catalogue all the present arrears. In four months, however, a great deal more music will have been received, so that the arrears will by no means have been got under, nor will my time have been given to placing, hand cataloguing, preparing work for the binder &c.

If I were permitted to devote myself, for a few months, entirely to the musical collection, I should save the time lost by passing from one kind of work to another, which according to Adam Smith & my own experience 'is much greater than at first view one should be apt to imagine'. I feel almost certain that by foregoing the remainder of my vacation, I should be able to catalogue all the music received up to the present time, before the end of the year.

The binding, placing, hand cataloguing &c would take but a short time longer & the titles might be transcribed in less than a month by two transcribers. By the beginning of Spring it is probable that I should have no music to catalogue but what was received from day to day, which is, however, more than formerly on account of what is received by international copyright. I might then devote my spare time to the revision of the music catalogue, the cataloguing of books, or any work you might deem necessary.

With regard to the assistance I give Mr Clarke I really think that an intelligent attendant—Kesson for instance who is already well acquainted with the Periodical Publications—could well supply my place, the work, though important, requiring nothing but care, no more abstruse question ever arising than whether certain parts of a work have been received, and every query being carefully revised by Mr Clarke.

At all events, whether I work 3 or 6 hours a day at the Music, I shall work equally <u>con</u> <u>amore</u> & do my utmost to bring the collection, as soon as possible, to the highest state of efficiency, So, leaving the matter to your consideration, I remain

Dear Sir

Yours respectfully

E A Roy

Obviously, arrears had accumulated since Oliphant left, and Roy, likewise working single-handed, at least initially, and only part-time, was hard-pressed to overtake them. It is revealing that Roy makes no mention of any time spent in purchasing music. This suggests that there was, at least in his early years, no policy for continuing and extending what Oliphant had begun. Roy was clearly burdened by time-consuming attention to detail, as he reveals in a second letter to Panizzi, written in the museum on 28 August 1854:

Dear Sir,

One of the most troublesome duties connected with the collection of music, is the arrangement of the different pieces for binding.

It is my wish to arrange and place the music, as much as possible, according to the classification already adopted, & also to render the latest pieces received at once available to the readers. It is, however, impossible to unite both these advantages under the present system of binding on account of the number of volumes which are too small to be bound, even in temporary binding. I wish therefore to obtain your authority to have them merely stitched & covered with a <u>paper</u> <u>cover</u> for the

present in order that I may be enabled to place them
& send all their titles for transcription.

Believe me,

Dear Sir,

Yours respectfully,

E Roy

Here he draws attention to a difficulty which has always
plagued music librarians—the conservation of thin pieces of
such awkward and diverse sizes that they cannot be conveniently bound with others to make a substantial volume.
Roy's solution of a 'temporary' binding in strong paper,
with a label bearing a hand-written title pasted on the front
cover, instead of gold lettering impressed on the spine,
remained in use for nearly a century, but with limp cloth
instead of paper. Roy gradually realised what Panizzi must
always have known but would not admit—that part-time
work on music was quite insufficient to avoid arrears. So he
wrote again, on 9 March 1855:

Dear Sir,

The experience of nearly a year and a half convinces
me that three hours a day are not sufficient to keep the
collection of music in proper order & to render every
new acquisition available to the public, even within a
moderate time from the date of its reception. If my
duties consisted merely in cataloguing, three hours
would doubtless be enough & I might perhaps have a
little time to spare, but there are many other operations
such as revising the titles, preparing the music for
binding, giving the volumes a place & a press-mark,
entering them in the hand catalogue, taking an account
of incomplete works, &c all of which are performed by
different persons in the book collection but which, with

regard to music, devolve upon me. The arranging of music for binding, from the number of pieces bound together, is an operation requiring great care and much time, & which (since pamphlets have been separated instead of united) has no parallel in the collection of books. Since the music has been under my care, I have catalogued a great quantity of arrears, consisting primarily of incomplete collections: I have recently discovered another mass of music which has not yet been catalogued.

Should you consider it desirable, I should be most happy, in order to accelerate the work, to devote more time to it during the period the Museum is open till 5 & 6 o'clock.

Believe me,
Dear Sir,
Yours respectfully,
E Roy

Panizzi's reply to this, as to the previous letters, is not extant. Roy, whose devotion to his work is evident, seems to have kept on good terms with his imperious Keeper, who was promoted to Principal Librarian in March 1856 and was succeeded by John Winter Jones, a man of more equable temperament, though an incomparably less forceful administrator.

Under Roy the music made steady progress. The number of titles he wrote was not, judged by the standard of some of his successors, very large, understandably so as he only worked part-time. For a short period in the later 1850s, he had help from John Kemp, then 'Assistant Clerk for receiving Copyright Books'.[11] Roy's purchases were more extensive than might have been expected in the circumstances, although the Trustees were not always sympathetic. At a Standing

Committee on 24 July 1858 they declined an offer from Dr Georg Heinrich Pertz, on behalf of the Royal Library of Berlin, of 237 musical works for £400. (Presumably these were duplicates.) In 1861, however, Roy reported the purchase of 1688 musical works in the previous year, a considerable haul, although some 1500 of them were accounted for by nine vellum-bound octavo volumes all containing French songs of the late eighteenth or early nineteenth century. These were offered by Asher of Berlin, as was also a large antiquarian collection of over 1000 items, including many part-books, for £878. This offer was actually accepted by the Trustees on 18 July 1861, but as they were reluctant to pay the bill then, Asher agreed that it be deferred for a year. Roy had another success in 1865, when on 21 June the Trustees bought from Asher thirty-nine choice sets of part-books, all duplicates from the Royal Library of Berlin, and possibly a residue of those which Dr Pertz had offered seven years before.

It is perhaps worth remarking here that the statement, in the first edition of Grove's *Dictionary*, (sv 'Musical Libraries') that in 1863 a notable purchase was made of duplicates from the Berlin Library, consisting mainly of old German and Italian madrigals, and church music, valued at about £1000, is an error. The author of the article, Russell Martineau, was a member of the Department of Printed Books, but he must have conflated the purchase of 1862 with that of 1865. His error went through to the fourth edition of 1940, and was repeated, in 1946, by Esdaile.

In addition, Roy built up the collections from English sources. Besides purchases from Oliphant, in 1863 he procured antiquarian music from two London dealers, G A Davies of Wardour Street, and W Hamilton of West Hammersmith. For some years to come, the latter continued to send in increasingly large offers. Again, when on 28 January 1863,

Puttick & Simpson sold the entire stock of John Hedgley, a music dealer in Ebury Street, Roy picked up some useful early nineteenth century items.

But in spite of all these efforts, there was much ground to be made up, and Winter Jones, who certainly appears to have been sympathetic to music, knew it. For on 10 October 1865, when submitting his financial estimates for 1867-68, he drew the Trustees' attention to the need to 'build up' the music. A year later, on 22 October, Jones reminded the Trustees again: 'The collection of music in the Museum is one of the collections most in need of attention and augmentation'. But these improvements lay in the future. Meanwhile little effort was made to bid at any of the numerous important auction sales of private libraries of music that were taking place in London in the 1860s.

The monthly statistical returns show that there was steady progress in the maintenance and improvement of the catalogues. In January 1861 it was reported that they had become so crowded that the slips needed to be relaid and respaced. The work seems to have been well on the way to completion by February 1862 when 28,780 slips in the first copy, 50,010 in the second, 26,743 in the third, and 13,512 in each of the three copies of the words catalogue, had all been relaid. Clearly the arrears of this work had mounted rapidly and a lot of men must have been concentrated on it. What the administration had then failed to realise, however, was that it was acting like King Canute in vainly trying to stay the ever rising tide of the transcribed moveable slips. Before twenty years were out, it was to engulf all the catalogues of the department.

Meanwhile, an important subsidiary music catalogue had been brought up to date. The monthly returns on 11 September 1861 reported that '21,420 title slips of the 4th copy have been mounted on cartridge paper for the carbonic hand catalogue of this collection [ie music], and the whole of this catalogue . . . has been arranged according to pressmarks and amounts to 62,539 slips'. Such intensive work must have entailed a good deal of supervision for Roy, in addition to cataloguing, incorporating and checking transcription.

After Roy had spent some twelve years on this work, he was the subject of an ambiguous report by Winter Jones, who wrote, on 8 November 1865, that he was 'extremely attentive' to his duties, but was 'of ordinary merit'. He could not therefore recommend him for promotion. The Trustees, however—presumably on the advice of Panizzi—over-ruled Jones, and promoted Roy to the upper section of the First Class of Assistants on 3 January 1866. Panizzi was wise, for Roy was destined for even higher things. On 15 February 1871 he was appointed Assistant Keeper in charge of the General Catalogue, a post which he held until his retirement twelve years later. He supervised the final phase of the amalgamation of the titles comprised in the 82 volumes of the 'old' interleaved catalogue of 1813-19 (still in use in 1872) with its transcribed successor. He also took an active part in planning the great *General catalogue of printed books* whose publication in parts began in 1881. Roy was thus one of the few men actively working on its early stages who had also seen the appearance of the abortive letter 'A' volume, its distant predecessor, printed in 1841.[12]

It seems fairly safe to assume that Roy's promotion in 1866 marked his move from the music back to the General Library, even if it did not happen earlier. His successor in charge of music was John Campbell Clarke (generally known as Campbell Clarke, already mentioned by Roy—see p83), who was educated at Bonn University and had joined the department on 10 April 1852, when still under eighteen, as an exceptionally young Assistant. He became musical correspondent of *The daily telegraph* and *The Sunday times*.

Practically nothing is known of his career during his first thirteen years of service, and nothing at all of his musical qualifications. That he was an able administrator, however, is suggested by the fact that in December 1864, in succession to George Hogarth (father-in-law of Charles Dickens), [13] he was appointed secretary of the Philharmonic Society. His letter of 8 February requesting permission[14] said: 'access to the valuable library of the Philharmonic Society will enable me to acquire information that will assist me greatly in my present occupation at the British Museum'. (This indicates that Clarke had been working with Roy on music, at least part-time, before the latter's promotion.)

Clarke's letter was the subject of an immediate report to the Trustees, which stated that he was ready to resign the Philharmonic post after six months if it were to take up more time than he anticipated. In fact, he held it for only some nineteen months. His date of succession to Roy is not recorded in any departmental document, though the fact is mentioned by Cowtan and is confirmed by Clarke's own letter. There is also the evidence of Clarke's handwriting as a cataloguer of music, and of the initials which he wrote on titles when revising the work of others. But here too the dates are inconclusive. Little of note seems to have happened during Clarke's superintendence of the music, which took place during a period when there are reasons for suspecting that whole-time work on it was still considered neither practicable nor desirable. Arrears began to accumulate.

Clarke's responsibility probably came to an end a year or so before he retired, on 7 June 1870.[15] The man who took his place was Charles John Evans, one of those whose cataloguing he had revised. Here again, there is no departmental report on the matter, but some facts about Evans's career and interests can fortunately be supplied from official and other sources. He was born in December 1839 and graduated at the University of London in 1858, in Latin and modern languages. Having entered the museum on 7 October that year as a Transcriber (or Junior Assistant), he gained promotion on 10 July 1867 to Senior Assistant, Lower Section. He supportee his application to the Trustees with a brief *curriculum vitae*, in which he said he had a good command of Latin, French, Italian and German, and had worked for four years on the music catalogue, having thus served successively under Roy and Clarke, and probably part-time.

Boase[16] says Evans was a bassoon player in the orchestra of the Wandering Minstrels, an amateur body with strongly aristocratic connections. It flourished from 1860 to 1898, and raised £16,657 for charities by giving concerts all over the home counties. Its complete records were fortunately presented to the British Museum in about 1925.[17] They show that Evans was elected on 4 July 1861, and played the first bassoon regularly until 24 April 1884. His election was celebrated in part of a doggerel poem describing members of the orchestra written by Henry Robley, one of its violoncellists:

> . . . For months we sought the priceless boon
> Of a real amateur bassoon.
> At last, just what we wanted, come is
> From amongst Egyptian mummies.

Some of the music the orchestra played was quite difficult. A chamber concert included part of Beethoven's Piano and Wind Quintet, Op 16, which has a taxing bassoon part. This suggests that Evans had a sound technique, but where he was taught remains a mystery. Apart from his bassoon playing, nothing is known of his musical expertise.

It was in the later 1860s that the Assistants working on music received regular help from a man in a lower grade, who relieved them of some of the mechanical part of their duties, which had irked Oliphant and Roy so much. This is known from three documents which date from October 1870, and relate to vacancies for attendants. A memorandum written by the Keeper, William Brenchley Rye, stated that one of the applicants, a binder's man named Frederick Kingston, then twenty-six years old, had been 'arranging and labelling music under Mr Evans'. The latter warmly supported his application. Kingston's own letter said that he 'had worked with Mr Clarke and Mr Evans for three years, arranging titles for transcription, finding unbound music for the Reading Room, pressmarking'—a much more comprehensive statement than the Keeper's. This does not, unfortunately, make clear whether Clarke and Evans were working the whole-time together on the music from 1867, or whether Kingston worked with each successively.

But Clarke may well have trained Evans and then returned to other work in the general library part-time for a year or so before his retirement. For it is improbable that two assistants would then have been on music together for very long. (This is rather borne out by a subsequent letter of Evans's, written in 1878, and quoted on p95). Kingston's description of his duties is most interesting. It is most unlikely that such help would have been confined to music, and it implies that the tradition of seconding binders' men was then established in the department as a whole. As will be seen later, this tradition lasted for many years.[18] It may be assumed from later developments that after Kingston finally won his promotion, on 22 September 1873, another binder took his place, but his name is not recorded in the reports, and there is no list of men seconded from the bindery to the department at any date.

From the 1870s onwards, there is a welcome increase in the number of documents in the reports and minutes relating to music. There are, however, no more long, detailed letters of the kind which Roy wrote to Panizzi seeking guidance.

Henceforth, if such guidance was sought, it was given orally. But though there is less information of a personal kind, much more is recorded about the growth of the department and about all aspects of its management, including music.

Evans, like Oliphant and Roy, was industrious and totally devoted to his work. His reports are admirably concise and lucid, and he was clearly held in high regard. He was certainly faced with heavy arrears. R E Graves, (who was appointed Assistant in 1854) is reported in *The musical times* for 1907 (p782) as recalling that when Evans was appointed 'nothing had been done', and that there were 'enormous stacks of music' waiting to be catalogued. When, however, Rye retired as Keeper in 1875, his final report said that the music was 'very satisfactory' under Evans. At some time before 1878 (as is revealed solely in the answer to criticisms made by the Musical Association, which will be mentioned later), he was joined by another cataloguer, whose name is unfortunately not known. This would account for the remarkable, sustained rise in the number of titles written annually. But it is unlikely that Evans would have been given this assistance until he had been in charge for a few years, and there is little doubt that his own early output of cataloguing was very high, as can be seen in appendix 4. After training his fellow cataloguer, Evans could give more of his time to purchasing important early music, in which, despite the efforts of Oliphant and Roy, the collections were still sadly deficient.

It may well be that Rye and George Bullen, the successive Keepers under whom Evans served, were more actively sympathetic in this respect than Panizzi and Winter Jones had been to Roy and Clarke. A statement accompanying the estimates for the purchase grant, submitted on 16 October 1874, drew particular attention to the music. It pointed out that while important editions of modern works, French, German, Italian and Russian, had been acquired, more money was needed to improve the collection of early music, which was still defective. Evans's energy was astonishing. Besides securing a sream of instrumental and vocal music, principally of the late eighteenth and early nineteenth century (notably from a London dealer called Crampton), he concentrated on earlier rareties of the highest importance.

His first notable attempt, however, was rather an unhappy one. At the sale of Edward Rimbault's very rich library, held 31 July to 7 August 1877, the museum bid for numerous lots. But in nearly every case, it was outbidden by Sabin who secured almost 400 lots, mostly destined for Joseph W Drexel, the distinguished American collector, who bequeathed them to New York Public Library. On 1 September *The musical times* remarked gloomily: 'All [the English *unica*] should have been purchased for the British Museum'. But in December 1877 Evans submitted an offer made by William Chappell, comprising eighteen editions of *The dancing master*, a unique opportunity, which the Trustees accepted. Among Evans's other purchases in this year were Aron, *Thoscanello de la musica* (1523), and Gafori, *Practica musicae* (1512).

Whether successful or not in his efforts to secure rare music, Evans took the most scrupulous pains over everything. There survives only one letter from him[19] of the many which he must have written about acquisitions. He addressed it to Bullen on 8 May 1878. It deserves quotation in full:

> Sir,
>
> I beg to report that in pursuance of your instructions, I have carefully examined Mr Rosenthal's[20] list of printed books, music, manuscripts, &c, &c, and find that the library already contains a large proportion of the former, and nearly the whole of the music. With regard to the

prices charged, I consider them far in excess to [*sic*] those usually paid by the Museum to any other dealer.

I can confidently assert this in the case of the music, and presume that it applies equally to the books. During the last ten years, I have examined many similar invoices, both for Mr Watts,[21] Mr Rye and yourself, and am fully persuaded upon examination you will find my opinion correct.

I am, Sir, your obedient servant,

Charles J Evans

He had surely well deserved his promotion to First Class Assistant on 16 February 1878, after just over twenty years' service.

Early in 1879, Evans reported a list of thirty rareties of German and Italian music, part-books, song-books and tablatures, ranging in date from 1547 to 1648, as a sample of what he purchased from the great Berlin dealer, Albert Cohn. Evans also mentioned Tovar's *Libro de música práctica* (Barcelona, 1510), Giovanni Guidetti's edition of the *Directorium chori* (published by Pustet of Ratisbon) and an Italian Gradual of the very early sixteenth century. (These are interesting because they show that Evans had some responsibility for acquiring liturgical and theoretical works.) He remarked that many of these items were 'unknown to bibliographers': not a few have since been found to be unique. Even more impressive was the museum's acquisition of 293 items, of great importance and scarcity, from the great library of Franz Gehring (a lecturer in mathematics at Vienna University), which was auctioned in Berlin in November 1880. Cohn acted for the museum. Submitting a selected list, Evans said: 'In addition to these, many other important purchases have been made, including R Dowland's "Varietie of lessons", . . . rare harpsichord music by Jeremiah Clarke,

Le Begue, Dandrieu, Couperin and Du Phly . . . 2 sets of
J S Bach's "Clavier Ubungen [*sic*]" said to have been engraved
by the hands of the composer, guitar music by A M Bartolotti
(unknown) and F Corbetta, a book of lute music by Francesco da Milano, 1562, Monteverde's "Scherzi", Frescobaldi's
"Ricercare [*sic*]", numerous works of chamber music of the
last century, and many scores of ballets &c &c'. These and
many other items represented an astonishing achievement for
one man.

Evans reported further splendid purchases in 1882, including all six books of Rontani, *Varie musiche* (1614-22); Fro-
berger, *Partite musicali* (1696); Agricola, *Musica instrumen-
talis Deudsch* (1532); Amerbach, *Tabulaturbuch* (1575);
Ochsenkun, *Tabulaturbuch* (1558); Sanz, *Instrucción de
música* (1697); and Keiser, *L'Inganno fedele* (1714). Evans
added: 'A large number of works, including opera, oratorios,
church music, etc was purchased at the second sale of the library of the late Dr Müller of Berlin' (this was Joseph Müller,
Secretary of the *Königliche Hochschule für Musik*). On
21 June 1883, Bullen obtained Trustees' sanction to purchase, from Cohn, 'a valuable collection of early Italian
church music, consisting of motets and psalms by well known
composers' (Constantini, Catalano, Sabbatini, etc), for
£103.5.0. A note was added to the report: 'It is specially
desired to make the antiquarian portion of the musical collection in the Museum as complete as possible in view of the
requirements of students of the Royal College of Music and
other institutions'. Pursuing this policy, Evans sought,
and was given, permission to bid up to £200 at the London
sale of Julian Marshall's fine library, held in July 1884.
Quaritch secured for the museum 84 lots for £89.13.4.
Here, as at the Rimbault sale, a good deal went to America.

On 12 January 1884, purchasing procedure was much simplified when the Trustees altered a long-standing regulation,

123	Leoni. Introduction to the Manoline	Lond.
4	Chabran Instructions for Guitar	" "
5	Wake. Practical first Opera Piano	
6	Russell. Instructions German Concertina	
7	Howell. Key to Musical Reeds (see a.80)	
8	Double Flageolet Instruction Books	Lond.
9	Briggs. art of playing on Doub. Flag.t	"
130	Roy (C.E.) Méthode pour la Flageolet	
1	Converse. Pt. 1 Banjo Instructor	
2	Collins. Instructions for French Flag.t	Lond.
3	Hyde. Preceptor for Trumpet &c.	"
4	Forster. Anleitung zum General bass	
5	Trumpet & Bugle Sounds &c. (R.A.7.)	
6	Bugle Horn Major's Companion	Lond.
7	Gilbert. Bugle Horn calls	"
8	Pashen. Kent Bugle Preceptor	"
9	Konigsburg. Cornopean Instructor	
140	Violin made easy	
1	Flute made easy	
2	Accordion made easy	
3	Travis (C.) Organ & Harmonium	
4	Accolaris. Orgel oder instrument Tabulatur. Leipzig &c. 1571	
5	Hiles (J.) Voluntaries for the	
6	Times (J.V.) Der katholische Organist	
7	Gottmann (G.) 15 kurze Orgelstücke	
8	Volkmann (G.) Choräle	
9	Rebel (C.) Der angehende praktische Organist	
150	Radlard (H.) Universal Organist	
1	Smart (H.) Organ Pieces	
2	Tuct (G.) Der praktische Organist	
3	Volkmann (C.) Orgelvorspiele & Nachspiele	
4	Brutishill (J.) Extra Piece	

Plate 3: A page of the Hand-List of Instrumental Music (for the identity of some of the hands, see note 4 to chapter 2).

L.

L. . . . , Mlle. DE. Si d'un grand nez au milieu du visage. Paroles de Mlle. de L. . . . *See* RÉPERTOIRE. Répertoire des Pensionnats, *etc.* No. 33. Conseil de grand'mère. Musique de L. Streabbog. [1875, *etc.*] fol.
H. 2833. a. (19.)

L., L. E. To-morrow, to-morrow thou loveliest May . . . By L[etitia] E[lizabeth] L[andon]. *See* WALMISLEY (T. F.) The First of the May. [1845?] fol.
H. 2831. j. (44.)

L., L. E. 'Twas sweet to look upon thine eyes. By L[etitia] E[lizabeth] L[andon]. *See* ROBINSON (F.) [1830?] fol.
G. 809. c. (6.)

L., L. E. When should lovers breathe their vows. By L[etitia] E[lizabeth] L[andon]. *See* PURDAY (C. H.) [1830?] fol.
G. 809. b. (68.)

LABARRE (LÉON) and **GRANCEY** (J.) Dans ton hamac aux nids pareil. Paroles de L. L. & J. G. *See* CHAUTAGNE (J. M.) [1883.] fol. H. 1793. a. (5.)

LABITTE (ALPHONSE) Connais-tu l'heure enchanteresse. *See* BROUTIN (C.) [1882.] fol.
H. 1793. (49.)

LABITTE (ALPHONSE) Quand les pommiers seront en fleurs. *See* RUPÈS (G.) [1880.] fol.
H. 2698. (43.)

LABLACHE (FANNY) O'er dreary plains and hills of snow. *See* PINSUTI (C. E.) Moorish Serenade. [1881.] fol.
H. 2680. h. (30.)

LABOUROT (J.) Une femme timide. Scène comique. *See* POURNY (C.) [1881.] fol. H. 1612. (16.)

LADIMIR (JULES) Dieu tout puissant. *See* MÉLODIES. Mélodies, *etc.* No. 13. Notre Père. Musique de J. B. Wekerlin. [1878.] fol.
H. 2833. a. (18.)

LADY. Blithe Strephon, the airiest of the gay throng . . . By a L. *See* WEIGH (J.) [1799.] fol.
G. 808. h. (42.)

LADY. O give to me those early flowers. . .By a L. *See* EULENSTEIN (C.) [1874.] fol. H. 2345.

LADY. Oh! who would think the time so long. . .By a L. *See* WELSH (T.) Jenny Gray. [1825?] fol.
G. 809. c. (61.)

LADY. O think not by my eyes betrayed. . .By a L. *See* GROSVENOR (J.) [1810?] fol. G. 809. a. (17.)

LADY. O where is my boy to-night. . .By a L. *See* WHITTEMORE (J. H.) [1874.] fol. H. 2345.

LAFITTE (ALPHONSE) Ernest, Jules, Léon, Dodore. *See* POURNY (C.) Les Adorateurs de Jeanneton. [1880.] fol. H. 1612. (10.)

LA GUARDIA (HERACLIO MARTIN DE) Venezuela! tus claros laureles. *See* PERÉZ (R.) Himno. 1878. 4°. 8180. i. 7.

LAMARTINE DE PRAT (MARIE LOUIS ALPHONSE DE) Pourquoi me fuir, passagère hirondelle. *See* JERVIS (E. R. S.) L'Hirondelle. [1881.] fol. H. 1787. i. (9.)

LAMARTINE DE PRAT (MARIE LOUIS ALPHONSE DE) Pourquoi, Seigneur, fais-tu fleurir. *See* RUPÈS (G.) Roses sous la Neige. [1881.] fol. H. 2698. (41.)

LAMARTINE DE PRAT (MARIE LOUIS ALPHONSE DE) Toi que j'ai recueilli sur sa bouche expirante. *See* WOUTERS (A. F.) Dix Mélodies, *etc.* No. 10. Le Crucifix. [1880.] fol. H. 1786. i. (33.)

LA MOTTE FOUQUÉ (FRIEDRICH HEINRICH CARL DE) *Baron.* Sleep calmly. *See* CROWDER (C. F.) [1882.] 8°. E. 308. l. (9.)

LAMY (FRANÇOIS) La Dame aux impairs. Scène comique. *See* POURNY (C.) [1880.] fol. H. 1612. (4.)

LANCASTER (GEORGE ERIC) Oh! would that I could tell my tale. *See* CASANO (E. P.) A Lover's Wish. [1881.] fol. H. 1787. d. (16.)

LANDON (LETITIA ELIZABETH) The muffled drum rolled on the air. *See* KETTLE (C. E.) The Soldier's Funeral. [1882.] fol. H. 1787. i. (44.)

LANG (A.) Now the white lily blows. *See* STANFORD (C. V.) Sweeter than the violet. [1882.] fol. H. 1960. (7.)

LANG (GEORG) Der Frühling ist da. *See* ABT (F.) Sechs Lieder, *etc.* Op. 585. No. 3. Mein Herz überfliegt sie alle. [1882.] 8°. F. 585. f. (2.)

LANG (GEORG) *See* ABT (F.) Neun Kinderlieder. [No. 4, 6–9 written by G. L.] [1882.] fol. H. 2092. g. (11.)

LANGAT (D.) Hier si vous m'aviez vu. *See* SERAENE (N.) La Feuillette pleine. [1881.] fol. H. 1786. h. (34.)

LANGBRIDGE (FREDERICK) Ah! me, the wet wind. *See* BLUMENTHAL (J.) My Heart. [1880.] fol. H. 1499. a. (14.)

Plate 4: A page of Part 1 of British Museum. Catalogue of music. Words. *1884.*

and decided that instead of all purchases of old books and music having to be reported before payment could be sanctioned, they required details only of those exceeding £20 each, or of those which were of special interest. That limit (which actually remained in force, however, until about 1950) eased considerably the work arising from large-scale acquisition. Had the change come earlier, it would have helped Evans a great deal, for in less than ten years his time-consuming labours had added immeasurably to the prestige and quantity of the collections in his care. Besides the treasures of the sixteenth and seventeenth centuries, he had augmented them with a very large amount of printed music of later date, much of which has since been found to be as rare of its period as were the more spectacular items of earlier times. Two works may be cited as a tribute to Evans's flair and judgement of rareties—the symphonies, Op 1 and Op 2 by Baron Ernst Wanczura, which he bought in 1874. They were printed at St Petersburg in about 1795: no copy of either is recorded in any European or Russian library. During all this period, music had also been coming in steadily by English copyright and by international copyright. The great bulk of this intake soon produced acute problems of storage, and the resultant stream of titles caused great pressure on the catalogues.

At this point, the question again arises—where in the library was the growing collection of printed music kept during Evans's time and that of his immediate predecessors? As already mentioned (p59), it is likely that Oliphant had to shelve the collection in one or more rooms in the basement of the North Wing. There it may well have remained until the mid-1860s. These dark rooms—electric light did not reach the museum until after 1879—must all have become very overcrowded, making orderly expansion far from easy. Though no report mentions any difficulties in respect of music, they were surely intense. But in the end a solution was found, and it was one that lasted for well over half a century.

The obvious place for rehousing the music ultimately was in one of the two reading rooms in the North Wing, which fell vacant after Panizzi's new Reading Room was opened in 1857. But it is not known when the decision to create a Music Room was taken and put into effect. Nomenclature, in a large building like the British Museum, dies hard, and so it is not surprising to find, in the annual estimates for works and fittings, right up to 1882, that the apartment in question is still referred to as 'the western Old Reading Room' (plate 1), or by a similar name. But it is quite clear that though this designation persisted, this room had been assigned to music some time before. For on 3 December 1880, Evans drafted the following report to be submitted to the Trustees:

> Mr Bullen has the honour to report to the Trustees that the Music Collection has so greatly increased during the last ten years that it has at length become absolutely necessary to provide increased accommodation for the volumes. At present there are 62 presses, containing about 16,000 vols, all of which are crowded. Besides these there are 2286 vols for which no space can be found and which are lying on and beneath the tables in the Music Room, causing great delay in finding works required by the Readers.
>
> To meet this want it would be advisable to construct new presses which could be moveable and could stand at right angles to those now existing. They should be of the same dimensions as these, and might consist of iron standards with deal shelves. There is sufficient space for 80 of these presses, which would contain about 24,000 vols and which would at the present

rate of increase afford accommodation for the next twenty years.

Bullen redrafted the last paragraph rather more cautiously:

> Mr Bullen is of the opinion it would be advisable to construct new presses in the Music Room projecting from the walls in a manner similar to those in the two supplementary rooms of the Library, forming alcoves or recesses. These would afford accommodation for about 24,000 volumes, and have a handsome appearance. Should it be deemed advisable, however, by the Trustees, to have recourse to moveable presses, of iron with wooden shelves, these would afford considerable accommodation, and should be constructed of the same dimensions as the iron presses in the new Library. At the present rate of increase this would afford accommodation for the next 12 years.[22]

The clear inference is that this room must have been used for music a good deal earlier, for the accumulation of such a quantity of unshelved volumes must have been gradual. It is known from a document headed 'Order and position of presses' which covers the whole library and was drawn up on 23 May 1892, that only the presses below the lofty gallery in the Music Room (see plate 1) were assigned to music.[23] Even in March 1884 there were 170 presses of music, containing 13,870 volumes on 1381 shelves.[24]

Pressure on shelf-space reflected increased accessions, which in turn caused a substantial increase in the size of the catalogue.[25] In 1850 Oliphant left it ready in 57 volumes—45 of music and 12 of words—containing together just over 31,000 entries. By the late 1880s, it had grown more than six-fold, to over 320 volumes of music in all, containing about 165,000 entries, and some 70 volumes of words containing over 25,000 entries. This had entailed very extensive relaying, all of which, as the monthly returns show, had been done in Evans's time. Some economy of shelf-room had been achieved by reducing the number of copies of the catalogue from three to two: this seems to have happened by about the end of 1878.[26]

These difficulties were of course identical with those of the General Catalogue of Printed Books, but on a much smaller scale. In 1882 Richard Garnett (who was to succeed Bullen as Keeper in 1890) stated[27] that in 1875 this catalogue occupied 2000 volumes, and was expected to grow to 9000 by the end of the century, which would have been impossibly cumbrous in both the Reading Room and the staff working areas. The solution approved by the Trustees in 1880 and blessed by the Treasury (with whom the matter had been discussed some time earlier) was to substitute print for transcription, and at the same time to publish a revision of the entire catalogue. This, the first since 1819, began to appear in 1881. Exactly the same decision was reached with the Catalogue of Maps, which was issued complete in two volumes in 1884. But the music catalogues, because of their greater size and complexity, and the relatively small staff available, could not be treated in the same way. Publication entire and revision were quite impracticable, but at least printing could be introduced.

In July 1883 Evans sent Bullen a report on the state of his arrears and added to it an illuminating statement of the costs of printing compared with those of transcription, as follows:

July 6 1883
I beg to report that the number of titles written for
the Music Catalogue during the last two years and now

awaiting transcription amounts to about 20,000. These titles represent the greater part of the musical works received under the English and International Copyright Acts during the years 1881 and 1882 besides a large number of works acquired by purchase many of which are of considerable importance.

As it is desirable that the Catalogue should be kept up to date as nearly as possible, I beg to apply for the services of a Writer, in order that the transcription may proceed without further delay.

I am,

Sir,

Your obedient servant,

Charles J Evans

Comparative Cost of Printing and Transcription

Printing a sheet of 8 pages in double column costs £3.1
A sheet will contain about 130 Music Titles
20,000 Titles require 77 sheets

$$£3.1 \times 77 = £234.17$$

A Writer working 7 hours a day will transcribe 100 Titles
20,000 Titles will require 200 days
His payment at 10d. per hour is 5s.10d.

$$5.10 \times 200 = £58.6.8.$$

Cost of material	20
„ mounting	40
	118.6.8.

Cost of Printing	£234.17	
„ Transcription	£118. 6.8.	
Difference	£116.10.4.	

Bullen obtained the sanction of the Trustees to proceed with printing in December 1883, and in his report increased Evans's estimate of the arrears from 20,000 for two years to

25,000 for three! The first Accession Part which Evans sent to press consisted, however, not of music, but of entries for the catalogue of words (plate 4).[28] The first Accession Part of music followed later in 1884. When ultimately the entries for music were incorporated, it produced a very odd, and rather complicated catalogue for the readers to use, because the two different elements in it gradually became grouped in three different ways. Many folios bore solely transcribed entries, and these still exist intact in many nineteenth century headings today (plate 5).[29] In these the sequence obviously ran from the top to the bottom of the page. This was also the principle governing those folios which ultimately consisted solely of new printed entries divided, by a vertical pencilled line, into two columns (plate 6). But there were also many folios on which both printed and manuscript entries appeared (plate 7). Here, two columns were impracticable, and whenever printed entries were intercalated with one or more transcribed entries, the resulting sequence was intended to be read across the page.

The new process of printing the accessions must have entailed a considerable extra burden for Evans and his small staff. But he seems to have kept most of the routine going as he had in earlier years. Although Evans worked at a time when music was more liberally treated in the department than ever before, to the outsider it still seemed to leave a lot to be desired. On 3 December 1877 the eminent music antiquarian and collector William Hayman Cummings (1831-1915) read a paper to the Musical Association entitled 'The formation of a national musical library'[30] He drew attention to the defects of the catalogues of printed and manuscript music in the British Museum, and to the supposed lack of any policy for acquisition. Cummings said plaintively: 'Music appears to have been regarded by the Trustees as a very poor relation of very little consequence, and therefore but just tolerated, with a distinct understanding that as little money as possible should be spent on her'. This was clearly based on inadequate information, and he went on to admit that the museum's holdings were of such unique quality that they ought to be expanded to form a collection worthy of the nation.

A rambling, confused discussion followed the paper, in which a number of eminent gentlemen talked inaccurate nonsense. Among them were William Chappell, who reminded the meeting that the very existence of a catalogue of the printed music in the British Museum was due to his efforts in 1841, and Edward Augustus Bond, the then Keeper of Manuscripts, who referred to Oliphant as 'Keeper of the manuscripts': 'he offered to make a catalogue and his offer was accepted'! Grove, who was in the chair, talked sense and pleaded for a 'temperate' memorial to be submitted to the Trustees, and the following motion was passed: 'That the Council be requested to prepare a memorial to the trustees of the British Museum, calling their attention to the deficiencies and imperfections in the collection of manuscript and printed music and musical literature in that museum, and the great want of an indexed catalogue and other means of more ready reference than at present exist'.

On 14 June 1878 Bullen wrote to the Principal Librarian, Winter Jones, making a detailed reply to all the points in the association's memorial. The letter deserves to be quoted in full because of the light it sheds on Evans's work, and on the department's attitude to music. It also furnishes details of policy which would otherwise be quite unknown:

Dear Mr Jones,
   . . . On the suggestions contained in the Memorial I beg to remark:—
   1. That for the last few years, every effort has been made to enlarge and improve the Music Collection. In

1874 the sale catalogues of the principal music sellers throughout Europe were procured, including even those of Russia and Spain, and a large and important selection was made. Many hundreds of works have since been purchased at public auctions by our agent, who regularly attends every sale of interest, and a large number from private dealers. About 4,000 new works are obtained annually under the Copyright Act, and about 3,000 through International Copyright, including nearly all important foreign works. The Music Collection now comprises above 17,000 volumes, containing about 75,000 works. As a test of its completeness, in the present year 376 Nos in Lonsdale's auction of old English music were marked for examination, and only 39 were found not to be in the Museum. Also, from Cohn's catalogue of rare music, out of 138 Nos examined 35 only were wanting, of which 31 were subsequently purchased.

2. The Museum already possesses a special Catalogue of Music, and has had one for many years. In the year 1858 it consisted of only 22 vols, it now comprises 372 vols, containing about 185,000 entries. It employs the services of two cataloguers and two copyists, and at least 10,000 new entries are made annually.

It is true that there is still a considerable arrear of titles to be transcribed in the Catalogue, but this is owing to the want of Transcribers, none having been appointed for some time past to fill vacancies. Recently, however, a number of copyists have been employed to fill their places and there is, consequently, no doubt that in a short time the arrear of untranscribed titles will be cleared off.

Works on musical literature are not included in this division, but are to be found in the New General Catalogue.

3. With respect to the printing of the Music Catalogue I cordially approve of the suggestion made by the Musical Association that this should be done, and I venture to hope that the Trustees will give it their sanction.

With reference to the paper by Mr Cummings I beg to observe that:—

Whatever remissness in former times there may have been in the interests of the Music Collection, for years past it has received a due amount of attention. Every auction catalogue is carefully examined, dealers in printed music are encouraged in offering works for sale, and nothing worthy of acquisition is rejected. With regard to the instances cited by Mr Cummings, Mr Oliphant did propose offering his library for sale to the Trustees; but on examination it was found to contain so many duplicates of works already in the Library, that it was not deemed advisable to purchase it as a whole. Mr Oliphant then consented to a selection being made, and this was actually in progress at the time of his death. At the ensuing sale, however, the Museum purchased no fewer than 152 works, many of great rarity.

The Sterndale Bennett library consisted entirely of ordinary works, most, if not all of which are in the Museum.

At the Rimbault sale our agent attended with a duly marked & priced catalogue, and made several purchases; but, owing to a large American commission, the prices were so high that he did not feel justified in buying the lots marked.

In conclusion it may be stated that all Music sent to the Museum is available for Readers within one week of its reception, and that every assistance is afforded to students in their researches. During the time that I was Superintendent of the Reading Room, I frequently called in the aid of Mr Evans, the Assistant in charge of the Music Collection, to answer the enquiries of Readers on musical subjects, and that practice is still continued by my successor, Mr Garnett.'

One or two matters require brief comment. The figure of 22 volumes given for the size of the catalogue in 1858 is clearly an error (see p175). The statement about the lack of Transcribers suggests that this grade was being reduced as the time for printing the accessions to the General Catalogue drew near. Bullen's hope that the Trustees would sanction the printing of the music catalogue was destined, as will be seen, to be hope deferred for many years. Finally, it is worth noting that the speed with which music could be made available to readers—within seven days of reception—has never been approached since. As it could not possibly have been catalogued in that time, this statement must imply that Evans had devised some system of temporary alphabetical filing, presumably under the name of composer or editor, by means of which any piece requested could be easily produced.

As has been indicated, Evans continued to build up the collections for six years after the memorial was submitted to the Trustees. All through this time he had been remarkably healthy, as the departmental records of sick-leave show, but in late November 1884 he fell ill with acute bronchitis. He died on December 8, in his home at 150 King's Road, Chelsea, when just forty-five years old. Normally, he would have continued in charge of the music for another fourteen years, until he became 60, in 1899, perhaps even continuing into the early years of the twentieth century. On the other hand, there are one or two reports written by Evans and dating from the late 1870s, which deal with other matters than music. This suggests that his undoubted ability might possibly have induced Bullen ultimately to move him back to the general library, as had happened with Roy. At all events, Evans's early death was a very severe loss. For some seventeen years he had dedicated himself zealously to the collections of printed music, to their great benefit. It is not too much to say that without his zeal, his successor's task would have been far more difficult than it was.

NOTES

1 So stated by Roy himself, in his letter of 1846, and in the Trustees' Archives, applying for promotion to Transcriber.

2 Frederic Boase, *Modern English biography*, Truro, 1892, vol 3, col 335. 'Rolandi' was probably P Rolandi, the well-known bookseller of 20, Berners Street, who had many dealings with Panizzi.

3 Panizzi Papers, 1849-50, f349.

4 Panizzi Papers, 1849-50, f454. These Papers, 1851, f131 foll, show that Cooke, as a reader, soon had a heated argument with Panizzi.

5 Standing Committee, 12 March 1853, p8525.

6 Original Papers, vol 49.

7 Panizzi Papers, 1853, f145, 150.

8 He does not seem to have been a member of the main line of the musical Bachs, nor was he apparently any relation of Edmund Bach, who was appointed Assistant to the Superintendent of the Reading Room in January 1838, and transferred to Printed Books in February 1842. He worked there as a specialist in German until his death on 21 October 1848. (Notes in Oldman papers. See also Cowtan, p362, 363).

9 Officers' Reports, no 122. Department of Printed Books, 3 February 1853.

10 Cowtan, p423.

11 Cowtan, p424, gives this information, and says that Kemp was 'a musician all his life-time, and . . . an able violinist'. His work as a music cataloguer is corroborated by the identity of his handwriting on title-slips dating from these years with his signed returns written after he became a Second Class Assistant in charge of the Copyright Office in 1864.

12 Roy died in 14 August 1884, of heart disease. See the *Athenaeum*, 23 August 1884, p237.

13 Robert Elkin, *Royal Philharmonic*, London, [1946], p136. Clarke is also mentioned by Myles Birket Foster, *The history of the Philharmonic Society*, London, 1912, where his name is twice given hyphenated, 'Campbell-Clarke'.

14 The Minutes of the Directors' Meetings (Department of Manuscripts, BL, Loan 48/2) show that Clarke began his duties as Secretary on 3 December 1864 and ended them with the Meeting of 29 June 1866. Clearly, he only told the Trustees after his appointment. In this context it should be remembered that in the British Museum throughout the nineteenth century any outside office—even that discharged by a clergyman working almost whole time on the staff and wishing to preach an occasional Sunday sermon—could only be held subject to the approval of the Trustees.

15 Cowtan, p424, says this was due to ill-health, and this is confirmed by Clarke's letter of resignation, 9 June 1870 (Original Papers, vol 4, May-June 1870. Reg no 6321), in which he stated that he suffered 'from some functional derangement of the heart'. In February 1870 Clarke had taken an extended vacation near Nice, with a 'Mr Prowse', perhaps William Prowse, a partner in the famous music publishing firm Keith, Prowse & Co. Clarke's career over the next thirty-two years was remarkable. He became Paris correspondent of *The daily telegraph* in 1872, and served as a member

of the jury for the Paris exhibitions of 1879 and 1889. He wrote plays, and was a noted art collector. He held seven foreign orders, was a member of the Athenaeum, the Garrick Club and the Reform Club, and was knighted in 1897. He died in 1902.

16 *Modern English biography*, Truro, 1892, vol 1, col 1001. Boase also states that Evans was a contributor to the first edition of Grove's *Dictionary*, but his name does not appear in the lists of them.

17 In three volumes and four miscellaneous collections, comprising programmes, accounts, photographs, cartoons, a manuscript catalogue of music and the like; pressmark K.5.e.1-7. Vol 2, f16r has a photograph of Evans as a young man.

18 It remained in the General Library for many years. The incorporators working on the General Catalogue in the 1920s and 1930s (including the present writer) had much help from a binder's man named J Richbell, who arranged and numbered the titles for the monthly Accession Parts sent to the printer, checked all cross-references for 'settled-queries', inserted the printed slips in batches ready for marking into the relevant volumes of the catalogue, and, like Kingston and his successors, was invaluable.

19 Minutes, Reports, Letters, etc, Supplementary volume (nd). Evans's letter is bound at the beginning of Section IV.

20 Ludwig Rosenthal of Munich, 1840-1928. (See Bernard M Rosenthal, 'Cartel, clan or dynasty? The Olschkis and the Rosenthals. 1859-1976', in *Harvard library bulletin*, vol xxv, no 4, Oct 1977, pp381-398.) But on 26 September 1904 he sold to the museum for only £2.10s. the unique and highly important fragment of a broadside with music printed by John Rastell c1525.

21 Thomas Watts, Keeper from 1866 to 1869.

22 In due course these alcoves were constructed and remained as part of the shelf-space of the Music Room (after

1922 the 'Old Music Room') until it was entirely rebuilt in 1936.

23 Reports, etc from 1893, vol 2, f20c. The gallery itself still contained the presses with their original numberings of 1838.

24 From a list drawn up in March 1884 by John R Anderson, a Senior Attendant, and bound with the estimates in the volume of reports, etc for 1882.

25 See appendix 3 for details.

26 The returns for one month, September 1880, mention *three* copies, but this seems to be a clerical error. The fourth copy shelf-list was apparently discontinued in the early 1880s, and was subsequently destroyed, at an unknown date, in order to save space. No trace of it now remains. The returns for 5 January 1879 mention a 'fourth copy' of the words catalogue, which is an odd contradiction in terms.

27 'Printing the British Museum Catalogue', in his *Essays in librarianship and bibliography*, 1899, p72.

28 This, and the second 'Words' part of 1886, comprising together some 4,500 entries, are the only surviving trace of that catalogue. The returns for 1886 show that in that year Squire incorporated barely 200 of these printed entries. For the subsequent history of the words catalogue, see pp78, 148.

29 These transcribed entries are now (1979) gradually being replaced by typed copies. The only other place in the Department of Printed Books where transcribed entries are found is in the Map Library, where a catalogue of charts in this form is still in use. In the Department of Manuscripts, the catalogue of the Sloane MSS 1091-1598 is still in use in its original transcribed form. (Its entries were, however, written on sheets, and not on moveable slips.) See T C Skeat, *The catalogues of the manuscript collections in the British Museum*, 1951, p4.

30 *Proceedings*, Session 4, 1877-78, pp13-26.

4

SQUIRE:
THE CATALOGUE AND THE SUCCESSION
1885 to 1908

BULLEN QUICKLY asked the Trustees to fill the vacancy caused by Evans's death, but the matter did not go as he wished. The minutes, which he received on 17 January 1885, give the bare outline of what happened.

> Assistant in place of Mr Evans, deceased.
>
> 1 With reference to Trustees' Minute of 13th December authorising the filling up of the vacancy for an Assistant caused by the death of Mr Evans, the Principal Librarian made enquiry of Mr Bullen as to the qualifications specially required, Mr Evans having for many years taken charge of the cataloguing of music in the Dept of Printed Books.
>
> 2 Letter from Mr Bullen, 14 January, recommending that an Assistant already on the staff, Mr Birch-Reynardson, be entrusted with the duties formerly discharged by Mr Evans: the appointment of a specialist from outside being, in his opinion, unnecessary.
>
> Resolved, that it is preferable to apply for a specialist.

Fortunately, this can be amplified from other sources. But first, the rejected candidate deserves brief mention. Herbert Frederick Birch-Reynardson, educated at Eton and Christ Church, had entered the department as a Second-Class Assistant on 24 February 1883. He had some talent as a composer. Between 1880 and 1892 there were published five of his single songs, one group of seven songs, and one group of Sussex folk songs which he edited. In December 1883, a

111

list of Assistants' duties mentions that he was engaged part-time in cataloguing music. Apart from these meagre facts, nothing is known of his work or of his general musical capacities, and there is no way of judging whether Bullen's recommendation of him would have been justified. Birch-Reynardson developed weak lungs, and retired on grounds of ill-health on 12 October 1889.

It was unusual for the Trustees to over-rule a Keeper in a matter of the succession to a specialist post. What Bullen did not know whas that Squire, Evans's destined successor, happened to be already waiting in the wings. Bond, the Principal Librarian, certainly knew this, and had probably told the Trustees informally without delay. The papers relating to Squire's application are preserved in the Trustees' Archives, and establish the remarkable chronology of events. Squire, who had had a ticket of admission to the Reading Room since April 1878, wrote to Bond on 27 September 1884, asking if there was a vacancy for which he might apply. In his letter he said he was 'well known' to Grove [1] and Colvin [2] and went on: 'by the death of my father, I found myself at liberty to follow what I have always regarded as my special subject, the study of music and musical literature'. There is no note of Bond's reply, which was presumably in the negative.

Then Evans died, as we have seen, on 8 December. Squire must have heard of this very quickly, for he took speedy action. On 11 December Grove wrote to Bond, strongly recommending Squire, and describing him as 'a good scholar, an accurate man, a gentle man and a well conditioned person'. On the very same day, Arthur Duke Coleridge (grand-nephew of the poet, and a founder of the Bach choir) wrote on Squire's behalf to Arthur Wellesley Peel (later Viscount Peel), Speaker of the House of Commons and one of the Principal Trustees. Fortified by an introduction from Colvin, Squire

called to see Bond on 12 December, and sent further testimonials on the 16th.[3] Not long after this, Bond asked
Bullen, whom obviously he kept in the dark, about the
necessary qualifications for the post, and on 14 January the
latter recommended Birch-Reynardson. Bullen can hardly
have been pleased with the manner and timing of the Trustees'
rebuff.

Once Squire's appointment was approved, extraordinary
steps were taken to get him in quickly, partly because of the
lapse of time since Evans's death, and partly because Squire
was, at 30, well beyond the normal age of entry. The minutes
of 14 November 1885 read:

Appointments by Principal Trustees of
I. Assistants, Second Class.
  Mr William Barclay Squire
                         12 October
  Dept of Printed Books — to take charge of music
collections, in succession to late Mr C J Evans.
Mem
  Mr Squire was specially certified by Civil Service
Commissioners under clause 7 of Order in Council of
4 June 1870, as sanctioned by Treasury letter of 30 July
1885.
                 Mr Squire. Assistant.
Letter from Mr Bullen, 12 November, with enclosure
from Mr Squire, Assistant, asking permission to come
at 10 o'clock, instead of 9, during probationary year of
service.
  Mr Bullen recommends that the request be granted.
Mem
  Mr Squire has entered the Trustees' service under
special circumstances, being already trained to his work.
Allowed.

Squire made his request barely ten days after he began work, on 3 November. Clearly, even as a young man, he could exercise considerable powers of persuasion. So began a new era in the history of the collections of printed music. But it is worth remembering that Squire would never have entered the service of the Trustees at all if Evans had lived to work until 1899. For by then Squire would have been forty-four and well advanced in his profession.

William Barclay Squire was born in London on 16 October 1855, and was first educated privately, then at a school in Isleworth sponsored by the Prince Consort. Later, he was sent to Frankfurt-on-Main to learn German.[4] In 1875 he entered Pembroke College, Cambridge, where he read history, and graduated with third-class honours in 1879. At one time, he had considered taking holy orders, but changed his mind, and joined a firm of solicitors in 1883. At Cambridge, he fostered his strong interest in music through friendship with Stanford[5] and J A Fuller-Maitland[6], who later married one of his sisters. It was doubtless through one of these men that Squire's evident gift for musical research became known to Grove. For his *Dictionary of music* Squire wrote nearly sixty articles between 1879 and 1884, half his ultimate total contribution.

By the time he entered the Museum Squire[7] certainly enjoyed repute as a musicologist, largely through the articles he had written for Grove's *Dictionary* and for the *Dictionary of national biography*. But in what sense he was 'already trained for the work', as the Trustees' minutes stated, is rather obscure.[8] In 1878 he had been librarian to the Cambridge Musical Society, but this could not have given him very wide experience. Before he started work in the Music Room, he must presumably have received some instruction in cataloguing, but the name of his mentor is unrecorded. Squire was, however, a born cataloguer. His first task was to overtake the arrears of music, both those which had accumulated since Evans's death and whatever the latter had left on one side during his last busy years. The state of progress is shown clearly in the table in appendix 4. The totals of titles written in 1884 and 1885 were the lowest recorded since 1861.

Evans had done little cataloguing in the eleven months before his death, because of the burden of proof-reading. It is recorded that Birch-Reynardson was again engaged temporarily on music at the end of 1884, but obviously Squire was faced with a mass of copyright music. There were also some useful purchases awaiting him. One notable invoice, of 14 February 1885, from Asher of Berlin, included the 1545 Wittenberg Hymn Book and Schein's *Cantional*, 1645. In 1886 Squire wrote 18,335 titles, not far below Evans's highest total of 1871 (20,080). In 1889, however, the total reached 27,031 titles, reflecting the benefit of some assistance, which proved however all too transitory.[9] Squire also had the loyal help of John Lister, a binder's man who was seconded to the department a little before 1885, and, like Kingston before him, and Kingston's unknown successor, was responsible for all pressmarking, care of titles, and presumably filing of unbound music.[10]

Squire also took great pains to acquaint himself with the collections. At the end of 1886 he submitted a report [11] in which he wrote as follows:

> During the past years the Music Collection has been carefully examined and partly re-arranged, the most valuable works being removed from the shelves and placed in glazed cases under lock and key. By this means increased space has been obtained and several extremely valuable works have been found, the possession of which by the British Museum had apparently

been overlooked. The most important of these discoveries has been that of no less than twelve works printed at Venice and Fossombrone by Ottaviano dei Petrucci between 1503 and 1519. The books of this printer are of extreme rarity and the possession of so large a number places the collection in the first rank among European musical Libraries.

In what sense the Petruccis had been 'overlooked', it is hard to see. Reference to Oliphant's shelf-list shows that eleven of them were entered in it, and that only one, the superius part of *Missae de Orto*, was retrieved by Squire from somewhere in the General Library. (It bears no previous museum pressmark, and has a black 'lozenge' stamp, probably indicative of uncertain provenance.) Evans had presumably left the Petruccis as Oliphant placed them, because there were no glazed cases at his disposal. Squire went on to point out that the complete edition of Palestrina, issued at Ratisbon since 1862, had now been purchased. He then enumerated some very important recent antiquarian purchases—two Portuguese treatises by Matheo de Arauda (1533 and 1535), early editions of masses by Porta and Palestrina, motets by Gombert, some lute tablatures, a fine collection of 111 volumes printed by Phalèse, and Beethoven's sonatas Wo047 (Spire, 1783).[12]

The next fourteen years were to see a growing wealth of similar purchases, equal numerically to what Evans had achieved, and distinctly exceeding it in quality. Only a representative selection can be mentioned here. In 1888 Squire bought madrigals by Merulo, Marenzio and Gabrieli. The single acquisitions for 1889 included Byrd's masses in 3, 4 and 5 parts, and Gerle, *Tablatur auff die Laudten* (1533), while in April of that year Leo Liepmannsohn (apparently the earliest appearance of this famous Berlin firm in the museum's papers) offered a variety of early theoretical works and liturgies. From the same source a year later came Narvaez, *Delphin de música* (1538). On 13 April Squire bought from Baron Hugh Bludowsky of Vienna some early Venetian madrigals, and on 14 June, from G Linnell of London, the c1615 issue of *Parthenia* and some Monteverdi part-books. In 1891 Richard Bertling of Dresden offered a complete copy of Praetorius's *Syntagma musicum* and a copy of J S Bach's *Clavier-Übung* part 2 corrected by the composer. In 1894 one batch of treasures from the Borghese library was offered by Liepmannsohn and another by Ludwig Rosenthal, while Leo Olschki of Florence provided a copy of the superbly printed Masses of Soriano, book 1, 1609, sumptuously bound for Pope Paul V. Squire acquired four Petruccis—one on 14 July 1894 from Howell Wills (the *Motetti de Passione* of 1503), and on 9 November 1896 three books of masses from Bludowsky (those of Alexander Agricola, 1503, of Jean de Orto, 1505— the bassus part—, and of Gasper, 1506). From Liepmannsohn again, in 1895, came forty-three important compositions of the sixteenth and seventeenth centuries—Landi, Sabbatini, Verdelot, Willaert, Caccini, Schütz and Ingegnieri. In the same year Squire himself presented 253 miscellaneous pieces from the library of his close friend Sir George Scharf (Keeper of the National Portrait Gallery), who had bequeathed them to him. 1896 brought Cohn's offer of a score of rarities from the Borghese and Heredia collections. One of the great jewels of all Squire's acquisitions, on 11 June 1897, for £75, was Cavazzoni, *Recerchari* (1523), besides which only one other, imperfect, copy is now recorded. In 1898 he reported the purchase of 236 sets of part-books of madrigals and motets. All this, on top of single-handed routine work (except from April 1888 to May 1890), must have taken up a lot of time in correspondence and reporting. Throughout the early 1900s, the stream of fine purchases continued, though on a diminishing level—some more Petruccis, for example, various parts of two famous publications of John Day, *Certaine notes* (1560) and *Mornyng and Evenyng Prayer* (1565) and numerous rare theoretical works. It was a truly remarkable sustained effort.

As a way of making these treasures better known, the Trustees decided in 1899 on a kind of trial run, and published a special Accessions Part devoted to music printed before 1800 and acquired, according to the preface, since 1885. It also contained, as the preface also said, some reprints of previous entries, and titles of theoretical works, such as a few Gaforis, transferred to the Music Room from the General Library. But while this publication marks a superb achievement in the intensification of the policy of acquisition begun by Squire's predecessors, it was not an isolated phenomenon. For in fact it represented an aspect of the two main preoccupations of the early and middle years of Squire's career—how to get part, at least, of the music catalogue published, and how to find—and keep—the staff essential to him. 'My only assistance', he reported in December 1887, 'is a binder's man'. This was to remain largely true for the next thirteen years.

As already mentioned, the question of publication was raised in 1878 by the memorial received from the Musical Association, of which Squire can hardly have been unaware. But all such questions were governed by rapid developments in the department as a whole, which may appropriately be summarised here. The decision to print and publish the entire General Catalogue of Printed Books from 1881 onwards affected the work of the department for two decades, for it became a priority which made heavy demands on the time and energy of the staff, and restricted their employment for special purposes. This immense task was well under way when Squire entered the museum in 1885, and gathered pace until the final supplementary volume appeared in 1905. As the General Catalogue was phased out, other postponed or starved projects were taken up. Such were the catalogue of the Thomason Tracts, the Catalogue of Incunabula, and work on the Subject Index. Consequently, the competition for staff within the department was intense, as Squire discovered early in his career. This was especially so in a subject like music, which, however fine the collections, lacked the status of maps, which included the King's Topographical Collection.[13] In spite of Squire's great and growing reputation, music in general, and particularly printed music, long remained not quite respectable in the eyes of authority. Cummings's words (p102) were echoed in different terms, as late as 1904, by Sir Edward Maunde Thompson, the Director and Principal Librarian[14] who, when interviewing the young J V Scholderer on the first day of his service, told him that 'too many of the staff wasted their time on music and such-like flummery'.[15] Indeed, even after this, in April 1919, Squire said, when looking back on his career: 'It was always understood that music was not to be encouraged'.[16] It was long before music became accepted as a suitable subject for scholarly study in England, and this attitude was reflected by the relatively modest status of the libraries serving its needs.

It was within this tradition that Squire began his campaign for more staff. In December 1887 Bullen submitted to the Trustees three proposals from him, 'for printing the catalogue of music in the museum library'. Squire suggested first 'a simplification of the system of cataloguing music'; second, 'the printing of the catalogue of authors of words in the form of an index to the General Catalogue of Music'; third, 'printing a catalogue of music published before 1800'. Squire pointed out that a complete revision of the catalogue was necessary, because it had been begun 'on too large a scale' (whatever that may mean), and kept up by insufficient staff (which was rather unfair to Evans). The 'simplification' which he proposed was just not to catalogue most of the music received by copyright, but to shelve it, space permitting, in such a way as to be readily available. This would presumably have lasted only as long as it took to prepare the pre-1800 catalogue. Squire estimated that two to three years would be needed to deal with a probable total of some 40,000 entries.

For the catalogue of words, Squire submitted an additional, separate report, which was accompanied by a specimen page (now, unfortunately, not traceable), and an estimate from Clowes which worked out at £4.13.0 per sheet for 250 copies, or £5.2.6. for 500 copies. Squire thought that the whole index would be complete in about 40 sheets, presumably using a small type, and that the 58 volumes of the transcribed entries, plus the two printed accession parts, would be reduced to two. (The catalogue of words was never mentioned again.) Bullen's report ended thus: 'Mr Squire asks for the help of an additional skilled assistant to the catalogue accessions &c. Mr Bullen recommends the proposals to the favourable consideration of the Trustees'. On 10 December the report was minuted: 'Consideration postponed'. Clearly the magnitude of the proposals caused some concern.

Nevertheless, they were not fruitless. On 14 January 1888 Bullen returned to the charge and repeated his request for an assistant, and the Treasury conceded the post. On 29 February Bullen took the very unusual step of sending to Bond a letter (drafted entirely in Squire's hand), of which the first part reads as follows:

> Mr T W Bourne, B A of New College, Oxford, who is a candidate for the post of Assistant in the Printed Books Department, with the special view to his being employed on the music catalogue, is strongly recommended on

account of his general acquaintance with music and his special knowledge of early music and musical literature, by Dr J H Mee, of Merton College, (President of the University Musical Union and one of the chief contributors to Sir George Grove's Dictionary of Music), and by Mr C H Lloyd, organist of Christchurch [*sic*], Oxford.

Besides their testimonials, Squire also mentioned a letter written to Russell Martineau (then an Assistant Keeper in the Department) by no less a person than Friedrich Chrysander, stating 'that he has chosen Mr Bourne as his collaborator in part of the work of the Handel Society'. Thomas William Bourne, who had been educated at Shrewsbury, and whose degree was a third class in Classical Moderations, was duly appointed and entered the department on 14 April 1888. It was doubtless his work which contributed to the total (already mentioned) of 27,031 titles written in 1889. Perhaps because of the initial help that Bourne gave Squire, Garnett, who was Bullen's senior Assistant Keeper, was emboldened to express optimism in public. For in October 1888 Garnett wrote an article in *The universal review* on 'The past present and future of the British Museum Catalogue', [17] in which *à propos* of its being printed, he said: 'The four hundred and fifty MS volumes of the catalogue of music, it is hoped, are on the eve of undergoing similar treatment'.

But all Squire's hopes, and Garnett's, were soon to be dashed. For on 28 May 1890 Bourne resigned. No reason was given when the matter was reported to the Trustees on 14 June: presumably he found the work boring. Bourne, who lived until 1948, seems to have retired into private life. Though no cooperation with Chrysander is known, he himself edited and published the orchestral parts of Handel's *Messiah* (no vocal score is recorded), *Nisi Dominus* (the first complete edition, 1898), and *Psalm 42* (1900, in the preface to which he mentions Chrysander as 'so great a friend'). Bourne also edited *Three fugues* (1937), wrongly ascribed to Frescobaldi—in fact by Gottlieb Muffat—and published two compositions of his own for organ, *Three fugues* (1896) and an *Introduction and fugue* (1901).

After reporting Bourne's resignation, Garnett wrote to the Principal Librarian, Maunde Thompson, on 6 June recommending 'that the vacancy should not be filled by the appointment of an assistant, but that a person of lower status should be engaged who could perform the mechanical work of incorporating slips into the Music Catalogue, and who should be competent to assist in clerical labour, as checking bills, entering books for the binder, making out donation lists, &c'. The Trustees' minute read: 'Referred to the special sub-committee appointed to consider the present condition and future prospects of the existing establishment of assistants in the British Museum'. Unfortunately, although the sub-committee approved in principle the employment of 'a person of lower status', no action followed, and the idea was dropped as a practical proposition for ten years. The designation 'of lower status' simply meant 'non-graduate'.

But the idea was not entirely forgotten. On 12 June 1891, Garnett wrote again to Maunde Thompson, setting out Squire's needs in the context of the department in general:

> I enclose a letter which I have received from Mr Barclay Squire respecting the condition of the music catalogue. The ordinary work upon this catalogue is, from the cause pointed out, necessarily in an unsatisfactory state, and the printed catalogue directed by the Trustees to be undertaken is, of course, entirely in abeyance. Mr Squire refrains from alluding to his own exertions. The fact is that he works much harder than he is fit to do

and I am in constant apprehension of the break-down of
his health, which would throw everything into hopeless
arrears. I have endeavoured to help him by letting him
have Mr England's services occasionally: but in the state
of general work arising from the recent transfer of two
assistants to other departments, and the ten unfilled
vacancies, very little assistance can be afforded. The
arrears which existed when I became Keeper remain
untouched, and threaten to be greatly increased by the
recent acquisitions of tracts and pamphlets, which are
as troublesome to catalogue as larger books.

Garnett continued by saying he was not against filling the
vacancies 'by persons of an inferior grade', and went on: 'it
is of course a sine qua non that [one of the two vacancies]
should be filled by one person able to assist Mr Squire, to
whose recommendation that Mr England should be employed
upon the music I am unable to assent in the present state of
the department'. Garnett ended by expressing his fear that
'we shall drift into a condition of chronic arrear and ineffi-
ciency'.

It is ironical to find that even if Squire had secured the
whole-time assistance of 'Mr England' and pinned his faith
on him, his hopes would have been dashed again. For Paul
England, to give him his full name, developed other ambi-
tions. Educated at Queen Elizabeth Grammar School,
Crediton, and Christ's College, Cambridge, he had entered
the British Museum as a Second Class Assistant on 15 May
1887, but resigned in August 1891. He then studied singing
in Germany, became well known as a singer and teacher, and
added to his reputation by translating numerous song texts
from French, German and Italian. He published a few songs
of his own, and died in 1932.

It seems unlikely that Squire received any assistance in the 1890s. Nevertheless, as appendix 4 shows, the output of titles remained quite high and he must have worked very hard. Garnett was certainly right to be concerned about Squire's health. In 1894 he contracted scarlet fever; in 1899 'throat disease and bronchitis'; in 1909 he had a long course of medical treatment for an unspecified illness, and in 1910 underwent the then fashionable appendectomy which entailed three months' absence. He needed all the leave he could get, and having private means was able to take unpaid leave as well—14 days in July 1889 to study the Trent Codices 'apparently proving the invention of counterpoint by Dunstable'(!); three weeks in 1892 for research in the Biblioteca Estense, again in connection with Dunstable as the 'inventor of counterpoint'; and an unspecified period in October 1896 to visit Delphi, during a Greek holiday, to study newly discovered inscriptions relating to music.[18]

Despite the pressures of work in the museum, Squire still had reserves of energy for other tasks. In June 1894 Garnett reported that he had received an invitation to catalogue the printed music in the Royal College of Music. This task was to engage much of Squire's leisure for the next fifteen years. He used to visit the college regularly on the way back from the museum to his home in South Kensington. The fine catalogue ultimately appeared in 1909, and amounted to 368 pages, double column. He then began work at once on a catalogue of the college's manuscripts, which engaged him intermittently until 1926; it was issued in four typed copies in 1931. In 1903 he issued a small, but valuable catalogue of the printed and manuscript music in Westminster Abbey. He also found time to write scholarly articles in periodicals, contributed some excellent musical criticism to several London journals, and did much important editing of early music, notably the Fitzwilliam Virginal Book, which he published in collaboration with J A Fuller-Maitland.

During the early 1890s Squire must have given renewed thought to the increasing problem of the music catalogue. There are extant two proposals in his hand, which show how his mind was working. The first, dated February 1896, deserves quotation in full:

The music-catalogue at present consists of 314 volumes, each averaging some 100 folios of printed and transcribed titles. Having regard to the small value of the greater part of the musical works catalogued, it is hardly advisable to go to the very large expense of printing the whole catalogue as it stands. A selection from it, however, might be well printed and would be likely to be of general use and interest. This selection could in the first instance take the form of printed copies of the most voluminous and important headings, leaving the early music, which forms the most valuable portion of the collection, to be dealt with in a separate manner at some future time. The following is a list of the headings (with the approximate amount of space they occupy) which it would be advisable to have in print:

Abt	2	volume(s)
Auber	$1\frac{1}{4}$	,,
Bach family	$\frac{3}{4}$	,,
Balfe	1	,,
Beethoven	2	,,
Bellini	$1\frac{3}{4}$	,,
Bishop	1	,,
Callcott family	1	,,
Donizetti	3	,,,
Glover (S)	$1\frac{1}{3}$	,,
Gluck	$\frac{1}{4}$	,,
Gounod	2	,,
Handel	2	,,

Haydn	$1\frac{1}{2}$	volume(s)
Hook	$1\frac{1}{2}$	,,
A Leduc	1	,,
Linley family	1	,,
Macfarren	1	,,
Mendelssohn	2	,,
Meyerbeer	2	,,
Mozart	3	,,
Offenbach	1	,,
Richards (B)	1	,,
Rossini	$2\frac{1}{2}$	,,
Schubert	1	,,
Schumann (H)	$\frac{3}{4}$	,,
Smart (G T) & (H)	1	,,
Verdi	4	,,
Wagner	$\frac{3}{4}$	,,
Wallace	1	,,
Weber	$1\frac{1}{2}$	,,

The printing of these headings would effect a large saving of space, and reduce the catalogue by some 40 or 50 volumes. It would be advisable to print the headings as much as possible in the same form as those of the General Catalogue, and also (wherever possible) to add to the lists of purely musical works the books &c relating to the various composers to be found under their names in the General Catalogue. In this way each heading would probably meet with considerable sale. It would be well to begin by printing headings of general interest, such as *Beethoven, Wagner, Mozart* or *Handel*; the ['simultaneous' added in 1897] publication of these would be likely to attract attention in the musical press & consequently to lead to a sale which might partly defray the cost of printing.

Wm Barclay Squire

Exactly a year later, Squire wrote another draft which was substantially the same as the above, but added a reference to the growing 'flood' of Americana, and mentioned the difficulty of identifying the source of excerpts and arrangements.

The basic ideas of these drafts were sound and ingenious. But it is rather curious that Squire, unconsciously echoing the opinion expressed by Oliphant in 1850, belittled the 'value of the greater part of the musical works catalogued'. (Ellis's view, expressed fifty-five years before—see p39— was far more judicious.) Though their musical value may have been slight, nineteenth century English publications contain much information of social interest, and are bibliographically useful for establishing dates on the basis of plate numbers and publishers' addresses. (Squire was himself a pioneer in the study of music publishers' numbers.) It also implies that trivial items issued before the end of 1800, which became his later dividing line for 'early' music, have an interest which is lacking in similar ones issued after that date. Moreover, while it was a sensible idea to start by selling three of the most important composers, it was surely unlikely that anyone who bought them would later wish also to buy, for instance, Leduc or Brinley Richards.

Neither plan was ever put to the Trustees: perhaps Squire was only flying a kite within the department, and in any case the plan was surely impracticable. But reflection did not essentially alter his mind. Two years later he returned to the charge, and Fortescue, his new Keeper, sent this report to the Trustees on 2 June 1899:

> Mr Fortescue has the honour to submit to the Trustees a proposal suggested by Mr Squire, to print separately a selection from the Music Catalogue consisting of a series of monographs of eminent Musical Composers, incorporating with the headings in the Music Catalogue

the titles of all the biographical and critical works relating to each composer from the General Catalogue, as well as lists of the Manuscript Music and the portraits in the Departments of Manuscripts and Prints and Drawings.

This plan would not merely reduce the great bulk of the existing Catalogue of Music, but would also bring into a useful and compressed compass the portion of that Catalogue which is most used by readers.

It would be desirable to issue each of these Monographs separately and if printed in a handy octavo form, Mr. Fortescue believes they would be fairly remunerative.

An estimate has been supplied by Messrs Clowes from which it appears that the cost of printing in the form of the accompanying specimen pages will be £3.16.0 per sheet for 250 copies and £4.3.6. for 500 copies.

The headings it is proposed to print are as follows:

Abt—2 vols [deleted]	Linley—1 vol [deleted]
Auber—1 vol 22 fol	Mendelssohn—2 vols
Bach—67 fol	Macfarren—1 vol
Balfe—1 vol	[deleted]
Beethoven—2 vols	Meyerbeer—2 vols
Bellini—1 vol 67 fol	Mozart—3 vols
Bishop—1 vol	Offenbach—1 vol
Callcott—1 vol [deleted]	Richards—1 vol [deleted]
Donizetti—3 vols	Rossini—$2\frac{1}{2}$ vols
Glover—$1\frac{1}{3}$ vols	Schubert—1 vol
[deleted]	Schumann—1 vol
Gluck—26 fol	Smart—80 fol [deleted]
Handel—2 vols	Verdi—4 vols
Haydn—$1\frac{1}{2}$ vols	Wagner—44 fol
Hook—$1\frac{1}{2}$ vols	Wallace—1 vol
[deleted]	Weber—$1\frac{1}{2}$ vols
Leduc—1 vol [deleted]	

Verdi (Giuseppe Fortunino Francesco)

H. 479 b / 51 [La Traviata] Parigi, o cara, duett. London [1856] fol.

Verdi (Giuseppe Fortunino Francesco)

H. 479 b / 47 [La Traviata] Bride of the ocean (Parigi, o cara) duett. The English words by C. Wyatt. London [1856] fol.

Verdi (Giuseppe Fortunino Francesco)

H. 479 b / 52 [La Traviata] Now the early morn, song (adapted to "Parigi o cara"). London [1856] fol.

Verdi (Giuseppe Fortunino Francesco)

H. 479 b / 46 [La Traviata] O lov'd Italie, duet (Parigi, o cara) written and arranged by G. Linley. London [18--] fol.

Verdi (Giuseppe Fortunino Francesco)

H. 479 b / 53 [La Traviata] Sweet is spring time after winter (Parigi o cara), duet, the poetry by D. Ryan. London [1856] fol.

Verdi (Giuseppe Fortunino Francesco)

H. 479 b / 44 [La Traviata] The merry swveyards, the favorite duet "Parigi o cara" from La Traviata, adapted to English words [begins: "Far from our native clime,"] by S. Williams. London [1857] fol.

Verdi (Giuseppe Fortunino Francesco)

H. 479 b / 50 [La Traviata] Night's gentle queen (Parigi o cara), duet [Begins: "Like a fair bride," written and arranged by E. Ellison]. London [1857] fol.

Plate 5: A page of transcribed entries in the Catalogue of Music printed after 1800.

If the Trustees should approve of the proposal, it would seem desirable to begin with Beethoven, Handel and Wagner, the simultaneous issue of which would be of sufficient importance to attract public attention and secure a good sale.

Apart from the deletion of the nine names as indicated, the proposal was rendered far more ambitious and complex because of the inclusion of the related material in the Departments of Manuscripts and of Prints and Drawings. It is also difficult to see how the idea of printing and selling these headings as separate books in octavo could be reconciled with the need to keep copies of them up to date within the framework of an expanding catalogue, as used in the department and by readers. But the Trustees approved the proposal, which is surprising, considering how unrealistic and ill thought-out it was, as Squire himself soon discovered. Apart from this, it never seems to have occurred to him to wonder how he could possibly prepare the catalogues unless he had reliable help with the routine work of cataloguing the current intake of music. In June 1899 no such help was in sight, nor had he reason to expect it. He could not possibly have then forseen that in little more than a year a new post would be allotted to him.

Progress in a large library such as the Department of Printed Books tends to be cyclical. An idea or a proposal is put forward, but the circumstances are unpropitious, or the conception is proved wrong, and the whole thing has to be dropped. But after a time circumstances change: the idea is revived, often in a better form, and it succeeds. So it was to be with the music catalogue, and so also it was now with the question of assistance for Squire. Some nine years after the proposal to employ a person 'of lower status', Fortescue reported to the Trustees on 10 July 1900 that there were three vacancies for Assistants in his department, two of which he proposed to retain: 'In the case of the third he is of the opinion that it would be to the advantage of the department to substitute for an Assistant a Second Division Clerk'. Fortescue continued: 'There is a considerable quantity of work such as the cataloguing of English books and music received by copyright which can be as efficiently performed by a Clerk as by an Assistant', so that the Assistant so replaced could be 'free to undertake cataloguing of a higher and more difficult class'. The Trustees liked the idea of this post because, as Fortescue pointed out, they could obtain for an Assistant's salary both a Clerk and an extra Commissionaire for warding in the King's Library, thus releasing an Attendant for work in the library.

Treasury sanction was sought and obtained, and on 3 September 1900 the clerkship created by this ingenious piece of bargaining was filled by William Charles Smith, who was transferred from the Scottish Education Department, having previously worked in the Inland Revenue.[19] Smith was educated at Woolwich High School from 1895 to 1898 and had studied the violin and pianoforte privately.[20] The reports on staff state that from 1900 to March 1903 he was engaged in cataloguing books as well as music received by copyright. Thereafter he worked full time on music alone. The benefit to Squire was great, as can be seen from the figures for titles written in the years up to 1916. From 1907 onwards Smith did incorporation as well. It is in the reports dating from Smith's early years that there is mentioned a 'Special Hand Catalogue of music'. This frequently occurs in section V of the monthly returns from 1901 to 1907, but no trace of it now survives. Its nature, extent and purpose are quite unknown, but it is likely that Smith worked on it.

Another member of the staff who assisted Squire at this time was Richard Alexander Streatfeild, educated at Oundle and Pembroke College, Cambridge, and appointed Assistant on 9 February 1889. During the mid-1890s he helped Squire by checking the invoices of purchases. In 1899, presumably while Squire was busy with his Accessions Part of pre-1800 acquisitions, and again in 1901, Streatfeild catalogued music. He was a critic and scholar of some repute. In 1907 he was allowed to transfer eight days annual leave to 1908, for the purpose of going to Italy to do research on Handel, on which composer his distinguished and still valuable book appeared in 1909. Streatfeild also wrote a good book on opera (1897), of which a fifth edition, by E J Dent, appeared in 1925, and his *Masters of Italian music* (1906) was a creditable piece of work. Together with Squire, Laurence Binyon of the Department of Prints and Drawings, and other colleagues, Streatfeild was a regular member of the 'Anglo-Austrians', a lunch club which met almost daily at the Vienna Café in Oxford Street. [21]

On 2 September 1907 the department recruited as a Boy Attendant Charles Humphries (1892-1978), an invaluable member of the staff, [22] who in 1910 was assigned to Squire full time, and worked in the old Music Room up till 1922 with Squire and Smith, then with Smith in its new quarters in the King Edward VII Building from 1922 to the latter's retirement in 1944. Another recruit during this decade was Francis Walter Jekyll, of Eton and Balliol, appointed an Assistant on 25 April 1906. Reporting on him after two years' service, Fortescue told the Trustees he had 'excellent abilities' and added that he was 'a student of musical literaure and bibliography'. [23] He went on: 'At present, as the Trustees are aware, the collection of music is in the hands of Mr W Barclay Squire, of whose work Mr Fortescue cannot speak too highly. It is however desirable that there should be in the library at least one younger assistant, capable, in the course of time, of succeeding to Mr Squire's duties, and in this respect Mr Fortescue hopes that Mr Jekyll may at some future date be of special service to the library. Mr Fortescue has no hesitation in recommending the Trustees to confirm Mr Jekyll's appointment.' The somewhat ironic significance of this document will become clear later, for Jekyll failed to fulfil his Keeper's hopes.

There now occurred an example of Squire's musical influence, which ultimately benefited the museum, although the episode caused him some temporary embarrassment. He enjoyed the acquaintance of Miss Harriet Chichele Plowden, an elderly lady whose father had bequeathed to her the autographs of Mozart's last string quartets. Squire had persuaded her to leave them in her will to the museum. At her decease the manuscripts were duly made over, but on 15 August 1907 an old friend of his, the collector and musical connoisseur Edward Speyer (1839-1934), wrote an over-hasty letter to the *Times*, in which he estimated the value of the autographs as not less than £6000, and extolled the generosity of the bequest. This induced Miss Plowden's heirs to sue the Trustees in order to upset the bequest. Squire must have been immensely relieved when the court upheld it.[24]

Such an episode was surely an unwelcome distraction in Squire's busy life. Having at last secured the assistance of two thoroughly dependable men, Smith and Humphries, and still supported by the reliable Lister, he could now see his way clear to concentrate his energy on the problem of the catalogue and finally solve it by partial publication. At this time the department was stable and well organised. Throughout, work was of a high standard, based on wide scholarship, supported by 'that undeviating mechanical accuracy which good administration endeavours to achieve'.[24] In November 1909, it was reported to the Trustees that there were no arrears of uncatalogued books in the General Library and that the fortnightly Accessions Parts included all current additions and were incorporated within fourteen days of publication. This remarkable momentum was soon to be broken by the first world war, never to be regained.

NOTES

1 George Grove, knighted in 1883, was at this time editor of *Macmillan's magazine*, and also heavily involved with his great *Dictionary of music*, which was being issued in parts. From 21 June 1878 onwards he exchanged numerous letters with Squire, asking his advice and help on a wide variety of matters connected with the *Dictionary*. Squire preserved Grove's letters to himself, most of which precede his entry into the museum, and later presented them to the Department of Manuscripts, where they are Add MS 39679.

2 Sidney Colvin, knighted in 1911, was Keeper of Prints and Drawings from 1883 to 1912.

3 Supplied by Leslie Stephen, W S Rockstro, C V Stanford, J F Bridge and W H Husk. None of their testimonials can now be traced.

4 Details of Squire's early life and of his subsequent multifarious career as scholar, editor, music critic, connoisseur, organiser of exhibitions and conferences, are given in my article 'William Barclay Squire, 1855-1927, Music Librarian', in *The library*, ser 5, vol 12, no 1, March 1957, pp1-10, and with fuller references in my article on him in *The new Grove*. In the present book I have mentioned his work outside the British Museum only when it is related to his official duties, or when it concerned music libraries. There are three known portraits of Squire. The earliest is a photograph by H S Mendelssohn, cut from an article in an unidentified magazine and presented by him, with other portraits of contemporary musicians, to the Department of Prints and Drawings, on 6 October 1894. It shows him wearing pincenez, and is wrongly described in the *Catalogue of engraved British portraits* as 'a photograph of a bust'. The second is

from a drawing made in 1904 by Sir William Strang (now in the Royal College of Music), and reproduced in my earlier article. The third is a photograph, probably taken in the 1920s, and reproduced in the supplementary volume to Grove's *Dictionary of music and musicians*, 1940, pl xv.

5 Charles Villiers Stanford, knighted in 1901, was Professor of Music at Cambridge from 1887 to 1924.

6 John Alexander Fuller-Maitland (1856-1936) was music critic to the *Times* from 1887 to 1911.

7 Before 1885, Squire does not seem regularly to have used his second name, 'Barclay'. It was said that he did so in order to avoid possible confusion with a certain George Squire who was an attendant in the same department. In 1904 the latter was promoted first class attendant and was put in charge of provincial newspapers at the Hendon Newspaper Repository, having already made a catalogue of them (report of 18 January 1904).

8 The then Keeper's report of 1 October 1920, on the subject of Squire's impending retirement, said that when he entered the department, 'he was already a fully equipped antiquary'. A volume of letters, now Add MS 39680, ranges from 1879 to 1909, and reveals a very wide acquaintance. Among Squire's correspondents were Ouseley, Leslie Stephen, Edmund Gurney, Scharf, Eitner, John Addington Symonds, Augustus Manns, Alberto Randegger, Henry James and Jacques Blumenthal.

9 See below p120 and p121.

10 There is no doubt that Lister did this, though it is not specified in the section dealing with his work in a report of 19 January 1894 on the duties of men seconded from the bindery. See Smith, *A Handelian's notebook*, 1965, p36. Lister seems to have served until towards the end of Squire's time.

11 Reports, etc 1887, vol 2, 'Returns of progress'.

12 For many years the museum remained strangely weak in first and early editions of the Viennese classics. Smith began purchasing them from 1929 onwards, and in 1937 acquired a useful quantity of duplicates from the library of the Gesellschaft der Musikfreunde, in Vienna, but the gaps were not thoroughly filled until the purchase of the Hirsch Library nine years later.

13 A separate Department of Maps, Plans and Charts, comprising both manuscript and printed material, existed under its own Keeper, R H Major, from 1867 to 1880. Before and after those dates printed maps were kept in the Department of Printed Books and manuscript maps, with few exceptions, in the Department of Manuscripts. See Miller, *That noble cabinet*, 1973, pp129-131, 267-8.

14 The expanded title, which lapsed in 1973, was created in 1898.

15 Julius Victor Scholderer, *Reminiscences*, Amsterdam, 1970, p20. He later became the most distinguished incunabulist of his generation.

16 'Musical libraries and catalogues', *Proceedings of the Musical Association*, session 45, pp97-111.

17 Reprinted in his *Essays in bibliography and librarianship*, 1899, pp87-114.

18 Probably the two fragmentary paeans of the late 2nd century BC, discovered in 1893. See *The Oxford classical dictionary*, Oxford, 1949, p590.

19 Smith mentions the transfer in the autobiographical section of *A Handelian's notebook*. This gives a useful description of his early years in the department, but it suppresses some matters and the account he gives of others is at variance with the facts and dates as recorded in the departmental reports and other documents. Smith later achieved a great reputation as a bibliographer of Handel. (See also note 22 infra.) Smith's *A bibliography of the*

musical works published by John Walsh during the years
1695-1720, London, 1948, is a pioneer work.

20 Grove, *Dictionary of music and musicians*, 5th edition,
1954, vol 7, p859.

21 Miller, *That noble cabinet*, p278, quoting Sir Henry
Newbolt's *My world as in my time*, London, 1932, pp209-
210.

22 From 1945 until his retirement in 1957 Humphries
worked with the present writer. Together with Smith,
during the latter's retirement, he compiled *Music publishing
in the British Isles*, first edition, 1954, second edition 1970.
He also collaborated with Smith in *A bibliography of the
musical works published by the firm of John Walsh during
the years 1721-1766*, London, 1968, and assisted him in
Handel. A descriptive catalogue of the early editions, London,
1960. Humphries rose to become a Higher Executive Officer.

23 Jekyll was a close friend of his fellow Etonian George
Butterworth, the composer and folk-song collector. With
Butterworth, and on his own, Jekyll collected a number of
folk songs and dances from 1906 onwards. There is a summary of his work in this field in an article by Michael
Dawnay, 'George Butterworth's folk song manuscripts', in
Folk music journal, 1976, vol 3, no 2, p100. It is interesting
that Birch-Reynardson, another Etonian, had also collected
folk-song.

24 See Edward Speyer, *My life and friends*, London,
1937, pp208-9.

25 Letter from Garnett to Rye, 28 October 1872. The
phrase was even more applicable to the conditions of 1909
than to those of the time when it was written.

5

SQUIRE'S YEARS OF FULFILMENT:
1909-1920

AGAINST THIS background, Squire began the preliminary work on his catalogue, perhaps about 1908. In February 1909 Fortescue submitted his report, very nearly ten years after the earliest proposal:

> On the 10th June 1899 the Trustees approved of a proposal made by Mr Fortescue to print a Catalogue of the works of the great composers. Mr Barclay Squire began the formation of this Catalogue, but as the work proceeded he found that it was open to several grave objections, the most serious being the fact that the original works of these composers formed only a very small proportion of the entries under their names; the great bulk of each heading being composed of selections, abstracts and adaptations, which possessed no musical or bibliographical value.
>
> Before reporting the failure of this scheme and expressing his regret for having recommended it, Mr Fortescue concurred with Mr Squire's suggestion to select from the existing Catalogue of Music all titles of musical works from the invention of music printing to the close of the eighteenth century.
>
> Mr Squire has now selected and entirely recatalogued their titles, in number about 42,000 and is of opinion that they would form a thoroughly useful and practicable catalogue which would be of great service both to the British Museum and to musical libraries and collections throughout the world.

Such a catalogue would greatly reduce the enormous bulk of the existing catalogue, which consists of 322 interleaved volumes, by substituting printed titles for the present transcribed slips and would also command a ready sale from libraries, collectors and dealers in Music.

The number of entries ultimately amounted to 43,835[1], which reduced the bulk of the volumes by rather less than a tenth. In order to find the main titles, Squire had to read through the entire music catalogue, which by then comprised well over 600,000 entries. He did not, of course, have to consider composers such as Spohr or Weber, none of whose music was printed in the eighteenth century though they were born well before its close. But composers such as G G Ferrari or James Hook, whose published work spanned the dividing line, had to be investigated carefully. Having made his selection and found the main titles with all the cross-references, Squire scrutinised all of them and recatalogued most. He also scoured the *General catalogue of printed books* for periodicals, in all languages, which contained supplements consisting of musical works. For these he wrote new titles. Following Oliphant's procedure of some sixty-five years before, he included numerous works of musical theory. One of the most time-consuming processes involved the more precise dating of the undated pieces (the majority being so issued) which were published at the end of the eighteenth century and the beginning of the nineteenth. In the many cases of uncertainty, difficult decisions of inclusion or rejection had to be made. Squire had also to devise special schemes of arrangement for the headings of large composers, and provide title-indexes for them.

The original plan was to publish the whole in one volume,[2] but this would obviously have been far too bulky. When the catalogue appeared, on 6 July 1912, it was in two volumes, royal octavo, of which 500 copies had been printed at a cost of £845.   The titlepage ran: *Catalogue of printed music published between 1498 and 1800 now in the British Museum*, while the head-title on page 1 read 'Catalogue of old music printed down to the end of the eighteenth century'. Vol 2 included a first supplement comprising music purchased while the work was in progress.   It was a pleasant gesture that Fortescue's preface (drafted, as museum prefaces generally were, by the compiler) mentioned the work of 'the late Thomas Oliphant'.   Clearly his name was not forgotten even sixty years after he left the department.

The Trustees agreed to present copies of the catalogue to Streatfeild and Smith, in recognition of the help (unspecified) which they had given Squire.   This was undoubtedly his finest achievement.   The catalogue soon became—and has remained—a standard work of musical reference.   It was, as can now clearly be seen, the only possible solution to a very difficult, protracted problem.   But the result of this solution was simply to create new difficulties both for the staff who succeeded Squire and for the generations of readers who have used the music catalogues in the museum itself.   For what was right for a finite catalogue in book form was really incompatible with the needs of an expanding catalogue organised on traditional lines for use in the museum itself.

It was the typography of the 1912 catalogue which caused the first difficulty.   Ten copies had been printed on one side of the sheet only, and two of them were cut up, so that each page produced two separate columns.   These were laid down on the left hand side of folio sheets which were of the same size as those of the rest of the music catalogue.   (This procedure had been followed with the published volumes of the *General catalogue of printed books*.)   The new laid-down catalogue of music amounted to ten bound volumes.   But the type-width of the columns was very narrow, and left little space for handwritten corrections to be made legibly. When the second supplement was issued in 1940, it too was printed in narrow columns to match those of the 1912 catalogue. Consequently, when after 1940 accessions of pre-1800 music began to multiply rapidly, and the need for space for subsequent manuscript correction and for greater general uniformity was foreseen, it was decided to print the entries in the same type-width—nearly double that of the 1912 columns—as had long been standard for both the *General catalogue of printed books* and for the post-1800 music catalogue. Thus there arose a most confusing visual difference. A lot of the trouble could have been avoided if Squire had used for the 1912 catalogue the larger typography of his 1909 Royal College of Music Catalogue, the column-width of which differed little from that of the museum's Accession Parts.

The division at 1800 caused difficulties of a different kind. Readers studying a composer such as Haydn, the editions of whose music spanned this date, had to consult two catalogues. Most of the contemporary first editions were in the earlier catalogue, but the later ones, often equally important, and those of numerous works not printed in his lifetime, were in the post-1800 catalogue. Readers did not always grasp this point, and were further confused by the fact that in many headings—Palestrina, for instance—in the pre-1800 catalogue the entries were arranged on principles which were quite different from those governing the same heading in the post-1800 catalogue.

Unintentionally, the break at 1800—though vaguely marking, as Fortescue's preface said, 'the division between the earlier and the modern schools of music'—fostered the fallacious notion that the music published before that date, being 'old', was somehow more important than what was published after it. Granted that Squire had to make some such division, and granted also that after about 1800 the quantity of music published increased very rapidly, it was nevertheless an unfortunate precedent, which was followed in some catalogues of other music libraries. Only now, after some seventy years, is this barrier being gradually broken down. It is doubtful whether Squire and Fortescue ever thought of the consequences of the decisions which they took on these matters of typography and chronology. Their task, as they saw it, was to make the treasures of the museum's 'early' printed music as widely known as possible, through a published catalogue. Posterity has certainly been grateful for the success of their undertaking, and for Squire's pertinacity.

Not content with the effort of preparing the 1912 catalogue, he began yet another one at about the same time. On 2 February 1914 Arthur William Kaye Miller, who had succeeded Fortescue as Keeper, mentioned in a general report on the work of the department that in 1909 Squire had begun a catalogue of the libretti of operas, oratorios and cantatas, having for this purpose read through the entire *General catalogue of printed books*. One cannot help wondering why he did so at that particular time. Perhaps the idea originated in an important purchase made from Ludwig Rosenthal of Munich on 3 April of that year. This was a collection of 950 libretti of Italian, French and English operas, mainly of the eighteenth century and cost £25.11.7. By 1914 the work was done, amounting to some 10,000 slips arranged by titles, but it lacked indexes. On 10 January 1917 George Frederick Barwick, Miller's successor, reported that Miss Cecilia Stainer, daughter of Sir John Stainer, had completed the two indexes, one of composers, the other of authors, and recommended that in recognition of her voluntary services the Trustees should present to her a copy of

Hughes-Hughes's three-volume *Catalogue of manuscript music in the British Museum*, 1906-09. Proposing that the printing of the now complete libretto catalogue be postponed until the next financial year, Barwick also expressed the hope that it would ultimately be printed. But unfortunately because of the war it never was. It remains in slip form as another remarkable monument of Squire's activity, and seems to have been one of the earliest compilations of its kind.

During the very time when Squire's work on the 1912 catalogue was coming to fruition and his labours on the catalogue of libretti had just begun, there occurred an event which was to engage his attention for the rest of his life. This was the deposit, on loan, of the 'Royal Collection of Music', as it was described in a letter written by Sir Walter Parratt, the Master of the King's Musick, on 17 January 1911, stating that he had the King's permission to transfer the collection from Buckingham Palace to the British Museum. Both as a piece of diplomacy and a practical step of immense benefit to posterity, this was the greatest triumph of Squire's career. The royal collection, containing the priceless autographs of Handel, a wealth of other manuscripts, and a large quantity of rare printed music, had previously been scattered in various royal residences. In about the middle of the nineteenth century it was brought together in Buckingham Palace, but was stored in a damp basement room, to which scholars could gain access only with considerable difficulty.

Squire, who had connections in Court circles, tried without avail to have the collection transferred to the British Museum during the reign of Edward VII. Soon after the accession of George V his renewed efforts were crowned with success, probably through the good offices of Countess Gleichen.[3] (Although the royal music, as already mentioned, was rich in manuscripts, by far the larger part of it comprised printed works, with some musical literature. It was this fact, coupled with Squire's expertise and influence, which caused the care of the collection to be entrusted to the Department of Printed Books.) On 6 April 1911 Fortescue reported that the collection was 'temporarily deposited in a room which is perfectly dry and fit for the storage of valuable books fitted with glazed cases in the basement of the White Wing'.[4] One of the conditions of the deposit was that the Trustees should publish a catalogue, but this was delayed by the outbreak of the war.

The work of making a preliminary inventory of a collection of some 5,000 volumes, as a check against loss or mislaying during transfer, was considerable. The colleague whom Squire took to the palace in February 1911 was Jekyll, and the extant list, still preserved with the royal music, is largely in his hand. This might suggest that the cautious hopes expressed by Fortescue in his report of 1906 (see p000 above) were in course of fulfilment. But unfortunately they were soon to be frustrated by Jekyll himself. In about March 1913 Miller gave him an unfavourable report, on the grounds that he failed 'to keep an accurate diary and to observe the rules and customs of the department'. Some improvement was noted on 30 September, but on 11 July 1914 Jekyll resigned. Barwick reported tersely: 'he finds the hours and regulations of the museum very irksome'. Clearly he lacked application and could not fit in to the routine of the department. But in view of his undoubted abilities and the hopes entertained by Fortescue eight years before, and having worked with Jekyll personally, Squire must have viewed his departure with some dismay. Once again, the succession was as uncertain as ever.

On 4 August 1914, England declared war on Germany. Squire was then 59. Lister too was well over military age.

Smith was 34, and was not called up until the end of 1915. Humphries, who had been promoted to Attendant on 8 February 1913, was released for the services as a territorial on 23 April 1916. Thus, for Squire, as apparently for the rest of the department, the effect of the first two years of the war was limited to restriction of the book-supply to readers and difficulty with foreign purchases. But thereafter things went very badly with work on the collections of music.

From 1916 onwards the whole department was drained of its manpower, either into the services or other government offices. Those who remained were moved round to work in various sections of the library. The general drop in production is also clearly reflected in the shrinking return of titles written for the music. Two Assistants were put to work on cataloguing it as and when they could be spared. They were Frederick Charles William Hiley, a member of the Bach choir, writer of light verse, translator of Horace and Catullus, and George Dean Raffles Tucker, a distinguished linguist and violinist and an enthusiastic mountaineer, astronomer and croquet player.[5]

Squire's duties during this difficult period were many and various: only some of the most important can be mentioned here. In 1912 he had been appointed Assistant Keeper, and in 1919 he became the senior in this grade in the whole department. Already in 1913 he had deputised as Superintendent of the Reading Room when Barwick visited America to study methods of book-conveying and the like in a number of libraries. In 1915, like Roy before him in more peaceful times, Squire assisted in the general management of the whole department, and—incidentally—in the same year he narrowly escaped serious injury when he was working on general duties in the First Supplementary Room and part of its lofty ceiling fell on him.

VERDI (FORTUNINO GIUSEPPE FRANCESCO) Aida...
Hymne, Marche, Danse, pour deux pianos. Transcrits
... par G. Pierné. Paris, [1883.] fol.
h. 3291. (28.)

VERDI (FORTUNINO GIUSEPPE FRANCESCO) Aida...
Hymne, Marche-Danse transcrits pour le piano à 2
mains ... Édition simplifiée par H. Hausser.
A. Leduc: Paris, [1887.] fol. h. 3281. a. (48.)

VERDI (FORTUNINO GIUSEPPE FRANCESCO) Aida...
Hymne, Marche, Danse, transcrits pour le piano à ...
4 mains ... Édition simplifiée par H. Hausser.
A. Leduc: Paris, [1887.] fol. h. 3290. j. (17.)

VERDI (FORTUNINO GIUSEPPE FRANCESCO) Aida...
Ballet Music and Grand March. (Arr. by M. Leslie.)
[P. F.] G. Ricordi & Co.: London, etc., 1929. 4°.
g. 1125. cc. (28.)

VERDI (FORTUNINO GIUSEPPE FRANCESCO) [Aida.]
Suite from Aida ... Arranged by S. Robinson. Piano
Conductor [and Orchestral Parts]. G. Ricordi & Co.:
London, 1940. 4°. h. 3210. h. (803.)

VERDI (FORTUNINO GIUSEPPE FRANCESCO)
— Aida ... "Easy-to-play" piano arrangements by Denis
Wright. pp. 15. Ascherberg, Hopwood & Crew: London,
[1961.] obl. 4°. c. 60. l. (4.)

VERDI (FORTUNINO GIUSEPPE FRANCESCO) [Aida.]
L'Abborrita Rivale. She, my Rival detested. ... Aria
...Arranged by H. R. Shelley. G. Schirmer:
London, New York, etc., 1915. fol. H. 1793. tt. (5l.)

VERDI (FORTUNINO GIUSEPPE FRANCESCO)
— [Aida.] Ballabile .. Arranged [for military band]
by Norman Richardson. [Conductor's score and parts.]
36 pt. Boosey & Hawkes: London, etc., [1952.] 4°.
[Q.M.B. Edition. no. 187.] h. 3211. b.
The part for euphonium is in duplicate.

VERDI (FORTUNINO GIUSEPPE FRANCESCO) [Aida.]
Celeste Aida. See BATTMANN (J. L.) O céleste Aida.
... Transcription. [P. F.] [1884.] fol.
h. 3009. b. (30.)

VERDI (FORTUNINO GIUSEPPE FRANCESCO) [Aida.
Gloria all'Egitto.] Grand-Chorus, Finale Act II ...
Arranged by A. Thornley. Concert Edition.
G. Ricordi & Co.: London, 1942. 8°. F. 1744. f. (15.)

VERDI (GIUSEPPE) Aida...Marche des Trompettes.
Transcription très facile pour Piano par J. L. Battmann.
Paris, [1880.] fol. h. 3272. r. (11.)

VERDI (FORTUNINO GIUSEPPE FRANCESCO) [Aida.]
March. See BATTMANN (J. L.) Marche des Trompettes
tirée d'Aida, etc. [P. F.] [1884.] fol.
h. 3009. b. (11.)

VERDI (FORTUNINO GIUSEPPE FRANCESCO) [Aida.]
Marche des Trompettes ... arrangée pour le piano à
6 mains par H. Hausser. A. Leduc: Paris, [1887.] fol.
h. 3290. j. (18.)

VERDI (FORTUNINO GIUSEPPE FRANCESCO) [Aida.]
Triumphal March...Arranged by H. Hind...for 1st
and 2nd Violins and Pianoforte, with ad lib. parts for
3rd Violin, or Viola, 'Cello, Bass and Wind, etc.
[Parts.] G. Ricordi & Co.: London, 1934. 4°.
h. 3219. h. (480.)
The Authentic School and Amateur Orchestra Series,
No. 6.

VERDI (FORTUNINO GIUSEPPE FRANCESCO)
— [Aida.] Grand March ... Arranged by David Stone.
Orchestral score. pp. 22. Boosey & Hawkes: London,
[1964.] 8°. g. 1630. ll. (5.)
Hawkes School Series. no. 96.

VERDI (FORTUNINO GIUSEPPE FRANCESCO)
— [Aida.] Grand March ... Arranged by David Stone.
(Piano conductor [and orchestral parts]. 25 pt. Boosey
& Hawkes: London, [1964.] 4°. h. 3210. i. (904.)
Hawkes School Series. no. 96.

VERDI (FORTUNINO GIUSEPPE FRANCESCO)
— "Aida." Grand March for Pianoforte Solo. (Arranged
by S. Crooke.) G. Ricordi & Co.: London, 1943. 4°.
g. 1125. nn. (23.)

VERDI (FORTUNINO GIUSEPPE FRANCESCO) [Aida.
Possente, possente Fthà.] Hear our pray'r, oh Lord!
For Mixed Voices, Soprano or Tenor Solo. Adapted
... by Wayne Howarth. Gamble Hinged Music Co.:
Chicago, 1937. 8°. F. 1176. l. (57.)

VERDI (FORTUNINO GIUSEPPE FRANCESCO) [Aida. Su!
del Nilo.] Till Victory be won...Chorus for soprano,
alto and baritone. (Words by G. Purcell. Verdi-
[Arranged by R.] Kountz.) M. Witmark & Sons:
New York, 1928. 8°. F. 585. rr. (39.)

VERDI (FORTUNINO GIUSEPPE FRANCESCO)
— [Aida.—Su! del Nilo.] The Nile Chorus .... For male
voices, T.T.B.B. English words by H. Proctor-Gregg.
pp. 8. G. Ricordi & Co.: London, [1952.] 8°.
F. 369. d. (2.)

VERDI (FORTUNINO GIUSEPPE FRANCESCO) [Aida.
Vieni o diletta.] The Mercy-Seat. Sacred Song for
low voice with Piano accompaniment, words by W.
Cowper, adapted... by W. H. Neidlinger.
G. Schirmer: New York, 1903. fol. G. 517. p. (22.)

VERDI (FORTUNINO GIUSEPPE FRANCESCO) [Aida.]
See ALARD (D.) Aida ... fantaisie pour Violon, etc.
[1881.] fol. h. 1814. c. (8.)

VERDI (FORTUNINO GIUSEPPE FRANCESCO) [Aida.]
See ALDER (E.) Aida ... Trio pour piano, flûte et
violon. [1885.] fol. h. 2551. f. (2.)

VERDI (GIUSEPPE) [Aida.] See ARBAN (J. J. B. L.)
Aida...fantaisie pour Cornet, etc. [1880.] fol.
h. 3219. e. (1.)

Plate 6: A page of printed entries in the Catalogue of Music printed after 1800.

VERDI (FORTUNINO GIUSEPPE FRANCESCO) Aida . . .
Partitura. *G. Ricordi & Co.: Milano, etc.*, [1872.] fol.
Lithographed throughout. K. 16. a. 11.

VERDI (FORTUNINO GIUSEPPE FRANCESCO)
—— Aida. Opera in quattro atti di Antonio Ghislanzoni . . .
Partitura d'orchestra. pp. 444. *G. Ricordi & c.:*
Milano, [1913.] 8°. Hirsch II. 915.

VERDI (FORTUNINO GIUSEPPE FRANCESCO)
—— Aida. Opera in quattro atti. Versi di A. Ghislanzoni . . .
Canto e pianoforte, *etc.* (Riduzione di Franco Faccio.)
pp. 283. *Edizioni Ricordi: Milano, etc.,* [1872.] fol.
H. 3915. g.

VERDI (FORTUNINO GIUSEPPE FRANCESCO) Aida.
Opera in quattro atti di Antonio Ghislanzoni . . .
Partitura d'Orchestra. *G. Ricordi & C.:*
Milano, etc., 1913. 8°. E. 190. u.

VERDI (FORTUNINO GIUSEPPE FRANCESCO)
—— Aida . . . (Partitura d'orchestra.) Nuova edizione
riveduta e corretta. pp. 444. *G. Ricordi & c.: Milano,*
1953. 8°. [*Partiture Ricordi.* 153.] D. 265.

VERDI (FORTUNINO GIUSEPPE FRANCESCO)
—— Aida. Opera in quattro atti. Versi di A. Ghislanzoni.
(Riduzione di Franco Faccio.) [Vocal score.] pp. 289.
Edizioni Ricordi: Milano, [1872.] 8°. E. 190. d.

Verdi (Fortunino (Giuseppe Francesco)
F. 125. m.   Aida. Complete arrangement for voice and Pianoforte by
M. Saladino with English and Italian words. London, [1877.] 8°.
Note. Ricordi's edition".

VERDI (FORTUNINO GIUSEPPE FRANCESCO)
—— Aida. Grand opéra en quatre actes, paroles françaises
de MM. Du Locle & Nuitter . . . Partition chant et piano,
etc. pp. 307. *Léon Escudier: Paris,* [188c.] 8°.
F. 125. dd.
*The fly-leaf bears a MS. dedication to Massenet in the
composer's autograph.*

VERDI (FORTUNINO GIUSEPPE FRANCESCO)
—— Aida. Opera in quattro atti. Versi di A. Ghislanzoni
. . . Pianoforte solo. (Riduzione di Luigi Rivetta.)
pp. 158. *Edizioni Ricordi: Milano,* [1871 ?] fol.
h. 1492. k.

VERDI (FORTUNINO GIUSEPPE FRANCESCO)
—— Aida . . . With new English translation by Humphrey
Procter-Gregg. Adapted for concert performance by Sir
Malcolm Sargent. [Vocal score.] pp. 246. *G. Ricordi*
& Co.: London, [1951.] 8°. E. 190. v. (1.)

VERDI (FORTUNINO GIUSEPPE FRANCESCO)
—— Aida. Opéra in quattro atti, *etc.* [P.F. solo.] (Riduzione di Luigi Rivetta.) pp. 155. *Léon Escudier: Paris,*
[c. 1875.] fol. h. 1492. n. (1.)

Verdi (Giuseppe Francesco)
f. 300.   Aida, opera . . . Riduzione per Pianoforte nello
stile facile di G. B. Pagnoncelli. Milano, [1875.] 8°?

Verdi (Giuseppe Francesco)
f. 250. a.   Aida . . . Complete arrangement for the Pianoforte by M. Saladino.
London, [1876.] 8°.
Note. One of Ricordi's editions of complete operas
for Pianoforte.

VERDI (GIUSEPPE FRANCESCO) Aida. Opéra in quattro atti . . .
Pianoforte solo . . . Riduzione di H. d'Aubel. *Paris,*
[1884.] 8°. f. 300. c.

VERDI (FORTUNINO GIUSEPPE FRANCESCO) Aida . . .
Partition piano à 4 mains. Nouvelle réduction . . . par
H. d'Aubel. *Paris,* [1887.] 8°. f. 300. e.

VERDI (FORTUNINO GIUSEPPE FRANCESCO)
—— Аида. Опера въ четырехъ дѣйствіяхъ . . . Полное
переложеніе для одного фортепіано. (Восьмое изданіе.)
pp. 130. *у П. Юргенсона: Москва,* [c. 1900.] 8°.
f. 540. jj.

Plate 7: *A page of transcribed and printed entries in the Catalogue of*
Music printed after 1800.

Next year, on 19 February, he was transferred to the Admiralty War Staff Intelligence Division, which worked under great pressure. Not surprisingly, he was ordered two months' rest in November 1917 because he suffered from insomnia and chronic bronchitis. It was in 1916 that Squire's astonishing range of knowledge, which included geography, [6] was put to new use. For in that year the Admiralty published anonymously, as a 'secret' document, his *Tunisia. Tribes*, a masterly historical and ethnographical survey. Throughout these years he also organised the loan from the museum to the Admiralty of the books needed for the purposes of naval intelligence. In December 1918 Squire began to work on peace conference documents; a year later, and throughout the spring of 1920, he was engaged part-time in the Foreign Office on a series of peace conference handbooks.

Only a man of exceptional stamina could have kept up this pace while maintaining his other duties in the museum. In October 1917 Barwick submitted to the Trustees a long report in Squire's hand drawing attention to the 'large and increasing amount' of American music deposited by copyright through agents, but not bearing any United Kingdom address printed or stamped on it. Much of it, said Squire, was 'of the most worthless description, consisting largely of music-hall songs, dance music, band-parts, hymn-tunes, &c'; he asked the Trustees to seek counsel's opinion as to whether the museum, so hard pressed for lack of space and staff, might not refuse it. The Treasury Solicitor pointed out (what is still often not understood) that deposit 'is not a condition to the acquisition of copyright' and opined that 'the American publishers need not send, and the British Museum need not accept, unless it chooses, the music in question'. The amended circular sent to publishers by the Director and Principal Librarian, Sir Frederick Kenyon, may have reduced the flood temporarily, but within a decade it had risen again.

Two events occurred during this time to lighten the cares of the war. One was in November 1916, when the apartment, known later as the King's Music Library, situated at the west end of the future Music Room on the mezzanine floor of the King Edward VII Building, was fitted up to receive the royal collection, and it was moved there without further delay. (The most valuable manuscripts were stored in a basement safe until the air-raids were over.) The second event took place in 1918 when Lady Dorothea Ruggles-Brise deposited on loan in the museum the collection of rare Scottish music formed by John Glen of Edinburgh. After his death in 1904, the collection had not been available for study until it was acquired from his executors by Lady Ruggles-Brise. This deposit was doubtless due to Squire's influence, though not so stated in the report.[7]

The invoices show that during the war years fewer than 350 pieces of printed music were added to the collections. Most of it was by modern composers, but there were some splendid early works. The most notable comprised a collection of twenty-six mint Venetian and Flemish part-books, of the sixteenth and seventeenth centuries, purchased from Lincoln Cathedral for £450 in October 1914. Two other fine purchases were Senfl, *Liber selectarum cantionum* (1520) and Porter, *Madrigals and ayres* (1622). About a dozen good pieces were secured at the Cummings sale in 1917 and at the Aylesford sale in 1918. At the latter Squire himself bought over a score of Handel manuscripts which he added, by permission, to the royal collection. All in all, considering the pressures and distractions of Squire's life at this period, it was remarkable that he could do much purchasing at all. But he also found time to prepare for publication a second supplement to his 1912 catalogue. This amounted to 34 pages, comprising perhaps some 1500 or so titles, but although an estimate of the cost of printing was duly submitted to the Trustees on 6 February 1919, publication was delayed for over twenty years. Compiled by William C Smith, it ultimately appeared in 1940, and included such pre-1801 items as had been acquired after Squire's time, and entries for various plays with music and works of musical theory which had come to light in the general library.

Knowing that retirement was not far away, Squire summarised the philosophy of his life's work in a paper which he read on 8 April 1919 to the Musical Association on 'Musical libraries and catalogues'.[8] This wide-ranging survey of libraries in the British isles included some points of great interest about the British Museum. Repeating the view expressed in his report of 1917, Squire complained that the museum alone of the 'copyright' libraries had to preserve all the music it received. 'What this burden is', he said, 'I know only too well . . . It has—during the last ten years—been increased to an enormous extent by the abolition of registration at Stationers' Hall, and the importation for copyright purposes of tons of American rubbish, all of which has to be preserved and arranged in the museum.'[9] He went on to complain that this source of intake consumed too much space, which is rather curious since he must have known that ample room had been allowed for music in the King Edward VII Building.

Squire pointed out that while separate classes were devoted to fine arts and architecture, musical literature was placed in the museum among books on games and pastimes. This accorded with what he was told at the time of his entry, that (as already quoted) 'it was always understood that music was not to be encouraged', and made him all the more appreciative of the liberal support which successive Keepers had given to his purchasing policy. He then gave a reasoned statement of the advantages and disadvantages which would arise if the museum, following the Royal Library in Berlin and the Library of Congress, were to form a department of music containing both printed and manuscript material. He hoped that such a development would take place in any future reorganisation, following the precedent of the Department of Oriental Printed Books and Manuscripts. Squire finally pleaded eloquently for a national catalogue of music, to include all important uncatalogued collections throughout the country—a vision which was to wait nearly forty years for its fulfilment.

Another instance of Squire's arbitrary turn of mind (exemplified in his dismissive remark about 'American rubbish') is found in his cavalier treatment of the catalogue of the authors of words set to music. This had probably fallen into abeyance about 1886, when a few of the entries from the first printed Accessions Part were incorporated. After it proved impracticable to have the fifty-eight volumes reduced to printed form, it is doubtful if any more titles were written, and to Squire the two copies of this catalogue became a space-consuming encumbrance. At some time during the war, he decided to have all the volumes (and presumably the titles) destroyed. Smith records[10] that when he returned from military service, this catalogue 'had been destroyed for space reasons, or maybe as salvage'. He went on: 'I never dared ask. It would have been considered an impertinence'. As a unique record of well over half a century of prolific song-writing, it would have been invaluable to posterity.

As a last example of Squire's duties outside the Music Room may be mentioned the legal proceedings which were threatened in May 1919 against the firm of T Werner Laurie for default under the Copyright Act. This seems to have fallen to his responsibility, and one cannot imagine that he found it very congenial. Far more so was a performance of

English madrigals which was arranged at his suggestion in the museum in June 1920, in connection with the private view of an exhibition mounted for a conference of professors of English literature.   Then on 4 November, exactly thirty-five years after he entered the service of the Trustees, Squire retired, having been granted permission to extend it by a few weeks after his sixty-fifth birthday.

During these events, the department was slowly reverting to normal.   Humphries returned on 12 May 1919, having achieved high NCO rank in the army of the Rhine occupation. Smith, who had become a lieutenant in the Army Service Corps, was demobilised on 10 October.   The question of a successor to Squire was now as much in the official mind as it had long been a matter of concern to him personally. The wheel of history had come full circle, for all Squire's endeavours to ensure a successor of his own grade had failed. Bourne and Jekyll, each of whom in turn had been so designated, had resigned. So too had Paul England, whose services Squire had been anxious to obtain, and on whom the mantle of succession might well have fallen in due course. Another obvious possibility was Streatfeild. But in June 1917 he had three months' sick leave for a 'nervous breakdown', which was prolonged, after a brief recovery, to mid-November. On 12 January 1918, he retired, being unable to work again full-time. He was re-employed, however, part-time at 3s.6d. an hour, on 12 October. But on 6 February 1919, he died, still only in his fifty-third year. To Squire, a member of the same Cambridge college, a friend and fellow scholar in music for over twenty years, his death must have been another sad and very personal blow, the more so if, as is very likely, he had regarded him in turn as his successor. Now Smith alone remained.

From the beginning of his service he had received good reports for efficiency and hard work. In 1907 he was said to have 'a fair ['elementary' deleted] knowledge of French, German and Italian', and it was further reported that his acquaintance with musical history increased with experience. Above all, he understood the relation of the music section to the department as a whole, and he had the merit of having stuck to his work, whereas those members of the higher grade who had been working wholly or partly in the same field had not.

It is perhaps significant that on 4 April 1919, only a month after Streatfeild's death and six months before Smith's return from military service, Barwick put forward his name for promotion in a report on the post-war reconstruction of the department.[11] He also drew attention to a perennial problem—the promotion prospects of men who, by circumstance or rank, find themselves doing work very little different from that of men in a senior grade: 'The efficiency of the Dept,' Barwick wrote, 'will certainly be increased if for young men certain to become discontented in middle life & whose aptitude for their work has only been tested by examination, there can be substituted older men of proved aptitude'. No action followed Barwick's report, but his recommendation was endorsed by his successor Alfred William Pollard in January 1921: 'Mr William C Smith has been carefully trained by Mr Squire in the work of the music section in the department, and has spared no pains to qualify himself further by acquiring a good knowledge of the history of music & several foreign languages. Mr Pollard cordially recommends him for promotion.' This recommendation was approved by the Trustees, and in March 1921 Smith was appointed Assistant (the term 'Assistant Keeper' had not yet been substituted for the older designation).

There remained the fulfilment of two important projects, both of which had been delayed by the war. The first was the removal of the books from the hopelessly congested

Music Room[12] to their new quarters in what was originally known simply as 'the extension'. The foundation stone of this edifice was laid by Edward VII on 27 June 1907 and the public galleries were formally opened by George V on 7 May 1914. Space in the 'King Edward VII Building', as it became known, was allocated some time before its completion. On the mezzanine floor, the area relevant to this narrative, the western part was given to music, the middle portion to maps, and the eastern area to the Department of Prints and Drawings. A request for some furniture for the music room was included in the estimates for 1914, but eight years were to pass before all the books were in place. As already mentioned, the King's Music was installed in November 1916. The bulk of the map collection was moved in January 1917. But doubtless because of the growing exigencies of the war, the music had to wait, although some of the shelving was provided.

This was a time of extreme difficulty for the General Library and there had to be many shifts to find space for accessions. One such had occurred at some time before April 1919 when it was recorded that the new presses intended for music had been filled with old novels. There they stayed until about the end of 1921; the annual report stated that the novels then filled 200 presses. But in the end, the room was given over to its own purpose, and the job was done. In 1921 the remainder of the shelving was included in the 1922-23 estimates, and the removal of the music was effected in 1922.

Two points in the planning deserve comment. One was the extraordinary decision to place the locked, glazed cases containing the most valuable books not at the north end of each row of presses, but at the south where they stood in the full glare of the sun blazing through large unprotected windows on the other side of the corridor. The second point was the failure to provide space for readers to consult the music *in situ*, as seems originally to have been intended, [13] and as was done in the adjacent Map Room in about 1923. As it was, extra staff had to be provided to collect the books from the Music Room and convey them to the Reading Rooms, either by hand down some seventy-five stairs or on barrows using erratic, ill-sited lifts. Moreover, the responsibility for the issue and return of case-books remained as previously with the North Library and not with the Music Room. In 1923 Pollard reported that the new Music Room was 'at an inconvenient distance from the rest of the department'. One cannot help remarking that some more realistic early planning would have paid handsome dividends by reducing wear and tear on books, and by saving valuable time for several generations of readers.[14]

Squire must soon have realised that the move of the music collection would not take place until after his retirement, and in any case he had little time during the war to plan for its arrangement and future development. The one exception was, of course, the King's Music. He must surely have supervised the planning of its special apartment and the design of the luxurious locked and glazed cases designed to contain the books.[15] To house that collection was one thing: to make it available for students was quite another. The conditions of deposit in 1911 had enjoined the Trustees, *inter alia*, to produce a catalogue 'as soon as convenient'. This was, however, an immense task. It is doubtful whether, even if there had been no war, Squire could have accomplished it before he retired because, in the last seven years of his service, general departmental duties made increasingly heavy demands on his time. Only in retirement could he find the necessary leisure and concentration.

On 1 October 1920 Pollard reminded the Trustees that Squire was due to retire, and asked for the short extension of the age limit already mentioned. He also submitted a memorandum from Squire on the subject of the King's

Music, in which the latter set out his proposals for cataloguing it himself. Squire estimated one volume of 200-300 pages for the printed music and musical literature and a second of 400-600 pages for all the manuscripts together. Pollard summarised these proposals thus:

> Mr Squire is uniquely qualified for the task, and Mr Pollard cordially recommends that his offer be accepted on the following terms (i) that Mr Squire be engaged in the first instance to compile the catalogue of the Manuscript portion of the collection for a fee of Four hundred pounds payable in such manner as the Treasury shall approve (ii) that Mr Squire be further engaged to compile or edit with any help he may require from members of the Staff of the Music section of the Dept of Printed Books, a catalogue of the Printed portion of the collection, for a further fee of One hundred pounds; (3) [*sic*] that it be understood that Mr Squire will do his best to complete both portions of the catalogue within the next three years, and that during this time he be allowed to retain his house key, and do his work in the King's Music Room in the Mezzanine.
>
> Mr Pollard believes that such an arrangement would be in every way advantageous & begs to recommend that application be made to the Treasury for the necessary leave, and that meanwhile as Mr Squire is willing, if funds are not forthcoming, to work gratuitously, he be permitted to begin whenever he wishes.

The Trustees endorsed these proposals and Squire began work, but without, it seems, at any time receiving payment. (Squire was appointed the first Honorary Curator of the collection in 1924.) He soon found that his plan would not do. It proved quite impracticable to catalogue the Handel manuscripts and the other manuscripts in one and the same volume. The former were an entity and all of one period, easily susceptible of uniform treatment. The others, however, ranged over some four centuries, and were of greatly differing types requiring various forms of treatment, and so would be better dealt with in a separate volume. When Squire reached this decision is not known. But in the event, the Handel manuscripts taxed Squire's energies to the full, and though he saw the volume through the press, he died, after an operation, on 13 January 1927, shortly before its publication. The printer's copy for this volume, written in his small, neat hand, survives, and has been preserved with the royal music as a record of what was his final service to the Trustees. On the Handel volume alone Squire had spent more than double the time he had estimated for the whole task.

It was not enough, of course, for the royal music just to be catalogued. Every single piece in it had to be clearly stamped for identification and security. But first a stamp with the appropriate wording had to be designed and made. The departmental papers contain two letters written to Squire on this topic by George V's Private Secretary, Lord Stamfordham. The first, dated 6 February, 1923 reads thus:

> How would it do to have on the stamp the words, "Royal Music Library, Buckingham Palace", surmounted with the Royal Arms as represented in the blue specimen enclosed in your letter, which I now return? Or it might be "Lent from the Royal Music Library, Buckingham Palace"; or "The Royal Music Library, Buckingham Palace, lent to the British Museum by King George V"?

Squire presumably pointed out that the last two suggestions, which ran to eight and fifteen words respectively, were incompatible with the design of a stamp which had to be compact enough for its impression to fit into the small space at the foot of a page, this being in many cases all that was available, apart from the verso of a titlepage. In his second letter, of 10 February, Lord Stamfordham raised a different point:

> With regard to the Stamp—"Royal Music Library" does not in my opinion sufficiently denote that the manuscripts really belong to the Soverign but have been lent to the British Museum. I would suggest, "The King's Music Library"—please let me know what you think.
>
> I think it would be advisable to keep the words "Buckingham Palace".
>
> Please note it should be "Music Library", not "Musical Library".

The blue stamp which was ultimately used simply bore the words: 'Royal Music Library. Buckingham Palace'.[16]

Besides attending to such details, Squire had split some of the volumes of the Handel autographs—making 97 out of the original 88—in order to re-assemble scattered portions of various works. He had also had many loose sets of printed parts of miscellaneous instrumental music bound. While Squire was still very busy with the Handel collection, he planned the principles on which the miscellaneous music[17] was to be catalogued, and this was accomplished by Hilda Andrews.[18] It appeared as Volume II in 1929, in which year volume III, comprising the printed music and musical literature, was also published, having been completed by William C Smith, who had begun the work under Squire's supervision. At the time of Squire's death, as just mentioned, the Handel volume had just passed through the press, and Robert Farquharson Sharp, the then Keeper, completed the preface before the end of January, and wrote: 'The whole work will remain as the final monument of his many services to musical history'. Nearly twenty years had passed since Squire made his first, unsuccessful, attempt to have the royal collection deposited in the British Museum.

Squire was fortunate in his generation. He served under a series of Keepers who were sympathetic to music, and could thus enrich the collections at a time when earlier rarities were still available for purchase in fair quantity. In expanding and altering the shape of the catalogues, he was able to build on the excellent foundations laid by his prede-cessors. Moreover, he enriched his skill as a music librarian with wide repute as a musicologist in a period when the first waves of musical scholarship were reaching England from the continent, and international contacts were being actively developed.

He was by no means free from faults and limitations. Although he had an exceptionally quick mind, it sometimes led him into impatience and an arbitrary lack of judgement. This latter defect can be seen throughout his career, as he consistently failed to assess the length of time needed to carry out a plan and to devise the best method of doing it. Squire also showed a limited understanding of the nature and needs of musical research. Regarding music entirely in terms of quality and historical importance, he remained unaware that the ephemera of any one generation, including what he so scornfully referred to as 'American rubbish', become the rarities of the future, susceptible of use and study in ways which the contemporary librarian can hardly imagine. But Squire's virtues and achievements far outweighed his faults. His industry was matched by a great tenacity of purpose, and he used his influence and powers of persuasion to the in-calculable benefit of the collections. He largely succeeded in the museum's traditional aim of making them the best for the printed music of every country outside that country itself. There can be no dispute about the high quality of his vision of the needs of musical scholarship as he understood them. Like Oliphant and Evans, Squire was entirely dedicated to enhancing the prestige and usefulness of the collections of printed music in the British Museum, and the cumulative effect of their efforts, sustained over some eighty years, provided a sure foundation on which their successors might build anew.

NOTES
    1 Undated report, 1912, f166.
    2 Report of 9 July 1910. The extra cost was about £25.
    3 Full details about the royal music are given in the present writer's *Some British collectors of music. c1600-1960*, Cambridge, 1963, pp103-129. The Royal Music Library, as it is now known, was presented outright to the British Museum on 27 November 1957 by Queen Elizabeth II, to mark the bicentenary of George II's gift of the Old Royal Library. Without Squire's original initiative, this ultimate act of munificence might never have taken place. That Squire had some connection with the royal music as early as 1904 is shown by an incident involving Vaughan Williams. In that year the composer, who was editing Purcell's *Welcome songs* for the Purcell Society, had to consult the autograph. Wearing an everyday suit, not a top hat, Vaughan Williams was conducted to Buckingham Palace by Squire, who was much upset, and 'because he was wrongly dressed, took him in and out through the kitchen premises' [ie the 'tradesmens' entrance']. See Ursula Vaughan Williams, *R.V.W.*, London, 1964, p68.
    4 The White Wing is on the south-eastern side of the museum, looking on to Montague Street. It was completed in 1885, and took its name not, as is sometimes thought,

from the colour of the stone, but from the surname of William White, whose bequest, made in 1823, provided the funds. See Miller, *That noble cabinet*, p285n.

5 Their work on music is unrecorded in official reports, but is known from the evidence of the titles they produced, their handwriting being familiar to the present writer. In 1937 Tucker published a clever volume entitled *Some croquet verses*, which is now very rare. The entire publisher's stock was destroyed when Paternoster Row was bombed out in 1941.

6 Squire had been elected a Fellow of the Royal Geographical Society in 1894.

7 The Glen collection was finally presented by Lady Ruggles-Brise to the National Library of Scotland in 1927.

8 *Proceedings*, session 45, 1918-19, pp96-111.

9 The consequences of this 'burden' were far-reaching. Its origin went back some twenty years. After succeeding Evans in 1885, Squire was compelled through lack of staff to begin selective cataloguing of copyright instrumental music. He continued to catalogue all copyright vocal music up to the end of 1889, but thereafter had to introduce selection for this also. Writing in *Grove* (2nd ed, 1906, p705, 706, vol 2) about the museum, in his article 'Libraries and collections of music', Squire stated that much of this secondary music was 'indexed in [*sic*] slips'. In the 1920s Smith extended and improved the system of indexing, and organised the uncatalogued music to form a ten-yearly series of parcels (1890-99, 1900-09, etc), arranged according to date of copyright receipt. Within each decade the pieces were filed alphabetically under the composers' names. Smith made two sequences of parcels, one for vocal music, another for instrumental. The latter was not indexed, but the former was, under title or first word (other than the article), followed by the name of the composer and the

date of copyright receipt. Any piece could thus be easily found in the parcels.

But this long established principle of segregation produced an ever-growing mass of 'secondary' music, including a huge quantity of American publications, which reached a peak in 1938-39. None of it was fully catalogued until August 1959, when Edward Claud Sington, OBE, a retired civil servant, joined the Music Room staff as a voluntary part-time worker. When he retired again, in 1975, in his eighty-third year, he had catalogued all the uncatalogued 'secondary' music, vocal and instrumental, published before the end of 1909, and all such vocal music by composers A to D in the decade 1910 to 1919. Sington wrote 62,254 titles, including cross-references, which were printed in nine individual Accession Parts. He read the proofs, did most of the press-marking himself, and made up the sheet music into batches of a suitable size for binding, which produced a total of some 490 folio volumes, besides a long series of boxes for unbindable band-parts.

10 *A Handelian's notebook*, pp38, 39.

11 This fact, and Pollard's recommendation nearly two years later, should be compared with the account which Smith gives of the background to his promotion in *A Handelian's notebook*, p30.

12 Smith wrote that a good deal of the collection 'was badly housed in other parts of the library', *A Handelian's notebook*, p30.

13 The annual return, 5 July 1915 (Accounts and Papers (18) 1914-1916. LV. p568), stated that the mezzanine floor in the King Edward VII Building was intended for 'the storage and study of maps and music'.

14 It was not until 1977 that a music reading area could be provided. By then the Music Library (as it became known in 1975) was too overcrowded to be able to accommodate

readers. Space was found directly beneath it, two floors down, in the erstwhile State Paper Room, then restyled the 'Official Publications Library', which is situated in the basement of the King Edward VII Building. However erratic the behaviour of the lifts, the much shorter journey substantially reduced both wear and tear on the books and the interval between application and delivery.

15 It is curious that there is no mention of these cases in the estimates.

16 A good many volumes also bear the words 'The King's Music Library' (without 'Buckingham Palace') impressed with a yellow stamp at some unknown date.

17 She was strongly recommended for this work to Elgar, then Master of the King's Musick, by Granville Bantock and by Sir Richard Terry. Their letters, dated respectively 1 March and 8 March 1927, are in BL Archives, Reference Division, Department of Printed Books, 5 Bed. Sq. 6 b.

18 A few more shelves of music, mainly manuscript, came to light at Windsor Castle in about 1921. Humphries conveyed it thence to the museum.

Appendixes

APPENDIX 1
The administration of the Department of Printed Books

THE PURPOSE of this appendix is to describe in outline the management of the department within the framework of the museum as a whole, to enumerate the various grades of the staff, and summarise their work. The period is that from the 1830s onwards, which, roughly speaking, represents the time when printed music began to develop into a significant entity.

The British Museum was governed by Trustees, who were of three kinds. The *ex officio* Trustees were a score or so in number, and included most of the highest officers of state. Among them were the three Principal Trustees—the Archbishop of Canterbury, the Lord Chancellor, and the Speaker of the House of Commons. The second category comprised the nominated Trustees, representatives of the families from whom the foundation collections (and some notable later additions) were acquired. From 1832 onwards this group included a Sovereign's representative. The *ex officio* and nominated Trustees elected fifteen others, all men outstanding in intellectual attainment and public affairs. It was these, together with the Principal Trustees and some of the nominated Trustees, who formed the Standing Committee that undertook the management of the museum's affairs. From its members it appointed sub-committees to be responsible for the various departments. The Trustees dealt directly with the Treasury on all matters concerning establishments and finance, over which they exercised the most stringent control.

The link between the Trustees and the heads of departments was the Principal Librarian (in 1898 re-named 'Director

163

and Principal Librarian') who was also the chief accounting officer. The head of each department was a Keeper, whose right-hand man, in the larger ones, was an Assistant Keeper. (Their numbers increased as the staff grew, and this designation lasted until about 1921 when it was changed to Deputy Keeper.) The next grade was that of the Assistants, who were divided into two sections, the 'upper' and the 'lower'. Below them came the Transcribers, and then the Attendants. The grades of Keeper, Assistant and Attendant were common to all the departments of the museum: Transcribers were found only in Printed Books and in Manuscripts. Later in the nineteenth century, Boy Attendants were recruited, as were also Second Division Clerks. On 14 July 1917, the grade of Attendant was re-named Museum Clerk.

The Assistants, from whom the higher posts were generally filled, were university graduates, originally with a bias towards the older public schools, and to Oxford and Cambridge. In time, London University added its quota. Graduates were also found, however, among the Transcribers, and some of the most able among them won promotion to higher rank. The Attendants, one of the oldest grades in the museum, were described by Smith thus: 'Recruited without much regard to education, but carefully chosen from the families of servants of the Trustees, or other well-to-do people, the attendants as a class were distinct and exceptional. Most of them, very carefully dressed, endeavoured to carry themselves with a dignity of fussy importance intended to convey that they were not as other folk'.[1] They too occasionally won promotion, and became Transcribers. Vacancies among the Attendants were sometimes filled from the bindery.

The Keeper organised the work of the department, and was responsible for staff discipline. At various times throughout the year, he submitted to the Trustees through the Principal Librarian reports on the work and conduct of all members of his staff, and recommended that they be granted an increment of pay. He made further recommendation for promotion as vacancies occurred. The Keeper also compiled monthly and annual reports of general work and progress, supported by full statistics. The annual report was co-ordinated with those of other departments, printed and submitted as a Return to Parliament, which also approved all estimates for staff, works, printing and the like, for the coming year. All proposals for publication of catalogues, with estimates of cost and all matters of policy (even sometimes the minutiae of cataloguing) were likewise submitted to the Trustees by the Keeper, who also had to obtain sanction for purchases. In the Department of Printed Books, the Assistant Keeper acted as a general co-ordinator and revised some of the cataloguing, which was the principal task of the Assistants, who also undertook book purchasing and 'incorporation' (which is described in appendix 2). Cataloguing was divided between the two 'sections' of the Assistants, according to the type of book, taking into account period, language and complexity. This grade included men of outstanding intellectual capacity such as Russell Martineau, the author of part of the article on 'Musical libraries' in the first edition of Grove's *Dictionary of music*. He was a polymath who served from 1857 to 1896 and knew, besides Greek, Latin and the principal European languages, Hebrew, Sanscrit, Arabic, Armenian and Hungarian. (He was largely responsible for the revision of the heading BIBLE in the first edition of the *General catalogue of printed books*, 1881-1905.) Men of this calibre rendered invaluable service throughout the nineteenth century and the early twentieth, when the boundaries of linguistic knowledge were more widely drawn than they have been since.

The grade of Transcriber probably goes back to the 1830s. Their work seems originally to have been writing out the entries for new accessions on the sheets of the interleaved copies of the 1813-19 catalogue. This they did by copying the 'title-slips' (see appendix 2) bearing the catalogue entries written by the Assistants. As the latter's handwriting varied in legibility and as the entries were in an immense range of languages, the Transcribers had to work, under supervision, with intelligence and accuracy. (The material change that took place in their work after 1849 is described in appendix 2.) After November 1866, their name was changed to 'Junior Assistants'. On 3 October 1870, it was reported that two of them knew oriental alphabets: others knew continental languages, which became a requirement for the grade on 13 January 1879. They seem to have been badly housed. In the 1850s they worked in a cramped, dark room under what is now the staircase at the north end of the King's Library. On 14 April 1872 they protested about their poor working conditions in the basement of the 'Iron Library' (ie the book stacks round the Reading Room), which they had occupied since early 1859. By 1875 they were housed in a room in the 'North Library' (ie the North Wing) formerly used as a reading room: this must have been the easternmost room on the ground floor, known until c1950 as the Catalogue Room. Right up to the 1880s, the work of the Transcribers was fundamental to the expansion of the catalogues and to making accessions quickly available to readers.

The Attendants were one of the oldest grades in the museum. In the Department of Printed Books, they were first employed to fetch volumes from the shelves for readers and replace them when done with, keeping a written record of each volume issued and returned. As the work of the department expanded, so did their duties. On 8 April 1861 it was reported that Attendants—rather surprisingly, it may now seem—were searching the catalogue for the titles of books proposed for purchase. Their range of duties is set out in a long report made on 23 June 1869 by the then Keeper, Winter Jones. Besides searching and book-supply, they also include the stamping of all new accessions, marking the pressmarks on the books and on the title-slips, interfiling the latter into the ever-growing main alphabetical series, and marking invoices. Since both the number of readers and books acquired increased rapidly, it is hardly surprising that the number of the Attendants grew more quickly than that of any other grade.

During most of the nineteenth century, the system of recruitment to an established post for all grades was by a nomination from one of the Principal Trustees. Such nominations were only valid of course when there was a vacancy or when the Treasury sanctioned a new post. A nomination was also often required when any member of the staff applied for a vacancy in a higher grade, as for instance in 1850, when Roy, then a Transcriber, sought promotion to an Assistant's post (see pp79, 80). All appointments were subject to ratification by the full Board of Trustees, and to approval by the Treasury. The system of nomination continued for many years, but was gradually replaced by a competitive examination conducted by the Civil Service Commissioners. [2] This examination could sometimes be waived for applicants of mature years with qualifications for a specialised post, as in the case of Squire (see p113). All entrants, whatever their grade and method of entry, were appointed subject to a probationary period of two years, after which the Keeper could recommend that the appointment be confirmed.

NOTES

1 Smith, p18.

2 The examination was introduced in the early 1860s, when the museum staff became pensionable within the civil service.

APPENDIX 2

The nature of the music catalogues and the
processes of their maintenance

IN ONE WAY or another, the work of all the grades mentioned in appendix 1 was derived from or contributed to the great catalogues of the department—the General Catalogue of Printed Books, and the separate catalogues of the music and the maps. The physical nature of all three catalogues was the same, and the processes used to maintain the music catalogues differed only in minor details from those used for the General Catalogue.

When the systematic cataloguing of the collections of printed books began towards the end of the eighteenth century, it was decided to write each entry on an oblong slip of paper of the most durable quality, measuring approximately 10 by 4 inches. This size gives ample space for setting out distinctly the various components of the entry— the author's name or the heading, title of the book, imprint, date of publication, format, any note required, and, at the left hand side (but not for printing) the date of copyright receipt, of purchase, or donation and sometimes, for the two last, the name of the seller or donor. Slips of approximately the same dimensions have been in use ever since. They were originally known as 'title-slips', a phrase which was soon abbreviated, somewhat ambiguously, to 'titles'. (This usage is apparently peculiar to the British Museum.) It was from these titles that there were printed the two-volume General Catalogue of 1787 and its six-volume successor of 1813-19. From the titles written for all books acquired from 1819 to 1848 were made the manuscript entries written on the

168

sheets of the two interleaved copies of the six-volume catalogue (see above p53 note 28).

But hand-written accession entries were, at best, a clumsy method of keeping a catalogue up-to-date. Long before 1848, when it was discontinued, the sheets had become overcrowded and the entries could not be made in the correct alphabetical order. The ensuing chaos, and the great public controversy that raged round the General Catalogue of Printed Books, cannot be given here in detail.[1] Suffice it to say that the constricted nature of the catalogue early became a matter of continuing concern to the Trustees, as indeed, for rather different reasons, its development was to be to their successors for over a century. Its obvious inconsistencies and general inadequacy, coupled with the ill-conceived decision of the Trustees to begin to print a catalogue of the entire library (which began and ended with one volume, letter A, published in 1841), cleared the way for Panizzi to proceed in 1849 with a new 'manuscript catalogue', as it was called. This was based on a revolutionary principle, by which each title was transcribed, in quadruplicate, on to folio sheets of thin, tough, carbonised paper, probably about six entries to a sheet.[2] The process used was presumably that which Panizzi alluded to, in connection with the music, as the 'Wedgwood Manifold Writer'.[3]

The transcribed entries were cut up into single slips, and laid down on large folio sheets of cartridge paper, from six to eight on each side of the sheet (see plate 5), each slip being pasted down lightly along the upper and lower edge only. This left each end of the slip open, so that a paper knife could be deftly inserted to lift the slip undamaged from the sheet. The slips could thus be moved about, respaced, and pasted down again to allow for accessions. The task of marking each slip into its correct place, by a simple system of

sequential numbering in pencil, required a thorough understanding of the principles of arrangement.   In the large
headings of a rapidly expanding catalogue, these principles
were complex and the work, known as 'incorporation', was
entrusted to an experienced Assistant.   The tasks of cutting
up the transcribed sheets, pasting down the slips and lifting
them for respacing, were done by a group of binders' men,
who worked in a room known as the 'catalogue shop'.   The
large sheets which bore the slips were bifolia, made up into
sections of four or eight leaves, and were bound, in the
museum bindery, into stout volumes of about 100 to 120
leaves per volume.   They were provided with an ample
number of stubs, or 'guards', on which extra single leaves
could be pasted, as required in expanding headings.   When
the volumes became too bulky, they could easily be split,
rebound and relettered, for throughout the nineteenth
century, and well into the twentieth, materials and binders'
labour were cheap.

The idea of the moveable slip, as providing a simple basis
for an orderly, flexible and infinitely expandable catalogue,
seems to have occurred almost simultaneously, probably in
the latter part of 1848, to two men, E A Roy,[4] then a Transcriber in the department, and John Wilson Croker,[5] the
politician and essayist.   This innovation, combined with the
carbonic copying in quadruplicate, meant that four copies
of the new 'manuscript catalogue' could be provided, a great
improvement on the two copies only of the old interleaved
catalogue.   Now there were three copies, one for the Reading
Room and two for the staff, one of which was regularly drawn
on to replace volumes of the Reading Room copy when they
were removed for incorporation.

The slips of the fourth carbonic copy were mounted on
thin cards, which were stored in boxes and arranged in an
order of pressmarks corresponding exactly with the sequence

of the books on the shelves throughout the entire library. The 'fourth copies', as they have always been called, served many purposes—for instance as a check on any missing book. They were also invaluable when corrections had to be made to a main entry in the catalogue and to all related entries, of which there might be many, of several kinds, for a single work. Because the fourth copies were all stored together at the one pressmark, all the corresponding titles scattered throughout the alphabetical sequence could easily be traced whenever an alteration which affected all the titles had to be made.

As already stated, in its physical nature and in all the processes of maintenance, the Music Catalogue was identical with the transcribed General Catalogue of Printed Books. (It did not discard its third copy and the fourth copy shelf-list until well into the 1880s.) But, unlike its vastly larger companion, the Music Catalogue was fully retrospective. This was because by 1849 Oliphant, having catalogued all the arrears then traceable of music received by copyright from about the 1790s onwards, had accumulated all the titles and was able also to add entries for all music acquired during his term of office. He had recatalogued much of the early music in the foundation and other special collections. Thus, until 1912, the reader who sought printed music had only one catalogue to consult, but anyone searching for printed books had to look in two catalogues, which were totally different in form and principles.

The immense task of revising all the entries in the old interleaved catalogue according to the Ninety-One Rules of 1839, and transcribing them for incorporation into the new catalogue, dragged on for nearly thirty years, the later stages —ironically enough—being in charge of Roy, one of the inventors of the system. This prolonged transcription and revision proved to be a continual drain on staff of all grades, and was one of the reasons why the provision of new special catalogues and the improvement of old ones was so long delayed. After compact printing superseded space-consuming transcription as the method of producing accession entries, the principle of the moveable slip was still retained as the means of keeping all the catalogues of the department, including the Music Catalogue, up to date.

NOTES

1 Particulars are given in the books by Esdaile and Miller, and in the lecture by Oldman, as cited in the list of sources.

2 That large sheets, rather than separate slips, were used is proved by the extant early catalogue of the Sloane Manuscripts 1091-1598, mentioned in note 29 to chapter 3.

3 This appears to be a development of an invention patented by Ralph Wedgwood, printed in 1856 as 'AD 1806 . . . 2972. Producing duplicates of writings'. It describes a 'carbonated paper' on which by using a 'style (ie stylus) made of agate, ground and polished to a smooth round point' two or more copies could be produced. It is curious that part of the phrase 'Wedgwood's Manifold Writer', used by Panizzi, is identical with the running title of another invention patented by Wedgwood, printed in 1856, as 'AD 1808 . . . No. 3110. Manifold Writer'. It describes 'An apparatus for producing several original writings or drawings at one and the same time which I call a Pennœpolygraph or pen and stylograph manifold writer'. This employed a complicated system of two pens held at the same time, in one hand. This patent does not mention carbonised paper. Wedgwood also patented 'AD 1810 . . . No. 3362. Character for language, numbers and music' which, for the last, involved a stave of twelve coloured lines, each representing a tone or semi-tone.

4 Esdaile, p366, states that Roy was one of the devisers of the moveable slip, but gives no source for this statement. Roy was given charge of the music some four years later.

5 Croker mentioned his idea, quite casually, on 21 March 1849, in the course of his evidence (8718) to the Royal Commission.

APPENDIX 3
The size and growth
of the music catalogues

THE SIZE OF the music catalogues in terms of volumes, and their rate of growth during the period covered by this books, are rather obscure subjects. But they are of interest because these catalogues were, and still are, by far the second largest in the department. Consequently the space which the three copies occupied—two (up to about 1890) in the staff working area and one in the Reading Room—was a factor which must have contributed materially to the general problem of overcrowding. The evidence for growth is scattered and rather contradictory, for the subject was not one that was really relevant to regular reporting. But the table on the facing page gives all the available evidence and does show a fairly consistent pattern over nearly seventy years, during which the catalogues grew nearly sixfold.

NOTES
1 The names of the authors given in this column correspond to those of the books given in the list of sources.
2 Statement in reply to Musical Association's memorial. See above p104.
3 A forecast, made while the entire music catalogue was being relaid and rebound.
4 A forecast, made while the words catalogue was being relaid.
5 Statement in reply to Musical Association's memorial. See above, p104.

Date	Source[1]	Total volumes, music & words	Volumes of music alone	Volumes of words alone
1850	Annual Report	57	45	12
1854	Sims, p164	57	45	12
1858	letter of 14 June 1878[2]	22 (an error)	—	
1859	Cowtan, p421	57	45	12
1866	Nichols, p62	126	105	21
1871	Cowtan, p299, 421	126	105	21
1872	Departmental Report of 5 July	126	105	21
1875	Rye's report, on his retirement	360[3]	—	—
1876	Annual Report	—	326	70[4]
1878	letter of 14 June 1878[5]	372 (c185,000 entries)	—	—
1887	Squire's report of 10 Dec, *re* printing (see above, p120)	—	—	58
1888	Garnett, p104	450	—	—
1906	Squire, article on 'Libraries and collections of music' in Grove, 2nd ed, vol 2, p704-705.	—	314	—
1912	Preface to Squire's 1912 catalogue	—	313	—

Statistics of entries in the music catalogues

THE NUMBER OF titles, representing both main entries and cross-references of various kinds, written for the catalogues of printed music is given in the British Museum's annual return to Parliament. The yearly figures, from 1841 to 1920, are as follows:

1841	245[1]	1863	6315
1842	4631	1864	4070
1843	9958	1865	4364
1844	9077	1866	5065
1845	647	1867	6145
1846	1796	1868	7313
1847	2283	1869	11825
1848	1891	1870	18578
1849	1661	1871	20080
1850	1689	1872	12620
1851	752	1873	12777
1852	1070	1874	6983
1853	4629	1875	13943
1854	4238	1876	11509
1855	3351	1877	17744
1856	5344	1878	19002
1857	2521	1879	19478
1858	4220	1880	14013
1859	4917	1881	14148
1860	177	1882	10848
1861	545	1883	10590
1862	6263	1884	1667

1885	1896	1903	9654
1886	18335	1904	11429
1887	9884	1905	11591
1888	11586	1906	9409
1889	27031	1907	12221
1890	11387	1908	13815
1891	6054	1909	16420
1892	7497	1910	14940
1893	12643	1911	9367
1894	9486	1912	16612
1895	8398	1913	11145
1896	11642	1914	7170
1897	10464	1915	11737
1898	13488	1916	4771
1899	11617	1917	—[2]
1900	11803	1918	—[2]
1901	15710	1919	7517
1902	11507	1920	8096
			706,304

For various reasons, the above total does not correspond to the actual number of entries in the music catalogue at the end of 1920, and even allowing for the war-time gap (explained in note 2) some adjustment is necessary. The total includes titles written for the fairly large heading Liturgies, which Squire abolished, probably when preparing his catalogue of 1912. This heading might well have contained some 2,000 titles. The total also includes titles written for the catalogue of words, which, by the time it fell into abeyance in about 1885, probably amounted to some 26,000. Further allowance must be made for entries for periodicals without musical content, which likewise have been removed, to a total, perhaps, of 100. On the credit side, there should be added the titles written before 1841 for the music in the

foundation collections, and scattered in the general catalogue of 1787 and its enlarged successor of 1813-19, to a
total of perhaps 500. The result works out thus:

Additions		Deductions	
Entries written		Words catalogue	26,000
before 1841	500	Liturgies	2,000
Estimated titles		Periodicals	100
written in 1917			28,100
and 1918	8,000		
	8,500		

Deductions	28,100		
less Additions	8,500		
	19,600		
Total of titles in annual returns			706,304
less total deductions			19,600
			686,704

NOTES

1 This figure represents the titles which Oliphant wrote
between the date of his appointment, 25 November 1841,
and the end of that year. Prior to 1841 no return was made
of any titles written for any of the catalogues of the department.

2 In these two years, 1917 and 1918, the reports state
that war-time conditions precluded all statistical returns.
Nevertheless, the cataloguing of music continued (see above
p00), and probably produced about 4,000 titles each year.

APPENDIX 5

The reckoning and growth of the collections

DURING THE first sixty years or so of the British Museum's existence the idea of regularly counting all additions to the collections hardly seems to have existed. This would have been specially difficult in the Department of Printed Books, where the staff was small in relation to the rate of expansion. But as the museum developed, the administration realised the need to record details of growth, and the first hesitant steps in print were taken with the issue of the *List of additions made to the collections of the British Museum in the year MDCCCXXXI (– MDCCCXXXV)*, published 1833 to 1839 (see p30 above). From 1842 onwards the museum's annual return to Parliament included figures for acquisitions made by the Department of Printed Books,[1] based on monthly cumulations reported by the Keeper. Separate totals were given for books and other material received under the new Copyright Act, and for purchases and donations. Of these by far the largest total was that for copyright, which was derived from figures recorded in the Copyright Receipt Office. From December 1856 onwards, these figures were entered in registers which were meticulously maintained until 1922 and are still preserved in the archives. Their covers bear the title 'Daily statistics'.

It might therefore be thought that it was a matter of simple arithmetic to reckon the growth and size of the collections of printed music during the eighty years effectively covered by this book. Unfortunately this is not so, and the reason lies largely in the chronic difficulty of consistently defining a unit of music. To define a unit was not easy with

179

books, having regard to those issued in one or more volumes, to parts of periodicals and to the great variety of different forms of publication. Nor was it simple for maps, considering the relation of atlases to single sheets of various kinds. But music was more complex than either, because besides works issued in score there were compositions printed complete as single sheets, others—of an educational nature—printed as cards, games, or rolls, and others again printed in parts which might not correspond numerically or musically to bibliographical criteria. There were also a vast number of series in progress, any single number of which might comprise one or more musical parts. The difficulty of defining a unit was compounded by erratic counting, which was due to the fact that within a decade this work could be assigned to different men who often counted in different ways.

How complex and varied was the presentation of the figures can be seen in the five following entries taken from the annual returns:

1847. The number of volumes of Music amounts to 126, of which 38 were presented, and 88 purchased. Besides this, 1,604 detached pieces of Music, comprehending 1,217 works, have been acquired by copyright.

1848. The number of volumes of Music amounts to 68, of which 13, comprising six works, were presented, and 55, comprising 39 works, were acquired by copyright. Besides these, 1,240 parts and numbers, comprising 1,016 complete works and 306 parts and numbers in progress, have been acquired by copyright.

1854. The number of pieces of Music, each comprising a complete work (including 234 titles received under the International Copyright Act), is 2,632, of which 1 was purchased, 5 presented, and 2,626 were acquired by copyright. 1,341 parts and numbers of works in progress (including 9 received under the International Copyright Act) have been acquired by copyright.

1860. The number of pieces of Music, each comprising a complete work (including 151 received under the International Copyright Treaties) is 3,408, of which 65 were purchased, two presented, and 3,341 acquired by copyright. 395 parts and numbers of works in progress have been acquired by copyright, and also 154 works, not included among the pieces of music, of which 15 were presented, and 139 purchased.

1870. 3,905 pieces of Music have been acquired, each piece complete in itself, of which 1,826 were received by English and 689 by International Copyright, and 1,390 purchased. Of 1,350 portions of musical works in progress, 1,052 have been received by English and 198 by International Copyright. 1,172 works of Music of greater extent than single pieces have also been acquired, comprising 630 by English and 226 by International Copyright, and 316 by purchase.

In historical terms it is clear that the difficulties of enumerating and describing musical accessions were realised quite early in the nineteenth century. The sequence of improvement is known solely because on 26 July 1872 the Trustees called for a complete return of all books received by copyright up to that date. The figures, going back to 1814,[2] were supplied by the Keeper, Rye, on 25 September. The original departmental copy in the hand of John Kemp is preserved in the reports for that year. The second column of this list is headed for each year up to 1841: 'Number of parts of volumes including music'. After the figures for 1841 there is a note reading: 'Previous to 1842, pieces of music, of which no separate account was taken, were received, but not claimed, until the passing of the Copyright Act 5 & 6 Vict c45'. From 1842 to 1856 there is a third column, solely for music, headed: 'Number of pieces of music'. After the entries for 1856, Kemp inserted yet another note, which reads: 'From this date, a more exact method was adopted, by distinguishing volumes from pieces of music'. Thenceforward Kemp gave two columns to the figures for music, and these were the basis of the returns to Parliament.

But the registers maintained in the Copyright Office give a much clearer and more consistent picture. From their inception in 1857 they contain two sets of four columns, one set for English copyright, the other for international copyright. The columns in each set are headed: 'works', 'volumes', 'pieces', 'parts'.[3] From 1860 onwards each column for international copyright is subdivided so as to contain two groups of figures, one headed 'F' for French, the other 'G' for German. A study of the totals in the columns of the registers reveals one important tendency. If in both categories the totals for 'volumes', 'pieces', 'parts' are added together, the aggregates correspond in varying degrees to the respective totals for 'works'. In some years the correspondence is not very close, but in others it is much nearer, and in others again it is exact or very nearly so.

Such an approximation seems always to have been the intention of the enumerators although, as mentioned, their methods were erratic at various times. The total of 'works' may therefore be taken as generally the most reliable figure for the number of items of printed music in the collections received by copyright, although the margin of error persisted right up to the 1890s. In 1899, Squire, having realised the inconsistencies and having understood the intention of the enumerators of earlier times, must have decided that if the breakdown by four categories was to continue, the sum total for 'volumes', 'pieces' and 'parts' should always equal that of 'works'. For in 1900 the equalisation becomes exact (as it had been earlier for some sporadic years in the late 1880s and 1890s), and continues so right up to 1922, the year when the Registers were discontinued. Music received by colonial copyright presents no difficulty, because only one figure is available, that in the annual returns, and the description 'publications' is consistently used. (If any was received before 1900, the quantity is unrecorded.)

There remains the question of establishing figures for music received by international copyright for the years prior to the consistent pattern of grouping begun in 1857 and also for purchases and donations for the whole period. Although the returns specify 'works' for the English copyright, they mention only 'pieces' for the first three years of international copyright (1854 to 1856). But as the figures are of the same order as the 'works' for the next three years, it seems reasonable to adopt the figures for 'pieces' for the earlier, defective, years, marking them with an asterisk.

The same difficulty arises with purchases, of which only 'pieces' or 'volumes' were recorded in the returns (the sole source of figures) for a number of years between 1843 and 1859. A similar lacuna is found in Evans's last years, when from 1879 to 1884 only 'pieces' are recorded, although both 'works' and 'pieces' appear for twenty two years previously. (Squire continued his system in his first few years, but then devised systems of his own, as is explained below.) For purchases, therefore, the same method of an asterisked figure will serve. Donations, being relatively such a tiny quantity, are a 'special case', as is explained on p188. This partial adjustment is admittedly a somewhat arbitrary way of providing a statistic. But given the over-riding value of a 'work' as best constituting a unit, such an adjustment probably does not distort the final total unduly and provides a necessary element of continuity in reckoning.

The material can be conveniently tabulated in two groups, one containing all three types of copyright accessions (see pages 186-187), the other (below) setting out the figures for purchases.

Purchases

1842	26	1865	878
1843	181	1866	202
1844	48	1867	255
1845	*154	1868	162
1846	*53	1869	103
1847	*88	1870	316
1848	—	1871	547
1849	90	1872	195
1850	2	1873	1587
1851	1	1874	2516
1852	4	1875	1635
1853	*44	1876	182
1854	*1	1877	1013
1855	*43	1878	653
1856	*108	1879	*138
1857	*40	1880	*358
1858	*146	1881	*551
1859	*1688	1882	*270
1860	139	1883	*444
1861	87	1884	*1123
1862	944	1885	*149
1863	833	1886	*133
1864	234	1887	—[4]
		1888	—[4]
			18,354

From 1889 onwards the method of enumerating music in the returns changes.   Until 1902 the subheading 'music' gives only figures for copyright accessions.   The quantity of music purchased is unspecified, but is included in a category of 'books of music' as part of a general total of 'volumes and pamphlets' acquired by the whole department.   This category must also have included substantial works (such as compositions printed in score or vocal score) received by copyright, because in 1896, for example, 'books of music' total 1714. But examination of the invoices shows that purchases in that year amounted to barely a quarter of that number.   For thirteen years, therefore, no valid total can be produced, but in 1902 and for the next five years the Returns give a separate figure for purchased 'books of music', thus:

1902	307	1905	337
1903	56	1906	32
1904	41	1907	153
			926

After this, Squire introduced another change and broke down the purchases into 'books' and 'parts', as follows:

1908	*books*	63	*parts*	90
1909		65		1170
1910		56		140
1911		31		132
1912		47		323
1913		86		267
1914		59		282
1915		45		33
1916		2		76
1917		—		—[5]
1918		—		—[5]
1919		23		128
1920		178		128
		625		2709

	English Copyright	International Copyright	Colonial Copyright
1842	550		
1843	1031		
1844	1137		
1845	1033		
1846	1008		
1847	1217		
1848	1016		
1849	1074		
1850	1142		
1851	1129		
1852	1329		
1853	1379		
1854	2626	*234	
1855	2304	*314	
1856	2239	*264	
1857	2581	251	
1858	4092	183	
1859	3424	267	
		1513	

		French	German
1860	2942	69	67
1861	3422	188	76
1862	2792	261	144
1863	2883	427	176
1864	2904	275	214
1865	2270	300	236
1866	2699	373	206
1867	1851	533	197
1868	1945	660	213
1869	2182	822	223
1870	2456	593	322
1871	2461	23	214
1872	2691	743	606
1873	3628	854	547
1874	6077	778	906
1875	2591	1122	1077
1876	5604	1035	961
1877	4369	1357	1186
1878	4743	1156	1082
1879	5186	1170	1297
1880	4432	1335	1404

	English Copyright	International Copyright		Colonial Copyright
		French	German	
1881	4469	1230	1242	
1882	3528	1316	1105	
1883	4506	1705	1554	
1884	3810	1526	1510	
1885	3116	1319	1554	
1886	4444	1382	1273	
1887	4463	1213	1297	
1888	4016	261	395	
1889	5083	10	27	
1890	3625	28	9	
1891	3878	24,064	21,320	
1892	6472			
1893	6560			
1894	6830			
1895	5795			
1896	6604			
1897	6735			
1898	7493			
1899	6952			
1900	7114			275
1901	8063			257
1902	8198			282
1903	8667			318
1904	7929			200
1905	9113			580
1906	8092			452
1907	10,744			341
1908	9779			513
1909	10,331			522
1910	11,121			706
1911	10,418			669
1912	11,577			530
1913	11,325			533
1914	11,436			594
1915	10,319			351
1916	9496			331
1917	7768[6]			—[6]
1918	6352[6]			—[6]
1919	9024			310
1920	11,141			774
	396,810			8,538

Clearly, the radical changes in the method of reckoning make it impossible to give any general total for purchases after 1886. Moreover, in some early years before annual reckoning began, substantial purchases were made. For instance, in December 1838 the museum bought from Thomas Rodd (one of its regular rare-book dealers) eleven volumes containing some 2,700 English folio sheet songs. They had all been the property of Dr Charles Burney[7] and ten of them have indexes in his hand. A similar collection, also probably Burney's, was bought in 1842. But none of them was included in the annual reckoning.

Accessions by donation were relatively few, and so irregular that they hardly merit tabulation. The recorded total from 1842 to 1920 does not exceed 2,000, and this total includes both Sir George Scharf's bequest to Squire in 1895 and 1377 pieces, mostly sheet music of the eighteenth and nineteenth century, presented in 1907 as duplicates from the Royal College of Music. (The latter was presumably a form of return for the duplicates which the college had received from the museum at Squire's suggestion.)

The difficulties of reaching any valid, comprehensive total for the collections, whatever the source, are further increased by a statement which appears, with some variation of wording, in many of the annual returns. That for 1870 reads thus: '5,827 articles have been received in the department, not included in the foregoing enumeration of volumes and parts of volumes, comprising Playbills, single pieces of music, Broadsides, Songs and Ballads'. The extent of this additional category of music over much of the eighty-year period, though not perhaps very great, cannot now be determined. But it adds another element of uncertainty to those already mentioned. Nevertheless, the tabulated figures are of some value in denoting the progressive growth of the collections, and the relationship between this growth and the number of titles written annually shows how much was achieved by the small staff available.

NOTES

1 The returns for both 1840 and 1841 include figures for printed books and for material in other library departments, but none for music.

2 It is hardly a co-incidence that the figures supplied by Kemp begin in 1814, the year in which an important Copyright Act (54–Geo III c156) became law. Whatever records Kemp used for the years 1814 to 1842 are no longer extant. For an earlier period, however, some figures are available from a transcript of the musical entries in the Stationers' Hall Registers. (William Hawes, the London music publisher, had this transcript made, and it is now in the Newberry Library, Chicago, Case MS 6A 36. I owe this information and the basic figures to Professor Donald W Krummel.) This transcript runs from 1700 to 1818, and it seems quite likely that from about the mid-1750s onwards most of the copies entered at Stationers' Hall were deposited in the British Museum. The total number of entries from 1785 to 1818 was 4951, giving an average of a little under 146 per year. This may be compared with the increase of some 33 per cent in the average total of copyright music received by the Museum from 1831 to 1835, as recorded in the *List of additions*, etc quoted on p30.

3 Figures for international copyright first appear in the returns for 1852, presumably due to the passing of the International Copyright Act in that year (15 – Vict c12). This source of deposit began to lapse after the Berne Convention was drawn up on 9 September 1886. This convention was intended 'for the creation of an international union for the protection of literary and artistic works'. It was ratified

by the United Kingdom on 5 September 1887, and came into force three months later.

4 No purchases of music at all are given in the 'Additions' section of the annual returns for 1887 and 1888. But in both years the final section on notable acquisitions mentions some important rare music. This is yet another example of inconsistency in reckoning.

5 Because of war-time exigencies, no statistics were given in the annual returns for 1917 and 1918. See also note 6.

6 No statistics were returned to Parliament in 1917 and 1918, but the Copyright Office maintained its 'Daily statistics'.

7 Now placed at G.304, G.305, and G.306-314 (placed in Montagu House at 13 V a). Only G.305 lacks a manuscript index. The hand can be identified as Burney's by comparison with his note bound in the autograph of Handel's *Ezio*, R.M. 20. a.12, f.92v. The volumes of songs tally with those in the Burney sale catalogue of 1814, lots 74, 75 and 77. The volume of Dibdin songs described in lot 77 was probably discarded by the museum because it duplicated his numerous songs received by copyright. Though the invoices for December 1838 are lost, the register of accessions, 1837-1849, shows that Rodd sold these songs to the museum with a large batch of 163 other pieces of mainly eighteenth century music.

LIST OF THE PRINCIPAL LIBRARIANS
OF THE BRITISH MUSEUM AND
OF THE KEEPERS
OF PRINTED BOOKS AND MANUSCRIPTS[1]

Principal Librarians
(From 1898 onwards Director and Principal Librarian)

1799	Joseph Planta
1827	Henry Ellis (Sir Henry Ellis, KH)
1856	Antonio Panizzi (Sir Anthony Panizzi, KCB)
1866	John Winter Jones
1873	Edward Augustus Bond (Sir Edward Bond, KCB)
1888	Edward Maunde Thompson (Sir Edward Maunde Thompson, GCB, ISO)
1909-1931	Frederic George Kenyon (Sir Frederic Kenyon, KCB, GBE)

Keepers of Printed Books

1812	Rev Henry Hervey Baber
1837	Antonio Panizzi (Sir Anthony Panizzi, KCB)
1856	John Winter Jones
1866	Thomas Watts
1869	William Brenchley Rye
1875	George Bullen
1890	Richard Garnett
1899	George Knottesford Fortescue
1912	Arthur William Kaye Miller
1914	George Frederick Barwick
1919	Alfred William Pollard
1924-1930	Robert Farquharson Sharp

Keepers of Manuscripts

1812	Henry Ellis (Sir Henry Ellis, KH)
1827	Rev Josiah Forshall

Keepers of Manuscripts (continued)

1837   Frederic Madden (Sir Frederic Madden, KH)
1866   Edward Augustus Bond (Sir Edward Bond, KCB)
1878   Edward Maunde Thompson (Sir Edward Maunde
            Thompson, GCB, ISO)
1888   Edward John Long Scott
1904   George Frederic Warner (Sir George Warner)
1911-1929   Julius Parnell Gilson

NOTE
    1 This list includes only those who held office from the time of the Rev James Bean, the first officer known to have been concerned with printed music.

OFFICERS IN CHARGE OF THE
COLLECTIONS OF PRINTED MUSIC

1812-1826 Rev James Bean (part-time)
1827-1840 none
1841-1850 Thomas Oliphant
1850?-1853 Johann F von Bach
1853-1866? Eugene Armand Roy
1867-1870 John Campbell Clarke (Sir Campbell Clarke)
1870-1884 Charles John Evans
1885-1920 William Barclay Squire
1921-1944 William Charles Smith

LIST OF SOURCES

1 Official

(a) Manuscript sources in the archives of the Department of Printed Books, Reference Division, British Library.

Panizzi, Sir Anthony. Official correspondence and papers, 1837-1855. (The 'Panizzi Papers'.)

Draft minutes, 12 January 1861, etc.

Miscellaneous departmental draft reports, 2 April 1856, etc.

Registers ('Daily statistics') of the Copyright Receipt Office, 1856-1922.

Two alphabetical series of title-slips, (i) Department of Printed Books, (ii) Music Library.

Invoices of purchases 1835, etc.

Register. Printed Books. 8 October 1837 – 10 November 1849. (Lists, arranged by year, month, day and number, giving the source of all accessions.)

Hand-lists of instrumental music and vocal music, 1844, etc.

(b) Manuscript sources in the archives of the British Museum.

Board of Trustees. General meetings. Minutes, December 1753, etc.

Committee minutes, January 1754, etc.

Sub-committee minutes, March 1828, etc.

(c) Printed.

Accounts relating to the income and expenditure of the British Museum.—Annual accounts, etc. [1803-1921.] Issued under various titles, and conventionally known as the 'annual returns' to Parliament.

194

Copy of a representation from the Trustees of the British Museum to the Treasury, on the subject of an enlarged scale of expenditure for the supply of printed books, with the Treasury minute thereon. Ordered . . . to be printed, 27 March 1846. (Parliamentary Papers 1846, vol xxv, p229. Copy also in W B Rye's collection of official papers, British Library, Department of Printed Books archives.)

Librorum impressorum, qui in Museo Britannico adservantur, catalogus. [Edited by Sir Henry Ellis and H H Baber.] 7 vol Londini, 1813-19.

List of additions made to the collections in the British Museum in the year MDCCCXXXI (-MDCCCXXXV). Printed by order of the Trustees, 1833-39. A *List of additions to the printed books* for 1836 to 1838 was published in 1843 but, according to the preface, the volumes 'were never completed in type'. That for 1836 finished at 'Luther', for 1837 at 'Cynosure', and for 1838 at 'Czerny'. Thus the information about 'Music', presumably in the same summary form as in the earlier Lists, is lost.

Report of the Commissioners appointed to inquire into the constitution and government of the British Museum with minutes of evidence. (Appendix. Index.) 2 vol 1850.

Synopsis of the contents of the British Museum. Printed by Cox, Son, and Baylis: [London,] 1808. Includes 'Analytical syllabus of the Library of Printed Books'.

2 Miscellaneous

Barwick, George Frederick *The Reading Room of the British Museum.* Ernest Benn: London, 1929.

Briggs, William *The law of international copyright.* Stevens & Haynes: London, 1896.

Cowtan, Robert *Memories of the British Museum.* Richard Bentley and Son: London, 1872 [1871].

— Index to Cowtan's 'Memories of the British Museum'. [Manuscript, compiled by F C W Hiley.] [1947.]

Crook, Joseph Mordaunt *The British Museum*. Allen Lane, The Penguin Press: London, 1972. Reprinted in Pelican Books, 1973, with the sub-title 'A case-study in architectural politics'.

Cummings, William Hayman 'The formation of a national musical library'. In: *Proceedings of the Musical Association*, session 4, 1877-78, pp13-26.

Esdaile, Arundell *The British Museum Library. A short history and survey.* George Allen & Unwin: London, 1946. 2nd impression 1948.

Garnett, Richard *Essays in librarianship and bibliography.* George Allen: London, 1899. Includes 'The printing of the British Museum Catalogue', and 'The past, present and future of the British Museum Catalogue'.

Hill, Francis John *Shelving and classification of printed books in the British Museum, 1753-1953.* [1953.] Typescript. A thesis, submitted for the Fellowship of the Library Association.

King, Alexander Hyatt 'The Music Room of the British Museum. 1753-1953'. In: *Proceedings of the Royal Musical Association*, session 79, 1952-53, pp65-79.

King, Alexander Hyatt 'William Barclay Squire, 1855-1927, Music Librarian'. In: *The library*, ser 5, vol 12, no 1, March 1957, pp1-10.

Miller, Edward *Prince of librarians: the life and times of Antonio Panizzi.* André Deutsch: London, 1967.

Miller, Edward *That noble cabinet. A history of the British Museum.* André Deutsch: London, 1973.

Nichols, Thomas *A handbook for readers at the British Museum.* Longmans, Green & Co: London, 1866.

Oldman, Cecil Bernard 'Panizzi and the music collections of the British Museum'. In: *Music, libraries and instruments*

. . . Editors: Unity Sherrington and Guy Oldham, pp62-67. Hinrichsen Edition: London, 1961 (Hinrichsen's Eleventh Music Book.)

Oldman, Cecil Bernard 'Sir Anthony Panizzi and the British Museum Library'. In: *English libraries 1800-1850. Three lectures delivered at University College, London. By C B Oldman, W A Mumford, Simon Nowell-Smith*, pp5-32. Published for the College by H K Lewis & Co: London, 1958.

Scholderer, Julius Victor *Reminiscences.* Vangendt & Co: Amsterdam, 9 October 1970.

Sims, Richard *Handbook to the Library of the British Museum.* John Russell Smith: London, 1854.

Smith, William Charles *A Handelian's notebook.* A & C Black: London, 1965.

Squire, William Barclay 'Musical libraries and catalogues'. In: *Proceedings of the Musical Association*, session 45, 1918-19, pp96-111.

INDEX